# MENCKEN

*Publisher's Note*

Works published as part of the Maryland Paperback Bookshelf are, we like to think, books that are classics of a kind. While some social attitudes have changed and knowledge of our surroundings has increased, we believe that the value of these books as literature, as history, and as timeless perspectives on our region remains undiminished.

*Also Available in the Series:*

# MENCKEN

A Life

FRED HOBSON

The Johns Hopkins University Press
Baltimore and London

Originally published as a hardcover edition in 1994 by Random House, Inc.
Published by arrangement with Random House, Inc.
Maryland Paperback Bookshelf edition, 1995
05 04 03 02 01 00 99 98 97 96 95    5 4 3 2 1

The Johns Hopkins University Press
2715 North Charles Street
Baltimore, Maryland 21218-4319
The Johns Hopkins Press Ltd., London

Library of Congress Cataloging-in-Publication Data

Hobson, Fred C., 1943-
Mencken : a life / Fred Hobson.—Maryland paperback bookshelf ed.
        p.     cm.—(Maryland paperback bookshelf)
Originally published : New York : Random House, c1994.
Includes bibliographical references and index.
ISBN 0-8018-5238-2 (alk. paper)
1. Mencken, H. L. (Henry Louis), 1880-1956—Biography. 2. Authors,
American—20th century—Biography. 3. Editors—United States—
Biography. I. Title. II. Series.
PS3525.E43Z467   1995
818'.5209—dc20
[B]                                                                 95-12735

A catalog rocord for this book is available from the British Library.

Owing to limitations of space, acknowledgements of permission to
quote from unpublished and published materials will be found
on pp. 649-50, following the index.

Book Design by Susan Hood

For my father
Fred Colby Hobson
And in memory of my mother
Miriam Tuttle Hobson
1909-1994

# CONTENTS

# Contents

# PRELUDE

# THE ELUSIVE MENCKEN

The American social and literary critic Henry Louis Mencken has experienced several deaths and resurrections over the past six decades. Called by Walter Lippmann in 1926 "the most powerful personal influence on this whole generation of educated people," by the mid-1930s he had fallen so far, and so quickly, that he was sometimes referred to as "the late H. L. Mencken." After experiencing a revival of popularity in the late 1930s and early 1940s with the publication of his autobiographical *Days* books and the monumental final edition of *The American Language*, he suffered in November 1948 a stroke so devastating that in the 1950s he referred to himself as having "died" in 1948. If we consider Mencken the author and editor, that was indeed the case since the stroke took the ability to read and write from this man for whom reading and writing seemed nearly everything.

When death, long anticipated and greatly desired, came at last in January 1956, it appeared that Mencken, at seventy-five, had indeed (to use his expression) reached the end of the chapter. But even then, if we consider Mencken as cultural force and object of national attention, such was hardly the case. For he had spent most of the last years before his stroke, in a very real sense, preparing to die—and then to live again as a writer through the release at stipulated times, after his death, of his correspondence, his diaries, and his recorded impressions of American life and letters in the first half of the twentieth century.

If to live again through his writing was Mencken's intent, he has succeeded spectacularly. Following the opening in January 1971 of his massive literary correspondence in the New York Public Library, he was indeed resurrected as literary force, through his letters to and from nearly every major American writer of the first half of the century—and through several books that drew heavily on that correspondence. If the letters helped to revive him, such was the case even more with the release in 1981, twenty-five years after his death, of other confidential materials, including the diary he had begun in 1930 at the age of fifty and kept until the month of his stroke in 1948. The publication of a substantial portion of the diary in 1989 created a furor that has yet to subside—an outpouring of reviews and essays, heated charges, and eloquent denials and defenses, revolving around the question of whether Mencken was or was not anti-Semitic, racist, misogynist, disloyal to friends and associates, and generally misanthropic.

That the politically insensitive H. L. Mencken would be resurrected a second—or third—time in an age of cultural and political correctness would have both amused and delighted him. He could not have anticipated the spirit of the age in which he would resurface, thus could not have guessed the exact form a response to his posthumous revelations would take. There is little doubt in my mind, however, that he expected the eventual publication of his diary and both expected and desired the publication of two final documents that he placed under lock and key for thirty-five years and that were at last released to researchers in January 1991. The most important of these final manuscripts, "My Life as Author and Editor," Mencken hoped would be "the most copious and accurate literary record" of the twentieth century; if it was not altogether that, it was a work—edited by Jonathan Yardley and published in 1993—guaranteed both to enlighten and to offend. Although Mencken could hardly have been aware of the sensibilities of the audience that would receive his secret writings a half century later, it is clear that, until the end, he was seeking to reach that later audience, albeit at a time long after his death, when, as he once wrote a friend, "there will be no more secrets, no more confidences." A posthumous revival is indeed an appropriate form of immortality for a man who professed to believe in no other kind.

⸺⸺

One result of the release of thousands of pages of manuscripts over the past twenty years is the need for a new examination of Mencken and his role in American life and letters. That the role was a significant one is indisputable, although many have disputed the area in which his significance principally lies. Best known in the 1920s as editor of the iconoclastic *American Mercury* and author of the controversial *Prejudices* books, in the 1930s and 1940s he was known principally as autobiographer and philologist. He was also a dazzling stylist—"the best prose [writer] in America during the twentieth century," Joseph Wood Krutch once remarked—and, when he chose to be, a spectacular public personality.

Both more and less than literary figure in the purest sense, not solely social and cultural critic, yet not precisely journalist, Mencken is as difficult to define now as he was in his own lifetime. He has been called variously, and with at least some justification, the American Voltaire, the American Swift, and the American Shaw. Other European figures from Rabelais to Dr. Johnson to Nietzsche have been used to "explain" him. "If Mencken had never lived," Alfred Kazin has written, "it would have taken a whole army of assorted philosophers, monologists, editors, and patrons of the new writing to make up for him." But to other Americans, particularly in the 1920s, Mencken was "the most universally hated man in the United States."

It is no accident, then, that such a figure has been the subject of several biographies before—the first of which, by Isaac Goldberg, appeared in 1925, when Mencken was but forty-five years old, and the most insightful and most reliable of which are those by William Manchester (1950) and Carl Bode (1969). But the most recent biography, Bode's, is now a quarter century old, and no biographer until the present has been able to take advantage of the recently released manuscript revelations, impressions, and judgments.

In these new materials we discover a private Mencken who had been largely concealed by the carefully constructed public persona, the buoyant and often bombastic Mencken. The material suggests a much more complex and ambiguous man, a darker figure, than we had previously known. We see, particularly in the diary, a man preoccupied with illness and—as he grew older—with his own mortality. We see a man capable of expressing emotions he never expressed publicly: great joy and sorrow when he considers the life and early death of his wife, Sara Haardt; despair when he dwells on the deaths of his friends; great sadness when he sees the deterioration of his Hollins Street neighborhood in Baltimore. We are also given in the diary and in the recently released "My Life as Author and Editor" often devastating portraits of his contemporaries Theodore Dreiser, Sinclair Lewis, F. Scott Fitzgerald, and, to a lesser extent, William Faulkner and Thomas Wolfe. All, he believed, led disorderly lives, and were given to excesses of either the bottle or the flesh (or both) that not only damaged their literary careers but made them, much of the time, unsuitable companions. In expressing this disapproval of many of his friends and acquaintances, Mencken reveals a great deal about himself.

What he reveals most strikingly is a certain rage for order in his own life, both in the living of it, as we shall see, and in his preparation for death. For Mencken was, in his private life, the most orderly and responsible of men—forever cautious, leaving nothing to chance—and from his fifties on he was also actively engaged in the business of posthumous image management.

At first, his careful record keeping and confidential commentary seem a great benefit to the biographer. "There is, indeed, probably no trace in history of a writer who left more careful accounts of himself and his contemporaries," he wrote of himself in his diary in 1945, and Charles Fecher, the author of a book on Mencken's thought and the editor of his diary, contends that with one possible exception Mencken indeed "left the most complete collection of manuscripts, letters, miscellaneous papers, and other memorabilia of any writer in the English-speaking world." He left as well—to the Enoch Pratt Free Library of Baltimore—dozens of scrapbooks of news clippings about himself and voluminous autobiographical notes, and to a larger reading public he left the autobiographical series, *Happy Days* (1940), *Newspaper Days* (1941), and *Heathen Days* (1943). In his collection at the Pratt he placed schoolboy grades, commencement accounts, bank statements, records of earnings, medical histories (including an exhaustive hay fever diary), and much else. All this is, of course, in addition to the more than ten million words in print, including journalism, which in 1940 he estimated he had produced and the more than one hundred thousand letters he wrote in his lifetime. As Fecher remarks, Mencken "went out of his way to simplify matters for future biographers and critics."

I would agree to an extent—but yet . . . Rarely has a person written so much about himself, saved so much, and still, in certain areas of his personal life, revealed so little—at least by intent. "I have tried hard to tell the truth," Mencken wrote in his diary, and in most respects he did. But in certain other regards he has (in the words of Emily Dickinson) told it "slant"—not so much through distortion of the truth as through omission. "I have always destroyed purely personal letters, especially when they came from women," he acknowledged in the 1940s, although in fact that was not always the case. In any event, this deficit is remediated by the letters Mencken wrote *to* various women who did not destroy them and, in recent years, have deposited them in numerous libraries.

Thus, Mencken preserved and recorded selectively. He saved thousands of Christmas cards, which we find in his correspondence in the New York Public Library, but he destroyed certain sensitive letters from close friends and probably lovers. He kept voluminous autobiographical notes, diaries, and journals, but these notes and diaries are sometimes as important for what they do not contain as for what they do. They focus on the world Mencken sees and hears and (especially in his case) tastes, but except in those few cases when the diarist drops his guard, they do not show him revealing his feelings and emotions (as distinct from his impressions and his prejudices) or describing delicate situations into which those feelings and emotions led him. Still, in spite of Mencken's strategies of concealment and diversion, the private life comes through, largely because, in tens of thousands of letters and thousands of pages of diary entries and autobiographical notes, even a cautious man occasionally slips; because, in other cases, his silence on a particular subject speaks volumes; and finally because, as I have suggested, many of those friends to whom he wrote did not burn or return sensitive letters, as he himself was wont to do, but rather preserved them, shared them, and thus, long after his death and theirs, ensured themselves a reflected kind of immortality.

But much of this has come about in the past two decades, and before that time Mencken played, in certain respects, the role of adversary—or at least that of elusive prey, teasing, showing and retreating—for his inquiring biographer. He still plays that role to some extent. Indeed, in making selected materials available and placing others under lock and key until 1971, 1981, and 1991, he encouraged his first biographers to paint a picture not radically different from that he himself would have painted. Goldberg's early biography was based in large part on a two-hundred-page typescript prepared by the subject himself. And Mencken's own memories of his youth in the *Days* books, on which all biographers have drawn heavily, are highly selective. We find not a rounded picture of young Henry Mencken but a sort of Tom Sawyer in Baltimore in the 1880s and 1890s living an altogether pleasant life.

The author concluded *Happy Days* in 1891 in his eleventh year, a point at which—he writes in the preface—"existence began inevitably to take on a new and more sinister aspect." Yet nowhere in his published work, or even in the unpublished material available to researchers before 1981, did he explore that "more sinister aspect." Bode tells us in his 1969 biography that Mencken at seventeen "was at least playing with the notion of committing suicide." We are little prepared for that revelation, and Bode is able to devote no more than six lines to it. He had little more to go on. The release in 1981 of Mencken's manuscripts, "Additions, Corrections and Explanatory Notes" to *Happy Days*, *Newspaper Days*, and *Heathen Days*, as well as the release of the letters in 1971, helps us understand more fully the conflict with his father that led to that state of mind. Why had Mencken withheld so much material from the published version of the *Days* books? In part, one suspects, because the inclusion of such somber matter would have altered the generally light tone of the works. Henry Mencken was hardly Henry Adams: he was not given to confession and introspection in public and, in particular, did not want to reveal too much while he and his family and friends still lived.

Even with the release of more revealing materials, Mencken presents a formidable challenge, partly because—as before—a biographer must be careful not to fall under the spell of the spectacular persona, partly because Mencken is still difficult to place in American life. He is more in the American grain than has generally been recognized, but he is also, in American civilization, *sui generis*—an original who approached the national life with a detachment and relentless honesty unlike that of any other critic or satirist before or since. He has, thus, no true American literary ancestors and no true descendants. As a forebear, Mark Twain comes closest, resembling Mencken in a number of ways: from the happy, adventurous childhood and the early death of an authoritarian father to a joyful, rebellious young manhood to the bitterness and melancholy of late years and a welcome death in his mid-seventies; in his ridicule of America but his love of the American language, his distaste for romance and his devotion to realism, his abhorrence of (and delight in) sham, fraud, and hypocrisy, and his love-hate relationship with the American South. But Mencken is different from Mark Twain, too, in numerous ways—among them, in his distaste for the American hinterland and, despite his American grounding, at times nearly a European point of view. Mencken has never been adequately explained. As Louis D. Rubin, Jr., has written, "Of all our important literary figures he has been the most taken for granted, the least investigated."

Among the most intriguing aspects of Mencken is the number of paradoxes in the man. He was at one and the same time a sort of literary Horatio Alger, shrewd, resourceful, industrious, self-educated, a product of the streets of Baltimore who started at the bottom of the world of journalism and rose quickly and decisively to the top—*and* the descendant, as he often pointed out in his late years, of one of the proudest and most accomplished families in German intellectual circles of the eighteenth century, a family resplendent with the very Ph.D.s he himself ridiculed.

In his own period of greatest influence, in the early twentieth century, this archfoe of the Victorian Genteel Tradition was himself, particularly in sexual matters, often Victorian; this most famous twentieth-century opponent of "puritanism" was, in many respects, a puritan himself. He was a famous South hater who, on more than one occasion, proclaimed himself a southerner; a conservative who, in the 1920s, was lionized by liberals; a man who spoke of "niggeros," "blackamoors," and "coons," yet (and this as a half southerner) had black writers into his home as dinner guests and championed more African-American writers than any other editor of his time. He was, as I have suggested, an apparent anti-Semite in much of his writing, both public and private, yet a man *most* of whose closest friends and associates for a time were Jewish, as well as one who gave a great deal of time and effort to helping individual Jews escape Hitler's Germany. He was a reformer who hated the notion of reform. And he was the American writer of the twentieth century who would seem to be most nearly devoid of what Mark Twain called "the moral sense," yet was a man always guided by fixed notions of right and wrong.

A biographer, then, particularly one with access to the material released in recent years, must examine these and other paradoxes of Mencken. That biographer, as well, must attempt to answer certain questions that Mencken himself was often reluctant to answer. To what extent, for example, did his early years depart from the idyll depicted in the *Days* books? Was his father altogether the genial prankster presented in *Happy Days?*—a portrait that seems inconsistent with the man who put his eldest son to work in the family cigar factory at fifteen and so frustrated his hopes of being a writer that the son considered suicide. How do we explain an attachment to home and mother that was so deep and abiding that Mencken lived with his mother and his unmarried brother and sister in the Hollins Street house until he was forty-five and married—at age fifty—only after his mother's death? To what extent did Mencken's pride in his German ancestry—his youth in a city with a large German-American population but an Anglo-American power structure, his silencing by the Baltimore Sunpapers during World War I—contribute to his rebelliousness in the early 1920s? And to what extent was Mencken's much-touted German consciousness present in his early life? What was his state of mind after 1935? What accounts for his virulent hatred of Franklin D. Roosevelt, a hatred that went beyond political differences?

Finally, what accounts for his nearly compulsive attitude toward work? Throughout his life Mencken worked indefatigably, exercising extraordinary self-discipline, turning out a massive amount of copy each day as well as answering ten or twenty letters most days, holding himself to a Puritan-like standard of accountability. Yet, at age sixty-four, reflecting on a career of more than two dozen books, thousands of essays and newspaper articles, and more than a hundred thousand letters written, he noted in his diary: "Looking back over a life of hard work . . . my only regret is that I didn't work even harder." Why was he so driven to work? What motivated him— particularly if life, as he often maintained, was meaningless?

Most important, perhaps, how much deep resentment and hurt were concealed by Mencken's bombastic public persona? No biographer has focused on what Alistair Cooke has called in passing a "strain of cruelty" in his work. It is, at times, more than a strain. He is often vicious when he writes of William Jennings Bryan, Woodrow Wilson, and Roosevelt; and his unpublished remarks on Roosevelt, contained in the miscellaneous notes in the Enoch Pratt Free Library, go far beyond anything he published.

Mencken once wrote that his basic thought, after an early age, never substantially changed, and I believe that to be the case. His means of expressing and defending that thought changed, but not the thought itself. His was an example of a first-rank mind put to the task of validating and justifying the prejudices of his family, his heritage, his community. For all his rebellion against his father, suppressed and thus all the more powerful—for all his exposure to ideas and various ways of viewing the world—Mencken held as a mature thinker nearly all of his father's views, attempted to justify them philosophically, and worked mightily to convince others of their merit. He was as rigid a thinker as the American Puritans he so vilified, and there was, despite the apparent contradictions in his character, a remarkable consistency in his thought.

It is not principally with that thought, however—at least not in any systematic sense—that I am concerned in this biography. Rather, it is with thought as one of many functions of time and place, of heredity and cultural environment, the relationship between ideas and personality—with what Mencken himself called his "prejudices" and with the role they played in his life. For despite his essentially valid claim that he was a creature of thought, not emotion, Mencken was a man of strong feelings, one for whom inclinations preceded ideas. He believed that he himself was "temperamentally" incapable of certain beliefs and attitudes, as he often said, and temperamentally bound to hold others. But he was also aware that those who would write his life after he was gone would have their own sets of prejudices, and that must have been, in part, what he had in mind when he once pronounced the verdict: A biographer is an unjust god.

In fact, in his choice of gods, Mencken has fared exceedingly well, for with the exception of Charles Angoff—his assistant on *The American Mercury* whom we might call Mencken's dark Boswell—his biographers have indeed been just. Now that all his manuscripts are released, all letters available, all returns in, he faces another with his own set of views and beliefs, his own "prejudices." On the surface, Mencken's chances would not appear to be good—since this biographer (as Alistair Cooke, writing on Mencken, also once said of *himself*) is many things for which Mencken sometimes expressed utter scorn: in my case, a southerner, a professor of literature, a political liberal, and an admirer of Franklin D. Roosevelt. Despite these liabilities, I am also of the opinion that H. L. Mencken was, for better or worse, a remarkable man who led a life that was rich, full, complex, historically significant—above all, fascinating.

May this god also be just.

# MENCKEN

# Chapter 1

# THE FATHERS

> What a small space in time a family usually marks off! The
> American Washingtons, scarcely heard of in the world before
> the 1760's, vanished before the end of their first century.
> . . . Jefferson's progeny are heard of no more, and neither are
> those of Lincoln, Sherman and Roosevelt I. . . . The Menck-
> enii, on their humbler level, have lasted a bit longer, but their
> end is in sight. . . . *Sic transit!*
>
> —*H. L. Mencken, "Autobiographical Notes, 1941–"*

This is the story of a family as well as the story of an individual.
H. L. Mencken himself always framed his life in such a way,
rarely escaping the knowledge that he was part of, indeed the end of,
a continuum. Nearly as important, the story of the Menckens in
America, by turns proud and undistinguished, exceptional and representative, casts light on a family that, despite the prominence of
one of its members, never quite took hold in America. "People of my
blood . . . have been in the country for more than a century,"
Mencken wrote in his sixties, "but I still feel and think of myself as
a stranger." "I have lived in the United States all my life without
becoming, in any deep sense, an American." "I often regret," he
wrote a distant German cousin in 1932, "that my grandfather did not
stay in Saxony."

These were only occasional musings. At other times, as we shall
see, H. L. Mencken felt himself very much an American. But his
sentiments show the degree of his alienation from twentieth-century
America (at the same time as he was deeply immersed in it), as well

as his ties to a Germany, often as much mythic as historical, to which he sometimes returned in his imagination. Particularly in his later years, he reflected often upon place and destiny, change and loss— perhaps the fate of a man who seized fame in his thirties, gained international celebrity in his forties, and was largely dismissed in his fifties. The story of the Menckens in America is a story of exactly one hundred years; at the time of Henry Mencken's cruel stroke in 1948, the family had been in the United States exactly that long. Other branches of Mencken's family had arrived somewhat earlier, but his father's family, as we shall see, was the branch that mattered most, and his grandfather Mencken had landed in Baltimore a century to the month before this most famous Mencken was silenced forever and the Mencken family as force and influence in American society ceased to exist.

That was the kind of historical coincidence, the kind of symmetry, that H. L. Mencken, if he had possessed the wit to appreciate it fully after 1948, would have relished. He had earlier pondered such coincidences and ironies in abundance, as well as detected a certain drama in the story of the Mencken family. In his late fifties and his sixties, he turned time and again to the past, collecting boxes of materials about the Menckens, planning to write a history of the family and its long line of *gelehrten*. In a land in which nearly all of those who claimed distinguished Old World origins were frauds, Mencken believed he was the real thing. Thus it was chiefly the European phase of the family on which he planned to focus. He would say little in autobiographical notes, diaries, and letters about his other forebears, the Abhaus, the Gegners, and the McLellands. Certainly the materials for the Menckens were more abundant than for the others, but that was only part of it. The Menckens were also the only branch of distinction. Besides, H. L. Mencken believed in patriarchy: it was the world of the *fathers* that mattered most.

Finally, he saw a certain poignancy in the rise and decline of the Menckens, for, taking the long view, it was during the decline of the family that he himself had been born. He was thus one of that notable company of American writers born in the nineteenth century— Emerson, Hawthorne, and Melville among them—who were products of families whose proudest days lay in the past. If Mencken did not at first set out precisely to revive the family name, at least, once he had revived it, he took no small measure of pride in his accomplishment. The pride lay not only in his measuring up to the earlier Menckens but also (since his own success was achieved before his keen interest in family set in) in their having measured up to him. He was astonished that they *resembled* him so greatly.

We must look, then, at Mencken's antecedents in some detail, always keeping in mind that it is not only the past but also Mencken's view of it that is important here. What he wrote about his ancestors tells us as much about his views on politics, history, class, education, religion—and self—as anything he ever wrote on the America of his own time. We learn above all that H. L. Mencken was just as fully a determinist (though a vastly different sort) as Cotton Mather or any other of the Puritans he so despised and ridiculed. Biological determinism—heredity—explained nearly all:

> How did I get my slant on life? Heredity. My ancestors for three hundred years back were all bad citizens. They weren't moral—in the conventional sense. They always were against what the rest were for. . . . I inherited their traits, and I am what I am today . . . just because . . . I am a mechanism, the product of heredity. . . . It was set for me which way I'd jump as I met my environment. . . . I was prejudiced when I came into the world.

Henry Mencken was not, like his beloved Huck Finn, "brung up to wickedness." He was born to it.

------

Just what sort of "bad citizens" the early Menckens were became evident shortly after they emerged from obscurity about the end of the sixteenth century. The earliest members of the family (then spelled Mencke) had lived without distinction for at least two or three centuries in and around Oldenburg, some thirty miles west of Bremen in what is now northwest Germany. But no member of the family came to true prominence until Eilard Mencke (1614–1657) moved to Prussia, "took to the Protestant pulpit"—as H. L. Mencken later wrote—and became archpresbyter of the cathedral at Marienwerder (now Kwidzyń). It was another of those historical ironies, the later Mencken must have noted, that the first prominent figure to bear his name had been a man of the cloth. Eilard also looms large in family legend as a benefactor of subsequent Menckes and Menckens. The owner of property in Oldenburg, in 1657 he established a university scholarship that would aid numerous members of the family and tempt others, including possible American claimants, as late as H. L. Mencken's time.

It was not to the direct line of Eilard Mencke, however, but to that of his cousin Helmrich that H. L. Mencken belonged. And it was principally in that line, and that of Helmrich's brother, Johann, that the "bad citizens" lay. Helmrich Mencke was a merchant in Oldenburg, but his son Lüder (1658–1726)—in the first act of a family drama that would be played out again two centuries later—left the family enterprise for the world of books and ideas. Lüder traveled to Leipzig, took his Ph.D. in 1682, and taught law for forty-four years at the University of Leipzig, becoming rector of the university and judge of the Saxon high court as well as the author of a number of books. His son Gottfried Ludwig (1683–1744) also became a professor of law, at Wittenberg. Gottfried's son and grandson—in the line of descent of the Baltimore Menckens—taught and practiced law as well.

The earliest notable ancestors, then, of that most famous twentieth-century adversary of preachers and pedagogues were themselves preachers and pedagogues—and lawyers—although H. L. Mencken might have added that the paths to prominence in other fields were severely limited in those days. If the preachers in the family died out quickly, the pedagogues remained for nearly two centuries, although more so in a line of collateral descent than in H. L. Mencken's own line. Helmrich's brother, Johann, was the progenitor of an even more notable branch, one with which, in its seventeenth- and eighteenth-century days, H. L. Mencken identified even more closely than he did with his own. For it was Johann's son, Otto (1644–1707), even before Lüder Mencke, who (H. L. Mencken later wrote) "broke away from the family business" and "took to the higher learning." It was he, rather than Lüder Mencke, who began the dynasty of Mencken professors at Leipzig, Wittenberg, and Halle.

The most notable figure in this dynasty, "the best of all the Menckens," was Otto's son, Johann Burkhard Mencke (1674–1732), a figure about whom Henry Louis Mencken was to write at length and with whom he was to identify most closely. Johann Burkhard, the prodigy of the family, took his A.B. at Leipzig at age eighteen and his

Ph.D. when he was barely twenty. He traveled to England and was elected a member of the Royal Society when he was but twenty-four, after which he returned to Leipzig as a full professor of history at age twenty-five and assumed the editorship of the *Acta Eruditorum*, the first learned journal in Germany, which his father had helped to found in 1682.

Thus proceeded the early career of Johann Burkhard Mencke—as chronicled by his spiritual, if collateral, descendant two and a half centuries later. We have no reason to question the accuracy of that account, nor the excitement reported by that descendant when he discovered that Johann Burkhard, like himself, had always thought on a grand scale. Johann Burkhard had conceived in his early twenties "an enormous work upon all the ancient historical manuscripts then known in all languages" and had produced a great number of books, including in his later years a magnum opus in three volumes, totaling 6,381 pages. But it was not these volumes that excited Henry Louis Mencken so much as a single volume that Johann Burkhard Mencke had published in 1715, a satire, *De Charlataneria Eruditorum* (*The Charlatanry of the Learned*), which was aimed at scholars and pedants. In reading that satire, H. L. Mencken later wrote, he was delighted "to find that a man of my name . . . had devoted himself so heartily to an enterprise that had engaged me . . . the tracking down of quacks of all sorts," quacks who were "still flourishing mightily" in twentieth-century America. When he first encountered the volume, Mencken wrote a friend, "It gave me a great shock. All my stock in trade was there—loud assertions, heavy buffooneries, slashing attacks on the professors. It really was uncanny."

Johann Burkhard Mencke had indeed lashed out at the "inclination toward fraud" in "the world of scholarship" and the great amount of learning that is "empty of significance." He had remarked, in particular, on self-promoters, pseudogrammarians, orators, scholars with inflated egos, and academic charlatans of all stripes. He also lampooned preachers, whose "outstanding aim seems to be to terrify the rabble by the wonders they invent." Johann Burkhard's distant cousin was so impressed that, more than two centuries later, he arranged for a translation of *De Charlataneria Eruditorum* from the Latin to the English and wrote a lengthy preface himself. The task, he wrote, took on "a sort of filial character."

Johann Burkhard Mencke, whatever his appeal to Henry Louis

Mencken, can hardly be said to have served as a model. H. L. Mencken did not read *Charlataneria* until his mid-thirties, long after he was launched on his own career of attacking quacks and frauds, particularly among the pedagogues. In any case, the later Mencken would have said, it was all in the blood. But the Mencken family had reached its peak of power and influence in Johann Burkhard. The author of *Charlataneria* had a son who, like his cousins, studied and practiced law and who, like his father, edited the *Acta Eruditorum*. But the son, Friedrich Otto Mencke, had but one son of his own, and that child died as a student. Thus ended this particular line of Menckens.

The late seventeenth century and the first three quarters of the eighteenth marked the golden age of Menckens in Germany, the period during which, H. L. Mencken later wrote, "my family reached its highest point." It was, indeed, in the eighteenth century that the modern spelling of the family name was first employed—Mencke being latinized to Menckenius and then shortened to Mencken. At least thirteen Menckens produced books between the mid-seventeenth century and the early nineteenth: "for nearly a hundred years . . . seldom a year passed that did not see some new Mencken book or pamphlet." The Menckens knew and associated with numerous leaders in the cultural and intellectual life of Germany and greater Europe in the eighteenth century: from Bach, whom Lüder Mencke may have helped to bring to Leipzig to serve as cantor of the Thomasschule and organist of the Thomaskirche, to those leading men of mind—Leibnitz, Descartes, Locke, Halley, Boyle, Pascal, Leeuwenhoek, and Newton—who contributed to the *Acta Eruditorum* during the sixty-eight years the Menckens edited it.

The Menckens made their mark in several cities, but in Leipzig it was especially pronounced. There is to this day the Menckestrasse, a major road leading into the city center, named for H. L. Mencken's direct ancestor, Lüder Mencke. In the Thomaskirche there remains a memorial window to the Menckes. One finds no streets by that name in Baltimore, no memorial windows, nor anything else that is likely to endure three centuries. The Menckens flourished in Baltimore, after all, for less than a century—but in Leipzig for nearly two. There was for them a sort of permanence there that they found nowhere else.

It is little wonder, then, that the eighteenth century came to assume such importance for H. L. Mencken, or that he referred to it on several occasions as "that most glorious" of times. Indeed, he later wrote, he *belonged* "to the pre-revolutionary Eighteenth Century." A rage for order, a predisposition toward reason, a religious skepticism, an emphasis on conduct, manner, and being a "gentleman": all characterized both H. L. Mencken and the eighteenth century. That century, Mencken wrote, was a time

> when human existence, according to my notion, was pleasanter and more spacious than ever before or since. . . . It got rid of religion. It lifted music to first place among the arts. . . . It took eating and drinking out of the stable and put them into the parlor. . . . It invented the first really comfortable human habitations ever seen on earth.

Such an estimate by Mencken was more than just historical preference or even a function of personality and temperament—although it was that in part. The eighteenth century was the greatest of centuries, among other reasons, because it was the greatest of centuries for the Menckens.

But that century saw the height of their prominence and influence. After 1800 the family declined. One line, to be sure, continued to prosper and even acquired a certain wider fame in nineteenth-century Germany: the Menckens who moved to Berlin numbered among their sons and daughters the beautiful Luise Wilhelmine, who became the mother of Bismarck, the Iron Chancellor. But this was not the line of the Baltimore Menckens. The decline of that line began, H. L. Mencken wrote, with the "hard times" in Wittenberg just after the turn of the century, "dreadful" times caused by the Napoleonic wars and the occupation of the city by French forces. The years between 1806 and 1815 were "years of terror in the town": the university was closed in 1813, the same year that saw a great fire as well as a renewed bombardment and occupation by the French that nearly destroyed the city.

It was during this period that H. L. Mencken's great-grandfather, Johann Christian August Mencken (1797–1867), came of age, and he was the first in his line for a century and a half to reach manhood without a university degree and a profession. He became a stock raiser near Laas, a country town in Saxony between Leipzig and

Dresden, and married a miller's daughter. When the stock farm failed, Johann Christian moved to another country town, bought and operated an inn, and acquired a great deal of other property. But it was still, in the eyes of his great-grandson, a significant demotion for this descendant of professors, authors, and lawyers. After the Napoleonic wars, the "*cacoethes scribendi* seem[ed] to have died out in the race"—not to be resurrected (except for an occasional reprint or family history) until nearly a century later, and then in America, in Baltimore, where the great-grandson of Johann Christian took to scribbling, and not in German.

Thus, in nineteenth-century Saxony, the Menckens were transformed from a family of writers and thinkers to one of businessmen, and if such was at first a drastic descent, the family soon seemed to take to the one as naturally as they had taken to the other. Johann Christian August Mencken lived for seventy years and had six daughters and one son—H. L. Mencken's grandfather, Burkhardt Ludwig, born in Laas in 1828. The family tradition of high callings gone, Burkhardt at age fourteen was apprenticed to a cigar manufacturer in Oschatz, a small city between Leipzig and Dresden, and there he learned the cigar maker's trade. Times were still hard in Saxony: it had barely recovered from the Napoleonic wars when there began the ferment that led to the revolution of 1848. Both because of the difficult economic times and because of a desire (his grandson later wrote) "to clear out for some more comfortable and amusing country," Burkhardt Mencken set sail for America.

His grandson's fuller description of his motivation tells us perhaps as much about the grandson as about the grandfather. It was common among "the Germans of that day," H. L. Mencken later wrote, "especially those above the rank of workman," to come to America "in much the same spirit that adventurous New Englanders, at the same time, were going to California." In fact, Burkhardt—regardless of the distinction of his forebears—was himself very little above the rank of workman, but he did have at least limited means. As his grandson continued, in notes written in 1925 for the use of his first biographer:

It will be observed that he was not the typical immigrant of legend. He had a *Fach* [a trade], he had money in hand [at least one hundred thalers], and he had a very considerable pride in his race.

He had taken no part in the political events of 1848 in Saxony. He was, indeed, no democrat.

It was very important, writing in 1925, that the grandson—who was more interested in matters of class and rank than has sometimes been supposed—make that point. It was especially important because H. L. Mencken, as a man without the usual trappings of inherited standing and privilege (social position, university education, old *American* family name) and with the reputation, in many circles, of a street fighter, would have no other way to communicate that family distinction to the world at large. So much more would have been the case, so much greater the anxiety about rank and class, in the mid-nineteenth century for young Burkhardt Mencken, who, after all, was himself but a cigar maker, who had no interest at all in books, art, or high culture, and had no other way to demonstrate the superiority he felt.

It was certainly not for that reason alone, but it may have been partly for that reason that Burkhardt Mencken, after landing in Baltimore in November 1848 and becoming solvent, began to detach himself from his fellow Germans. He was, his grandson later observed, a "generally confident and even somewhat cocky" man, short in stature (about five feet, five inches) but showing an independent spirit from the beginning, as well as a certain defiance of civil authority. On his naturalization certificate, signed in Baltimore in October 1852, Burkhardt had a witness swear that he had been in the United States "five years at least," when in fact he had been in America fewer than four. He was far from the helpless immigrant, then, overwhelmed by the New World. To the contrary, he made his way quickly, applied himself so diligently to his work as cigar maker, then storekeeper, that he was soon able to buy and run his own store. Later he turned exclusively to the wholesale trade in tobacco and eventually prospered in that line.

But he continued to have little to do with other Baltimore Germans, most of whom, his grandson wrote, were "ignoramuses of the petty trading class." He refused to join their societies, declined to attend their churches, had "no apparent taste for [their] *Biergemütlichkeit*," considered "nearly all of them nobodies by his standards." In short, he "kept away from them." There was, to be sure, a small class of "superior Germans" in Baltimore, "but they were richer than he was, and hence he had little truck with them." When he married, in 1851, he chose not another German but rather Harriet McLelland, of English and Scottish descent. Thus, the language of Burkhardt Mencken's household became English, not German: his five children, his grandson later wrote, "never learned more than the rudiments of his mother tongue." And when the time came to baptize the children—though an unbeliever, Burkhardt held to such conventions—he had them baptized in the Protestant Episcopal church, not the Lutheran.

It would appear at first that Burkhardt Mencken was just following that tried-and-true pattern of most nineteenth-century American immigrants: he was assimilating, although in his case with a vengeance, greatly accelerating the process, doing in ten years what other immigrants took thirty or forty to accomplish. But that was not altogether the case either, for he did not truly assimilate. He remained at least as alienated from the native population of Baltimore as from the German, in fact more alienated because he was, of course, by national origin and culture, German, whatever his opinion of other German Americans.

Thus, from the beginning, the Menckens found themselves doubly detached from their society, cut off both from mainstream American culture, particularly the Anglo-American power structure of old Baltimore, and also from their fellow Germans, both the "petty tradesmen" and those few wealthy Germans in the city. The one form of separation—from English Baltimore—was inevitable, but the other was and would continue to be a separation by choice. For no matter how certain of their position back in Germany, once in America the Menckens realized that the traits that distinguished them from other Germans were not as obvious, especially to non-Germans, as the traits they had in common. From the beginning the Menckens *had* to remain apart in order to remind native-born Americans, their fellow Germans, and, most of all, themselves, just who and what they were. Burkhardt instilled a habit of detachment that would be hard to break.

If the Menckens of Baltimore were a family with a heightened consciousness of origins, H. L. Mencken's other forebears—the McLellands, Abhaus, and Gegners—virtually sprang from nowhere, it seemed, in early-nineteenth-century America. We know little, as Mencken knew little, about their European origins. The McLellands, the family into which Burkhardt Mencken had married in 1851, had come to Baltimore from Jamaica (and, before that, Northern Ireland) in the first half of the nineteenth century. From all indications, they cut no great figure. When Mencken's great-grandfather McLelland died in Baltimore in 1844, his widow returned to Jamaica for a time but came back to Baltimore in 1846, bringing with her a nine-year-old daughter, Harriet. Harriet McLelland would seem to have assured herself a bright economic future when at age fourteen she married the up-and-coming Burkhardt Mencken. Within ten years they had five children, the second of whom—and the first son—was August Mencken, who was to become the father of H. L. Mencken. When August was eight years old, Harriet McLelland Mencken died of tuberculosis, just short of her twenty-sixth birthday. She was buried in Baltimore's Western Cemetery under a tombstone reading "Leaving a Husband and Four Children to Mourn Her."

We know even less about the Gegners, Mencken's maternal grandmother's family, than we do about the McLellands. Primarily, we are aware that they came to America in the 1830s from lower Bavaria, where they had operated coach lines. But we have somewhat more knowledge of the Abhaus, his maternal grandfather's family. More representative German immigrants than the Menckens, they were poor, amiable, and without an elevated sense of their own importance in the scheme of things. Mencken's grandfather Abhau had been born in Hesse in 1827, descended in part—family lore had it—from French Huguenots who had fled to Hesse in the seventeenth century. H. L. Mencken *knew* about the Menckens; he could only hypothesize about the Abhaus, and on one such occasion he concluded that, since *kohlenabbau* meant "coal mining" and there were numerous mines in Hesse, it was not unlikely that some aboriginal Abhau had been a miner.

In any case, in the early nineteenth century, one Carl Heinrich Abhau, having been orphaned as a child, was turned over to an uncle who trained him as a cabinetmaker. He then ran away from home at age twenty and took to sea as a ship's carpenter, finally settling in Baltimore and marrying Eva Gegner in 1852. He had a tougher time of it than Burkhardt Mencken, carrying more heavily the burden of being a foreigner in this era of the Know-Nothings in American politics. According to his grandson, Abhau was stoned "several times" on the streets of Baltimore. Nor did he flourish economically: he was poor all his life, and his sons eventually had to support him. But his grandson H. L. Mencken was to be exceedingly fond of him, and if that grandson identified himself principally with the loftier Menckens, he also found a part of his identity in the Abhaus and Gegners. "I am myself partly a peasant, and glad of it," Mencken wrote in 1921 to one he considered a bona fide peasant, Theodore Dreiser. "If it were not for my peasant blood, the Mencken element would have made a professor out of me. . . . Thank God that my mother's grandfather was a Bauer, with all of a Bauer's capacity for believing in the romantic."

Thus the two families, the *bauern*-turned-workers-and-craftsmen and the *gelehrten*-turned-tradesmen, lived, both rather obscurely, in the Baltimore of the 1860s and 1870s. The Abhaus, pure German, entered fully into the life of the German-American community, speaking German, attending the Lutheran church. The Menckens, half German and that sometimes reluctantly, held themselves at a distance from the German community, speaking only English and attending no church at all except for ceremonial baptisms. The Menckens' son August was educated in a private school, where he excelled in mathematics, but he left school in his early teens and traveled to Pennsylvania, where he worked at various jobs. He then returned to Baltimore, learned the cigar maker's trade, and worked as a journeyman in West Virginia before returning a second time to Baltimore to work in his father's small tobacco business. Desiring more independence and full of ideas he could not implement in his father's firm, about the time he turned twenty August followed a family tradition by striking out on his own. With his teenaged brother, Henry, he established the cigar manufacturing firm of Aug. Mencken & Bro. at some point between 1873 and 1875. Burkhardt Mencken apparently supported his sons' effort, at least materially, for according to his grandson he staked them with a supply of tobacco and, probably, a certain amount of cash. August Mencken was in charge of the factory and office. Henry—"a very indolent fellow," his nephew later wrote—was in charge of sales. The new company struggled for a couple of years, but by its third year it was beginning to make a profit.

Although August Mencken broke from his father's business, he retained many of Burkhardt's attitudes, particularly toward other German Americans. August, too, was "inclined to be anti-German," H. L. Mencken later wrote, indeed seemed at times to have "had an active distaste for [Germans]." If anything, August Mencken carried his apostasy one step further than his father's. Although Burkhardt had rejected other German Americans in Baltimore, he had retained great pride in Germany and in the position the Menckens had held there. In 1867 he had traveled to his old home and returned with a great store of documents of family history. But August disdained both the Germans around him *and* the family heritage. As H. L. Mencken later wrote, his father's "indifferent if not to say Philistine attitude" toward German *kultur* and the family glories was suggested by the fact that he registered the family coat-of-arms as the trademark of his business. August Mencken might have considered that appropriate, but to his son it was vulgar. "An oval bearing [the coat of arms] was pasted on every box of cigars that issued from his factory . . ." Moreover, the coat of arms as it appeared on the label was "incorrectly blazoned."

August Mencken was also a more affable man than his father, a rather handsome figure about five feet nine inches tall, with dark brown eyes. He looked, his son later wrote, "far more the Celt than the Teuton." In his early twenties August lived, among other places, in a Baltimore hotel that served as headquarters for the city's professional baseball team, and there he developed an interest in the sporting life that was never to leave him. He also enjoyed the *gemütlichkeit* his father rejected, and on one festive occasion—a picnic probably, Henry Mencken was later told—August met young Anna Abhau: "he struck her as a kind of comic character and [she] laughed at him for some time afterward. I assume he attempted to entertain her with clowning . . ."

She laughed, but she also began seeing August Mencken, and on November 11, 1879, they were married. August was twenty-five, Anna twenty-one. It was the only marriage among his children that Burkhardt Mencken did not play some part in arranging, and even in this case he probably determined the place—not the Lutheran church of the Abhaus but rather St. John the Baptist Episcopal Church—and he apparently chose the minister. It must have seemed

15

a good marriage for Anna Abhau. August Mencken's cigar business was beginning to prosper, and the Menckens, even in the New World—if for reasons different than in the Old—were a family of some relative standing. It was a wise marriage, but most of all, Henry Mencken later insisted, it was "a love match."

# Chapter 2

# HAPPY DAYS

H e was born under a lucky star, H. L. Mencken sometimes said, and from the beginning there seemed little doubt that he was indeed a favorite of the gods. A *stammhalter,* the eldest son of an eldest son to at least the fifth generation, he was the plump, healthy child of the self-satisfied Baltimore bourgeoisie, and he felt special for another reason as well. He entered the world on September 12—the proudest holiday of the state he came to call "incomparably the loveliest"—in the city he came to believe the most livable of any on earth and in a year, 1880, he believed the best of all times to have been born.

September 12 was Defenders' Day, marking the triumph of the besieged Baltimoreans over the attacking British in the Battle of North Point during the War of 1812. Throughout Henry Mencken's childhood the holiday was to be marked by parades, fireworks, and the cancellation of school. The only reason Defenders' Day was not so observed on the day of his birth was that this particular September 12 fell on a Sunday and the festivities were scheduled for the following day. Henry Mencken was born at 9:00 P.M.—just before "the police raided ten or twelve saloons," he later wrote—and his single greatest stroke of good fortune, given Mencken's later penchant for ill omens, may have been that he was not born three hours later. For much of his adult life H. L. Mencken was to dread the 13th, the date on which both his father and his mother died as well as the date of many other unpleasant events in his life. Although he never remarked on his particularly narrow escape in 1880, he invariably took note of other occurrences on the 13th. For this most rational of men was, in many ways, among the most superstitious.

The circumstances of the birth itself were largely unremarkable, at least for the child. Henry Louis Mencken—named for his uncle Henry and for one of his grandmother's sons who had died in infancy—was born at 380 West Lexington Street, in a small three-story house his father had rented for sixteen dollars a month. The house, in a respectable residential district inhabited chiefly by Germans, was in a section of West Baltimore not far removed from the country. Henry was delivered, at a charge of ten dollars, by an old German doctor with muttonchops who had, the newborn later wrote, "the reputation for being far from gentle in his handling of patients." It was not for that reason alone that the birth was somewhat difficult for twenty-two-year-old Anna Mencken. Mrs. Mencken was a small woman and Henry a large child.

The first few months of the life of Harry Mencken (for such he soon came to be called) were spent in the house on West Lexington, less than a half mile from the grave of Edgar Allan Poe and nearly as close to the birthplace, fifteen years later, of the only Baltimorean whose fame would come to exceed H. L. Mencken's own: George Herman (Babe) Ruth. At some point during Harry's first year the Menckens moved to another rented house, a mile south on Russell Street. It was there, in 1882, that their second son, Charles Edward, was born. As for young Harry Mencken, he continued to be—he later wrote—"encapsulated in affection, and kept fat, saucy and contented." He was baptized when a few months old in the Episcopal church; again the half-British Menckens won out over the pure German Abhaus. He was photographed for the first time at five months, and he learned to talk early.

The Menckens remained on Russell Street for about two years before August Mencken bought, for $2,900, a handsome, newly constructed row house a dozen blocks northwest on Hollins Street—"not a German neighborhood," H. L. Mencken later wrote, although there were German families in it. Harry first became aware of the cosmos, he later remarked, on his third birthday, in 1883, sitting on his mother's lap, looking out the second-floor window of his father's factory on Baltimore Street. What he saw was a great burst of light—gaslights and marchers carrying torches—although later he was uncertain whether the occasion had been the celebration of the Battle of North Point or, more likely, the Summer Nights Carnival of the Order of Orioles.

Other impressions were soon registered on his consciousness, and most of them involved his mother. Anna Mencken was pretty, with blue eyes and light hair; her son resembled her more than he did his father. Anna ran the house with a firm hand—a later son said she was not a woman "to be trifled with"—but she was gentle with her children, and Harry always took his troubles to her rather than to his father.

Mencken never wrote as much about Anna as he did about his father, but he wrote enough in *Happy Days* and in unpublished manuscripts, autobiographical notes, and letters to friends that we can construct a rather full portrait of her as a young mother. She emerges as one who attended faithfully to wifely and motherly duties, who was greatly supportive of her children, who was a "great worrier" with "a generally jittery disposition," who had set ways of doing things and was intolerant of those who deviated from those ways. That is, she was very little different from any other Victorian housewife. Given to propriety in speech and manner, she always used "clear and excellent" English, her son later wrote. She was also fluent in German, although she spoke it rarely except to the hired girls and to market men and repairmen who dropped by. When her father came over, he would speak German but she would reply in English. She liked to sing to her children, was especially fond of ballads she had collected as a girl, and was given to proverbs and maxims in both English and German. Although she did not read a great deal—other than the *Ladies' Home Journal* every month "from end to end"— she was generally well informed and often demonstrated a sense of humor, laughing at the foibles of people in the community.

Anna was the center of the world of young Harry Mencken, the confines of which in his preschool years did not extend much beyond the Hollins Street house and yard. The long, narrow backyard— nearly a hundred feet long but only twenty-five across—seemed "a strange, wild land of endless discoveries and enchantments," with its assortment of peach, cherry, plum, and pear trees as well as a grape arbor. Since the trees had not yet reached great heights, the backyard was often a "blaze of sunlight." Harry watched as Anna Mencken planted and nurtured zinnias, petunias, geraniums, dahlias, and sun-flowers, as well as radishes, carrots, and tomatoes.

His brother, Charles, twenty months younger, was Harry's companion by day and night: in their early years they slept together and by day they explored house and garden. They were forbidden to play in the cellar before it was cemented in 1885, but they sneaked downstairs anyway whenever their mother was away. Upstairs, they slid down banisters and played with the family cat. In winter Harry and Charlie played store, usually selling books. They also enjoyed the company of the hired girls, some Irish, some German, and they later remembered one in particular—"the least intelligent but most faithful"—who played Parcheesi with them on winter evenings and looked the other way while they raided the kitchen.

Harry Mencken was introduced to the world of books long before he started school. His mother often read to him stories such as *Robinson Crusoe, Wild Animals for Children,* and *Buffalo Bill's Wild West.* One book in particular he remembered: "My first recollection of beautiful letters has to do with 'The Story of Simple Simon.' " He recalled "very vividly" sitting with his mother "at an upstairs window in Hollins street, looking down upon a snowstorm," hearing of Simon and reflecting on what a comic rustic he was: "Indeed, I sometimes suspect that my lifelong view of the American yokel was generated by poor Simon. . . . I still know half of his saga by heart." By the time he was seven Harry had his own copy of "Simple Simon," self-inscribed "Harry Mencken, 1887."

All in all, life at Hollins Street was pleasant. There is no reason to challenge Mencken's own characterization of these early childhood years as "happy days." Rewards "for good conduct," he later wrote, were abundant, and "the system of criminal justice . . . very mild": he was paddled for misdemeanors, "but always gently," and even paddling ceased by the age of six or seven. He was surrounded by compatriots and admirers. Next door lived his uncle Henry and two cousins very close to his own age. His grandfather Mencken lived not far away, in a big house on West Fayette Street, and Mencken later recalled Burkhardt Mencken, dressed in a long-tailed black coat, coming by in his one-seat carriage to take Harry and the other grandchildren for a ride: "He drove at a violent pace, and driving with him over the cobblestoned streets of . . . Baltimore [was] exciting." On Christmas morning Harry and Charlie and their two cousins always paid a visit to their grandfather's house and were greeted with abundant gifts. Christmas, in general, was a "gaudy festival" in the Mencken home. Preparations began immediately after Thanksgiving, and Anna gave much attention to the selection and the trimming of the tree. But even then Mencken—who later came to dread Christmas above all other times of the year—recognized the transient joys of the season: "Before Christmas afternoon was half over, I always came down with violent pains in the stomach from overeating and had to go to bed."

If there was a dark side to life on Hollins Street in the early 1880s, it was the shadow hanging over every American childhood in the nineteenth century—the threat of serious illness and death. In Baltimore of the late nineteenth century, typhoid and smallpox were annual threats, and nearby marshes and mosquitoes made malaria a threat as well. "At night in summer," Mencken wrote later, "I slept under a hot and dreadful mosquito-net, for there were no fly screens on the windows, and at mealtime the flies swarmed over the dinner table." Mencken escaped most of the serious diseases, including diphtheria and scarlet fever and, for the time being, malaria, and fell prey mainly to routine afflictions such as measles and chicken pox. But he had from his earliest years respiratory and throat infections, including tonsillitis, and he faced frequent unpleasant moppings of his throat with ferric chloride, which, he later suspected, did permanent damage.

Thus, home and garden, the world of 1524 Hollins Street, was ruled by Mencken's mother, and Anna Mencken was a benevolent despot. In that particular, H. L. Mencken's case may have been precisely the opposite of that facing the alienated artist of legend, misunderstood by family, never finding the security of place. In fact, in those early years, he was blessed with a superfluity of place, an overabundance of support and understanding: he was made to feel so secure in the scheme of things that the world beyond 1524 Hollins would never quite measure up. Even his next-door cousins, Pauline and John Henry, would soon be found wanting: John Henry, he would decide, was a "numskull." No better were their younger brother and sisters, their "stupid and lazy" father, Uncle Henry, and Harry Mencken's other relatives, save one. "Dislike for a cousin . . . is natural and probably almost universal," Mencken later wrote. "He is a faint simulacrum of one's self, and hence tends to be a burlesque." But more than that, no cousin was an inhabitant of Harry Mencken's own household. Throughout his life Mencken was to feel, even more strongly than most people, that what was believed and affirmed in his childhood home was the only truth.

When Harry, after age four or five, did begin to circulate in the world beyond 1524 Hollins Street with some regularity, his guide to that larger world was principally his father. August Mencken gave his son that same sense of security in the outside world that Anna Mencken had ensured at home. "There was never an instant in my childhood," Mencken once wrote, "when I doubted my father's capacity to resolve any difficulty that menaced me, or to beat off any danger."

August Mencken, in his modest realm, was a supremely confident man, neither a worrier, as Anna was, nor a stickler for detail—or propriety. "He was usually pretty placid, not to say complacent," H. L. Mencken recalled, "though on occasion he could yield to his feelings and swear fluently." By his late twenties August had become a successful businessman and high-tariff Republican (breaking with his father, a Democrat with southern sympathies). "A curious mixture of snob and Philistine," his son later described him, he was "always the center of his small world, and in my eyes a man of illimitable puissance and resourcefulness." He also seemed at times an amusing figure to young Harry, combining an informal house language with negligent grammar, "barbarisms" of English that would later "outrage" the schoolboy Harry. August Mencken, as his son described him, seems an unlikely combination of other traits as well. On the one hand, he was playful with his young sons, on the other "always . . . a little remote." On the one hand, he was something of a klutz, too clumsy to shave himself, too inept to perform routine household tasks; on the other, he was a captain of industry, if an exceedingly modest one, an authoritative figure who met his obligations, believed he was good to his employees, and possessed, in some measure, the habit of command.

August appears to have been a good husband to Anna Mencken, as judged by the standards of the day, but his business interests and other outside activities attracted most of his time. When Harry was five years old, Aug. Mencken & Bro. moved out of their quarters in Baltimore Street into a new, larger four-story warehouse, constructed at the cost of $15,000, not far away on Paca Street. When he was in town, August would come home for dinner, the large meal of the day, shortly after noon, and afterward would take a short nap and return to work until 5:30 or 6:00 P.M. But he was often out of town, taking two or three trips a year to tobacco-growing regions of Pennsylvania and, on other occasions, to Ohio and Connecticut, as well as traveling nearly weekly to Washington, where he had opened a branch in 1879. Occasionally he went to Cuba, from which he returned loaded down with gifts and full of tales of excitement and enchantment that made Harry Mencken curious about an even larger world. The young Harry loved his father's tobacco business, the "romantic place" he found the cigar factory to be, the smell of fresh tobacco that was always to delight him. He loved to go with his father to Washington, beginning at age five or six, to visit the saloons his father called on. He would sit at the bar, drinking sarsaparilla and eating pretzels as August Mencken talked baseball and passed out complimentary samples of his wares. On one occasion a Supreme Court justice patted Harry on the back and gave him a quarter.

But August was busy with far more than tobacco. A faithful reader of the *Sporting Times,* a baseball organ of the 1880s, he became a stockholder in the Washington baseball club, then for a time its vice president, establishing a sort of informal baseball headquarters in the Washington branch of his business. Unlike his father, August Mencken was a joiner, belonging to the Knights Templars and the Shriners, both Masonic orders, wearing their exotic regalia, and attending their conventions. August Mencken belonged not only to the King David's Lodge but also to the Phoenix Royal Arch Chapter and the Boumi Temple of the Ancient Arabic Order of the Mystic Shrine—an impressive fraternal résumé for one whose son was later to make his reputation debunking all such brotherhood and its whooping.

H. L. Mencken later suspected that some of these fraternal activities were undertaken for the good of his father's business, and that much of the time spent in such activities was given to friendly drinking, an activity August pursued outside fraternal confines as well. Receipts in H. L. Mencken's scrapbooks reveal that August bought a great deal of whiskey from one John F. Reus on Columbia Avenue; he bought even more beer, partly for business customers who stopped by Hollins Street, mostly for his own consumption. Much of his time at home in warm weather he spent in the "summerhouse" built by Grandfather Abhau in the backyard, talking and drinking with his brother, Henry.

When Harry Mencken was not accompanying his father to Washington or to the plant on Paca Street, or going on family outings to Schützen Park and various German beer gardens in West Baltimore (for, in matters bibulous and culinary, the Menckens were still at least half German), he was out exploring the world on his own. At about age six, he later wrote, "I began journeying every day from what was then the farthest reach of West Baltimore to [the city center]. . . . I came to know all the principal buildings and all the main streets." He began with the area around 1524 Hollins Street, first Union Square—just across the street—and the alleys behind his house.

Union Square, south of Hollins Street, was a garden spot of West Baltimore. Opened in 1847 on land given to the city, the square gave the young Mencken a feeling of spaciousness not always to be found in an eastern seaboard city. As he looked out the front windows of his house he saw the trees of the square, and those of the House of the Good Shepherd, a convent and home for wayward girls to the southwest. This "enclosure in green," Mencken later wrote, "may have had a good deal to do with formulating my view of life. I have never had any sense of being hemmed in . . ."

When he looked out the back windows of his house, however, Harry saw something quite different—a world less serene and less orderly than Union Square, but one more intriguing, much more exciting, and even more important to his education. The small houses in the alley behind Hollins Street had black inhabitants, and Harry and Charlie found playmates, mentors, tale tellers, and characters of unending fascination among them: a one-eyed man named Scotty who lived a life of ease, kept by a number of women; another black man, Wesley, who served as alley philosopher; an ancient woman, Aunt Sophie (who lived near if not in the alley), whose days were spent going to funerals, white and black, all over West Baltimore; another black woman, a hard worker who lived with "her worthless white lover and their family of six or seven mulatto children . . . poor creatures with yellow, stupid faces"; and, most enlightening of all for young Harry Mencken, a plethora of black evangelists, male and female, often in action seven days a week, preaching, praying, and singing. He heard hundreds of their sermons and was particularly struck by a female evangelist dressed in purple who made such a noise that the white inhabitants of Hollins Street called in the police. All this was spectacle, pure delight for Harry, but he was also genuinely moved by much of what he saw behind his house. The alley dwellers, he recalled, "were extremely kind to their children, and devoted a great deal of their time to looking after them." Mencken remembered in particular the sight of a black worker, in worn and dirty clothes, greeting his daughter: she looked at him "proudly . . . it was obvious that there was great affection between them."

As a young child, then, Harry Mencken literally faced onto two worlds—the one the orderly Anglo-American and German-American world of Hollins Street and Union Square, the other the folk culture of African Americans up from the hot South. It was partly because of the world of the alley—the world of tall tales, evangelical religion, and southern foods and speech and manner—that the later Mencken, on several occasions, claimed he was a southerner. Such was a dubious claim in most regards and one that will later bear closer scrutiny.

Indeed, most of the world Harry Mencken encountered in the mid-1880s, when he left the alleys behind Hollins Street, was, with certain exceptions, anything but southern. Two blocks west of 1524 Hollins the open lots began. But walking east, toward the center of Baltimore, Harry would have encountered a bustling, raucous, prosperous place, with all the sights and sounds and smells of an up-to-date eastern seaboard city. If it was a city still tied to the past in many ways (so close to the early days of the Republic, we should remember, that the day after Harry Mencken's birth more than a dozen veterans of the War of 1812 had paraded through its streets), it was also a city with its eye very much on the future. Baltimore in the 1880s numbered some 400,000 people, nearly one fourth of whom were German Americans, mostly of recent vintage. The city thus had numerous German schools, churches, societies, and newspapers. It was, H. L. Mencken later wrote, a "charming place," with horsecars and streetcars, neighborhood shops, beer gardens, theaters, and restaurants, as well as freedom from moralists and antivice crusaders. In short, it had a "talent for Gemütlichkeit," with the Irish as well as Germans enlivening the old Anglo-American Baltimore.

It was also a place and time in which youngsters like Harry Mencken still classified people by ethnic and national origins—a habit that would be difficult to break in later years. "It was believed by every boy of that era," Mencken later wrote, "that Chinamen ate rats and were all opium addicts. It was also believed that they were so frugal that they lived on eight cents a day." His own grandfather was "violently anti-Semitic," Mencken wrote a friend many years later, and Grandfather Mencken was hardly alone:

At 1403 W. Baltimore Street, between the oyster-bay and the tea-store, was a china and tinware store kept by a Jew whose name I forget. He was a hideous creature with sore eyes. One day a woman customer ran out of his store crying that he had tried to kiss her. He was arrested on a charge of assault, and the magistrate at the watch-house . . . fined him $20. Ever thereafter, until he finally moved away, he was known as the $20 Jew in the neighborhood. My mother never spoke of him in any other way. She refused to patronize him, and so did most of the other housewives in Hollins street.

Such memories—included not in the published *Happy Days* (1940) but in the unpublished manuscript "Happy Days: Additions, Corrections and Explanatory Notes," released in the 1980s—perhaps tell us more about the prejudices of Mencken's childhood Baltimore, and of Anna Mencken, than he intended to reveal. The Baltimore of that era he himself later pictured as a nearly perfect place in a nearly perfect age, a city, he would contend, at a particularly fortunate juncture in its history, after the first great wave of European immigration which brought the Germans and the Irish—to one of which he belonged, the other of which he approved—but before the second great wave which brought, in Mencken's later words, the "flood of Italians, Russian Jews, Greeks, Lithuanians, and other half-civilized foreigners" who "submerged" both the Anglo-American and the German-American cultures of his youth.

Such words reveal a great deal about this grandson of a German immigrant who had been, in the 1850s, the target of stones thrown by Know-Nothings in the streets of Baltimore. When he considered the more recent immigrant groups, this later opponent of nativism, of insularity in American culture, was in certain respects a nativist, a Know-Nothing himself. It was as if, looking back, H. L. Mencken wanted all time frozen at some point in that charmed era of the 1880s, a time when the Germans and Irish (and, he would add, Jews, if of German origin) had given their richness and flavor to American life—that is, a time when his *own* people had arrived and were secure—but before the Italians and Slavs and Russian Jews had arrived in force and before the "low-grade native whites" had come to Baltimore from the Appalachian slopes. That, to Mencken looking back, had been a magical period, never to be recaptured or duplicated in his lifetime.

The education of Henry Mencken—absorbed through Simple Simon, back alleys, and the world his father showed him in Baltimore and Washington—was well under way when he began the formal phase of that education at age six at Knapp's Institute. That institute, begun in 1852 by Friedrich Knapp, a German schoolmaster of the old style, had flourished in the mid-nineteenth century before declining somewhat with the competition of the public schools in the 1880s. It was Harry Mencken's grandfather, Burkhardt, who determined that he should attend Knapp's Institute, although August agreed in large measure. He himself was opposed to the public schools, particularly the "German-English" public schools, in which German was the primary language. He believed that German Americans should not have their children educated in German at the taxpayers' expense.

Although Knapp's Institute itself was largely for German Americans, it also included various other ethnic groups, including Jews, in addition to native-born Americans of English and Scots-Irish descent. The latter group, in fact, performed least well at Knapp's, indeed seemed to Professor Knapp "intellectually underprivileged"—one of many early observations that helped to convince Mencken that "the average American of the old stock was an idiot." The school was located, when Harry began in 1886, two miles east of Union Square near the center of Baltimore; in 1890 it moved west to Hollins Street. Knapp, who was already an old man when Harry first encountered him, seemed at first an intimidating presence, wearing the uniform of the German schoolmaster, a black alpaca coat with long tails, a white string necktie, and a plug hat. Overseeing all aspects of his school, he opened each day by playing his violin, conducted a sort of military inspection in the courtyard, and handled administrative duties from caning to pulling teeth.

Yet Harry Mencken liked the old man and later recalled the school routine with pleasure. He would travel by streetcar or horsecar from Hollins Street each morning, in winter wearing heavy flannel underwear and a polo cap. His schoolroom was heated by a stove, which roasted those who sat too near, and left chilled those too far away—as a probable result of which Harry Mencken caught five or six bad colds a winter. After a plump and healthy early childhood, he had become thin and rather weak by the age of seven or eight, had become round-shouldered, and, for a time, wore shoulder braces. According to his report cards, for a time he missed school rather frequently because of illness. But he was vigorous enough to like baseball; though a poor hitter with a weak throwing arm, he was a good base runner. And, like the other boys at Knapp's, he was smitten by a "small, straight-backed, black-haired, dark-eyed" German girl named Anna Encke, the daughter of a dressmaker.

From the beginning Mencken excelled academically—in everything, curiously, except German—and his report cards also contain outstanding marks in "Deportment," "Industry," "Advancement," and "Cleanliness." One report also contains a remark by Friedrich Knapp: "A good boy and a good scholar." Harry used the McGuffey *Reader*, although he did not like writing compositions until a red-haired orphan girl, Mary Schilling, taught him "that concocting them might be stimulating." After that his interest in writing accelerated. His composition books, signed "Harry Mencken," include essays on coal, electricity, rapid transit, forests, the circus, Washington, D.C., Baltimore, Fort McHenry, and the U.S. Navy. They also include the draft of an address he delivered on Friedrich Knapp's birthday in 1892, in which the dutiful student presents the old professor an easy chair as a "token of esteem and love." The essays are generally well written, marked by close observation and attention to detail if hardly by a style in any way distinctive.

But Harry Mencken was already demonstrating a keen interest in language. One Knapp composition book contains, as Mencken later described it, a "boyish effort to record the equivalents of the word *man* in 26 foreign languages"—some of which Harry Mencken invented. He also picked up Yiddish phrases from Jewish students at Knapp's and, following that, sat in on a class in Hebrew given for the Jewish students and learned the Hebrew alphabet. "There was no enmity between the Chosen and the *Goyim* in the old professor's establishment," Mencken later wrote, and in general he was right. All the Jews were of "German-Jewish origin, and came of well-to-do families."

Harry's learning between the years of six and twelve was hardly confined to Knapp's Institute. A good deal of it continued to occur at 1524 Hollins Street. In the summer of 1887, before he was seven, he had "got down [his] first book," and by age eight he had felt "the powerful suction of beautiful letters." In 1886 the Enoch Pratt Free Library had opened a branch in Hollins Street, and soon Harry was checking out books with regularity, as well as pulling his father's books down from the shelves of his secretary at home.

By the time he was nine Harry Mencken had already acquired a critical taste of sorts, one that was never to change. Upon trying *Grimm's Fairy Tales* at age eight, he discovered that he was "born . . . without any natural taste for fairy tales, or, indeed, for any other writing of a fanciful and unearthly character." He had an equal distaste for the stories of Horatio Alger and other such "hortatory" juvenile fiction of the time. But early in 1889 he pulled from his father's secretary a volume the discovery of which—he later wrote in the kind of overstatement that marked him as more a product of his time than he would have liked to admit—was "probably the most stupendous event of my whole life." The volume was *The Adventures of Huckleberry Finn*. His father was not a bookish man, but he did like Mark Twain and had eight or ten other Twain works in his modest library. Harry soon read them all. He had found his early literary idol, and one of his idols for life.

Indeed, the young Mencken might have considered himself a kind of urban Huck Finn—even at an early age, independent of spirit, skeptical in nature, with a "highly literal mind." But in truth, rather than Huck, he was more nearly Huck's adventurous but respectable friend, Tom Sawyer—the product of good family, still more conventional than not. No Huck Finn would have given his teacher a "token of esteem and love," but Tom Sawyer would have. Like Tom, Harry was well fed, clothed, and sheltered, faithfully attending school and sometimes even church, still with a number of romantic notions, and more a spectator of than a participant in a life of adventure and danger.

And like the leader of "Tom Sawyer's Gang," the young Harry tried to conjure up that adventure and danger which was missing in his own life. He joined the Hollins Street Gang, a crew made up largely of prepubescent schoolboys of respectable family but including a few older boys "who instructed the rest of us in riot and infamy." Despite Mencken's later remark that the Hollins Street neighborhood was not predominantly German, most of the gang members were in fact German American; and no member, according to Mencken, "ever reached any genuine distinction in later life." Their various activities—to which they often invited the black boys in the alley—included not riot and infamy but rather setting off fireworks, following fire engines, stealing boxes to build election-night bonfires, raiding vegetable stands, and taking fruit and nuts from the B & O warehouse.

At least H. L. Mencken, looking back nearly a half century later, recalled such activities. He also recalled exploring the treacherous territory west of Union Square, including the lime kilns and slaughterhouses of Steuart Hill and the large gully known as "the Canyon." The Hollins Street Gang was not nearly so tough as its rivals in working-class neighborhoods, not nearly so expert in fighting. But it, too, had its territory to defend, and its members invaded other territories at their peril. Mencken later recalled the time at age ten when he was robbed of his handkerchief and pocket knife by "two boy highwaymen" carrying a "cat-and-rat rifle" and a knife. "It was a thrilling affair for all hands, including the victim."

Such was life for this Tom Sawyer of Hollins Street. When Harry Mencken was not stirring up trouble with other members of the gang, he was seeking adventure with his younger brother Charlie—sledding at great speeds on hills in West Baltimore, roughing up cats and rats "and other such fauna" in back alleys. Once, accompanied by Charlie, he sneaked into a funeral parlor to see the corpse of a black man who had been hanged, an image that haunted him for many nights. He also had a few close calls. Once he fell into a pile of burning leaves and had to be rescued by a friend. Another time, on the spring morning the Druid Hill Avenue cable line began operation, he was hit and knocked down by the side of a cable car rounding a bend. "Why my legs were not cut off by the front wheels," he recalled much later, "I do not know to this day." He remembered only the screams of a nearby woman who had seen the accident—and the good luck he always seemed to carry with him in those early days. He and Charlie roamed the streets, watching workers at their tasks— bakers, waffle men on the streets, tombstone cutters, wheelwrights, and, most exciting of all, the iron molders in the shops of the B & O railroad. Most of the workers Harry saw in the streets were Irish immigrants. As he put it in the unpublished "Happy Days: Additions, Corrections and Explanatory Notes," "The Italians and other such anthropoid strangers had not yet arrived."

While Harry and Charlie explored much of West Baltimore, their favorite place was the livery stable near Paca Street where August Mencken kept his horse. The boys got to know the black hostlers and carriage washers, though none of the Paca Street contingent quite measured up to Jim, the black carriage washer near Hollins Street. Harry found another early hero in Felix Cohlens, cousin and employee of the stable owner, who taught him to drive August Mencken's horse and buggy: "I believe I admired Mr. Felix more than I admired any other man then extant, save, perhaps, it was my father himself." He admired nearly as much Sam Morrison, the blacksmith, and put in a great deal of time "marvelling at the skill of the smiths." After an afternoon at the stables and blacksmith's shop, he and Charlie often stopped by Ehoff's saloon nearby, where they ate pretzels out of the bowl on the bar. They visited much less frequently the nearby saloon operated by William Ruth, soon to be the father of Babe. His establishment, with the words "Union Bar" over the door, was frequented mainly by laborers. August Mencken did not approve of it.

When Harry and Charlie were confined to 1524 Hollins, they now had to share the house and yard with a sister and another brother— Gertrude, born in 1886, and August, named for his father, born in 1889—but they found much to occupy them there as well. Although Mencken later remarked on how mechanically inept he was as a child, he and his brother built railroads and constructed ponds in the backyard, even rigged up a telephone. They kept a series of animals—always a dog and a cat, occasionally rabbits, guinea pigs, frogs, once even a goat. But most important was their pony, Frank. For a time, when Harry was twelve or thirteen, they also took up boxing under their father's tutelage. Charlie, stronger and more aggressive, usually emerged the victor.

The Mencken brothers were envied in the neighborhood because, on summer Sunday mornings, 1524 Hollins was often full of professional baseball players who had come to see their baseball-executive father. As August and the players talked in the backyard summerhouse, Harry and Charlie would let the Hollins Street boys look through the back gate, a privilege that was all the greater if heavyhitting Matt Kilroy, Baltimore's greatest baseball hero, were present. Even then it must have seemed to Harry, baseball fan though he was, that his father, in fact, was more powerful than the baseball stars—even than Kilroy, after whom he named a cigar. Baseball, too, was a business, and August Mencken was management. Indeed, by 1890, August looked the part of the minor magnate, with his $200 watch and his massive watch guard, diamond stud, and seal ring.

As he neared his teens, Harry Mencken continued to be the dutiful son. He bought gifts for his parents with his own money and, from his earliest days at Knapp's, was in the habit of writing Christmas and New Year's letters expressing his love and devotion. It is clear that the letters (preserved in Mencken's scrapbooks) were in part academic exercises, with stilted language and conventional sentiments. "My dear Parents," he had written at age seven, at New Year's 1888, "With a grateful heart I write you this letter to show my gratitude for your great kindness to me during this past year. I pray to God that he may spare you many more years, and give you health and happiness." As Harry grew older the letters also demonstrated a highly conscientious, nearly contrite tone. "I will try my utmost to please you in future by being a studious and obedient child," he had written at age eight. The next year he had thanked his parents for cautioning him "not to get into the path of doing wrong." Then, at age ten, he had assured them that his expressions "spring from a heart which is a stranger to deceit." However conventional his words, Harry Mencken undoubtedly meant it—at this point.

As the Menckens grew more prosperous, August was able to take more time away from his business. He took the family on weekend excursions to the shore east of Baltimore, sometimes traveling as far south as Annapolis and beyond. In the summer of 1889 August and his brother, Henry, also rented a double house in rural Ellicott City, ten miles west of Hollins Street by the National Pike, and they returned there the following summer. Such a place in the hills above the Patapsco River, a small town with nearly an Appalachian flavor, was a delight for young Harry. He hiked the hills with Charlie and his cousin John Henry, and the neighboring Reus boys introduced him to country ways and country people. "It was my first wilderness," he later wrote, "and from it I got my first notion of the rich and glorious loveliness of nature." Uncharted territory, wildlife, tales of dangerous half humans in the forest: this was different from the orderly nature Harry had known before, the unthreatening green of Union Square.

After two summers of renting at Ellicott City and the summer of 1891 back at Hollins Street, in 1892 August Mencken bought a summer house on four acres of hilly terrain at Mount Washington, just north of Baltimore, seven miles from Hollins Street. He paid $3,000 for the house and spent another $1,500 renovating it, and in late spring 1892 the Menckens moved out for the summer—a routine they would follow through Harry Mencken's teens. On moving day a driver would load a wagon with kitchen gear, bedding, clothing, and other items. August and Anna Mencken would follow in a second wagon, with Gertrude, young August, and the hired girl in tow. Harry and Charlie would follow in their pony cart.

In *Happy Days* and in the unpublished "Additions," Mencken wrote at great length about life at Mount Washington, although it was about the early years, 1892–1894, that he principally wrote. His education in the ways of the country, begun at Ellicott City, continued there, his guides now being the next-door Lürssen brothers, friendly sorts who became, Mencken later wrote, "like brothers to me." Harry and his cohorts explored the woods behind his house, "largely primeval forest" with "all sorts of wonders," and the even wilder region down near Jones Falls. Harry collected rocks, gathered berries and nuts, set out a few lines for fish, and hunted bullfrogs and turtles—once, with Charlie, beheading a turtle, only to see the victim, headless, crawl away. He had other adventures worthy of an 1890s Tom Sawyer—making rafts for navigation in Jones Falls (Baltimorean for creek), stealing grapes from an old German farmer, watching as a friend stole a stick of dynamite and blew up a carp in the creek, and himself once narrowly escaping a freight train by clinging to a steep bank beside a railroad bridge. Harry and his friends undertook more civilized sports as well, primarily baseball

and, for a time, cricket, which they learned from watching the players at the nearby Baltimore Cricket Club. They soon dismissed the
sport as "slow, clumsy and idiotic" compared to baseball. They
dismissed tennis, too, as "a rather effeminate game."

Nearly every summer day Harry went to Mount Washington village, often driving his pony cart along the Falls Road or the North
Central railroad tracks. Soon he and his friends were ranging far and
wide, occasionally by bicycle but usually on foot. They walked northeast to Towson and Loch Raven, some five miles distant, they explored the forests of what would soon become Roland Park and took
the Roland Park trolley into Baltimore. By his early teens Mencken
had explored all of Baltimore's suburbs, east, west, north, and south.

Although Harry Mencken was an active and sociable sort, by the
age of twelve or thirteen he had also begun to detach himself, emotionally at least, from many of his friends and companions, assuming
a certain critical stance that was to become a habit for life. To him,
nearly everyone outside his immediate family seemed flawed—not
only, as we have seen, Uncle Henry's family but also many of Harry's
neighbors and friends, both on Hollins Street and in Mount Washington. Mrs. Eckhardt, next door at Hollins Street, was "a very vixenish
woman"; her successor at that address, Mrs. Hancock, was equally a
"virago." A third neighbor, Fortenbaugh, was an "assiduous boozer"
whose wife "often belabored him with shrill screams." A fourth, who
later occupied Uncle Henry's house, was "very stupid" and given to
"idiotic talk."

At Mount Washington the neighbors were little better. One, Otto
Mattfeldt, was "an amiable but extremely indolent fellow" whose
laziness "filled my mother with amazement, not unaccompanied by
indignation." Another neighbor named Bartz was a "poor fish."
Even Harry's constant companions, the Lürssen brothers, he soon
decided, were of "subnormal intelligence." When he and Charlie
became "painfully aware of their low mental visibility," the Mencken
boys "had to keep away from them."

These were the words of the sixty-year-old H. L. Mencken reporting the twelve-year-old boy's views after a half century—words entered into a manuscript that would not be released for nearly another
half century—but the judgments were those of twelve-year-old
Harry, already possessed of a critical cast of mind. Even at twelve he
could not abide people whom he judged to be either stupid or lazy.

He himself was bright, industrious, and ambitious, and he had little patience for those who were anything else.

---

The first summer or two at Mount Washington marked an end to H. L. Mencken's childhood, if by childhood is meant that period of relative security within family and home that is little threatened by the outside world, or a capacity for living in the moment with little regard for the passage of time and the long-range consequences of choice—most of all, if childhood means a period in which the words and actions of one's parents by and large escape critical scrutiny. A number of things happened in Harry Mencken's life just before he entered his teens, none of which in itself was particularly disastrous but all of which contributed to a sometimes somber and not altogether welcome maturity.

In 1891, the year before Mencken completed his work at Knapp's Institute, he also made his first extended trip outside the Baltimore-Washington area. Accompanying his grandfather Abhau on a trip to northern Ohio, he visited relatives who had settled in Cleveland and in the country outside Toledo. According to the account of the trip in his school composition book, he and his grandfather traveled from Baltimore to Washington by train, then continued overnight to Pittsburgh, of which Harry wrote: "The City of Smoke was that morning also the city of mist and fog. In the darkness huge flames shot from the chimneys of the iron works." When he reached Cleveland he was impressed by the Standard Oil Works and the millionaires' mansions on Euclid Avenue, but he was even more fascinated by life on his relatives' farms, where he remained nearly two weeks, helping with chores, attending church, and getting to know his country cousins.

What we see in most of Harry Mencken's recorded observations of his trip is the mind more of the budding engineer than of the budding writer. He remarks on the use of natural gas in Ohio, on the use of wood as a building material in Cleveland (sometimes spelled "Cleaveland") and Toledo, on the farmers' methods of draining their land. He found his country cousins more to his liking in many ways than his cousins back in Baltimore. They were "rich farmers, living in fine brick houses"—but they were rich, he was informed, largely because one of them had won a lottery shortly after arriving in

America. Harry believed what he was told. If such were indeed the case, it must have seemed that the family luck extended far beyond West Baltimore.

It was an eye-opening trip for young Harry Mencken, a movement away from the predictable world of Hollins Street, Knapp's Institute, and the streets of Baltimore. What he found when he returned home was another departure from that known world. For while he and his grandfather Abhau were away, his grandfather Mencken had died, and Harry was greeted by black crepe on the door at 1524 Hollins. At the time he was not particularly moved: the "wicked thought" that ran through his mind, he wrote in *Happy Days*, was "No school tomorrow!" But later he realized what his grandfather's loss meant— for Burkhardt was the patriarch, the grandparent who mattered most, the keeper of whatever ties the Mencken family had to a distinguished past in Germany. If Burkhardt had lived longer, H. L. Mencken later wrote, he himself would have taken a keen interest, much sooner than he did, in his German ancestry.

Burkhardt's death was followed shortly by other events which shook, though hardly shattered, the secure childhood world of Harry Mencken. The Panic of 1893 seriously damaged his father's tobacco company, reducing its resources and nearly ruining the trade with the southern states on which the company depended. During that same period, on a Saturday evening in December 1893, the physical plant of Aug. Mencken & Bro. was completely destroyed by fire. The handsome building was partly insured, but insurance did not cover all the $40,000 loss. By 1894 the company, which had numbered more than fifty employees in the early 1890s, was facing its darkest period.

It was not by chance that H. L. Mencken, writing in the late 1930s, ended his book *Happy Days* just before this point. He concluded it with the trip to Ohio and the death of his grandfather, which would be followed a year later by his graduation from Knapp's Institute. Not only did ominous economic times threaten, but—he wrote in his introduction to *Happy Days*—"I was then at the brink of the terrible teens, and existence began inevitably to take on a new and more sinister aspect." The teens would not be all burden and frustration— the summers at Mount Washington offered reminders of the old, carefree life—but what Mencken later called "childhood's happy hour" was past. Like Samuel Clemens before him, he would later try to recapture, through the force of words, what seemed to be a golden age of innocent pleasure, but by that point he would be all too aware of time and change and loss. "Those were the days indeed," he wrote more than a half century later to an old friend. "What a swell time we had—and how little we realized that it would soon be over."

# THE EDUCATION OF
# HENRY MENCKEN

H L. Mencken's teenage years, specifically the period between
thirteen and seventeen, constitute the period of his life we
know least about. It is the only period, before his disabling stroke in
1948, that he did not describe in great detail, through either published reminiscences or, more often, unpublished autobiographical
notes and diary entries.

But from what he does tell us—and does not tell—we can surmise
that these were, by far, the unhappiest years of his life, save of course
the seven bitter years after his stroke. In letters to friends and in
discussions of what he would and would not include in the *Days*
books, he often mentioned this unhappiness. He was given to making
such general observations as "Youth is the time of real tragedy" and
"School days, I believe, are the unhappiest in the whole span of
human existence." In his particular case, he wrote Theodore Dreiser
in 1939, *Happy Days* "sets a mood that it would be impossible to
keep up in the later years. My teens . . . were full of loud alarms, and
it would sound idiotic to treat them as I deal with my first ten years."
Later, he added:

> The teens are at once too grotesque and too pathetic to be dealt
> with in the mood of the three "Days" books. They belong, intrinsi-
> cally, to pathology, and it is no wonder that they offer a happy
> hunting ground to quack psychologists. The individual passing

38

through them has lost the artlessness of childhood but is still far from the rationality of maturity.

Still, for a time, Mencken considered including a volume on his teens—"much more serious in tone"—in his autobiographical series, before he returned to his earlier conclusion that they "were generally unpleasant" and should be skipped altogether. Thus we miss Mencken's official version of these years, but that is about all we miss. From school reports, various later letters, and miscellaneous notes, as well as hints and silences which reveal as much as they conceal, we are able to piece together a rather full picture of the teenaged Henry Mencken.

We know that Mencken entered the Baltimore Manual Training School (soon to be called Baltimore Polytechnic) in September 1892, one week before his twelfth birthday, and about his academic life at the Polytechnic the later Mencken is, in fact, forthcoming. Less certain than his academic performance is the reason his father decided to enroll him in a "manual training school" in the first place. In those days the Polytechnic occupied "an extraordinarily hideous building," H. L. Mencken later wrote, and, according to the testimony of another Baltimore schoolboy of the 1890s, "only roughnecks" went to the school.

So why Henry Mencken? He had been a star pupil at Knapp's, excelling in reading and composition, and he came from a family of some financial, if not social, position. Besides, he had very little interest in or aptitude for mechanics and little manual dexterity. It would have been logical, then, for him to attend, if not a private academy, at least the Baltimore City College, a high school that stressed liberal arts and university preparation. But his father had other ideas, possibly because the neighbors at Mount Washington, the Lürssen boys, attended Polytechnic, more likely because August himself as a youth had had an ambition to be an engineer and believed his sons should follow that line. (The younger two did, in fact.) Henry Mencken had no interest at all in engineering, but he was a dutiful son—if one who by this point should have had some doubts about the father who, he had earlier felt, could "resolve any difficulty . . . beat off any danger." And as a dutiful son he gave it a good try.

Although Mencken later remarked that he forgot all he had learned at the Polytechnic within a year of his graduation and could not "imagine a more useless education than that I received there," in fact he encountered a curriculum that was rigorous in many areas. If he was forced to take electricity, steam engineering, and black-smith shop, he also took English, mathematics, physics, chemistry, and German. His marks were among the highest ever recorded at the Polytechnic (save in declamation, blacksmith shop, and—curiously—German), and his absences were fewer than at Knapp's. In mathematics he enjoyed challenging and surpassing his father, who was very proud of his own mathematical ability but in fact knew nothing beyond arithmetic and became indignant when his son knew more than he did. In English composition Henry turned out well-crafted, if uninspired, essays—now sometimes signed "H. L. Mencken"—on a number of subjects, including the monkey, "who, according to Darwinian Theory, is the beast from which we are descended."

Despite Mencken's verdict that most of the teachers at the Poly-technic were incompetent, he did encounter two "drunken and dis-reputable" English instructors, Edward S. Kines and William Blake, who had a "passionate love of sound literature" and who exerted some influence on him. "Two evil fellows" who soon left teaching, they introduced him to Rabelais, *The Spectator,* and Thackeray. But a more lasting mark of quite another sort was left by his chemistry teacher, "a pedagogue pure and simple" whose "two years of . . . inept tutelage confused and disheartened me." "He had a great influence on my life," later wrote the social critic who numbered pedagogues and professors among his favorite targets. "He taught me the useful lesson that fools are often potent in this world."

If it had not been for that teacher, H. L. Mencken might have become a chemist, not a writer. He had developed a keen interest in the subject by twelve or thirteen, and for a time his greatest ambi-tions lay in that area. He spent much of his leisure time between thirteen and fifteen conducting experiments at Hollins Street, often filling his room with fumes. As a result, he soon became more expert than his teacher, and the other students—and finally, if we are to believe Mencken, the instructor himself—came to him for help.

He was able to combine his interest in chemistry with another early passion, photography. Henry had been given his first camera at Christmas when he was twelve and a better one the following Christmas. He had subscribed to *Photo-American*, had read everything else about photography he could find, had learned to do his own developing and printing, and by the time he was thirteen had devised a platinum toning solution for photographs. At Mount Washington in the summer of 1894 he put his results into an article, sent it to *Photo-American*, and received his first rejection slip. But his study of photography and chemistry yielded lasting rewards—the former, a series of pictures (extant) taken by Mencken in 1893 of Union Square and other Baltimore sights; the latter, a certain rigor of thought, a scientific cast of mind.

But the arts were competing with science for Henry Mencken's attention. By twelve or thirteen he had produced drawings and watercolors of Jones Falls, near Mount Washington, as well as the Patapsco River and other scenes in and around Baltimore. More important, he had become interested in music, a pastime that had begun with piano lessons at age eight and later became much more than a pastime. Having become adept at playing marches and waltzes, by his early teens he was also composing on the piano, as well as selecting and arranging numbers and playing piano for a musical comedy performed at the Polytechnic. He also made notes for a comic opera libretto based on *Bluebeard*.

Mencken later expressed a belief that music was the most sublime of arts and wished that he had been given the talent to match his interest and desire. But he was aware by his early teens that his future lay elsewhere, either in chemistry or in those twin callings—journalism and literature—that had fascinated him since he had been given a printing press for Christmas when he was seven or eight years old and, shortly afterward, had read *Huckleberry Finn*. With the press he had printed personal cards (his own reading "H. L. Mencken" only because his father, with characteristic agility, had smashed the lowercase *r*, making "Henry" or "Harry" impossible) and had also begun his own four-page newspaper. This interest in newspapering had grown stronger during his first summer in Ellicott City, when he had looked through the window of the *Ellicott City Times* and had seen the weekly being printed. Later, at eleven or twelve, he overheard his father's Washington agent say that "the real princes of Washington" were not senators or congressmen, who "were mere passing shapes," but instead were newspaper correspondents. By the time he entered the Polytechnic, Henry Mencken was as smitten with newspapering as young Sam Clemens had been with the idea of piloting on the river.

But his plans to write for the Polytechnic newspaper or student magazine were frustrated by the student politicians who controlled the publications. So he kept his desires to himself, made a mental note of the ways of politicians, and turned instead to his other passion, belles lettres. By the time he was fourteen he was writing poetry with a vengeance, for a time producing a poem a day. Some of the poems were experiments in French forms then popular, others were imitations of Kipling. By his mid-teens Mencken knew what he wanted to be. Chemistry was no longer an option: his teacher had ruined that for him. So if he were free to pursue his own course, independent of parental interference, he would turn to either journalism or the world of letters—or both.

The furious writing of Mencken's early and mid-teens was accompanied by an equally furious period of reading. Indeed, he later boasted, "I doubt that any human being in this world has ever read more than I did between my twelfth and eighteenth years." After finishing all the books in his father's library, he turned to the Hollins Street branch of the Enoch Pratt Free Library, and after exhausting the limited resources of the branch library, at about fourteen he turned to the main Enoch Pratt, a mile or so east of Hollins Street. During the winter he visited the Pratt nearly every weekday, and between 1893 and 1898, he later estimated, he read an average of three books a week, often four or five, outside of school. The Pratt gave him "whatever education I may be said to have."

What Mencken read, almost exclusively, was English literature. He had plunged into the novels of Dickens when he was nine, and by his early and mid-teens he was reading Chaucer, Shakespeare and the Elizabethans, Herrick, and Pepys, as well as Addison, Steele, Pope, Swift, Johnson, Boswell, Fielding, Smollett, and Sterne. He did not care for Spenser or Milton, nor for Samuel Johnson, the English writer with whom he would later be compared. According to the later Mencken, Johnson was "the first Rotarian" (D. H. Lawrence was to say the same of Benjamin Franklin), "the [Theodore] Roosevelt of the eighteenth century," a writer who left "such wounds upon English prose it was a century recovering from them." If Mencken rejected Johnson, he embraced the other eighteenth-century writers, as well as most of the reigning English writers of the nineteenth century—the Romantics, as well as Arnold, Macaulay, George Eliot, Tennyson, and Swinburne. But Thackeray, whom he began to read at fourteen, was a greater influence than any of the others. His discovery of Thackeray, Mencken later wrote, "completely reorganized my view of literature. Here was richness indeed. . . . I read the whole of Thackeray in one Winter."

It was not Thackeray, however, so much as two other nineteenth-century English writers who became, along with Mark Twain, Mencken's early literary idols and models. In his early teens, he later wrote a friend, he became "a violent Kiplingmaniac," absorbing Kipling's subjects and settings, imitating his cadences, in every respect finding his first true literary hero. Mencken spent much of his spare money buying books and pictures of Kipling, at one time having no fewer than ten Kipling portraits on his bedroom walls.

Kipling was his hero, but T. H. Huxley was a greater and more lasting intellectual influence. "The greatest Englishman of the nineteenth century," Mencken came to call him, "perhaps the greatest Englishman of all times." At fifteen he read Huxley's essays in the Pratt library and greatly admired his rigor of thought, his attack on convention and moral certainty, his combative style. Huxley was a truth seeker, a scientist with a touch of the poet—as Mencken hoped to be a poet with the skeptical temper of the scientist.

The notable fact, again, about those writers Mencken read in his early and mid-teens—particularly considering Mencken's later anti-English feelings—is that nearly all of them *are* English. He read a few contemporary American authors besides Mark Twain—Howells, Crane, Richard Harding Davis, and some Henry James—but he did not particularly care for the American classics, including Hawthorne and Emerson, or for those writers from the mid-nineteenth century whose works would later be pronounced classics. He felt a "sort of antipathy" toward Thoreau—he later wrote Theodore Dreiser—"probably because [Thoreau] was a New Englander and something of a transcendentalist"; much of Whitman he found "trivial"; and Melville, whom he got around to reading later, he did not care for either.

But at least he read some of the Americans. What he did not read in his teens—curious for one who later led the charge against an exclusively English and Anglo-American literary tradition—was

European literature, most of which he could have found in translation and much of which was being touted by reigning American
literary critics and editors such as William Dean Howells. Aside from
Rabelais, he read virtually no French literature and, aside from
dipping into Tolstoi, no Russian. Particularly to the point, in his
teens he read no German literature, past or present.

Such an omission is significant, all the more since Mencken is often
believed to have come out of a staunchly German and German-
American family background and to have been intensely conscious of
that background from his schooldays on. But the fact is that not only
Henry Mencken's literary background but his entire cultural consciousness (save in those visceral matters of food, drink, and music)
was almost exclusively English and Anglo-American. In most respects, thus, he was as fully a product of the Anglo-American Genteel
Tradition—as well as its Kiplingesque variant of muscular Christianity—as those writers he was later to condemn. "The most massive
influences of my life have all been unmistakenly English," he himself
later acknowledged, and such was the case from the beginning. His
mother, pure German though she was, greatly admired Queen Victoria (and not for *her* German blood), and her regard for Victoria and
the prince consort made her determined to name her third son
Albert. She was overruled by Grandfather Burkhardt Mencken, who
insisted that his grandson, like his son, be named August.

The young Mencken, then, was hardly cut off from the Anglo-
American cultural tradition; neither was he consciously alienated
from the America of his own time. He was, as he later wrote, a
"patriot" as a boy, approving of the Spanish-American War (the only
American war of his lifetime that he would approve), cheering when
Dewey defeated the Spanish fleet in 1898—just as, the following year,
he would root for the British in the Boer War. Even when, just after
his teens, he began to express criticism of many aspects of American
life, he doubted, as he wrote much later, "that my German blood had
anything to do with this reaction, at least on the conscious level."

In fact, the young Mencken—following the lead of his father and,
in certain respects, his grandfather—was at least as critical of German Americans as he was of other Americans. "My opinion of [them]
was always very low," he later wrote. "The plain fact is that the
overwhelming majority of German-Americans are of the lower and
more backward classes, culturally speaking . . ." At first he hardly

considered himself one of those German Americans—both because of the Menckens' loftier origins and because of their apparently successful assimilation into American life. Long afterward, in his unhappy sixties, Mencken would question whether he had ever been truly American, whether his grandfather should have come to the United States. But he would not have expressed such doubts in his youth. The Menckens *were* American, first and second generation. Henry Mencken was not aware, and would not be for twenty-five years, of any living relatives in Germany, any binding ties to the Fatherland. He had, he later recalled, "little contact or sympathy with Germans, and my acquaintance . . . with German history was of the meagerest." If his grandfather Mencken had not died before Henry was twelve, he might indeed have absorbed more of this history (along with, however, an even greater disdain for most German Americans). But his own father had no interest at all, save in the fact that Bismarck's mother had been a Mencken.

As it was, Mencken's first interest in Germany was sparked not by his family or by German literature or music or mythology—but by Mark Twain, whose *A Tramp Abroad* he read in his teens. Even after that, the German culture was far more alien than the English and the German language, spoken by some of the servant girls, an "awful language" that became one of his weakest subjects at Knapp's and the Polytechnic. His identification with Germany and its culture would come in time, as would his greater alienation from American culture. Events to come—and a recognition by Mencken of certain facts he had not recognized as a youth—would make all the difference.

If there was any group, in fact, in the Baltimore of his youth that Mencken seemed to admire, and with which he sometimes even identified, it was not German Americans but a species he later gained particular fame for defaming—southerners, or at least a particular subspecies of southerner. "In so far as I am an American at all," he was to write in 1921, "I am a Southerner." On another occasion he referred to himself "as one of Southern birth, and of Southerners born. . . . I thus qualify as a Southern gentleman, or, at all events, as a Southerner." He knew such claims were debatable, and he knew his feelings about the American South were complicated: "Why do I denounce the southern *kultur* so often and so violently?" he was to ask at the height of his later war with the South. "Send a postcard to professor Dr. Sigmund Freud, General Delivery, Vienna, and you will get the answer by return mail."

Mencken was kidding only in part. His feelings about the South, and more particularly about himself as a kind of southerner, were complex indeed. Certainly, for reasons we have seen, a case could be made for Baltimore as a southern city, not only because of the influx of African Americans from the South that gave the back alleys a southern flavor but also because of its history. Before the Civil War the city had certainly considered itself southern, and some of its southern character remained. It was the home of journals with names such as the *Southern Magazine* and *The Southern Review,* and it published organs of southern industrial boosting such as the *Manufacturers' Record.* In 1895 three quarters of the city's trade (including much of the trade of Aug. Mencken & Bro.) was with the South.

To say that Baltimore was, in part, a southern city is not to say, however, that Henry Mencken was southern. Only the rather superficial fact that his grandfather had been in sympathy with Southern Democrats and his father had grown up using "southern speech" (by which Mencken meant poor grammar)—and, of course, that he himself lived near the Hollins Street alley—linked Mencken in any way to the South. In almost all important respects *his* Baltimore was not southern, and he was—if, to a small degree, southern bred—not at all southern born. It was he himself who said that heredity, not environment, made all the difference—and the Menckens, the Abhaus, and the Gegners had come straight from Germany and, once in Baltimore, had not in any substantial way absorbed the city's southern flavor. Henry Mencken's reasons for making such claims about his southernness were curious indeed, particularly given his well-publicized distaste for the South, and they bear close examination.

To begin with, the nineteenth-century immigrants to Baltimore whom Mencken regarded most highly came not from across the Atlantic but from across the Potomac—not from Germany but from Virginia—and to understand his feelings toward Virginians is to understand a great deal about his idea of himself. Those Virginians had come, he later wrote, "with good manners and empty bellies" to Baltimore after the Civil War and had brought to the city "a talent for civilized living, a spacious and amiable view of the world." The Virginians were "first-rate people," Mencken believed; indeed, in the late nineteenth century "they did more for the town than any other group." It was these Virginians—certainly not the "anthropoids" who he believed populated the lower South and the Appalachian slopes—Mencken had in mind when he told a correspondent in all seriousness in 1936, "Life in this country would have been much pleasanter if the South had won the Civil War."

It is at first glance a curious statement, even if Mencken did have the Virginians in mind—because the Virginians, as well as the older Marylanders who were southern in manner and sentiment, were precisely that group, in Mencken's youth, to whom German Americans were most suspect and against whom the German Americans had to battle. When Henry Mencken was a boy, these Virginians and Marylanders of English descent were entrenched in power in Baltimore, controlling the city's political and social institutions. Theirs was the Baltimore of horses and hunts and balls, the Baltimore to which H. L. Mencken, even in his most powerful days, would never really belong—to which, in his youth, he could hardly have imagined belonging and to which he said he did not want to belong. Yet, from his earliest days, he was more lavish—and unreserved—in his praise of this group than of any other.

The reasons for this near adulation have something to do with Mencken's idea of his own family. For he would have said that the Menckens, though German immigrants themselves, had far more in common with the Virginians and the older Anglo-Marylanders than with their fellow German Americans. The Virginians and the older Marylanders represented to Mencken a certain Old World grace and charm. So, Mencken would say, did the ancestral Menckens. The Virginians and English Marylanders were gentlemen who gave some attention to the art of living, to good food and drink, to a civilized leisure. So, he would say, did the Menckens. The Virginians and Marylanders had inquiring minds, lived orderly lives, embraced religious tolerance—which is to say, skepticism. So did the Menckens. The Virginians and the earlier Marylanders of English descent, that is, were not so greatly different from Mencken's idea of what the Menckens had been—in Leipzig and in Wittenberg.

In an essay written in 1922, Mencken was to praise the world of the colonial Maryland planters, a civilization that "in its best days" must have been even *more* charming than that of the Virginians but was founded on the same principles. In the Tidewater society of both colonies "the upper classes founded their life upon that of the English country gentry." It was an eighteenth-century world of order and civility, and it is no coincidence that it was also the eighteenth century in which the Menckens had flourished. The Virginians and the English Marylanders were the last aristocrats in a land overrun with democracy. When Henry Mencken praised their world, he felt he was, in great measure, praising the world of his own fathers.

The young Mencken, of course, could hardly have identified all these forces at work, although he could have identified some of them. What he did know even then was that he felt somehow different. He spoke of a feeling of "apartness" he had from an early age, and he sometimes wondered if that feeling did not spring from his "unusual surname"—although in fact the name was no more unusual than a number of others. Neither would it be correct to say, at least in those years, that he suffered from that cultural double detachment his grandfather and, to a lesser extent, his father had experienced— alienation both from the German-American community of Baltimore and from the older, predominantly British Baltimore population. "I grew up entirely devoid of the usual immigrant's inferiority complex," he later wrote a friend, and in a deeper sense he was right: it was *superiority* he felt, at least culturally and intellectually, both to the German Americans and to the older Americans. He may have had a certain insecurity regarding class, coming from a family financially well off (if a little shakier after 1893) but without social standing, but there is no evidence at all of the "psychic damage" from Mencken's schooldays of which Gerald W. Johnson later spoke, damage stemming from a "bruising disdain of his Teutonic origins." There would be damage—later. But in his youth, Mencken himself wrote much later, "I certainly did not think of myself as a German, though I was already conscious of my differentiation from the common run of Americans. If I ever pondered that differentiation at all, I probably thought of it, in the egoistic way of youth, as no more than an evidence of my superiority as an individual." Or to state it even more accurately: If as a schoolboy Henry Mencken experienced any detachment, it was not because he was a German American. It was because he was a Mencken.

In the course of schooldays, of course, pedigree counts for less than looks and cleverness, less than athletic ability and social success, sexual prowess and boasting ability. It is those tangibles, as much as family station, we must examine if we are to understand Mencken during those years he tried to obscure. Later he wrote that adolescence in general was marked by a certain "groping imbecility." He experienced his share of that imbecility, as well as insecurity.

Mencken was a year younger than most of his Polytechnic classmates, although a year ahead academically, and according to later faculty lore at the Polytechnic, he was not particularly well liked. We can trust pedagogues in such matters, long after the fact, no more than we can trust Mencken's own veiled testimony. But it is a fact that he came to the Polytechnic with certain liabilities, none of which matter greatly in later life but all of which are of enormous significance when one is thirteen or fourteen. Henry Mencken was small and slight and even somewhat sickly from a chronic sore throat. He had poor coordination and manual dexterity (inherited from August), and he had no expertise in the mechanical courses the school stressed. He had friends—one the son of a draftsman for the Baltimore & Ohio Railroad, another, three years older, the son of the B & O librarian, and a third, his closest Polytechnic friend, Arthur Hawks, who shared his literary interests and ambitions—but he was not close to the student leaders at the Polytechnic. Besides, he had lost touch with most of his old friends in the Hollins Street Gang. In the life of this most sociable of men, the teen years were doubtless his least sociable time.

Male friends were one thing. Girls were quite another. Females to the young Mencken already existed in that realm of mystery and secrecy they were to occupy for the rest of his life: here, as later, he tells us very little about female acquaintances. The little we do know makes it clear that Mencken had already begun, in some fashion, that habit of dividing women into two camps—the seductive and the romantically chaste. Only twice in all his letters and autobiographical notes does he mention schoolboy sexual experience, once in a letter to Edgar Lee Masters and once in a diary entry in 1945. "I was seduced at fourteen by a girl of my own age," he wrote at age sixty-five, "and she had thrown off the pall of virginity before I tackled her." To Masters he wrote that he was but thirteen. We have no particular reason to doubt Mencken's account, although for this slight, uncoordinated boy with the innocent look, it must have been an impressive conquest. What is more important—and anticipatory—is that Mencken, at about the same time, fell in love and conducted a chaste romance with the blond daughter of a neighbor. "This highly virtuous and romantic affair went on for four or five years, and produced a good deal of bad poetry," he wrote in 1925, his only written reference to his youthful love. "Since then, I fear, I have never loved so nobly."

Mencken had at least limited success with love, but he had none at all on the athletic field, and this was a failing that must have been difficult to absorb for the son of the vice president of the Washington baseball club. In the days before high school he had experienced minor triumphs. If nothing else, he had been fleet afoot, later claiming that, at nine or ten, he had been able to run the hundred-yard dash in 12.4 seconds—and if that claim seems somewhat exaggerated for a boy of nine or ten, it is not altogether out of reach. But by the time he reached the Polytechnic, Mencken's best days as an athlete were behind him. He was still a "violent fan" of the Orioles and went to their games whenever he could come up with a quarter for the bleachers. When the Orioles won the pennant in 1894, he and Charlie and the Lürssen boys rode in the triumphant parade. The interest in baseball was still there but not the ability, and by sixteen even the interest was gone. Football was even worse. Mencken tried to play at the Polytechnic, had no success, and soon gave it up. He later dismissed the sport as "a combat of gorillas."

By this time Henry had decided that he belonged to a higher species of animal in any case and had already begun to develop what he later told a friend was "a violent antipathy" to sports in general. On one level, he was to retain a certain fondness for baseball: it was at least, when compared to football, "a game for gentlemen," and Mencken never lost the habit of pitching baseballs, not counting sheep, when he had trouble sleeping. "The scene is Oriole Park," he wrote in the 1940s, "and I see the green sward, the packed grandstand, and the long shafts of the setting sun as clearly as if I were back in 1892."

But that, after all, was nostalgia for boyhood, not for sport, and for sport and those who cared about it the mature Mencken was to have nothing but contempt. "I still . . . hate all sports as rabidly as a person who likes sports hates common sense," he was to write on one occasion. "Very little," he wrote elsewhere, "is to be said for the man who develops virtuosity at games. . . . It is better to be an even second-rate bricklayer than to be the best polo player on earth." It is worthy of mention that Mencken, when he jotted that note in 1939, had become a backyard bricklayer, but the sentiment he expressed was just as true in 1895. What he had decided early was that most of those activities in which he did not excel were hardly worth pursuing anyway, were (in the case of sports) full of "unbearable boredom," and that—conversely—most of what Mencken had a talent for was worthwhile indeed. It was a view of life that, psychologically, was more salutary than not.

But at age fourteen Henry still had a father to please, and sports continued to be important to August, if not to his eldest son. Seeing that his son was "already a bookworm and beginning to be a bit round-shouldered," he encouraged Henry to enroll in the west branch of the Baltimore YMCA, largely for the use of the gymnasium upstairs. Mencken hated the calisthenics and, predictably, soon convinced himself that he was superior to the athletes. What drove him out of the YMCA, however, was not the calisthenics but rather the "Christian endeavor" of the place—in particular, a pious boy in the library who was given to reading aloud from inspirational literature.

The reaction of the young Mencken was hardly surprising. In the realm of religion he was, in the tradition of his grandfather and father, already a confirmed skeptic. As he later explained to a nun with whom he corresponded, he was "born without any religious impulse whatever." It was not that his family was antagonistic to religion. Indeed, when Mencken was a child, a family Bible rested on the center table in the parlor, although no one ever opened it. The untouched Bible epitomized the Menckens' religious sensibility: religion was "simply not a living subject in [my] house. . . . I grew up believing finally that it was unimportant . . ." His mother attended church infrequently and his father not at all, although August Mencken felt it his obligation to make financial contributions to that institution that christened, married, and buried people. A genial agnostic, he was particularly friendly toward the Jesuits and certain other Catholics. And when Henry and Charlie had become of school age, he had sent them to a Methodist Sunday school four blocks away, although, as it later came out, he had wanted them out of the house so he could take his Sunday nap undisturbed.

Nonetheless, the two years of Methodist Sunday school had an effect on Henry similar to that of the incompetent Polytechnic chemistry teacher: if he were not already predisposed to flee from religion, this experience assured it. He liked the singing, but like his hero Huck Finn he resisted being civilized. The Methodists made such an impression, however, that thirty years later, when Mencken became the most famous American critic of organized religion, particularly its southern varieties, it was not the rawer forms of southern Calvinism but Methodism that he ridiculed most of all.

Although he soon attended Sunday school infrequently, Mencken was not through with organized religion yet. At about the time he was quitting the YMCA in protest of its excesses of Christian endeavor, he was also preparing for his confirmation in the Second English Lutheran Sabbath school, to which August had transferred his sons from the Methodists. Confirmation, too, was a part of family tradition. As Mencken's brother August later explained it, the children in the house "tend[ed] to belong to the church" when they reached a certain age. Thus when he was fourteen Mencken began a series of catechism classes, although he never looked at the catechism until he arrived for each session and could never answer the pastor's questions. On Palm Sunday 1895 "Harry L. Mencken" was one of the forty-three scholars confirmed in the church. His entire family, including August Sr., attended.

After his confirmation, the successful candidate hardly darkened the door of a church again. He had taken to reading T. H. Huxley by now—during the time he was supposed to be studying the catechism—and the English scientist, he later wrote, "gave order and coherence to my own doubts and converted me into a violent agnostic." Not an atheist, since atheism, Mencken felt, was as much "nonsense" as belief: the universe was "governed by law, and if there is anything plain about law it is that it can never be anything but a manifestation of will."

Though he was to remain an "infidel" to the end of his days, Mencken would always find a certain beauty and charm in religion, particularly Catholicism. As he looked west from his upstairs window on Hollins Street into the convent garden of the House of the Good

Shepherd, he would see the nuns moving about and, on occasion, would reflect on religious faith: "It gives me a quick trip, when the mood is on me, into far countries and a remote time. . . . Its basic doctrines are plainly preposterous and it [*sic*] hopes are pathetically futile, but nevertheless it continues in being and perhaps serves a genuine need."

H. L. Mencken graduated from the Baltimore Polytechnic Institute on June 23, 1896, three months short of his sixteenth birthday. He finished at the head of his class by virtue of a performance on final examinations which was the best recorded at the Polytechnic to that date. He made marks in the 90s in all subjects except one—an 81 in German. For his achievement his father gave him a hundred dollars, part of which Henry used for a new bicycle and part of which he put into the bank. "Harold B. Mencken," wrote the head of the Polytechnic to the alumni association president, was entitled to the Polytechnic Alumni Medal of Honor, given to the student with the highest examination average. But in fact the award went to another student who had earned the highest marks over the entire four-year period.

Nonetheless, Mencken was asked to be the class's honorary speaker at graduation, and he arrived at Ford's Opera House on June 23 dressed in rented finery and frightened by the prospect of giving a talk to his twenty-five classmates and their families and friends. His was not the only speech of the evening: the salutatorian held forth on "the evils of the modern novel." Mencken's own speech, produced on his father's typewriter, was, if largely conventional, also somewhat prophetic. He foresaw the "noiseless motor-car" which would "soon supersede the puffing locomotive" and "airships" which would become "formidable rivals of the craft that ploughs the seas"— although he believed that both motorcar and airship would be powered by electricity. After the speeches were completed and the diplomas awarded, the class of 1896 gathered at the Ganzhorn City Hotel for a banquet that included turtle soup and soft-shell crabs and ended with cigars. With that, Henry Mencken, academic prodigy, athletic failure, and social mediocrity, was through with school forever. He was not to prove a loyal alumnus. "Though I pass the Polytechnic buildings very often," he wrote a friend exactly fifty years later, "I have entered them only once since I left. . . . I . . . have no affection for . . . the place."

But the Polytechnic years, though less enjoyable than the years preceding them, were to be vastly better than the three and a half years that followed. Upon graduation, Mencken's prospects would appear to have been bright. Although he had the disadvantage of education at a manual arts high school, he had the advantage of high achievement at that school and the added advantage of a father with the means to send him to college or university. Indeed, August Mencken occasionally spoke of sending Henry to the Johns Hopkins University to study law. In addition, Henry was still operating under the assumption that he was eligible for Eilard Mencke's stipend to attend a German university under the seventeenth-century Mencken family trust. He did not know at that time that the family council in Germany had ruled in 1869 that no American Menckens need apply. Mencken later believed that if his grandfather had still been living he would have looked closely into the trust, would have successfully challenged any barring of Americans, and might have sent Henry to Leipzig.

But with his grandfather dead, no talk of higher education appears to have been taken very seriously. Certainly, a genuine belief in a seventeenth-century trust sounds unworthy of a hardheaded realist such as Henry Mencken; and August Mencken, for his part, was halfhearted at best in his discussion of university education. In fact, Henry had no interest in law, medicine, or any other university curriculum except possibly chemistry. What he had in mind was newspaper work. But August Mencken had other plans. "My father," Mencken later wrote, "had his heart set upon taking me into his tobacco business. There was no apparent way of escape."

As he had with Henry's education at the Polytechnic, August Mencken got his way. Henry went to work for Aug. Mencken & Bro. immediately upon receiving his diploma. His father's plan was that his son would learn all facets of the business and eventually succeed him as head. Henry began at three dollars a week and, that first summer, ran errands, helped as a janitor, and soon graduated to the bench to learn cigar making. Before long he was making seven dollars, and besides had taken his father's suggestion that he learn to smoke as the best way to learn about tobacco. He went on to other tasks, at times calling on his skills as a chemist in an attempt to improve the leaf. He proposed moistening cheaper Pennsylvania tobacco with scuppernong wine in order to give it the aroma of genuine Havana. He tried to design a machine that would paste up containers for cheroots. In addition, his father assigned him the task of learning Spanish so he could deal with the Cuban market.

Mencken did not particularly mind the factory work, in fact was to retain a fondness for its smells and colors, as well as a lifelong habit of chewing a cigar while he worked. But he loathed the rest of the tobacco business, both office work and sales. When his father promoted him to the bookkeeper's office, he became "intensely unhappy." "Keeping books seemed to me to be a horrible way to put in one's days," he later wrote. "When I was sent to the bank with checks to deposit I made mistakes; when I had bills to make out, I made worse ones."

Selling cigars was "even more terrible than the office." His father sent him out early, in 1896, to tobacco and grocery stores and kept him at it until the summer of 1898. "I was a bad hand at it," Mencken recalled, and he is supported by the evidence of his meager sales preserved in his commissions scrapbook. In eight months in 1896 he sold $171 worth of cigars. In August he sold $3.50 worth. "I hated to shine up to people, and argue with them," he later wrote. "I detested approaching customers."

The entire experience was devastating for Mencken. After having been the star pupil at Polytechnic, he later wrote, "I was soon deflated . . . it quickly appeared that I knew nothing." An inferiority complex—which, as we have seen, he kept at bay throughout his nonage—threatened, and for reasons that had nothing at all to do with his being German. Viewed from a later vantage point, Mencken's failure in his father's factory is curious. In his references to the experience in autobiographical volumes and elsewhere he always gave the impression that, quite simply, he was incompetent. But it was more complicated than that. Even then, Mencken had personality, charm, wit, all those characteristics required in an era of gregarious salesmanship. Even then, he was a talker, and it would be difficult to imagine a time at which he did not relish what he said he detested—"to argue with [people]." Similarly, it is difficult to picture his failing so dismally as bookkeeper and manager of money. He was later to become a nearly compulsive record keeper, a meticulous financial manager, a shrewd businessman.

Why, then, did he fail? In part, as a salesman, because a certain sense of self—a dignity of person and a disinclination to demean himself—kept him from playing the game, from doing all he could to please customers. But even more, in the office as well as in sales, he did not succeed because he had no *will* to succeed, no real interest in what he was doing, no incentive to do well—and, beyond that, because he had a wish to escape more than anything else. He was "fully determined to leave the cigar business for newspaper work," he later wrote, "but I knew that it would be difficult to break away."

He expressed his unhappiness to his father, but to little avail. When he first made it clear to August that he did not want to stay at the factory, his father was "understanding," Mencken later wrote, and confided in his son that he too, as a youth, had not wanted to go into business. But August "was so plainly dashed by my desire to leave him that I said no more about it until 1898." Henry was bitterly unhappy, despairing to the point of contemplating suicide when he was seventeen. Though he later dismissed such thoughts of suicide as "the green sickness of youth," he was indeed miserable, concluded "more than once . . . that death was preferable to life," and, as he had always done when he was troubled, he went to his mother for consolation. She was "well aware," he recalled, "that my father's plans for the future were all grounded on the assumption that I would remain with him," but she gave him moral support nonetheless. By the summer of 1898 Mencken had "fully made up [his] mind to escape, amicably if possible but if necessary by open rebellion." Again he approached his father, and again he found August "plainly full of hope that I would change my mind." So Mencken "shut up again."

These could have been happy years for Mencken. He was young, with a measure of financial independence, living in a booming city in fin-de-siècle America. But the Gay Nineties were anything but gay for him. Finding no source of personal well-being, satisfaction, or pleasure in the cigar business, he looked elsewhere. For a time he became a regular theatergoer, sitting in the galleries of Baltimore's two theaters and smoking the cigars he had rolled during the day. He also frequented a burlesque house in West Baltimore. He had lost interest in music, however, and was not to regain it until he left the cigar factory. He still lived at home, at Hollins Street most of the year and in Mount Washington in the summer. He had at least casual friends, among them his father's bookkeeper, with whom he took numerous bicycle trips on summer evenings and occasionally Sundays. But nowhere in his remarks about these three years does he mention seeing women, although the infatuation with the blond neighbor seems to have continued.

What Henry Mencken turned to increasingly in his off-hours in those years between fifteen and eighteen was the world of his imagination. If he was not allowed to approach that world on his job, he would doggedly pursue it on his own time. He continued his reading of English literature but also read contemporary American fiction. He was struck in particular by one novel, Stephen Crane's *The Red Badge of Courage*, which came in 1895 "like a flash of lightning out of a clear winter sky; it was at once unprecedented and irresistible . . ." He was breaking somewhat from Thackeray and from the Genteel Tradition, now spending much of his money on the *Tendenz* magazines of the 1890s and finding special delight in *M'lle New York*, which featured a young iconoclast named James Gibbons Huneker.

Reading was not enough. Although Mencken later claimed that he "wrote next to nothing" during his years in the tobacco business, the material in his scrapbooks tells a far different story. Not only did he continue to write poetry, mostly under the influence of Kipling, but he also began writing fiction in earnest. The poems he sent to the Baltimore *American*, and during his first summer at Aug. Mencken & Bro. he had a satiric piece, "Ode to the Pennant on the Centerfield Pole," accepted. A mock tribute to the weathered pennant won by the Orioles in 1894 and 1895, the poem bore the mark of Kipling less than that of William Cullen Bryant's "To a Waterfowl," of which it seems nearly a parody: "Thy wasted form / And hungry, homeless air / Seem sad in one / Who erstwhile was so fair." Mencken's baseball "Ode" was his first published piece, and thus it should be duly noted not only that this eventual decrier of poetry began his literary career as a poet, but also that this arch-hater of sports began his journalistic career as a kind of sportswriter.

A year and a half passed before the *American* accepted a second poem, "The Gordon Highlanders," inspired by what would seem for Mencken another unlikely subject: British gallantry in the Tirah campaign on the Indian frontier in October 1897. So fanatical an admirer of Kipling had he become that, he later wrote, "I swallowed his imperialistic politics along with his poetry."

By 1898, however, Mencken's primary interest had shifted from poetry to fiction. He had dabbled in short-story writing before, producing his first story, "Idyl," in a single evening during his final year at the Polytechnic. It was a "dreadful piece," he recalled, a love story with a twist, and it was best left unpublished. After this story, he wrote no more fiction until, nearly two years later, his uncle Charlie Abhau called his attention to a correspondence course in writing operated by *Cosmopolitan*, and he promptly enrolled. He wrote several stories in 1898, but it is obvious that he had not at first learned the lesson of his favorite novel, *Huckleberry Finn:* his correspondence school instructor warned him, with reason, against "fine writing" and "pompous and bookish expressions." Mencken learned quickly. His fifth submission, "An Alley Case," was a story of low life near the Baltimore wharf. That story and the one that followed were "very good," the instructor wrote, "as excellent work as we have received here."

At the same time Mencken was learning to write fiction through correspondence courses, he embarked on a similar plan for a career in journalism. He went to the Pratt library, checked out every book he could find on newspaper writing, and pored over a volume, *Steps into Journalism*, by an editorial writer for the *Chicago Tribune*. Then he completed an application for the Associated Newspaper Bureau School of Journalism, a correspondence firm in New York from which he hoped to take courses. Under "Occupation" he wrote "Clerical work in factory" and under "Expectations," "Expect to begin as a reporter and after that trust to hard work & luck for something better." For age he wrote nineteen, although he was in fact only seventeen or eighteen.

All this—reading voraciously, writing stories, preparing for newspaper work—was carried out in virtual isolation. As Mencken later noted, his early life was spent in an "amazingly unliterary environment." His family showed little interest in his work, and only one of his friends had any literary or journalistic ambitions. By day he worked in the cigar business, and at night and on weekends he read, wrote, and planned for the future in newspaper work or literature that he was now determined he would have. But he still had little idea when and how he would have it. After his talk with his father in the summer of 1898, Mencken had let the matter lie. "It was understood between us," he later wrote, "that we were to resume the discussion in a year or so."

That moment never came. On the last day of 1898, as August Mencken stretched out in his characteristic after-dinner fashion on the walnut lounge in the sitting room, he suffered convulsions and lapsed into unconsciousness. Anna Mencken immediately summoned Henry, who himself lay ill upstairs with influenza. August's eldest son raced out to find the family doctor, Z. K. Wiley, and as he ran the eleven blocks through the freezing night he kept saying to himself—he later revealed—"that if my father died I'd be free at last." Although Dr. Wiley was not at home, his mother had found another doctor by the time Henry returned. After they put August to bed, Wiley did arrive, examined the patient, found an acute kidney infection, and sent Henry out a second time to a druggist on Baltimore Street for a prescription. While Mencken waited for the druggist to appear, he shivered outside in the cold.

Thus began a watch that continued around the clock at 1524 Hollins Street. Anna Mencken, Henry, and Charlie took turns sitting with August, who soon was diagnosed as having acute nephritis. He improved somewhat after two or three days and became rational again, only to grow worse after about a week. When Dr. Wiley decided to apply leeches to the patient, he sent Henry out to fetch them from a German barber. When that and other remedies failed, August again fell into unconsciousness and suffered convulsions. Mencken later recalled having to hold him down in bed, with Charlie's help, as August raved. At the end of the second week Henry and his mother and brother were exhausted. Henry was asleep in the next room when August Mencken died at 10:45 P.M. on Friday, January 13. His uncle William Abhau awakened him. Later Mencken could not fully recall his feelings at that moment: he was drained physically and emotionally, and he returned to bed in a few minutes.

August Mencken was buried on Sunday, January 15, at Loudon Park Cemetery, barely two miles west of Union Square. August had earlier bought stock in the Cremation Company of Baltimore, and Henry tried to persuade his mother that cremation was "much more civilized" than burial, but Anna Mencken had her way. The Freemasons put on a "considerable show," Mencken later recalled: "Just before their march into the house, a bugler at the corner of Hollins and Gilmor streets let go with a fanfare." Then August Mencken's family and friends proceeded to the gravesite for the afternoon burial. After the ceremony Henry came back to the house, took a florid pastel portrait of his father out of its frame, and burned it in the backyard. "My mother made a formal protest," Mencken wrote a friend nearly forty years later, "but it was easy to see that she was greatly relieved." No matter how curious his action might appear— Oedipal at most, bizarre at the least—he meant no disrespect to his father, Mencken insisted in that same letter. He just disliked the picture.

Indeed, the emotions Henry Mencken experienced that cold bright day in 1899 must have been conflicting and powerful. He grieved and, besides, was aware of the heavy responsibilities of being head of household. But the death of his father had also meant his "deliverance," as he wrote a half century later. His later accounts of the conflict with his father attempt to place August in the best possible light: his father, he said, was sympathetic to his plight, indeed in time would have relented and let him leave the family business, "if only because of his vivid memory of his own disappointed ambition."

But the facts suggest a somewhat different interpretation. At least twice between 1896 and 1898 Henry had appealed to his father, only to be turned away each time with the promise of another talk later, and each time he was made to feel that he had injured his father severely. He "made no formal protest," Mencken wrote of one of the occasions, "but neither did he give his formal consent, and I feared that there would be a considerable family debate before I could be set free." August seems essentially to have been buying time, holding out until Henry eventually came around to his way of thinking. It would have been, for Henry, the course of least resistance. It would have also been the course of the dutiful son he had always proved to be. "If he had lived," Mencken later wrote Edgar Lee Masters, "I'd have stuck on in the tobacco business for at least a few years longer, probably to my permanent damage."

But sooner or later Mencken would have rebelled, and it was this outward rebellion—this challenge to his father's authority and the resulting confrontation—that he dreaded. August's death, he wrote Masters, was a "tremendous relief to me." His "departure for parts unknown," he wrote elsewhere, saved Mencken "from what must have been a painful unpleasantness, for even if he had consented to my leaving it would have been at the cost of his long-cherished plans." Despite Mencken's later insistence that the 13th, particularly Friday the 13th, brought only bad luck to him, this particular Friday the 13th, he later acknowledged in letters, notes, and manuscripts, brought an unlikely and bizarre "stroke of [good] luck." Indeed, looking back near the end of what he considered a lucky life, Mencken wrote, "His death was the luckiest thing that ever happened to me, though we were on good terms and I missed him sorely after he was gone."

But August Mencken had left his mark on his son, a mark more pronounced than any other person was ever to leave. August was always to be a source of fascination, far more than Anna Mencken, to whom Henry was, in fact, much closer. Henry saw a certain poignancy, a drama of the missed life, in his father's brief existence. He once compared August to Abraham Cahan's fictional hero David Levinsky, a man who "fail[ed] to achieve the goal of his life," who "succeed[ed] in winning headway in all other fields save the one which was secreted in the innermost chambers of his heart and mind"—in August's case, mathematics and engineering. His father was taken by "the realities of life" to "more practical activities, in which he succeeded," but "he never could remain contented." "My father was a 'David Levinsky,' though of a different race, of a different mould, and different circumstances."

Was the example of his father's life the reason Henry Mencken was so determined not to be sidetracked—to be delayed, perhaps, but not deterred—from his own ambitions and dreams? It would not have been August's only legacy. "The main elements in my body of ideas," Mencken later wrote a friend, "were picked up as a boy, and largely from my father." There were exceptions: his father did not admire the genteel Virginians as Henry did, and the two occasionally disagreed on the merits of individual politicians. But on balance Mencken was correct. His views on business, labor, religion, government, education, various ethnic groups, and any number of other matters he drew from his father, although he argued those views more persuasively than his father ever could have.

We must wonder if those views would have gone so completely unchallenged if August Mencken had lived, if his son had indeed been forced to defy his authority. The death of Mencken's father, completely unexpected, when he was but forty-four years old, served in some measure to freeze August Mencken in time, to make sacrosanct the beliefs and prejudices of a rather narrow and limited man. His death came just at the moment when Henry was marshaling his resources for such a rebellion, which of course never came.

Henry Mencken never spoke of guilt as being among the emotions he felt at his father's death; it was a commodity in which he rarely dealt. He did refer to other legacies of that two-week ordeal, particularly of his several ventures into the midwinter Baltimore night to seek medical help that, interestingly, "left me with a cough that persisted for years." In a letter to Masters he later explained his differences with his father in this manner: "No really intelligent boy gets on with his father." But the fact remains that there were profound and irreconcilable differences between the two that Mencken never fully acknowledged. The several pages of reflections on his father's illness that he included in the manuscript "Newspaper Days: Additions, Corrections and Explanatory Notes" demonstrate a certain dispassionate quality, a curious lack of pain and sorrow. Since that tone may be explained partly by the passage of time between the events of 1899 and the writing, it is even more fruitful, as we shall see, to consider Mencken's course of activities in the days immediately following the death itself. What is certain is that Mencken felt, most of all, great relief. He had wanted to escape August's relatively gentle but firm hand, and now, almost miraculously, he had—and without having to take any action himself. His luck indeed had held. Of all the debts Henry Mencken owed his father, the greatest of all was August's early death.

# Chapter 4

# HIS YALE COLLEGE AND HIS HARVARD

It is the fate of man, I believe, to be wholly happy only once in his life.

—*H. L. Mencken,*
*Baltimore* Evening Sun,
*January 10, 1927*

Whether it was the day after his father's funeral that H. L. Mencken climbed to the fifth-floor newsroom of the Baltimore *Morning Herald* to apply for a job—or four days later, or two weeks later—we cannot be sure. In his autobiographical notes Mencken himself gave conflicting accounts, although he usually invested the occasion with the kind of drama reminiscent, say, of the young Ben Franklin entering Philadelphia nearly two centuries before. It was "the most important moment of my life," he once wrote a friend, and it was central in the making of the legend of H. L. Mencken, ex–cigar manufacturer released by his father's death to follow his destiny.

This much is clear. Immediately after his father's death Mencken told his mother that he wanted to apply for a newspaper position at once, and he was surprised that she did not protest. The reason she did not, he later realized, was that she did not want him to continue working with his uncle Henry, whose industriousness and business acumen were suspect. Moreover, she encouraged him to apply for a position on the *Morning Herald,* a lively newspaper that occupied a rung in prestige beneath that of the solid, respectable *Sun.* He himself was inclined toward the *Herald* because his Polytechnic friend Arthur Hawks and Hawks's brother both worked for the newspaper and could put in a good word for him.

In any case, on the evening of January 16, 1899, or shortly thereafter, Henry Mencken shaved, put on his best suit, parted his hair in the middle as was his wont, and traveled the fifteen blocks to the *Herald* offices at the corner of Fayette and St. Paul to ask Max Ways, the city editor, for a job. We cannot be sure what Ways thought of the "slim and even cadaverous youth" standing before him. But Ways was polite. He told Mencken there were no openings and little chance for openings anytime soon. But he added that Mencken might stop by on other nights if he wanted, on the chance there might be trial assignments—for no pay, of course.

That was all Mencken needed. For the next few weeks, after a day's work at Aug. Mencken & Bro., he showed up in the *Herald* newsroom. At last, on February 23, he was sent out on snowy streets to the far northern suburb of Govanstown to see what he could find. There he came up with his first news story:

> A horse, a buggy and several sets of harness, valued in all at about $250, were stolen last night from the stable of Howard Quinlan, near Kingsville, in the Eleventh district. The county police are at work on the case, but so far no trace of either thieves or booty has been found.

The next night Mencken was sent to Waverly, another northern suburb. Other assignments followed. The city editor introduced him around the newsroom as "Macon," and his newspaper career was under way.

It was not, for some months, much of a career. Through the winter and spring of 1899 Mencken roamed the outer reaches of Baltimore looking for news. Still unpaid and having to use his own funds for trolleys, he was losing money. But soon he was given assignments closer in, covering church meetings, concerts and recitals, high school commencements, and minor political rallies. On July 2 Ways made him a salaried reporter at seven dollars a week.

Thus began at age eighteen, Mencken later wrote, the best three or four years of his life, "gaudy and gorgeous days" that followed on the heels of the most miserable. It was "the maddest, gladdest, damndest existence ever enjoyed by mortal youth. . . . I had yet to taste the sharp teeth of responsibility. Life was arduous, but it was gay and carefree. The days chased one another like kittens chasing their tails." It was also, he recounted forty years later, the best education he could have had:

> At a time when the respectable bourgeois youngsters of my generation were college freshmen, oppressed by simian sophomores and affronted by balderdash daily and hourly by chalky pedagogues, I was at large in a wicked seaport of half a million people . . . getting earfuls and eyefuls of instruction in a hundred giddy arcana, none of them taught in schools. . . . I was . . . laying in all the worldly wisdom of a police lieutenant, a bartender, a shyster lawyer, or a midwife.

The streets of Baltimore thus became—to quote Herman Melville's Ishmael—Mencken's Yale College and his Harvard or, perhaps more accurately, his equivalent of the Mississippi riverboats on which Samuel Clemens had served his apprenticeship.

Max Ways assumed the role of Clemens' mentor, Horace Bixby, teaching Mencken the newspaper trade as Bixby had taught Clemens the river. A charming man, Ways was also a shrewd, tough boss who directed "withering denunciation" at incompetent or careless reporters. Mencken worked for Ways twelve hours a day, six and sometimes seven days a week, often writing more than five thousand words of copy a day. For a time, as police reporter, he covered crimes routine and bizarre, viewed the victims of murder and suicide, witnessed autopsies—in one instance saw a decayed body explode. In his first month as a full-time reporter he covered the hangings of four black men in the yard of the Baltimore city jail, the first of nine hangings he was to witness. Several older reporters took it hard, Mencken wrote, "but I was unperturbed." Before his first year was over he had been promoted from the police beat to City Hall, and his salary had increased to $10 a week and, within the next year, to $14, then $16, then $18.

Mencken later said he was not a good reporter, but in fact he was an excellent one, attentive to detail and crisp in style. He also contended that, in those days of crusading reporting, he would have nothing of uplift, that his "true and natural allegiance was to the

Devil's party": "I was born, happily, with no more public spirit than a cat . . ." That too was a characterization of the older Mencken looking back. In fact, as the young reporter saw the victims of industrial accidents, dead and mutilated, he became a strong supporter of industrial safety, workers' compensation, and other such departures from the strict laissez-faire of his father. And the hangings may have had more of an effect than he thought: he also came to oppose capital punishment.

In the autumn of 1900, after little more than a year at the *Morning Herald*, Mencken was given a weekly column on the editorial page. In some of these columns he found an outlet for his unpublished schoolboy verse, of which the *Herald*'s editor, Colonel A. B. Cunningham, was fond. In other columns we find hints of both the substance and the style to come. Mencken begins to poke fun at the evangelical clergy and certain politicians, and on November 4, 1900, he makes a prophecy that must have startled those who read it at the time: "Some day [Mark Twain's] critics will awake to the fact that his 'Huckleberry Finn' is the greatest novel yet produced by an American writer."

The young Mencken threw himself into his work on the *Herald*, sitting at his desk in the newsroom, chewing a cigar, and turning out copy in his one-finger typing style. He reveled in the cast of newspaper characters he encountered, including two imposters worthy of Mark Twain who "were content to let it be known that they were cadets of French families running back to Charlemagne. . . . One, when in his cups, called himself Jean-Baptiste du Plessis de Savines, and the other . . . Jacques de Corbigny." Heavy drinking was a way of life at the *Herald*, a newspaper numbering but one teetotaler, and Mencken attended to the bottle at selected times. He also frequented the black dives of Hawk Street and other establishments of the Baltimore night.

At first Anna Mencken was alarmed by his company—his aunt Pauline had told her that large numbers of newspapermen ended up in the gutter—but soon she accepted her son's unusual habits and hours. On summer nights he got home as late as 3:00 A.M., slept until ten the next morning, and was gone again by noon. But she must have been impressed with how much he was accomplishing, and how quickly. Aside from his *Herald* work, by 1900 he was serving as a correspondent for *The Philadelphia Inquirer* and other out-of-town newspapers, including several papers in Japan and China, and was contributing an occasional piece to magazines such as W. C. Brann's monthly, *The Iconoclast.* He was also writing free-lance advertising copy, including an oleaginous promotion booklet for Loudon Park Cemetery, where his father lay and where he himself would land a half century later. For all his childhood distaste for Horatio Alger stories—and his later debunking of the American success myth— Mencken seemed to be a real-life Alger character, bright, streetwise, self-reliant, and practical. In nineteen months he rose from the lowest apprentice to the highest-paid young reporter on the *Herald* staff.

But there was a side of Mencken's life during 1899 and 1900 that was darker than the "gaudy and gorgeous" period depicted in *Newspaper Days.* Chronic bronchitis, which he believed was a result of his exposure to cold while running after doctors and pharmacists during his father's illness, grew increasingly worse. His health, in fact, had concerned him for the past three or four years; between ages sixteen and eighteen he had suffered from malaria, almost certainly acquired through mosquitoes that bred in the marshes outside Baltimore, and he had been cured only through "heroic doses of quinine." He had also suffered from a painful case of urethritis, relieved, after it became chronic, by application of silver nitrate. Finally, and as psychologically disturbing as it was physically, he had apparently paid the price for his ventures into the Baltimore night, although the exact time and the source of his affliction are unclear. He had, he told a physician friend much later, contracted gonorrhea on one occasion, and although he was quickly treated and cured, his experience may have reinforced his division of women into virgins and whores.

All these encounters with physical misery he apparently bore stoically—or at least silently—but events in the spring of 1900 were of even greater concern. He had a very bad cough, he had begun to lose weight, and he felt exhausted much of the time. Since his family physician, Wiley, suspected tuberculosis, Mencken saw a specialist, who made no precise diagnosis but suggested he take a sea voyage to the Caribbean. In late June he sailed for Jamaica on a banana boat chartered by the United Fruit Company, stayed on the island nearly a month, and came home on a Danish tramp, still not fully recovered. "I was probably doomed to early death," he later wrote of his feelings at that time, no doubt exaggerating but still capturing something of his anxiety. Doomed anyway, he determined to take to smoking and beer drinking with a vengeance.

The illness subsided in time, and the most notable legacy of the tuberculosis scare was the Jamaica trip itself, with its abundance of new experiences. For this journey was Mencken's first outside the United States, indeed his first of any length except for his trip to Ohio with his grandfather when he was ten, and it opened his eyes to a new people and a new culture. After the short sea voyage, he left the banana boat at Port Antonio on the northeastern shore of Jamaica and went ashore just before daylight. "I'll never forget the sounds and sights of that tropical morning," he wrote a friend much later. He had read Lafcadio Hearn's *Two Years in the French West Indies* and was primed for "the sweet tropical smells . . . the palms . . . skiffs full of niggers . . . the blinding, pea-green water."

He was equally impressed by what he found when he explored the rest of Jamaica over the following two weeks. He listened to tales of plantation owners, made the acquaintance of the natives, and—if we are to believe the often unreliable Charles Angoff—made a sexual conquest among the West Indian women. He gave his impressions of Jamaica in three articles written for the *Herald* and in a long letter to his sister, Gertrude. The articles are conventional travel pieces, generally romantic in their descriptions of the landscape. The beauty of Jamaica struck him "dumb," although the natives themselves were "dishonest and lazy." His letter to Gertrude suggests another reason for Mencken's interest in Jamaica. For a time in the early nineteenth century, it had been the home of his paternal grandmother's family, the McLellands, and he was determined to discover all he could about ancestors other than the Menckens.

What he discovered most of all about the Jamaican McLellands, after three days of questioning newspaper editors and the elderly inhabitants of Kingston, was that—he wrote Gertrude—"*they are mulattos*" [Mencken's italics]. With that information in hand, he went to Spanish Town, the former capital of the island, looked up McLelland records, examined the will of his great-granduncle, and verified that many of Jeremiah McLelland's progeny were indeed of "almost burnt cork complexion."

That discovery did not disturb Mencken in the least. Many early Irish and Scots-Irish settlers had cohabited with slaves and ex-slaves in Jamaica, and besides, demonstrating that combination of racial tolerance and racial insensitivity he was always to display, Mencken added, "A nigger here, if he is decent, is as good as a white man. The mayor of Kingston and most of the city council are coons . . ." Indeed, he rather delighted in his discovery. He had found some ancestors other than Menckens worthy of interest. Besides, he must have realized, he had something more—black relatives—in common with many of the Virginians he revered. In later years, in correspondence, Mencken regularly spoke of his Jamaican cousins, "rang[ing] in hue from a pale coffee color to a rich purplish black."

The trip to Jamaica, as well as a train trip ten months later to Jacksonville, Florida, to represent the *Herald* in the aftermath of the destructive 1901 Jacksonville fire, opened up to the young reporter a larger and more varied world. On the trip to Jacksonville he saw in the backwoods and the spare, ugly towns of the Carolinas and Georgia a South vastly different from that he had imagined from observing the expatriate Virginians—and a South that would later provide material for some of his most biting social commentary. The assignment in Jacksonville itself he viewed with amusement. His primary role was to wait for the *Herald* relief train to arrive from Baltimore, to report the *Herald*'s efforts, and to obtain a statement of gratitude from the Jacksonville mayor.

When he returned to Baltimore, Mencken continued his education in metropolitan journalism, his instructors being, besides Max Ways, two managing editors, Robert Carter and Lynn Roby Meekins. Carter, a New Englander and Harvard graduate, Mencken found a "highly civilized man," a knowledgeable student of music and drama, and a man who kept his young reporter from yielding to the growing philistinism in Baltimore journalism. Meekins, who succeeded Carter in 1903, was a less urbane, more sober sort—a Methodist—but Mencken greatly respected his competence and appreciated his personal kindness. Mencken was assigned a variety of tasks. He went to Annapolis to cover state politics, to Washington to cover the U.S. Senate, and, shortly before President McKinley's death, to Antietam to cover the president's speech. He began to write editorials, holding forth on subjects from South Africa to June brides, finding his primary stylistic influence an obscure editorial writer for the New York *Sun* named Charles Kingsbury.

But most important, in his signed column Mencken found the sort of editorial freedom that would characterize his later writing. In a series entitled "Untold Tales," running through 1901 and early 1902, he demonstrated a sense of the ridiculous, a delight in the eternal human comedy. In scenes supposedly set in Rome, circa A.D. 150–250, he remarked on Roman—or Baltimorean—graft and corruption and, in particular, lambasted J. Bozzo Puritani, three-term mayor of Rome and the "brood of he-she parasites known as reformers." In two other long pieces, unsigned but unmistakably his, he assumed the role of a staff member of "Prince Henry" of Germany, who traveled around the United States and recorded his impressions to send back to Germany.

Mencken soon had other responsibilities as well, in 1901 becoming both Sunday editor and theater critic for the *Herald* and in 1903 becoming city editor. With the city editorship, at age twenty-three, he had fully arrived as a journalist, and he enjoyed his new authority. At Meekins' suggestion, he fired a number of incompetent reporters, cracked down on others, and emphasized a kind of brisk writing the *Herald* had not known before.

But Mencken's interests during this period were hardly confined to journalism. He still considered himself an imaginative writer as well, and during his first two or three years on the *Herald* he devoted a good deal of time to writing and submitting short fiction. He worked in his third-floor bedroom on Hollins Street, writing on his secondhand Remington and often laboring long into the night. His first acceptance had come in April 1900, just before the Jamaica trip, and that story, "The Cook's Victory," had appeared in *Short Stories* in August, a month before his twentieth birthday. Other early stories drew on the month in Jamaica. "The Fear of the Savage," which dealt with the mistreatment of a Jamaican stevedore, turned into Mencken's commentary on black psychology. A second story, "When Magic Met Muscle," treated the Jamaican *obeah* man, a conjurer who threatens but in the end is defeated by a white American dentist who intrudes on his territory.

*Short Stories* had accepted two other stories in 1901 and an additional four in 1902 and 1903. Mencken sold other stories to *Frank Leslie's Popular Monthly*, the *Criterion*, *The Bookman*, *The Youth's Companion*, and other magazines. Although he could not crack major magazines such as *Harper's*, the *Saturday Evening Post*, *Cosmopolitan*, *Red Book*, and *The Smart Set*, he nonetheless made as much as fifty dollars a story—or three or four times his weekly salary. In all, he sold some fifteen or twenty stories to popular magazines during his days on the *Herald*.

Mencken's fiction showed greater promise than he himself later suggested. "The Outcast" (1900), the story of a leper shunned by his community, bears a resemblance to Stephen Crane's "The Monster," which had been published a year earlier. Other tales also suggest Crane in style and particularly in subject matter. In stories of low-life Baltimore that were essentially naturalistic in setting and incident and often ironic (if occasionally sentimental) in tone, Mencken demonstrated a true narrative confidence. Other stories, such as one tale of the British Army in Africa, showed the old influence of Kipling, and still others suggested that of Mark Twain. One story in particular, "The War and Providence," resembled Twain's "The Man That Corrupted Hadleyburg" in its depiction of the ridiculous ends to which the inhabitants of two warring towns allow pride and other frailties to lead them. Mencken attracted some praise as a short-story writer and through his fiction found his first literary champion, Ellery Sedgwick, editor of *Frank Leslie's Popular Monthly*, later to be editor of the *Atlantic Monthly*. Sedgwick first accepted a Mencken story in the spring of 1901, accepted another that summer, and by the autumn of 1901 was asking for more. "I really believe," he assured Mencken, "you have a talent for [fiction]."

Mencken's short-story writing was appreciably more successful than his one attempt at a novel. Most of his short stories were realistic, tough-minded, and contemporary in setting and subject matter, while his one longer work, a historical novel set in Elizabethan England, departed from realism into something approximating romance. Mencken's fifty-two-page trial at a novel was not, however, the complete disaster the author later described it as being. Displaying a keen narrative sense, an admirable attention to detail, and a lively if sometimes antiquated prose style, the author also demonstrated a sure comic touch in his depiction of a boy growing up near Stratford in the late sixteenth century. The boy is not William Shakespeare, although he meets "Will" at a young age, beats him in a fight, and becomes his friend. Mencken's aborted novel in many ways resembles certain of Mark Twain's ventures into earlier European history, particularly *The Prince and the Pauper*. He creates a somewhat autobiographical protagonist—the son of gentlefolk and a precocious child, he is close to his mother, fond of his pony, and filled with curiosity about the world—who absorbs tall tales worthy of Twain's yarn spinners and teams up with a clever friend both to do mischief and to undertake chivalric deeds.

Mencken later said that he abandoned his novel because of a lack of historical knowledge—although, in fact, his portrait of the Elizabethan age, though stylized, is at least as convincing as that of numerous other historical novelists. His real problem was not historical inaccuracy but an ill-chosen genre. In the year after Theodore Dreiser published *Sister Carrie*, just after Stephen Crane had published *Maggie, A Girl of the Streets* (1893) and Frank Norris had written *McTeague* (1899)—all classics of American naturalism written in contemporary American English and set in bustling and often raw contemporary American cities—Mencken had embarked on a historical romance, written partly in archaic English, set in Elizabethan England. The future foe of the Genteel Tradition was himself, in his long fiction if not his short, still very much within its grasp. The champion of the American language, as opposed to British English, had yet to emerge.

At about the time Mencken was working on his novel, he received a letter from a Boston publisher, Richard Badger, who had seen his first story in *Frank Leslie's Popular Monthly* and inquired whether "you have other stories, as good as this, to form a volume." If so, "we think we can make you a proposition for their publication that will please you." Within a week Mencken's stories were in Badger's hands, and for a few days he basked in the glory of anticipated publication—only to learn in Badger's next letter that the publisher expected Mencken himself "to advance $300 towards the expense of publication." The young author had stumbled upon a vanity press, but even at that, Mencken later wrote, "I must have been sorely tempted." He did not subsidize the publication only because he did not have the three hundred dollars to spare. The next year Mencken submitted his stories to a more reputable publisher, promptly had them rejected, went back to Badger for one more round of negotiations, and finally gave up his efforts to publish a volume of stories.

Shortly after Mencken ceased his efforts with Badger, another opportunity for book publication came from a totally unexpected source. Mencken had continued to write poetry during his early days with the *Herald*, although not at the frantic pace of his teen years, and had published poems in *The Bookman, Life, Leslie's Weekly*, the *National Magazine*, and the *New England Magazine*, as well as in his own *Herald* column. Much of this verse had continued to be influenced by Kipling, both in subject matter and in style. But he had about given up writing poetry—although he still had an abundance of it, both published and unpublished, on hand—when, in 1903, three friends on the *Herald* proposed to publish a volume of his poetry as the maiden effort of a printing business they were setting up. Although Mencken had suggested a collection of his stories, they believed they could exercise more printerly creativity with verse. Running short of funds, they successfully appealed to Mencken for the last thirty dollars, and in April 1903, when the poet was still twenty-two, *Ventures into Verse* appeared. He was given half the one hundred copies printed; he gave half of his volumes to friends and sent the others to reviewers.

Mencken began *Ventures into Verse*, which ran to forty-six pages, with a "Warning" that some of the poems were "imitations—necessarily weak—of the verse of several men in whose writing [he had] found a good deal of innocent pleasure." He followed that notice with a poem dedicated to the leading of those men, Kipling—"Prophet of brawn and bravery: / Bard of the fighting man!"—and demonstrated Kipling's influence in the poems that followed:

Oho! for the days of the olden time,
When a fight was a fight of men . . .
When lance broke lance and arm met arm—
There were no cowards then . . .

He continued with other imitations of Kipling, poems with titles such as "The Spanish Main," "The War Song," "The Orf'cer Boy," and the poem he considered perhaps his best, "The Ballad of Ships in Harbor":

Here is a bark from Rio,
    Back—and away she steals!
Here, from her trip, is a clipper ship
    That showed the sea her heels—
South to the Galapagos,

Down, due south, to the Horn,
And up, by the windward Passage way,
On the breath of the balm-wind borne.

He concluded with several rondeaux and love poems that broke with Kipling's influence.

While Mencken was not altogether truthful when he wrote later that "every paper which noticed [*Ventures into Verse*] at all praised it as good," he was not far wrong. Most of the reviews were indeed favorable, and the notices were abundant as well, with the *Boston Herald*, the Cleveland *Plain Dealer*, *The Kansas City Star*, the *Los Angeles Times*, the Minneapolis *Tribune*, and the venerable Baltimore *Sun* all taking note of his book, most identifying Mencken as a "Kiplingite." If the *Brooklyn Eagle* was critical of the Kipling imitations and the Chicago *Record-Herald* found the poems "salable rather than sincere" (a rather questionable charge since only three copies sold), the Cleveland *Blade* praised Mencken's humor, the New York *Telegraph* called him an "eccentric genius," and the *Deutsch-Amerikanes* of Baltimore, recognizing one of its own whether the poet acknowledged German kinship or not, was boundless in its praise of "this Maryland Genius." Not only was Mencken the finest poet in Maryland, but "we compare him advisedly with the great German poets." *The Nation*, more on target, described the poet as "anglicized."

Mencken's family took some pride in having a poet in its midst, although a letter from brother Charlie to sister Gertrude perhaps best pronounced its literary verdict: "I received Harry's 'Ventures' and think they are fine. I have been reading reviews in the papers that he sent. He must be becoming a sport, wearing all those fine clothes." The reaction in the *Herald* office was more enthusiastic. Indeed, a number of *Herald* staffers had encouraged Mencken's literary ambitions and had provided him with at least a tenuous tie to the world of letters he had missed altogether in his years at Aug. Mencken & Bro. The *Herald* writers were hardly central in the Baltimore literary community, that privileged circle presided over by such refined souls as Lizette Woodworth Reese and Edward A. V. Valentine. But at least they were interested in writing and being published, and in some cases had already been published. Mencken had become close friends with Leo Crane, a *Herald* employee who had sold several stories to *Harper's*—one of Mencken's own elusive targets. But it was Lynn Meekins who inspired him most. A former managing editor of the *Saturday Evening Post*, he himself had written three books of fiction. Meekins had operated close to the highest levels, and it was those levels Mencken wished to reach.

Much of his social life in the *Herald* years was spent drinking and fraternizing with other budding writers as well as with people involved in drama and music. He became close friends with Channing Pollock, drama reviewer for *The Smart Set*, with Will A. Page, a theater press agent and former drama critic, and with Paul Armstrong, a popular playwright with whom he later became particularly close. The support of these and other friends was important in two ways. First, the contacts he made helped him to be published and reviewed and in general helped him learn his way around the world of letters. But even more important, they gave him a certain assurance about self, vocation, and masculinity that he had not always possessed in abundance.

To be sure, there had been men of letters in the Mencken family before. But that had been in another country, in another age, long before what Mencken saw as the feminization of Anglo-American letters in the late nineteenth century. In the world of the *American* Menckens, the pursuit of letters—and particularly the writing of poetry, to which Mencken was devoted in his mid-teens—was a rather suspect calling. Was it, after all, manly work? Henry Mencken, nonathletic son of baseball club vice president and then failure in the masculine world of business, had been, by age eighteen, already deficient by his father's standards. He had spent his nights reading and writing and had posted pictures of a poet, not an athlete, on his bedroom wall. Now, after his father's death, he found himself in his early twenties living at home with his mother, sister, and younger brother in a house controlled altogether by Anna Mencken: the feminization of American culture brought home in the most tangible of ways.

But the young Mencken wanted to write, and it is interesting the form that his writing took. The poet whose pictures he posted and whose verse he imitated was, he believed, the most masculine of poets, Kipling. The prose writers he admired or shortly came to admire were also advocates of a cult of adventure and experience, a certain vigorous ideal of manhood—Stephen Crane, Joseph Conrad, and Mark Twain. (Mencken did not yet realize the extent to which Twain was himself a product of the feminization of American culture.) And the philosopher he came to champion, as we shall see, was Nietzsche—whom Mencken associated with the words "Be hard!"—and the views he himself came to espouse on the strenuous life were worthy of Theodore Roosevelt. As he later wrote a lover, "The joy of life comes in overcoming difficulties."

Similarly, in 1899, when Mencken began his job on the *Herald*, the kind of reporting he relished at first was that which introduced him to the raw and violent life of the Baltimore streets: he witnessed hangings and autopsies, as we have seen, without flinching. Such newspaper work was writing, but it was a long way from the genteel world controlled by (to use a phrase employed by one of Mencken's friends) "old women of both sexes." As he sat at his newspaper desk Mencken chewed cigars—both a practice of most hard-bitten reporters and a very real legacy of the masculine world of Aug. Mencken & Bro.—and after work he drank, joked, frequented the seamiest parts of town, boasted of whoring, and apparently still accomplished it on occasion. Although he had departed from the particular masculine world of his father, Mencken willed himself to manhood all the same, and in those early years on the *Herald* he gained a sense of self and vocation he was never to relinquish. He would always see himself as the newspaperman (in a man's world) rather than the belletrist.

The profession of letters was permissible, then, because it was entered through the door of rough turn-of-the-century metropolitan journalism. As Mencken later wrote, during this period "the heavy reading of my teens [was] abandoned in favor of life itself." In fact, that was not altogether true, but such a statement projected the image Mencken wanted to project, as well as expressed that same preference for "life" over "literature" voiced by Frank Norris and others during that vigorous age. With such a self-image in mind, he plunged into a strenuous world, frequenting saloons, burlesque houses, and occasionally bawdy houses, combining life and literature, preparing himself to write the kind of literature that is grounded in life. "The Mauve Decade was just ending," he later wrote of that period, "and the newer era of standardization and efficiency had not come in. . . . Life was unutterably charming." Writing in 1927, he recalled the "romantic waterfront," "sinister alleys," "the pervasive rowdiness and bawdiness of the town," and added, "I believe that a young journalist, turned loose in a large city, had more fun than any other man." He "was almost completely his own man."

Although Mencken considered himself the self-reliant man in his early twenties, he was also becoming an eminently clubbable man, acquiring for himself that habit of joining that he later ridiculed in others, including his late father. About 1900 he became a member of a drinking group called the Stevedores, so named because "it devoted itself to the unloading of schooners." Nearly every night after work, the members met in a saloon near City Hall, drank for an hour or two, and roared choruses from German stein songs led by reporters from a German-language daily.

More important to Mencken was a dinner club he joined in 1904, the Vagabonds, because this group numbered among its members several writers, including George Bronson Howard, a creator of popular fiction who introduced Mencken to Dreiser's *Sister Carrie*. The club included lawyers and businessmen as well. The Stevedores were given to drink and song, but the Vagabonds existed for "the avowed purpose of mutual improvement" of its twelve or thirteen members, although Mencken later took pains to point out that "the club was not at all pedantic or arty." Given to the promotion of both learning and "digestion," at each session the members first ate and drank, then got down to the discussion of a matter of literary, historical, or political importance raised in a paper by one of the members. Mencken was the second youngest of those whose brief biographies were given in a program for the Vagabonds' meeting of January 1, 1905. His autobiographical sketch identifies him as a journalist and short-story writer whose published work had "reached 5,500,000 words." He also exaggerates his height—he lists 5 feet 10¼ inches—and reports that he weighs 172 pounds "and is not beautiful." Finally, he insists that he has "tested all forms of dissipation except gambling," professes to dislike "all forms of sport except prize-fighting" (his fondness for baseball having diminished), and concludes that he is "unmarried and glad of it."

If the Vagabonds served Mencken's interests in literature and general erudition, the *Herald*'s music critic, W. G. Owst, and copywriter Joseph Callahan revived his interest in music. Callahan introduced Mencken to Albert Hildebrandt, a Baltimore violin maker, and in 1902 or 1903 Mencken, Hildebrandt, and another *Herald* staffer, Emanuel Daniel, began to play trios in Hildebrandt's shop. Hildebrandt played the cello, Daniel violin, and Mencken the piano. Others joined in the playing, and by 1904 the group was meeting regularly. Out of those sessions came a group to which Mencken would be devoted for a full half century and to which he would owe greater allegiance than to any body other than his own family—the Saturday Night Club.

From its beginnings this club was devoted to more than music; it specialized as well in hearty eating and drinking and boisterous fun, all of which (along with Mencken's occasional piano playing in Baltimore bawdy houses) made music at least as manly an activity for Mencken as baseball had been for his father. At first the group gathered on weeknights, not Saturdays—meeting in members' homes as well as Hildebrandt's shop—and the musicians soon fell into the habit of proceeding, after the playing, to a nearby drinking place for two or three hours. Mencken's customary position was second piano, not first, and, he later wrote, "My piano technique is dreadful, I have no talent for the instrument." In fact, he was better than that, but he was correct in his estimate that he was less an accomplished musician than a "happy music lover." Music to him was the one "wholly satisfying," "absolutely pure" art, and his prejudices concerning this subject were just as deeply held as those involving literature or politics. Although he was slow in coming to an appreciation of most things German, in music he was a Germanophile from the beginning. As he once wrote, "There are, indeed, only two kinds of music: German music and bad music." Among the Germans and Austrians, his gods were Beethoven, Schubert, Mozart, and Brahms.

Mencken's musical interests took him in other directions as well. Through Joseph Callahan he met Baltimore brewer and amateur flutist Frederick Gottlieb and attended dozens of Gottlieb's lavish parties, affairs—he later wrote—"which began with music, proceeded to eating and drinking, and ended in venery." "On many a night Al Hildebrandt and I, after playing for and toasting the female guests, entertained them in a more confidential manner in the bedrooms. They ranged all the way from ladies belonging to the first social circles of Baltimore to the kept women of police captains."

We might wonder if many of Gottlieb's guests indeed belonged to "the first social circles of Baltimore" or if Mencken, a stranger to those first circles, simply assumed—rather like a Dreiser character—that they did. In fact, he was nearly as alienated from Baltimore's social elite as he had ever been, and further he professed not to care. When Gottlieb and Dr. William H. Welch, members of the University Club, invited him to join, he declined for two reasons. First, he did not like Welch, and "second, if I was ever to go into a university club I did not want to be proposed by a Jewish brewer."

Socially, then, in these *Herald* days, Mencken appears to have been a curious combination of egalitarian and (as he later described himself) "incurable snob." The figure he cut was an impressive one in many ways: he was bright and witty, usually nattily attired in tailor-made suits, looking out on the world with striking china blue eyes and a look of constant astonishment on his face. He entertained women when and as he chose, but he remained staunchly a bachelor. "The worst burden that a competent and ambitious man can carry is a stupid wife," he remarked after observing the lot of a close friend, and in his own case he seemed to mean (as he suggested in his autobiographical sketch for the Vagabonds) any wife at all. He was still hard to please when it came to choosing friends and associates as well, preferring not to keep company with those newspapermen he found to be "poor fish . . . mere ciphers" or with those writers he deemed "failures." He had a low opinion of Colonel A. B. Cunningham, the editor in chief of the *Herald*, and of Alexander Bechhofer, the former president and general manager—"a highly dubious fellow . . . the worst type of pushing unscrupulous Jew." He refused to join the Journalists Club because "it was mainly composed of shyster lawyers, quack doctors, brewery collectors, minor jobholders and dubious politicians." Even his good friend Arthur Hawks—who had helped Mencken land his job on the *Herald* and at whose wedding he was best man—Mencken finally concluded was "extraordinarily indolent and not a little stupid."

As always, then, Mencken maintained his high standards. As always, he was sharper, quicker, and wittier than most of his associates, and he felt especially good about himself as he reached his midtwenties. As he wrote a friend thirty years later, "My life in 1905 was pretty pleasant. After a number of years of indifferent health I was feeling brisk and vigorous again. I had a good job, knew everybody worth knowing in Baltimore, and spent my evenings in the theatres, breweries and other cultural establishments of the town."

79

Again we might question Mencken's assessment. At twenty-four—
not yet acquainted with many of the luminaries of the Johns Hopkins, not to mention the Baltimore Virginians he admired from
afar—*did* he know "everybody worth knowing" in Baltimore? Could
he have spent all his evenings as he described and still have had time
to turn out the massive amount of writing—fiction, essays, public
relations copy, and free-lance journalism, not to mention the heavy
*Herald* work—he was producing? The truth is that Mencken, although he did enjoy music, drama, and *biergemütlichkeit*, probably
claimed to have been more of a hedonist than he actually was. In fact,
during this period—with his "mutual improvement" club, his self-
study, his emphasis on work, his consciousness of time, and his eye
on the future—Mencken conducted his life with a Ben Franklin–like
standard of accountability. It is no accident that he later found
Franklin one of only three "absolutely first-rate Americans" (Jefferson and William Tecumseh Sherman were the others). The eighteenth-century author of *Essays to Do Good* and this most famous
twentieth-century opponent of do-gooders—the secular Puritan and
the great opponent of Puritanism—had more in common than
Mencken at first quite realized.

In 1904, just as he was beginning to tire somewhat of the routine of
newspaper work and was growing particularly weary of the "imbecile
mismanagement" of the *Herald*'s owner and general manager,
Mencken again found himself the recipient of that notable luck he
had always enjoyed. On Sunday morning, February 7, the great
Baltimore fire broke out. The most destructive fire in an American
city since that in Chicago in 1871, it was to mean for Mencken one
of his two most glorious moments as a reporter and editor. It was also
to mean the beginning of the end of the Baltimore *Morning Herald*,
and thus—eventually—a means of escape for its star writer and
editor.

Mencken had covered dozens of fires before, and when he was
roused out of sleep about 11:00 A.M. Sunday he could not have
imagined that he would not sleep again for nearly three days or come
home again for a week. He had been out until 3:30 or 4:00 A.M.,
participating in the late Saturday night drinking exercises of the

Stevedore Club. Now he rushed downtown to Hopkins Place, where the fire was raging out of control. Mencken described the fire and his role in covering it in great detail in *Newspaper Days:*

> The wind had . . . begun to roar from the West. In ten minutes the fire had routed [the Baltimore firemen] and leaped to a second block, and in half an hour to a third and fourth, and by dark the whole of downtown Baltimore was under a hail of sparks and flying brands, and a dozen outlying fires had started to eastward. . . . The fire raged for a full week, helped by that bitter Winter wind, and when it fizzled out at last the burned area looked like Pompeii, and up from its ashes rose the pathetic skeletons of no less than twenty overtaken and cremated fire-engines . . .

In his description Mencken told some stretchers—the fire did not rage for an entire week—but the facts themselves were striking enough. The fire destroyed some one hundred fifty acres in the heart of downtown Baltimore, consuming nearly every office building and hotel, including the *Herald*'s offices and those of every other newspaper but one.

In his account Mencken focused on the reporting heroics of the *Herald* staff, which he, as city editor, and Meekins directed. They "went to work with the enthusiasm of crusaders shinning up the walls of Antioch, and all sorts of volunteers swarmed in, including three or four forgotten veterans who had been fired years before, and were thought to have long since reached the dissecting-room." They had to print the paper in Washington, then Philadelphia, and Mencken worked nearly nonstop until Wednesday morning, then carried on with little sleep for the remainder of the week, commuting by train between Baltimore and Philadelphia. "It was brain-fagging and back-breaking," he later wrote, "but it was grand beyond compare . . ." He went into the fire "a boy" driven by "the hot gas of youth"; he came out, he recalled with customary hyperbole, "a settled and indeed almost a middle-aged man." Mencken's Baltimore underwent a similar transformation. The old "rowdy and bawdy" city, "unutterably charming," also "passed with the fire of 1904. . . . The new Baltimore that emerged from the ashes was simply a virtuoso piece of Babbitts."

Or at least that is the way Mencken saw it, and himself, looking back a quarter century later. In fact, the spirit of Baltimore had not been changed radically by the fire, nor had Mencken himself, but he was to remember the fire as a great turning point in his own life and to depict himself as the courageous young newspaperman resembling no one so much as the sailor in Joseph Conrad's "Youth," "remember[ing] [his] youth and the feeling that will never come back any more—the feeling that I could last forever, outlast the sea, the earth, and all men. . . . The silly, charming, beautiful youth!"

Mencken began to lose interest in daily journalism shortly after the events of February 1904, and the fire itself was certainly part of the reason. What could possibly match its excitement and challenge? Less than a week later, in fact, he received a letter from Ellery Sedgwick, editor of *Frank Leslie's Popular Monthly*, asking if he would be interested in coming to New York to work for *Leslie's*. "The whole matter has been in my mind for some time before the fire," Sedgwick wrote. "Now that you are burnt out, and reconstruction of the Herald's business is inevitable, perhaps it would be a good time for you to pull up stakes."

Mencken seriously considered Sedgwick's proposal, traveled to New York immediately to discuss the assistant editorship of the magazine, and missed talking with Sedgwick only because the editor had confused the time Mencken was to come up and had left the city for the day. For the next week or two Mencken weighed the offer—and the munificent sum of sixty dollars a week, double his *Herald* salary—but on February 29 he wrote Sedgwick that he could not accept the position. He was "sorely tempted"—he was to tell Sedgwick nearly forty years later—and it was mainly "the desire to remain by my mother here in Baltimore" that made him say no. Mencken wondered, in that same retrospective letter to Sedgwick, how his life would have been different if he had accepted: "I suspect now and then that staying here cut off some good opportunities." In fact, the decision made little professional difference at all: the opportunities still arose. The only real difference is that Mencken would continue to live in Baltimore, and, when he at last tackled New York, he would encounter it on his own terms.

After rejecting the *Leslie's* offer—an unwise decision, Sedgwick wrote him—Mencken settled back for a time into his work on the *Herald*, soon to be in rebuilt quarters. His final two years on the newspaper, if not as exciting as covering the great fire, were rewarding in other ways. In the summer of 1904, he covered the first of his national political conventions, seeing the Republicans nominate President Theodore Roosevelt in Chicago and witnessing his future adversary William Jennings Bryan for the first time at the Democratic convention in St. Louis. At age twenty-three he had somewhat more compassion for the unsuccessful nominee Bryan than he would have twenty years later: "With his voice a mere whisper, his collar a rag, his hair disheveled, his eyes sunken and his face pallid and deep-lined, the old leader rose before his old retainers and his victorious foes, an imperial and mighty figure . . ."

When Mencken returned to Baltimore, he wrote editorials attacking or ridiculing Roosevelt as well as others critical of reformers, professors, Henry James, the American South, and Russia's treatment of its masses: "What a day it will be when [the Russian peasants] arise to have their revenge—what a day of massacre, slaughter and judgment! Then, indeed, the Slav will stagger humanity." He wrote other editorials praising Mark Twain and looking back nostalgically—already, at twenty-four—at his Baltimore boyhood: "Gone . . . are the boys of those days."

Mencken continued to have fun on the job. In 1905, realizing a battle was imminent in the Korean strait but impatient for the results, he fabricated a story announcing a great Japanese naval victory in its war with Russia—a victory that came about several days later as he had described it. But he also assumed more responsibility on the *Herald*. In 1905 he was promoted from city editor to managing editor, and early in 1906 he became editor in chief. Thus, at age twenty-five, he found himself editor of a major, if crumbling, newspaper, having completed the first phase of that ascent that had begun when he had first climbed the *Herald*'s steps at age eighteen. He was impressed with his position, and so were others. Reflecting on Mencken's lofty post, his fiction, and his other writing, Sedgwick wrote from New York: "I hesitate to imagine were [*sic*] you will be at fifty if you are where you are at twenty-five."

Three months after Sedgwick wrote, the *Herald* folded, but for Mencken this was good fortune rather than bad. He was ready to move on. Earlier he had rejected not only Sedgwick's offer but some from other Baltimore dailies as well. Now in the summer of 1906, released from any obligation to the *Herald*, he was in a position to listen carefully to all offers. First he accepted a position as news editor of the Baltimore *News*, at forty dollars a week, and six weeks later moved over to the *Sun* as Sunday editor. The *Sun* was still the newspaper of record in Baltimore, although Mencken believed it was in a period of slight decline, and he felt besides that he would have more time to write for the *Sun*.

He had another chance to move three months later. *The New York Times* offered him a job, primarily upon the recommendation of Lynn Roby Meekins. He declined the offer, largely for the same reason he had turned down Sedgwick's offer two years earlier: he preferred to remain with his mother in Baltimore. Besides, Mencken had settled in at the *Sun* and was already content in what was to become the longest professional association of his life: he was to serve the Sunpapers in various capacities for the next four decades. In November, when the *Sun* moved into new quarters at Charles and Baltimore streets, he was given a comfortable office overlooking Charles Street. He soon he got along well with Walter Abell, president of A. S. Abell Co., owner of the *Sun*, and also discovered that he had a great deal of freedom as Sunday editor.

By the end of 1906 Mencken was writing editorials as well, and in the following year he was holding forth on such familiar topics as the decline of the American South and the advantages of bachelorhood. Mencken later dated the beginning of his distinctive prose style to 1906: it was "in full flower," he wrote, "by the end of that year." In fact, there had been a gradual development of that style during the *Herald* days, but he was correct that he had largely found his voice by late 1906. In a piece on marriage dated December 30, he discussed, in what approached vintage Mencken style, the obstacles facing the man who wants to remain single: "It is more difficult than being a Republican in Mississippi or a reformer in Philadelphia. Against such a man stands the whole female sex, in one vast and horrible phalanx."

Mencken greatly enjoyed what he called "the placid and lordly life of a Sun man" under the early Abell regime. "There was never on this earth a more pleasant newspaper office . . . more a good club than a great industrial plant." But at the same time he was convinced, as he later wrote a friend, that journalism was "a fleeting thing, and the man who devotes his life to it writes his history in water." He already had a certain sense of his own importance—as early as 1903, in order to collect reviews of his work or other mentions of himself, he had begun to subscribe to a clipping service—and he was careful not to take his eye off the larger world of letters. That world, to Mencken, no longer meant primarily the writing of fiction and poetry. He continued to publish his earlier stories in *Criterion*, the *Monthly Story Magazine*, and *Red Book* up through 1906, receiving as much as seventy-five dollars a story, but he had written little or no new fiction since 1902 and was searching for other areas in which to make his name. "I began to be conscious of a lack of direction," he later wrote of this period, "and tried a number of times to decide formally what I really wanted to do, and to get on with the doing of it."

What he had settled on about 1903 or 1904 was the critical discussion of literature, society, and ideas. He had come to this conclusion partly through the success of his polemical and satirical writing for the *Herald* and partly through his writing for Sedgwick at *Frank Leslie's Popular Monthly*, *The American Illustrated Magazine*, and *McClure's*—writing that had gradually turned from fiction to nonfiction. Sedgwick saw Mencken as his "discovery," and the young writer was grateful for the attention. Well connected in publishing circles, Sedgwick was "a Brahmin of the Brahmins," and Mencken—who never met Mark Twain, William Dean Howells, Henry James, Frank Norris, Jack London, Stephen Crane, and other reigning authors of the day—was very much in need of a champion in New York.

Aside from Sedgwick and the few *Herald* associates who were fiction writers, Mencken's firsthand acquaintance with something approaching the world of letters had come through his position as drama editor. The world of the Baltimore theater was in most respects middlebrow, and most of the plays Mencken had reviewed were moralistic and sentimental. But out of his reviewing—despite, or perhaps because of, the low quality of the plays—he had arrived at an aesthetic, a preference for a drama of ideas, for realism, and for the playwright as iconoclast and rebel. Holding to this standard, he had come to embrace the playwright of that era who most fully embodied those qualities: George Bernard Shaw. "Through Shaw," Mencken later wrote, "I found my vocation at last."

He had been introduced to Shaw's work by his friend Will Page, had read and delighted in the plays, and had begun to collect material on Shaw in his *Herald* clippings file. By late 1904 he had begun work on a book about Shaw and had approached Shaw's American publisher, Brentano. When Brentano had expressed no interest, he wrote to a Boston publisher, John W. Luce, who had earlier brought out a pirated edition of Shaw's *On Going to Church*. To Luce he proposed a descriptive and critical work of some twenty to thirty thousand words, giving Sedgwick as a reference. Again, Mencken's luck held. For Harrison Hale Schaff of Luce already had in mind a book on Shaw and others of the new playwrights, and in March he wrote to Mencken, urging him to send a prospectus and to proceed with the book. Mencken plunged into the writing, sending Schaff parts as he went, only to learn in a letter of July 11 that Schaff had some doubts about the book as written: it had too much summary of plays and not enough analysis. But a reader to whom Schaff sent the manuscript had a higher opinion of it, and, with certain revisions, the book was placed on the fall list. When Mencken received the proofs of the book in late September, he was congratulated and given the day off by Lynn Meekins. Late in 1905 Mencken's first real book appeared.

The book was a modest one, scarcely more than a hundred pages, and its aims were modest as well. Mencken intended not a "novel interpretation" but a general examination of Shaw. The brief introduction, in which he saw Shaw as a product of late-nineteenth-century iconoclasm, is perhaps most revealing. He began by praising Charles Darwin, Thomas Huxley, and Herbert Spencer, whose influence he detected in Shaw: "Darwin made this war between the faithful and the scoffers the chief concern of the time, and the sham-smashing that is now going on . . . might be compared to the crusades that engrossed the world in the middle ages." An analysis of the plays followed—plays dealing "almost wholly with the current conflict between orthodoxy and heterodoxy"—and in the individual chapters, particularly that on *Man and Superman*, Mencken was fascinated by the sham smashers.

What we get in *George Bernard Shaw: His Plays*, of course, is as much Mencken as Shaw, although a Mencken greatly influenced by his reading of Shaw as well as the works of Darwin, Huxley, and Spencer. In fact, Shaw was not a Darwinist as Mencken had claimed, although few if any of the reviewers corrected him. Most of the reviews were favorable—including those in *The New York Times*, the San Francisco *Bulletin*, *The Boston Globe*, the *Brooklyn Eagle*, and the Baltimore *Sun*—but the *New York Post* claimed that Mencken was too easily taken in by Shaw, and *The Nation*, in a long review, found Mencken's style "rather too colloquial for elegance."

The book did not sell well—Mencken made no money from it at the time—but the author did not particularly care. In December he sent Shaw a copy of the work and wrote a note: "In case you come to the United States shortly I shall give myself the pleasure of calling on you—to make my apologies [for any mistakes]." Shaw did not reply, and Mencken's fears that he did not like the book were reinforced later when he was told that Shaw believed the tone flippant. In fact, Shaw had been favorably impressed, but Mencken did not make this discovery until 1920, long after he had ceased to admire the man he came to call "The Ulster Polonius."

Shortly after he completed the Shaw book, Mencken proposed to Harrison Hale Schaff another study of contemporary drama, but the publisher was not interested. He did suggest, however, that the young author undertake a subject that Schaff had suggested much earlier but that Mencken, at the time, had felt himself unprepared to tackle—the philosophy of Friedrich Nietzsche. In the Shaw book Schaff had originally wanted Mencken to connect his subject with the iconoclastic spirit of Nietzsche, and Mencken to some extent had done so. He had taken his epigraph from Nietzsche and had referred to the philosopher's thought at several points. But up until that time Mencken had known virtually nothing about Nietzsche, and—significantly for one who was to become known as the American Nietzschean—his interest in Nietzsche, when it came, came rather reluctantly, was more a product of Schaff's urging than of his own fervor. "I was not enthusiastic," he later recalled.

Schaff wanted Mencken to make the Nietzsche book somewhat like the Shaw, a review of Nietzsche's life, beliefs, and influence. But this book would be a far more difficult undertaking. Only a small portion of Nietzsche's work had been translated into English—a major problem for a writer who did not trust his command of German—and besides, Mencken had no historical grounding in philosophy. He had a *view* of mankind and the cosmos: that the Judeo-Christian God did not exist, that human life was without meaning, that man was highly flawed and without dignity but was an amusing creature whose vain strivings and self-delusions created an eternal comedy, a spectacle in which Mencken, for one, delighted. He had a point of view, then— partly inherited from his father, partly based on observation—but he had no philosophical position except, as he once said, "common sense." The nearest he came was his wholehearted approval of Dar-

87

win and Huxley, his belief in an unbridled individualism, and his endorsement of a creed akin to positivism—although, as Charles Fecher has pointed out, Mencken was not particularly influenced by Auguste Comte and would not have called himself a positivist. He did call himself, at least later, an Aristotelian, not a Platonist, but in fact he knew very little about the great tradition of European philosophy. In particular he knew little about German rationalism.

Armed, then, with an inadequate knowledge of German philosophy—and, to the degree he needed, the German language—Mencken plunged into Nietzsche, and it was a plunge he discovered, once immersed, it was time to have taken. His German consciousness had indeed been in the making for the previous two or three years, as demonstrated by his editorials and columns in the *Herald* and the *Sun*. In his earliest columns he had demonstrated no interest at all in German politics, history, or literature, and if, by the time of his final years on the *Herald*, 1904 to 1906, he had developed some slight interest in those subjects, it was an interest that any other American editorial writer, watching the expansion of the new Germany, would have shown. Germany had taken Russia's place, Mencken had insisted in 1905, as the bully of Europe; indeed, the Germany of Kaiser Wilhelm was becoming the European "nightmare."

He had voiced that sentiment in several other pieces in 1905, but in 1906, in editorials for the equally pro-English *Sun*, he sounded a different note. In August 1906 he issued a qualified defense of the kaiser and later went on record with an unabashed defense of the German people, "the surpassing . . . vitality of the race; its perfect balance and strong common sense, its industry, its love of beautiful things, its vein of poetry . . ." He also proposed to Sedgwick an article on Kaiser Wilhelm for *The American Illustrated Magazine*, only to be turned down because Sedgwick said the magazine's readers were more interested in American subjects than German ones.

The immersion in Nietzsche was very much part of the making of the self-conscious German, and Mencken worked harder on this book than on any other he had undertaken. First he prepared himself by reading German philosophy, although he found most of it "dull . . . not to say repulsive." Then he turned to Nietzsche himself, for whose "shock" he was prepared by having read Huxley and Spencer. When he could, he commuted to Washington to work in the Library of Congress. He found in Nietzsche a kind of German language that was "extremely difficult, at least until I got used to it," but he kept at his work "resolutely" and returned to Hollins Street to write at night.

By writing furiously Mencken completed the book in the summer of 1907. He had worked at a pace that, for him, was to become commonplace: in eight or nine months he had dug into German philosophy, had read all of Nietzsche, mainly in German, and had written a book of more than three hundred printed pages—all the while working full-time for the *Sun*. *The Philosophy of Friedrich Nietzsche*, published in 1908, was the first book in English on the philosopher. It was also *Mencken's* Nietzsche, just as *George Bernard Shaw* had been his Shaw. He stressed the iconoclast, the Darwinian materialist, "the high priest of the actual," and largely ignored Nietzsche the mystic, out of touch with the actual. His study was an attempt to present the philosopher to an American reading public that had, since about 1900, on occasion heard Nietzsche denounced as a Teutonic monster but in fact knew little about him.

Mencken was obviously in sympathy with his subject. He saw Nietzsche as "prophet," as "king of all axiom smashers and the arch dissenter of the age," the great foe of the "slave-morality" of Christianity. But he was not uncritical. He spoke of Nietzsche's "incredible intolerance, jealousy, spitefulness and egomania." He saw contradictions in the philosopher's thought, pointing out in particular that this advocate of "the will to power" was himself a determinist, denying free will. At times, indeed, Nietzsche seemed the "mad German," and at those times Mencken saw in him "the traditional German tendency to indulge in wild and imbecile flights of speculation."

For more than three quarters of his book Mencken was essentially the scholar, presenting the details of Nietzsche's life, tracing his development as philosopher—particularly his debt to Schopenhauer—and discussing his central ideas. He was particularly fascinated with Nietzsche as Dionysian and with the conflict between Dionysian and Apollonian impulses that he saw at the heart of *The Birth of Tragedy* (1872). But ideas to Mencken were never to be treated in isolation, and near the end of his study he turned to Nietzsche as philosopher for his, and Mencken's, own time. He saw in Theodore Roosevelt an example of Nietzsche's philosophy transferred to a larger stage. "In all things fundamental the Roosevelt-

ian philosophy and the Nietzschean philosophy are identical," he
wrote, although in so contending he too closely identified Nietzsche's
idea of "the strenuous life" with Roosevelt's own version, which in
fact drew more on turn-of-the-century muscular Christianity. In a
larger sense, Mencken saw Nietzsche as the voice of a new age of individualism, scientific inquiry, and Social Darwinism. "The age is
dionysian," he wrote. "The civilized world has disposed of super-
naturalism and is engaged in a destructive criticism of the old faith's
residuum—morality."

*The Philosophy of Friedrich Nietzsche* was reviewed more widely
than Mencken's Shaw book, but the response was not universally
favorable. The New York *Evening Sun* and the Chicago *Post,* among
other newspapers, found fault. Numerous other American newspapers as well as the London *Standard* and the London *Telegraph*
thought highly of it. *The New York Times'* reviewer praised
Mencken's "clear, forceful, and even ardent style," his "keen and
thorough-going intellect," and his "sense of humor." But the review
that pleased Mencken most was written by Nicholas Murray Butler,
president of Columbia University, in the *Educational Review:*
". . . we do not know who Mr. Mencken is. . . . Nevertheless, he has
written one of the most interesting and instructive books that has
come from the American press in many a long day. Mr. Mencken can
write. In addition, he has something to write about."

Few of the reviewers leveled the charge that Mencken was to hear
increasingly in the following years: that he was Nietzsche's spokesman and disciple. There is little question, however, that as he
reached the final quarter of his book he became less the scholar, more
the defender. His own voice came to the fore, or rather the two voices
merged, and the author nearly identified with his subject. He must
also have identified in ways that were not so clear to the reader. By
the time he wrote his *Nietzsche* Mencken had already become—if not
yet to America at large, at least to readers of the *Herald* and the *Sun*
in and around Baltimore—what the young Nietzsche had been in
Germany: a critic of religion and democracy, an enemy of public
morality, sentimentality, and middlebrow culture—in short, an
iconoclast. He must also have given at least brief attention to certain
superficial personal resemblances. Like the Menckens, Nietzsche had
been a native of Saxony who had studied at Leipzig. He had never

married, he had been devoted to his mother, and he had found his passion in music.

Nietzsche's German identity, for this newly awakened German American, was a more complicated matter. For the philosopher, though German born, had roots in Poland and, as Mencken wrote, "regarded himself as a Polish grandee . . . among German shopkeepers." But this revelation, rather than distancing Mencken from Nietzsche, would in fact have made him identify with Nietzsche the more. For what else, in 1908, was Mencken coming to consider himself— what role had his grandfather assumed—but a sort of *German* grandee among American shopkeepers, one of high birth who dwelled among the Philistines?

In his later life Mencken dismissed his Nietzsche book as "a work of my youth" and tried to distance himself from his subject as well. "In my own mind my debt to Nietzsche seems very slight," he was to write in 1937, "though I confess that other people seem to have put a larger value on it." Indeed, there were great differences in the thought of the two men, differences that became clearer to Mencken in time. But in 1907 and 1908, when he was "working out [his] own ideas for future use," there is no doubt that he was greatly drawn to the philosopher. The ideas he settled on, he later wrote a friend, "were plainly *based* [his italics] on Nietzsche; without him I'd never have come to them."

Mencken was overstating his debt. Most of his ideas were in place before he ever encountered Nietzsche. But what Nietzsche offered him was *certification* of those ideas, a philosophical framework into which to place them. And Nietzsche offered as well a model who, whether he considered himself German or not, was assumed by the English-speaking world—and by Mencken himself—to be German, who moreover had been accepted, whether correctly or not, as the philosopher of the new, bold, strong, self-reliant Germany. Nietzsche offered that, and he also offered a manner, an extravagant, hyperbolic style, unleashing a torrent of metaphors and similes. He was the iconoclast telling the truth magnified by ten diameters.

Mencken in fact was never the true Dionysian he celebrated in Nietzsche and professed to see in himself. He was rather, in some respects, the Apollonian, ordered, controlled, rarely (as we shall see) plunging incautiously into life. He was, in his personal life, too much the sober citizen who believed that one's highest responsibility was to pay one's debts and meet one's daily obligations. But Mencken determined early that he would, in the mask he wore, in the voice with which he spoke, be Dionysian, dancing "with arms and legs." "Like Nietzsche," he wrote later, "I console myself with the hope that I am the man of the future, emancipated from the prevailing delusions and superstitions. . . . I thus represent a kind of posterity. But it will be a long time displacing the race of believers that now pollute the earth."

# Chapter 5

# STIRRING UP THE ANIMALS

M encken received his first widespread national recognition with the publication of *The Philosophy of Friedrich Nietzsche*— lengthy newspaper reviews accompanied by photographs, as well as discussions in *Current Literature* and other magazines. He suddenly found himself in *Who's Who in America*, principally on the strength of *Nietzsche*, and was also treated as a serious critic of ideas. Indeed, in several reviews he was identified as a former "fellow at the Johns Hopkins University." Although he later said he was embarrassed by this misinformation, which had been distributed by Schaff in an advance notice, his embarrassment must have been mixed with a certain malicious pleasure. At twenty-seven, never having entered a university classroom, he found himself assigned a place of honor in the seat of higher learning of his native city.

He celebrated the reception of his Nietzsche book by taking his first European trip in the spring of 1908. Traveling alone, he sailed for Liverpool on the Cunard *Laconia* and spent several days in London. He then proceeded to Germany, using Mark Twain's *A Tramp Abroad* as a guidebook, and visited Munich as well as the ancestral home of the Menckens, Leipzig. When he arrived he set out to find the Menckestrasse, named for his ancestor Lüder Mencke. But despite his immersion in Nietzsche, Mencken was at this point still more Anglophile than Germanophile. The highlight of his trip, he later wrote, "was not my visit to Leipzig . . . but that to London."

There he ran into a Baltimore friend who introduced him to Simpson's in the Strand and showed him much of the old city. Seeing the graves of Goldsmith and Thackeray made a powerful impression.

When Mencken returned to Baltimore, he resumed his duties as Sunday editor and editorial writer for the *Sun*. His prestige there, too, had risen with the publication of *Nietzsche*, and he found he was now admitted to "the inner circle of dignitaries." He believed, however, that the influence of the *Sun* was declining—because of Walter Abell's caution and because of the aggressive challenge from the Baltimore *Evening News*—and he was not altogether unhappy when, in 1910, the Abells gave up management of the newspaper. When he learned, however, that the new editor and publisher was to be Charles Henry Grasty, he had second thoughts—for Grasty had been the publisher of the *News* when Mencken had joined that paper in 1906 only to resign six weeks later, when Grasty was abroad, to join the *Sun*.

He was prepared to be dismissed, a prospect not altogether displeasing since he had many other options. But he found that Grasty did not hold the earlier departure against him after all and in fact had greater things in mind for him. He had in mind, in particular, the creation of an afternoon daily, the *Evening Sun*, and he immediately made Mencken second-in-command of the newspaper. Mencken's duties were to write two editorials and an initialed column each day, to review plays, and to handle letters to the editor. His editorials, as Edward A. Martin has noted, were to differ little from those of most other progressive journalists of the time: he favored an expansion of the electorate, favored controls on Standard Oil and other industrial giants, and came out against capital punishment. He had kind things to say about such future foes as William Jennings Bryan and Woodrow Wilson. He even supported Wilson's candidacy for governor of New Jersey in 1910 and, two years later, his presidential candidacy— although his public praise for Wilson might be explained in part by Wilson's friendship with Grasty, who, in 1910, had offered Wilson the editorship of the Sunpapers.

The essential Mencken emerged not in the unsigned editorials but in the initialed columns, in which he was allowed freer rein. He devoted one column to the "expurgators" who trimmed indelicate parts from great books to make them "suitable" for the young:

Why print such bleeding fragments . . . ? Why cut the whiskers from Homer and put him in an eton jacket? . . . Boccaccio, Chaucer and the incomparable Doctor Francis [Rabelais] did not write for sucklings. They were men of free speech, living in an age of free-speaking, and they were addressing audiences of their adult contemporaries. Why try to convert them into Twentieth-century kindergartners? As well attempt a condensed version of *The Critique of Pure Reason*, in words of one syllable: As well put the Constitution into couplets and Leviticus into limericks!

He devoted another signed piece to the joys and glories of alcohol:

What would become of romance if there were no alcohol? Imagine a teetotaler writing *Much Ado About Nothing*, or the Fifth Symphony, or *Le Malade Imaginaire*, or *Peer Gynt*, or the Zend-Avesta, or the Declaration of Independence or any other great work of feeling and fancy! Imagine Wagner, bursting with ginger-pop, at work upon *Tristan and Isolde*. Imagine Leonardo, soaked in health drinks from Battle Creek, fashioning the unfathomable smile of Mona Lisa!

The marks of the mature Mencken were evident: the sense of the outrageous, the catalogues, the cadences. Having begun to find his voice, he so impressed one of the *Sun* owners, Harry Black, that Black suggested the young columnist be given an even freer hand. The result was "The Free Lance," a daily column that began in May 1911 and was to continue for more than four years. Mencken was given permission to fire away at anybody he chose except Baltimore ministers, and when he lured the preachers into attacking him, they became fair game too. From the beginning his primary targets were Baltimore politicians, boosters, prohibitionists, antivice crusaders, and moralists and reformers of all stripes. All the while, he was a kind of reformer himself, calling for such public health improvements as public ambulance service and citywide typhoid inoculation.

But his characteristic mode was humor, and his weapons were satire and ridicule. If his style was not always so engaging as it had been in the earlier signed columns—he now often wrote in spurts and fragments and his subjects were often of local interest only—he mastered in "The Free Lance" the art of confrontation with those close at hand. The column "launched me as a general assassin," he later wrote a friend, and within months he was Baltimore's Bad Boy, his rebellious nature given truly free rein for the first time. The readers of Baltimore wrote in, wondering what motivated these outbursts against authority. Was that motivation what he once called his "mere love of combat"? Was it a resentment of authority stemming from an unresolved and unacknowledged anger toward an authoritarian father who died too soon to be the object of that anger? Or did the rebellion come simply from his belief, as he wrote a friend in 1910, that "the noblest of all sports is stirring up the animals"? Whatever the reason, the result was one of the most outspoken and irreverent onslaughts against the powers that be that Baltimore had ever seen.

The earlier signed columns and "The Free Lance" were important not only for the fireworks they created at the time but also for what they presaged. One of Mencken's great assets as a writer is that nothing was lost on him, nothing wasted. His pen—or typewriter— was an extension of his mind: to think something was to write it down, to preserve it for later use. The *Evening Sun* columns, which were usually insights and prejudices rather than crafted essays, provided such a trying out of ideas, as well as voices and styles. If the columns themselves were far from his best work, they were suggestive of that best work to come.

Though now a local celebrity, Mencken continued to look beyond Baltimore, indeed—he later wrote—was "fearfully aware" during the "Free Lance" days that he "might become a mere local worthy." Following his books on Shaw and Nietzsche, he turned to a third iconoclast, Ibsen, and collaborated with Holger A. Koppel, the Danish consul to Baltimore and a fellow member of the Vagabonds Club, on English translations of *A Doll's House*, *Little Eyolf*, and *Hedda Gabler*. The first two translations were published by John W. Luce in 1909 to generally favorable if limited reviews and modest sales. *Hedda Gabler* was never published at all, and Mencken felt the entire enterprise was a failure.

He soon had other projects under way. Shortly after the publication of the Ibsen translations, Harrison Schaff had proposed that he put together a collection of Nietzsche's writings. Though reluctant to work with Schaff and Luce any further, he nonetheless made selections from Nietzsche and added two pages of introduction, all in a week or less. Luce put the book out immediately. Although the volume received generally favorable reviews, Mencken believed it a "lousy affair" and wrote a friend, "I am done with Luce."

At the time he wrote that, March 1910, he had already signed a contract with Henry Holt & Co. for a book of a quite different sort. A year or two before, he had begun what became a lengthy correspondence with Robert Rives La Monte, a wealthy socialist who took issue with Mencken's indictment of socialism and defense of individualism. Later in 1909, at La Monte's suggestion, they agreed to publish the correspondence, and Holt came to Baltimore in January 1910 to discuss the matter. Mencken at first liked the arrangement with Holt. "The connection promises a lot," he wrote a friend, and the book did give him an opportunity to restate, in systematic fashion, his belief in "natural castes" and other of his guiding principles:

> I believe [socialism] overlooks certain ineradicable characteristics of the human animal, and certain immutable laws of the biological process. . . . Every comfort that we have to-day was devised by some man who yearned to get more out of life than the men around him. . . . Just as every micro-organism in the sea ooze fights for that pin point of space which will give it life while its fellows die, just so every man fights for that microscopic degree of superiority which gives him eminence over his fellow-man. . . .
>
> Such is the law of the survival of the fittest, and so it stands immutable. Socialism is only one of a hundred plans for ameliorating it, and since all of the others have failed, I believe that Socialism will fail too.

Despite his hopes for it, *Men Versus the Man*—the title Mencken and La Monte gave their 250-page debate between socialism and capitalism—was a failure, with poor sales and mixed reviews.

In 1910, Mencken collaborated on still another book, a most unlikely undertaking, this time with Dr. Leonard K. Hirshberg, a Baltimore physician and another member of the Vagabonds. A guide to infant care, *What You Ought to Know About Your Baby*, seems a strange work for this twenty-nine-year-old bachelor who was childless and destined to remain that way. But Mencken was a pen for hire, and Hirshberg, who provided the medical knowledge, needed the services of a skilled writer. With the publication of the baby book, Mencken had produced—written, cowritten, edited, or helped to translate—no fewer than seven books between 1905 and 1910. He had turned them out while holding a demanding newspaper job and for part of that time, as we shall soon see, another editorial position that would have been nearly full-time for anyone else. "Work is a curse," he wrote a friend shortly after this, but in fact for Mencken it seemed more a stimulant—and was to remain so the rest of his life.

He was often to reflect on his commitment to work, that drive that kept him writing most of every day, stopping only late at night for beer and conversation. The need to work was a part of his makeup, he believed: he was afflicted with a "conscientiousness" which was "one of the curses of this family," as he wrote his uncle. Besides, he was endowed with "an extraordinary amount of reserve energy." It appeared no contradiction to Mencken that he was also "by nature, an indolent man," for a "conscientious" man who knows he is inclined toward indolence is driven all the harder to work.

In any case, "this thing of writing seems to be an incurable disease," he concluded, and the words of his brother August, looking back at Mencken's life after his death, suggest just how afflicted he was: "His life was based entirely on work. Everything else was supplementary to it, but work was the important thing, and everything else had to revolve around it and fit into it, [and] nothing must be let to interfere with it." Or, as Mencken himself put it, also looking back: "no other enterprise ever gave me the same pleasure" as "a hard day's work . . . the flow of my own ideas." At other times he dug more deeply. "Why do I work?" he asked, and gave his answer: "No man can face the boredom of life; he escapes accepting its futility by working. . . . We work to live; it saves us from contemplating futility."

———※———

Work, for Mencken, was a means of avoiding the abyss, of keeping the emptiness at bay. It became as well, particularly after 1908, a rich breeding ground of close personal associations, the unlikeliest professional undertakings sometimes leading to close friendships. Such was the case with the baby book he wrote with Hirshberg, for through that enterprise he met Theodore Dreiser, and thus resulted one of the most intriguing literary friendships of the century. It was a friendship in many ways as improbable as the book that brought them together: Dreiser, thirty-six, the ponderous, earnest midwesterner of low birth, a mystical bent and—Mencken wrote—"a fundamentally believing mind," and Mencken, twenty-seven (when they met) and well born, the city smart aleck, the rationalist and skeptic. Dreiser, in 1907, was the enterprising editorial director of B. W. Dodge & Co., and Mencken, as always, was ready to write anything, even an instructional book for the mothers of America.

He had known of Dreiser since 1902, when he had encountered *Sister Carrie*, but he first heard from the novelist—in Dreiser's capacity of editorial director—in August 1907. At first Dreiser was interested not in child care but rather in a popular edition of Schopenhauer that he hoped the author of *Nietzsche* would undertake. Mencken had been suggested by his Baltimore friend and fellow Vagabond George Bronson Howard. He was not interested in pursuing the Schopenhauer volume, but he did interest Dreiser, who was also editor of *The Delineator*, in one of the medical articles that he and Hirshberg were writing and publishing in other mass-circulation magazines. The result was that Mencken and Hirshberg produced a number of the articles on baby care for *The Delineator* in 1908 and 1909. It was those articles, along with pieces Mencken wrote on childhood diseases, that made up *What You Ought to Know About Your Baby*.

He did not meet Dreiser until the spring or early summer of 1908, some eight or nine months after they had first corresponded, and Dreiser's first impression of the young reporter from Baltimore— who had dropped by his office in New York to discuss the medical articles—is perhaps the most memorable description of the young Mencken. Dreiser later recalled that

> there appeared in my office a taut, ruddy, blue-eyed, snub-nosed youth of twenty eight or nine whose brisk gait and ingratiating smile proved to me at once enormously intriguing and amusing. . . . More than anything else he reminded me of a spoiled and petted and possibly over-financed brewer's or wholesale grocer's son who was out for a lark. With the sang-froid of a Caesar or a Napoleon he made himself comfortable in a large and impressive chair . . . and from that particular and unintended vantage point

he beamed on me with the confidence of a smirking fox about to devour a chicken. . . . After studying him in that almost arch-episcopal setting which the chair provided, I began to laugh. "Well, well," I said, "if it isn't Anheuser's own brightest boy out to see the town."

Despite differences in age and temperament, Mencken and Dreiser soon found themselves in agreement on any number of subjects. Mencken continued to contribute to Dreiser's magazines in 1909 and 1910, writing a series of humorous pieces for the "man's page" of *The Delineator* as well as short, humorous editorials for another of Dreiser's publications, *The Bohemian*. In April 1909 he declined Dreiser's offer to join the *Delineator* staff at fifty dollars a week, but by that point the two were already fast friends. Mencken often had dinner with Dreiser in New York, and afterward they would seek out beer halls and lively parties in Manhattan. At Thanksgiving 1909 he invited Dreiser to Baltimore for dinner at Hollins Street. Mencken asked his friend to stay over for "a demon rum party" given by Hirshberg on Thanksgiving night.

The friendship with Dreiser proved valuable to Mencken in another way. In 1908 he had received a letter from Fred Splint, editor of *The Smart Set*, offering him the position of literary reviewer for the magazine. Splint had heard of Mencken through Dreiser, with whom he had worked closely, although the actual suggestion of Mencken as book reviewer—as he would learn thirty years later—apparently came not from Dreiser (as Mencken would long assume) but rather from Norman Boyer, assistant editor of *The Smart Set* and former reporter with Mencken on the Baltimore *Morning Herald*. Mencken was greatly surprised by the offer. He had never published in *The Smart Set*, although he had had three or four dozen poems rejected by the magazine six or eight years before. Neither did he consider himself a book reviewer. But he was interested enough to go to New York to meet with Splint and Boyer. He was offered fifty dollars a month, and he could remain in Baltimore. He returned home with the job and an armful of books.

A somewhat racy magazine with an indecorous past, *The Smart Set* was far from the top rung of American literary journalism. It was at least a step below such magazines as the *Atlantic Monthly*, *Scribner's*, *Century*, and *Harper's*. Founded by Colonel William

D'Alton Mann in 1900, it needed new blood in 1908, and the hiring of Mencken as well as George Jean Nathan as drama critic was intended to serve that purpose. Mencken was assigned one lengthy review essay each month, and in his first essay, "The Good, The Bad and The Best Sellers" for November 1908, he dealt with no fewer than eighteen books. After that piece, which he later confessed feeling "stage-fright" in composing, he settled in and wrote nearly a million words of criticism for *The Smart Set* over the next fifteen years, producing 182 essays in which he reviewed some two thousand books.

Mencken discussed books on a wide variety of subjects—politics, social and cultural commentary, medicine and psychology, music criticism, poetry—but fiction became his primary interest, and it was as critic of fiction that he made his name with *The Smart Set*. From the beginning he had a firm idea of the sort of literary critic he wanted to be—the critic as iconoclast, as rebel against the Genteel Tradition. He found models in Percival Pollard, who wrote for *Town Topics* and had been associated with the avant-garde *Criterion* in New York in the late 1890s, and in James Gibbons Huneker, a critic of the arts who wrote for *The Bookman* and the New York *Sun* and had also been part of the *Criterion* group. Pollard, who had earlier written fiction, plays, and travel pieces, had turned primarily to criticism after 1900. He appealed to Mencken because of his wide reading in European literature and his revolt against moralism—in short, his embodiment of the rebellious literary spirit of the 1890s. Huneker, who also took an aesthetic rather than a moral approach to letters, was even more important to Mencken. He was the first American, Mencken felt, to write intelligently of Mencken's own passions—Ibsen, Nietzsche, and Shaw—and he wrote with gusto. As Mencken later remarked of Huneker, "He emancipated criticism in America from its old bondage to sentimentality and stupidity . . ."

With these iconoclastic models in mind, Mencken soon warmed to the task. Since his early immersion in English literature, he had broadened his reading to include several French writers, including Flaubert and Zola. He was also reading the contemporary Germans Hermann Sudermann and Gerhart Hauptmann—although curiously, even with his new enthusiasm for things German, he never could overcome his early disinterest in Goethe. Among American writers Mark Twain still reigned supreme, for Mencken if for no one else. At

Twain's death in 1910 he hailed "one of the most notable figures in the whole range of English literature," a writer in the company of Cervantes, Thackeray, and Fielding. In *The Smart Set* three years later he saw Mark Twain as "the one authentic giant of our national literature" and described *Huckleberry Finn* as "one of the great masterpieces of the world." He did not think so highly of Twain's contemporary, Henry James, whom he found "quite without any sense of the profound wonder and mystery of human life." "Still," he wrote a fellow critic in 1911, with James "the artist is there. . . . He led the escape from the old novel of external incident . . ."

Mencken gained a reputation in his early *Smart Set* days as a demanding critic, a "killer," as he later wrote. He was hard on such reigning writers as Upton Sinclair and Hamlin Garland as well as such guardians of the Genteel Tradition as William Allen White, F. Marion Crawford, and Meredith Nicholson. He was also critical of the new Imagist poets, particularly Amy Lowell, "the fair Trotsky of the movement." But he valued the experimentation and gusto of Ezra Pound's poetry, found Pound "a poet with something to say and with the skill to say it in a new way." Among fiction writers he praised the Virginia satirist James Branch Cabell, the late literary naturalist Frank Norris, and English realists Arnold Bennett and, particularly, H. G. Wells—although his enthusiasm for Wells waned after 1912 or 1913. But the writer he came to admire most, who finally surpassed even Mark Twain in his mind as "the greatest of them all," was Joseph Conrad.

In *The Smart Set* Mencken lauded Conrad more frequently and more lavishly than any other writer. He was drawn to the novelist for a number of reasons, not the least of which was that, as a Pole living in England and writing in English, Conrad was within English culture without being fully of it. He was, as well, a chronicler of the strenuous life, but in a manner far more honest, far darker, than Mencken's early hero Kipling. Conrad appealed to both the romantic and the skeptic in Mencken, setting "romance . . . free from sentimentality," he wrote in 1912, and, more important, penetrating "to the central fact of human existence . . . that life is meaningless."

When, several years later, Mencken devoted a lengthy essay to Conrad in a larger work on contemporary literature and sent a copy of the book to the novelist, he received a lengthy and friendly response along with a photograph. But he had little correspondence with Conrad after that and was not to know of the novelist's respect for his own work until, after Conrad's death, G. Jean-Aubry's *Joseph Conrad: Life and Letters* was published. In that book he found lines from a letter Conrad had written to a book collector in New York: "Mencken's vigor is astounding. It is like an electric current. . . . My debt of gratitude to him has been growing for years." But Mencken was never to meet Conrad, and, as was the case with his early idol Shaw and with Mark Twain, he made no attempt to see him when he had the opportunity—in Conrad's case when the novelist visited America in 1923. In general, the young Mencken was curiously hesitant about meeting those writers whom he had known and admired as forces before he had the chance to encounter them in the flesh. But of all his British and European literary idols—Kipling, Shaw, Nietzsche, Conrad—only Conrad endured.

Although Conrad was the writer he regarded most highly, the *Smart Set* critic soon realized he would have to champion some other, more obscure novelist—and one closer to home—if he were to affect the literature of his own time and place. Since his earliest days as a literary critic in 1908 and 1909, he later wrote,

> I had been on the lookout for an author who would serve me as a sort of tank in my war upon the frauds and dolts who still reigned in American letters. It was not enough to ridicule and revile the fakers they admired and whooped up, though I did this with great enthusiasm: it was also necessary, if only for the sake of the dramatic contrast, to fight for writers, and especially for newcomers, they sniffed at. . . . What I needed was some American, preferably young, to mass my artillery behind, and I gave a good deal of diligence to the search for him.

Mencken considered Cabell the Virginian, for whose work he had great personal regard, but Cabell—writing about his mythical realm of Poictesme even while remarking on the vices and foibles of the American South—was too sophisticated and remote. "What I needed," Mencken continued in "My Life as Author and Editor," "was an author who was completely American in his themes and his point of view, who dealt with people and situations of wide and durable interest . . . who was . . . simple enough to be understood by the vulgar, and who knew how to concoct and tell an engrossing story." Mencken then thought he had the "tank" to "mass [his] artillery behind" in David Graham Phillips, a realist whose novels *The Hungry Heart* and *The Husband's Story* he praised lavishly in *The Smart Set* of April 1909 and January 1911. But just as the January 1911 review appeared, under the title "The Leading American Novelist," Mencken lost his writer. That same month Phillips was shot and killed, and the *Smart Set* reviewer resumed his search for a "tank."

Mencken found him three months later, when he received a package from his friend Dreiser containing the manuscript of Dreiser's second novel, *Jennie Gerhardt*. He had long admired *Sister Carrie*, although the novel was still little known by others, and he once told Dreiser that it was precisely the novel he himself would like to have written. Indeed, just the month before he received Dreiser's package, he had remarked in the *Evening Sun* that "not many better works than Sister Carrie have been written in this fair land of ours" and had added that "Dreiser, perhaps, will be the man of tomorrow." He also knew Dreiser had been at work on another novel about a working girl, and he had consented to read the manuscript. When he received it, he got to it immediately, and, as he wrote fellow literary iconoclast Harry Leon Wilson, "it floored me." When the novel was published six months later, Mencken praised it extravagantly in *The Smart Set*, calling it the finest American novel he had read "with the lonesome but Himalayan exception of 'Huckleberry Finn.' " Despite its lack of grace and polish, he believed it had the same power Dreiser had brought to *Sister Carrie*. For the next five years Dreiser was to join Conrad in his book column as Mencken's most esteemed writer. The *Smart Set* critic would become known as Dreiser's champion, and, after Dreiser was accepted by other reviewers, Mencken's own position as a literary prophet would be considerably enhanced.

By this point, in fact, Mencken had already built up a considerable following as—in his words—"the chief fugleman of a new criticism, principally aimed at overturning the old American idols." His national reputation, which had blossomed with his book on Nietzsche, continued to grow, and in a fashion Mencken approved. The *Smart Set* critic, wrote the *Los Angeles Times*, "has much to say and he talks in a loud voice. . . . By his brutality, his assertive masculinity, his bellowing rages, he has done much to quash the effeminacy which for a half century has devastated our literature." In Mencken's "virile and ruthless attitude," his "free and fearless spirit of criticism, lies the only hope for the future of American letters."

Mencken undoubtedly relished the rhetoric of manliness, and the fact that the author of those words was probably his friend Willard Huntington Wright, another Nietzschean and devotee of the strenuous life, would not have diminished his delight. Neither would the ignorance demonstrated by another Los Angeles newspaperman who, in 1913, identified him as "R. L. Mencken, a distinguished writer from abroad." What was important to Mencken was that, with the response to his pieces in *The Smart Set*, he had indeed accomplished his earlier goal of becoming more than "a mere local worthy." He was "America's first satirist," remarked the *Los Angeles Times* (again, probably Wright), and in the East he was reaping the benefits of his new position as well. He had begun to visit New York often for business and pleasure, and if he had originally felt the city to be "unliveable"—and would continue to express that belief as long as he lived—he was also coming to find it a place of great excitement. He greatly enjoyed the life of bookman-as-celebrity, the good friends he made among writers and other editors, the long lunches and dinners, the conversations over beer.

According to a close friend, Mencken had the reputation in New York, "chiefly with those who did not know him well . . . of being a burly, loud, raucous fellow, rough in his speech and lacking in refined manners." But in fact, as Edward A. Martin has observed, there were two public Menckens, one of whom was indeed somewhat crude but the other a "dignified, Edwardian gentleman, striving to be proper, a little awkward but traditional in dress and manners." In either case, there was the disarmingly friendly Mencken described by another acquaintance at that time: "Implacable enemies would find themselves capitulating within the first few minutes; the coldest hate would have to thaw before any such warmth."

One of Mencken's closest friends in New York, an old acquaintance with whom he often stayed when he was in the city, was the popular playwright Paul Armstrong. A figure completely forgotten today but one to whom Mencken gives a great deal of attention in his unpublished reminiscences, Armstrong had served, even before Mencken took the *Smart Set* position, as a virtual guide to the gaudy world of theater and theater stars. Some ten years older than Mencken, a burly ex-boxer who loved sports as much as

Mencken disliked them—and a man with little real interest in ideas—Armstrong had little in common with his young friend except a certain zest for living and, as Mencken said, a "delight in the human spectacle and the everyday imbecilities of man."

But that was enough, and not long after Mencken, as drama critic of the Baltimore *Morning Herald,* met Armstrong in 1902 the two men had become close friends. When the playwright and his wife bought an estate near Annapolis in 1907, Mencken saw him even more frequently, both in Baltimore and in Annapolis, to which Armstrong would sometimes invite theater guests from New York. Between 1910 and 1912, when he was in his heyday on Broadway, Armstrong would often put Mencken up at his apartment on West Fifty-seventh Street and accompany him around New York. "I never took him seriously," Mencken later wrote of Armstrong, but nonetheless his friend interested him as an object of study. A flashy dresser and heavy drinker, inventing his past and out to impress the world, he was a simple man infected with an increasingly virulent strain of the American dream. "It was his great sentimentality that attracted me to him," Mencken recalled. He was "a yokel at heart," and Mencken was already interested "in learning something about yokels."

Dreiser—from whose pen Armstrong might have sprung—was an even closer companion in New York during Mencken's days as *Smart Set* reviewer. In 1909 and 1910 Dreiser was the editor and Mencken the writer, Mencken reporting in March 1909, "I want to write a couple of books for you within the next few years." Soon the roles were reversed. In 1910 Dreiser was dismissed as editor of *The Delineator* because of his infatuation with the eighteen-year-old daughter of an editor at Butterick Publications, and he turned all his attention to the writing of fiction. At times Mencken had dinner uptown with Dreiser and his wife, Sara—"a small and meagrely made woman," Mencken later described her, with a manner "suggesting the country environment from which she had come." More often Mencken and Dreiser met in the city for food, drink, and conversation, often accompanied by women who, however improbably, seemed to find Dreiser irresistible.

Dreiser's sexual adventures fascinated Mencken from the beginning, and he often remarked on the subject in his unpublished reminiscences. "A polygamist on a really wholesale scale," Mencken wrote; "during the years of our association I saw almost as much of his women as I did of him." Mencken was hardly exaggerating in his accounts of this corn-fed Lothario, who was reputed, on occasion, to have retired to the bedroom between courses of a dinner party to entertain one of the guests. Mencken marveled at how a man so "reckless in his amours," who made no "attempt to protect his partners," stayed out of the paternity courts. Dreiser, he concluded, must be sterile.

For his part, Mencken had always had, he acknowledged, "a prejudice against adultery, if only because it involved a breach of faith," although he "certainly had no desire to inflict" his prejudices "upon the entire human race." In considering Dreiser, however, the issue sometimes seemed more than adultery: the novelist's indiscriminate bedding involved a breach of taste as well as faith. Mencken himself, of course, was no celibate, but he was also excessively discreet, as we shall see, about the details of his own sexual life. It was bad form to say too much—unless, of course, one was engaging in Mencken's equivalent of locker-room bragging and inventing, in which case individual names were not named. As for Dreiser, despite Mencken's closeness to his friend, the issue touched on the basic difference Mencken felt between himself and Dreiser nearly from the beginning. The difference, as much else with Mencken, was a matter of class, although he would not usually have called it that. Both he and Dreiser were German Americans, but there the similarity ended. As Mencken was the well-born child of the *gelehrten*, at least if he dug back far enough, Dreiser was the "peasant," Mencken believed, little different in origin from those Baltimore German Americans his father and grandfather had taught him to view skeptically. Dreiser's numerous sexual encounters and his lack of discretion about reporting them betrayed not only a certain deficit of honor—in Mencken's mind, the mark of a gentleman—but also the peasant's lack of manners.

But in Dreiser's case Mencken also felt a certain ambivalence, and he felt it in particular when he was approached by Sara Dreiser, who asked for his help in putting an end to her husband's extramarital affairs. Despite his theoretical opposition to adultery, he concluded that Dreiser might be justified after all:

[I]t was unhappily clear that [Sara] had failed dismally in the prime duty of every wife, which is to be charming to her lord. . . . "How," I asked myself, . . . "would *you* like to be married to a red-haired Christian Scientist from the Great Plains? How would *you* like to go home to her every night . . ." Who, indeed, was I to pronounce judgment upon a man who was my elder and my better—a great artist, and, in the history of the Republic, almost incomparable? If the needs of his extremely difficult and onerous trade required him to consume and spit out a schoolma'm from the cow country, then it was certainly to be lamented—but that was as far as I could go in logic, or in such ethical theory as I subscribed to.

It is clear, as was often the case when he pondered Dreiser, that Mencken was having fun in his analysis. Among other things, he thought of no man as his "better." But it is also clear that his allegiance was to his friend rather than to his friend's wife; that the role of Sara Dreiser, as he saw it, was to keep her husband happy; and that the work of his friend—the rigors of the writer's trade—justified whatever he did. Mencken also detected in Sara a "pervasive jealousy of her husband's growing fame." Thus:

I dismissed her from my mind with hardly more than formal regret, and took my stand with the devil's party, which is to say, with Dreiser. . . . So far as I was concerned, she was merely a minor and non-essential function of a man whose activities in other directions I greatly admired, and I was thus easily resigned to letting him work his wicked will with her.

Dreiser's will, by 1912 or 1913, required separation from Sara, at least the majority of the time, and Mencken continued to view Dreiser the social creature with some amusement. He must have recognized in him that same tendency evident in certain other chroniclers of the American dream, from Mark Twain to Sinclair Lewis and F. Scott Fitzgerald—that tendency to become in one's own life what one dissects, understands, and often even rejects in one's fiction.

But it was the fiction, after all, that mattered most to Mencken, and his *Smart Set* praise for *Jennie Gerhardt* in 1911 was simply the public expression of an admiration he had often expressed privately to Dreiser. He had, from the time his friend was dismissed from

Butterick, served as Dreiser's great supporter behind the scenes as well. When Dreiser had written him, a month or two after he finished *Jennie Gerhardt*, that he was not making a good living, Mencken had answered, "Give the game a fair trial; you have got the goods, and soon or late the fact will penetrate the skulls of those who have anything within." When Mencken had read the manuscript of *Jennie Gerhardt*, before he had gone public in his praise, he had written Dreiser: "The story comes upon me with great force; it touches my own experiences of life in a hundred places; . . . altogether I get a powerful effect of reality, stark and unashamed." In other letters, written between his reading of the manuscript and the publication of the book, Mencken had told Dreiser that *Jennie Gerhardt* was "a novel of the first rank—the best ever done in America" and then, a week later, remembering an older allegiance, had modified that to "the best American novel ever done, with the one exception of 'Huckleberry Finn.' "

The two men's literary relationship became even closer during the next two or three years. When Dreiser wrote in November 1912 asking if Mencken would serve as his literary executor "in case of my death," Mencken responded that he would consider it a high privilege. In fact, he was already overseeing his friend's literary affairs. After reading Dreiser's next novel, *The Financier*, in proof, he suggested changes that Dreiser then made. Mencken was not as enthusiastic about this study of wealth and power, based on the life of business tycoon Charles T. Yerkes, but he still found much to commend in the novel, and he said as much in *The New York Times Book Review*.

Dreiser came to Baltimore the following year to discuss with Mencken his sequel to *The Financier*, entitled *The Titan*, and when Mencken read the novel in proof he wrote Dreiser, "It is the best thing you have ever done, with the possible exception of 'Jennie Gerhardt.' . . . It is the best picture of an immoralist in all modern literature . . ." *The Titan*, he added a few days later, was "a great Nietzschean document." Although the novel did not fare so well with other reviewers, Mencken was equally glowing in *The Smart Set*, comparing Dreiser with Conrad in one important particular: "To each the salient fact of life is its utter meaninglessness, its sordid cruelty, its mystery."

Not only did Mencken serve as advance man for Dreiser (thus

reversing the original order since it was Dreiser who was to have been *his* "tank") and advise him on the direction of his fiction, he also counseled the novelist as to publishers, recommending George H. Doran and Mencken's own earlier publisher Henry Holt—only to conclude later, as he wrote Dreiser, that Holt "was not for you." In short, Mencken did about everything an increasingly influential critic and reviewer could have done for an emerging novelist, and Dreiser was grateful. In 1914 he offered Mencken the "original pen copy" of any one of his manuscripts. Mencken thanked him for his generosity and chose *Sister Carrie*. The two men, at this point, saw themselves as a team, united in their opposition to the American bourgeoisie and the Genteel Tradition. "The philistines will never run us out as long as life do last," Dreiser wrote in March 1914. "Given health & strength we can shake the American Jericho to its fourth sub-story."

If Mencken found with no other friend quite the sense of common purpose he found with Dreiser between 1909 and 1914, he found with any number of other men a mutual enjoyment of life. He got along especially well with George Jean Nathan, the expatriate from Indiana who had begun as drama critic for *The Smart Set* shortly after Mencken became literary critic. The two men were at least as different, personally, as Mencken and Dreiser were. Nathan was Jewish, slight, elegant, polished, and interested not in politics or even in ideas but exclusively in beauty and art, especially the theater. It would not be quite accurate to say that he was to Mencken as Mencken was to Dreiser—it infuriated Mencken when Burton Rascoe once suggested that *he* was the "peasant" to Nathan's aristocrat—but he was indeed cruder than Nathan, louder and earthier. The two men had in common, however, a sense of irreverence, a distaste for reformers, and a love of good beer and conversation, as well as defiant bachelorhood and confirmed agnosticism. In his private thoughts—as was always the case even with his closest friends—Mencken kept a certain distance from Nathan, finding himself amused by his friend's self-importance, his self-consciousness about his lack of height and bulk, and his attempts to conceal that lack of size by appearing in public only with women who were shorter than he. But in their early *Smart Set* days Mencken was also exceedingly fond of Nathan and would become even closer to him after 1914.

Mencken encountered numerous other men in his late twenties and early thirties whose company he enjoyed or came to enjoy, including poets Edgar Lee Masters and Louis Untermeyer, budding novelist Ben Hecht, and Herbert Bayard Swope, editor of the New York *World*, all of whom later recorded their vivid impressions of the young critic. They hardly found Mencken an imposing physical presence. When he first met Mencken in 1912, Untermeyer gazed on a "chubby, moon-faced" man with an "impudent" snub nose. The same year Hecht, then only eighteen years old but already a newspaper reporter, met Mencken and decided he resembled "a city alderman": the critic "looked like a man who had never played a physical game of any sort . . . not fat or ill shapen but seemingly without muscles." Hecht changed his mind the following year, when he saw Mencken at the piano in his home in Baltimore, "his forearms, hands, and fingers . . . obviously as powerful as a blacksmith's." Mencken was to Hecht the "hero-mind of my youth," "my alma mater." "No single American mind . . . influenced existence in the Republic as much as he did."

In New York and sometimes Baltimore, Mencken encountered not only younger writers but also more established figures whom he had long known by reputation or through correspondence. Although Percival Pollard had been one of his heroes in the 1890s and he had corresponded with Pollard since 1906, Mencken did not meet Pollard until October 1910. Shortly before their meeting he had praised the critic in *The Smart Set*, remarking that "a man of Mr. Pollard's assertive masculinity stands forth like a truth seeker in the Baptist college of cardinals." If Mencken in that review had been attracted to Pollard's revolt against the feminine—a prevailing theme, as we have seen, in Mencken's early criticism—when he met Pollard they principally discussed a book Pollard currently had under way, to be entitled *Masks and Minstrels of the New Germany*.

Mencken had long been drawn to Pollard as a cosmopolitan critic. Born in England of English and German descent, Pollard had come to America in his teens, but he returned to Europe each year, visiting Berlin and Munich in particular. "A thorough-going Germanophil [*sic*]," as Mencken described him, he served as a catalyst for Mencken's "dawning race consciousness." The young critic sent Pollard clippings and other materials for his book, and when *Masks and Minstrels of the New Germany* appeared, Mencken praised it highly in the *Evening Sun* and *The Smart Set*. When Pollard returned to the United States from Berlin and Vienna in May 1911, he and Mencken spent a great deal of time together, drinking and talking in Baltimore, to which Pollard had come for a long visit. "I looked forward with pleasant anticipations," Mencken later wrote, "to fighting by his side in the rough-and-tumble literary battle that was just joining." That battle was against the Genteel Tradition and against an exclusively English political and cultural influence in America.

Pollard's death at forty-two, later that same year, robbed Mencken of a close friend and ally, but, in a fashion both bizarre and humorous, he was to become more closely acquainted with his old hero dying and dead than he had been alive. As Mencken told the gruesome story in "My Life as Author and Editor," when Pollard became seriously ill in December 1911 he returned to Baltimore for treatment at a small homeopathic hospital. When his condition became truly grave, Mencken and a friend checked him into the Johns Hopkins Hospital. There Pollard died of a brain tumor two days later. Taking charge in the absence of Mrs. Pollard, Mencken arranged for the funeral and cremation, making certain that an Episcopal priest showed up to say a few words—and then had Pollard's ashes on his hands for the next eight months while Mrs. Pollard, who had come to Baltimore for the funeral but had left immediately afterward, decided what to do with them. On Christmas morning, a week after Pollard's death, Mencken and his brother August visited the Loudon Park Cemetery—where Mencken was paying fifty cents per day storage—and were shown the ashes, with the larger bones not yet fully disintegrated and the skull still clearly visible. A few months later, after Mrs. Pollard determined that the ashes, now fully ground up, should be buried in Iowa, where Pollard had lived in his teens, Mencken tried to mail them. He was turned away by an express clerk on the grounds that the ashes constituted a corpse and consequently could not be mailed without a permit. Mencken finally paid an undertaker fifteen dollars to take care of the permit and the shipping.

It was a story worthy of Pollard's good friend Ambrose Bierce, who showed up in Baltimore for the funeral and entertained Mencken with "cynical witticisms" as they drove to the cemetery. They made two of the funeral party of five. It was the first time Mencken had met "the Bitter Bierce," who was then sixty-nine, although he knew Bierce's work well and agreed with much of what Bierce said about the dismal state of American life and letters. The two men were to have some contact over the next two years, corresponding about the possibility of Bierce's contributing to *The Smart Set* and about Bierce's high regard for Mencken's writing. In April 1913 Bierce wrote that he was planning to "go West later in the season, or rather Southwest—and may go into Mexico (where, thank God, there is something doing) and to South America . . . if, in Mexico, I do not incur the mischance of standing against a wall to be shot." That may have been precisely what happened. When Bierce disappeared in the Mexican Revolution, Mencken had little immediate reaction. But the tribute he penned to the bitter satirist in a later essay could have served, as he must have known, as his own epitaph:

> What delighted [Bierce] most in this life was the spectacle of human cowardice and folly. . . . Out of the spectacle of life about him he got an unflagging and Gargantuan joy. The obscene farce of politics delighted him. He was an almost amorous connoisseur of theology and theologians. He howled with mirth whenever he thought of a professor, a doctor or a husband.

Between 1910 and 1914 Mencken's life was turning toward that dual existence he was to live for the next two decades—spending a few days each month (more after 1914) in the literary spotlight of New York, living the greater part of the time a more subdued life as son, brother, and family caretaker in Baltimore. Even in Baltimore, to be sure, there was a dual identity of another sort—the flamboyant and rebellious author of "The Free Lance" on the one hand and, on the other, the proper citizen of 1524 Hollins Street who lived with his mother, met all his obligations, and found his greatest pleasure in playing Beethoven with his friends every Saturday night.

In 1910 Mencken had been happy to move into his fourth decade. "The thirties are vastly more stimulating and productive," he wrote a friend, "and hence vastly more happy, than the twenties." He was also more satisfied with his health than he had been at any time in his adult life. "I was ill all through my later teens and early twenties," he wrote in his diary, "and it was not until I was 30 years old that I ever felt really brisk and lively." With Mencken, however, good health was always relative, and if we take his word that his early thirties was a period of physical well-being, we can only wonder at the bodily horrors of his twenties. For by 1910 he had already fallen into that lifelong habit of filling letters to friends with details of his deteriorating corpus. From those letters, as well as his autobiographical notes and reminiscences, we know that he suffered during this "brisk and lively" period from, at the very least, hemorrhoids, hyperacidity, neuralgia, "flabbiness," hay fever, tonsillitis, sore throat, and, especially, "tongue trouble," a mysterious and uncomfortable sensation that began about 1912 or 1913. On one particular morning he listed these additional ailments:

A pimple inside the jaw
A sour stomach
Pain in the prostate
Burning in the gospel pipe (always a preliminary of the hay fever season)
A cut finger
A small pimple inside the nose (going away)
A razor cut, smarting
Tired eyes

It would be easy to call Mencken a hypochondriac, although two of his primary physicians, in interviews, maintained that he was not truly hypochondriacal—focusing on ailments that were not there—but rather was bothered by an unusual number of actual ailments. Indeed, in the period between 1909 and 1914 he had a hemorrhoidectomy and a tonsillectomy, as well as surgery for the removal of his uvula, performed with little finesse by his friend Hirshberg. If these operations and several other minor surgeries at various points in his life were not absolutely necessary, they were deemed medically advisable.

As Mencken himself knew, however, he was unusually attuned to unpleasant physical sensations that might not have troubled someone else—was hypersensitive, if not hypochondriacal. "The slightest pain sets my whole perimeter to trembling," he wrote a friend, "and I am unfit for human society until the chiropractors* relieve me." The hypersensitivity was, in part, attributable to the writer's trade. As his

*Mencken's favorite word—along with "quacks"—for physicians.

brother August later remarked, "He was always working at such a pitch that a slight discomfort or a slight ailment that wouldn't disturb the normal person at all, to him was of enormous proportions." Or, as Mencken himself said to a fellow writer, "A man who sits in a room alone trying to fetch up ideas out of his own gizzard seems bound to be more or less unhealthy."

At times his ailments interfered with the writing itself—for example, the "sore tongue" he withstood for nine months, he complained to Dreiser early in 1914, kept him "from all save routine work"—and Mencken's astounding literary output is all the more remarkable for that reason. If his work suffered from that hardship, however, it undoubtedly benefited from his particular living situation in Baltimore, with all his physical needs, and many of his emotional ones as well, being met by his mother. "I owed to her, and to her alone," Mencken later wrote, "the fact that I had a comfortable home throughout my . . . early manhood."

A number of Mencken's friends and acquaintances attributed his continued bachelorhood, as well as that of brother August and the spinsterhood of sister Gertrude, to that comfortable arrangement. Anna Mencken was, in her way, a "dynamic personality," Mencken's cousin W. C. Abhau later noted, poised and pleasant to be around but nonetheless controlling. She was still "an extraordinarily good-looking woman, something to write home about," Mencken's friend the novelist James Cain remarked in a letter to a mutual friend, "and very possibly . . . furnished these Mencken children with all they needed in the way of female emotion." She took pride in her eldest son's journalistic and literary achievements, and although she might at times have been disturbed by some of his more outrageous writings, she was also somewhat amused. In any case, she never discussed such matters with Henry.

If Mencken enjoyed the life of privileged eldest son, he was still the dutiful son as well, in many ways taking the place of his father. He took very seriously the role of head of house, became nearly the patriarch in his father's manner. He had never had to fill the role of primary financial provider for the family, since August Mencken, in his will, had taken care of Anna and her younger children, but Henry did contribute a significant amount to meet family expenses and at age twenty-one transferred to his mother his share of his father's inheritance. He had taken on numerous other responsibilities as well, including the rental and sale of the Mount Washington house, the handling of certain legal entanglements related to the Mount Washington property, and now, in his early thirties, the renovation of much of the Hollins Street house. He also took his mother, as well as Gertrude and young August, on at least one trip to Jamaica, accompanied his uncle Charles A. Abhau on another, and, when his grandfather Abhau was at the point of death, was the family member "summoned to his house," Mencken later wrote, where "he died, in fact, in my arms." "The one obligation I recognize in this world is my duty to my immediate family," Mencken was to write in his diary. "We should go out of the world at the end having paid our way in it in full."

Besides his care of his mother, that obligation was demonstrated most clearly in his concern for his brother August. For a time after the death of August Mencken, Sr., W. C. Abhau has noted, Henry assumed the role of father for young August, who was only nine years old when his father died. When August became ill with tuberculosis during his junior year at the Polytechnic and was forced to go to a sanitarium in Pennsylvania for treatment, Mencken went to see the head of the school to ask for a furlough. He was met with such a lack of understanding and sympathy that he departed in disgust and never returned to the school after that. August later had a relapse, and his uncertain health probably made him even more dependent on his older brother than he would otherwise have been. Although he recovered and became an engineer, he continued to live at home much of the time, although frequently traveling on business.

Mencken devoted less attention to his sister, Gertrude, and his other brother, Charlie. Gertrude also remained at home most of this time, worrying her mother with an antisocial attitude and a certain negative streak, but she was not primarily Henry's concern. Charlie, the playfellow of his youth, was the only one of the children who moved out and left the family circle. "A rather wild fellow," as Mencken described him, he was also the only family member, according to W. C. Abhau, who seemed to regard Henry with no awe at all. Carefree, sometimes irresponsible and undependable, he was the antithesis of his older brother—a figure, in that respect, giving support neither to Mencken's cherished idea of heredity nor to the power of environment, except that, as a second child, he might be said to have reacted against his conscientious, successful older brother.

Nonetheless, like the younger August, Charlie had applied himself sufficiently to realize his father's frustrated dream of becoming an engineer and had gone to work for the Pennsylvania Steel Company and then the Pennsylvania Railroad, usually based in the Pittsburgh area. In 1909 Charlie had married in Pennsylvania and further loosened his ties to the Baltimore family. Six years later his wife gave birth to the only child the four children of August and Anna Mencken would produce.

Even closer than his brothers in certain respects, and certainly closer than most of his New York associates, continued to be Mencken's old Baltimore friends—very few of whom were writers, at least of the creative variety, and very few of whom were assertive or highly visible figures, although most were professionally successful. Among those closest friends, principally but not exclusively of German descent, were Albert Hildebrandt, the violin maker who had been in on the beginning of the Saturday Night Club, and Heinrich Buchholz, the head of a Baltimore company that published educational books and journals. Mencken often had lunch at the Rennert Hotel with Hildebrandt and Buchholz and found Buchholz a fine nighttime drinking companion as well. In his early thirties he also became close to Max Brödel, an anatomical artist at the Johns Hopkins who had been trained in Leipzig; Carl Schon, a meticulous craftsman and defiant agnostic; and Willie Woollcott, brother of the New York critic and wit Alexander Woollcott and, in Mencken's opinion, a far better man. The qualities Mencken most appreciated in these friends and others were not brilliance and flamboyance but rather steadiness, modesty, generosity, and humor. Hildebrandt was unassuming, dependable, and, Mencken said, the happiest man he had ever known. Schon, a childless widower, was a "man of great charm and . . . courtly manners." Woollcott was kind, tolerant, a man with "less malice in him [and] more charm" than anyone Mencken ever met. And so on.

Most of Mencken's Baltimore friends were involved professionally in music, medicine, or craftsmanship of some variety, all callings which required a high degree of precision and professional competence. This quality drew Mencken to them as well. All, whether professionally involved in music or not, were attracted to music in their off-hours. Most were members of the Saturday Night Club, either as participants or, as in Woollcott's case, as listeners. And many belonged as well to the much larger Florestan Club, which took its name from a character in Schumann's *Carnaval*. Organized in 1910 with Mencken as a charter member, the Florestan in turn gave rise to a much smaller Sunday dinner club, also featuring good food and music, which met every other week either at the Florestan Club on Charles Street or in the suburban homes of Woollcott and another member. In his correspondence with Max Brödel in 1913, Mencken spoke of still another dinner club, which met once a month at the Rennert Hotel, and elsewhere he referred to a picnic club that took to the country on summer weekends. The point is that this "Free Lance" of Baltimore, the scourge of Rotary and other fraternal organizations, was himself, in his private life, a very sociable man. The difference, he would have said, was that *his* clubs did not presume to undertake good works.

As he approached his mid-thirties, Mencken cast off some of the friends of his Baltimore youth. Leonard Hirshberg, for one, no matter how bright and amusing, proved to be a liar and a sponge. But old Sunpaper friends, though not as close as his musical comrades, still served as superb lunch and drinking companions. Mencken particularly enjoyed A. H. McDannald, who was both *Sun* political reporter and a nonplaying member of the Saturday Night Club. When he made plans in 1911 and 1912 for a second European trip, he included the portly Virginian.

That trip, like his first to Europe in 1908, was concentrated on Germany and England, Munich and London, almost as if the former half Anglophile, now Germanophile, were testing the two cultures, comparing them back to back. He and McDannald sailed on April 16, 1912, from New York on the *Kronprinz Wilhelm*, Mencken rereading *Huckleberry Finn* as they crossed on generally smooth seas. They set out across the North Atlantic the day following the sinking of the *Titanic*, and Mencken, in a letter written at sea to Gertrude, spoke of the impact of the *Titanic* on those aboard. Several passengers tried to sell their tickets at the pier, others stayed up all night watching for ice, and the *Kronprinz Wilhelm* sailed a hundred miles south of its usual course to avoid ice fields. But Mencken himself felt secure "with the Titanic affair on every captain's mind."

Mencken and McDannald landed at Bremen and caught a train down to Munich, where they were shown the city by the British consul. They also attended concerts in massive beer halls, heard

Richard Strauss's *Elektra,* and frequented beer gardens. The weather, the beer, and "the gals," he wrote Dreiser, were perfect. In May, after calling off a walking tour in the Tyrol because of raw, rainy weather, they traveled north to Heidelberg and the Rhine and then moved on to London. There Mencken called on Nietzsche translator Oscar Levy and enjoyed the city as he had four years before. But his London visit this time was brief. If England had captured his affection in 1908, Germany wooed him now.

Mencken had embarked on his European trip under the assumption, unlikely as it may seem, that when he returned in six weeks he would be a candidate for vice president of the United States and thus a celebrity at the Democratic convention in Baltimore in July. Such a scheme had been hatched just before he sailed. Charles Grasty, editor of the Sunpapers, wanted to embarrass Baltimore's mayor, James H. Preston, who himself wanted the Democratic nomination for vice president but wanted to avoid paying the $270 filing fee. The fee would not be necessary if no other Marylander filed. So Mencken agreed to allow the Sunpapers to enter him as a candidate and pay his filing fee, all to take place while he was at sea. Grasty's scheme failed only because Preston heard of the scheme and filed just minutes before the *Sun* agent showed up to file for Mencken.

The aspiring candidate had received the wireless message "Everything is off" while he was still at sea, so he returned to New York in early June knowing that he would not be a mock vice presidential contender after all. (He could not have been, in any case, since he was underage.) But he returned to more serious matters as well. First, he found August in the hospital with pneumonia, and although his brother soon recovered, the incident again reminded Mencken of the grave responsibility of heading a family. Second, and less easily resolved, *The Smart Set* was in equally poor health, and its affliction, if not terminal, would require strong medicine.

Since Mencken had taken over as *Smart Set* reviewer in 1908, the magazine had undergone a change of ownership, Colonel William Mann having sold out in 1911 to John Adams Thayer, who had earlier had great financial success with *Everybody's Magazine.* But *The Smart Set* was losing money under Thayer's control. Mencken liked Thayer well enough personally—and attended lavish parties at his New York apartment and his country place in Connecticut—but had little respect for his ability to run a magazine of the arts. He thought

119

no more highly of Mark Lee Luther and Norman Boyer, who served as coeditors of the magazine after Fred Splint resigned in 1911. Thayer had come to Mencken on occasion asking that he himself consider editing *The Smart Set,* but Mencken's disinclination to work closely with Thayer and, especially, to leave Baltimore always made him decline the offer.

When Thayer approached him again in 1912, this time more insistent than before, Mencken had a suggestion. He had been corresponding since 1908 or 1909 with Willard Huntington Wright, a Virginian in his late twenties who had attended Harvard briefly before winding up in Los Angeles. Mencken had been grateful for Wright's glowing review of his Nietzsche book and had met Wright at least once in the East. It was also Wright, in all likelihood, who in 1910 had praised Mencken's "assertive masculinity," his "free and fearless spirit of criticism." Mencken expressed an equally high regard for Wright as critic, and for some of the same reasons. "You have got into English the thing that Nietzsche got into German—a loud heart beat, an assertive clang," Mencken wrote him in October 1909. "*Keep* that style. . . . Guard it, by all means, from feminization." Mencken liked Wright for reasons other than his "electric style." The critic was also such good company that in 1911 Mencken had urged him to join McDannald and himself on their upcoming European trip.

Theodore Dreiser's regard for Wright was less elevated than Mencken's, and for once Dreiser saw the situation more clearly than his friend did. "To me Wright is about a third impression of Henry L. Mencken," Dreiser wrote him. "He is so overcome by your spirit that he even uses your language—almost verbatim and I think unconsciously." Nathan's opinion of Wright was higher than Dreiser's but still mixed. Nonetheless, Mencken wanted Wright to come East. "Once you are in New York," he wrote in January 1912, "I think I can get you in on the ground floor of the Smart Set. . . . There are lots of chances ahead for both of us, and I believe that some of them will open quicker if we work together." Wright indeed came to New York shortly after that, principally to assume Percival Pollard's old place as literary editor of *Town Topics,* and met with Mencken, who took him to talk with Thayer. Thayer hired Wright as an "associate editor." Mencken's man soon assumed the duties of editor in chief.

In certain ways Wright was an excellent editor, although his reign lasted hardly more than a year. He brought in a number of British and European writers, including Conrad, Yeats, D. H. Lawrence, August Strindberg, Robert Bridges, and George Moore, and began what William H. Nolte has called the "golden age" of *The Smart Set*. Mencken fared well under Wright, who got Thayer to increase the payment for his monthly book essays from $50 to $100. As a result of that increase, as well as payment for the additional writing he was now undertaking for the magazine, Mencken's *Smart Set* income nearly doubled, to $1,750, in 1913. He also served as primary adviser to Wright, rounding up potential contributors, including Ezra Pound, and discussing in some detail the direction of the magazine. "Be very careful with the sexual stuff, at least for the present," Mencken warned him in June 1913.

It was pushing the limits of sexual license, among other things, that spelled trouble for the new *Smart Set* editor. Wright's own life was hardly conventional: he had left his wife and daughter behind in Los Angeles and was living with various women in New York. Mencken enjoyed the numerous parties at his apartment on Forty-fifth Street and also invited Wright down to Baltimore for sessions of the Florestan Club—which Wright must have considered tame and sober affairs. But at the same time, Mencken found fault with Wright's poor judgment and "infantile recklessness." Thayer disapproved not only of Wright's sexual openness, personally and professionally, but of his financial extravagance with the magazine. He was particularly disturbed in the spring of 1913, when he discovered that Wright, along with Mencken and Nathan, was plotting an even more risqué magazine, to be entitled *The Blue Weekly*, and had drawn up the dummy for the new magazine at Thayer's expense.

Matters came to a head late in 1913, and Thayer enlisted Mencken's help in getting rid of Wright. Mencken resisted at first, but after Thayer made a trip to Baltimore one Sunday in December to discuss the matter, he realized it was useless to hold out. "From [Thayer's] talk I conclude that the situation is hopeless," he wrote Wright on December 14. "The only thing for you to do in decency is to clear out." In fact, Mencken had advised Thayer to dismiss Wright, but only because it was clear that Thayer wanted his magazine to be only for "right-thinkers," and Wright could never work to achieve that end. A few days later, after a conversation with Thayer in New York, Wright felt Mencken had betrayed him. So he too came to Baltimore for a talk, was assured that Mencken had worked in his best interest once Thayer had become adamant, and departed on good terms. Wright left *The Smart Set* early in 1914, and Mencken helped him find a job on the New York *Evening Mail.*

Mencken and Wright, who remained close friends, continued to make plans for another European trip that Wright had conceived in 1913, ostensibly to seek out European authors for *The Smart Set* but, in fact, to sample European nightlife. This trip in the spring of 1914 was Mencken's third to Europe, and it was, he later said, his most pleasurable. It would also mark an end, in more ways than one, of his days of innocence.

He and two Baltimore companions, McDannald of the *Sun* and Edwin Moffett, a fellow member of the Saturday Night Club and Sunday dinner club, sailed from New York to Naples on the Cunard *Laconia.* Their plan was to link up with Wright and Nathan in Paris. En route to Naples they stopped off briefly at Gibraltar and drove into Spain, where, Mencken wrote his mother, "a general filthiness . . . was over everything." He pronounced Naples at least as dirty, and then proceeded to Capri, Pompei, Rome, Venice, Florence, Munich, and Lucerne before winding up in Paris for—Mencken wrote his sister—"a sort of Smart Set reunion." Throughout, Mencken and his companions looked for a good time, and in their various shenanigans—serving as escorts for a mock wedding aboard ship, sneaking into a group of pilgrims for an audience with Pope Pius X, playing pranks on Moffett, putting in a "riotous week" in Paris—they resembled no one so much as the untamed Americans of Mark Twain's *Innocents Abroad,* irreverent New World ruffians paying no heed to the dignity of the Old.

When they returned from boozing their way across Europe, Mencken, Nathan, and Wright put together a book—based more on previous excursions than on the one just completed—on European nightlife, entitled *Europe After 8:15.* Nathan wrote essays on Paris and Berlin, and Wright did a section on Vienna as well as serving as editor of the manuscript, which was brought out by the American representative of the British publisher John Lane. Mencken's primary contribution, a piece on Munich that focused on beer and food, had first appeared in *The Smart Set* in April 1913, even before his most recent European trip. In "The Beeriad" (now entitled simply "Munich") he wrote with a new confidence and authority:

I am by nature a vulgar fellow. I prefer *Tom Jones* to *The Rosary*, Rabelais to the Elsie books, the Old Testament to the New, the expurgated parts of *Gulliver's Travels* to those that are left. I delight in beef stews, limericks, burlesque shows . . . and the music of Haydn, that beery and delightful old rascal: I swear in the presence of ladies and archdeacons. When the mercury is above ninety-five I dine in my shirt sleeves and write poetry naked. . . . As I have said, I joy in vulgarity, whether it take the form of divorce procedings or of Tristan und Isolde, of an Odd Fellows' funeral or of Munich beer.

Munich beer, then, was "unique, incomparable, *sui generis* . . . consummate, transcendental, *übernatürlich*," and Munich food— "schnitzels and bifsteks, those mighty double portions of sauerbraten and rostbif"—was equally magnificent. Mencken launched into a catalogue of cafés and bierkellers—the Luitpold, the Odéon, the Pschorrbräu, the Mathäserbräu, and at last the Löwenbräukeller and the Hofbräuhaus, on which he lavished his most excessive praise:

Ah, the Hofbräuhaus: A massive and majestic shrine, the Parthenon of beer drinking, seductive to virtuosi, fascinating to the connoisseur, but a bit too strenuous, a trifle too cruel, perhaps, for the dilettante. The Müncheners love it as hillmen love the hills. . . . There, when [the Münchener] has passed out . . . his pallbearers in their gauds of grief will step to refresh themselves, and to praise him in speech and song, and to weep unashamed for the loss of so *gemütlich* a fellow.

In his contribution to *Europe After 8:15* Mencken had hit his stride. But he also had more serious business at hand when he returned from his travels in late spring 1914. After dismissing Wright, Thayer had again asked him to take over as editor of *The Smart Set*. When Mencken again had declined, Thayer had once more put Boyer and Luther in charge of editorial affairs but had continued to pursue Mencken. When Mencken still said no, Thayer turned to Nathan, who also refused him. The magazine had begun to slide back into that mediocrity from which Wright had rescued it. "Thayer is wholly unfitted to run [*The Smart Set*]," Mencken wrote Harry Leon Wilson in February 1914. "I have never met a man with less appreciation of good writing."

Seeing the magazine lose circulation and feeling somewhat desperate, Thayer sold out in 1914 to one of his creditors, Eugene F. Crowe, and Crowe soon appointed Eltinge F. Warner, successful publisher of *Field and Stream,* as his own publisher. "John Adams Thayer has vanished from the *Smart Set* to a low comedy tune," Mencken triumphantly announced to Ellery Sedgwick, and "new owners are in charge." Warner, as it turned out, had become acquainted with Nathan when the two returned from Europe on the same ship a few months before. Now he thought of Nathan, offered him the editorship, and this time, with Thayer out of the picture, Nathan was interested—but only if he could talk Mencken into serving as his coeditor.

Mencken was also interested. "I am at work on a plan which may give me editorial control of Smart Set . . ." he wrote Dreiser on August 22. "George Nathan is with me." He went to New York later in the week to meet with Nathan and Warner and was assured he could remain in Baltimore most of the time. "My chief job," he told Dreiser, "will be to get and read ms. and negotiate with authors." All terms were satisfactory. In August 1914 Mencken and Nathan became editors of *The Smart Set.*

In early August 1914 Mencken's attention was focused largely on New York, although he could hardly ignore the outbreak of war in Europe during those same days. At the time it seemed that his primary concern, when he considered events in Europe, was the role the beginning of hostilities and the resulting unstable American stock market had played in Thayer's decision to sell quickly. But the entangling alliances of Europe would soon serve, even more than he recognized at first, to ensnare him as well. He did realize from the beginning that the coming war meant that his recently acquired pride in the new Germany would be put to the test. But he did not yet realize how severe that test would be.

The year 1914, in all its ramifications, would be the most momentous in Mencken's life to that point. Such was particularly true of the first eight months of that year. He had made a farewell trip to the old Europe of grandeur and empire and had had the gaudiest time he would ever have across the Atlantic. He had returned to America and helped put out, that same summer, a book about the Europe of beer halls and theaters and elegant restaurants, a clever, frivolous book that had appeared just as the Europe it described was about to be altered forever. He had—he reflected accurately thirty years later—"by 1914, pretty well established [himself] as a literary critic, and was beginning to be quoted and discussed." He had become coeditor of *The Smart Set* in August 1914, just at the moment the Great War was breaking out.

And early in 1914 he had met Marion Bloom.

# Chapter 6

# LOVE AND WAR

enry Mencken met Marion Bloom, a twenty-two-year-old aspiring writer, in February 1914, when Marion and her sister Estelle came to the Baltimore *Sun* to inquire as to the whereabouts of Estelle's missing husband. A native of rural Maryland, Marion had gone to Washington in her late teens to find work and whatever excitement the city had to offer. When she met Mencken, she was still living there with her sister. She was immediately taken with Mencken and he with her. Within the month he had seen the small, dark, and lively Marion in Baltimore and was writing to her in his customary courtly and mock-heroic manner: "I may visit your fair city [soon] and when I arrive I shall certainly call you up and crave the privilege of calling on you." By summer Mencken was traveling to Washington often to see her. By autumn he and Marion were almost certainly lovers.

Marion Bloom is not only Mencken's first great—documented—love but is also an interesting character in her own right. Indeed, both the irony and the poignancy of the case of this ambitious, independent woman lie in the fact that whatever small fame she might claim is entirely of a reflected nature, acquired not because she wrote stories deemed memorable but because she wrote hundreds of letters to H. L. Mencken, who wrote her hundreds in return. Mencken, as was his wont, destroyed her letters to him, but Marion did not destroy his, despite Mencken's customary request that his

126

loves, when they became ex-loves, do so. Through these letters, which wound up, fifty years after their love affair and twenty years after Mencken's death, in the Enoch Pratt Free Library of Baltimore—and through Marion's and Mencken's letters to her sister Estelle, which found their way to the New York Public Library—we know far more about their relationship and about Marion herself than Mencken, who orchestrated the interpretation of his life for posterity, would ever have wanted us to know.

Marion Bloom is a compelling figure not so much because she is unique as because, in many respects, she is representative—another of those several figures revolving around Mencken in his twenties and thirties who could have come from the pages of his friend Dreiser. She was the prototypical small-town girl, emerging from hardship, poverty, and religious piety, who went to the city to pursue her own idea of the American dream. But Marion was never fully able to determine what version of that dream she wanted most—whether to succeed as a new woman, self-reliant professionally and emotionally, or whether to play a more traditional role and become the wife of a powerful man such as H. L. Mencken. She could not easily, in her time, have both, and she ended up having neither. But for at least fifteen years—and, if we judge by her later letters, probably always— she found the emotional center of her life in Henry Mencken.

Just what sort of life Marion Bloom lived before she met Mencken is suggested in a twenty-one-page autobiographical sketch Estelle Bloom once wrote. The suicide of their father, a pious country schoolteacher who had begun a dairy, left the seven-year-old Marion, her mother, and her five brothers and sisters in desperate financial shape. From that point on the Blooms led a hard, drab life, the older children working in the dairy and in a cannery, none of the children seeing much of the world beyond the small town of New Windsor and Carroll County, Maryland. When Estelle left home for Baltimore in her late teens, she lived in a series of cheap boardinghouses. When Marion left several years later, the two lived together in Washington and hoped for something better.

It was the same story that could be told of thousands of other working girls in the early years of the century, and Marion Bloom, attractive though hardly beautiful, must have thought in early 1914 that she suddenly had within her grasp a dream beyond imagining: the well-fixed and already famous Henry Mencken, charming, courtly, and fascinating, was smitten by her. She became Mencken's sole serious romantic interest by the end of 1914, and they frequently saw each other in Washington and New York—although, as they became more intimate, less so in Baltimore. Mencken filled his letters to Marion with the same combination of mock formality, chivalry, and good humor he was later to employ with other women he cared for deeply. He expressed his affection, but he always held something back. "I kiss your hand with sentiments of the highest esteem," he would say, or "O lovely Mary Ann . . . I . . . regard you . . . with sentiments of the highest veneration. Ah, that we two were Maying." Or "Need I say that your aspect yesterday was extremely pleasing to the eye."

He kept Marion posted as to his health, he advised her on living arrangements and clothing, he kept her informed on the progress of *The Smart Set*, and he sent her gifts. Assuming a dual role he was to play several other times in his life, combining courtship with literary encouragement, he employed her as a contributor of epigrams to *The Smart Set* and assured her that she was capable of much greater literary achievement: "You are 80 times as clever as most of the literary wenches who are pictured in the public prints, with long crepes hanging from their nose-glasses, and a melancholy, nobody-will-betray-me air about them."

As always, Mencken strove to please, but all the while he kept a certain distance, at least on paper. Some of his letters suggest that Marion was frustrated both with their relationship and with her professional progress. "But if you'll be home Monday, I'd like to drop in and talk it over," Mencken wrote on one such occasion. "I dragged you out of such a mood once before." By 1915, as their liaison moved into its second year, he was occasionally willing to commit to paper his thoughts about Marion's continued fears and doubts. But still he employed the familiar distancing device of humor as well as a certain platitudinizing, playing Polonius, as he once acknowledged, to her Werther. "Away with your croakings about the futility of life," he wrote in the summer of 1915. "That it is meaningless I grant you, but surely not futile. So long as there is the joy of a job well-done—whether an epic, a fried egg or a murder—there will be plenty of excuses for remaining alive." Other weighty matters he preferred to discuss face to face rather than in correspondence: "Your long letter deserves an answer in detail, and by voice. We shall review it at our next meeting. . . . Meanwhile, I certify in writing that you were super-charming yesterday. Such fair and genial wenches as thou are rare in this imperfect world. In fact, I can think of no other . . ."

What disturbed Marion, among other things, was precisely that—Mencken's tone of mock formality, his refusal to let down his guard. She was grateful for his attention. On one letter she later jotted, "Henry was writing me almost daily for nearly the year of 1915," and that was not much of an exaggeration. She was also grateful for Mencken's genuine regard for her work and her determination to succeed professionally. Most important, as she later wrote her sister, she relished in him a "tenderness which he as a lover could not conceal when he cared for me." But they disagreed on many matters, among them the degree of control Mencken sometimes tried to exert over her life, although he was usually whimsically philosophical rather than direct in his advice. When, in June 1915, Marion decided to move from Washington to New York, he mused:

> Well, have your own way, old top! Far be it from me to say what is wise for you and what is not wise. If you find New York an impossible place you can always come back to Washington. . . .
>
> I yield so easily, not because I am not intensely interested, but because I long since came to the conclusion that it is wholly impossible for one human being to understand another's point of view. Each of us is eternally isolated.

As it turned out, Mencken came to prefer Marion's being in New York, both because he was often there for his own work and because he and Marion felt a greater freedom there than they felt in Washington and certainly in Baltimore. Even there, however, Mencken was often a creature of propriety. So great was his desire to keep up appearances that when he slept with Marion at the apartment she and Estelle shared at 274 West Nineteenth Street, he always wanted Estelle to remain overnight as escort. If such an arrangement amused Marion and Estelle, it absolutely astounded the libertine who would shortly become Estelle's lover: Theodore Dreiser. Mencken was sensitive to the accusations of excessive conventionality brought by both Dreiser and Marion. He was not, he insisted, what both, at various times, called him: a "moralist." Such would put him in league with his bitterest enemies, the bluenoses. It was the worst epithet he could imagine.

As he and Marion moved into their second year, Mencken continued to take refuge in humor and flattery, employing in his letters the same kind of consciously inflated rhetoric he used in his newspaper columns. "You were most amicable and charming yesterday," he wrote in April 1915. "Spring, a decent meal, near-beer and a pretty girl—what more had Caesar, Caligula, King Edward. . . . I salute you in the Austro-Hungarian manner with a kiss upon the velvet hand." "You grow more pleasing as a spectacle as the years chase one another down the dim corridors of illimitable time," he wrote three months later. "At 34 or 35 you will be a charmer, indeed." He played equally light with a matter that was to become sensitive indeed: "I note the shameless exposure of your plot to kidnap and marry me." Mencken adopted a persona in his correspondence with women just as surely as in his printed work, and that persona with Marion was the gracious, accommodating gentleman—and, as time went on, the well-born German gallant of refined sensibilities: "Ach, Frühling, wie bis Du so schön!"

By the summer of 1916, after a relative lull, the love affair between Mencken and Marion had grown more intense. They spent a great deal of time together in New York, and on one occasion Marion wrote her sister, "Henry has been here since Thurs and I have never been happier. I know certainly that he cares a great deal about me, even if it never goes any further. . . . He can be the tenderest person I ever saw." Like Mencken, Marion preferred remaining in New York, she told Estelle, "because we are fixed so pleasantly." By this time she had also come to realize that Mencken, rather curiously, connected his love for her with a certain idea of her as a serious writer. He constantly urged her to keep at her work. "Otherwise he must wash his hands of me," Marion wrote Estelle. "It seems very little to ask to make complete the harmony between us, and God knows I want to do it, because I love him so much."

It was obvious, then, that Mencken had certain requirements that Marion had to meet. He frequently advised her to dress conventionally and act conventionally, and he put certain checks on her spontaneity. By the fall of 1916 these differences and others were causing the two to quarrel a great deal. Although (lacking Marion's letters) we cannot grasp completely the issues at stake, we can tell a great deal both from Mencken's letters *to* Marion and from one letter in particular that Marion wrote and believed important enough to copy. She wrote on November 1, in response to a characteristically flippant letter from Mencken, written four days earlier, in which he had remarked, "I am so sorry that I managed to offend you again. Let me know how many days I am to serve in jail . . ." We don't know precisely what Mencken had said when they were together to offend her, but in Marion's letter—which she began by responding angrily to remarks he had made about a close female friend of hers—we can tell a great deal about the dynamics of their relationship. "Your approval of my 'getting what I deserved' . . . is so charmingly German!" Marion wrote. "I had forgotten, almost, your genius for hurting me. . . . If you accidentally drove your motor into the river, I can't imagine my gleeful delight that you got what you deserved!"

In the same letter Marion turned to another quality of Mencken's she always found objectionable: "You infuriate me by hiding a tenderness behind your cruelty. Why, then, be either? Why be so ungracious and irritated because you find that you can care for someone beside [*sic*] yourself?" Marion insisted that she had "tried so hard to be what you want me to be and the result is you hurt me." She had looked to Mencken "for light and sympathy, because you see so clearly and are so wise." But "as it is, I was a fool."

Such a letter, of course, presents only Marion's side. And such words hardly meant the end for Mencken and Marion, nor even an interruption of affection, since Marion still planned to see Mencken that weekend—unless "you want to be childish and get mad"—and in fact she concluded the letter, "I love you very much, in spite of yourself." By the next month, if not sooner, they were as close as before, Mencken sending Marion gifts—a watch as well as jades in a Chinese setting—and making plans to see her, saluting her on producing "two very creditable short stories," and reminding her that "life is too short for rowing."

But the problems Marion had identified—and others—would continue to plague them the remainder of their time together. Mencken wanted Marion to become the image he had of what she could be, and that image included Marion as woman of sophistication and writer of merit. He encouraged her toward those ends, in fact more than encouraged. An especially fine piece of her work—he wrote a mutual friend—"only goes to show what the unspeakable Bloom could do if she'd once rid herself of her follies and settle down to work." "Nothing could prove more plainly," he wrote Marion herself after she had sent him stories he thought particularly fine, "how easy it would be for you to make a success." She tried, but she could not always live up to his expectations. She was "built of the real, simple and genuine," she wrote of herself, and Mencken, though also possessing a "real and genuine streak," buried that streak beneath a "smart aleck" pose. That difference—and the greater problem of constructing a self of which Mencken would unreservedly approve—would continue to preoccupy Marion. Over the next five years things would become both better and worse.

---

If Marion Bloom made inroads to Mencken's heart between 1914 and 1916, the war in Europe not only engaged his mind but, from the time the fighting began, was a highly visceral matter as well. It was in his remarks on the war, not in his letters to Marion, that his passion was evident. "God's benison upon the Kaiser," Mencken had written Dreiser the month the war broke out. "He will lick 'em all." Thus, love and war coexisted quite well for Mencken in these years. Both meant living dramatically, testing oneself—a creed to which he had subscribed, at least in theory, since he had encountered Kipling long before.

In matters tied less to temperament and more to reasoned position, Mencken had undergone a remarkable transformation in the two or three years before the war began in 1914. Despite his immersion in German *kultur* through Nietzsche and then Percival Pollard, and despite his occasional praise of the German people in the Baltimore *Evening Sun,* he had in many of his public expressions in 1910 and 1911 still been a critic of Germany and an admirer of the English. In several editorials for the *Evening Sun* he had seen Germany as the greatest threat to the peace of Europe. In others he had been critical of Germany's treatment of its working class, insisting that the workingman fared better in England. In still other editorials he had praised the "clear-headedness and self-control" of the English as well as their steadfastness: "few powers will venture into the Sea of Strife so long as our country and England shall say to them, 'Peace. Be still.' "

If those words were hardly vintage Mencken—and if these were, after all, largely unsigned editorials rather than signed columns—they were still indisputably Mencken's and he had hardly been forced to write them. In fact, although, as we have seen, he had come in the years between 1908 and 1911 to identify himself intellectually and culturally with the new Germany, he still distrusted it politically. Even more important, he still viewed Germany nearly as an abstraction, not yet feeling any deep personal connection with the Fatherland. He was not yet aware of any living relatives in Germany, and he later said, overstating the case somewhat, that he did not in 1914 "know a single man in Germany save the British consul in Munich." Although he was predominantly of German blood, he thought of himself rather, as he later wrote, as not "actually" German at all but rather an "international mongrel," a "melting pot American," with "Scotch, Irish and even French blood."

We can picture Mencken in 1912 and 1913, then, as a man still more defined by local than by national loyalties, still identifying himself by family, neighborhood, city, and state—to all of which he bore happy allegiance—rather than by nation, whether that nation was the United States or the kaiser's Germany. He was more a Baltimorean and a Marylander than he was an American, more a Baltimorean than a German. As for the sentiments of the American people at large, he was so ill informed on the eve of World War I that in 1913 or 1914 he jotted a note, presumably intended for use in *The Smart Set*, which maintained "Americans dislike Germans, but as between G. and Eng., are for G."

The war changed all that in Mencken's mind, although at first he was forced into the German camp as much as he chose it. As his fellow Nietzschean Oscar Levy wrote him from London only two months after the war began, in England Nietzsche was being denounced as "the intellectual author of the war," and America soon came to the same opinion. Thus Mencken, as the most prominent American Nietzschean, was implicated from the beginning. It was hardly a position he rejected. He was already starting to lean that way, largely because of his talks with Pollard in 1911 and his reading of I.A.R. Wylie's *The Germans* the following year, as well as his growing admiration for the new Germany and his objections to the English propaganda machine, already cranking up in 1912 and 1913.

But, as Mencken would later write in "My Life as Author and

Editor," "it remained for the shock of World War I to carry me all the way." The war focused his thoughts, brought disparate elements together into a clear position:

> Even in its preliminary rumblings I saw the beginnings of an inevitable struggle to the death between the German *Weltanschauung* and the Anglo-Saxon *Weltanschauung*, and it was quickly apparent which side I was to take myself. I, too, like the leaders of Germany, had grave doubts about democracy. . . . It suddenly dawned on me, somewhat to my surprise, that the whole body of doctrine that I had been preaching was fundamentally anti–Anglo Saxon and that if I had any spiritual home at all it must be in the land of my ancestors. When World War I actually started I began forthwith to whoop for the Kaiser, and I kept up that whooping so long as there was any free speech left . . .

Mencken omitted one motive for the enthusiasm with which he greeted the war and the relish with which he took sides. That is, the war gave him an intellectually defensible reason to do what, temperamentally, he was already inclined to do—detach himself even further from prevailing American values (which were largely Anglo-Saxon values, after all) and, culturally speaking, go to war with the majority of the American people. Detachment was his natural position intellectually, he had concluded—a superior detachment from the herd—and now he was justified. "I am for the hellish Deutsche until hell freezes over," he wrote Dreiser in November 1914. To which Dreiser, in full sympathy, replied that it would benefit the world if "the despicable British aristocracy—the snobbery of English intellectuality were smashed and a German Vice-Roy sat in London." "My one hope is to see [the Germans] in London," Mencken agreed. "English pecksniffery must be crushed."

Mencken continued to indulge himself in his private war lust. "On to London," he wrote Dreiser. "May all Englishmen roast forever in hell!" But Dreiser, after all, was a sympathetic ear, and Mencken took even more delight in pronouncing the same sentiments in "The Free Lance" for the benefit of the citizens of Anglophile Baltimore, including the descendants of his admired old Virginians, the most English of Baltimoreans. If in his editorials of 1910 and 1911 he had appeared largely pro-British, in "The Free Lance" of 1913 he had become decidedly pro-German. In March he had praised the "new Germany" of "enormous practicality . . . sharp common sense . . . straightforwardness and ruthlessness" (as compared to the "muddle-headed and pedantic" old Germany), and in other columns we see that he had come to take Germany's side for reasons beyond politics. For when he compared the Germany he had seen in his travels in 1912 with the Baltimore he encountered upon his return, he came down on the side of a Germany that, he maintained, let its citizens *enjoy* life. "Munich has never seen a vice crusader; and has never had a raid on the Hofbrauhaus. . . . In all Munich there is not a single uplifter, social server or other such moral bichloride tablet."

What Mencken had in mind, then, more than a year before the war began and nearly four years before the United States would enter it, was his own version of a *kulturkampf*. He had embraced German culture absolutely and rejected "moralistic" American culture. He had continued to pursue this theme in "The Free Lance" in late 1913 and the first half of 1914, framing his own private war just before the larger war to come. It was the Baltimore Anglo-Americans, pious and prudish, versus the Baltimore Germans, "unanimously opposed to blue-nosed snoutery in all its forms."

Once the fighting began in the summer of 1914, Mencken was ready to plunge in. In August "The Free Lance" was devoted almost entirely to a discussion of the war. Mencken's initial response was regret that the United States was not involved. "More than any other people, we need the burden of resolute and manly effort," he wrote, echoing Nietzsche or Roosevelt, or both. "A foreign war—and, in particular, a foreign war in which we got the worst of it—would purge the national blood of the impurities which now pollute it." Mencken continued, speaking of the "craving" for conflict, "this eternal will to power," in all people:

> War is a good thing because it is honest, because it admits the central fact of human nature. . . . A nation too long at peace becomes a sort of gigantic old maid. . . . A war would do us good. It would make us healthier in body, cleaner in mind. . . . At this moment the peoples of Europe are preparing to fight out the great fight that must inevitably select and determine . . . the fittest to survive . . . [the] re-enactment of the law of natural selection.

135

Thus spoke the Nietzschean, by turns the Social Darwinist, demonstrating reasons for war madness other than patriotism or love of virtue. A "manly effort" lest the nation become an "old maid": again, the fear of feminization motivated Mencken. A fifty-year peace, broken only briefly in the 1890s, had been detrimental to America, he argued, because the luxury of peace had given rise to excessive moralism, sentimentality, and hypocrisy—a reformist and uplifting mentality accompanied by a people's cowardice in the face of a government that enforced petty laws and put checks on natural appetites.

Soon, in "The Free Lance," Mencken moved away from a general consideration of war to a discussion of the war at hand. He was enlivened as he pored over the war news, nearly gleeful as he contemplated affairs beyond the Atlantic. As always, it was as if a great spectacle had been staged for his own entertainment and amusement, and he was an unabashed cheerleader for Germany. Shouting "Deutschland, Deutschland, gegen alles," he ridiculed the French and the Belgians cowering before the Germans. At other times he was more solemn, defending the Germans as a people "whose one genuine desire [was] for peace" but who were "doomed to do battle for [their] very life." Soon the *Evening Sun* was receiving stacks of letters protesting Mencken's unrestrained German loyalties. This response, in addition to the general anti-German feeling prevailing in Baltimore and the pro-British stand of the Sunpapers themselves, made the experience all the better. As long as the pilsner held out in Baltimore, Mencken was happy. There was nothing he adjusted to more cheerfully than a siege mentality.

He continued to fire from his entrenched position during the remaining months of 1914. In a number of columns he attempted to state the German case. In another—in response to a reader's letter—he insisted that he himself was "not a German and . . . not bound to Germany by sentimental ties" or personal associations. Rather, he had been born in Baltimore of Baltimore-born parents, read German "very imperfectly," and—he maintained erroneously—did not write or speak German at all. But on other days, in "The Free Lance," he could hardly restrain himself:

What! Neutral? Not on your life! I am no more neutral in this war than the Hon. Winston Churchill or Gen. Joseph Joffre. Convinced, after long and prayerful consideration, that the Germans are wholly right, and that they deserve to win, and that they *will* win, I go, as the saying is, the whole hog. That is to say, I swallow not only the Germans themselves, but also and more especially the Kaiser, and not only the Kaiser, but also the whole war machine. [To be called neutral would be] the last, the awfullest, the one wholly unbearable insult!

For once in his life, Mencken was dropping his pose as scoffer and cynic and adopting the role of enthusiast. It was as if, after years of reading and absorbing Kipling and then Nietzsche, at last he had *his* opportunity to live boldly and recklessly, to lead the manly life and fight a war, if only at a typewriter. He insisted at first that, however pro-German, he was not by nature anti-English, that in fact the England of old had been a proud and distinguished realm, in great contrast to the contemporary England "of puerile moralizing and silly pettifogging . . . mobocracy." A victory of present-day England over a Germany it feared and envied "would be a victory for all the ideas and ideals that I most ardently detest." Against that England "I wage a battle with all the strength that I can muster" and to that England "I pledge my unceasing enmity."

Mencken was more romantic than he knew, venerating the "England of old" as he had earlier celebrated the Baltimore of old and the older American South. But among the new nations, he embraced only Germany. As he wrote, he continued to view the war in Europe as a sort of Nietzschean drama. If others had cast it in that light, he also would, although he knew well that Nietzsche had been anything but a German patriot. In the dozens of "Free Lance" columns devoted to the war he mentioned hardly at all the death and suffering the conflict was bringing, except once to plead for funds for wounded, widowed, and orphaned Germans. He preferred rather to view the war in a larger context—and to depict it in a manner that would be certain to further antagonize his readers. Autocracy and democracy were doing battle, he announced, and as for himself, "Down with mob rule! . . . Down with democracy!" As for the outcome of the war, Mencken at times suggested that it came down not so much to a matter of right—since each side could make its case—but of might. In that most Bismarckian of phrases, "This is an affair of blood and iron."

Just how long Mencken would be allowed to continue his polemic was uncertain. The letters continued to pour in, many of them anonymous and, Mencken later said, "not a few of them threatening me with violence." In the columns for 1915 he was somewhat less gleeful than before, but he was no less defiant. In May he defended the German sinking of the *Lusitania,* in which more than a thousand passengers, including 128 Americans, had been killed, on the grounds that the ship was transporting munitions and would have escaped if the Germans had hailed it before firing. On the brink of what seemed certain to be American entry into the war, he attempted to reason with his readers: if the United States were in Germany's position, with hostile neighbors on all sides, it too would respond aggressively. Most of all, he sensed a "Germanophobia . . . sweeping America," and when he saw an imminent American declaration of war he declared in June 1915, "There are bitter days ahead for all men of German blood in the United States . . ." Four months later, when America had not entered the fray after all, he announced that the war was "entering upon its last stage." England and France would soon cease fighting and ask for peace.

In fact, as he wrote in October 1915, it was not the war but "The Free Lance" that was entering its last stage. Two weeks after his prediction of German victory the column was suspended. There was no announcement of the suspension, and Mencken later contended that time constraints rather than the *Sun*'s opposition caused him to give it up. For the present he may have been partly right. He continued to write occasional signed pieces on the war over the next couple of months for the *Evening Sun,* and in these pieces his fervor was hardly diminished. Several days before "The Free Lance" had ceased he had written Dreiser, "There can never be any compromise in future between men of German blood and the common run of 'good,' 'right-thinking' Americans. We must stand against them forever, and do what damage we can do to them, and to their tin-pot democracy." And in the *Evening Sun* he ridiculed the pretense of official American "neutrality," and again framed the struggle, rather grandly, in Nietzschean terms. The morality of England and the United States—"sentimentality and hypocrisy"—was that "anaemic offspring of the slave morality of the post-exodus Jews. The German's ideal morality . . . is a sturdy reassertion of the master morality of the Periclean Greeks." "It is right for the German people to aspire to a place in the sun," he concluded, "it is right for them to seize it if it is denied them by envious moralists across the channel. . . . Germany is strong, and fearless, and ruthless, and resolute. *Ergo*, Germany must, shall and will prevail."

These words, and similar ones in a column the following week, were Mencken's valedictory as war commentator to *Evening Sun* readers. He continued to write on a variety of subjects for nearly another year, but virtually none of these pieces dealt with the war. In less direct ways he reiterated his position—by attacking English culture and "Anglo-Saxons," by praising the German-American Dreiser, and by proclaiming himself "a foreigner psychically." But he resisted remarking on the war itself. As he explained in May 1916 to readers who wondered why he had stopped, "Four months ago, for good and sufficient reasons, I resolved to write no more . . ." His reasons would "be set forth at length at the proper time, and in plain English, though probably not here."

Whatever Mencken later suggested, one of the reasons was indeed the *Evening Sun*'s discomfort at his boldness. For a time at least, he had other outlets for his polemical pieces. His old friend and admirer Ellery Sedgwick was now editor of the *Atlantic Monthly*, and Sedgwick, though a committed Anglophile, nonetheless wanted Mencken to write on the war. In August 1914 he had written, acknowledging that "you are (presumably) on the wrong side of this war and . . . Münchenerbrau in your veins keeps you German," but still expressing interest in an essay connecting Nietzsche and the war. In suggesting that particular subject, Sedgwick must have known he was asking Mencken to reinforce American prejudices about Germany. But Mencken had risen to the challenge nonetheless, replying the next day that if Sedgwick indeed wanted to "stir up the animals" he would be happy to oblige. He set to work on an essay on Nietzsche, the new Germany, and "the cult of efficiency." Within a week he had completed a piece that Sedgwick called "as extravagantly immoral as I had hoped."

"The Mailed Fist and Its Prophet," which appeared in the *Atlantic Monthly* in November 1914, set forth Mencken's position to a much larger audience than any he could hope to reach in Baltimore. He also did greater justice to Nietzsche than he had in his *Evening Sun* pieces, acknowledging that the early Nietzsche had been more critical of Germans—particularly religious, patriotic, and sentimental Germans—than of anyone else. But that, Mencken contended, returning to one of his favorite themes, had been the old Germany, and when Germany began to change in the 1880s and 1890s—and when Nietzsche published *Thus Spake Zarathustra* in 1892—the philosopher became its prophet. The new Germany was "contemptuous of weakness" as well as piety, mysticism, and sentimentality, and so was the author of the words "Be hard!" Germany's effort in the war, Mencken declared, was the "supreme manifestation of the new Germany . . . Germany becomes Nietzsche; Nietzsche becomes Germany." And Mencken becomes Germany, he might have added, as he was carried along by his own argument in his final lines: "Do we see again those grave blond warriors of whom Tacitus tells us—who were good to their women, and would not lie, and were terrible in battle? Is the Teuton afoot for new conquests . . . ?" For once Mencken's characteristic overwriting was not intended altogether in fun. He meant it, and in the most important single piece he wrote on Germany during the war, he left no question about his own position.

"The Mailed Fist" met an unfriendly reception in most quarters, but that had been expected. Moreover, Mencken was eager to write another essay, he told Sedgwick, this one "an indictment of England." "It would be red-hot. The war discussion down here has been extraordinarily furious, and I have been bombarded daily." Although Sedgwick did not want this piece—it was apparently *too* hot—a few months later he was again urging Mencken to write an essay, apparently an even hotter piece, to be entitled "After Germany's Conquest of the United States," which would "lay the civilization of Germany over that of the United States."

As before, Mencken took to the task enthusiastically, delighted that he had found such an unlikely coconspirator among the Brahmins. Shortly after the *Atlantic Monthly* received the piece, however, came the sinking of the *Lusitania* in May 1915 and the strong possibility of an American declaration of war. Mencken and Sedgwick agreed that under the circumstances it would be unwise to use the article, Sedgwick because "I have no desire to foment treason." Many months later he returned the piece to Mencken.

Mencken and Sedgwick continued to discuss possible essays for the *Atlantic Monthly*, Sedgwick once requesting "an onslaught upon democracy." Mencken declined because he would have to bring the *verboten* subject of the war into the piece. In any case, he had resolved by the end of 1915 to study war no more, at least in a public forum. For the time being that was no great sacrifice because he had a great deal more to keep him busy. What occupied him most of all was *The Smart Set*, which he and Nathan had agreed at the outset would carry no discussion of the war. They had held to that resolve.

At the beginning Mencken had not believed *The Smart Set* would require a great deal of time. As he had written Sedgwick in September 1914, his primary responsibility on the magazine would be to use his connections to bring in good writers and then to choose among manuscripts from those writers and others. Nathan was to handle the copyreading, makeup, and other in-office editorial work.

For the first couple of months, however, Mencken found it a more demanding job than he had anticipated. He and Nathan discovered that former editors Norman Boyer and Mark Lee Luther had on hand a number of mediocre manuscripts as well as a large and mediocre staff. They set about disposing of both. Their takeover was made no easier when the dismissed editor, Boyer, committed suicide in September. It was to Boyer that Mencken owed his first job on *The Smart Set* (although he had not been aware of that fact at the time), and he was upset, but hardly guilt-filled. "If anybody was responsible for Boyer's loss of his post," Mencken wrote later, "it was not us, but [John Adams] Thayer." "In any case, [Boyer] was a foolish fellow," he added, with little compassion. "His suicide . . . was quickly forgotten."

Financially, at first, matters were just as uncertain as they were editorially. Circulation had declined greatly since Willard Huntington Wright's editorship, and the magazine was in debt when Mencken and Nathan took over. That condition was soon remedied under the shrewd financial management of Eugene R. Crowe and Eltinge F. Warner. Crowe moved the *Smart Set* offices from the high-budget Knox Building on Fifth Avenue to less expensive quarters, where they remained until spring 1915, when the magazine moved to somewhat better offices on Fourth Avenue. Mencken was nearly as shrewd in his negotiations as Crowe. Although he and Nathan had begun working for no salary, each was given a one-sixth financial interest in the magazine as a result of Mencken's hard bargaining. Mencken continued to draw his $100 monthly for book review essays, and in March 1915, after some more negotiations with Crowe, the editors were given an extra $50 a week as salary after all.

Mencken always insisted that he did not approve of the name "The Smart Set"—which, for reasons beyond his control, could not be changed. But in fact, according to a three-page "Note to Authors" he and Nathan drew up, they hoped to "interest and amuse the more civilized and sophisticated sort of reader" the magazine's name would suggest—"the man or woman who has lived in large cities, and read good books, and seen good plays, and heard good music." Putting their personal stamp on the magazine, the editors added, "and is tired of politicians, reformers and the newspapers." Their magazine would have nothing to do with "the uplift" and would not "pretend that it is made sad by the sorrows of the world." *The Smart Set*, rather, was for the "well-fed," for people "more interested in their own class than they are in the struggles and aspirations" of laborers and do-gooders. It was in this appeal to smug class superiority—though hardly in the appeal to elegance or affectation—that Mencken felt more at home with *The Smart Set* than he admitted.

He and Nathan soon settled into a routine, Mencken reading manuscripts in Baltimore and going to New York at least once a month for five or six days. A negative reading by either editor would kill a manuscript, and Mencken usually read submissions first. *The Smart Set* could not afford to pay much—in most cases, only a penny a word for prose and fifty cents a line for poetry—but the editors prided themselves on paying promptly. Since at first they did not have much publishable material to work with and were particularly pressed to put together the first issue for November 1914, they fell into the habit of writing material for the magazine themselves, under pseudonyms (often "Owen Hatteras"). Mencken filled nearly forty of the 156 pages of their first number, in that issue and in those to follow utilizing the unsold stories and poems he had produced, largely under Kipling's influence, in his early twenties, as well as more recent fiction he had written. More important were his continued duties as literary reviewer. He was by this point not so much literary critic as literary force, not merely remarking on but helping to shape the nation's letters.

The free rein he was given at *The Smart Set* also gave Mencken an opportunity to try out in longer essays for a national audience the voice he had begun to develop in his *Evening Sun* columns. By 1913 he was producing magazine essays such as "Good Old Baltimore" that let him, in Nietzsche's phrase, "dance with arms and legs":

> The old town will not give you the time of your life; it is not a brazen hussy among cities, blinding you with its xanthous curls, kicking up its legs, inviting you to exquisite deviltries. Not at all. It is, if the truth must come out, a Perfect Lady. But for all its resultant narrowness, its niceness, its air of merely playing at being a city, it has, at bottom, the one quality which, in cities as in women, shames and survives all the rest. And that is the impalpable, indefinable, irresistible quality of charm.

More significantly, in 1913 and 1914 he undertook a series of *Smart Set* essays on "The American" in which he entertained ideas to which he would return often in the next decade. For the first time addressing a national audience, he fulminated at length about his countryman:

> that sub-brachycephalous and sentimental fellow, with his brummagem Puritanism, his childish braggadocio, . . . his elemental humor, his great dislike of arts and artists, his fondness for the grotesque and melodramatic, his pious faith in quacks and panaceas, his curious ignorance of foreigners, his bad sportsmanship, . . . his weakness for tin pot display and strutting, his jealous distrust of all genuine distinction, his abounding optimism, his agile pursuit of the dollar.

As editor of *The Smart Set,* which he and Nathan now labeled "The Aristocrat Among Magazines," Mencken was also able to solicit stories and poems from writers he had earlier lauded, as well as from undiscovered writers who were suggested to him. He corresponded with and published fiction by James Branch Cabell, Sherwood Anderson, Sinclair Lewis, Willa Cather, Waldo Frank, and Ben Hecht as well as Dreiser, and, somewhat later, twenty-three-year-old F. Scott Fitzgerald—whose first published story, "Babes in the Wood," was to appear in *The Smart Set* for September 1919. Among poets, Mencken published Ezra Pound, Edgar Lee Masters, Sara Teasdale, Stephen Vincent Benét, Elinor Wylie, Louis Untermeyer, and John Hall Wheelock. He became acquainted with the plays of twenty-nine-year-old Eugene O'Neill when Untermeyer dropped "Bound East for Cardiff" and other work by the *Smart Set* offices for him to consider—although Nathan, in fact, was more responsible than Mencken for O'Neill's three appearances in *The Smart Set* in 1917 and 1918. Mencken also published such literary and cultural critics as Ludwig Lewisohn, Joseph Wood Krutch, Lewis Mumford, and his own mentor James Gibbons Huneker.

It would not be accurate to call most of these writers Mencken's "discoveries"; some had made reputations, if minor ones, by the time he approached them or they him. And his relations were better with certain writers than with others. Mencken had heard of Sherwood Anderson through Dreiser and had written to him in 1915 asking to see some of his stories. Of the two stories Anderson sent, Mencken and Nathan accepted one, "The Story Writers," for the January 1916 number. The one they rejected, later to be included as "Queer" in *Winesburg, Ohio,* was perhaps the better one, but Mencken returned the story because he felt it was, in fact, simply a sketch. Anderson was quite clearly courting the favor of the influential editor. In those days, he later wrote, Mencken was "our great hero . . . in Chicago we would have delivered the town over to him." When *Winesburg* appeared in 1919, Mencken praised the volume, both in *The Smart Set* and in letters to friends. Yet, he wrote later, he really "did not like" Anderson, and Anderson for his part came to feel that Mencken had embraced his work only after other critics hailed *Winesburg* and that he later claimed more of a role in Anderson's success than was merited.

Mencken's correspondence with Ezra Pound, who had taken up residence in England, proved to be more beneficial for both parties. Pound sent Mencken a number of poems from England in 1915, although Mencken did not publish as many as he would have liked because Nathan did not care for Pound's work. Pound was an "extremely imprudent fellow," Mencken wrote Edgar Lee Masters, and he and Pound disagreed on what constituted good literature. But Mencken liked Pound's poetry, which he had reviewed favorably in 1911 and 1913 and, of course, had recommended to Wright. "It was plain from the start," he later wrote, "that we had many ideas and prejudices in common—for example, our violent dissent from the orthodox American credo and from that moral order of the world on which it was so innocently based."

Pound was even more valuable to Mencken as literary contact in England than he was as poet and fellow dissenter. From the beginning of their correspondence in 1914 he had been suggesting various writers, including "the prose writer I am really interested in . . . James Joyce." Joyce was then in his early thirties, living in Trieste, beginning to work on *Ulysses*, and publishing stories in little magazines in England. Even before Mencken became coeditor, Pound had sent him some of Joyce's published work to examine. Now he sent, in manuscript, Joyce's "The Boarding House" and "A Little Cloud," both of which Mencken accepted and used in May 1915. The stories (both of which were included in *Dubliners*, which had just appeared in England) were Joyce's first published work in an American magazine. Mencken wrote Joyce that he would have liked to take more stories, but the upcoming publication of *Dubliners* in America prevented him from doing so.

Joyce was grateful for Mencken's attention, in March 1915 writing to thank him for the introduction to an American audience. He also suggested that Mencken consider publishing in serial form parts of *A Portrait of the Artist as a Young Man*, then appearing in England in the *Egoist*. Mencken was "tempted," he later wrote, but he and Nathan had earlier decided "to print no serials, and resolved to stick to it." He and Joyce had little contact after that. When in 1917 Mencken passed through Zurich, where Joyce then lived, he considered calling on the novelist but was too busy to follow through.

In Mencken's search for writers abroad, he was aided not only by Pound but by his own growing international reputation. He corresponded with and published a number of British and Irish writers of some reputation, including novelists Hugh Walpole and Frank Harris, poet Padraic Colum, critic Arthur Symons, the Abbey Theatre playwright Lord Dunsany, and—somewhat later—Somerset Maugham and Aldous Huxley. He found in Harris, in particular, a fellow rebel, although Harris's contributions to *The Smart Set* were limited by the meager payments Mencken and Nathan could offer. An Anglo-Irishman who had spent part of his youth in America, Harris had been a friend and biographer of Oscar Wilde. When Mencken met him in New York in 1915, he found Harris a vain and rather "dubious" figure with "a touch of the sinister in his appearance" but also an amusing drinking companion, enjoyed his frequent conversations about sex, and, most of all, shared his skeptical attitude toward the English and their war aims. That, for Mencken, during the war years, was a basis for friendship, no matter how dubious one's character.

After two years on the job, he had begun to put his own mark on *The Smart Set*. The magazine had become a curious combination of iconoclasm and propriety, of established writers and young unknowns. "Whenever a volunteer showed the slightest sign of talent," Mencken later wrote, "I wrote to him encouragingly, and kept on blowing his spark so long as the faintest hope remained of fanning it into flame." In some cases that spark would never catch fire; in others only Mencken saw it flaming. With the exception of Pound and one or two others, the poets he published and praised were mostly conventional versifiers, chief among them the much-lauded but now-forgotten Robert Loveman of Georgia and Muna Lee and John McClure of Oklahoma. Some poems by T. S. Eliot (sent to him by Pound) he rejected, but he accepted almost everything from McClure, whom he once called "the best lyric poet the United States has produced in fifty years." Other poets, such as Maxwell Bodenheim, he not only rejected but criticized in print. "It may be possible," a wounded Bodenheim wrote Mencken, "that future generations will recall nothing of you save the fact that you persisted in spurting your clumsy venom at the few, original creatures of your time."

Many of the young writers whom Mencken particularly encouraged were women, a number of whom became personal acquaintances in New York as well as contributors. He was sensitive, however, to the charge that his interest in female contributors was not always entirely professional. As he wrote to Edgar Kemler in 1948, looking back on the *Smart Set* years, "My servicing of lady contributors was, of course, Nathan's invention"—although he hardly helped his case by adding, "I can recall climbing into the hay with very few of them."

In fact, Mencken had a genuine appreciation for such writers as Amanda Hall, a "young and lovely" poet whom he came to know in New York in the years before 1920, Zoë Akins, who contributed plays, poems, and stories and became a lifelong friend as well, and

Leonora Speyer, a tall blond German violinist, somewhat older than he, who was married to a wealthy pro-German Jew and whose poetry and fiction he published. He had an especially high regard for the fiction of two discoveries, Thyra Samter Winslow and Lilith Benda (or Lucia Bronder). Winslow, an ex–chorus girl sometimes called "Siren Thyra," he regarded so highly that she appeared more often in *The Smart Set* than anyone except Mencken and Nathan themselves in the years they were editors. Benda, who lived in Brooklyn with her parents, was as shy and retiring as Winslow was outgoing. The author, Mencken felt, of some of the best fiction published in *The Smart Set,* she was at least as interesting to him for her "strangely elusive personality." She remained no less elusive after Mencken had lunch with her several times and was invited to her Brooklyn home for dinner. Tubercular—and an eventual suicide— she is one of numerous writers who looked very promising to Mencken for a time but was soon forgotten.

After he landed on his feet at *The Smart Set,* Mencken found the work anything but onerous. In later letters to friends he described his first two or three years as editor as one of the happiest periods of his life. Financially he was doing well, not so much because of *The Smart Set* as because of the success of the *Parisienne* and *Saucy Stories,* pulp magazines featuring hack writers that he and Nathan had begun with Crowe's support. He quickly sold his interest in the two magazines—for nearly $15,000—but for the year or two he ran them he enjoyed the work. He made far less money at but had nearly as much fun with *The Smart Set.* "Nathan and I never took [the magazine] seriously," he later wrote. "Our main purpose was to have a pleasant time—and we always had it." He was not overstating his case by much. The editors gaudily decorated their new offices at 331 Fourth Avenue, played practical jokes on visitors (particularly Dreiser), and took long lunches at a nearby German restaurant when they did not head for Delmonico's. They put in long nights eating, drinking, and talking, usually accompanied by women of their acquaintance. When Marion Bloom was not available—or when Mencken sought diversion—there was no shortage of company.

Two of their most interesting dinner companions in their early editorial days were Marguerite Clark, a successful early movie star, and Kay Laurell, the girlfriend of movie actor (later producer) Edgar Selwyn. Clark, small and pretty, often invited Mencken and Nathan for rides through Central Park in her automobile or for dinner in her apartment on Central Park West. Laurell, as Mencken described her in his reminiscences, was even more memorable, "a slim, not too young and far from beautiful woman" with "all the arts of the really first-rate harlot"—who was, in fact, "the most successful practitioner of that trade of her generation in New York." To Mencken and Nathan, Laurell was appealing not primarily for that reason but because she was a capital source of New York scandal: "Once she had become convinced that we had no designs on her professional stock in trade she gave us her confidence and was very amusing." Mencken insisted that he was not even interested in her sexually; her physical appearance "damped" his "natural fires" to such an extent that "more than once I have lain in a bed with her at her apartment without having the slightest impulse to use her carnally." But Laurell—as suggested by the four or five pages Mencken devoted to her in "My Life as Author and Editor"—obviously fascinated him. In telling him tales of her trade, including stories of encounters with wealthy clients such as *The Smart Set*'s principal owner, Eugene Crowe, she "contributed not a little to my education."

Mencken and Nathan spent many other evenings in 1915 and 1916 in the company of John Williams and Tom Smith, two literary and theater friends, and occasionally with Dreiser—of whom Nathan was not particularly fond. Mencken's own friendship with Dreiser had undergone hard times since their halcyon days of 1910–1913. The first signs of disharmony appear in their correspondence of October 1914, at first for purely professional reasons, shortly afterward for personal reasons as well. When Dreiser sent three plays to *The Smart Set* that Mencken believed vastly inferior to his past fiction, he said he would rather have part of Dreiser's new novel, *The "Genius."* After it was clear that Dreiser's tender feelings had been hurt, Mencken avoided the truth and insisted that he himself thought the plays were "excellent" but that *The Smart Set* still had to please "the Thayer audience," who would prefer the fiction. Dreiser was conciliatory in his response, promising some episodes from *The "Genius."* But the friendship between the two had been damaged for the first time.

The following two years Mencken and Dreiser remained in close contact, with alternating periods of harmony and disharmony. They quarreled over what Dreiser felt to be, and in fact was, Mencken's disapproval of the direction his friend's career was taking. In 1915 and 1916 Mencken turned down several poems and plays Dreiser sent and also, as it turned out, did not care for The "Genius," Dreiser's semi-autobiographical story of a persecuted young artist. When Dreiser sent him the manuscript of the novel in late 1914, he had cautiously expressed disapproval, and in early January 1915 the two met in Dreiser's Greenwich Village apartment to discuss the novel. The result was an argument so heated that it caused a rift in their friendship the first months of 1915. When Mencken reviewed The "Genius" in The Smart Set in December 1915, for the first time he was severely critical of Dreiser in print. Under the title "A Literary Behemoth" he charged that the novel amounted to "more than 300,000 long and short words, most of them commonplace, many of them improperly used." Although the story was compelling in some respects, he wrote, Dreiser had nonetheless produced a novel "as devoid of aesthetic quality as an article in the Nation."

Despite such a response to Dreiser's latest work, Mencken tried with some success to maintain their friendship. He and Dreiser could agree on the war, and Mencken still felt a vast sympathy for his friend. The month after he had first expressed dissatisfaction with the work of the "new Dreiser," he had written Sedgwick of the Atlantic Monthly that "the poor fellow is now down in the dumps, and talks of giving it up. I rather think a careful article on him would attract some attention." Indeed, the very month after his harsh review of The "Genius" appeared in The Smart Set, Mencken observed to Dreiser that several poems the novelist had sent him were "truly excellent." And the following year he read in manuscript Dreiser's travel narrative A Hoosier Holiday, sang its praises privately to the author, and reviewed it favorably in the October 1916 Smart Set.

But these kind words could not disguise the fact that things were no longer as they had been. The criticism was hardly one-sided. For his part, Dreiser disapproved of the way The Smart Set was being run. "Under you and Nathan," he wrote Mencken in April 1915, "the thing seems to have tamed down to a light, non-disturbing period of persiflage and badinage. . . . It is as innocent as the Ladies Home Journal." Mencken responded, more kindly than he might have, that the magazine represented "a compromise between what we'd like to do and what the difficulties that we face allow us to do." He added that in any case the magazine was *intended* to be light, not revolutionary.

Mencken believed that Dreiser's criticism of *The Smart Set* resulted from his own criticism of Dreiser's private life, and no doubt that did play some part in their dispute. For with Dreiser and Mencken the professional could never be separated from the personal, and Mencken disapproved of the life Dreiser was leading in Greenwich Village after he left Sara. Mencken had always been skeptical of writers who congregated in the Village, finding fault with both their fashionable radicalism and their unconventional lives, and he had felt especially betrayed when Dreiser moved to Tenth Street with a twenty-two-year-old actress, Kirah Markham, in mid-1913.

For a time Dreiser had kept his liaison a secret from his friend, and even after Mencken found out Dreiser at first preferred not to talk about Kirah, although Mencken later came to know her well. No doubt Mencken had preferred, as he later wrote, the "thoroughly bourgeois life"—aside from extramarital affairs—Dreiser had led uptown, and he disapproved in every particular of the "life of art" the novelist was now living.

He found fault with Dreiser's apartment, his furniture, even the way Kirah preferred candles to bright lights at meals. He detected something "third-rate" about Kirah herself and felt she "came very near making Dreiser third-rate too." Mencken poked fun at Dreiser's "own grotesque transmogrification—a German peasant turned Bohemian," and his ridicule irritated both Dreiser and Kirah. When Mencken was invited over—he accepted partly because he liked Kirah's cooking—it was understood that none of their Bohemian friends was to come.

Dreiser blamed much of Mencken's disapproval on the narrow and rigid standard by which Mencken lived his own life and measured the lives of others. "I sometimes think that because I have moved into 10th Street," he wrote in 1915, "and am living a life not suitable to the home streets of Baltimore that you think I have gone over to the red ink family." "Pish!" replied Mencken, sensitive as always to a charge of moral virtue. "What slush is this . . . ? Do you take me for a Methodist deacon—or a male virgin?"

Mencken's rejection of Dreiser's life, then, was consistent with his rejection of the "new" Dreiser's writing. In both, the lowborn Hoosier was departing too boldly from convention, and in the latter case—by including material in *The "Genius"* and other works that would be seen as sexually provocative—he was needlessly tempting the censors.

Nonetheless, when the New York Society for the Suppression of Vice moved to ban *The "Genius"* in July 1916, Mencken jumped to Dreiser's defense. As soon as the novelist apprised him of the situation, he began to offer advice and to write hundreds of letters on Dreiser's behalf. Mencken also drew up a manifesto for other authors to sign and rounded up members of the Authors League of America to sign it. He financed most of the operation himself, later estimating that it had cost him at least three hundred dollars. Part of his fervor was stirred by the cause—Mencken abhorred censorship—and part because of Dreiser's particularly vulnerable position as a German American in a country of English sympathizers. "A man accused of being a German has no chance whatever in a New York court at this time," he wrote his friend.

Mencken had some success with his efforts, getting signatures for his petition from such mainstream figures as Sedgwick and Booth Tarkington as well as Willa Cather, Amy Lowell, James Branch Cabell (who was soon to have his own trouble with the censors), Edgar Lee Masters, Sherwood Anderson, Sinclair Lewis, and, in England, H. G. Wells and Arnold Bennett. Those literary progressives of an earlier time Hamlin Garland, Ellen Glasgow, and—as Mencken described him—that "notorious coward" William Dean Howells refused to sign.

Dreiser should have been grateful, but he was not completely. During the protest he and Mencken were often at odds, primarily because Mencken insisted on handling matters his own way and Dreiser had other ideas. At first Mencken cautioned moderation and even compromise, while Dreiser wanted to fight recklessly, saying he would go to jail if necessary. And while Mencken was appealing to the members of the American literary establishment, he feared Dreiser would bring in radicals who would alienate mainstream writers as well as the courts. "For God's sake, don't start making speeches at the Liberal Club," he warned in September 1916. "This organization consists of all the tinpot revolutionaries and sophomoric advanced thinkers in New York." The following month he chided Dreiser for adding the names of "four or five tenth-rate Greenwich geniuses" to the protest.

Dreiser resented these directions, responding that Mencken's objection to the names he had included seemed

> to me to be curiously animated by something which does not appear on the surface. . . . Recently, on several occasions you have gone out of your way to comment . . . on my supposed relationship to this band of "jitney radicals" . . . to whom you think I am wedded. . . . Have I tried to supervise your private life or comment on any of your friends or deeds? What's eating you, anyhow? . . . Your letter smacks of something I do not like & if you have any real downright grievance come across.

"I haven't the slightest right or desire to question your private doings," Mencken replied in a manner both righteous and mocking. "They are, I am informed, of a generally immoral nature, and hence abhorrent to a right-thinking man." But, he added, "I would be a false friend if I stood idly by and let you do things certain to injure you, and some of your most faithful partisans with you."

For the present, Mencken's protest on Dreiser's behalf did little good: the New York ban on *The "Genius"* was not officially lifted until 1922. But Mencken and Dreiser found a great deal more to quarrel about as well. Mencken's belief that Dreiser was a "fearful ass"—as he wrote a mutual friend—was reinforced in December 1916, when Dreiser sent him a play, *The Hand of the Potter*, which Mencken immediately read and found wanting. The story of a sexually depraved murderer, it was a work "of sexual perversion," he wrote Dreiser, "a cheap piece of pornography," he told the publisher Ben Huebsch. "Frankly," he wrote Dreiser, "the play seems to me to be hopeless." He found it unacceptable both because of its subject matter, child molestation, and its technique:

> I say the subject is forbidden on the stage, and mean it. It is all very well enough to talk of artistic freedom, but it must be plain that there must be a limit in the theatre, as in books. You and I, if we are lucky, visit the bowel-pot daily . . . you, at least, have been known to roll a working girl on the couch. But such things, however natural, however interesting, are not for the stage. The very mention of them is banned by that convention on which the whole of civilized order depends.

With such an objection, Mencken pointed to the primary deficiency he detected in his friend: Dreiser was simply *uncivilized*, refusing to abide by, perhaps even unaware of, the proprieties that civilized people observed. Mencken knew quite well the charge that Dreiser, for his part, would bring in return: "you will accuse me of a lingering prudishness. Accuse all you please; it is not so. If the thing were possible, I'd advocate absolutely unlimited freedom of speech, written and spoken." Again sensitive to a possible charge of moralism, he wrote that such an accusation would be "as intelligent as your treatment of your subject in your play." The play was simply "a very bad one," Mencken wrote, but after receiving a Christmas Day suggestion from Dreiser that they lay "aside this argument for the time being" he agreed to an armistice. "I surely hope you will keep its terms and not foully murder me when I am not looking."

One reason Mencken was happy to call off his private war with Dreiser in December 1916—and to lay aside his *Smart Set* work as well—is that his attention was being drawn, even more than before, to the larger war in Europe; just two days after he and Dreiser concluded their peace he was at long last off to Germany to cover the war.

It was an assignment he had wanted for some time and one that he had been discussing with the Sunpapers since the summer of 1916. In October he had ceased all other writing for the *Evening Sun* and had begun to make plans for the German trip. He had received official authorization not only from the Sunpapers but also from the Wheeler Newspaper Features syndicate, for which he would also be writing, then had traveled to Washington to apply for a German visa and had cleared matters with the U.S. State Department. After wrapping up all necessary *Smart Set* business and saying good-bye to Anna Mencken, on December 27—the night before his departure—he put in a "gay and somewhat boozy evening" with Marion, Estelle Bloom, the recently reconciled Dreiser, Nathan, and a woman of Nathan's acquaintance. Afterward, he bid Marion a particularly affectionate farewell.

Mencken was being sent to Europe, the Sunpapers announced, "to get the true inwardness of the German situation":

He does not go as a pro-German or as pro anything else. [At other times the *Sun* acknowledged that Mencken was indeed "pro-German."] Just what the situation is in Germany has been a great deal of a puzzle to most people in this country. . . . His intimate knowledge of the country and of its people . . . will enable him to do this probably better than any other newspaper man from this side of the water.

Mencken's own reasons for going were less noble. He went, he later remarked, "to get some excitement and new experience into a life that had begun to grow unendurably stagnant."

He sailed three days after Christmas on the Danish steamship *Oscar II*, with the intention of returning in a little more than two months. His first day out he wrote Marion an uncharacteristically endearing letter, assuring "Dear Marionne" that he was "more crushed than ever" to leave her and signing the letter, for the first time, "With love." As was often the case with Marion, Mencken's tenderest written expression came just at the moment he or she was taking off—in this case, on a "damned depressing" voyage, he wrote her—and he would not see her again for some time.

The adventures at sea, or at least the potential for adventure, began as soon as he left Hoboken. Sailing on a small, cold ship across the North Atlantic on a far northern route close to Greenland, he faced the possibility of stormy weather, British searches, and encounters with German U-boats. Mencken made the best of the slow seventeen-day trip, finding humor in the essentially humorless Danes, Norwegians, Swedes, Germans, Swiss, Russians, and Americans on board. He was especially amused by a haughty Russian general with a Hindenburg mustache who sat at Mencken's own table at meals, not uttering a word but eating prodigiously while the assembled diners (who assumed, incorrectly, that he did not understand English) speculated about him. Mencken also observed closely the rest of the "excessively mixed and belligerent" population, nationalistic and rowdy, on this particular ship of fools.

On New Year's Eve he sent his mother a telegram and in letters to Anna Mencken described what turned out to be a generally smooth crossing, a discordant New Year's Eve party, and a cold, bleak couple of days in Norway. In Christiania he found the temperature below zero and "little to see save the Ibsen monument and the Grand Cafe, where Ibsen used to sit." He wrote Anna from Copenhagen as well but did not tell her—as he told several other correspondents—of a riotous party during which he and several other Americans had been arrested and charged with deceiving a waiter. Mencken had talked his way out of the trouble. He wrote several letters to Marion as well, remarking on the "poor old tub" of a ship—a "horribly cold, damp and silent" vessel—and the "godless censor with a hard heart" who read every line of every letter or dispatch that crossed the Atlantic.

He stayed in Copenhagen between two and four days, then traveled down to the Baltic, crossed to Germany, and traveled to Berlin by train. It appeared, he wrote his mother, that he was the only American correspondent going into Germany at that time. When he arrived in Berlin, he was gratified to learn that, because the recent Bismarck centenary had reminded Germans that Bismarck's mother was a Mencken of Leipzig, his "name got [him] extra politeness." He had first considered applying to go to the Austrian front, then applied instead for the Turkish front, to which, he was told, only one correspondent had preceded him. But when the Germans offered to let him go immediately to Lithuania and the eastern front, he accepted.

Mencken spent only five days at the front, but it was a period he would describe in some detail, both in dispatches back to the *Sun* and in later letters to friends. In the trenches, only several hundred yards away from Russian troops and within reach of enemy gas, shrapnel, and shells, he was as close to military action as he ever came in his life. In autobiographical notes made in the 1940s, he would refer to "a moment in a German switch trench when it seemed to me to be all up with Henry." He was probably recalling a moment when the Russians briefly opened fire on him and the Germans accompanying him. But in fact his greatest danger seems to have come not from enemy fire but from an "appalling and incomparable" cold, which went as low as forty degrees below zero and left him with a temporary case of frostbite. At night he slept by stoves in the houses of peasants, "always expecting," he later wrote, "to be cremated before morning."

Life at the front was not all hardship. After inspecting the trenches by day, Mencken ate and drank with German officers by night. Both the food and wine, he reported, were acceptable. It is obvious from his reports in the *Sun* that he admired the Germans and their resourcefulness as much as he pitied the "stupid" Russians. He described a small Lithuanian town—which he called "Russian"—that had been captured and "civilized" by the Germans: "It will seem a pity to turn this lovely country back to the Russians, once the war is over."

Mencken returned to Berlin at the end of January "tired, rheumatic and half-frozen." He awoke the morning of February 1 to newspaper announcements of Germany's new policy of unrestricted submarine warfare, a move that was almost certain to bring the United States into the war. He remained in Berlin another ten days, during which time he kept a detailed diary remarking on a German people at war with much of Europe and on the brink of war with America. He was amazed at the calm, even "cockiness," of the Berliners. He spoke with German officers, walked the Unter den Linden at night, saw a light opera, and found Berlin, "once . . . full of gaudy night life, as quiet as Blue Boston." Other nights the Unter den Linden was more crowded, but still calm. He marveled at the stoicism of the people.

What was chiefly on Mencken's mind as he wandered around Berlin was how he might be able to leave it. Since war with the United States now seemed imminent, correspondents who had been to the front were being detained. Mencken, who was the last American correspondent to return from the front, seemed to face the longest detention of all, up to eight weeks. He and the other Americans were treated with great politeness, even after February 4, when news came that the United States had broken off diplomatic relations with Germany. Mencken, who by this time could not send anything but bare-bones dispatches out of Germany, took the opportunity to make notes for future use. He spent time with several German friends, dined with a German-American Jewish friend two or three times, and weighed the invitation of a German woman acquaintance to go to Munich for a week. "The Bavarians are far better fellows than these cold-blooded North Germans," he wrote.

He continued to be amazed by the lack of anti-American feeling among the Germans. In his diary he himself was remarkably objective as well, expressing far less opposition to British and American policy than he had back in the United States and in fact commenting several times on the "stupidity" of certain aspects of the German war effort, particularly its inept propaganda. Nor was he as buoyant and excited about war as he had been in "The Free Lance." "It depresses me to think of what is ahead," he wrote in his diary, "the misunderstandings, the lunacies, the bitter, unending hatreds." As for his German friends: "It is hard to think of them as enemies." They agreed to meet after the war "and crack a magnum of Pilsner . . ."

He was ready to flee the cold, gray city that now suffered not only from war deprivation but also from an influenza epidemic. Refusing to believe the report of the American ambassador, James W. Gerard, that all journalists were now virtually "prisoners," he petitioned German authorities to waive the travel restriction, and he was granted permission to depart by General Ludendorff, who personally heard his appeal. He left Berlin the night of February 10 on a train with Gerard, and as he traveled south through snow-clad Germany he observed the nearly deserted stations. Missing were the beer booths on the platforms, the boys with trays of sandwiches. There was, he found, little activity except "soldiers everywhere." "The war changes all things," he wrote in his diary. "It is a new Europe, and a much duller and sadder one."

Mencken crossed into Switzerland the afternoon of February 11 and was struck by how prosperous and brisk Zurich appeared compared with war-torn Germany. He was also struck by the rabid anti-German tone of the British newspapers he found—in comparison to the "dignity" of the German papers. His diary, which had been largely nonpartisan while he was in Germany, soon began to take on a distinctly anti-British, pro-German quality. But his primary concern now was getting his German pamphlets and papers and his own notes across the French border, and he finally decided to destroy some papers and to leave others in Switzerland until after the war. His strategy was successful: he was allowed into France, although four other Americans were held up at the border. After a cold day in Paris, he was off to Spain on an overnight train. When he awoke the morning of February 16 in southern France, he caught his first sight of the sun, "hearty and undimmed, for nearly two months."

He was happy to leave war-torn northern Europe, "skittish, under pressure, constantly fatigued," and as he moved into Spain the tone of his diary became lighter, more irreverent, more the *Innocents Abroad* voice of his 1914 European trip. In Madrid, where he found carnival season, the war seemed "infinitely remote"—as he wrote a friend in New York—and in La Coruña even more so. He sailed from

La Coruña on February 21, bound for Cuba on the *Alfonso XIII,* the only correspondent on board and thus the first to be able to report fully what he had seen in Germany. For most of his nine days at sea, while many of the Spanish passengers fell seasick, he worked up his material, typing on deck and in the smokeroom, producing five thousand words a day. He was invigorated by the sun, the tropical warmth, the increasingly blue seas, and his passion against the English. His diary now became a defense of Germany against British propaganda—a denial, in particular, that Germany was experiencing famine because of the British blockade. The urban masses were indeed facing food shortages, food distribution was a problem, and the Germans were facing a shortage of labor and an overloaded train system. But their plight, Mencken reported, was not nearly so dismal as the British suggested. When he read the English claims, he wrote his mother, they "made me yell with mirth."

Mencken had thought as he approached Cuba that his work was nearly complete. "The retreat from Berlin is over," he wrote in his diary the day he was to land. But in fact he was going from one war into another—a Cuban revolution in progress, of which he had heard some news as he left Spain—and the day before he landed he received a telegram from the *Sun* instructing him to file reports from Havana. He arrived, quickly wrote a 2,500-word piece on Germany for the *Sun* and the New York *World* and then turned to his next war.

For the next week he reported from Cuba the rebellion of former president José Miguel Gómez against the conservative president Mario García Menocal, at the same time as he continued to revise and dispatch his German material. In his reporting on Cuba he was aided greatly by a well-placed Danish friend, resident in Cuba, who arranged interviews with both Menocal and a spokesman for the rebels. From the beginning Mencken saw the Cuban uprising as a kind of mock war, a parody of graver events in Europe, and his reporting suggests his half-comical approach to it. By his fourth day in Cuba, José Miguel Gómez had been captured and this "very tame affair"— as he characterized it to his mother—was nearing its end. On March 12, nearly eleven weeks after he had sailed from Hoboken, Mencken set out for Florida and then took a train back to Baltimore. "The retreat ended," he noted in his last diary entry, "in a drizzling rain."

# Chapter 7

# UNDER SIEGE

M encken was exuberant when he stepped off the train in Baltimore on March 14, 1917. He had seen and experienced the European war without having undergone total immersion, and he had escaped, ahead of the rest, to tell his tale. The darkness and depression of the Berlin winter now seemed far away. "I had the time of my life in Europe," he wrote a friend. "The tale of my late wanderings would fill six books and kill the world with mirth," he wrote another. "In eight weeks I have lived 19 or 20 years. These days are truly gigantic." Or, as he had written his mother from Cuba, "The trip was one continuous show. I never enjoyed anything more in my life."

What Mencken was to find on his return to Baltimore, however, was something quite other than mirth and joy, and he seems to have been aware of what awaited him even before he sailed from Cuba. For the first time in his two-hundred-page diary he raised the plight of German Americans: "No one appears to think what a tragedy the whole business is and has been to them. . . . Democracy will have a chance to prove itself in the way they are treated." The next day, as he sailed to Florida, he glimpsed what was to follow. A man overheard speaking German was rumored to be a spy. To Mencken he seemed "a quite harmless fellow . . . he looks the Hollander far more than the German." Nonetheless, the man was detained upon landing

159

at Key West. "A curious foretaste," Mencken noted, "of what all Germans must be facing at home!"

When he arrived, war hysteria was indeed at fever pitch. "Mobs are already afoot here," he reported to Dreiser in late March or early April. "Last night they raided a pacific meeting and raised hell. It is very likely that there will be some smashing of windows and other delicate heroics when war is declared." He needed to come to New York, he reported, but "[I] don't know how long I can stay. My mother and sister are here alone, and I don't want to leave them unprotected." When, on April 6, the United States at last declared war on Germany, he wrote Dreiser, "Confidentially, I think it well to be near home at this moment."

Thus began a long period of suspicion and uncertainty. Mencken had, the previous month, stopped writing for the pro-British Sunpapers, although parts of his Berlin diary had run daily during March. He had planned to publish the diary as a book but found he could not because of the censors. Instead, fearing his house would be searched, he put the diary, along with other sensitive materials, into a large box which he buried in the backyard at Hollins Street. There the diary would remain until late 1918.

Some of his fears may have been justified. Although mob hysteria subsided somewhat with the actual declaration of war, he found that his own German associations made him suspect. He had been joking when he wrote Dreiser in 1915, "I expect to go to jail with the first batch of Baltimore suspects. Maybe we can contrive to be incarcerated in the same dungeon." That prospect was still unlikely, although Mencken did see several of his friends imprisoned. He himself received dozens of threatening letters, had his international mail opened, and was watched and visited by government agents. He soon found himself the subject of investigation by the Justice Department and the American Protective League, a notorious anti-German group.

He was suspect for a number of reasons—not only his German ancestry but also his openly pro-German articles in the *Evening Sun* in 1914 and 1915, his trip to Germany in early 1917 (which, some charged, had been undertaken for subversive purposes), and his early departure from Germany in February 1917, particularly since he had been aided by General Ludendorff. In addition, despite his occasional statements to the contrary, Mencken had a number of German friends. Although he made it a point to stay away from known German agents, he maintained his acquaintance with Captain Paul Koenig, the commander of the unarmed submarine *Deutschland*, and with Dr. Wilhelm Sohler, an ophthalmologist and ship's surgeon whom he had met in 1914. He saw Koenig on several occasions, once in New London, Connecticut, in late 1916. Sohler he saw in Baltimore and Norfolk. He was also friends with Victor Hugo Erpf, a Baltimore businessman and member of the Florestan Club arrested in 1917 and interned as a suspected German spy, as well as Grete Egerer, an Austrian teaching at Goucher College who was also suspected of illegal activities.

Thus he expected the visits from government agents who wanted information about his friendships with these and other Germans and Baltimore German Americans. Neither was he particularly surprised when the American Protective League set out to investigate him. In fact, he was rather amused by its investigation, which was assigned to *Smart Set* publisher Eltinge F. Warner, a member of the league. Warner told Mencken about the investigation, asked him to draw up a report exonerating himself, and then submitted the report under his own name.

Mencken, then, was aware of these and certain other activities. As he wrote later, "There has never been an occasion when the agents of the United States showed any awareness of . . . the individual citizen H. L. Mencken that they did not try to do me in." But he was not aware of the full extent of the effort—if not to do him in—at least to keep close checks on him. According to a rather extensive Justice Department file, he was more closely watched than he knew, largely because of his association with Sohler and Erpf.

When Sohler was sent to an internment camp at Fort McPherson, Georgia, in 1917, Mencken wrote him frequently and sent clothing, tobacco, and—when he was allowed—books. After reading his letters, the military censor at Fort McPherson recommended that Mencken's mail be "carefully watched" and further determined that future letters should be sent "to the War College, regardless of their content." Another government official determined that none of his letters to Sohler should be delivered since "they are thought to contain veiled information." Still another official was ordered to place a cover on all his mail. That Baltimore official, Billups Harris, filed a report in which he labeled Mencken "notoriously pro-

German" and identified him as an "intimate friend" of the now-imprisoned spy suspect Erpf. Although Harris added that Baltimore sources believed Mencken's "pro-German slant a sort of affectation," he maintained that their subject still should be watched and his mail in New York, as well as Baltimore, covered.

There were other complaints, some even more serious. In November 1917 a colonel of the General Staff of the Military Intelligence Section reported to the chief of the Justice Department's Bureau of Investigation (the forerunner of the FBI) the contents of a particular letter from Mencken to Sohler in which he had suggested that he was working for Sohler's release. "It might be well to lock him up," the colonel advised, "to determine what his efforts in that direction have been." The bureau chief, Bruce Bielaski, in turn wrote to Harris in Baltimore and asked him to "ascertain if there are any reasons to suspect that H. L. Mencken is a dangerous alien enemy." Again Harris reported his association with the "German spy" Erpf and "others of sort of a would-be high brow pro-German set of which Mencken was the center." "Most of Mencken's former friends in Baltimore have broken off anything like close relationships with him on account of his pronounced pro-German feeling," Harris added, "but hardly any of them think that Mencken himself would engage in any activity against this country. . . . Of course that's problematic," he concluded.

Other allegations about Mencken were amusing—that he had paid one million dollars for *The Smart Set*, that he and Nathan were "one & the same," that he was a man of "Ludendorfian & Nietzchean [*sic*] tendencies," even that he was "an intimate friend" of "the German monster, Nitsky," now dead seventeen years. Mencken later took delight in such charges (although he was never to know the extent of the material in the Justice Department file), and even though he had stopped writing on the war, he made no effort to conceal his sympathies. The "fundamental charge" against him, he later wrote Dreiser, "was true, at least in a general sense": he had indeed sought "to poison the wells of the Republic." Moreover, he "was in great hopes until near the end that [the German army] would chase the American army into the sea."

Indeed, it was during the war years more than at any other time that Mencken allowed himself to identify, if only in their common plight, with other German Americans in Baltimore. He accepted honorary memberships in the Germania Männerchor and several other German societies, memberships he resigned shortly after the war. Although he attended very few of their meetings, he did appear before a packed house of the Germania shortly after he returned from Germany in March 1917 to give his impressions of the war. The Germania, founded in 1840, included the "more civilized Germans of Baltimore," and he did not object strenuously to their company. But even during the war—as he was to report in his posthumously released manuscript "Thirty-Five Years of Newspaper Work"—he rejected the embraces of the "petty trading classes," those "simpleminded and much-troubled" Baltimore Germans who invited him to their gatherings and "insisted upon regarding me as a German patriot." Class consciousness remained with this child of the privileged even in the face of a common enemy: the "gratitude" of the lowerclass Germans, he said, bothered him far more than the attacks by English Baltimore.

The Germania shut down shortly after the United States entered the war. So did other organizations much closer to Mencken's heart. Friendships and professional associations (as Baltimore sleuth Billups Harris had suggested in his report) were affected as well. Certain of his friends at the very least compromised their friendship—at the worst, betrayed him—in ways he would never fully discover. His old friend and collaborator Dr. Leonard K. Hirshberg, a dubious character in any event, may have been a government informer, and a more recent friend, Lieutenant Colonel Fielding H. Garrison of the Surgeon General's office in Washington, filed an unfavorable report on Mencken at one point.

In fact, Garrison's close friendship with Mencken lay more in the future than in the present: they were to become frequent correspondents, discussing music, books, and ideas, and Garrison was to be a visitor to the Saturday Night Club and the Sunday dinner club. But that friendship might never have developed if Mencken had known all the details of a report Garrison made to military intelligence officers in August 1918. As a means of avoiding the draft, Mencken had shown interest in a position as coeditor of a medical history of the war. When he was recommended to Garrison, a medical librarian, for the post, Garrison was greatly suspicious. Mencken was aware of some of his suspicions, since Garrison had written him indicating that he had "queered" himself with the government with his pro-

German writing. "May I inquire," Garrison had asked, "what is your object in seeking government work?" In his response he had assured Garrison, distorting the truth, that he had no "loyalty" to Germany "as a state or a nation" and had not "even a friend there." In fact, Garrison had already reported his suspicions to the authorities. He was of the opinion that Mencken wanted regular employment as a writer in the Army Medical Service and believed that in such a position he would be a security risk. His reason was that Mencken would have access to confidential information, such as sailing dates for officers.

Far more disturbing to Mencken, both because he knew the details involved and because the friendship had been much closer, was what he considered a betrayal by Willard Huntington Wright, his old *Smart Set* collaborator. The two men had remained friends after Wright's dismissal from the magazine and after their joint European trip in 1914. Mencken had visited frequently at Wright's Lexington Avenue apartment in New York, had lent him money on several occasions, and in 1917 had helped him gain employment as literary editor of the New York *Evening Mail*. His disagreement with Wright now came not because his friend held opposing views on the war—Wright, in fact, was at least as pro-German as Mencken was— but rather because he expressed those views in a manner certain to bring trouble. In the summer of 1917 he published a book critical of England, a manuscript Mencken had warned him not to publish, and as a result he was targeted by the British Secret Service operating in New York. What Wright did next angered Mencken greatly: when the Secret Service planted a spy as a secretary in his office, he suspected her role and dictated a seditious letter to test her. She fled the office with the letter and called police, who—along with the U.S. Secret Service—questioned Wright. Before the day was over, Wright had been fired, the completely innocent man to whom he addressed the letter—another friend of Mencken's—was in serious trouble, and the New York newspapers gave the story a great deal of attention. Mencken himself was questioned.

Mencken broke off the friendship immediately. He had put up with Wright's borrowing money, his drug addiction, and his general instability; but stupidity, as always, Mencken could not abide. When Wright wrote him a long letter of explanation and apology, he did not reply. "It is impossible, in the circumstances, to have anything to do with him," he wrote a mutual friend. "A man so silly is a public nuisance." A quarter century later he was still referring to Wright's "almost incredible imbecility." Mencken did not forget easily. "When I am done with a man, I am done with him," he wrote the friend who had suffered because of Wright's action. "I was surely friendly enough to him, and yet in the end he deliberately betrayed my confidence. Such things are not to be forgiven."

If such a dismissal seems overly harsh—Wright had not, in fact, "deliberately betrayed" his confidence—such was the way Mencken often operated. He valued friendship even more highly than most people do, in part because he gave to friends the time and loyalty another man might have given to wife and children—and, even more, because he prized a camaraderie grounded in shared beliefs and prejudices, in an active interplay of ideas, and, most of all, in good judgment. "I have never met anyone to whom the tending of his friendships was more precious," an English acquaintance wrote later, but in fact, as he demonstrated in several later instances as well, Mencken made a habit of breaking off long-standing friendships if he felt betrayed, as he did with Wright. When such friendships were interrupted, they were very rarely renewed.

Mencken saw his rigorous standards as a personal strength, not a weakness. "A man of active and resilient mind," he wrote, "outwears his friendships just as certainly as he outwears his love affairs, his politics and his epistemology. They become threadbare, shabby, pumped-up, irritating, depressing." Particularly during the war years he cast off friends, most of whom (unlike Wright) had British sympathies. "I had to live among people whose view of the events of the time seemed almost insane to me, and whose concept of honor . . . was violently at war with my own. . . . I lost a great many friends . . . but though I missed them . . . it would be going too far to say that I regretted them." When the war was over and some wanted to renew their friendship, "I refused to go along."

The war was the period, Mencken later wrote, of "my withdrawal into myself," but it was also the period in which most of the deep friendships of his life were formed or solidified. In some cases such relationships were forged *because* of common adversity, because of shared feelings about the war and American dishonor. During the war Mencken also spent more time in New York and, through his work, came into contact with increasing numbers of like-minded people.

He had not changed his mind about New York as a place to live. He never would. "For some reason or other, the town irritates me beyond expression," he later wrote. "It is associated in my mind with unpleasant duties and unpleasant people." But in fact during the war years he seemed to enjoy the city immensely. About 1918 he made the Algonquin Hotel his New York headquarters, taking a suite at six dollars a day. There he made the acquaintance of several film stars. "The squads of lovely movie gals," he later wrote, "to my bucolic eye, looked like princesses or even like angels." He was less favorably impressed with the Algonquin Round Table, that group consisting of Alexander Woollcott, Heywood Broun, Robert Sherwood, and other "hollow frauds," all "literati of the third, fourth and fifth rate." He continued to prefer the company of Nathan, Edgar Selwyn, John D. Williams, and Tom Smith. They often gathered in the late afternoon at Delmonico's or Sherry's for cocktails, then moved on to Lüchow's, the Beaux Arts, or the Kaiserhof for dinner.

Mencken made the acquaintance of numerous other writers during these years, but no friendship was more gratifying than that with his old hero, James Gibbons Huneker. Although he had corresponded with Huneker since 1905, the two men had not met until 1914, when Willard Wright brought them together. Mencken was fascinated with Huneker: "plainly no ordinary man," he concluded in the memoirs in which he devoted some forty-five pages to Huneker. Not only had Huneker been America's boldest literary and cultural critic of the 1890s, but as a conversationalist and beer drinker he surpassed Mencken himself. Their frequent lunches at Lüchow's, which would begin at 1:00 P.M., often ran until 4:00 or 5:00. Now in his mid-fifties, Huneker had lived fully and had known a great number of people, but his prime had clearly passed. During the war years, except when he appeared in Manhattan to meet Mencken or to pursue his own work, he led a rather secluded, even lonely, life in Brooklyn, writing for two or three New York newspapers, battling diabetes, and closer to death (which came in 1921) than anyone realized. But to Mencken he was still a larger-than-life figure, one of those few men of his acquaintance who seemed to illustrate the possibilities of a life lived with even more gusto—and much less restraint—than he himself brought to it.

Another such figure Mencken met during the war—and one who was to be his closest companion in New York over the next fifteen years—was advertising man, aspiring publisher, and eventual theatrical producer Philip Goodman. A huge man of enormous appetites weighing nearly three hundred pounds and exhibiting even more gusto than Huneker, Goodman became an eating and drinking companion sans pareil, a worthy Falstaff to this particular Prince Henry. Introduced to Mencken in 1917 by their mutual friend John Williams, Goodman first wanted to be Mencken's publisher, and Mencken consented to let him produce two small books in 1918. He was interested in Goodman's idea of selling books in drugstores and other mass-distribution outlets as well as bookstores.

A failure as a publisher, Goodman was a great success as a friend. Mencken was drawn to him not only because of their similar tastes in food and drink but also because of their shared passion for other things German. The product of a German-Jewish background in Philadelphia, Goodman traveled to Germany frequently and was, Mencken later wrote, "in love with all things German." In his frequent letters to Goodman in 1918 and 1919 Mencken recounted stories, largely apocryphal, of his own German-American upbringing in Baltimore, recalling and inventing characters, putting himself into the anecdotal frame of mind to which he would return twenty years later when he began to write about his childhood. The letters suggest the rollicking, irreverent tone of the friendship between the two men. Only beer was treated seriously. If Mencken had a true soul mate during the late war years and just afterward, much closer than Dreiser and Nathan ever were, it was Goodman. That closeness survived the war and the following decade only to become a casualty of another war, one in which it would be far more difficult for a Jew to be a Germanophile as well.

But the friendship that was to last longest of all—that also began during the war years and was to endure a lifetime—was that with Alfred A. Knopf. In fact, Mencken had met Knopf some years before he met Goodman—in 1913, when the twenty-one-year-old employee of the publishing firm of Doubleday, Page stopped by the *Sun* offices to talk about Kipling and wound up talking about Joseph Conrad.

But he had not been as immediately drawn to Knopf, a somewhat colder specimen, as he would be to Goodman. Indeed, in 1914 he had warned Dreiser—whom the publisher apparently had approached— "Beware of Knopf: he is representing himself as your intimate friend." And when, the following year, Knopf established his own firm and wanted Mencken as one of his authors, Mencken resisted. When he did consent to join forces with Knopf in 1917, it was largely because Scribner's, Macmillan, and Harper's showed no interest in him.

He was initially skeptical of Knopf, at least as a publisher, for several reasons. Knopf was very young and inexperienced. He seemed to have no money of his own and thus was forced to depend on his father for capital. And, Mencken later wrote, "there was the fact that he was a Jew." "I had little if any prejudice against Jews myself," he hastened to add in his posthumous memoir, "and in fact spent a great deal of my leisure in their company, but they were rare in the publishing business and rather resented by the *Goyim*, and there was little indication that they would ever be successful." He had in mind, in particular, Horace Liveright, of whom he had a "very low opinion." Liveright "was a loud, bold, unpleasant Jew who got into publishing by way of Wall Street."

It would be easy to dismiss Mencken's statement that he himself had few if any negative feelings about Jews and did not at first reject Knopf on those grounds. But, as concerns Knopf as publisher, he was probably right. There was little in Mencken's life to this point to give any evidence of anti-Semitism. As he maintained, during this period as afterward, much of his leisure was indeed spent with Jewish friends—Goodman, Nathan, Louis Untermeyer, and Edgar Selwyn, among others—and he had numerous other, less intimate Jewish friends, including Benjamin de Casseres, Ludwig Lewisohn, and Abraham Cahan, editor of the *Jewish Daily Forward* and the author of one of Mencken's favorite contemporary novels, *The Rise of David Levinsky*. At least two members of the Saturday Night Club were Jewish (as, a quarter century earlier, a number of members of August Mencken's lodge had been Jewish). It was even assumed— erroneously—by many, including some of Mencken's close friends, that Marion Bloom was Jewish. In his written work as well, to this point, Mencken had appeared anything but anti-Semitic. As early as 1906, in the *Sun*, he had suggested the "experiment" of a Jewish state in British East Africa, and on another occasion in "The Free Lance" he had defended Jewish shopkeepers against Baltimore authorities who had raided their establishments and forced them to close on Sundays. These merchants and their patrons, Mencken had written, "keep their own Sabbath very scrupulously on Saturday, and it is certainly unfair to make them outlaws for refusing to keep two Sabbaths in succession."

All this Mencken could have offered to support his claim that he had "little if any prejudice against Jews," and he would have been largely justified. He could have added Knopf's own claim that he was no more "anti-Semitic [than] most liberal Jews tend to be." And yet now and later—in ways he never fully recognized—he could not completely escape those prejudices of his youth. If there had been Jews in August's lodge, there had also been Mencken's "violently anti-Semitic" grandfather and the "$20 Jew" in his neighborhood whom his mother refused to patronize. If he had admired the fine houses of some of Baltimore's German Jews, he had also as a young reporter seen the Jewish ghetto of East Baltimore and pronounced it "almost unimaginably filthy . . . [I] was appalled by what I saw." In remarking on his first impression of Knopf—in that same posthumously released manuscript in which he was to defend himself against anti-Semitism—he also referred to Knopf's possessing "a certain amount of the obnoxious tactlessness of his race." In the same manuscript, in which he generally spoke with great affection of Nathan, he also referred to the "typically Jewish inferiority complex," which he believed Nathan possessed. And when he turned to his other frequent companion, Selwyn, he noted, "There was but little suggestion of the Jewish in his appearance and manner, and I got on with him very well."

Regardless of whether Mencken was anti-Semitic (and the issue later becomes even more central), the salient fact is that he was, and increasingly would be, highly *conscious* of Jews and of what he considered Jewishness. Indeed, he was aware that he himself was often assumed to be Jewish. Perhaps it was not surprising that he was thus identified by many of his critics, particularly those in the South and Midwest who believed that any eastern critic of American life, especially one with a German name, was perforce Jewish. But he was also thus identified by Jews themselves: on three or four occasions he was listed in *The Jewish Year Book*, and at other times he was identified in print as a Jewish member of the Authors League of America. The same assumption had often been made about the Menckens in eighteenth- and nineteenth-century Germany: Bismarck's mother, Luise Wilhelmine Mencken, had often been said to be Jewish. Even closer to home, Mencken's brother August (in this case, being altogether serious) once said, "There is no doubt a trace of . . . Jewish blood" in the Mencken family. There was not the slightest evidence for such a conclusion.

Mencken's suspicions about Alfred Knopf had long since vanished by 1917, when he decided to cast his lot with the fledgling publishing company, and except for the brief interlude with Goodman in 1918 he was to remain with Knopf for the remainder of his career. The story of the subsequent years of their friendship, however, belongs to later stages of Mencken's life. For during the war years Knopf was hardly the partner in *biergemütlichkeit* that Huneker, Goodman, and Nathan were. Neither was he then the close friend that two other companions, Ernest Boyd and Joseph Hergesheimer, were.

Mencken had first met Boyd in 1913, when the slight Irishman with the reddish brown beard had come to Baltimore as British vice consul. The two men had spent a great deal of time drinking and talking, and Mencken had enjoyed the company of Boyd's French-born wife, Madeleine, as well. In time Mencken introduced Boyd to his New York friends, and this "Matterhorn of learning," as Mencken called him, quickly carved out a reputation for himself. Van Wyck Brooks later remembered him as "an impenitent rationalist," an "acidulous Orangeman" who "recalled to me the literary gladiators of the Grub Street of the age of Pope and Swift." What Mencken prized most in this British vice consul was his anti-British views: he and Boyd enjoyed ridiculing British censors and propaganda efforts. But he also valued Boyd as a skilled literary critic and translator, a cosmopolitan figure who spoke several languages. During part of the war Boyd was back in Dublin—from which he conducted as lively a correspondence with Mencken as the censors would allow—and when he returned to New York Mencken recommended him to Knopf as a man who could help with international authors. Knopf took him on.

In the long run Boyd proved a "false friend," as Mencken later wrote—one who was eventually destroyed by the excesses Mencken both relished and ultimately rejected in certain of his companions. A far steadier and more enduring friendship was that with Hergesheimer, soon to be a widely popular novelist. Their acquaintance had begun shortly after Mencken wrote a generally unfavorable review of Hergesheimer's novel *The Lay Anthony* in *The Smart Set* of December 1914. Then largely unknown, Hergesheimer had written Mencken a long letter defending his novel, discussing literature in general, and concluding by inviting Mencken to Pennsylvania for a visit. "You matter, and I intend to," Hergesheimer had concluded, "and we should know each other." Mencken liked Hergesheimer's approach, found in the novelist a kindred "civilized spirit," and responded that he would indeed like to visit Hergesheimer. Thus began a lively correspondence and a close friendship, with Mencken recruiting Hergesheimer for *The Smart Set* and (even before he himself signed on) for Knopf, and with the two meeting frequently in Philadelphia, Baltimore, and New York. In time Hergesheimer was to become, along with Knopf, Mencken's closest personal friend outside Baltimore. Indeed, Hergesheimer was, he later wrote, "the only professional author I ever became genuinely intimate with."

That included Dreiser, of whom Mencken earlier might have said the same, but with whom his relations remained strained between 1917 and 1920. In his posthumously released memoirs, Mencken insisted that relations between the two men "continued friendly" during most of this period, but letters to and from Dreiser—and from Mencken to others about Dreiser—tell a different story. To Boyd in Dublin he complained that Dreiser was growing "more and more asinine" and that his old friend had "some obscure complaint against me . . . and so I don't see him." In December 1917 he told Boyd about encountering Dreiser by accident in a New York restaurant; the two "solemnly" shook hands, Mencken reported, but "I think I am done with him." Shortly afterward he reported that he and Dreiser were "now definitely at war. The business gives me a sense of relief." But with Willard Wright also "excommunicated," Mencken confessed to Boyd that he was, at least for a brief period, leading "a very lonely life in New York."

What Mencken continued to find highly objectionable in Dreiser was his dissolute life, particularly his sexual license. If earlier he had believed Dreiser unwise and indiscreet, by 1917 and 1918 he had come to consider his old friend completely out of control. During that period—after Dreiser's breakup with Kirah Markham in the summer of 1916—he had multiple lovers, sometimes entertaining two or three women in a single day. He spent most of his time with Marion Bloom's sister, Estelle (called "Gloom" by Mencken and Marion because of her disposition and her love of heavy Russian novels), but he was also involved sexually with, among others, a twenty-seven-year-old woman in New York, a somewhat older woman in Philadelphia, and Kirah herself when she was back in town. He recorded all of it in detail in a diary he kept from May 1917 through March 1918.

Mencken did not have access to the diary until 1925—when Estelle, who found the diary in Dreiser's desk, typed a copy and gave it to him. At that time he read with alternating disgust and amazement, jotting notes as he went. After reading about a particularly strenuous day in 1917 in which Dreiser claimed to have serviced the Philadelphia woman four times in a single afternoon rendezvous in Trenton and then returned to New York and made love to Estelle twice more, Mencken exclaimed: "This made six in one day—and Dreiser was forty-six years old." Another time, some months later, he noted, "This is three, with three different women, within 24 hours—and Dreiser was 47!" He must have been amused by other Dreiser entries—"Feel that I must give up so much screwing or I will break down"—but if so he didn't record his response. After reading the diary, he put it into a vault in his cellar with the instructions "To be destroyed unread at my death." Later he concluded that it should be read, after all, when he and Dreiser were no longer around. He made the diary part of his posthumous memoir "My Life as Author and Editor."

In fact, Mencken hardly needed access to the diary in 1918 to express, in letters to numerous friends, great disapproval of Dreiser's sexual conduct. He was in close touch with Estelle and of course with Marion, and he and Nathan still saw Dreiser occasionally. To Boyd he wrote, "Dreiser is going on with women like a crazy college boy; his place is full of them all day and all night." He was "such a hopeless ass that he falls for any flatterers. Let some preposterous wench come in in a long blue smock, and call him 'Master,' and he is immediately undone." Dreiser was doing little writing, Mencken reported, but "devotes himself largely to the stud." When he heard that, after all, his old friend was at work "on a philosophical book," he added, "You may well guess that fornication will be defended in it." On another occasion, when Dreiser drew up a manifesto protesting "puritanical" standards and calling for an "American critical society," Mencken refused to cooperate. He believed such a society would be taken over by "advanced thinkers . . . especially the Sex Boys."

Mencken's criticism was not simply, as Dreiser would have it, prudery. Nor was it jealousy. It was rather, in large part, that he had lost much of his respect for his friend and could no longer separate the artist from the man. Knopf shared Mencken's views. When he learned in 1917 that Dreiser was looking for a new publisher, Knopf (who earlier had sought Dreiser out) would not even consider taking him on. He too—at least by Mencken's account—was wary of Dreiser as "a stalker of women." "I don't want any author on my list," Mencken reported him as saying, "that I'd hesitate to invite to my house."

But his friend's philandering disturbed Mencken for a reason that went beyond respect or decorum. It was simply that in his debauchery Dreiser was hurting Estelle Bloom, whom Mencken also valued as a close friend. She had become Dreiser's "slave," he felt, doing secretarial work, cooking and washing, and making herself available sexually, all the while he was being unfaithful. "The trouble with Dreiser is that he is a Christian," Mencken wrote Estelle. "He gets as much satanic joy out of a session with one of those wenches as a school-boy gets out of his first affair with a servant girl." Mencken and Estelle exchanged frequent letters about the man Mencken variously called "the Indiana Tiger," the "Warsaw [Indiana] Guinea Pig," and (somewhat later) "the Hollywood Fornicator." On several occasions he urged Estelle to leave. "You have allowed the old boy to make a doormat of you," he wrote in January 1918, "yet you have gone back every time . . ." One "roll of the evil eye" was enough for Estelle to return. On at least one occasion Mencken offered to help Estelle financially if she left Dreiser in New York and returned to Washington. "Why in hell a woman of your talents should be a slave of a man is beyond my comprehension."

Mencken felt his own relationship with Marion was altogether different, and for the most part he was correct. In comparison with

Dreiser, at least, he was certainly no philanderer; rather, he remained, as Dreiser sneered in the diary Mencken himself would later
see, "the cautious conventionalist." He and Marion continued to be
very close during the remainder of the war years, indeed closer
between 1917 and 1919 than they would ever be again. Mencken had
written to her frequently during his European trip in early 1917,
letters filled both with his usual mock gallantry and with a new
affection and devotion. Shortly after he returned to Baltimore he was
off to New York to see her, and that spring and summer they continued to meet in New York—although Marion complained to Estelle
that he came only every three or four weeks and she, meanwhile, was
"seeing [her] youth slowly and methodically eas[e] away. . . . It is so
painful."

She complained to Mencken as well, so much that the following
year he wrote Estelle:

> I had a long letter from Marion day before yesterday, so infernally
> martyred that I lost patience and wrote to her very sharply. The
> thing has really become unbearable. She lashes herself into a fury
> of self-pity and then empties the whole thing on me. . . . I am
> constantly ill, have a great amount of work to do, and am months
> behind on it. For six months this endless weeping and wailing has
> kept me on a red-hot stove. I simply can't go on with it any longer.

Mencken went on to complain of "heart pains," "constant . . .
discomfort," and low blood pressure. Although he wanted to continue helping Marion financially, he was ready to agree to her suggestion that they avoid each other for three months.

During the summer of 1918 Marion signed on as a military nurse,
and in September 1918 she was off to Europe. As always, Mencken
became more attentive and affectionate just before they were to part.
He made several trips to New York for farewells, and just after they
spent their last night together in New York he wrote with uncharacteristic tenderness: "I shall not forget, my dear—this last visit, nor
any of the others. You will believe how much I have loved you when
the bad dream is over and we are all secure and happy again. You
have been very good to me."

He wrote several other unusually affectionate letters over the next
few days. "New York, to me, is simply full of you," he wrote the day

after she sailed. "I'll be seeing your tracks everywhere, and wishing this and that—you know the fancies of a romantic young man." "All my thoughts are on the day you come back," he wrote two days later, "and we can start off with the sand out of your eyes. . . . I think of you always as coming back very soon, and unchanged." Other times he reiterated that sentiment—"Let us think only of the day you come back"—and still others he suggested that he would meet Marion in France after the war. He seemed to be astounded at his own condition: "I am infernally lonesome, and long for a glimpse of a certain gal. It is amazing that I should be so soft at my advanced age." "Ah, that I were less windblown and wheezy and could make love in true waltz time," he wrote another time. "As it is, you have it all."

It is obvious that Mencken was, as he put it, "mashed," was in love or as close to it as he had ever given evidence of being. He signed those September letters "With love," and Marion had every reason to look forward to returning. When she did come back, early in 1919, they resumed the discussion of marriage they had begun, if tentatively, before she had left. According to letters Marion wrote to Estelle (as well as the testimony of a weary and wiser Marion more than a half century later), in 1918 and 1919 Mencken suggested that she marry him and move into 1524 Hollins Street. They would live with Anna Mencken—"a pure German hausfrau," Marion later wrote—and with whatever other family would be in residence. She and Henry would take the top floor, and Mencken would have his office outside the house. He wanted both mother and wife, Marion later wrote, "at the same time, same place." Much more to Marion's taste was his next suggestion, that he and Marion take a house in the country.

Just how seriously he considered such a plan we cannot be altogether certain. He had long believed marriage to be incompatible with the life of a man of ideas. "A married Schopenhauer or Kant or Nietzsche," he had announced in *The Philosophy of Friedrich Nietzsche*, "would be unthinkable." In his own case, contemplating such a course of action while Marion was safely away in France, romantically inaccessible, was one thing; putting it into action upon her return was another. Even before she returned, the tone of their letters had grown less affectionate. In her letters, Mencken wrote Ernest Boyd, Marion was accusing him "of the usual atrocities." After she came back his ardor apparently cooled. Despite at least some talk of marriage, none of his letters in 1919 was to match the fervor of the letters he had written in September 1918. Now he rarely signed "With love."

Still, Mencken cared deeply for Marion. In letters to Estelle he expressed great concern about her health and well-being. Although he did not share the diagnosis of an army doctor that she might have tuberculosis, he did feel she was in "poor condition." He was also frustrated because she would not always heed his advice. She spoke of going abroad again, this time to Serbia, and she also spoke of other possibilities. "What is to be done?" he wrote Estelle. "I am at my wit's end. A remarkable girl, with an amazing talent for riling me." He was willing to try to get her a release from the Surgeon General's office, he was willing "to stake her until she can look after herself again," he was willing to do any number of things for her.

But he was not willing to marry her, and the reason he finally decided he could not—if he needed another reason—was her conversion to Christian Science not long after her return from France. As far back as 1908 Mencken had called Christian Science "that most grotesque child of credulous faith and incredible denial," and in 1919 it was still his "pet abomination." Yet Marion had returned from Europe "shattered" by what she had seen and experienced—"destituted spiritually," as she still expressed it fifty years later—and "searching for a God to explain the horrors of war." When she was introduced to the teachings of Mary Baker Eddy, she was ready to believe.

"What is this Christian Science stuff that Marion is unloading on me by the gallon?" Mencken asked Estelle in September 1919. "Has she really fallen for that buncombe? I am amazed . . . the thing is pishposh. Its fundamental ideas are idiotic. . . . Is she simply kidding me? I surely hope so." Not only was Marion serious, but for a brief time she even had hopes of converting Mencken himself. He soon convinced her of his adamant opposition. "He . . . scorned me and ridiculed me and talked against me to family and friends," she later charged, and she was largely correct. The "Christian Science stuff" in the fall of 1919 "sent me scurrying to the sewers," he later wrote Estelle. For several months he tried to convince Marion that it was "quite idiotic," but she "stood pat, and so there was nothing to do but shake hands and call it a day." Christian Science "riled me intolerably," he added. "I can't bear to hear it mentioned. . . . All this makes me sick. I thought I had a nice girl, but she turns out to be an evangelist."

On several later occasions Mencken suggested that Christian Science was the primary if not the sole reason he did not marry Marion Bloom. But it is likely that he would have found others if that had not existed. Marion later insisted that it was she who broke off any serious discussion of marriage and that she did it because she was "horror-stricken" that marriage would "destroy" Mencken's "gift or talent." She had stressed to him, she later maintained, that she was an abominable cook and housekeeper as well as a woman who did not want to be tied down—all this to discourage any marriage plans. She also contended that she was miserable over her own failures and did not want to afflict him with them. She insisted, finally, that she was tired of "being the man in H's and my case." She was tired of making decisions, of having to "go forth to 'make good,' to 'prove myself.' " "You utterly lack that bravado and deviltry in speaking of marriage so dear to a woman," she once wrote him. She refused, in particular, to take "him by the back of his neck and [lead] him to the altar."

What Marion said was partly true. It was probably true as well, as she later claimed, that she broke off their relationship in late 1919 because of her "discouragement." But there was much more to the failure of their relationship than either she or Mencken fully realized—much that is to Mencken's discredit—although Marion comes close to the truth at times in her letters to Estelle. A great part of the truth was that Mencken did not marry Marion because, quite simply, he believed Marion was not fine enough for him. She was not sufficiently well bred, not well educated, well dressed, financially well off: she was not sufficiently *successful.* As with so much else about this son of a prosperous but socially undistinguished family, this descendant of *gelehrten* who attended an industrial high school and no university, it came down, whether he admitted it or not, to a matter of class.

Marion understood this in part. She recalled, at least twice in later letters, an incident in late 1919 or early 1920 in which, after an "idyllic afternoon," Mencken "had swatted [her] cold in Union Station with the statement that if I had a background, financial security, in brief, our affair might be different." Mencken had "explained this calculation on the ground that he was a high-born German and had it in him to desire his wife to make a fine showing before his world."

"Oh that January night," she wrote either of that incident or another shortly after it, "when he said I was unlucky, unfortunate, and that he couldn't bear unfortunate people—and I struggling like a wounded animal to emerge from the tragic fogs a war had blinded me with overlong." Mencken, Marion had concluded, was "a shallow man who judges a woman by what she possesses." "I know that merely writing famous books doesn't make a gentleman in my definition of the word."

We must consider that these words came from a rejected woman, yet one who in many respects, even after her rejection, was often very generous in her estimate of Mencken. In one important particular, her words have the ring of truth. We know from other sources that propriety and appearance—the appearance that money, particularly old money, could buy—meant a great deal more to Mencken than he often acknowledged. Indeed, at times he did acknowledge their importance—at least once in the notes he left at his death and, more to the point, in a statement in *The Smart Set* just months after he and Marion had parted in late 1919: "To one ineradicable prejudice I freely confess, and that is a prejudice against poverty. I never have anything to do, if it is possible, with anyone who is in financial difficulties. . . . Such persons do not excite my compassion; they excite my aversion. . . . The blame, so far as my experience runs, always lies within." It is not surprising that Marion, who read Mencken's remarks and sent the piece to Estelle, took these words personally. "It was these very thoughts, uttered," she wrote her sister, "that caused me in my discouragement to separate from him."

Indeed, both in his relationship with Marion in 1919 and 1920 and in his association with her afterward, Mencken appears in a more unfavorable light than he was perhaps ever to appear elsewhere. With her, this man who was capable of great kindness, consideration, tenderness, and loyalty (each of which he demonstrated toward her some of the time) verged on occasion, whether intentionally or not, on cruelty. It was, then, far more than Christian Science that caused him to reject her, and to the extent that Christian Science did play a part—and it did—its role was predictable. Mencken considered it intellectually dishonest, certainly, but as much as that, he considered it bad *form*. To his thinking, Christian Science, like Dreiser's whoring, betrayed a lack of discrimination, a breach of decorum. It was, in Mencken's eyes, somewhat shabby—like Marion's poverty and her occasional residence in boardinghouses. It was one of many reasons why Marion finally felt—overstating her case but grasping part of the truth—that Mencken "despised me as a 29-cent bargain."

That may also explain in part why Mencken, in later years, distanced himself from even the memory of Marion Bloom. In the more than two thousand pages of his posthumously released memoir "My Life as Author and Editor," a work that thoroughly covered the years 1914–1923, when he knew Marion best and in which he mentioned dozens of other women of his professional and personal acquaintance, he referred to Marion but once. That was in a single line, in a footnote to an appendix, as "a woman with whom Wright, Claire Burke and I used to dine in the Italian restaurant in Lexington Avenue." In the tens of thousands of letters he wrote after 1925 he hardly ever mentioned her (save to Estelle) except when—as in a letter in 1948—he was responding to an inquiry: "How the Bloom lady got that manuscript . . . I simply can't tell you." Even more remarkable, in a letter of 1971 from Alfred Knopf—Mencken's close friend during the entire period he knew Marion—to Betty Adler of the Enoch Pratt Free Library, Knopf remarked, "As for Marion Bloom, yours is the first mention of her name that I have ever heard." Either Knopf, recalling his late friend's passion for confidentiality, was concealing the truth, or Marion, even during the period when she was closest to Mencken, hardly figured in other compartments of his life. And this was the woman he loved more than he ever loved any other woman, except one.

Much more than discretion or protection of a romantic relationship was involved here. The fact is that, except among their few mutual friends, Mencken later hardly acknowledged knowing Marion Bloom on any level. As years went by she became a figure nearly anonymous. But Mencken remained much more than that to her, as she had known he would. In a four-paragraph sketch she contributed to *The Smart Set* for March 1917—despite all Mencken's efforts, her only signed piece in the magazine—she had depicted a woman, obviously herself, listening to a man, obviously Mencken, with a "matronly figure" and an "awkwardly fitting suit." "How I love him," the woman realizes as she listens to his voice. "But Heavens, how much I will find to hate about him when I have ceased to love him!"

In late 1919 she had not ceased to love him, if indeed she ever would. She was hurt deeply, she felt altogether rejected, and in the next few months she fell into such a depression that she considered suicide. She feared that Mencken "might be in love with . . . some successful woman and joyously happy to be free of me." Such was not entirely the case: at least he was in love with no other woman, successful or not.

In fact, the tortured relationship between Mencken and Marion was to last, in its active phase, another three years, and in some manner for much longer than that. Despite his disapproval, he could not give her up, and Marion, for her part, as she wrote her sister, "had a habit of making access to me easy." Although "mortal enemies," Marion wrote Estelle, again overstating her case, "suspicious of ourselves and therefore of each other," they would remain linked antagonists, and sometimes lovers, for the better part of another decade. But the chances for a life together had come and gone in 1918 and 1919. Much of what remained after that would consist of recriminations and regrets.

# Chapter 8

# MARKING TIME

S ince most of the time Mencken spent with Marion Bloom between 1917 and 1920 was spent in New York—as well as nearly
all the time with Dreiser, Nathan, Knopf, and Goodman—it is easy
to forget that during this period, as in any other period of his life, he
lived the majority of his days in Baltimore. Despite being out of a job
with the Sunpapers from early 1917 through 1920, his devotion to his
family and long-standing friends kept him there. Working at home,
he seldom went by the *Sun* offices. In the morning he usually read
manuscripts and handled business and correspondence, after 1918
assisted by a secretary. In the afternoon he often worked on and
around the house: he had begun renovations at Hollins Street in
1914, and he continued with the job during the war years. He
managed some writing during the daylight hours, but most of his
writing he did at night. He stopped about 10:00 P.M. for conversation,
drink, and reading.

After the anti-German hysteria of March and April 1917 there was
little overt threat to himself or his family. Mencken learned to live
with opened mail and occasional questioning by federal agents. In
September 1918, on his thirty-eighth birthday, he was at last required to register for the draft, and for a time he believed he would
be called up. As a bachelor, he felt particularly vulnerable. For the
most part, he now viewed the war with detachment and even good
humor, but at times he would grow somber. "There is constant snow,

great cold, and hence much suffering," he wrote Ernest Boyd in January 1918. "Coal is short, food is high, and every day seems to be meatless, wheatless, beerless, porkless or sugarless." Later that year, in the midst of the "amazingly deadly" autumn influenza epidemic, he reported to a friend in California, "All these parts are ravaged. . . . An undertaker's wagon gallops by my house every few minutes." "It amounts to a pestilence," he wrote Boyd. "Five and a half columns of death notices in the Sun this morning. . . . Last night, at Union Station, I saw about 50 coffins in the train shed." Nathan had been "floored" in New York, he told Boyd, and "I feel wobbly myself." In fact, Mencken escaped influenza altogether in the fall of 1918 and even, with his characteristic good luck, benefited from the epidemic. The influenza meant that army camps had to be quarantined and preinduction physicals curtailed. He had been given a "reprieve," he wrote Boyd in October.

As before, he took seriously his duties as head of household for 1524 Hollins Street. He felt especially responsible for August, who petitioned for an exemption from military service because of his arrested case of pulmonary tuberculosis. A few months after that petition, August's car was hit and severely damaged by a freight train; according to a newspaper account, August and a passenger "miraculously" escaped. Mencken took care of his extended family as well. He entertained his four-year-old niece, Charlie's daughter, Virginia, when she visited from Pittsburgh, and in September 1917 he arranged for Dr. Joseph Bloodgood of the Johns Hopkins to operate on Charlie's wife, Mary. It was the first of many medical procedures he would arrange for her.

Although his own health was sound enough during the war years—partly because, under doctor's orders, he had lost nearly twenty pounds in 1915 and had kept most of it off—we might assume from his complaints to friends that he was often at death's door. He complained at various times of a bad cough, "sleeping fits," sore eyes, hay fever, "beer-drinker's liver," the old "uncomfortable sensation of the tongue," and, in a single letter of March 14, 1917, "a splinter under the fingernail . . . laryngitis, and piles" as well as—the previous week—"a skinned thumb, a sour stomach and vague pains in the shoulders." Twice—aside from the epidemic of late 1918—he had what he felt was surely influenza, once in early 1918 and again in late 1919. And he had his normal quota of operations, among them one on his nose and another to remove a mole from his neck. Since the mole had begun to grow and was found to be "on the very edge of malignancy," Mencken credited Bloodgood with saving his life.

His principal Baltimore diversion during the war was, as always, the Saturday Night Club. At times Mencken feared the club's "days [were] numbered." One member, Theodore Hemberger, he wrote Boyd in 1918, was "an enemy alien, and as a result there is a great deal of watching, spying, solemn reporting, etc." In fact, the Saturday Night Club continued to flourish, an Englishman and a Belgian sitting weekly, Mencken wrote, "with four or five Germans, and alongside them . . . half-a-dozen Americans of sharply differing opinion." Mencken's own closest friend in the club during these years was Hemberger, the staunchest German. Mencken and Max Brödel also indulged themselves in discussions of German ancestry, beer, and music. Club members did not hesitate to discuss and disagree about the war. But no one dropped out. All, Mencken noted, were "civilized men."

He did not find that to be the case with the Florestan Club, that other convivial group of ombibulous musicians he had helped to found in 1911. It broke up in 1916, largely because of the war: certain members were strongly pro-German and others vocally pro-English. Mencken's old friend and music mentor W. G. Owst, despite his education in Germany, was "a true Englishman," he wrote, "and did some pious ranting against the Hun." Mencken terminated that friendship shortly after the outbreak of war, and Owst was hardly the only casualty among his old Baltimore companions. "I acquired a long blacklist of Baltimoreans who offended me in one way or another," he later wrote, "and during the years since I have avoided them as much as possible."

Financially, he suffered little because of the war. Although he sometimes gave the impression that he was financially troubled—in August 1918 he complained to Ernest Boyd that his situation was "so damned bad that I must either take to the trenches before long, or go back to cigar-making"—in fact, his situation was never desperate and most of the time was comfortable. It made little difference that he was not writing for the Sunpapers, since from 1914 his outside income had surpassed his newspaper earnings. Although 1917 was not a good year for *The Smart Set* and much of the year Mencken received no salary, 1918 was better: from magazine income and other sources he earned nearly $7,000.

In fact, he never needed a great deal of money, especially not in Baltimore, and despite his statement that he always liked to give the "impression" of being wealthy, he never sought money. Just before and during the war he turned down numerous lucrative opportunities—once declining an offer, as he wrote Dreiser, "to make a lot of money by acting as a sort of literary attorney for a crowd of pirates," another time rejecting the offer of a group of brewers to write advertising, and still another time, if we are to believe him, turning down a $30,000 offer to write anti-Prohibition speeches for various senators and congressmen.

"I can recall no year since I was 20 when I couldn't have doubled my income if I had been so disposed," Mencken wrote later in life, and there is no reason to doubt him. But as long as he had money for household expenses, food and drink, and occasional travel, he was happy. The Studebaker he bought in 1915 for $900 he sold in late 1918 for $300, having discovered that he was mechanically inept. He invested the $300 in beer, wine, and liquor. About the same time he took up home brewing, finding in that art the same satisfaction he found in undertaking his own home improvements. In his careful records of income and expenditures, in his delight and pride in doing many of his own home repairs and much of the renovation at Hollins Street, in his belief that "the most durable delights of life are cheap," in his nearly compulsive accountability: in all these ways there was something nearly Thoreauvian about Mencken. He liked to reflect on the joys derived from his fireplace at 5½ cents per night. Even the $300 spent on potables was not altogether inconsistent with Thoreauvian economy: he was storing up, hoarding, preparing for the dry days ahead.

———※———

If he took great satisfaction in his self-reliance during the war years as well as pride in his ability to prosper without the Sunpapers, Mencken was also frustrated by his enforced silence on the subject of the war. From 1917 until late 1919 he had to "mark time," he later wrote. "For the first and last time in my life, I suffered from a feeling of bafflement." Not only could he not write on the war (his only contribution being a purely factual article, "Ludendorff," in the *Atlantic Monthly* in 1917), but an amendment to the Espionage Act seemed for a time to make "*all* discussion of American culture impossible." Thus a series of books he had outlined in a letter to Boyd in 1916, writing that was to have engaged him for the following five or six years, had to be largely put aside. In particular, he had to delay his "short history of the American effort to maintain neutrality in the war," as well as books on democracy and war in general and a "detailed account of events that these eyes witnessed."

He turned increasingly to satire, parody, and other lighter work, as well as the literary criticism he continued to produce for *The Smart Set*. Much of the lighter work appeared in the New York *Evening Mail*, for which he began in the spring of 1917 to write a thrice-weekly column. Here Mencken wrote about a number of subjects, including Prohibition, women, food, and language, and produced two of his most famous newspaper pieces. "The Sahara of the Bozart" (here in its early and shorter version) was his lament for the fallen American South, and "A Neglected Anniversary" his mock-serious history of the bathtub. In the former piece, in some of his most memorable prose, he suggested that the late Confederacy, once "a civilization of manifold excellences," had now become a desert of the beaux arts, barren and hopeless:

> That vast region south of the Potomac is as large as Europe. . . . And yet it is as sterile, artistically, intellectually, culturally, as the Sahara Desert. It would be difficult in all history to match so amazing a drying-up of civilization. . . .
>
> In all that gargantuan empire there is not a single picture gallery worth going into, nor a single orchestra capable of playing a Beethoven symphony, nor a single opera house. . . . When you come to composers, historians, critics, scientists, painters, sculptors and architects, you will have to give it up, for there is not one between Alexandria and the gulf.

In "A Neglected Anniversary" he made the claim, repeated to this day, that the first American bathtub had been installed in 1842 and that Millard Fillmore had placed the first bathtub in the White House in 1850:

> On December 20 there flitted past us, absolutely without public notice, one of the most important profane anniversaries in American history—to wit: the seventy-fifth anniversary of the introduction of the bathtub into these states. Not a plumber fired a salute or hung out a flag. Not a governor proclaimed a day of prayer. Not a newspaper called attention to the day.

His bathtub hoax, he must have thought, was no less true than the accounts of the war reaching the American people in 1917. In believing the one they were no more gullible than in believing the other.

Not all of his writing for the *Evening Mail* was satirical. In "Mark Twain's Americanism" he wrote his most perceptive essay yet on Samuel Clemens, focusing on the nihilistic posthumous works, *The Mysterious Stranger* and *What Is Man?:* "For Mark Twain dead is beginning to show far different . . . colors than those he seemed to wear during life, and the one thing no sane critic would say of him to-day is that he was the harmless fireside jester, the mellow chautauquan, the amiable old grandpa of letters that he was once so widely thought to be." In this piece the thirty-seven-year-old Mencken not only discussed his favorite American novelist but also penned what could have been, later in the century, his own lengthy epitaph:

> He was a destructive satirist of the utmost pungency and relentlessness, and the most bitter critic of American platitude and delusion, whether social, political or religious, that ever lived. . . . Bit by bit as his posthumous books appear, the true man emerges. . . . He put into them, without concealment, the fundamental ideas of his personal philosophy—the ideas which colored his whole view of the world. Then he laid the manuscripts away, safe in the knowledge that they would not see the light until he was under six feet of earth.

The primary difference is that Mencken was determined, in his own case, that much of the "true man" appear before posthumous works came to light, that the truth-telling iconoclast not be concealed until death—or even until the end of hostilities in Europe.

In his writing for the *Evening Mail* he did not escape the war altogether. Occasionally he could not resist writing a piece such as

"Why Free Speech Is Impossible During War"—a column that, however moderate, was suppressed by the newspaper. And his connection to the *Mail*, however tenuous, brought the war home when, in 1918, the pro-German publisher of the newspaper, Edward A. Rumely, was harassed by spy hunters, arrested, and forced to relinquish control to a pro-English group. To his new bosses Mencken was suspect as well. His contract was canceled, and although he threatened a lawsuit—and received some financial compensation—he was not unhappy to end the relationship. He had made more than $2,100 from his columns and had had a good deal of fun besides.

He also tried his hand as a playwright during this enforced vacation from more serious work. As far back as 1908 or 1909 he had worked on various plays, including "The Artist," a one-act drama that he later called "my satirical fling at the artiness hanging over from the '90s." Although he did not take the play seriously, he had been delighted when little theaters in Philadelphia and Baltimore, among other cities, had produced it in 1916. He had attended rehearsals and noted the favorable reviews. In 1918 and 1919 he and Nathan collaborated on several plays, including an English version of Ludwig Thoma's *Moral* for which he did nearly all the writing. In *Morals: A Satiric Comedy in Three Acts*, he took great liberties with Thoma's original script: he portrayed a European antivice crusader—host to an American crusader—who is greatly embarrassed when his name appears on a list of clients taken by police from a raid on a bawdy house. A study in hypocrisy and a well-crafted work with a keen sense of humor and timing, the play was never produced in the United States because of anti-German sentiment.

Mencken followed *Morals* with *Heliogabalus*, a three-act burlesque set in A.D. 221 in the court of "Heliogabalus, Emperor of Rome." Conceived as a joke by Mencken and Nathan as they sat in Rogers restaurant in New York and written by Mencken in four or five weeks, the farce depicted an emperor smitten by a beautiful Christian maiden whom he marries and then discards. Although the play was first rejected by potential producers who feared it would be judged obscene, Knopf published it in a limited edition that quickly sold out. One reader, Marion Bloom, took special note. *Heliogabalus*, she wrote a friend thirty-five years later, was "about my apostasy" and was written "to publicize my defection from the 'true worship' of HLM." With her turn toward Christian Science, she "brought him shame and ridicule" and *Heliogabalus* "was his way of showing me up."

That Mencken intended *Heliogabalus* primarily as a commentary on his relationship with Marion is doubtful. There can be no doubt, however, that he had Marion and himself in mind in the social comedy "The Goat," which he undertook next. In the scenario of the uncompleted play, he described a well-off bachelor, sociable, worldly, and exactly his own age (thirty-nine), who thinks he understands women. "A sentimentalist at heart" who "has escaped marriage by various acts of God," he has a younger girlfriend with six months' training in first aid during the war who is out "to land" him. He has proposed to her, but all the while he is flirting with other women. The man is obviously based on Mencken, the woman on Marion, but the play takes a twist that suggests the playwright had a greater talent for self-criticism than Marion realized. The bachelor, Lorimer, is exposed, his treatment of the woman is roundly condemned, and he winds up as the goat, the victim.

Mencken had collected several of his earlier short plays, including "The Artist," in *A Book of Burlesques*, a miscellany of drama, essays, and sketches published in 1916. Several reviewers, rather generously, had seen Mencken in the tradition of Swift, Thackeray, and Shaw, although in fact the book was far from his best work. He also produced several other light works during the war years. *A Little Book in C Major* (1916), a collection of witty epigrams on women, religion, and public life, was a failure commercially, as *A Book of Burlesques* had been. Among its offerings, few as clever as Mencken thought, were:

Love is the delusion that one woman differs from another.

Democracy is the theory that the common people know what they want, and deserve to get it good and hard.

Marriage: the end of hope.

Wife: a former sweetheart.

*Pistols for Two* (1917), published by Knopf, was a humorous, often ridiculous short biography of himself and Nathan, written by the two men under their favorite pseudonym, Owen Hatteras.

The next year Mencken let Phil Goodman publish a collection of his short essays, entitled *Damn! A Book of Calumny*. Again, sales were poor, despite Goodman's idea for drugstore sales and advertising through the mail, but reviews were plentiful. Although the tone of the book was essentially light, the author received a great deal of negative comment for his mild criticism of American institutions and his remarks on religion: "Granting the existence of God, a house dedicated to Him naturally follows. . . . But why praise and flatter him for his unspeakable cruelties?" "The terrible child of American literature," he was labeled in a New York *Sun* article entitled "H. L. Mencken and the Second Fall of Man." He was becoming a "veritable cult," Mencken's erstwhile employer, the *Evening Sun*, concluded. "His tribe is . . . rapidly increasing."

At the same time as he was producing slight and eminently forgettable books, Mencken longed to undertake more serious work. If he could not write about the war, he concluded, he could at least attempt to write seriously about the underlying American culture he believed responsible for America's role in the war. "All my work hangs together, once the main ideas under it are discerned," he once wrote, and nowhere is that truth better illustrated than in his several interests just before and during World War I. His crusades against Anglo-Saxons, democracy, Prohibition, religious fundamentalism, vice squads, censorship, and cant and sentimentality in American letters were all related to his growing distaste for, and then his outright abhorrence of, England. Such was also the case with his attacks on the American South, the stronghold of those who called themselves "pure Anglo-Saxons"—but, as Mencken pointed out, were more often Celts. The late Confederacy was the repository in twentieth-century America of what he believed to be the worst elements of the English cultural tradition. In particular, he believed the South had succeeded New England as the home of Puritanism in the Western Hemisphere.

Puritanism, indeed, now became the inclusive term, bringing together nearly all of Mencken's antipathies. He did not precisely understand the seventeenth-century Puritanism of the Massachusetts Bay; in particular, he underestimated its intellectual rigor and psychological complexity, confusing it on the one hand with genteel Victorianism and, on the other, with raw southern Calvinism. But in the period during and following the war he made "Puritanism" famous in a manner no American had for two centuries, redefining that term for twentieth-century Americans: it was "the haunting fear that someone, somewhere, may be happy."

He had hated Puritanism, to be sure, long before he had hated the England from which it came; it represented, quite simply, the antithesis of the *gemütlichkeit* he had long believed the basis of a civilized life. As a twenty-one-year-old newspaperman, he had burlesqued Puritanism through the story of "J. Bozzo Puritani" in the Baltimore *Morning Herald*. He had attacked it in editorials and columns of the Baltimore *Sun* in 1911 and 1912, in letters to Willard Huntington Wright in 1913, in "The Free Lance" of 1913 and 1914, in *Evening Sun* editorials of 1915, and in *The Smart Set* during all those years. At times he was good-natured in his remarks. "England gave us Puritanism," he had written in 1914; "Germany gave us Pilsner." But at other times he spoke with a nearly evangelical zeal. "My whole life, once I get free from my present engagements," he had written Dreiser in 1916, "will be devoted to combatting Puritanism."

Mencken acknowledged in himself a touch of what he identified as Puritanism—"In my case it takes the form of a dislike for smutty pictures," he wrote Fielding Garrison—but he could not abide it in others. He was constantly reminded of its sway in Baltimore in the person of Dr. Howard Kelly, the eminent Johns Hopkins physician and leading Baltimore moralist who was in frequent touch with him. On one occasion Kelly had invited him to meet his archenemy Anthony Comstock, the most famous of American censors and antivice crusaders.

More important, he was reminded of Puritanism in the person of Woodrow Wilson, the man who in the war years came to represent everything he detested. Wilson was an Anglo-Saxon and an English sympathizer, a rigid Christian, a southerner, a prohibitionist, an academic, and a moralist given to lofty sentiments and grand abstractions. To Mencken, he even *looked* the part of the Puritan. If in 1912 he had been not altogether unsympathetic to Wilson—and, after that, remained a friend of his sister-in-law Bertha Bolling, who was an occasional contributor to *The Smart Set*—he came to abhor Wilson as he would no other figure save Franklin D. Roosevelt. By mid-1914 he had begun to attack Wilson's "tendency to apply the concepts and principles of an outworn Puritanism to the daily business of a virile and ambitious nation." But he did not turn his full fury against Wilson until the war was well under way, the American policy of neutrality seemed a sham, and German Americans were under siege:

> The Germans among us, in those first soul-wracking days [of the war] needed a friend who stood above the tumult. They faced a mob aroused to intolerable fury, their every effort to defend themselves was denounced as treason and worse. Ah, that a genuinely first-rate man had been in the White House, with a first-rate man's sense of justice and a first-rate man's courage.

For that failing, in particular, Mencken would never forgive Wilson.

All the while, in the *Evening Mail* and *The Smart Set*, that Mencken was blasting Wilson and the Puritans, the South, and the Genteel Tradition, he was also working on a series of books treating those subjects, although he was not sure how much he could publish while the war continued. For a time he turned to a book to be entitled *The American*, a critical look at the American character that drew on the six essays on the subject he had published in *The Smart Set* in 1913 and 1914. The book, he had explained, would be "full of studied insult and may conceivably help me along." He also considered for publication after the war a study of the politically repressive climate in the United States during the war years. "The Anglo-Saxon Under the Terror," he called it in letters to Dreiser. In many respects this proclaimed enemy of crusaders had become a crusader himself. As he wrote in his memoirs, he realized he had attained a "following" among the younger critics: "I led them in a battle against false gods and false values."

The books on the American and the war were never completed, at least not in the form Mencken first intended them. But he did produce three other books of great importance during the war years, the first of which, *A Book of Prefaces*, Mencken later called "[my] most important book in its effects upon my professional career." Begun as a work that would set forth his "objections to the whole Puritan *Kultur* in a large and positive way," *Prefaces* itself was nearly a casualty of the war. Most of it had been written by early

1917, but when the United States declared war in April and the Espionage Act was passed, Mencken was forced to make a great many changes. Even at that, Knopf was concerned about publishing the book.

*A Book of Prefaces* included lengthy essays on Dreiser, Huneker, and Conrad, but the most bellicose section was an eighty-five-page discussion entitled "Puritanism as a Literary Force." This essay Mencken later called, with some justification, "the most headlong and uncompromising attack upon the American *Kultur* ever made up to that time." In it he challenged the "intolerable prudishness and dirty-mindedness of Puritanism" and set out to show how numerous American writers, including William Dean Howells, Henry James, and Mark Twain, had been victims of the Puritan spirit:

> The literature of the nation, even the literature of the enlightened minority, has been under harsh Puritan restraints from the beginning, and despite a few stealthy efforts at revolt . . . it shows not the slightest sign of emancipating itself today. . . .
>
> The Puritan's utter lack of aesthetic sense, his distrust of all romantic emotion, his unmatchable intolerance of opposition, his unbreakable belief in his own bleak and narrow views, his savage cruelty of attack, his lust for relentless and barbarous persecution—these things have put an almost unbearable burden upon the exchange of ideas in the United States.

He spoke of an American prejudice against beauty, of the Puritan's "moral obsession," and the "militant . . . new Puritanism" in the censorship of Anthony Comstock and his associates.

Mencken's book was certain to bring objections from those guardians of the American way already incensed by his pro-German sentiments, and it did. Not all of the reviews were negative. Burton Rascoe, in the *Chicago Tribune*, praised *Prefaces* lavishly and at length. Randolph Bourne, in *The New Republic*, recognized the power of the work, although he was far from completely favorable. Bourne believed, with reason, that Mencken was a "moralist contra moralism" and had overstated his case. Certain other reviews were downright hostile. The Los Angeles *Continent* called the author "the most dangerous man in America today, intellectually considered."

But the most forceful and most eloquent opposition to *A Book of*

*Prefaces* came from Stuart Sherman, professor of English at the University of Illinois and a scholar whom Mencken had attacked in the *Prefaces* itself. In fact, he had been engaged in an ongoing debate with Sherman since 1915, when the professor had denounced Dreiser in a widely publicized essay in *The Nation*. Sherman's piece, Mencken had written Dreiser, was "a masterly exposure of what is going on within the Puritan mind, and particularly of its maniacal fear of the German." He had vowed revenge on Sherman and other "degraded swine," and he had a measure of that revenge in *A Book of Prefaces*, although in words less harsh than Sherman might have expected. In his essay on Dreiser, Mencken ridiculed Sherman's "pompous syllogisms" and charged that what offended the professor was not Dreiser's art but his "shortcoming as a Christian and an American." Sherman was—what Randolph Bourne had said of Mencken, what even Dreiser and Marion had said of Mencken—"the moralist."

It was not surprising that Sherman struck back. He loved combat nearly as much as Mencken did, and his own vigorous style made him a worthy adversary. His review in *The Nation*, entitled "Beautifying American Letters," was belligerently sarcastic, focusing on Mencken's preference for European over American culture, particularly his pro-German sympathies. It was one of several Sherman attacks in the two or three years that followed. His essay "Mr. H. L. Mencken and the Jeune Fille" in *The New York Times Book Review* decried what Sherman believed was a tendency of the new reader to ignore classical American writing and to find inspiration only in continental European literature and the new American immoralists such as Mencken and Dreiser. Mencken "leaps from the saddle with sabre flashing," Sherman wrote, "stables his horse in the church, shoots the priest, hangs three professors, exiles the Academy, burns the library and the university, and amid smoking ashes, erects a new school of criticism on modern German principles."

Mencken did not mind such sparring in principle, but what he was never to forgive in Sherman—even when his adversary revised his position in the early and mid-1920s and wanted to make peace—was that during the war Sherman had played to the war hysteria. He had based his indictment of Dreiser and of Mencken himself on the fact that they were German American. When in the 1920s Mencken's friends Carl and Irita Van Doren tried to bring them together,

Mencken declined. When once they found themselves at the same dinner party and Sherman wanted to shake hands, he refused. He "seemed to me a swine," Mencken wrote Ernest Boyd, and he told the Van Dorens, "I'd prefer to pass into Heaven without having enjoyed the honor of Sherman's acquaintance." As always, he did not easily forget or forgive.

His battle with Sherman had the effect of reinforcing his long-standing animosity toward "professor doktors," particularly professors of literature. Men like Sherman—a "hayseed from Iowa," Mencken charged, albeit one educated at Williams College and Harvard—as well as Paul Elmer More of Princeton and Irving Babbitt of Harvard were indeed the guardians of that Genteel Tradition he was trying to destroy, the moralists who met the barbarians at the gate. He did not hold toward More and Babbitt the personal enmity he felt toward Sherman, but he believed they and others of the "New Humanists" were equally misguided. What they missed in their study of literature, he insisted, was *life:* while he had been roaming the Baltimore waterfront in his teens and twenties, their world had been limited by the boundaries of the university. They were the academic wing of Puritanism in American life, Mencken believed, focusing on the past, refusing to allow new growth and disparate views. "The curse of criticism in America," he wrote in *The Smart Set*, was "the infernal babbling of the third-rate college professor . . ." *A Book of Prefaces* was particularly gratifying because "it shook the professors as they had never been shaken before."

The *Prefaces*, then, was a deeply satisfying work to Mencken, but even more satisfying in immediately personal ways was the book he next began. Most of the research for *In Defense of Women* (1918) was conducted not in libraries but in saloons and restaurants with Marion and Estelle Bloom and in bedrooms with Marion and with Mencken's New York confidante, the harlot Kay Laurell. It was a book for which he had been preparing for some time. Much of the material in his several plays and in *A Book of Burlesques*, as well as in his "Free Lance" and *Smart Set* columns, had dealt with male-female relations, with desire and obligation, courtship and marriage. As usual, he had drawn a mixed reception to his newspaper and magazine pieces. Depending on the position of the reader, he was either a great defender of women's rights or, as a critic labeled him in 1916, "the greatest misogynist since Schopenhauer," "the country's high-priest of woman-haters."

As early as 1916 Mencken had written Ernest Boyd that he was contemplating "A Book for Men Only," a "critical consideration of la femme. Aphoristic, scandalous." When he got down to serious work on *In Defense of Women* in February 1918, he first entitled it "The Eternal Feminine." Recognizing that such a title suggested a mythic, even anthropological approach he did not intend to take, he also considered "The Infernal Feminine," then settled on the ironic "In Defense of Women."

He certainly intended his book to be ironic, and for the most part it was. But the matter was more complicated than that. For in certain ways that Mencken himself did not completely understand—since he had long decried the feminization of American culture, had embraced a code of masculinity and denied any "feminine" qualities in himself—he had a far greater sympathy, even identification, with women than he fully knew. He recognized the deep care and respect he had for his mother, a love so strong that he could not move from Baltimore. He recognized, too, the vast sympathy he had for the plight of certain individual women, whether fictional characters such as Dreiser's Carrie Meeber and Jennie Gerhardt (two of the most compelling characters he found in all fiction) or flesh-and-blood women such as Estelle Bloom and (even if he contributed to her plight) Marion. He was also a supporter of women's political rights, of suffrage, even if he often ridiculed the suffragette.

This much Mencken knew about himself. But what he did not seem to recognize fully was the extent to which his own point of view—the way he saw the world—had a great deal in common with what he defined as the woman's point of view. Women were superior to men, he wrote in *Defense*, intending to be ironic, but he was less ironic than he knew. For the qualities he assigned women in *Defense* were precisely those qualities he himself had always championed, defended, and, to a great extent, embodied. He had long prided himself on being a realist, one who saw clearly, who had no illusions about religion, love, or brotherhood. Women, he announced in *In Defense of Women*, were "the supreme realists of the race," creatures of common sense, hardheaded skeptics, and clever manipulators who refused to be duped—as opposed to most men, who were incurable romantics and sentimentalists. Mencken favored women's suffrage because woman "out of her greater instinct for reality . . . will make democracy safe for a democracy." And he believed women possessed (as he himself possessed) a detached and thus superior view of the mass of men. A woman, he wrote, must "always regard" a man "secretly as an ass." Or, as he had written Marion Bloom in 1915, "A man must always seem more or less childish and ridiculous to a woman."

To this extent, *In Defense of Women* was not ironic at all, as Mencken claimed it would be. It was as if he had begun his book with the understanding that such a defender of masculinity as he had previously announced himself to be *should* be ironic in his "defense" of women—but as he proceeded found a greater sympathy than he had intended. As a bachelor, he concluded, he possessed a "relative freedom from the ordinary sentimentalism of his sex"—that is, he possessed the clear-sighted vision he associated with women. He was not exaggerating when he spoke of what he considered to be the greater intelligence of women. In private he had occasionally remarked on men who occupied positions of power and influence but whose wives were infinitely smarter and shrewder. "Women in general seem to me to be appreciably more intelligent than men," he was to write in his diary. "A great many of them suffer in silence from the imbecilities of their husbands."

All this was true, Mencken maintained, and yet, if we read closely, we find that in ways he hardly intended his book was indeed an indictment of women. A woman's penchant for "realism," as he defined it, could also be taken for small-mindedness, pettiness, an inability to conceptualize on the grand scale. As Vincent Fitzpatrick has observed, as a determinist and Social Darwinist, Mencken *saw* that men were physically stronger: it was evident—or appeared to be—that women should not take charge. In this respect, Mencken's private correspondence is more revealing than *In Defense of Women*. In his letters women are assumed to belong on the periphery. "I am utterly against executive jobs for women," he had written Willard Wright in 1913, "either on magazines or newspapers." "A woman with a masculinized mentality," he wrote Estelle Bloom somewhat later, "must perforce be hard on the eyes." In the world beyond the workplace women were equally peripheral. "I have discovered that it is possible to get enjoyment out of women, alcohol and ideas," he maintained long after *In Defense of Women* appeared. "I get little enjoyment out of women, more out of alcohol and most out of ideas." Thus, as he wrote Dreiser on one occasion, "I am strongly against taking the fair ones on booze parties." Or, as he was to write another friend, "Let's have a session without any women to disturb us. There are so many things to talk of I'd begrudge the attention they demand."

Mencken would hardly have gone so far as his mentor Nietzsche— "Let woman be a toy, pure and delicate as a jewel. . . . Thou goest to women? *Forget not thy whip!*" But it is clear that a primary role of women, as he saw it, was to be attentive to men. As he was to write Sinclair Lewis: "I like women who appreciate their men. We bucks do a great deal for them. We defend them, support them, soothe their frenzies, and even admire them. I think they deserve that admiration—but not when they try to make slaves of men who are their betters. In any combat between superior and inferior I am for No. 1."

Allowing for Mencken's penchant for overstatement, he was indeed stating the situation as he saw it. As he was to write in a later edition of *In Defense of Women,* "Nine men out of ten would be quite happy, I believe, if there were no women in the world." Or, as he would write a female friend, "What men esteem most in women is a common politeness, and by common politeness, of course, they mean the highest degree of conceivable deference."

In his 1918 edition of *In Defense of Women* Mencken hardly addressed the matter of sex, a result partly of a wary eye on the censors but even more a result of his own belief that—as he later put it—"the lives of normal men are [not] much colored or conditioned, either directly or indirectly, by purely sexual considerations." He was representing his own view certainly, at least after his mid-twenties. It was not, as we have seen, that he had no interest in sex or did not enjoy it. He appears to have had a satisfactory sexual relationship with Marion (at least when he could find what he considered to be an appropriate time and place), and he may in fact, as Nathan maintained, have slept with several *Smart Set* contributors. He also had, as we have seen, a certain fascination with Dreiser's sexual adventures as well as the erotic tales of Kay Laurell—although we should probably take this fascination as more an example of Mencken's interest in the desires and strivings of the human animal than any great interest in erotica.

Indeed, in the total picture sex *was* relatively unimportant to Mencken. As one of his primary physicians maintained long after his death, he simply did not seem to have had "a particularly strong sex drive." "If I take a gal to bed," he himself wrote Estelle Bloom, "it is chiefly out of politeness. My thoughts are far more often on beer brewing and the things of the soul." As always, we cannot take Mencken altogether seriously—and we must allow for the fact that he might have been defending himself against Marion's charge that he was "wenching" in Manhattan—but as always there is more than a germ of truth in what he says. Similarly, his single description of the female body in *Defense,* though intended largely in fun, was nonetheless guaranteed to extinguish any sexual desire in the male reader: "even at its best . . . very defective in form; it has harsh curves and very clumsily distributed masses; compared to it the average milk-jug, or even the average cuspidor, is a thing of intelligent and gratifying design . . ."

Mencken believed, as he wrote Marion, that Freud "overestimate[d] sex," and he expressed the same opinion in numerous other places. Once or twice, in *The Smart Set,* he had expressed admiration for Freud's early work, but increasingly he was coming to reject Freud and his "sex flubdub" and was moving toward his later position that Freud was "nine-tenths quack," "the worst mountebank heard of in the world for a generation." But if he rejected Freud and the Freudians, he had long embraced the Englishman Havelock Ellis and his multivolume *Studies in the Psychology of Sex.*

In any case, it was more than prudery that led Mencken to object to overly clinical discussions of sex. The realist in other matters, when it came to relations between men and women, at least tender relations, he was largely the romantic. We read in the famous conclusion of *In Defense of Women* his depiction of the ideal situation involving a man and a woman:

It is the close of a busy and vexatious day—say half past five or six o'clock of a winter afternoon. I have had a cocktail or two, and am stretched out on a divan in front of a fire, smoking. At the edge of the divan, close enough for me to reach her with my hands, sits a woman not too young, but still good-looking and well-dressed—above all, a woman with a soft, low-pitched, agreeable voice. As I snooze she talks—of anything, everything, all the things that women talk of: books, music, the play, men, other women. No politics. No business. No religion. No metaphysics. Nothing challenging and vexatious—but remember, she is intelligent; what she says is clearly expressed. . . . I observe the fine sheen of her hair, the pretty cut of her frock, the glint of her white teeth, the arch of her eye-brow, the graceful curve of her arm. I listen to the exquisite murmur of her voice. Gradually I fall asleep—but only for an instant. . . . Then to sleep again—slowly and charmingly down that slippery hill of dreams. And then awake again, and then asleep again, and so on.

I ask you seriously: could anything be more unutterly beautiful?

Mencken's self-indulgent fantasy is significant for several reasons. First, sexual desire is altogether missing from the picture, at least in any overt way. What Mencken prefers in his ideal woman is not sensuality but rather cultivation, refinement, and charm. Her role is to offer contentment, not excitement. She is calming and soothing, not necessarily maternal but nonetheless comforting. She is indeed a creature whose function is to please her man—an appealing accessory, along with the cocktail and the fire. Mencken does not want her to speak of politics, business, metaphysics, or anything "challenging and vexatious." But, he reminds us, she is intelligent: she could perhaps speak of these matters if he wanted, but he prefers that she not.

And she is not Marion Bloom. Marion always thought she was—thought, having lost everything else, that she at least had that—and others have so identified her as well. But, Mencken revealed in his memoirs, his idealized woman was in fact an unnamed "half-Jewish lady who had been a successful actress and was later to have a brief time of glory as a movie star." Marion was destined to forgo even that bit of immortality.

Reviewers in 1918, in fact, did not have that "unutterly beautiful" scene to consider: it was added to the 1922 edition of *In Defense of Women*, published by Knopf. But they did have much more to weigh. Some women offered counterblasts, others were simply puzzled over what the author meant. But curiously, as Mencken himself later noted, most of the women reviewers took "my mock praises of their sex seriously." Most reviews appeared just before the advent of women's suffrage in 1920, and that timing caused the tone of many of the reviews to be anticipatory and celebratory. The advent of suffrage, as well as poor distribution and sales of the original edition by Goodman, was the reason Mencken felt a revised edition of the book was necessary. As the first edition appeared, he continued to ponder the subject in *The Smart Set:*

> The allurement that [women] hold out to men is precisely the allurement that Cape Hatteras holds out to sailors—they are enormously dangerous and hence enormously fascinating. To the average man, doomed to some banal and sordid drudgery all his life long, they offer the only grand hazard that he ever encounters. Take them away and his existence would be as flat and secure as that of a milch-cow.

Much as he would have liked to put out a new edition, however, he had no time for such a revision in early 1919. By that point he was wrapping up the third of his major books of the war years, a very different sort of work and one in which he was prepared to challenge the professors on their own grounds.

*The American Language* (1919) was the nearest thing to a scholarly work Mencken ever produced, one in which he proved to be as thorough and as painstaking as those Ph.D.s who were his usual adversaries. Like most of his other work during the war, it was the product of many years of observation and note taking. His fascination with American speech, he later wrote a friend, may have had its origins in the early boyhood trips with his father to Washington saloons, where he was charmed by "the argot of the colored waiters" and "a great deal [more] of philological interest." It may also have had roots in his love for the novels of Mark Twain and his early days as a reporter on the Baltimore streets.

In any case, by age twenty-one, in his Baltimore *Morning Herald* column for 1902, Mencken had already remarked on the language of vaudeville, the racetrack, and popular songs—"the queer words which go into the making of 'United Statese.'" By the end of 1910 he had written several *Evening Sun* columns on American speech, including a lengthy discussion, "The Two Englishes," in which he had seconded linguist Brander Matthews's contention that "the English people speak an English which differs enormously, in vocabulary and idiom, from the English spoken by Americans." That same month, October 1910, he had asked, "Why doesn't some painstaking pundit attempt a grammar of the American language . . . English, that is, as spoken by the great masses of the plain people of this fair land?"

He had asked the same question other times over the next few years, but it apparently had not occurred to him until sometime during the war years that he himself was the pundit to undertake the work. The idea may have come to him then for two reasons. Obviously he could not write on politics and international affairs. But also, during a period in which he was inveighing against an exclusively British cultural tradition, was insisting that writers other than British writers should capture the attention of American readers, it might be expected that he would question the supremacy of an exclusively *British* English language. As far back as 1908—a time when he was still, in some measure, an Anglophile—he had been made aware that his own English was not acceptable on the other side of the Atlantic. Reviewers in the London *Standard*, the Edinburgh *Scotsman*, and *Athenaeum* had denounced the "Americanisms" in his Nietzsche book.

Since no one else seemed willing and able, Mencken himself would become the champion of the American language, and such he would remain to the end of his days. As much as he would have deplored seeing himself in the tradition of certain revered New Englanders who championed American English, he was indeed their unlikely and unintentional successor. Like Noah Webster, who had produced his dictionary as a protest against English domination of the American language—or Emerson, who had urged Americans to find their own voices—Mencken would assume his role as definer and defender of the people's English.

Certainly he had no such lofty goals in mind when, in late 1917 and early 1918, he began considering a book on American usage, nor even in the spring of 1918, when he was hard at work on it. In fact, he was very modest in his original aims. "I am . . . neither teacher, nor prophet, nor reformer," he announced in his introduction, but "merely inquirer," one who attempted to "make a first sketch of the living speech of These States." In the 374-page study that resulted he discussed the beginnings of "American," its growth in the eighteenth and nineteenth centuries, and its considerable differences in pronunciation, spelling, and usage from twentieth-century British English. He was particularly interested in American names and slang. Throughout he was the scholar, carefully recording and observing, but he was also, in his manner, the partisan. American English, he maintained, was more colorful, more vivid, more creative and flexible than its counterpart in Great Britain. And the United States, in the twentieth century, was far more than a cultural colony of England.

The enthusiastic response to the first edition of *The American Language* somewhat surprised Mencken. Published in March 1919 by Knopf, it had sold nearly 1,400 copies by June—high by his previous standards—and it continued to sell; it became the first of his books to earn him more than $500 in royalties. Reviews in *The New York Times*, the New York *Tribune, The New Republic,* and other leading newspapers and magazines were overwhelmingly positive. Not only did journalistic reviewers praise Mencken, one calling him "the Christopher Columbus of Americanese," but most professors, including Brander Matthews, embraced him as well. Among the few dissenters were the *Atlantic Monthly,* which saw Mencken as something of a smart aleck, and Stuart Sherman. In his introduction to the book Mencken had anticipated Sherman's objections. "Certain American pedants," he had predicted, would argue that "to examine and exhibit the constantly growing difference between English and American" constituted an "anti-social act." Sherman rose to the occasion. *The American Language,* he maintained, was "designed as a wedge to split asunder the two great English-speaking peoples."

By the time he saw the publication of *The American Language,* Mencken had come to recognize that World War I, as far as his professional career was concerned, had been a boon, not a hindrance. Since he had found it impossible to write as much or as openly as he would have liked in newspapers and magazines, he had been forced to think of himself principally as an author of books—and books on subjects other than politics and public affairs. Even more important, as he observed in autobiographical notes and in letters to friends, the treatment to which he and other German Americans had been subjected during the war had set him "free": after having come under the suspicion of federal agents, informers, and censors, he was "purged of the last remaining vestiges of patriotic feeling." As he wrote Fielding Garrison (still not realizing the extent to which Garrison had been, in at least one instance, one of those informers), "The ensuing festivities filled me with new ideas, greatly changed my aims, and flooded me with such an amount of material that I'll never be able to use a tenth of it." It was Mencken's belief, dubious as it might have been, that he had been "going down hill" from 1914 to 1916, and that the events of 1917, 1918, and 1919 created a large audience that he otherwise would not have had: "I came in on the full tide of reaction against the war . . . and I had the advantage of not needing to establish my character. . . . In other words, I had the floor." He came out of the war with "a certain sureness and a desire for revenge."

The year 1919, then, proved to be a pivotal one for Mencken, the worst of times, professionally speaking, being transformed into the best. He was full of ideas, of energy, and he had a rage to explain. As soon as *The American Language*—and a translation the same year of Nietzsche's *Der Antichrist*—were out of the way, he contemplated just which of his many projects he might turn to next. He was eager to get to work on "a history of the American share in World War I," which would be largely a history of American spy-hunting, profiteering, and "patrioteering," and the role such institutions as newspapers, universities, and churches had played in these activities. He planned to recruit "a committee of like-minded persons," and, perhaps recalling the example of old Johann Burkhard Mencke and his magnum opus of 6,381 pages, he conceived the work on a grand scale. It would run "25 or 30 volumes, and perhaps more." Again, Mencken's luck held: the project fell through because of a lack of funding, and he could turn to more fruitful pursuits. In January and February 1919 he wrote Ernest Boyd and Dreiser that he had begun work on a book to be called "The National Letters" with another book, "On Democracy," to follow. By mid-February he was writing Dreiser about still another book: "a slaughterhouse. Absolutely no guilty man will escape."

The "slaughterhouse" was to become the first of Mencken's six volumes of *Prejudices*, a work he had envisioned in some form as early as 1916. The idea of such a series had not really taken shape, however, until a bookseller in Cleveland had proposed it to Knopf. Although both he and Knopf were skeptical, Mencken plunged into the writing. He reshaped a great deal of old *Smart Set* material, and by July he had finished. He had inserted "some rat-poison," he wrote Boyd, "in order to put an end to this new respectability" occasioned by the favorable academic reviews of *The American Language.* The rat poison took the form of attacks on H. G. Wells, Hamlin Garland, Thorstein Veblen, and William Dean Howells, among others.

On Veblen and Howells he was particularly rough. Veblen, whose *Theory of the Leisure Class* (1899) still exerted great influence, was "head Great Thinker to the parlor radicals," he charged, "Socrates of the intellectual Greenwich Village, chief star (at least transiently) of the American *Athenaeums.*" As for Howells, Mencken conceded that the former "dean of American Letters"—and still, at age eighty-two, a revered figure—was a fine prose stylist. But as a novelist he was

> a first-rate journeyman, a contriver of pretty things . . . [the author of] a long row of uninspired and hollow books, with no more ideas in them than so many volumes of the *Ladies Home Journal,* and no more deep and contagious feeling than so many reports of autopsies, and no more glow and gusto than so many tables of bond prices. The profound dread and agony of life, the surge of passion and aspiration, the grand crash and glitter of things, the tragedy that runs eternally under the surface—all this the critic of the future will seek in vain in Dr. Howells' elegant and shallow volumes. . . .
>
> The truth about Howells is that he really has nothing to say, for all the charm he gets into saying it. . . . He could no more have written the last chapters of "Lord Jim" than he could have written the Book of Mark.

In his *Prejudices* Mencken also took aim at the "New Poetry Movement"—particularly Amy Lowell ("the schoolmarm of the movement") and to a lesser degree Edgar Lee Masters ("for a short season, the undisputed Homer of the movement") and Robert Frost ("Whittier without the whiskers"). He trained his guns as well on professors ("an indistinct herd of intellectual eunuchs"), on the science of psychology, the sexual preoccupation of the Freudians, and the "literature of sex-hygiene"—to which he objected, he insisted, not "on moral grounds but on aesthetic grounds." Finally he turned against his old idol, George Bernard Shaw, whom he now saw as a Puritan, a moralist—"the Ulster Polonius."

In fact, *Prejudices, First Series,* taken in its entirety, was not as "rough" or as "cruel" as Mencken had written Fielding Garrison it would be. When the book appeared in the fall of 1919, the reviews were favorable enough, except for Sherman's in *The New York Times.* But this first volume of *Prejudices* was more important for what it anticipated than what it contained; the history of this remarkable series belongs more properly to the 1920s.

As the end of the 1910s approached, Mencken was confronted with an abundance of feelings about himself, his future, and the postwar world. On one hand, he was deeply pessimistic. Focusing on the "Hun-hating" and general xenophobia around him, he wrote Boyd in September 1919, "I see nothing ahead save race war to the death. In ten years every man in the world will hate every other man." Now that the war was over he was faced with a new enemy—Prohibition—which, if we are to judge by his remarks to friends, seemed every bit as ominous for civilization as the war itself. "The full force of Prohibition now oppresses me," he wrote Boyd in December. "It is indescribably damnable." The advent of Prohibition and the deaths of three Saturday Night Club members would do what the war could not, he wrote Boyd: the club "will probably pass out of existence within six weeks." As was often the case, Mencken was needlessly pessimistic: the club was to last another thirty years, surviving yet another war between England and Germany.

For a time, in 1919, Mencken at least mildly considered leaving the United States. As far back as 1914 he had mentioned to Dreiser, half in jest, that he would like to "spend my declining years in a civilized country." He seemed more serious when he wrote Dreiser in February 1919 that his scheme was "to move to Munich as soon as I can shake off my obligations" and when he later remarked, "The future of both of us, I think, lies on the other side of the water." To Boyd, too, he wrote of leaving "these Wesleyan haunts," of departing "these shores more or less permanently on the restoration of free seas." In July he told Boyd that he was "planning to get out of the United States as soon as possible, and to stay out."

It is hard to believe that Mencken seriously considered such action, and not only because he would never have permanently left his mother. If "active contact with American life" made writing difficult, as he wrote Dreiser, he also knew that the same contact gave substance and vitality to his work. And if Prohibition was a burden, it also summoned again the siege mentality, the state of being embattled in which he flourished. He had, of course, already stocked up on wine, beer, and spirits. "If a seizure act is considered," he wrote Boyd, "there will be time before it goes into effect to conceal the stocks. . . . Be assured that no Methodist will ever grab a single bottle."

Thus Mencken approached the American apocalypse with glee, and he would have had it no other way. "The close of 1919," he later wrote, "saw me in the midst of a kind of whirlpool, and it goes without saying that the exposure was exhilarating." Events of December 1919 looked both backward and forward. He got together with Marion in New York. He found himself the target of Stuart Sherman in *The New York Times*. He observed Wilson's deteriorating health and crippled presidency and in mid-December wrote Boyd, "I care not a single damn. I have a big stock of liquor, and am privy to a supply of illicit ale that is excellent." He would celebrate Christmas, he wrote Garrison, "in the ancient Christian manner, by getting tight."

Most of all, he would look forward to the new year. The 1920s, he seemed to sense, would be his decade. Wait until "after the show is over," he had written a friend in 1917. Now it was indeed over. "Think of the noble mark that American *Kultur* offers!" he wrote Garrison. "My hands itch."

# Chapter 9

# "A SORT OF HEATHEN MISSIONARY"

On January 1, 1920, Mencken rejoined the staff of the Baltimore *Evening Sun* at the salary of fifty dollars a week. He was ready to return, grateful to have a weekly column in which he could again hold forth on national affairs. American politics was in a "fearful state of inflammation," he wrote Ernest Boyd, Wilson's presidency was "in great distress," and, in general, "the show is excellent." He found himself inhabiting a new intellectual frontier created by the war: the resulting "chaos," he later wrote, "made things easier for me," and he was able "to let go *fortissimo*." If earlier he had considered taking up residence in Europe, now he was delighted to remain home. "Where, indeed," he wrote in the *Evening Sun* in October 1920, "is there a better show in the world?"

In fact, Mencken had never broken completely with the Sunpapers, despite his disagreement with their pro-British war policy. He had maintained cordial relations during the war with Harry Black, later to become chairman of the board of the A. S. Abell Company, and with Paul Patterson, the business manager who became president of the Abell Company in 1919. He had discussed with Patterson, in particular, plans to revive and reshape the newspapers after the war. Never was his interest in the Sunpapers higher than it was in 1920. He eagerly wrote a white paper proposing a newspaper "doubtful of politicians of all sorts, and devoted mainly to unearthing the facts underneath their pretensions." He had in mind a truly

207

"national newspaper," an "absolutely free agent," and he proposed as well a lively *Sun* weekly that "every American of any intellectual pretensions" would be forced to read.

Mencken did not get his weekly, partly because he himself was unwilling to become its editor, but overall he was favorably impressed with the vision and energy of the postwar Sunpapers leadership. He valued his friendships with Patterson and Black and, after 1922, Hamilton Owens, new editor of the *Evening Sun*. Although he found it impossible to forgive certain other *Sun* colleagues who he felt had betrayed him during the war—particularly morning *Sun* editor J. H. Adams, who had told him on one occasion that German Americans deserved any harsh treatment they received—in general he found himself working harmoniously even with men with whom he disagreed politically. After a brief period of discontent in the summer of 1920, during which he wrote Boyd that he intended to "break off any connection with the paper," he took to his job with his old abandon. He played an active and vigorous role in daily editorial conferences when he was in town, both for the stodgier morning *Sun* and the more iconoclastic *Evening Sun*, and he immersed himself in his writing.

Particularly, in the summer of 1920 he threw himself into the national political conventions, the Republican in Chicago and the Democratic in San Francisco. The Democratic convention in July, in which James A. Cox emerged as the nominee, was the "most charming" of all the more than two dozen such occasions he covered in his lifetime. The nearly ideal weather, the vigorous singing on the convention floor which "for a few minutes" caused him "almost" to "believe in democracy"—and, especially, the carload of good bourbon compliments of the mayor of San Francisco—all combined to create a political show he would recall more fondly than any other.

What impressed him most about the convention was San Francisco itself. All other American cities were shabby by comparison: Washington, "a hundred thousand miserable botches of ninth-rate clerks"; Philadelphia, "an intellectual and cultural slum"; New York, "a wholesale district with an annex for entertaining the visiting trade"; New Haven and Hartford, "blanks"; Boston, "a potter's field, a dissecting room." Even Baltimore brought to mind "mile after mile of identical houses, all inhabited by people who regard

Douglas Fairbanks as a greater man than Beethoven." But San Francisco was incomparable, "dazzling, exotic and curiously romantic."

Inside the convention hall the figure who fascinated him most—as he had at Mencken's first convention sixteen years before—was William Jennings Bryan. William Gibbs McAdoo, A. Mitchell Palmer, and, of course, the victorious Cox had their moments, and the spirit of the "sick man" Wilson was all about, but Bryan in defeat inspired Mencken's most spirited writing:

> Yesterday's session [he wrote on July 3] was devoted to the canonization of William Jennings Bryan and then to his murder in cold blood. They lifted him to the topless towers of Ilium, and then they sent him crashing and bawling down the eternal chutes . . . an earnest, a laborious and somewhat fly-blown and pathetic man. As he raged and leaped around the platform in his frayed alpaca coat, weeping for the orphans poisoned by whiskey, the widows debauched and brought down in infamy by absinthe and champagne, the felons fed to the gallows by malt liquors, light wines and gin, it was almost beyond human power to resist him. But to sob with him was one thing and to vote with him was quite another.

As always, Mencken delighted in what he witnessed inside the hall, but the part of his two weeks in San Francisco he most relished—and for which he had leisure since his reporting duties were not strenuous—was the time spent with his bohemian friend the poet George Sterling, and with Sterling's friends. A contributor to *The Smart Set* who had been a close friend of Jack London and Ambrose Bierce, Sterling was a self-indulgent figure with whom Mencken had been acquainted since 1914, and in Sterling's presence he departed from the role of responsible burgher he assumed back in Baltimore and even, to some extent, in New York. In San Francisco he spent several pleasurable evenings with attractive "sparring partners," he wrote Dreiser, and one morning, after an especially heavy night of drinking, he woke up in a strange bed with an unknown woman. Assuming at first she was a "low harlot," as he wrote Edgar Lee Masters, he then discovered that she was a "perfectly respectable woman" whom he had been too drunk and too tired to "use carnally at all." Another morning he awakened on the beach at Half Moon Bay with "a handsome Irish wench . . . [a] leading woman in a San Francisco stock company" named Jane O'Roarke. She was "lovely" to him, he reported to Sterling, during his two weeks in San Francisco.

Mencken paid for the excesses of San Francisco by suffering an attack of gastritis and spending much of the return trip in bed. He was content to return east: the hedonism of San Francisco he could enjoy for a short time, but by nature he belonged to a soberer realm. What he returned to in New York, however, was not altogether pleasant. By this point he had grown even wearier of the editorship of *The Smart Set*. A strike by the pressmen in late 1919, the illness of Nathan and several other employees in 1920, and "all sorts of conspiracies [and] atrocities" in the office discouraged him. Circulation had begun to decline after a slight increase following the war, and the magazine was barely making expenses. *The Smart Set* owed Mencken several months' back salary.

Even more serious, as he explained the situation to several friends in 1920 and 1921, was the fact that he had begun to "sicken of *belles lettres*." "All I have accomplished in literary pastures is this," he wrote Fielding Garrison. "I have made college professing a disreputable profession in America." Thus he had no interest at all in a proposition made about the same time by his old mentor James Gibbons Huneker that he take over the literary editorship of the New York *Sun-Herald*. "You are the big critical centre now," Huneker had written. "You should have a wider audience." Even the limited amount of literary work he now did for *The Smart Set* seemed "too trivial." "My work hereafter," he wrote Dreiser in October 1920, "will be a good deal more political than literary": "In Prejudices II I skin [Theodore] Roosevelt's carcass. In Prejudices III I hope to tear out the cold bowels of Woodrow [Wilson]. A pox upon all such swine! May they sweat in hell forever!"

In fact, Mencken's literary interest had not yet waned as much as he suggested. Earlier that year he had written Louis Untermeyer that he was considering the formation of a "small but effective organization of American authors, a defensive and offensive alliance," which would include, among others, Dreiser, Cabell, and Nathan. Though nothing specific came of that idea, he continued to entertain it.

Nor was his situation in general as grim as he described it. Financially, if he was not profiting from *The Smart Set* itself, he was still making a large amount of money for limited work from the pulp magazines he oversaw and from a scheme he and Nathan had devised to sell *Smart Set* epigrams to motion picture companies for display on the screen. Editorially, although he later said that he himself put "no hard work and thought" into the magazine after 1920 but simply "slogged along," a number of fine writers appeared in *The Smart Set* after that time. Some were holdovers from earlier years—James Branch Cabell, Sherwood Anderson, Willa Cather, and F. Scott Fitzgerald, as well as frequent contributors Thyra Winslow and Lilith Benda—but others, including Somerset Maugham and Aldous Huxley, appeared for the first time. Mencken also continued to cultivate young and undiscovered American writers. In 1921 he took a great deal of interest in Ruth Suckow of Iowa and Julia Peterkin of South Carolina after receiving stories and sketches from the two women. He published both in *The Smart Set* and recommended them to Knopf, who published their first books. He also hired Josephine Herbst as a reader for *The Smart Set* and the pulp magazines, encouraged her writing, and subsequently published her early fiction.

Through his monthly *Smart Set* essay reviews and through a new feature, "Répétition Générale," Mencken found he was able to articulate his growing social and political interests. He turned a review of John Dos Passos's *Three Soldiers* into an attack on the "dishonest and knavish" American conduct during the war, a crusade carried out "with no more gallantry in it than a lynching." In "Répétition Générale" he often focused on the American provinces, which he believed had given rise not only to Prohibition but to most of the other ills of American society. Widely identified as the archenemy of the South, he now trained his guns on the Midwest as well. In October 1920, after returning from his first transcontinental trip, he reflected, nearly in the cadences of "The Sahara of the Bozart," on the "intolerably bleak, lonesome and God-forsaken" American heartland: "Three days out from Chicago . . . and in those three days I did not eat a single decent meal, or see a single pretty village, or get a glimpse of a single handsome gal. What I remember most vividly, indeed, is the incredible hideousness of the whole show."

Having disposed of the South and the Midwest, he turned to New England. The ancestral home of Puritanism boasted a literature that, "even in its best days, was principally a cad literature. . . . There was very little if any beauty in it." In the twentieth century Ralph Waldo Emerson was important only as "the papa of the New Thought, the

211

favourite metaphysician of [Mary Baker] Eddy." And since Emerson's day, "the intellectual life in New England has moved steadily toward the estate and dignity of the intellectual life of Iowa."

Most of the United States, then, joined the South in constituting a cultural desert. The value of the tradition that had given rise to Hawthorne, Emerson, Thoreau, and Emily Dickinson was altogether lost on the postwar Mencken, as were the power and beauty of the American West. It was not that some necessary ingredient was missing from his imagination; it was rather, as he saw it, that New England produced only bluenoses and wowsers, while the hinterlands, south and west, had produced Woodrow Wilson, William Jennings Bryan, and Stuart Sherman as well as that narrow spirit that generated American intolerance in World War I. To a Mencken both angered and emboldened by the war, the only civilization in the United States seemed to rest in the Middle Atlantic states, from Maryland to New York, and perhaps that northern industrial belt between New York and Chicago—and, on the West Coast, San Francisco.

The fragments that Mencken published in "Répétition Générale" had another use as well: they served as raw materials for a series of books over which he labored in the early 1920s, books that would focus largely on what he called the American character. It was always difficult for him to find time for book-length works, and 1920 and 1921 were especially difficult. Not only was he occupied with the *Evening Sun* and *The Smart Set*, either of which would have been a full-time job for many writers, but he was overseeing the pulp magazines associated with *The Smart Set* and was serving as an unpaid consultant to Knopf. In addition, he was contributing articles and essays to other magazines (including *The Nation*, which he joined as contributing editor in March 1921) and was coerced into contributing to works such as Harold Stearns's celebrated *Civilization in the United States*. Putting in twelve to fourteen hours a day, he was "frightfully overworked," he complained to Dreiser. Besides, he was afflicted with a stomach disorder that at times made work impossible, as well as the occasional care of Charlie's wife, Mary, who spent several months in 1920 and 1921 in Baltimore for medical treatment.

Despite such obstacles, Mencken labored throughout much of 1920 on a second volume of *Prejudices*, all the while "cursing the Lord God Jehovah!" The formula of the *Prejudices* books was simple, he wrote Fielding Garrison: "a fundamental structure of serious argument, with enough personal abuse to engage the general reader, and one or two Rabelaisian touches." As critic, he was concerned with the grand sweep, the great and epochal movements of a national history, culture, and literature, and it was in the *Prejudices* volumes more than anywhere else that this essential Mencken emerged. The United States was his great subject, and if the Republic disgusted him, it also continued to fascinate him. Despite his immersion in it, the persona he affected in those *Prejudices* essays on American life was often that of an observer a bit incredulous, a bit amazed that he was offered an opportunity to gaze upon such a rich field. In one respect, as a friend of his observed, if Mencken as critic had been able to create his perfect world, it would have been the United States of the early twentieth century. He would have wanted nothing changed.

He delivered the manuscript of *Prejudices: Second Series* to Knopf in mid-1920, and it appeared in November. As usual, he had accepted no advance, believing, as he once wrote Dreiser, that "advances on royalty are immoral." Included in the volume were pieces on Theodore Roosevelt, Prohibition, love, death, and the agonies of writing.

But the most significant essays were a much-expanded version of his 1917 *Evening Mail* column "The Sahara of the Bozart" and a lengthy discussion of "The National Letters." In "The Sahara" he polished the prose of his 1917 indictment of the South and stepped up the hyperbole:

> Nearly the whole of Europe could be lost in that stupendous region of fat farms, shoddy cities and paralyzed cerebrums. . . . [Yet] there are single acres in Europe that house more first-rate men than all the states south of the Potomac; there are probably single square miles in America. If the whole of the late Confederacy were to be engulfed by a tidal wave tomorrow, the effect upon the civilized minority of men in the world would be but little greater than that of a flood on the Yang-tse-kiang.

What had happened in Dixie, he maintained, was that "the vast blood-letting of the Civil War half exterminated and wholly paralyzed the old aristocracy, and so left the land to the harsh mercies of the poor white trash." In Virginia, "the best of the south today," all was crassness: "a Washington or a Jefferson, dumped there by some act of God, would be denounced as a scoundrel and jailed overnight." The Old Dominion was "an intellectual Gobi or Lapland" in which "one could no more imagine a Lee or a Washington . . . than one could imagine a Huxley in Nicaragua." As Virginia was the best, Georgia was the worst, "the home of . . . the Methodist parson turned Savonarola and of the lynching bee." In between Virginia and Georgia in spirit "lies a vast plain of mediocrity, stupidity, lethargy, almost of dead silence."

In "The National Letters," nearly a hundred pages in length, he painted a picture brighter only by comparison: American literature was and always had been "chiefly remarkable . . . for its respectable mediocrity," its "timorous flaccidity, an amiable hollowness." Continuing the campaign he was currently waging in *The Smart Set*, he again blasted New England, with its stultifying Puritanism and its Genteel Tradition, but he also mocked the Greenwich Village revolt against the Genteel Tradition. In the American literary past he saw little of value except Poe and Whitman, who revolted against the "predominant English taste." Altogether, the primary problem was "the lack of civilized aristocracy, secure in its position, animated by an intelligent curiosity, skeptical of all facile generalizations, superior to the sentimentality of the mob, and delighting in the battle of ideas for its own sake." The result was that the United States was "a nation of third-rate men, a land offering hospitality only to fourth-rate artists." Again Mencken saw cautious and anemic professors as a large part of the problem, and he maintained that he himself had every right to pass such judgment: "There are more Ph.D.'s on my family tree than even a Boston bluestocking can boast; there was a whole century when even the most ignorant of my house was at least *Juris utriusque Doctor*."

*Prejudices: Second Series* was but one of several studies of the American character that engaged him in the early 1920s. He and Nathan coedited, also in 1920, *The American Credo*, which they subtitled "A Contribution Toward the Interpretation of the National Mind." Only Mencken's hundred-page preface justified that lofty description; in it he again remarked on the intolerance, the social insecurity, and the passion for conformity of the contemporary American.

Shortly afterward he was at work on two other volumes, one of them a third book of *Prejudices* to be published by Knopf in 1922. Most of the essays in this *Prejudices* were on subjects other than the contemporary United States—Mencken discussed education, economics, and literature, as well as the debased condition of mankind—but it was the lead essay, "On Being an American," that caught the attention of most readers. In it he sounded his familiar note: the American people constituted "the most timorous, sniveling, poltroonish, ignominious mob of serfs and goose-steppers ever gathered under one flag in Christendom since the end of the Middle Ages." He debunked the assumption that American immigrants had come from "brave, idealistic and liberty loving minorities":

> The truth is that the majority of non-Anglo-Saxon immigrants since the Revolution, like the majority of Anglo-Saxon immigrants before the Revolution, have been . . . the botched and unfit: Irishmen starving to death in Ireland, Germans unable to weather the *Sturm und Drang* of the post-Napoleonic reorganization, Italians weed-grown on exhausted soil, Scandinavians run to all bone and no brain, Jews too incompetent to swindle even the barbarous peasants of Russia, Poland and Roumania.

Why, then, given such a nation of misfits, did Mencken "remain on the dock . . . when [other] Young Intellectuals set sail" for Europe? He repeated the answer he had given earlier: America was the most amusing spectacle on earth. He preferred residence in this "glorious commonwealth of morons," "this Eden of clowns," to life anywhere else. Thus, he would remain, "contributing my mite toward the glory of the national arts and sciences, enriching and embellishing the national language, spurning all lures (and even all invitations) to get out and stay out." He was "well-fed, unhounded by sordid cares, at ease in Zion." And taxes were low: "I figure . . . that my private share of the expense of maintaining the Hon. Mr. Harding in the White House this year will work out to less than 80 cents. Try to think of better sport for the money . . ."

Such was the tone in much of Mencken's writing in the early 1920s. His delight in the American scene seemed to mitigate the distaste he felt for it, and he expressed that delight not only in the published volumes but also in *The Smart Set*, the *Evening Sun*, and numerous other places. The "show," he affirmed on several occasions, was better than any "since the Reformation": "It goes on daily, not in three rings, but in three hundred rings, and in each one of them whole battalions of acrobats tie themselves into fabulous knots and the handsomest gals in Christendom pirouette upon the loveliest and most skittish horses, and clowns of unbelievable limberness and humor perform inordinate monkey-shines."

He covered the Carpentier-Dempsey fight in July 1921 and, indulging himself in a love of sport he had not exhibited for twenty-five years, created epic—or mock epic—out of that "great combat, staged there in that colossal sterilizer beneath the harsh Jersey sun."

He was also fascinated by the American penchant, seen long ago in his own father, for rites and rituals, medals and ribbons and orders:

Rank by rank, [Americans] became Knights of Pythias, Odd Fellows, Red Men, Nobles of the Mystic Shrine, Knights Templar, Patriarchs Militant, Elks, Moose, Woodmen of the World, Foresters, Hoo-Hoos, Ku Kluxers—and in every new order there were thirty-two degrees, and for every degree there was a badge, and for every badge there was a yard of ribbon. The Nobles of the Mystic Shrine, chiefly paunchy wholesalers of the Rotary Club species, are not content with swords, baldrics, stars, garters, jewels; they also wear red fezzes. The Elks run to rubies. The Red Men array themselves like Sitting Bull. . . . There is a mortician in Hagerstown, Md., who has been initiated eighteen times. When he robes himself to plant a fellow joiner he weighs three hundred pounds and sparkles and flashes like the mouth of Hell itself. He is entitled to bear seven swords, all jeweled, and to hang his watch chain with the golden busts of nine wild animals, all with precious stones for eyes. Put beside this lowly washer of the dead, [John J.] Pershing newly polished would seem almost like a Trappist.

But most of all he delighted in observing and ridiculing the American presidents. He had already had his fun with Wilson—"the whole Wilsonian buncombe," "the Woodrovian style"—although at times he had been so indignant he had lost his ability to satirize. Warren G. Harding was more fun, "a third-rate political wheel-horse, with the face of a moving-picture actor, the intelligence of a respectable agricultural implement dealer, and the imagination of a lodge joiner

. . . a benign blank—a decent, harmless, laborious, hollow-headed mediocrity . . ." And Harding's speeches—pure "Gamalielese," Mencken reported after hearing his inaugural address in 1921— offered the finest delight imaginable:

> He writes the worst English that I have ever encountered. It reminds me of a string of wet sponges; it reminds me of tattered washing on the line; it reminds me of stale bean-soup, of college yells, of dogs barking idiotically through endless nights. It is so bad that a sort of grandeur creeps into it.

Presidents past as well as present fascinated Mencken. In *Damn!* he had described George Washington as a man who "would be under indictment by every grand jury south of the Potomac":

> He was not pious. He drank whisky whenever he felt chilly, and kept a jug of it handy. He knew far more profanity than Scripture, and used and enjoyed it more. He had no belief in the infallible wisdom of the lower classes, but regarded them as inflammatory dolts, and tried to save the republic from them. He took no interest in the private morals of his neighbors.

In *The Smart Set* he demythologized Lincoln as well:

> The varnishers and veneerers have been busily converting Abe into a plaster saint. . . . There is an obvious effort to pump all his human weaknesses out of him, and so leave him a mere moral apparition, a sort of amalgam of John Wesley and the Holy Ghost. . . . In point of fact . . . until he emerged from Illinois they always put the women, children and clergy to bed when he got a few gourds of corn aboard, and it is a matter of unescapable record that his career in the State Legislature was indistinguishable from that of a Tammany Nietzsche.

Even Grover Cleveland, hardly an American icon but in fact one of Mencken's own favorite presidents, was not to escape his pen: "His whole huge carcass seemed to be made of iron. There was no give in him, no bounce, no softness. He sailed through American history like a steel ship loaded with monoliths of granite." And ahead lay the

217

delicious era of Coolidge, of whom Mencken would say: "He slept more than any other President, whether by day or by night. . . . He had no ideas, but he was not a nuisance."

With the *Prejudices* volumes, the *Smart Set* columns and other works of the early 1920s, Mencken had become not only the most widely quoted but also the most widely discussed of American intellectuals. Joseph Wood Krutch, writing in *The Nation*, saw him as "a sort of heathen missionary zealously endeavoring to convert the barbarian Christians away from the false gods of Humility and Restraint." Edmund Wilson, five years out of Princeton and writing in *The New Republic*, saw him as the "civilized consciousness of modern America," a "genuine artist" of great honesty and courage, a "mind of extraordinary vigor and a temperament of extraordinary interest." Unlike past first-rank American minds, Mencken was "thoroughly familiar with, even thoroughly saturated with, the common life." Wilson repeated his praise the following year in *Vanity Fair*. Mencken was "a satiric creative artist of a very high order" with a "genuine magic" in his literary style. Wilson's former Princeton classmate F. Scott Fitzgerald was even more excessive in his praise. Mencken, he exclaimed in *The Bookman*, had "done more for the national letters than any man alive."

Not all estimates were so generous. Writing in *The New Republic* (and perhaps responding in part to unkind remarks by Mencken in *The Smart Set*), Walter Lippmann found him a "near Machiavelli," a philologist and literary critic of some talent but a misguided critic of democracy and a pretender to true intellectual leadership. But Lippmann acknowledged that Mencken had indeed become a force in American life, the "prophet"—even if a false one—"of a new aristocracy." His was a view shared by nearly all observers. Mencken was widely regarded as the critic who had penetrated the nation's vaunted and unwarranted pride, had exposed its self-deluded politicians and roaring evangelists, its literary boosters, romancers, and poetasters, and thus had emerged as the leader of the new American forces of liberation. He seemed, as Edmund Wilson had written, something nearly unprecedented in the national life. In a way Emerson would never have recognized, he was becoming that independent "scholar" for whom the New Englander had called—free, fearless, and disrespectful of the models of the past, particularly English ones.

At first Mencken was uncomfortable with the role in which he had been cast, but soon enough he acknowledged that role. He had become, he himself later wrote, "the symbol . . . of the revolt of post-war youth against the old American certainties." He insisted that he did not want the "leadership in dissent" he had been handed: "the messianic passion was simply not in me . . ." But, in fact, most of the time he reveled in the publicity, even promoted it. When a mocking but nonetheless flattering poem on "Mencken/Nathan/And God," appeared in the New York *Sun* in December 1920, he and Nathan had the poem printed and circulated in large numbers. He still subscribed to the clipping service he had used since 1903, and he marveled at the stories, both favorable and unfavorable, that poured in. "The dictator of American letters," he was proclaimed, or, less flatteringly, "the Billy Sunday of American literary criticism."

He noted the physical descriptions of himself in the frequent interviews he gave: "forty years lightly carried . . . the face broad, rather heavy-jowled; of the type known as 'honest' "; or "a stocky individual, with a convex waist, cordial, hospitable, unaffected, with faultless manners and perfect poise." Interviewers marveled that so fierce a polemicist was so congenial in person, not at all the "lean man with a hard face and sombre eye" one reporter expected. Those writers and editors who did not encounter him face to face tended to be more hostile, particularly if they hailed from a South stung by "The Sahara of the Bozart." Southern editors railed against the "German-born" Mencken, this "self-appointed emissary of the Wilhelmstrasse," and the president of the Arkansas Advancement Association urged Congress to begin deportation proceedings. But among most young readers and writers, even in the late Confederacy, the reception was not at all negative. In fact, Mencken wrote to Fielding Garrison, "nearly all" the southerners who wrote to him "agree with me, at least in general."

In the early 1920s Mencken's reputation abroad nearly equaled his reputation at home. "One of the curious literary phenomena of the time," an American reporter wrote in 1921, was "the remarkable growth in England and continental Europe of the fame of Henry L. Mencken." Particularly in Great Britain, the target of so much of his invective, was he praised. Indeed, he wrote Dreiser late in 1920, "Until I got a few good notices in France and England, I was sneered at at home. . . . My sales are now at least three times what they were a year and a half ago. The whole change began with a few favorable notices abroad." One British notice Mencken had in mind was that by the grandson of his old idol and mentor T. H. Huxley. The Baltimorean "turns a pair of civilized eyes on the extraordinary and fantastic spectacle which is contemporary American life," Aldous Huxley wrote in the London *Athenaeum.* "We should welcome his appearance among us here, for we have sore need of critics who hate humbug . . ." Within weeks of Huxley's remarks, he wrote to Mencken, asking to be "allowed, as an humble fellow-critic, to express my great admiration for 'Prejudices.' " Delighted, Mencken sent Huxley copies of his other books.

It was in part to capitalize on his British and European fame, as well as to meet British *Smart Set* contributors and "to have a look at the fruits of the Treaty of Versailles," that Mencken, in the spring of 1922, decided to make his first European trip since the war. The trip was delayed because he had a great deal of writing to complete for the Sunpapers and *The Smart Set,* as well as work on several books in progress, before he could get away: "I am driven absolutely frantic by work," he complained to Hergesheimer in July. He planned to spend a week or two in London, then push on to Germany. On August 8 he sailed. He was to remain through mid-October.

He approached England with a curious combination of feelings. It was the land of his youthful cultural and literary allegiance, the place he had felt most at home—more so than in Germany—when he had first visited in 1908. But England was also the spawning ground of Puritanism, democracy, and the Victorian Genteel Tradition, and it had been the enemy in the late war.

Toward its writers he also felt a curious ambivalence. Its novelists, poets, and essayists of the eighteenth and nineteenth centuries had been his models, and certain of its contemporary writers he admired. He had met H. G. Wells in Washington the year before and shortly afterward had met John Galsworthy at dinner at Alfred Knopf's. Through *The Smart Set* he had corresponded with and published a number of other English writers, including Hugh Walpole, Somerset Maugham, Aleister Crowley, and Lord Alfred Douglas. He would meet with some of these writers, and others, during his week in London.

But Mencken had reservations about spending much time in the company of these men and certain others known to him by reputation, and he frankly acknowledged the reason in his posthumously released memoirs: Walpole and Crowley, as well as Lord Douglas, Maugham, and a number of other English writers, were or were reputed to be homosexual, and Mencken felt very uncomfortable in the company of homosexuals. Or, as he expressed it with characteristic tact in his memoirs, "I have always had a loathing for homos . . ."

He had felt the same way, he revealed, about certain American writers of his acquaintance. He had a "very low" opinion of *Smart Set* contributor Djuna Barnes, a lesbian who seemed to him "revolting" because of her physical appearance. He thought little better of Margaret Anderson, editor of *The Little Review*, and "her arty and homosexual friends." But in London Mencken might expect to be thrown into contact with homosexual males more than he had ever been before. Lord Douglas, Oscar Wilde's friend and lover, Mencken referred to in his memoirs as Wilde's "old girl," a "filthy homo." Walpole was not only "reputed to be homosexual" but, Mencken later reported, had once "actually made an attempt" on Joseph Hergesheimer. Crowley "seemed to me [to have] the marks of the homosexual . . . all over him." Maugham he was to meet at least twice, once at a friend's apartment in New York, an occasion on which he and the novelist talked until 2:00 A.M., and another time in Baltimore for a pleasant conversation of an hour or two. Still, he maintained, Maugham was "reputed . . . to be a homosexual of the school of Hugh Walpole, and I was thus somewhat shy of his society." He felt even more strongly about the other English writers.

We can only imagine, then, the wariness with which Mencken had received an earlier invitation from Walpole: "Come over here and drink with me, eat with me, sleep with me (this in a limited sense of course) as soon as you can." Or the invitation extended in June 1922, two months before he sailed: "Will you stay with me from the 18th for a few days? I wish you would." Or, once in London, the invitation of Crowley—whom Mencken had determined to "steer clear of" but who had "looked me up" nonetheless—to "visit a 'temple' that he had established." Mencken wanted at all costs to avoid both the "temple" and the homosexual "disciples" Crowley was alleged to have.

His response to homosexuality was hardly unusual for a man of his time and place: homophobia was more deeply ingrained in him than was any racial or ethnic prejudice, and it is no accident that it is virtually the only one of his prejudices that he did not choose to reveal in published writing during his lifetime. We learn of such feelings only in the memoirs he locked away, not to be opened until thirty-five years after his death. In part, his homophobia was consistent with his essentially Victorian temper and its rage for order, with what he considered to be the natural order of things and thus a great revulsion for all that departed from that order. But homosexuality was, as well, a deeply personal threat to Mencken. More than anything else he encountered in the world of "feminized" belles lettres, indeed in an increasingly feminized American culture at large, he considered it to be an affront to the code of masculinity, to which, as we have seen, he had subscribed since the 1890s—a code that was, at first, somewhat threatened by his own entry into that world of letters, an entry that had revealed a "feminine" side of himself.

He had thus taken refuge in the solid masculine presences of Huneker, Dreiser, Goodman, and Hergesheimer—men of letters but still men of the world—but now, in London, he encountered a representation of that earlier impression of arts and literature. He solved the problem in the manner that seemed most logical: he avoided it. He "refuse[d] to visit [Crowley's] 'temple' or to see him again . . . I brushed him off as quickly as possible." As for Walpole, Mencken rejected all invitations except lunch "in his luxurious house" in Regent's Park. Neither Crowley nor Walpole, Mencken reported in his memoirs, made any advances to him. "Maybe," he added curiously, "that was because homosexuals always avoid me." Whether he believed they avoided him because they felt his hostility—or because they found him not sufficiently attractive—he did not explain.

It would be misleading to suggest that Mencken's entire week in London was spent tripping through what he imagined to be homosexual mine fields. That was only one occupation. In fact, he settled into a small hotel near St. James's Street, ate and drank with his usual vigor, met with journalists, and gave interviews. He let it be known that the United States was money-mad and "half-civilized"—a statement that appeared prominently in dozens of English and American newspapers. Several English writers, including Edith Sitwell and H. G. Wells, remarked on Mencken as a phenomenon of letters, and he received rave notices from the English press. "He and he alone," *The English Review* remarked, "has put America on the literary map."

In contrast to his first English visit, when he had reluctantly left London and proceeded to Germany, in 1922 he was eager to reach the Fatherland. On that earlier trip he had spent but a few days in Germany. This time he would remain in and around Germany nearly two months. By 1922 he had begun to acquire a substantial German reputation, largely through the efforts of his translator, Herman George Scheffauer, and on this trip, unlike those in 1908, 1912, and 1917, he had a large number of German friends to see. After a stay in Berlin—which he had last seen in the dark days of 1917 but which was now, he wrote Marion Bloom, "too big and too busy"—he traveled to Prague, where he met Adolph Torovsky, a Baltimore friend and fellow Saturday Night Club member who was a native of Czechoslovakia. After a pilgrimage to Pilsen—"the home of the best beer on earth and hence one of the great shrines of the human race"—he moved on to Munich, where he stayed two weeks with Dr. Wilhelm Sohler, his wartime friend whose internment in Georgia had brought Mencken great distress as well as the scrutiny of the Justice Department.

Mencken much preferred Munich to Berlin; he particularly liked his quarters in Sohler's apartment overlooking the Isar. When he arrived he found the Oktoberfest under way, and he immediately plunged in. "Great God," he later wrote an English friend, "I lost my left kidney there. . . . It is the grandest festival ever arranged on this earth by mortal man." Oktoberfest, he wrote another friend, was "the greatest thrill of my life."

From Munich he proceeded to Berchtesgaden, where he spent the night with a Baltimore acquaintance, Henry Wood, whose wife, related to the German aristocracy, knew the Hohenzollerns well. He then returned to Berlin for another week of what he found to be "its feverish, and indeed almost delirious life." There he spent a good deal of time with Scheffauer as well as a number of German authors. From Berlin he traveled across Germany to Oldenburg, seat of the earliest Menckens. Earlier in the trip he had visited Leipzig and had also met with a German genealogist who gave him abundant information about his family. For the first time he began to take a great interest in the world of his fathers. In Oldenburg he visited the crumbling tombs in the Saint Gertrud churchyard.

He had one more stop in Europe. The Sunpapers had asked him to interview the former crown prince of Germany, now confined to a small farmhouse on Wieringen, a small and remote island off the coast of Holland. He had arranged the interview with the aid of Mrs. Henry Wood, who had written the crown prince in advance. In early October he proceeded to Amsterdam and took a train to northern Holland, a car to the Zuider Zee, and a motorboat to Wieringen. There he was met by an aide, who took him by car to the crown prince. Mencken found the man who would be kaiser to be intelligent and amusing, possessing fluent English, and much more reasonable than his father, Wilhelm II. But the crown prince decried the "insane" Treaty of Versailles and the punishment it had inflicted upon Germany.

Mencken returned to Amsterdam and filed his story, which appeared in the Baltimore *Sun* in mid-October. Mrs. Wood had also offered to help arrange an interview with the former kaiser, but Mencken had little respect for Wilhelm II and did not care to remain longer in Europe to talk with him. He was ready to return home, and he sailed from Bremen on October 11. He had seen and experienced a great deal, much of it delightful. But Germany, taken altogether, he found a "confusing and astounding spectacle." On the surface "everything looks serene," he wrote Paul Patterson from Munich. But underneath, "every intelligent man looks for a catastrophe. If it comes, there will be a colossal massacre of Jews."

Mencken had begun to arrive at that conclusion even before his trip. His fellow Nietzschean Oscar Levy, a German Jew, had written him from England in 1919 that the Germans, in defeat, were united by "an intense hatred of Jews," and in 1920 and 1921 he had been reading numerous German pamphlets, "chiefly anti-Semitic." He had received letters and material from other Germans complaining about what one pamphleteer called "the so called peace treaty of Versailles." He himself had remarked to Fielding Garrison on the German habit of oscillating "between megalomania and défaitism." But his primary complaint with Germany had been the new democratic movement, "all the balderdash of democracy dished up again."

Thus his trip to Germany had not opened his eyes so much as it had reinforced certain impressions he already had. Workingmen and farmers were prospering, it seemed to him upon arrival, as well as "rich industrialists, particularly the Jews." But the "salaried man" was barely getting by, and, he wrote Hergesheimer, "the situation of the German authors, as of the whole German intelligentsia," was "fearful." In Munich, where in late September he joined "40,000 Müncheners [in being] soused," Adolf Hitler was feeding on German discontent. But Hitler was at that time still a minor figure, still a year away from his beer-hall putsch, and Mencken heard nothing of him.

Mencken's own attitude toward the German Jews was a mixture of sympathy and censure; at times he seemed to absorb the anti-Semitism of many of his German friends. Earlier, after reading anti-Semitic pamphlets, he had expressed to Fielding Garrison a measure of agreement with those who blamed the Jews for German labor unrest. He had also written Ernest Boyd that European Jews, besides being identified "with the Bolsheviki," had "robbed the plain people on a colossal scale during the war," and he had entered disparaging remarks (among many favorable ones) about Jews in his introduction to Nietzsche's *The Antichrist*. Now, in Germany, he reflected sadly on the plight of an old German friend who had "lived long enough to see the German republic fall into the hands of the Jews, but not long enough to see Germany revive, rearm and tackle its enemies once more." Like most of his friends, however, he placed the greatest blame for Germany's instability not on the Jews but on the Versailles treaty. He was "convinced that its imbecilities" could never "be corrected by argument," that "only" those Bismarckian remedies, blood and iron, could rectify them.

---

If the 1922 European trip, as a fact-finding mission, had been somewhat troubling for Mencken, most of what was disturbing had been, upon his return, put out of his mind. The trip had also served as a triumphal tour, one in which he had capitalized on his fame and reputation, as well as cultivated writers and reviewers for his future benefit. When he landed in New York in late October, he returned to a three-month accumulation of work, but he also returned to a routine under which he had come to thrive and which, despite his complaints of overwork, he largely enjoyed. In New York he was now at the center of the literary world; he had become a friend or acquaintance of nearly every American writer of the first rank and many of the second. Aside from Dreiser and Hergesheimer, he was, or shortly would be, well acquainted with Edgar Lee Masters, Vachel Lindsay, F. Scott Fitzgerald, Sinclair Lewis, and Carl Van Vechten, among others, as well as editors such as John Farrar of *The Bookman* and Robert H. Davis of *Munsey's Magazine*. Other writers, such as Carl Sandburg, Floyd Dell, Ring Lardner, and Edna Ferber, he corresponded with and saw when they could meet in New York.

But Mencken was far from universally popular. He later listed among the writers of this period who "disliked me intensely" Edna St. Vincent Millay, Irvin Cobb, and Heywood Broun, as well as Robert W. Chambers, an Anglophile who (he recalled twenty-five years later) had spread stories during the war that "Nathan and I were homosexuals and engaged in mutual carnalities." One writer who courted him for a time, was accorded less than an enthusiastic reception, and then became an adversary was the twenty-five-year-old poet Allen Tate, fresh to New York from Tennessee. After an encounter in which Mencken became "vulgar and admonitory"—according to Tate's version of the meeting in a letter to his friend Donald Davidson—Tate concluded that the older man was a "perfect ass," although also "doubtless a great man" who could "kill my literary reputation with one vulgar blow."

Other writers Mencken saw on occasion but disapproved of so strongly that they could never be friends. Upton Sinclair, whom he saw in Baltimore as well as in New York, he could not forgive for his socialist politics and, even more, for supporting Wilson and suppressing free speech during the war. Sherwood Anderson he still saw occasionally in New York, but he continued to find Anderson (as he wrote Masters) a "rather trying fellow," "extremely shabby," an "extraordinarily unreliable" man. He was friendly with Willa Cather for a time but fell out with her after he reviewed her novel *Death Comes for the Archbishop* unfavorably. She was "a 100% American," he decided, and besides had "succumbed to Catholicism." Ruth Suckow and Julia Peterkin, with whom he had also been friendly, he struck off his list after they left Knopf for other publishers. "My relations with women novelists," Mencken wrote in his diary, not altogether accurately, "have been somewhat unhappy."

His relations with fellow young intellectuals in New York were cordial enough, although he was politically to the right of most of them. He saw little of Randolph Bourne, who had earlier found fault not only with his *Prefaces* but with his treatment of Nietzsche, but he was friendly with Van Wyck Brooks, Carl Van Doren, and Harold Stearns, as well as with Joseph Wood Krutch and Ludwig Lewisohn. He also made the acquaintances of Walter Lippmann and Edmund Wilson, whose essays had helped give him intellectual respectability in the early 1920s. Although Lippmann had expressed interest in meeting Mencken as early as 1913, the two men did not get together until the early twenties. They saw each other occasionally in New York but found they disagreed on many matters, particularly the merits of democracy. In letters to friends, Mencken found much to criticize in Lippmann.

Wilson, as a student at the Hill School between 1908 and 1912, had seen Mencken as a literary idol. He had continued to read *The Smart Set* at Princeton and as a young soldier in France, and he met Mencken for the first time in 1920 or 1921 at a coffeehouse in Manhattan. Shortly afterward, Mencken summoned him to the *Smart Set* offices. Although he rejected several stories by Wilson and found fault with a book manuscript the young writer sent to Alfred Knopf, he continued to encourage his work. He was grateful for the praise Wilson lavished upon him; most important, he believed, Wilson *understood* his work. In his letters he always assumed the role of the authority, Wilson the polite young man wanting very much to please the literary arbiter.

Wilson's friend Fitzgerald continued to be eager to please Mencken as well, particularly after meeting the *Smart Set* editor for the first time in Nathan's apartment in New York, probably in the summer of 1919. Mencken's first impression of Fitzgerald was that of a "slim, blonde young fellow . . . so handsome that he might even have been called beautiful." Fitzgerald immediately fell under his spell: he usually addressed Mencken as "Sir," and in an inscription in Mencken's copy of *This Side of Paradise* he acknowledged that he had "adopted a great many of your views." The two men met at several other parties at Nathan's in 1919 and 1920, and after Fitzgerald and Zelda Sayre married in April 1920 Mencken and Nathan took them to dinner at the Plaza and got together with them in Manhattan on other occasions. About the same time, Mencken reviewed *This Side of Paradise*, praising it as an exceptional first novel.

Although he was interested in Fitzgerald's work, Mencken found him unsuitable as a friend for the same reason he rejected, or was to reject, numerous other literary acquaintances: Fitzgerald lacked discipline, both in his writing and especially in his personal life. Mencken disapproved of Scott and Zelda's heavy drinking and, in general, believed Fitzgerald to be a "foolish fellow." "A very amiable pair," he wrote about Scott and Zelda to James Branch Cabell in 1922, "innocent and charming," but Zelda talked too much about money and Scott's danger lay "in trying to get it too rapidly."

Another young novelist Mencken encountered about the same time he met Fitzgerald was Sinclair Lewis, and he was to find Lewis objectionable for many of the same reasons he rejected Fitzgerald's friendship. Although he had corresponded briefly with the young writer as far back as 1916, when Mencken published one of his early stories in *The Smart Set*, he had nearly forgotten Lewis when he encountered the lanky red-haired Minnesotan in 1920 at a friend's party on 105th Street. Intoxicated, Lewis had come up to him and announced that he had just written a great novel. After Mencken succeeded in getting rid of him, he told Nathan that it was unimaginable that such a boor had written a first-rate book. The next day he found advance sheets of the novel in the *Smart Set* office and to satisfy his curiosity took them with him to read on the train to Baltimore. He was astonished. By Philadelphia he was certain enough that he stopped and wired Nathan, "That idiot has written a masterpiece." The novel was *Main Street*, and Mencken wrote to Lewis, offering his congratulations: "It is a sound and excellent piece of work—the best thing of its sort that has been done so far." When it was published shortly afterward, he praised it highly in *The Smart Set*.

That first meeting on 105th Street established a certain tone for the relationship between Mencken and Lewis. "In drink," Mencken later wrote, the novelist was "noisy and hard to bear. . . . His heavy boozing alienated many of his most useful friends . . ." Sober, Lewis was even worse: "he was dull . . . Drinking soda pop and eating ice-cream, he was simply a bore." Nonetheless, Mencken saw him with some frequency in New York, found him at times "an extremely amicable fellow," one from whose company he "got a reasonable amount of pleasure." He recognized as well a sort of "genius" in Lewis the writer. From the beginning the two men felt in each other a shared sympathy and aim, a comic and satiric vision of American life. Lewis remarked that he often thought as he wrote, "Wonder if Mencken would like this." In those early years Mencken unfailingly did.

Lewis's next novel, *Babbitt* (1922), was "curiously associated with" Mencken, Lewis wrote him. In his review of *Main Street* the *Smart Set* editor had suggested that the "medium-sized" American city now needed to be treated—not New York or Chicago but the city of 200,000 to 500,000. "I was startled to read it," Lewis added, "because that was precisely what I WAS then planning, and am now doing." He had been considering two or three other topics for his next novel until he read Mencken's words. "Your piece helped me to decide on this particular one. . . . I think you'll like it." If, in part, Lewis was shrewdly soliciting Mencken's interest in his new novel and thus setting up a favorable review, he was also close to the truth. In any case, Mencken liked *Babbitt* very much. When the advance copy reached him, he read it at once. "It seemed to me," he wrote later, "to be the best American novel, saving only 'Huckleberry Finn,' that I had ever read." In print he accorded it similar praise.

By the early 1920s, then, Lewis had assumed the role Theodore Dreiser had once occupied for Mencken, his staunchest ally among American novelists in his war against convention as well as the novelist most closely identified with him in the public eye. The target now was not so much the Genteel Tradition in literature as the great American middle class, the mode was not Dreiser's earnest naturalism but Lewis's clever satire, and the novel *Babbitt* had succeeded Dreiser's *Jennie Gerhardt* as a worthy second to Mark Twain's masterpiece.

Mencken had not, however, completely lost contact with his old friend Dreiser in the early twenties. If anything, their relationship benefited from Dreiser's move to California late in 1919. They fell back into the habit of writing letters full of joking, spoofing, and sexual boasting. In other letters Mencken felt comfortable enough to pour out his troubles—the death of friends, a "very strict diet" on which he had been placed, his own work, which had "gone to pot," as well as the usual medical ills: gastritis, laryngitis, a sprained arm, hay fever, and other ailments. "I am in a low state of mind," he wrote Dreiser in March 1921. "I am surrounded by illness here, and full of troubles."

However outwardly cordial, the relationship with Dreiser was still strained. The novelist had taken with him to California Helen Richardson, an aspiring actress who was also his second cousin, and they had rented a house in Los Angeles. Knowing of Mencken's loyalty to Estelle Bloom, for a time Dreiser kept his arrangement and his address secret. Mencken was also indignant over his old friend's susceptibility to frauds and quacks of all varieties. Dreiser wrote him about a California acquaintance who possessed a "machine" that would cure "all the more serious diseases." He was certain Mencken's gastritis could be cured if he sent a drop of blood on a sheet of paper to California.

Mencken was equally critical of Dreiser's professional conduct, particularly a suggestion in a letter of January 1921 that he promote the novelist for "the Noble [sic] prize": "You are in a position to make a large noise looking to that result." It was a simple "business proposition," Dreiser explained. "Start the ball and if I snake the forty thousand [sic] . . . you get five thousand, or, between twelve and thirteen percent. . . . Where else can you pick up five thousand for a few kind words judiciously uttered?"

Mencken recognized that Dreiser was quite serious, and he wrote back, giving the impression that he would accept the offer. He would work through a Dane, he said, attempting to accomplish Dreiser's goal. "The Dane, of course, was imaginary," Mencken wrote in his memoirs, "and I did nothing whatever." In fact, he believed that, more than any other American, Dreiser deserved the Nobel, but now his friend "had made it impossible for me to undertake any propaganda for him." As for Dreiser's "scandal proposal," Mencken was not surprised. "He was . . . quite devoid of any sense of honor."

Mencken became further convinced of such a deficiency in 1921 and 1922, when he made a final attempt to ensure publication of Dreiser's novel *The "Genius,"* that questionable work of art for which he had fought unsuccessfully five years before. With Dreiser's approval, he negotiated with John Sumner of the New York Society for the Suppression of Vice to make minor deletions in the book without altering it substantially. He notified Dreiser of the cuts, the novelist approved, and Mencken sailed for Europe in August, assuming the matter was resolved. When he returned, he found that Dreiser was renegotiating with Horace Liveright for an unexpurgated edition of the novel. Mencken felt betrayed, was rightly upset, and concluded what he had long suspected: Dreiser was "essentially a German peasant, oafish, dour and distrustful of all mankind." "His customary attitude to the world" was "that of any other yahoo."

When Mencken tired of Dreiser, he turned to more patrician friends among novelists, men such as Hergesheimer and, on occasion, James Branch Cabell. He often visited Hergesheimer in West Chester, Pennsylvania, enjoying weekends in the novelist's two-hundred-year-old Dower House. In May 1923 the two men also made the first of Mencken's ten pilgrimages to the Bach Festival in Bethlehem, Pennsylvania—where they found "excellent beer," Mencken wrote Ernest Boyd, for ten cents a glass.

But the "most elegant" of their trips in the early 1920s, as Hergesheimer had predicted it would be, was to Richmond to visit Cabell and other Virginians with whom Mencken had been in close contact. The Richmond trip was the first of several he was to make in the twenties into a South that both repelled and fascinated him, and his attitude toward the Virginians in particular continued to be intriguing. In May 1921 he had begun corresponding with Emily Clark, the daughter of an Episcopal minister who earlier that year had begun a lively little magazine, *The Reviewer*. By the summer of 1921 he himself had taken an active role in directing the affairs of the magazine, and it was obvious that the editor wanted to please him more than any other literary figure. Redheaded, with green eyes and a southern drawl, Clark was one of several southern literary women who competed for Mencken's attention in the twenties. She was "homely," Mencken noted, but "interesting and energetic." With his help, she was to turn *The Reviewer* into a bold and critical southern voice, a harbinger of the South's literary renascence.

But it was not principally to see Emily Clark and to discuss *The Reviewer* that Mencken and Hergesheimer came to Richmond in November 1921. Mencken's larger fascination with Virginia and the old aristocracy drew him there. Cabell, the author of the slightly risqué and much-celebrated *Jurgen* (1919) as well as other novels often deemed "escapist," Mencken saw as the last aristocrat, "a lingering survivor [he had written in "The Sahara"] of the *ancien régime.*" The Virginian was the only southern novelist he had excluded from his searing indictment of the South.

Thus he was delighted when Cabell gave a party in his honor and later drove him to his country home, Dumbarton Grange, just outside Richmond. He was equally pleased by an invitation to Castle Hill, the home of novelist Amélie Rives and her husband, Prince Pierre Troubetzkoy. Rives, another product of Virginia's first families, and Troubetzkoy, a Russian painter, had lived abroad for a time and combined a certain international sophistication and southern charm of which Mencken approved. Although he could not accept their invitation in 1921, since Castle Hill was some miles away in the hunt country of Albemarle County, he was later to be their houseguest on several occasions.

The Prince and Princess Troubetzkoy of Castle Hill, Cabell of Dumbarton Grange (an estate, in fact, less grand than its name), and the other Virginians he met in 1921 reinforced for Mencken a certain ideal of the good life. But he wanted to see Cabell for reasons other than that. The Virginian was, quite simply, the contemporary American literary artist he respected most. A fabulist and satirist, Cabell was the creator of the mythical kingdom of Poictesme, a realm that seemed vastly remote from Virginia and the contemporary South but in fact was nearer to Cabell's own Virginia than his Richmond neighbors liked to think. Mencken was hardly alone in his esteem for Cabell. Fitzgerald had written him in 1920 that he considered Cabell, along with Mencken himself, "at the head and front of American letters," and various other writers, including Carl Van Doren and Burton Rascoe, shared Fitzgerald's assessment.

The Virginian would seem, on several levels, to be an unlikely writer for Mencken to admire—particularly the Mencken of the war years and the early twenties who was waging war against England, the "Anglo-Saxons," and the English tradition in American literature. For Cabell, as Mencken himself pointed out, was "an absolutely pure Anglo-Saxon," was "of pure English stock on both sides," and thought of himself as nothing less than an English gentleman. But the reason he could embrace Cabell and reject other Anglo-Saxons, not to mention southerners, was that he felt Cabell was the Englishman (or southerner) as cavalier, not as Puritan. He was, indeed, a "gentleman" in keeping with that eighteenth-century tradition Mencken himself revered.

But more than that, Mencken respected him, and had done so since they had first begun to correspond in 1916, because he believed Cabell was the artist pure and undefiled, the stylist and ironist, untainted by moral fervor or social concern. Despite the very different nature of his own work, he believed he shared with Cabell a certain vision, a view from afar of mankind as a "slightly foreign genus." In that respect he identified with Cabell perhaps more than with any other contemporary American novelist, even more than with Lewis. And more than that, in many respects he undoubtedly envied Cabell. There was a Mencken, after all, who in his youth had set out to write poems and stories, had experienced some small success, before he found a greater success in a more public arena. Although he relished that later success and reveled in the fame it brought him, there were times—when he read Conrad and Cabell—that he coveted the imaginative writer's private world, his awful solitude.

Mencken's relations with Dreiser, Lewis, and Fitzgerald, if not with Cabell and Hergesheimer, contributed greatly to his conclusion that notable novelists made unreliable and often undesirable friends. Although in the early 1920s he was publicly identified with Dreiser and Lewis, in fact his closest literary friends continued to be that group of editors, publishers, and critics in New York with whom he had been close during the war years, particularly Nathan, Goodman, Ernest Boyd, and Tom Smith, and much of the time he spent with these men in Prohibition-era New York was devoted to locating the ideal watering hole. After an extensive search, they found perfection a short ferry ride across the Hudson in Union Hill, New Jersey.

It is remarkable indeed how much time and attention Mencken expended on alcohol during these years, filling numerous letters with complaints about Prohibition or, when he was so ordered because of diet, complaining about the hardships of being on the wagon. He continued to devote a considerable amount of time and thought to home brewing as well. By the early twenties he had come to make "quite potable brews." In turn, he instructed Max Brödel and Phil Goodman in the art.

Goodman was still the friend whose company he valued most and whom he saw nearly every night he was in New York. When the two men were not setting out for the Alt Heidelburg in Union Hill or other drinking places in Hoboken or meeting at the Algonquin or at Nick's in Manhattan, they often had dinner at Goodman's Riverside Drive apartment with his wife and daughter. He prized Lily Goodman, who spoke good German, and to Goodman's young daughter, Ruth, Mencken seemed like a "second father"—she recalled much later—"an additional parent, only without the drawbacks." Sometimes Ruth went along with her father on his visits to Baltimore, where Goodman would accompany Mencken to the Saturday Night Club. Even as a girl she was struck by the contrast in Mencken's two worlds, particularly by the women in each. She found "a kind of dowdy dignity" in his mother and sister. They were "much less fashionable" than the women in New York.

Much of the correspondence between Mencken and Goodman in these years was filled with sexual banter. In fact, Mencken discussed sexual matters more frequently and more openly in his letters to Goodman than in any other written form, although even here he was usually hesitant to mention names and, compared to Goodman, was usually genteel, or medically clinical, in his language. He was now seeing a good many women in New York. "Your succession of gals bewilders me," his friend Paul de Kruif wrote him on one occasion. Sometimes he and Goodman took women along to Union Hill, other times Ernest Boyd arranged dinner companions and, when Mencken was in Baltimore, kept him informed by mail of the "amazing and charming" women, "exotic" creatures, who were asking for him. "Your lecheries are becoming fabulous," Boyd teased him, and Mencken was branching out to other cities as well. To a Baltimore friend he wrote of a particular bacchanal in Philadelphia, "such a party as the ancient Romans might have envied. The gin was brought on in gallon jugs, the eating lasted until 3 A.M., and the gals all had genito-urinary certificates over the great seal of the University of Pennsylvania . . ." Then he moved on to New York "and another gorgeous affair lasting all night."

In his social relations with women, even in these most adventurous of days, Mencken was in fact more refined than he suggested, at least with women whom he considered socially and culturally worthy of him. Alfred Knopf later recalled that his friend, whose barroom talk with men could be "ribald and scurrilous," was "perhaps the most polite man I have ever known . . . with women." Mencken himself acknowledged that he operated on a double standard. As he wrote Goodman, "I never drink what you might call freely under female scrutiny. I fear to cause pain by my gurglings and snortings." Such a resolve would explain the remark, long after Mencken's death, of a female friend, quite refined herself, who had never in thirty-three years seen Mencken even "slightly drunk" or known him to be "impolite, inconsiderate, or guilty of the slightest impropriety where any woman was concerned."

Among the women of whom Mencken was enamored in the early twenties was Jane O'Roarke, the actress whom he had met in San Francisco in 1920 and who was shortly to follow him to New York. He "genuinely fell" for O'Roarke, he wrote George Sterling, and with both Hergesheimer and Nathan he was even more direct: "I fell in love." If so, once O'Roarke was in New York his ardor cooled and he began to extricate himself from their entanglement. Within a year or two, his "handsome Irish-woman" was convicted of fraud and sent to prison. "A strange character and rather amusing," Mencken described her, appealing, "though somewhat too stout for my tastes." "It was generally assumed by everyone who knew us . . . that we were engaged in fornication," he felt compelled to add in a memoir twenty years later, "but, perhaps rather curiously, this was not true."

In the summer of 1920, just before he met Jane O'Roarke at the Democratic convention in San Francisco, he had made the acquaintance of Fanny Butcher at the Republican convention in Chicago. If Butcher, a literary journalist and bookstore owner, hardly inspired the kind of romantic fervor inspired by O'Roarke, she was to prove a far more enduring friend. For a time Mencken played the role of suitor, seeing her occasionally in both Chicago and New York, signing his letters with those words he reserved for a favored few—"Ich küss die Hand"—and assuming the rustic tone he often affected at such times: "Fanny, I wish you wasn't so far off. Fanny, we might set around when the shades of evening come busting down. . . ." Although he occasionally professed his love, Butcher believed he was kidding, and she was right.

Through Hergesheimer, Mencken met others, including a charming woman, Caroline Baird, whom he saw at Dower House in West Chester as well as in New York and to whom he wrote flirtatious letters in 1922 and 1923. In West Chester for long party weekends he often found, as Hergesheimer promised him on one of many such occasions, "a handsome gal or two, strong spirits and a pleasant air of the inconsequential." Still other women he saw in New York, usually in the company of Boyd and other friends. For a time in 1923, he kept company with Bernice Lesbia Kenyon, a poet and sometime contributor to *The Smart Set,* and received a steady stream of letters from "La Kenyon" that summer and fall. The newspapers printed news and rumors of his romantic entanglements, and on a particular Saturday night in April 1921 he emerged from a beer party to confront a report that he was engaged to be married. The rumor had appeared in the New York *Evening Post,* had been picked up by other newspapers, and, Mencken wrote Hergesheimer, "played hell with my chances with a certain fair creature. She won't listen to my denials."

In fact, the woman (excepting Anna Mencken) who continued to matter most in Mencken's life, even *in absentia,* was the only woman he had come close to marrying, Marion Bloom. Their parting in 1919 turned out to be a mutual retreat for a time into what both hoped would be emotionally safer quarters. But Mencken hardly forgot about Marion. He was "full of uneasy feelings" that she was "in difficulties," he wrote Estelle Bloom in February 1920. "With no news from her it worries me very much." He didn't want to write to her—Marion, in fact, had "forbidden" such correspondence—but he was concerned that she was in financial need and suggested that he send money to Estelle to give to her "without her knowing where it came from." Mencken wrote Estelle other letters in the late winter of 1920 remarking on what he saw as Marion's "martyr complex," confiding that he "couldn't bear to think of her in difficulties," and reflecting on events that had brought them to their "sorry finish." But the "whole business" was "closed, completely and finally," he insisted. "I think it would be insane to reopen it."

Reopen it they did, however, in some manner. By May Mencken was back in touch, again advising Marion to concentrate on her writing. For her part, she could not easily forgive him, she wrote Estelle, for "quit[ting] me when I was hitting a series of hard luck," and she was jealous of the women he was seeing in New York. But it was obvious that she missed him a great deal. In June she called and made arrangements to see him in Baltimore on a trip home to Maryland. She "accuses me of various atrocities, including a lewd affair with some imaginary cutie," Mencken wrote Estelle. But he would indeed see her.

Thus began another chapter in the Mencken-Bloom melodrama, an affair that continued to be agonizing for them both and drove Mencken, as he once wrote Marion, "almost beyond intelligent thinking." "I loved him enough to forget that we had passed the lover and mistress stage in planning marriage (or playing with the idea)," Marion wrote later, "and . . . I willingly re-entered the mistress stage." By December 1920 she reported to Estelle that Mencken had assured her "that he constantly needs me, and that if I actually showed a driving desire to marry, we'd do it. . . . We've both been through the fires and come out caring for each other," she reported him as saying.

But things were no easier than before. It is indeed curious testimony to the power of love, devotion, or carnal desire (which Mencken denied having in abundance) that a man who prized order and control above all things was in this particular so drawn to a liaison that promised only disorder and emotional chaos. He did not see Marion as often or as exclusively now as he had in 1919, but they remained in constant touch, "bombard[ing] each other with letters." He continued to lecture her on Christian Science and in his letters to Estelle referred to her as "the metaphysician," the "young [Mary Baker] Eddy," and "the New Windsor [Maryland] Jezebel." Marion continued to worry about "the Broadwayites," the "paradise birds," she feared were competing for his attention, all the while continuing to regret that he had not "held me close and sheltered me when I was hurt by war and life." She had come to believe that Mencken, like Dreiser, wanted "something for nothing."

At times—when he assured Marion that he cared for her more than for any other woman, when he came for a weekend, when he suggested a trip—she was exultant. She was delighted when he took her to a Sunpapers party and introduced her to Baltimore guests as "my girl." Maryland governor Albert C. Ritchie had been "violently attentive to her," she reported to Estelle, and Mencken had called her the belle of the occasion: "I think Henry was pleased with me." She was even happier when he told her that one guest from Washington had assumed she was his wife.

Marion also felt she had a more balanced view of Mencken now. She still loved him, even "worship[ed]" him, but she did not trust him. She reported to Estelle her expectations for a particular weekend in late 1921: "His visit will probably mean the reiteration that I am the only woman he cares for" to be followed by "a blank cartridge for months to come." She had not departed from her earlier view that he was among the most conventional of men: "He wants a virgin to [be his] wife, with all the dash of our broad thinking backed up with the exterior things of wealth, position, etc." Nonetheless, he had "been as good to me as he could be while respecting his personal inclinations."

In the summer of 1922 Mencken launched what appears to have been a last brief offensive in his reluctant crusade to win Marion. Before he went abroad in August, he spoke again of marriage. "I fell in joyously," Marion wrote her sister. Again, he was at his most attentive just before they would separate for several months. While he was in Europe he continued to write faithfully, just as he had when he sailed to Europe in 1917 and when Marion had sailed in 1918. "All the time," he wrote from Berlin in early September, he thought of seeing her again. "I do nothing here save drink beer and think of you," he wrote two weeks later from Munich. As he walked into the Leipzig railway station several days later, he caught sight of a woman "who was your exact duplicate . . . I was powerfully tempted to give her a royal buss . . ."

But in that last September letter he returned to one of the matters that had separated them earlier. Marion had just sent him an "essay" on the virtues of Christian Science, and he insisted, as usual, that she was in error. He continued in his familiar vein, combining humor with matters of consequence:

Good cooking is a damned sight more important in this carnal and loathesome [sic] life than accurate theology. . . . I give you fair warning that if . . . I come home in a bad humor, and find you with your nose in the Revelation of La Eddy (or Bergson), with cockroaches swarming in the kitchen and the beds not made—that, in such case I shall esteem it to be my duty to drape you over my knee and give you a good clouting.

When he returned the following month he had ceased to speak of marriage. He wanted to resume the former liaison. "I could not," Marion wrote Estelle. "And so we ended." This time it was over for good.

One reason for Mencken's abortive final campaign the summer of 1922 was his knowledge that she now had another suitor, one more committed than he himself was willing to be. As early as spring 1921 he had become aware that Marion, now living in Washington, was being pursued by a Romanian historian named Lou Maritzer, and that Maritzer wanted to marry her. In June he had written Estelle that he feared Marion would indeed "marry [Maritzer] some fine day, and be miserable forever after." In November 1922, after his own reluctant offensive of the summer and early fall, Mencken assumed the role of adviser: "If you should get yourself married to some plausible vacuum, with no money, I shall go into mourning for you. . . . For God's sake, don't let any fool delude you with speeches about what he is *going* to do." "Why don't you come over to Baltimore one evening," he asked, "and let me give you an old-time dinner, with a bottle of red wine?" She came.

When Mencken had occasion to meet Maritzer in February 1923, he jotted his impressions to Estelle: "He has merit, unquestionably, but it would be stretching the truth to call him handsome. I begin to suspect that the bride is an utter damned fool." Yet Mencken would not intervene. When in the summer of 1923 Marion told him that she was indeed planning to marry Maritzer, he did not appear to protest. When she proposed a meeting, he avoided it. Marion still loved Mencken a great deal, she wrote Estelle, and she could not get him out of her mind. Earlier, in describing Maritzer to Dreiser, Marion had written: "His complexion is certainly no lovelier than Henry's was. . . . I like his hands, but then Henry's were nice too." Mencken was the ideal against whom Maritzer or any other man was to be judged, and no one would ever measure up to him.

The spring and summer of 1923 were a very tense time for Marion. She felt pressure from Maritzer to marry and she despaired at the prospect of losing touch with Mencken, but she could take no more of his indecision. On July 28, "on an impulse," she married Maritzer. She notified Estelle, who in turn phoned Mencken. We have only Marion's version of what happened next. As Mencken sat in Estelle's home in New York and listened to her account of events, he wept openly. In spite of his own responsibility, he felt betrayed by Marion for not having been assertive enough to lead *him* to the altar, and for—he felt—having made a fool of him. In any case, after he left Estelle's, he went home and wrote Marion: "What am I to say? That I wish you the happiness that no one deserves so much as you do. That I have got out some old letters of yours, and re-read them, and burned them, and now sit down and smoke my pipe, and wonder what in hell it is all about."

The nine years of Mencken's deep involvement with Marion had come to an end, and two weeks after her marriage he reflected on it all in a letter to Estelle: "Well, such is human destiny in a world run by a jackass." He tried to be jocular: "Little will that gal ever suspect how near she came to cooking, washing and ironing for the next President of the United States." But at this point humor failed him. He attributed their dismal end to her Christian Science and to his "general rampaging in late years," which "scared her to death." Marion lived "in a world of dreams—many of them beautiful." As for himself, "I am 43, and all things begin to seem far off."

# Chapter 10

# "THE NEAREST THING
# TO VOLTAIRE"

I n August 1923, as Mencken was absorbing the news of Marion
Bloom's marriage, he was also seeing his editorship of *The Smart
Set* come to an end. Like his association with Marion, it had lasted
nine years, and by the summer of 1923 he was ready to move on. He,
Nathan, and, in his own way, publisher Eltinge F. Warner had made
attempts both to revive and to get rid of the magazine. Approaching
representatives of William Randolph Hearst, they had hoped to sell
*The Smart Set*, but with no success. Mencken and Nathan had also
encouraged Alfred Knopf and his father to approach Warner to see
if he were interested in selling, but Warner refused to consider
selling to the Knopfs. Finally, in August 1923 the editors contributed
to their own demise by writing for the September "Répétition Générale" a brief satirical piece on President Harding, who had died on
August 2 in California. When Warner killed the piece, Mencken and
Nathan were through.

The Harding satire, in fact, had been but the final episode in a
sorry story. Only three days before the president's death Mencken
had written Max Brödel that he was about to "assassinate the Smart
Set," and if Harding's death had not presented an opportunity for
the execution, something else would have. As Mencken told his
readers, he and Nathan had accomplished most of what they had set
themselves to do in 1908 and then again in 1914: "break down some
of the difficulties which beset the American imaginative writer . . . do

241

battle for him critically, attacking vigorously all the influences which sought to intimidate and regiment him." He and Nathan had not tired "of the combat," he insisted. But their interests and desires now led them "beyond belles lettres and so outside the proper field of THE SMART SET."

Mencken's interests led him, more specifically, to a new magazine, *The American Mercury*, which he and Knopf had been planning for some months. In fact, he had envisioned such a magazine, treating "the whole of American life," for more than a decade. As early as 1909 he had discussed a similar possibility with Willard Wright, and somewhat later he had envisioned a "Blue Weekly" to serve that function. Knopf had been thinking of Mencken as his editor since at least 1919, the two men were having discussions by 1921, and by late spring 1923 they were making firm plans. The idea, originally, was that Mencken and Nathan would also continue to edit *The Smart Set*. With the disagreement over the Harding satire, that plan became impossible, and for Mencken such an outcome was for the best. He was thinking only of the new magazine, "something far grander and gaudier," he wrote Brödel in July. "It is my hope . . . to stir up the animals. . . . The prospect makes me young again."

In letters to other friends, Mencken was equally enthusiastic. To Dreiser he confided his plans for a magazine "far above anything hitherto seen in the Republic." To Hergesheimer—who, he later discovered, tried to dissuade Knopf from making Nathan and himself editors—he remarked that it would be best if the *Mercury* were confined, "at least for the first year, to American themes." And to Carl Van Doren he explained his thinking behind the new *Mercury*:

> The scheme is to drive a wedge between the Liberals and their chasing of butterflies on the one hand and the New York Times Conservatives . . . on the other. There must be many young fellows in the country who baulk at Liberalism and yet can't go at the pace of the North American Review. . . . Well, I hope to bring them out, and to set them performing.

The magazine would represent "an educated Toryism," he wrote James Branch Cabell, "the true Disraelian brand."

To that end Mencken and Knopf labored over plans during the late summer and fall of 1923. According to Mencken's later account, Knopf wanted him to serve as sole editor. Mencken insisted, out of loyalty to Nathan, that his longtime friend be coeditor. It was agreed that both he and Nathan would be given one-sixth financial interest in *The American Mercury*, Inc. But the arrangement would be different from that of *The Smart Set*; this time Mencken's name would appear first on the masthead. The reason was not only that his fame now greatly exceeded Nathan's. It was also that the magazine, from the beginning, was essentially Mencken's creation. As he explained it, its subject matter, politics, and broad social and cultural issues "went far beyond Nathan's range of interest."

To all outward appearances, the *Mercury* got off to an exceptional start in January 1924. Intended for the "civilized minority" (as Knopf was quoted in many newspapers as saying, although the term was in fact Mencken's) and selling for fifty cents an issue, the first number included essays by Carl Van Doren, Ernest Boyd, and Harry Elmer Barnes, a story by Ruth Suckow, reviews by Mencken and Cabell, a series of letters by the late James Gibbons Huneker (who had died in 1921), and four poems by Dreiser. Mencken and Nathan also initiated several features which would become monthly staples of the magazine, including "Americana," which reported offenses against intelligence in all forty-eight states, and "Clinical Notes," which served the same function as "Répétition Générale" had in *The Smart Set*. The editors set forth their purpose in a four-page editorial. Not only would they tell the truth, they would also approach the truth with minds "entirely devoid of messianic passion." They would devote the magazine to the interests of "the normal, educated, well-disposed, unfrenzied, enlightened citizen of the middle minority." And they would laugh at frauds.

The January issue was greeted with great fanfare, and the February number, featuring a story by Sherwood Anderson and Eugene O'Neill's play *All God's Chillun Got Wings*, met with an equally enthusiastic response. By the second issue the circulation, over 15,000, had already far exceeded Mencken's earlier estimate for circulation by the end of the first year. But the trouble with Nathan that Mencken and Knopf had feared from the beginning soon made itself evident, and partly for the reason Mencken had anticipated: while he himself wanted social and political commentary, Nathan wanted literature. The two had even clashed over O'Neill's play: Nathan had wanted to accept it, Mencken had not. With Knopf's support, this time Nathan had won.

But Mencken's complaints with Nathan went beyond editorial control. By the spring of 1924 he was upset by his coeditor's inability or reluctance to take care of routine office business, as Nathan had on *The Smart Set*. Mencken was swamped with work, and by the summer of 1924 he had decided that Nathan was "completely incompetent," so "hopeless" that he would have to be dismissed. On October 15 he wrote the first of several letters, offering his assessment that the magazine was "full of defects" and "fast slipping into the formalism which ruined the Smart Set." He proposed a change in the editorship: "I will, as of January 1st next, take over complete control of the editorial department [and] put in a managing editor to run the place" or "will retire from all editorial duties." For the moment, he added, he was inclined toward the latter, although it is unlikely he meant that.

Several days later Mencken wrote another letter to Nathan, again forecasting a "round of dull drudgery" if the magazine remained as it was. His interests and those of Nathan were "too far apart," and they were drifting even "further and further apart": "I note an obvious proof of it: we no longer play together." The future of the magazine could be bright—it had an "opportunity to seize the leadership of the genuinely civilized minority of Americans"—but *only* if it had a single editor. To that end Mencken proposed a meeting with Knopf. He was not entirely sure, he wrote Nathan, "what is to be done," but he knew he could not continue as they were: "I am tired of routine, and much of it is routine and shouldn't be thrown on me. . . . I could work with a competent slave, but I can't work when I must be that slave myself."

Nathan was unhappy as well, but for far different reasons. He complained to Mencken of the "unreasonable and often insulting attitude you have displayed toward me in the last four or five months." He resented Mencken's assumption that the *Mercury* editorial department "must be run for your sole convenience." But he too was aware that something had to be done, and it was finally clear to him—since Mencken had Knopf's support—that he would be the one to give up the editorship. After discussing these matters, he, Mencken, and Knopf agreed that he would resign as coeditor as of the

February 1925 issue, although his name would remain on the magazine somewhat longer. And Nathan would continue to write "Clinical Notes" and "Theatre."

By early 1925 Mencken not only had complete editorial control of the *Mercury* but had found the "slave" to whom he could turn over office duties. In October 1924, the same month he had begun divorce proceedings from Nathan, he had received a letter from Charles Angoff, a young Harvard graduate and editorial writer for a small Massachusetts newspaper, in which Angoff inquired about a position on the Sunpapers. Mencken had responded that he could meet Angoff in New York, but to discuss a position on the *Mercury*, not the *Sun*. They had met for Sunday lunch, Mencken had been satisfied that Angoff could handle the routine work of managing the office and screening manuscripts, and thus he had hired him. Mencken would be able to return to his familiar *Smart Set* routine and come to New York only every third week.

He intended to make *The American Mercury* a "more serious and mature" magazine than *The Smart Set*, and it was soon evident that he had succeeded. Although he published fiction by Dreiser, Fitzgerald, Cabell, Sherwood Anderson, and Dorothy Parker and poetry by Carl Sandburg, Vachel Lindsay, Edgar Lee Masters, and Louis Untermeyer, it was clear from the beginning that the strength of the magazine lay in its essays. The list of nonfiction contributors for the first two years is impressive: Clarence Darrow, Charles Beard, Upton Sinclair, Carl Van Vechten, Waldo Frank, Margaret Sanger, Max Eastman, Emma Goldman, Joseph Wood Krutch, Carl Van Doren, Ernest Boyd, Arthur Krock, Josephine Herbst, Bernard De Voto, and Benjamin de Casseres. Mencken also published essays by Dreiser, Hergesheimer, and Lewis. He brought along others of his own discoveries, including journalists Gerald W. Johnson and James Cain, and several young southern women writers, among them Emily Clark, Julia Peterkin, and a twenty-seven-year-old Alabamian, Sara Haardt.

The subjects Mencken encouraged his contributors to tackle—which he, indeed, sometimes assigned—were usually controversial: birth control, racial purity, fundamentalism, Prohibition, and the Ku Klux Klan, as well as often iconoclastic portraits of political figures from Lincoln to Wilson and Coolidge and literary figures from Shakespeare to Whitman. He did not hesitate to accept essays representing positions different from his own. He published Max Eastman and Emma Goldman on the left as well as, from a son of the Massachusetts Bay, an essay entitled "In Defense of the Puritan." But he made his own position clear in review essays in the "Library" section and in lengthy editorials. Here he turned his critical eye on organized religion, American journalism, William Jennings Bryan, "The Coolidge Farce," Christian Science, and the American farmer. Mencken had at last found his forum, the pulpit he had dreamed of ever since, ten years before, he had envisioned the "Blue Weekly." He had all the editorial freedom of the old "Free Lance" but a vastly more sophisticated and sympathetic national audience.

The *Mercury* belonged, as he had predicted it would, to neither the liberal nor the conservative camp. In the area of arts and letters its editor continued to abhor the traditionalists, but neither would he fully embrace modernism. It was clear from his statements in the *Mercury*, as it had been in *The Smart Set*, that he rejected modern art, had little use for twentieth-century music, and, as he later wrote, "had but little truck with the Imagists, Dadaists, Expressionists, Vorticists, Futurists and other revolutionaries . . . !"

He continued to correspond with Ezra Pound, now concerning, in Pound's words, the "Murkn Mercury," and he still thought highly of Joyce (a view that was soon to change), but he completely rejected his fellow Baltimorean Gertrude Stein. She was—he later wrote, at his vitriolic worst, in his memoirs—"a psychopathic case, and her grotesque body was matched by a cretinous and homosexual mind. There was absolutely nothing in her incoherent ramblings." He had much more respect for but little understanding of T. S. Eliot, whom Pound had earlier recommended to him as "the last intelligent man." It was not that he disagreed with Eliot in all particulars—politically, both were not only Tories but monarchists—but his remarks suggested how far he was from fully grasping the form and substance of modernism: "In the doctrine that [Eliot] was both a great poet and a great thinker I could see nothing but nonsense. His poetry, in fact, was largely only prose sawed up into lengths . . ."

But the literary modernist, other than Stein, to whom he objected most—as much because of his personality as his work—was Ernest Hemingway. In the fall of 1924 he rejected stories the young writer sent to the *Mercury*, and Hemingway never forgave or forgot the rejection. For a time he sought Mencken out as a personal challenge, lampooning him in *The Sun Also Rises* (though not so harshly as Mencken believed) and placing an ironic dedication to him in his parody *The Torrents of Spring*. On another occasion, after reading Mencken's critical remarks, Hemingway sent word that he was coming to Baltimore for revenge. Mencken regarded Hemingway as "an extremely vain and petty fellow" who continued to demonstrate a "bitter and implacable hostility" toward him personally—or, as he wrote Jim Cain, a "dreadful ass" who could not "get rid of the yokel's desire to be regarded as a devilish fellow."

In fact, despite his rejection of the early stories, he felt that Hemingway as a writer "unquestionably had some talent" and that, indeed, some of his work was "excellent." And in matters of personality, he had more in common with Hemingway than either man acknowledged—not only a combative spirit and a devotion to the cult of masculinity but also an abhorrence of romanticism and a nearly compulsive desire for order. Mencken's creed, stated later in his memoirs, is a close cousin of Hemingway's own. "Competence, indeed," Mencken was to write, "[is] my chief admiration . . . and next to competence I put what is called being a good soldier—that is, not whining."

Although Mencken rejected Hemingway for the early *Mercury*—and the young writer vowed never again to send material to the magazine—the *Mercury* editor was more charitable to numbers of other new authors. In particular, he was receptive to black writers, without question more helpful than any other editor of his time. Both W.E.B. Du Bois and the poet Countee Cullen appeared in the *Mercury*'s pages during its first year, and in later issues poets James Weldon Johnson and Langston Hughes and future NAACP head Walter F. White were represented. Indeed, the black journalist George S. Schuyler, who contributed nine essays to the *Mercury*, was to appear more frequently in the magazine in the final six years of Mencken's editorship than any other writer, white or black.

Mencken's position on race is a most curious matter (particularly given the heated discussion of race after a substantial part of his diary was published in 1989), and that position in the 1920s continued to be the mixture of enlightenment, paternalism, and racial stereotyping he had always shown. "I am . . . almost devoid of race prejudice," he claimed in 1925, yet much of what he had written to that point suggests otherwise. If he fondly recalled his acquaintance with blacks

in the Hollins alley, he also remarked—in autobiographical notes—
that most of his family's black hired women were "sloppy, dirty and
incompetent," and we find in an early school composition notebook
a reference to gorillas, which "so closely resemble the woodsmen of
Africa that hardly any distinction can be found."

Although such a schoolboy sentiment might be excused—given
European and American ideas about racial supremacy, what white
American schoolboy in 1894 might not have said that?—as a young
newspaperman he seemed at times almost as harsh. He was still given
to almost all the epithets—coon, niggero, darkey, and blackamoor
were among his favorites—and, writing in 1911 in "The Free Lance"
on the subject of black crime, he had written that Americans of
African descent "constitute a class apart, a separate caste of abnor-
mally vicious and disorderly citizens." The year before, in *Men
Versus the Man*, he had maintained that the Negro

> brain is not fitted for the higher form of mental effort; his ideals,
> no matter how laboriously he is trained and sheltered, remain those
> of the clown. He is, in brief, a low-caste man [along with, Mencken
> had added, certain "European peasants" now coming to America]
> . . . and he will remain inert and inefficient until fifty generations
> of him have lived in civilization. And even then, the superior white
> race will be fifty generations ahead of him.

Even in the *Mercury*, in an essay praising black accomplishments, he
gave the impression that he had not departed a great deal from his
early sentiments. "The vast majority of the people of their race," he
wrote in 1926, "are but one or two inches removed from gorillas."

Such a record would seem to condemn Mencken outright, and yet,
if his utterances at times suggested severe racial prejudice, at other
times his words—and more particularly, his actions—seem, given his
time and place, a virtual testimony to racial enlightenment. If in his
early writing he had once depicted blacks as "a class apart," he had
also in early Sunpaper editorials and columns stood almost alone in
calling for humane treatment of Baltimore's black citizens, had in
1906 proposed to Ellery Sedgwick an essay on "What It Means to Be
a Negro," and in 1917 in the New York *Evening Mail* had praised
a black Howard University professor for speaking out against racial
wrongs and demanding political rights.

It was in the period during and after World War I, indeed, that Mencken had come to demonstrate a racial (if not linguistic) sensitivity that he had shown only occasionally before. That heightened awareness was suggested not only in his recruitment of black writers for the *Mercury* but in the aid he gave in numerous other ways. It was as if he had concluded that the literary suffrage, which he had fought to extend to Germans, Jews, and Eastern Europeans, should now be extended to writers of African descent as well. Because of his own experiences during the war, he had come to identify more closely with the oppressed and the silenced. Both he and black Americans had suffered at the hands of the Anglo-American establishment, and both possessed a particular abhorrence for the contemporary South.

Whatever the case, in the 1920s Mencken became a champion of black American literature and any number of individual black writers. He carried on a friendly correspondence with Du Bois, Schuyler, Cullen, James Weldon Johnson, Walter F. White, and the poet Claude McKay, among others, in most cases discussing essays they might write for the *Mercury*. With Schuyler he spoke of possible articles on Jim Crow, intermarriage, the black clergy, and black soldiers, as well as "the dear Nordic brethren." White he not only published in the *Mercury* but also urged to write a novel on southern race relations. The result was *The Fire in the Flint*, a work about lynching that reinforced Mencken's own picture of a benighted South, and he spoke with Knopf about the manuscript. When Knopf published the novel, White gave Mencken the "credit and thanks" for his book.

James Weldon Johnson he had known much longer. The two had met during the war, when the black poet, a great admirer of Mencken's work, had come to the *Smart Set* offices hoping to meet him but not feeling "entirely confident" that the white editor would come out to greet him. Mencken had not only appeared promptly, he had spoken with Johnson for thirty or forty minutes, far longer than Johnson had anticipated. The poet had left feeling "buoyed up, exhilarated," despite Mencken's rejection of the translation of a Spanish play he had hoped to publish. Later, Mencken not only published Johnson's work but recommended that Knopf consider publishing his memoirs.

His racial concerns in the twenties went beyond helping black authors to be published. He campaigned within the Sunpapers for the fair and adequate presentation of Negro news, insisting that black cultural activities be reported and a black reporter employed. In 1926, when the members of the Baltimore City Club invited Countee Cullen to speak at the Emerson Hotel "and then stood by without a protest," he wrote Hamilton Owens, "while he was kicked out of the Emerson," he was furious. "It would be hard to match in Mississippi," he wrote. "The City Club cads, knowing very well that Cullen was a coon, should have looked into the matter at length before inviting him. . . . Their guest was insulted, and Maryland was made ridiculous."

Mencken's statement captures the combination of moral indignation, sensitivity to decorum, and verbal insensitivity that would always be a part of his racial attitude. At times in the twenties the insensitivity went beyond the use of racial epithets. The man who could protest mightily when Countee Cullen was dismissed from the Emerson Hotel could also—as he put it in a letter to a Washington friend—hire "a Jew lawyer to induce the neighboring owners to sign an anti-coon agreement" when it appeared that blacks would move into the Hollins Street neighborhood. "I don't care a damn myself," he added. He had done it for his mother.

Mencken's black authors hardly knew that side of him. To them he was not only the most trenchant critic of a society that had treated them unjustly but also their friend and advocate. Johnson, White, Schuyler, and other writers publicly acknowledged their debt, and the black press often chimed in with its praise as well. Even to aspiring black authors whom he would never meet, he was a champion. In 1927, in Memphis, Tennessee, nineteen-year-old Richard Wright read in the Memphis *Commercial-Appeal* an editorial denouncing him for his criticism of the white South. This Mencken, Wright decided, must be worth reading. As he was to relate the story in his autobiography, *Black Boy*, he was able to borrow a library card from a white man and forge a note to the librarian: "Will you please let this nigger boy have some books by H. L. Mencken?" The suspicious librarian gave him *A Book of Prefaces* and one volume of *Prejudices*, and he read all night long. "I pictured the man as a raging demon, slashing with his pen . . . denouncing everything American . . . laughing at the weaknesses of people, mocking God, authority. . . . He was using words as a weapon, using them as one would use a club."

Wright dated his birth as a writer from that hour.

If Mencken had achieved a rather substantial fame by 1920, by the mid-twenties he had become, Walter Lippmann wrote, the most powerful influence on a whole generation of educated Americans. The circulation of the *Mercury* was now nearly 60,000, a remarkable figure for a magazine of ideas and cultural commentary, and it was still on the rise. Mencken's magazine was the most widely discussed in America, and on campuses the green-backed *Mercury* was carried as a mark of liberation. The *Prejudice* volumes were also having an influence far in excess of their sales figures, and Mencken was being hailed as a phenomenon unprecedented in the nation's cultural life.

His celebrity went far beyond the world of letters and ideas. His clipping service now sent two or three hundred items each month, including a piece from the New York *Daily News* that concluded through interviewing women, however unscientifically, that he was the third most fascinating man in the world. (He tied with Rudolph Valentino, Charlie Chaplin, and Douglas Fairbanks; another newspaper, somewhat later, had him as number one.) The newspapers were full of his activities and opinions, as well as attempts by editors to find exact parallels for him. "America's Dr. Johnson," one editor called him, "the nearest thing to Voltaire that America has ever produced," remarked another, "the most vital critic we have had." He was "the most civilized man in America" to one writer, "the Genghis Khan of the Campus" to still another. His fame extended to places he cared little for. He was already a "legend" in Greenwich Village, according to Klaus Mann, and Sherwood Anderson wrote him from New Orleans that he had captured "the back country as well. Everywhere I went they asked me first—what do you think of Mencken?"

Mencken was indeed a phenomenon. Perhaps for the first time in American life a critic, rather than a novelist or a poet, was the most famous and most influential American writer, and numerous were the attempts to explain him. To many he was what he sometimes called himself, a high Tory, but, according to one of his informers, in the books of at least one Justice Department official he was listed as a Bolshevik. To Rotarians and Kiwanians he was an outrage, casting doubt on the meaning of life as they perceived it, and to

Christian ministers, particularly Methodist, he was a "menace" who had his "ghastly fingers of death about the throats of so many young Americans," the dispenser of a "poison which will eat out their hearts and drag their souls down to hell." To Walter Lippmann he was an "outraged sentimentalist," a frustrated idealist who "calls you a swine, and an imbecile, and . . . increases your will to live." To a New York psychoanalyst, writing anonymously, he was a reluctant iconoclast whose "fundamental character-shaping wish" was "to join the ranks of the respectable." And to a wounded editor in Arkansas, searching Mencken's fulminations about Dixie for an explanation of his anger, he was simply a puzzle. "What," he asked, "has the South done to Menneken [sic]?"

Mencken-watching had become such a preoccupation by the midtwenties that two books were under way, one by his old friend Ernest Boyd, the other by an acquaintance and *American Mercury* contributor, Isaac Goldberg. Both works appeared in 1925. Boyd's brief critical study, somewhat short of a hundred pages, treated him as critic and "philosopher" but—from the Irishman's point of view—one very much in the American grain, a provincial Baltimorean in the homegrown traditions of individualism and optimistic good humor. Though Boyd had not hesitated to disagree with Mencken occasionally, particularly concerning Nietzsche, the subject thought highly of the product. It was, he wrote Boyd, "a quite extraordinary piece of synthesis."

But the book that truly engaged him in the mid-1920s was Goldberg's biography, so much so that he became virtual coauthor. In 1924 Goldberg—"the better sort of Jew," Mencken once remarked—had written a short pamphlet on him for E. Haldeman-Julius and, finding he was still interested in his subject, had set to work on a full-length biography for which he requested Mencken's help. Since Goldberg knew very little about his ancestry and early years, Mencken agreed to provide such material. What resulted was an autobiographical sketch of some two hundred typed pages, part of which Goldberg plugged into his biography, changing first person to third.

Their correspondence in 1925 demonstrates how fully Mencken was a participant, at times a controlling force, in the writing of the biography. Goldberg kept him informed every few days of its progress and sent him chapters as they came out of the typewriter. Following Mencken's suggestion, he rewrote certain passages and excised selected lines. Mencken passed on the entire manuscript before it went to the publisher, Simon and Schuster. Yet he rejected a suggestion from Goldberg that he sign one hundred copies of the book. He feared such an action would give the impression that he had played some part in it.

Goldberg's book proved less a conventional biography than a three-hundred-page encomium. Though a socialist and thus a critic of Mencken's political position—as well as of his "excessive mistrust of the emotions" and his occasional "critical masochism and sadism"—Goldberg was otherwise a great admirer. He saw the *Mercury* editor as the dominant intellectual force of his time, "the Lucifer of the American paradise, leading the revolt of the angels." Although a few reviewers called the biographer too much the sycophant, most praised the biography and several called its author "Mencken's Boswell"—with the understanding that his subject was indeed a sort of Dr. Johnson. One reviewer, noting the appearance the same year of both the Goldberg and Boyd books, was moved to observe, "The canonization of H. L. Mencken has begun."

It would have been heady stuff for any other forty-five-year-old, but by this time Mencken was accustomed to such adulation. He relished the attention (although he did eliminate one of Goldberg's references to his "greatness"), and while the biography was being written he was constantly in motion, adding to his legend. The year 1924, he later wrote, had been the busiest of his life, and 1925 was nearly as frantic. But his energy was also "at an all-time peak," and despite the usual physical complaints, he had never been, nor would he ever be, "in better form." He was unreceptive to an offer that would have paid him thousands to lecture across the country for six weeks, but he was occupied in numerous other ways. Aside from writing for the *Evening Sun* and the *Mercury*, he began a weekly column, for $200 an essay, for the *Chicago Tribune* and its syndicate. Although he had less time for writing books than he had just after the war, he did produce a fourth in the series of *Prejudices*. This volume, with essays on American literature, politics, Prohibition, New York City, the Anglo-Saxon, rural Americans ("Christian bumpkins" who "assemble in their Little Bethels to be instructed in the word of God, the plots of the Pope, the crimes of the atheists and Jews"), and numerous other subjects seemed less original than its predecessors.

In several events of the mid-1920s Mencken was able to combine the roles of reporter and celebrity. Indeed, when he traveled to cover a notable event, he often became part of the story himself. In 1924, as usual, he covered the national conventions, the Republicans in Cleveland and the Democrats in New York, although the Republican show, which came first, was particularly disappointing. He found "a parade of small town Rotarians in mailorder clothes," an "almost pathological stupidity," democracy at its "lowest recorded dip." Since the Cleveland convention, which nominated Coolidge, was bone dry—and the motorboatload of bottled beer, sent from Detroit by Mencken's brewing instructor, Harry Rickel, was drunk by the crew en route—proceedings were made bearable only by a supply of gin Paul Patterson had brought along, a chance to talk with Ring Lardner, and a trip just after the convention to Michigan to see Rickel and meet with British poet laureate Robert Bridges.

The Democratic show, better than the Republican as usual, led Mencken to reflect on the nature of such events:

> There is something about a national convention that makes it as fascinating as a revival or a hanging. It is vulgar, it is ugly, it is stupid, it is tedious, it is hard upon both the higher cerebral centers and the gluteus maximus, and yet it is somehow charming. One sits through long sessions wishing heartily that all the delegates and alternates were dead and in hell—and then suddenly there comes a show so gaudy and hilarious, so melodramatic and obscene, so unimaginably exhilarating and preposterous that one lives a gorgeous year in an hour.

The New York convention had three such "supreme shows," the final one occurring after two weeks, when "the whole company . . . went crazy in ten seconds" and nominated John W. Davis. As it turned out, Mencken missed those ten seconds. The convention as a whole could not compete with 1920 in San Francisco. But he nonetheless had his "fair share of fun—enough . . . to take me back in 1928."

He also continued to paint vivid pictures of the American scene in the *Mercury* and the *Evening Sun*. After covering a Ku Klux Klan rally in Washington, he came away reflecting on the spectacle:

> The Klansmen plodded bravely on, their eyes upon the starry future of the republic, purged of atheism and hyphenism at last. . . . Some were clad in billowy gowns of sea-green satin, with turbans on their heads set with synthetic rubies. Others were swathed in yellow, red and blue. They were, in the main, men of girth and so there was plenty of room for showing off their finery. . . . They were common folk, and their commonness radiated from them like heat from a stove. . . . The wheelbarrow handle, it was plain, was more familiar to the men in that long line than the golf-stick, and the washtub had engaged the women far oftener than the lipstick.
>
> But what of it? The klan is not a club for snobs, it is a device for organizing inferiorities into a mystical superiority . . .

And he continued his assault on university professors, to whom he showed far less compassion than to Klansmen: "Of a thousand head of such dull drudges not ten, with their doctors' dissertations behind them, ever contribute so much as a flyspeck to the sum of human knowledge." He kept blasting away at higher education in general, particularly the colleges "in the Cow States, where the peasants have long cherished a superstitious veneration for education, and credit it with powers almost equal to those of a United Brethren bishop or Lydia Pinkham's Vegetable Compound." As for Eastern universities:

> A Yale man, however he may snort and roar, can never get rid of the scarlet fact that, while he was being fattened for the investment securities business, he was herded into chapel each morning. It rides him through life like a Freudian suppression: he recalls it in the forlorn blackness of the night as a Y.M.C.A. secretary recalls a wicked glass of beer, or the smooth, demoralizing, horrible whiteness of a charwoman's neck. A Princeton man remembers the Fundamentalists at commencement—flies in amber, spectres at memory's feast.

All these American phenomena excited Mencken, but the spectacle that excited him most of all, and that gave him his greatest celebrity as a reporter, was the Scopes trial in Dayton, Tennessee, in July 1925. In many ways, indeed, the trial of a young science instructor for teaching evolution in the public schools was a prototypic event in American history, the single event of the 1920s that brought to the surface all the forces and tensions of postwar America and most dramatically illustrated the struggle between religious fundamentalism—and American provincialism in a larger sense—and the values of the modern, secular world. The trial was conducted in sweltering heat in a red-brick courthouse before more than two hundred American reporters and several others from Western Europe. It was an event created for Mencken, and the defendant, John Thomas Scopes, was more accurate than he knew when he remarked, some forty years later, "In a way it was Mencken's show."

Mencken had been in on the writing of the script nearly from the beginning. While visiting Cabell in Richmond in the spring of 1925, he had heard that the aging William Jennings Bryan, object of Mencken's attention at the 1904 and 1920 Democratic conventions and now a crusader for fundamentalism, would be going to Dayton to help prosecute Scopes. He and Hergesheimer had met with Clarence Darrow, who also happened to be in Richmond, and had persuaded Darrow to undertake Scopes's defense. He had not always thought highly of Darrow, who was on the left politically and who he also felt had been a "violent Hun-hater" during the war, but now he had joined forces with great delight. Later in the spring he had met at Hollins Street with an associate of Darrow and his cocounsel, Arthur Garfield Hays, in order to plan strategy for the trial; it was Mencken who suggested putting Bryan on the stand, thus shifting the focus away from Scopes. The *Evening Sun* provided bail for Scopes. And Mencken himself—who had earlier given the term "the Bible Belt" to the American language—gave the Dayton spectacle the label it has worn ever since, "the Monkey Trial."

The events in Tennessee could not have come at a better time. Earlier that year, even before the reports of Scopes's ungodliness, he and Patterson had discussed another "stirring up of the South," and Patterson had suggested that he take a southern trip of a week or ten days to see what he could turn up. The journey to east Tennessee would thus be a virtual field trip for the man who, in "The Sahara of the Bozart" and elsewhere, had described southern whites, particularly the Celts and Anglo-Saxons of the hills, as a nearly foreign species. For Mencken's greatest prejudice of all—far greater than any against blacks, Jews, "half-civilized" immigrants from Eastern Europe, or even Methodists—was that against the southern cracker. "The Southern poor white [is] a great deal worse than [the] Southern blackamoor," he believed; or, as he was to write his black friend George Schuyler, "[The poor white] seems to me to be hardly human. . . . There has never been a more miserable white man on this earth, nor black man, nor yellow man."

Thus the prospect of such an anthropological expedition to the Cumberland slopes—in addition to the prospect of encountering, in the flesh and in great abundance, the very fundamentalist preachers who had always fascinated him—made Mencken spit on his hands. "On to Dayton," he wrote sociologist Howard W. Odum of Chapel Hill in late June. "The greatest trial since that before Pilate!" "I'm leaving for the Hill of the Skull tonight," he gloated to Fielding Garrison on July 6. "I look for three or four days of excellent comedy."

In fact, Mencken was to stay nearly two weeks. Accompanied by four other members of the Sunpapers staff, he first found quarters in Chattanooga and commuted the fifty miles through the hills. After a couple of days he moved to Dayton and took rooms in the home of the town dentist and his wife, cautiously liberal folks who, Mencken wrote Hamilton Owens, he found "much superior to the common run of Daytonians."

At first, in fact, he found even that "common run" less benighted than he had anticipated. "I expected to find a squalid Southern village, with darkies snoozing on the horseblocks, pigs rooting under the houses and the inhabitants full of hookworm and malaria," he wrote in an early dispatch from Tennessee. "What I found was a country town full of charm and even beauty." But it was obvious to him from the beginning that it would be "no more possible in this Christian valley to get a jury unprejudiced against Scopes than would be possible in Wall Street to get a jury unprejudiced against a Bolshevik." The "exegetes who roar and snuffle in the town" saw only

blazing ratifications and reinforcements of Genesis. Darwin is the devil with seven tails and nine horns. Scopes, though he is disguised by flannel pantaloons and a Beta Theta Pi haircut, is the harlot of Babylon. Darrow is Beelzebub in person . . .

The day before the trial began, he ran into Bryan and had a good talk with the Great Commoner. Bryan at first was grateful to him for having written in *The Nation* that, whatever the merits of evolution, Tennessee had a right to determine what was to be taught in its schools. Mencken and his colleague Henry Hyde found much else to occupy them as well—debating the numerous fundamentalists who had poured into Dayton for the trial, passing out handbills announcing the appearance of "Elmer Chubb, LL.D.," and attending a camp meeting in the hills outside the town. He delighted in the street debate of the fundamentalists, most of whom (though hardly all) were "yokels from the hills, where no sound is heard after sundown save the roar of the catamount and the wailing of departed spirits, and a man thus has time to ponder the divine mysteries." But he delighted most of all in the "Holy Roller communion" he himself invaded on a mountainside outside town. To Mencken, the utter rationalist, the scene he beheld—a series of preachers and mourners male and female—was nearly unfathomable:

What followed . . . reached such heights of barbaric grotesquerie that it was hard to believe it real. At a signal all the faithful crowded up to the bench and began to pray—not in unison but each for himself. . . . The leader kneeled, facing us, his head alternately thrown back dramatically or buried in his hands. Words spouted from his lips like bullets from a machine gun—appeals to God to pull the penitent back out of hell, defiances of the powers and principalities of the air, a vast impassioned jargon of apocalyptic texts. Suddenly he rose to his feet, threw back his head and began to speak in tongues. . . . His voice rose to a higher register. The climax was a shrill, inarticulate squawk, like that of a man throttled. He fell headlong across the pyramid of supplicants. . . .

From the squirming and jabbering mass a young woman gradually detached herself. . . . Her head jerked back, the veins of her neck swelled, and her fists went to her throat as if she were fighting for breath. She bent backward until she was like half of a hoop. Then she suddenly snapped forward. . . . Presently her whole body began to be convulsed. . . . She would leap to her feet, thrust her arms in air and then hurl herself upon the heap. . . . The lady's [sensations] . . . were obviously contagious, for soon another damsel joined her, and then another and then a fourth. The last one

... was bounding all over the place, exactly like a chicken with its head cut off. ... Once she collided with a dark, undersized brother, hitherto silent and stolid. Contact with her set him off as if he had been kicked by a mule. He leaped into the air, threw back his head and began to gargle as if with a mouthful of BB shot. Then he loosened one tremendous stentorian sentence in the tongues and collapsed. ...

The heap of mourners was directly before us. They bounced into us as they cavorted. The smell that they radiated, sweating there in that obscene heap, half suffocated us.

Mencken reported such activities "as a strict behaviorist," he told his *Evening Sun* readers, but he was spellbound by what he saw, and his lengthy description was like no reporting he had ever done. Nothing had prepared him for what he encountered beside the mountain cornfield, nor for much else he witnessed in and around Dayton. The entire scene—the trial and its peripheral activities—would constitute "the Tennessee Circus," he had written earlier, and now he believed he had vastly underestimated its impact. It was "five times better than I expected," he wrote a friend in Baltimore. "That such a place as Dayton exists," he now decided, "is really staggering."

The trial itself was a subdued show in comparison with much else Mencken found, but he showed up daily, taking his place in the crowded courtroom, often standing on a table in the corner, fanning himself and staring incredulously at the events unfolding before him. He sent back to the *Evening Sun* nine daily dispatches, all of which were picked up by numerous other newspapers, including the nearby *Chattanooga News*. When Bryan read the dispatches depicting him as an "old mountebank," "mangey and flea-bitten," "full of . . . bitter, implacable hatreds," his attitude toward Mencken changed. At first he frowned, and by the end of the first week of the trial, Mencken reported in later autobiographical notes, "he was glaring ferociously every time he saw me." But most of the townspeople and visiting evangelists, Mencken wrote a friend, "treated me with the greatest politeness." One of their number, a Pastor Martin of Blue Mountain, Mississippi, was to write to him for years afterward, in hopes of landing his biggest convert. He went to his death, Martin's daughter later wrote Mencken, in full hope "of saving [him] soon or late."

Despite widespread stories to the contrary, Mencken was not run out of Dayton at the end of the two weeks. He left on his own, having to return for business, and thus missed Darrow's legendary cross-examination of Bryan—in which Bryan denied that man was a mammal—as well as the verdict: Scopes was convicted, and the *Evening Sun* paid his $100 fine. But Mencken was hardly through with the Scopes trial. As he wrote a friend in Baltimore, he would "be writing about it for the next 10 years." Indeed, he could not leave it behind for so much as a week. For five days after the trial concluded, Bryan died in Dayton, and Mencken turned to his typewriter to compose his dubious tribute for the *Evening Sun*. Given the circumstances—the death of a three-time presidential nominee and former national hero—it was to be perhaps the harshest prose he ever wrote.

It was evident in Dayton, Mencken wrote in his mock eulogy, that Bryan was "simply a walking malignancy," radiating hatred toward all intelligence and civility: "All sense departed from him. He bit right and left, like a dog with rabies." The silver-tongued orator of national legend had in fact been

> a vulgar and common man, a cad undiluted . . . ignorant, bigoted, self-seeking, blatant and dishonest . . . deluded by a childish theology, full of an almost pathological hatred of all learning, all human dignity, all beauty, all fine and noble things. He was a peasant come home to the dung-pile.

Bryan passed out of life "a pathetic fool," "one of the most tragic asses in American history."

Mencken should hardly have been surprised that the *Evening Sun* had doubts about using his piece—which it nonetheless printed—and in a letter to Fielding Garrison he reflected on the newspaper's initial reluctance:

> Sentimentality dies very hard. For two weeks I denounced him as a mountebank daily; now he must be praised. But not by me, by damn! He was a villainous old scoundrel, evil and greasy. I had a long gabble with him one day, and came away almost puking.

He reflected on Bryan's death in letters to numerous friends over the next few days, and hardly with the requisite high seriousness. "No doubt Heaven is in turmoil today, with Bryan just arrived," he wrote Garrison. "Today," he remarked to Hergesheimer, "he flaps his wings." As much of the nation praised Bryan, he continued his gleeful assault. "I shall have the book of Psalms in my pocket when I go to the Bryan funeral tomorrow," he wrote another friend, and the next day, to still another, "I stopped work today for an hour during the funeral of Bryan."

Mencken's treatment of the fallen Bryan, one of three obituary essays he would write on his adversary, brought down his readers' wrath as much as anything he had ever written. He simply was not observing the common courtesies and conventions: in death, one should say something kind or nothing at all. It was only the most obvious instance of his defiance of the rules by which others played— or, as he saw it, the most obvious display of an honesty and courage too long absent from the pages of American newspapers. He despised Bryan the fundamentalist, the Prohibitionist, the Anglophile, the defender of all those rural values that were anathema to Mencken himself. Besides, he was having great fun. He was in his mid-forties, full of energy and hilarity, delighted with his own malicious magnetism, internationally famous, and at the absolute peak of his form. The times were as good for him as they would ever be.

Mencken should have known, as he left Dayton and headed north in late July, that his mood of high hilarity and comic detachment could not last. If anything in life seemed certain, his experience told him, it was that nothing good endures, that particularly heady times are often followed by especially bad ones. Never was that truth clearer and most painful than in the second half of 1925. His most spectacular year was to wind down most dismally, and this time death could not be laughed away. December was to be, to that point, the cruelest month of his life.

He had some idea of what was to come when Dr. Louis Hamburger told him in the summer of 1925 that his mother, now sixty-seven, was suffering from "a rapidly progressive form of arteriosclerosis" and that nothing could be done other than to make her as comfortable as possible. He had remained extremely close to his mother, not only continuing to live at home but always taking her welfare into account

261

when he planned out-of-town trips. Now "it was dreadful to watch her sufferings," he wrote, although "her actual pain was never great." As he took nightly breaks from his work in his third-floor office, he would come to her second-floor sitting room to talk and find that "the sight and thought of her" made further work impossible: "My mind was filled with horrible imaginings, and I resented bitterly the fact that medicine could do so little for her."

Anna Mencken's condition deteriorated during the autumn. She experienced numbness in her hands and was unable to sleep without medication. On December 9 Mencken went into her sitting room, found her appearance particularly alarming, and discovered that she had a temperature of 103 degrees. What she was suffering from was not a complication of the arteriosclerosis but rather acute tonsillitis and a streptococcus infection, and Mencken wrote Alfred Knopf the following day that he would probably have to cancel an upcoming trip to New York. The next day, December 11, he took his mother to Union Memorial Hospital, where she underwent minor surgery for drainage. The following day, Saturday, he wrote Knopf that she was still "very ill" but seemed "a little better," and he felt she would recover. He repeated this hope in another letter to Blanche Knopf, the same day.

The following day, Sunday, at 6:00 P.M., Anna Mencken died. The date was the 13th, Mencken noted, the same date on which his father had died. His mother had died painlessly and peacefully, he wrote Philip Goodman. "She simply went to sleep," he recorded later. "Her last words to me were that she felt much better."

Mencken immediately notified other close friends of his mother's death, and to all he expressed the same sentiment: "She faced long illness and much pain" if she had lived, and thus her death had been merciful. He, Gertrude, and August placed a brief obituary notice in the Baltimore *Sun*, then followed Anna Mencken's wishes and planned a simple private ceremony. Three days later she was buried beside August Mencken in Loudon Park Cemetery. Not long after her burial, Henry placed at the head of their graves a new family tombstone of marble displaying the Mencken coat of arms and had his father's tombstone—"a hideous thing of granite," he wrote in his diary, "bearing the Masonic G and compass"—removed and "broken up."

Anna Mencken's will was probated immediately. According to a notice in the *Sun,* she left "all her property in trust to her son [and executor] Henry Louis Mencken," with the stipulation that Gertrude receive an annuity of $900 and free dwelling at 1524 Hollins Street. That business having been concluded, Henry, Gertrude, and August left for Pittsburgh to spend Christmas with Charlie. After a "ghastly holiday"—he wrote Dorothy Hergesheimer—he returned to Baltimore, where he and his sister planned "to keep the house going."

But 1524 Hollins now seemed "as empty as a cave," and Mencken felt "very much alone." "What a woman is gone! I feel like a boy of 6," he wrote Marion Bloom, making contact for the first time in more than two years. The death of his mother, he reflected much later, was "pure disaster for she had always stood by me loyally. . . . Her death filled me with a sense of futility and desolation," as well as an awareness of the "stupendous debt" he owed her. Or, as he wrote Dreiser several weeks after Anna's death:

I begin to realize how inextricably my life was interwoven with my mother's. A hundred times a day I find myself planning to tell her something, or ask her for this or that. It is a curious thing: the human incapacity to imagine finality. The house seems strange, as if the people in it were deaf and dumb. But all life, I begin to believe, resolves itself into a doing without.

# Chapter 11

# A TORY IN A
# DEMOCRATIC WORLD

H ard work, as always, was Mencken's most effective antidote to personal loss, although after the death of his mother, he wrote, "it was weeks before I was fit for any work beyond routine." In January and February 1926 he tried to resume writing his *Notes on Democracy*, the book he had labored over during Anna Mencken's illness. Although he had little success at first, he forced himself back into his routine. He also set resolutely to work on other projects. "I have finished two books since March 1," he wrote Hergesheimer in mid-June, "and am now hard at work on a third." By late July he told Hergesheimer that all three books, including *Notes on Democracy* and another volume of *Prejudices*, were "under my nose in proof."

*Notes on Democracy* examined a subject that had long fascinated Mencken, both in theory and in practice. From the time he had covered City Hall for the Baltimore *Morning Herald,* then in 1904 had covered his first national political conventions, he had been hooked. His distaste for politicians went back even further—to the time when he had been shunned by student politicians at the Poly-technic—but he also had a great fascination with men like Bryan and Theodore Roosevelt and, in time, a genuine affection for others of their species. He numbered among his friends Senator James Reed of Missouri, an occasional *American Mercury* contributor, and Al-bert C. Ritchie, the Maryland governor, who depended on him for advice. Among those who amused him were the late Harding and

264

Coolidge. He had voted for the departed "Gamaliel" in 1920: Harding was a "numskull," the worst candidate he had ever supported, but still superior, he believed, to Democrat James M. Cox. As Harding had lain gravely ill in late July 1923, Mencken had written Phil Goodman, "I fear that he will die, and that the succession of Cal Coolidge will tickle me so much that I'll come down with spasms." When Coolidge indeed ascended to the presidency two days later, he kept up a stream of laughter. But he greatly preferred both Harding and Coolidge to the "puritan" Wilson.

He had begun to make notes for a book on democracy as early as 1910, although he had not begun the writing until 1921 and then, after interruptions, continued in 1923 and, in earnest, in the autumn of 1925. After still other interruptions he completed it in June, and Knopf published the book in October. To those who had read Mencken in the previous decade, the message was hardly original. Democracy was "charming" in the abstract but impractical in fact: why should superior men be governed by their inferiors, by "peasants," by the "eternal mob"? Democracy was "based upon propositions that are palpably not true," primarily that "the lowly shall inherit the earth." It was "government by orgy, almost by orgasm," and worse still, it was a close cousin of Puritanism. Both were based on jealousy of one's betters. Democracy's only redeeming feature was that it was "incomparably idiotic, and hence incomparably amusing." The "true charm of democracy" was "not for the democrat but for the spectator."

Mencken knew he had written a flawed book—"probably the worst of all my books"—even before the reviews appeared, and he blamed its inadequacies on the "very unfavorable conditions" under which it had been written. In fact, most of the reviews, though hardly glowing, were not "furiously hostile," as he characterized them in autobiographical notes. Both Walter Lippmann and Edmund Wilson acknowledged the authority and power of the work, even if they disagreed with its author. To Lippmann, writing in *Saturday Review*, his "attack on the divine right of demos" was "an almost exact equivalent of the earlier attacks on the kings, the nobles, and the priests," and to Wilson, in *The New Republic*, it was "a portrait of Democratic man" that resembled nothing so much as the yahoos of Swift. But Wilson was more critical of Mencken than he had previously been—in many respects, he charged, the book amounted to

Mencken's "same old melodrama, with the gentleman, the man of honor, pitted against the peasant and the boob"—and other reviewers were even less charitable. Virtually the only unreservedly appreciative reader was the former German kaiser, who wrote Mencken with his congratulations and sent along two autographed pictures.

Mencken had no higher hopes for the three other books on which he labored in 1926. His fifth volume of *Prejudices* was not nearly as original as most of its predecessors; a sixth *Prejudices*, following on its heels, was "a hack job, done to get some money," and an edited volume, *Americana: 1926*, was a collection of ridiculous news items from the forty-eight states. The *Prejudices*, brilliant in the early volumes, seemed now to be growing stale. He had at first intended the series to stop at four volumes, and it might have been better if it had. The offerings had always been largely expanded and reworked essays, but now, though still dazzling readers with his style, Mencken seemed to be repeating himself even more than before.

For those who had not read his coverage of the Scopes trial, *Prejudices, Fifth Series* did offer two pieces on the events of July 1925, including "In Memoriam: W.J.B.," a longer version of his irreverent obituary column in the *Evening Sun*. The sixth and final volume in the series contained essays on many of the old subjects— Puritanism, journalism, literature, music, Christianity, and New York City—but none added much to what he had said before. To some reviewers he now seemed overly cute, straining for effect. "If you find so much that is unworthy of reverence in the United States," he had asked himself at the end of volume five, "then why do you live here?" "Why do men go to zoos?" he answered.

If hard work, however uneven, served in 1926 as one antidote to grief and sorrow, public controversy served as another. Mencken had known for some time that he and *The American Mercury* were asking for trouble from the censors, and it came in the spring of 1926 in the form of a fight with the New England Watch and Ward Society and its secretary, J. Franklin Chase. In the September 1925 *Mercury* he had published an essay, "Keeping the Puritans Pure," which was a direct attack on Chase and the latter-day "wowsers" of Boston. He had followed that essay with another, "Boston Twilight," written by Angoff for the December 1925 issue. Chase had been furious when he read the two pieces and, according to Mencken, vowed to bar *The American Mercury* from Boston and, if possible, from the mails. He possessed the power to accomplish such aims. Although holding no public office, he was able to intimidate Boston booksellers and news-dealers with the threat that the Watch and Ward Society would take them to court if they displayed and sold obscene or otherwise objectionable material.

Thus Chase was ready when the April *Mercury* appeared, featuring not one but two pieces to which he objected. An ex–Methodist minister, he was personally offended by "The Methodists," an iconoclastic essay written by Angoff under a pseudonym. But he knew he had a better chance if he focused his complaint on the second piece, a story, "Hatrack," by a young Missourian, Herbert Asbury, who happened to be a direct descendant of the patron saint of American Methodism, Francis Asbury. The story, which Mencken had selected from Asbury's iconoclastic work in progress, *Up from Methodism*, was in fact quite harmless. It told the tale of a small-town prostitute who, when rejected by the church, plied her trade with the parishioners, but it contained no language and no scenes that could in the least be called offensive. Nonetheless, Chase was determined to act. On March 30 he requested that Boston newsdealers, under threat of arrest, return their copies of the April *Mercury*.

At first Mencken thought little of the challenge. Most copies of the April issue had been sold by March 30, and all mailed copies had already reached subscribers. But after discussing the matter with Knopf, the two men decided to hire a member of the Scopes defense team, Arthur Garfield Hays, to fight the ban. Hays suggested that Mencken go to Boston, publicly sell a copy of the April *Mercury*, and dare Chase to have him arrested. "If my mother had been still alive," he wrote later, "I'd have been forced to let that outrage pass, for it would have been cruel to expose her to the anxieties of my trial." But as it was, he decided to risk arrest, with the possibility, unlikely though that might be, of as much as a year or two in prison. The more he considered the matter, the angrier he became. "I am against any further parlay with these sons of bitches," he wrote Knopf. "Let us tackle them as soon as possible." He would go to Boston.

The encounter with Chase turned into one of the most publicized moments of Mencken's career, one such as the Scopes trial in which the journalist was at the center of the story. At Dayton he had taken on one of the regions he detested, the contemporary South; now he could challenge the other, Puritan New England. He, Hays, and

Knopf notified reporters that he would appear in the Boston Common on April 5 to sell the April issue.

He left Baltimore by train the morning of Sunday, April 4, arrived in Boston Monday morning, and went to the Common at 2:00 P.M. to meet Chase. According to newspaper reports, more than a thousand people had gathered, including Chase's assistant but not, at first, Chase himself. When the secretary of the Watch and Ward Society at last arrived, Mencken sold him a single copy of the *Mercury*, biting his half-dollar for the benefit of the crowd. Chase ordered his arrest, plainclothes officers complied, and Mencken set off to police headquarters to be arraigned. After he pleaded not guilty to the possession and sale of indecent materials, a hearing was set for the following morning. He was certain he would be held for trial and reasonably sure he would be convicted, although he believed he would probably win on appeal. He felt little better when, the next morning, the judge said he would read the story and would hand down a decision the following day.

Thus Mencken was astounded on the morning of April 7 when Judge James P. Parmenter appeared, pronounced the words "No offense has been committed," and let him go without trial. With that, in the old Puritan paradise, he was an instant hero. He was taken for lunch to the Harvard Union, where students and a few professors cheered his victory, and then proceeded to New York for a celebration with the Knopfs and Hays and his first sound sleep for a week.

The next night, after drinking bootleg beer in Hoboken, he discovered in a short newspaper notice that the celebration was premature. The April *Mercury*, while available for public sale in Boston, had just been banned from the mails. Again, he, Knopf, and Hays conferred and decided not only to fight the ban but to bring action against Chase in the Massachusetts courts as well. They prevailed on both fronts. Although, after an April 15 hearing in Washington, the April *Mercury* was indeed ruled unfit for the mails, an injunction filed by Hays kept the Post Office from carrying out its order. And from Boston came a ruling that the Watch and Ward Society could no longer interfere with the *Mercury*.

Again Mencken's luck had held. He later discovered that both Boston judges he had drawn, Parmenter and James M. Morton, happened to be Unitarians and liberal thinkers, and Parmenter, besides, was the uncle of a young acquaintance in Baltimore. In addition, the "Hatrack" controversy had generated thousands of pages of free publicity for the *Mercury:* his clipping service sent enough newspaper pieces to fill two large scrapbooks.

But the victory over the censors had come at great financial cost to the *Mercury.* Hays alone was paid $7,500, and Mencken later estimated that the entire affair had cost the magazine some $20,000. He had felt it necessary to reprint the entire May issue, at a cost of some $8,000, because the action by the Post Office Department convinced him that he needed to remove an innocent enough article with an eye-catching title, "Sex and the Coed," written under a pseudonym by Bernard De Voto. Besides the financial expense, Mencken had been forced to resort to his wartime siege mentality, a condition he seemed to find less invigorating than before. "I had accumulated . . . a large crop of bitter enemies," he later wrote, and many of them now took advantage of him. Particularly he felt betrayed by American newspapers, many of which ran editorials against him for defending what he felt should have been their cause as well, freedom of speech.

He had been "nearly exhausted" by the "Hatrack" controversy, he wrote Boyd in late April. The "war against the Comstocks" had been "a hard sweat," and when it was over he was ready for his first holiday in four years. He would have to wait another four months— first he had to wrap up the three books in progress—but by midsummer 1926 he was planning what was to be his grandest American tour ever. He would head through the South, that lost region of "shoddy cities and paralyzed cerebrums" which he had described at length but most of which he had never seen, and would then proceed across the Southwest to California. The first part of the trip would have, in part, a professional purpose. He would call on various newspaper editors across Dixie. Most of the rest would be pure pleasure.

On October 13 he and Patterson, who would accompany him on the early southern swing, left Baltimore, made a quick stop in Richmond, where they dined with Emily Clark's stepmother, then pushed on to North Carolina. Since the early 1920s Mencken had been praising Chapel Hill, which he had come to see as the center of a new southern enlightenment. He numbered among his allies and frequent correspondents there Howard W. Odum, the noted sociologist who was giving the South "a whiff of the true scientific spirit," and Gerald W. Johnson, a newspaperman so liberated that Mencken had just lured him across the Potomac to the Sunpapers. Chapel Hill was a strange mixture of "plain living and high thinking," Emily Clark had written him, and he was eager to see it. His spirits held up over the weekend despite his being subjected to a college football game. Although he sat on the Carolina bench, the unsuccessful Polytechnic gridder had forgotten the rules and "couldn't make out what was going on."

After a weekend during which he met Fred and Betty Hanes of Duke University, shortly to take their place among his best friends, he and Patterson moved deeper into the "Christian abyss." In Atlanta he visited the Confederate memorial at Stone Mountain, accompanied by another of his great admirers, Frances Newman, whose soon-to-be-published Mencken-boosted novel, *The Hard-Boiled Virgin*, he was given to read on his way west. In Columbus, Georgia, he met with liberal newspaper editors Julia and Julian Harris and in Montgomery, Alabama, with Grover C. Hall, another liberal editor he had cultivated. After receiving magnificent treatment in New Orleans, he pushed off for the West Coast.

He had never seen the Southwest—indeed, the entire southern expanse from Georgia to southern California was new territory—and for one who held forth monthly on the American hinterland, particularly its southern reaches, it was a valuable experience. But the trip from New Orleans to Los Angeles was not a pleasant one. "These ghastly wilds, I fear, are not for me," he wrote a friend from Texas. "I have been riding through them since daylight, and had enough of them by 9:07 AM. I am a cockney, and love the comfortable saloons of great cities."

What he found in California, at least part of it, was more to his liking. He had never visited Hollywood, and by the mid-twenties he had acquired a great curiosity about the place. Although still highly skeptical of motion pictures—he had not seen his first until 1921 and by 1925 had still seen only half a dozen—he had come to know several film stars and thought rather highly of them. In June 1926, at Hergesheimer's home in West Chester, he had met Aileen Pringle, a star of stage and film, and he had found her not only beautiful but intelligent. "A very amusing movie gal," he called her. He had seen her again at Hergesheimer's in August. He, Pringle, and the Hergesheimers had entertained themselves by writing a one-act drama and had played it on the lawn while Hergesheimer filmed with his movie camera.

Through Pringle that same summer he had met Rudolph Valentino. The film star had sought him out because he thought Mencken would be able to give him advice on how to handle an often critical press. After he, Mencken, and Pringle had dinner in New York, the two men had had a long talk, and Mencken had found a great vulnerability, as well as "an obvious fineness" in Valentino. The star, he decided, was a "gentleman." He was strangely moved by his encounter with Valentino, and all the more so the following month, when Valentino died suddenly at thirty-one. He was able to joke to Boyd, "Valentino's death throws a heavy responsibility upon me. I am now the most powerful aphrodisiac in the Western World." He expressed truer feelings in a piece he included in *Prejudices, Sixth Series*. Despite all he possessed, Mencken observed, Valentino had been very unhappy.

Thus Mencken was expected when he reached Hollywood in late October, and his arrival was accompanied by great fanfare. Hergesheimer was to follow him shortly, and Mencken was primed for a good time. He submitted to interviews and posed for pictures with Pringle, Louis B. Mayer, and other Hollywood stars and producers, and since he himself had now achieved celebrity status his activities were widely reported in the eastern press. He was generally in good form, attending several Hollywood parties, going to two or three movies, having tea with Mary Pickford, and, after a late party, spending the night in Aileen Pringle's home—but not, he insisted, her bedroom.

He also spent an afternoon at evangelist Aimee Semple McPherson's famous temple. Although he had long been curious about the celebrated Aimee, what he saw, in fact, disappointed him. She employed the "oldest, safest tricks out of the pack of Dr. Billy Sunday, Dr. Gipsy Smith and the rest of the consecrated hell-robbers" but had few original ones of her own. Mencken attributed her "roaring success" to the spiritual vacuum into which she had moved. Los Angeles had long swarmed with "osteopaths, chiropractors . . . swamis, spiritualists, Christian Scientists, crystal-gazers and the allied necromancers," as well as "melancholy High Church Episcopalians, laboriously trying to interest retired Iowa alfalfa kings in ritualism," but it lacked the kind of spellbinding evangelists who worked the South and Midwest. Thus Aimee found her calling, "twice a day, week in and week out, caress[ing] the anthropoids of that dusty, forbidding region."

In nearly all respects, Mencken wrote Goodman, Los Angeles was "the damndest hole I ever saw," and to another friend he was even more emphatic: "This place is the one true and original arse-hole of creation. It is at least nine times as bad as I expected." What he found confirmed his belief that it was a land of quacks and frauds. But he had no complaints with what he later was to call "the gaudy sexual society" of Hollywood. He was making the acquaintance of "beautiful, intelligent" women, he wrote Goodman, and enjoying himself. "In truth," he later wrote another friend, "I never had a sweller time on this earth."

After several days in Los Angeles, he was ready to move on to San Francisco, where he looked forward to a reunion with George Sterling. In early August he had written his old bohemian friend that he was coming west, and throughout the late summer and early autumn the two had written back and forth planning festivities, similar to those in 1920, revolving around women and drink. Sterling was somewhat irritated when Mencken was delayed a day or two in Hollywood and he had to postpone a dinner he had planned for his guest at the Bohemian Club. By the time Mencken arrived on November 16 and registered at the St. Francis, Sterling had already drunk a great deal, had taken to his room, and was complaining of great pain. Mencken met with him briefly, but when he returned to the Bohemian Club later in the day to see his old friend there was no answer.

Mencken was disturbed by Sterling's condition. "A terrible spectacle," he wrote a friend in Baltimore. "I really fear for his life." He was more alarmed by Sterling's general instability, but he reluctantly went on with the evening's activities. He was hardly prepared for the news the next morning: Sterling had been found dead in his room. The poet had committed suicide by taking cyanide. But Mencken was equally disturbed by reports that he and Sterling had quarreled just before his death and that he, in some measure, was responsible for his friend's suicide. Certainly Sterling had greatly anticipated Mencken's arrival—"It will be dam [sic] wonderful to see you again, Hen," he had written in his last letter to Mencken a week earlier—

and certainly he was upset that his friend was late in arriving. But, Mencken insisted in a letter long after Sterling's suicide, "There was absolutely no quarrel between George and me." Nor, apparently, did he ever receive a note from Sterling that, according to an acquaintance of the poet, Sterling had left on his bed table.

Mencken could hardly have been blamed for Sterling's death: the poet, at fifty-seven, drank excessively, had long wrestled with private demons, was in frequent physical pain, and was known to carry cyanide. His former wife had preceded him by committing suicide with cyanide in 1917. But what surprised certain of their mutual friends was what to them seemed to be Mencken's heartless behavior after the suicide. Although he had planned to stay for the funeral, he left when he heard that the mayor of San Francisco had declared the ceremony a "civic occasion." What might seem even more callous is his remark two months later to a friend: "He was wise to bump off. Booze had him, and he was impotent. A charming fellow. He was 57, old enough to die."

If Mencken was "badly shaken" by Sterling's death, as another friend contended, he gave little evidence of his distress. Two days after he returned, he wrote Hergesheimer that the journey west had been "a gaudy and charming trip" and he believed that "in the long run it will do me a lot of good." Among other things, the cross-country trip had renewed his interest in the hinterlands, although his opinion of those remote reaches was no higher than before.

That opinion was not changed by what he found some eighteen months later when he traveled to Kansas City and Houston for the Republican and Democratic conventions. After a Republican gathering enlivened only by the supply of liquor that he and Patterson, as usual, had brought along, the two men had driven to Springfield, Missouri, and then ventured into the Ozarks of southern Missouri and Arkansas, where Mencken encountered "the most barbaric white people I have ever seen." After traveling through the backcountry for nearly a week, they arrived in Houston two days before the Democratic convention was to begin.

Mencken did not like Houston: he found the convention dull and the city unpleasant, and his first extended meeting with Franklin D. Roosevelt, a conversation of about an hour, was not memorable. More interesting to him were Will Rogers, with whom he had a pleasant talk, and a big Texan named Amon Carter, who displayed his pistol-wielding skills by firing through Mencken's window in the direction of a nearby hotel, nearly accomplishing Mencken's arrest. Mencken left Houston with "a considerable distaste" for it and for the entire state of Texas. "The Texans," he wrote, were "simply not my kind of people." No doubt Texans felt the same.

Although the conventions of 1928 had proved unpleasant, the campaign for the presidency was to prove altogether different. Al Smith had emerged from Houston as the Democratic nominee to run against "Lord Hoover," and in the candidacy of the Catholic wet from New York, Mencken saw the opportunity for a round of reporting reminiscent of the Scopes trial. He toured with Smith long enough to decide both that he was poor presidential material and that he could put on a "good show." In the *Evening Sun* he struggled to explain Smith's appeal, even to those "aurignacian men" of the hinterlands who did not agree with him. It wasn't Smith's looks: "Compared to him Dr. Coolidge seems almost a pretty fellow, and the late Dr. Harding was an Apollo." Nor was it even the fact that he, like the inhabitants of the hinterlands, sweated freely: "When he is fully in action the perspiration literally pours from him. It runs down his long nose and leaps into space." But Smith's fan appeal did not translate into support, and in order to fully understand the antipathy to Smith of the dry, Protestant South, Mencken subscribed to most of the Methodist and Baptist journals in Dixie. Now nearly every week he held forth in his Monday *Evening Sun* column on "the holy war against Al in the Confederacy." "On the one hand are the Ku Klux Klergy," he wrote, "desperately determined to put down Al and the Pope. . . . On the other side are the awakening [southern] intelligentsia . . ."

The Smith campaign was to be Mencken's last total immersion into southern affairs, as well as his last extended trip as a newspaperman for some time. He had long since decided that he was spending too much time on the road as a highly visible journalist and not enough back in Baltimore as a serious writer of books. Aside from the Smith tour, during the past three years he had made extended trips not only to Tennessee, California, Kansas City, and Houston but, in January 1928, to Havana to cover the Pan-American Conference. He relished the attention that came from being a celebrity journalist, but he was aware as well that in the eyes of many he was becoming a clever showman, a dispenser of witticisms, the nation's good-natured cynic. Was he falling into the trap into which his first hero, Mark Twain, had fallen—playing too much to the American public, being forced by that very superficial quality of American culture he himself had identified to become a funny man rather than a serious writer?

Marion Bloom, now in Paris, certainly thought so. "What *is* Henry up to?" she wrote her sister in 1927. "Once he stood for exclusiveness and aristocracy; these days he shows up as a clown." A number of newspaper and magazine editors agreed. That same service that in the early 1920s had sent laudatory clippings now sent news stories and editorials entitled "The Passing of H. L. Mencken," "The Decline of Mencken," "The Sorrows of Mencken," "Something Must Have Happened to Henry," and "Long Reign of 'King' Mencken Seen near End." His "ancient jibes at congressmen and pastors are grown stale and thin with repetition," noted a writer in *The Richmond News Leader* in 1926, the week he returned from his California trip. "He is . . . the enthusiasm of last year. . . . It is no longer fashionable to admire him, as it was in 1924."

He had become "the god of the sophomores," the *News Leader* added, and, if we believe an editorial in the Harvard *Crimson*, two years later he was not even that. Mencken had been a great influence on students "some years ago," according to the *Crimson* editor in a 1928 piece entitled "Was a Prominent Writer," but now he was forced to collect "his own obituaries." What the editor particularly had in mind was *Menckeniana: A Schimpflexikon*, a book in which the *Mercury* editor had collected from newspapers, magazines, and other sources 132 pages of epithets about himself. Included among the twenty-three categories—Zöological, Genealogical, Pathological, and so forth—were "literary hyena," "intellectual gorilla," "a clever and bitter Jew," "a Jew, or at least a German," "a Negro by inclination if not by birth," and "a very sick man." The book was clever indeed, and showed in addition that Mencken was able to laugh at himself. But it also played into the hands of his critics. Was he not, in a period of apparent decline, trying too hard to boost himself back into the center of controversy, to regain his position as the national bad boy who took pride in being scolded by authorities? The editor of the *Crimson* did not say that. He was content to note that the *Mercury* editor now took his place "among the great and late."

Mencken did not care a great deal what Harvard students said (although he had not minded, in April 1926, when they praised him), but he did care that *The American Mercury* was beginning to lose circulation, and he cared even more about what the most influential of his former admirers were saying. "The youngest of the younger literary generation . . . have thrown Mencken overboard," Edmund Wilson announced in 1926, and in England, where the boom had begun just after the war, the comments were no longer so favorable. Arnold Bennett, Hugh Walpole, G. K. Chesterton, Lytton Strachey, and Vita Sackville-West were among those who made critical remarks, some of which Mencken included in his *Schimpflexikon*. But he chose not to include Rebecca West's description in December 1926: "Appallingly feminine. Feminine, that is, in the old, abusive sense. He prefers to exploit his personality instead of doing the hard thinking he is capable of. He is continually shaking his curls."

Mencken may have been affected by this onslaught in the mid- and late twenties, but he gave little public sign of it. The rumors of his death, he knew, were exaggerated, and in certain quarters he continued to command great respect. In the same year in which editorials insisted that his "long reign" was over, the English critic St. John Ervine traveled around the United States touting him for the Nobel Prize in literature.

In addition, if now less frequently a practicing literary critic, he remained the nation's dominant literary force. He was still the reader the two most celebrated new American novelists, Sinclair Lewis and F. Scott Fitzgerald, wanted most to please, and on occasion he still dispensed assignments like a city editor. He discussed with Lewis the novel that became *Elmer Gantry* before Lewis began to write and then directed him to the Reverend L. M. Birkhead of Kansas City, the Unitarian minister who provided Lewis with a great deal of material. It was no accident that Lewis's novel of the go-getting evangelist, nearly a character out of one of Mencken's own essays, was dedicated to Mencken, "with profound admiration." Nor was it any surprise that Lewis the year before had, at his suggestion, refused the Pulitzer Prize for his novel *Arrowsmith*. Mencken felt such prizes were based on any number of political criteria, all unworthy, rather than on artistic quality.

Fitzgerald's respect still bordered on reverence. From France he wrote with lavish thanks for a Mencken review of *The Great Gatsby* that was in fact not altogether favorable. "I'd rather have you like a book of mine," he added, "than anyone in America." "After we come back," he wrote in 1926, "will you some time give me a chance to talk with you . . . ? I've never met you without being either shy or drunk."

It was not, then, so much lack of appreciation from without that caused Mencken to take stock in the mid- and late 1920s as it was a more reliable inner barometer. The pace of the past half decade had been maddening. In addition to professional demands, his family responsibilities had grown even heavier. Indeed, those who believed that his productivity stemmed from his being unmarried, childless, and thus free to write were sadly mistaken: he had most of the burdens of wife and family with none of the pleasures and benefits. He was the head of a family that still included not only August and Gertrude, both at home, but also Charlie and his wife and daughter and, on the periphery, two Abhau uncles and a younger first cousin.

He took these responsibilities very seriously indeed. In particular, he oversaw the health of his own brothers and sister and his sister-in-law. August still seemed accident- and illness-prone: in 1926 he was involved in a second serious auto accident, and on another occasion he had a near-fatal case of appendicitis, followed by an emergency appendectomy. Gertrude was ill at other times and, besides, was not easy to get along with.

But most draining of all was the attention he gave to Charlie's wife, Mary, for whom he continued to arrange medical care in Baltimore. She came from Pittsburgh on three occasions for surgery and long recuperations, twice in the early twenties, the third time in 1927. We find dozens of letters in the twenties about Mary's health, Mencken's attention to her condition, and the demands on his time that attention required. When Joseph Bloodgood first operated on her for appendicitis, Mencken actually saw the operation, which he described in great detail in a letter to August: after removing the appendix, the surgeon also found an inoperable though nonmalignant tumor near the right kidney. Mary remained in Baltimore at least two or three months on that occasion, and when a second operation a year and a half later uncovered a "huge cyst" that could not be removed, Mencken attended to her faithfully and kept the bad news to himself. Although he feared a "hemorrhage at any minute," he felt it best, for the time being, not to tell Charlie. Again Mary remained in Baltimore two or three months under his watchful eye, and when she returned to Pennsylvania he dutifully went up to check on her.

On a third stay of seven weeks in Baltimore in 1927, as well as during Mary's numerous trips back to Baltimore for treatment, he was similarly attentive. But he resented the time her illnesses forced him to spend away from his work. "My writing has gone to pot," he wrote on one occasion, "I scarcely get time to shave" on another. Mary was an "impatient patient," he reported, so much that Anna Mencken, while she still lived, finally refused to visit her in the hospital. But Mencken remained the responsible head of family. A call to duty was the strongest call he acknowledged.

Charlie's home in Pittsburgh provided minor comforts at times. It was a place to flee at Christmas, to escape a Baltimore that had become "impossible" during that season since his mother's death. He disliked the long train trip through the Pennsylvania hills, but at least, as he wrote Goodman, he could "get drunk with my two brothers." He could also see his niece, Virginia, who was both a delight and, as she grew older, another burden. On Virginia's trips to Maryland he took her to Baltimore shops and traveled to Washington to show her monuments and museums. But increasingly his letters contained complaints about the time her visits required. "My niece will be here the coming week," he wrote Max Brödel on one occasion, "and so I'll get no work done." "It will mean two or three days lost," he wrote Fielding Garrison before another visit. He took care of Virginia's surgical needs as well. "Virginia here for tonsillectomy," he jotted in his illness file. His Saturday Night Club friend Frank Hazlehurst performed the surgery.

The one part of his extended family that he ignored was his uncle Henry Mencken's. His preference for the Abhaus over the contemporary Menckens had been reinforced in December 1925, just two days before his mother's death, when his uncle had sent for him and told him that he himself was "virtually bankrupt" and that the old family firm of Aug. Mencken & Bro. was going under. The company had been in poor shape for many years. "My uncle and his son," Mencken later wrote, "were too stupid and lazy to breast the competition that was ruining all the old cigar firms of Baltimore." But the circumstance that had pushed Uncle Henry to the point of bankruptcy was a foolish investment in a mining venture in the West.

Mencken was furious at his uncle and his "numskull cousin" John Henry, the more so because he thought he would have to tell his mother of the company's failure. He knew "how proud she had always been" of her husband's firm and "how crushed she would be by its debacle." When the company closed its doors within a month, he vowed to have little more to do with his uncle's family. Not only, in late December and January, did he have to come to terms with his mother's death; he also had to sell the building at Pratt and Greene streets belonging to Aug. Mencken & Bro. and attempt to settle "without public scandal" the affairs of his father's company.

In every direction the old order was breaking up, and certain friends were part of that order. "Of the men I knew best when I first began going to New York, twenty-five years ago, not one is a friend today," he wrote in 1926, and the same could have been said of many friends of shorter duration. As before, his own feelings about friendship were partly responsible. When friends "begin to bore me," he wrote, "I get rid of them. . . . It is foolish to go on with people who have ceased to be interesting, and become nuisances."

Since casting out Nathan as coeditor of the *Mercury*, he had continued to keep his distance, outwardly cordial but uncompromising in professional matters. Even Knopf felt he was being too rough on his old friend. He "somehow never seemed to realize," Knopf wrote later, "that George couldn't just be wished or ordered off the premises." Nathan could not be dispensed with because he still owned a one-sixth share in the magazine and, besides, continued to write two monthly features. Mencken fully understood how "enormously" Nathan was upset and understood that he had put up a "furious resistance" to being dismissed. But he was adamant. He had Nathan's name removed from the directory in the lobby and moved his desk into the stenographers' office. He wrote Knopf that, under an agreement he had proposed to Nathan, he would "refuse absolutely to put his name on letter paper," and further, he wrote Knopf, he would prefer not even to publish Nathan's "Clinical Notes" and theater reviews. "In case you part with him as his publisher, I shall notify him at once that his reviews will be terminated . . ." Mencken wanted a "complete divorce," Knopf felt, and he would settle for nothing less.

He also now wanted a complete divorce from Dreiser, and he accomplished that as well in 1926. His grounds for a dissolution were far better in this instance: for once Mencken was justified in feeling that a friend had betrayed him. First, Dreiser, who had been finishing up his mammoth novel *An American Tragedy*, wanted Mencken to help him gain access to Sing Sing prison so he might more accurately describe the death-cell scenes near the end of the novel. After Mencken wrote friends at the New York *World* and obtained a pass for Dreiser, Dreiser refused, for anything less than $500, to write a story based on his interview with a death-row inmate. "This puts me in a nice hole indeed," he telegraphed Dreiser, and the novelist responded that Mencken's telegram was "an insult." He had not, he insisted, agreed in advance to write such a story.

That matter had barely been settled—as a compromise Dreiser agreed to be interviewed by the *World* on his Sing Sing experience—when the novelist showed up at Hollins Street on December 12, 1925, the day after Mencken had taken his mother to the hospital. He told Dreiser he feared his mother would die of her illness, but, according to Mencken in his diary, "he seemed uninterested, and offered no word of hope that she would recover." He was on his way, by car, to Florida and seemed concerned, Mencken reported, only about ac-quiring a bottle of Scotch to take along. After they talked a short time before the fire, Mencken asked if he were alone, and he replied that Helen Richardson was in the car. Indignant that she had been left out in the cold, Mencken went out immediately and invited her in. After the three of them talked for a short while, Dreiser prepared to leave, again saying nothing about Mencken's mother. When Anna Mencken died the following day, he sent no message of sympathy.

"This episode caused me to set him down as an incurable lout," Mencken wrote in his diary. Of all the "other evidences to the same end" during their acquaintance, none had been "so gross and dis-gusting." His account of the events of December 1925 ends at that point, but in fact there was more to the story, evidence that hardly exonerates Dreiser but makes him less culpable than Mencken sug-gested.

He may indeed have been guilty of leaving Helen Richardson in the car—that would have been characteristic Dreiser behavior—although, as Richardson wrote Mencken twenty years later, she did not remember it. (On another occasion she modified that to "only a few minutes.") He was guilty, too, of a failure to express to Mencken any hope for his mother's recovery. As for the offense that truly wounded Mencken, it appears that Dreiser had not written because he was "lost in the wilds of Florida," as he later explained it, and thus had not heard of Anna Mencken's death. In fact, he had written Mencken cheerily from Florida a month later, "Greeting. How is your mother?" When Mencken notified him the following week that "my poor mother died the day after you were in Baltimore," and shortly after that he heard the same news from Horace Liveright, he wrote Mencken a note of sympathy. Mencken responded with gratitude and spoke of his great debt to his mother.

But in that same letter Mencken had told Dreiser that in the March *American Mercury* he was "performing upon you without anaesthetics." He was referring to his review of *An American Tragedy* and was trying to forewarn Dreiser, as he also had in a letter a week before in which he had thanked his friend for an inscribed copy of the novel. When the review appeared, Dreiser saw that it was indeed harsh. He had produced a "shapeless and forbidding monster," Mencken had written, "a heaping cartload of raw materials for a novel, with rubbish of all sorts intermixed—a vast, sloppy, chaotic thing of 385,000 words—at least 250,000 of them unnecessary!" What Dreiser had written, Mencken acknowledged, "as a human document . . . is searching and full of a solemn dignity, and at times it rises to the level of genuine tragedy." But "as a work of art," it was "a colossal botch."

In fact, *An American Tragedy* was much better than that, even as a work of art. Dreiser's flaws were his earlier flaws, if here carried on at greater length, and in reviews of *Jennie Gerhardt* and *The Titan* Mencken had deemphasized if not overlooked them. But now he seemed in no mood to be charitable to his old friend. Dreiser had expected certain unfavorable remarks. "Who reads you?" he had written in a postscript to an otherwise friendly letter responding to Mencken's warning that an unfavorable review was to come. "Bums and loafers. No goods. We were friends before ever you were a critic of mine, if I recall. And . . . may remain so . . ." But that was hardly the case. Friendship could not stand the review that was to come *and* all that had happened over the previous three months. Dreiser's was to be the last letter the two men would exchange for nearly nine years.

# Chapter 12

# A LONELINESS
# AT THE CORE

Whether as a result of his mother's death, overwork, family burdens, broken friendships, a loss of public favor, an accumulation of these factors—or simply a belated recognition of the vanity of human wishes—in the mid- and late 1920s Mencken came as close as he had ever come to periods of depression. Despite the southern swing and Hollywood trip, despite pleasant weekends at Hergesheimer's and good times in New York, the year 1926, he maintained, had been an "unhappy one," and 1927 and 1928 were little better. As he wrote Irita Van Doren in September of 1926, even before the Hollywood trip, the preceding year had "nearly finished" him, and when he returned he wrote Nathan—in whom, despite their disagreements, he sometimes still confided—that he had come back from his cross-country journey "thoroughly disillusioned and disheartened": "I got an immense amount of notice but I believe that I could honestly say that ninety-nine percent of it was disgusting. It left me feeling lonely and miserable."

It was not simply that the world was too much with him. He was also increasingly aware of the passage of time and its consequences. In his twenties and thirties he had usually been carefree, he was later to write, "but since the age of forty I have been full of a sense of human sorrow." Particularly after his mother's death, he wrote a friend, it was hard to "reorganize" his life. He had already lived longer than his father had, and he too had intimations of mortality.

He was already, he wrote, "almost up to the average span of the Menckenii for three hundred years. We are, I suspect, a somewhat feverish race, launching out into life prematurely and wearing out before most [men] are full-grown."

His mood had not been brightened by the sudden death of Valentino, a month after he had been strangely "touched" by their conversation, and by the suicide of his host, Sterling, three months later in San Francisco. The next year, in *Prejudices, Sixth Series*, he included a short essay, "On Suicide," in which he concluded that life, stripped of illusion, "becomes unbearable," a "horror." Indeed, "Life, fundamentally, is not worth living," so man creates work and play to take his mind off it: "What could be more preposterous than keeping alive? Yet nearly all of us cling to life with desperate devotion, even when the length of it remaining is palpably slight, and filled with agony." Life now seemed a "progress . . . to the death house," a "gray emptiness."

His despair of 1927 was not altogether without precedent. In fact, Mencken had always concealed a deep reservoir of pessimism and doubt beneath the buoyant public persona. "I have had the blues steadily for thirty-five years," he was later to write a distant relative, for once dropping the jocular tone he usually assumed even in letters. "They are somewhat uncontrollable . . . but they don't seem to be fatal." In other letters he spoke of "doldrums" and "depressions," of being in a "bad state mentally," and in one of his later books he was to tell his readers that he had "suffered from recurrent depressions and despairs"—although he hastened to add that, for the most part, he had "had a fine time of it." Not only his *Mercury* "slave," Charles Angoff, but Sunpapers colleagues more sympathetic to him were later to speak of his "loneliness."

As Mencken took stock of himself in the mid- and late twenties, he saw himself in many respects as a man out of his time and place, not only a German devotee of *gemütlichkeit* in a Puritan paradise and a Tory in a democratic world but also a man in more tangible ways out of touch with his surroundings. "The only modern inventions that have been of any real use to me," he later said, were "the typewriter and the Pullman car." He disliked the telephone, hated the interruption of his work it brought, and kept one in his house only because he occasionally needed it and because friends often needed to reach him. He had got rid of the only automobile he ever owned, and, as we have seen, he cared nothing for motion pictures.

Even from the tumultuous decade for which he was widely pre-sumed to be spokesman he was, in many respects, alienated. In an age gone mad over sports and sports heroes, Ruth and Grange and Dempsey, he still detested sports—and heroes of any sort. "The Lindbergh business somehow leaves me cold," he wrote a friend in 1927. "The uproar suggested the reception of a movie actor." And in an age of mobility, a new suburbanization, and the increasingly nuclear family, all made possible by postwar prosperity and the automobile, he still lived in the old row house in which he had always lived, with his forty-year-old unmarried sister and his thirty-eight-year-old unmarried brother.

There was loneliness, but it was a loneliness at the core, carefully disguised by the exuberant outer man and his constant activity. It was a loneliness, in large measure, that was part and parcel of the trade he had embraced thirty years before. "The writing profession," he remarked in 1928, "is reeking with this loneliness, this melan-choly. All our lives we spend in discoursing with ourselves. . . . The loneliest people in the world we writers are. Except that, while we are conversing and laughing with ourselves, we manage to shed our loneliness . . . to scatter it as we go along."

On several other occasions he referred to the hardships of the writer's trade. "What a life!" he exclaimed to a friend. "I wish I had studied drumming and taken to the road. It is a dreadful thing to sit in a room alone . . ." To another friend he confessed that once, as far as serious writing was concerned, he had been "practically helpless for more than a year." Elsewhere he gave reasons for the writer's inevitable agony: "Every jangle of the telephone cuts him like a knife; every entrance of a visitor blows him up. Solitary . . . tired of himself . . . his every physical sensation is enormously magnified." It was hardly that this condition, in Mencken's case, was constant; in fact, he often wrote with a joy and exuberance that only the most gifted, the bravest, or the most innocent of writers can muster. But even upon this most confident and gregarious of writers the dark shadows fell.

The shadows fell, but much of the time he still kept them at bay. Even during this period of the mid- and late twenties—especially during this period—he gravitated toward the comic vision, preferred to observe and to think rather than to feel, to study mankind in the abstract rather than viewing too closely the sufferings of individual men and women. "I probably belong to the colder half of humanity," he had written Isaac Goldberg in 1925, and, despite lapses, it was that colder territory, a safer territory, he still preferred to inhabit.

It was a territory he could more easily control. Indeed, writing, for all its burdens, was itself a form of control, a means of ordering a world otherwise resistant to order. That rage for order, evident in Mencken since his earliest days as a writer, continued to be his ruling passion. Edmund Wilson, later relating an occasion in the twenties on which Mencken took him to meet with Ernest Boyd, was struck by his great need to arrive on time. "It's a mania with me," he had told Wilson. In his diary Mencken himself confessed to that need. When he traveled by rail—which, after 1918, was on virtually all occasions—he always arrived at the station at least fifteen minutes, often thirty, ahead of schedule. Of the hundreds, probably thousands, of trips he had made by rail to that point, he had missed a train only once—as a schoolboy traveling home to Mount Washington. He was not to miss another until 1943, a half century after his first lapse.

He desired order above all else, perhaps, because of his belief that there existed no inherent order in the universe, that all is random and meaningless and that any order must thus be provided by the individual. He was never so unsettled as when things were out of place. When matters were "so insecure" around him, as he once wrote Marion Bloom, "the whole thing seems a fantastic farce." In all areas, an English friend observed, he had both the great need and the ability to compartmentalize his life.

One part of life that was not susceptible to order and compartmentalization, that was by nature random and unpredictable, was physical frailty and illness, although he strove mightily to put even that into its place. Never, to this point, had that been more true than in the 1920s. What else was his "Illnesses" file—later assembled from notes to himself and copies of letters to others—but an attempt to combat the capriciousness, to record and understand illness and thus keep it at bay? The folder groans with entries from the 1920s, surpassing even the numerous complaints of previous years: influenza, bronchitis, bad colds, sore throats, laryngitis, hay fever, hiccoughs, "a persistent bellyache," "severe lumbago," an eye injury, an infected "left tonsil hole . . . filled with scar tissue and other muck," a sinus infection picked up on the Al Smith tour that made him "miserable for five months," a "warty tumor on the ball of the foot" that "must come out," "synovitis in my right wrist," "an infected cut on my left little finger," and, of course, when he was so ordered, the horrors of an enforced diet and the water wagon.

It was nearly a Whitmanesque catalogue, a virtual poetry of affliction, boasting and chanting of pain and illness, an off-key "Song of Myself." It was the kind of listing and totaling to which he also was given when numbering the faults of the Puritans or the sins of the South. And there was more in the file for the twenties: surgery for the foot tumor, surgery for the infected tonsil cavity, the removal of "two small moles from my left breast" and four other moles from unspecified locations, a sliver of material in his eye. All this does not include the meticulous entries in the separate hay fever diary.

It would not be accurate to say that Mencken took pleasure in suffering—although his letters are full of expressions such as "I am enjoying an attack of lumbago in the right shoulder" and "I've been entertaining my old friend, the hiccoughs." It is simply that he took a certain pleasure in *talking* about that suffering. He indulged himself in his afflictions, proclaimed them as evidence, in this most uncertain of existences, that he was *alive,* and filled his letters with complaints and lamentations worthy of Job. "Hay fever has me by the ear," he wrote Estelle Bloom; or, to Boyd, "God has me by the balls."

Nor would it be of use to probe further Mencken's fascination with the workings, or failings, of his own body. Such fascination was, in part, simply another function of the orderly, controlling personality. It was, as well, a function of the materialist who believed in nothing transcendent and thus noted and listed nearly all observable phenomena. It may have even been, in part, a product of living in Baltimore, the site of the most famous hospital in the country, and, beginning with Leonard Hirshberg in his twenties, of spending much of his leisure with doctors. In the early years of the century the seriously ill and the dying were drawn to the Johns Hopkins like the halt and the lame to Lourdes, and by the twenties Mencken did his share of the drawing—and not only for family. He had already begun his career as a sort of medical broker, attracting close friends to his city and placing them into the hands of physicians who were his friends. He was to perform such services for Blanche and Alfred Knopf, for Hergesheimer, even for casual correspondents who happened to mention that they were afflicted in some puzzling manner. His illness file went beyond his own maladies. It included, to a lesser degree, the sufferings of relatives and friends. Knopf had an entry. So did Rudolph Valentino.

If Mencken had faith in anything, then, it was in the scientific method and in the ability of physicians to use that method to diagnose and treat human ills. But this most rational of men saw no contradiction in the fact that he was also superstitious. Indeed, he said on several occasions, it was rational that a man such as he, with no religious belief but with a deep need to explain things, *would* be superstitious. There existed in all humans a desire to find some order or meaning in events, even if that order did not truly exist, and in lieu of religion, superstition was such an ordering device. Besides, Mencken believed he had grounds: his father *had* died on Friday the 13th, his mother also on the 13th.

There is, in fact, in the miscellaneous papers Mencken left at his death a curious six-page typescript entitled "Astrological Reading of Mencken," dated December 18, 1925, just five days after Anna Mencken's death. The detailed, personalized reading (one of two such detailed readings buried in his papers) is by an L. Pratt of Cleveland, Ohio, and there is no indication whether the astrologer in fact saw his subject, whether Mencken requested the reading (an unlikely possibility), or whether there is a reason the reading comes just after his mother's death. The reading itself is unremarkable: it was mostly right, partly wrong, in its insistence that the subject had strong biases, a great deal of energy, a materialistic temper, manual dexterity, a desire to serve, and "considerable sorrow in life." But Mencken was obviously interested enough to keep it, whether for enlightenment or amusement we cannot be sure.

Although he felt himself on guard against the gods in certain respects, he also continued to see himself as the recipient of uncanny good luck in others—opportunities arising and adversaries falling just at the moment he needed them to. "One of my superstitions," he wrote in his "Hatrack" scrapbook, "is to the effect that men who set out to do me evil not infrequently die suddenly," and never did that belief appear more valid than in the mid- and late twenties. "Of the six bitterest enemies I had two years ago," he wrote a friend in December 1927, "five are dead, all suddenly and unexpectedly." Three of the men he had in mind were Bryan, Stuart Sherman, and

J. Franklin Chase—Bryan a week after Mencken had confronted him in Dayton, Sherman at age forty-five in a drowning accident, and Chase, weary from his battles with Mencken and overcome by pneumonia. "I must have been born at a lucky hour," Mencken told an interviewer two months after Chase's death, and he must have had in mind, among other things, that efficient dispatching of his enemies.

His response to the deaths of his adversaries reveals as well a darker side that was increasingly evident in the mid- and late 1920s. "I am told," he wrote of Chase, "that worry over the case, especially over the reprisals we held over him, helped to kill him. I hope so." It was hardly the Mencken whom Goldberg had envisioned when he ended his 1925 biography with the suggestion that a "new Mencken" was emerging "from the old," a man with a diminished "ruthlessness" and a "greater willingness to feel." It was, rather, the man Carl Van Doren had in mind when he noted—as a judgment on Mencken's writing in a generally favorable review—that what he "most conspicuously lacks . . . is the mood of pity." That lack of pity was evident not only in his treatment of the late Bryan and Chase and in his unkind treatment of Nathan but also in his earlier statements about the salutary effects of war and such later remarks as that, in a letter to a friend, about alcoholism: "William Graham Sumner is quite right in his belief that [the alcoholic's] proper place was the gutter. . . . If [alcohol] knocked them off in, say, six months it would be an enormously valuable eugenic agent."

In making such statements Mencken was dealing with abstractions; it could always be contended that he was speaking in hyperbole, that when it came to the individual case, he did not quite mean it. More revealing of the "cold" quality he identified in himself is an account of a mid-twenties visit to Cabell's home in Richmond, an account made all the more striking because of his great respect for Cabell, virtually the only contemporary American writer of whom he was almost never critical. In an entry written twenty years after the event for his memoir "My Life as Author and Editor," he described a buffet dinner to which he had been invited in Cabell's home, an evening "made horrible by the presence of his son Ballard." Cabell's only son was physically deformed and mentally deficient: "either a cretin or a Mongolian idiot," Mencken wrote, "a dreadful spectacle . . . his features . . . coarse and repulsive, his speech . . . muddled and unintelligible, and he walked with the shambling gait of a gorilla."

Although Mencken "tried to avoid him as much as possible," the boy pressed "his simian attentions" upon him. To Mencken the affair was "exactly like going into an animal cage," and the aspect of the evening that shocked him most was that Cabell treated his son as if there were nothing wrong with him. It was, he wrote, "a truly appalling manifestation of family pride."

Mencken's description was undoubtedly reliable. Indeed, if he had been in one of his demythologizing moods, he might have taken the account even further and reflected on a favorite theme, southern decline and decay, the collapse of the old aristocracy—an especially compelling illustration of Southern Gothic. It is certainly not that failure, nor any question about the facts, that is remarkable. Rather, it is the *tone* of his description, a complete absence of sympathy or compassion for Cabell's son or for Cabell himself, for what his good friend must have felt as he considered his only child or why he might have wanted his son to be a part of the occasion. Mencken was, as ever, the stark and honest realist, stating bluntly, harshly, and accurately the facts as he saw them, announcing his revulsion, and letting it go at that.

It was not, as his remarks might suggest, that he was heartless. Deficient in sympathy he might have been, but not devoid of it, and certainly not in his private relations. It was rather that, in Mencken's view, Cabell, a "gentleman" and the most civilized writer he knew, should have shown better form. Allowing his son to mix with guests was a breach of decorum, a violation not only of propriety but of a certain standard of order—of things in their place—to which Mencken held. Indeed, during the same period as he was casting his critical eye on Cabell's son, or more publicly on Bryan and Chase, he was demonstrating an abundance of compassion in other areas— taking care not only of family but of friends, spending (as we shall soon see) even more time visiting others in the hospital than he spent in it himself. He was even becoming, on selected fronts, what some of his Nietzschean friends might have seen as a softhearted sentimentalist, petitioning for the parole of several prisoners, the commutation of a death sentence of another. He helped in such matters even after the incarcerated recipients of his goodwill had stopped writing for the *Mercury*.

But compassion had its limits, and when its demands conflicted with what Mencken considered appropriate and orderly behavior, there was no doubt where he stood. Not only Cabell, in an isolated instance, but Bryan and Chase in a more pernicious and pervasive way, had breached a certain standard of civilized behavior. When Bryan had told the courtroom in Dayton that man is not a mammal, he was to Mencken beyond the limits of compassion. When Chase, full of petty hurts and jealousies, attempted to abridge free speech, he too was beyond such limits. When even Cabell, in a rare departure from form and through whatever misguided sense of kindness, loosed his "idiot" son upon people of breeding and manners, even he was not immune. When Mencken confronted such offenses against his idea of civility and order, his indignation knew no bounds.

---

Such pondering of order and disorder, fortune and fate, time and mutability placed Mencken in 1927 and 1928 in a philosophical frame of mind. At the same time, he was more determined than ever, as he wrote a friend, "to make one good book before I die." All his previous works had been "transient and trivial," he had decided. "They will be forgotten in twenty-five years." Thus he would dispense with journalism as fully as he was able and turn to more enduring monuments.

In fact, for a time in 1927, he was putting time and thought into not "one good book" but two. The first was a study to be entitled "Homo Sapiens," a "complete treatise on Man"; the other was to be a treatise on religion. The study of man would begin "with his descent," proceed "through his body to his psyche," and end with "an examination of his principal habits and ideas." The study of religion, only somewhat more modest in scope, would trace the origins, development, and current manifestations of religious faith. Either book would be in keeping with a resolve Mencken had made two or three years before:

I have passed into the middle forties, and am no longer the artless youth I once was. That youth was chiefly interested in the gaudy spectacle of life, i.e., the superficial effects of ideas. The ageing man who now confronts you is chiefly interested in the immemorial instincts and emotions that lie under them. So this is a good time, perhaps, to draw a line. The show is not over, I hope, but there is a climax and a new beginning.

As it turned out, Mencken chose, wisely, to give up the "treatise on man," at first for the time being and eventually for good. He turned rather to his *Treatise on the Gods*. It was to serve, in some measure, as the second volume of an informal trilogy on government, religion, and ethics, a series begun with the hastily prepared and ill-received *Notes on Democracy*. But it was to be a much more ambitious work than that, would be based on original research and thought rather than scraps from the *Evening Sun, The American Mercury*, and other journalistic offerings. Indeed, it would be his first book since *The Philosophy of Friedrich Nietzsche* "made up wholly of new matter."

In some measure, the preparation for *Treatise on the Gods* had begun long before 1927. The book had been in the works all his adult life, from the time of his earliest fascination with religious psychology. For an infidel he was amazingly well read in the Scriptures, and for one who on occasion lifted Gideon Bibles from hotel rooms (giving them to friends inscribed "Compliments of the Author"), he took religion seriously indeed. He had made it his business, long before the Scopes trial and the Al Smith campaign, to become well acquainted with the Christian clergy, both Roman Catholic and Protestant, as well as with theology, Catholic, Calvinist, and Wesleyan. He had filled his writings, both public and private, with religious allusions, and, if a given reader had not known of his infidelity and his penchant for teasing, that reader might often have thought him a genuine believer. Frequently his letters were nearly a parody of the writings of Jonathan Edwards and those other Puritans he despised: "I have spent the whole day in prayer and soul-searching"; "I shall spend the day searching the Scriptures"; "I begin to believe seriously that the Second Coming may be at hand"; "The marvels of God constantly astonish me"; "Let us praise God from whom all blessings flow"; and "God will reward you." When he was so moved, he signed letters to selected friends, "Yours in Christ."

He had also been subjected to religious persuasion in his adult years more often than he had wanted to be. He was a lifelong target for the proselytizing of his pious acquaintance Dr. Howard A. Kelly of the Johns Hopkins medical faculty, who was given to writing him at various times: "I do hope as I pray you will become a Christian," and "May God our Father convert you to salvation by His Son and turn your talents wholly into nobler higher [*sic*] constructive channels." In 1916 he had gone with Kelly to hear Billy Sunday when the famed evangelist was conducting a revival in Baltimore. He had embarked on the evening's services with Kelly's fervent wish that "you'll be honest about it and not steel yourself against such truths as may appeal to you." In fact, Mencken had found he rather liked Sunday and was delighted when he had the chance to visit with the evangelist in his room.

Over the years he had complained of Kelly, but he could tolerate him. Much more disturbing had been the newfound piety of Marion Bloom in the years just after the war and Marion's attempts to justify her Christian Science to him. In a series of letters Mencken had played Mephistopheles, attempting to dissuade Marion from her "delusion":

> The God business is really quite simple. No sane man denies that the universe presents phenomena quite beyond human understanding, and so it is a fair assumption that they are directed by some understanding that is superhuman. But that is as far as sound thought can go. All religions pretend to go further. That is, they pretend to explain the unknowable. . . . Anyone who pretends to say what God wants or doesn't want, and what the whole show is about, is simply an ass.

"My skepticism is more thorough-going than you imagine," he had written on another occasion. "I doubt everything, including even my own doubts."

Mencken's disapproval of Marion's religious faith had not kept him from addressing the subject in his own writings throughout the 1920s. If he had defended his agnosticism and had seemed to strip the cosmos of meaning in a statement such as that in his *Prejudices* suicide essay—men were but "miserable and ridiculous bags of rapidly disintegrating amino acids"—he had also written in the *Mercury* that "atheism, properly so-called, is nonsense":

> I can recall no concrete atheist who did not appear to me to be a donkey. To deny any given god is, of course, quite reasonable, but

to deny *all* gods is simply folly. For if there is anything plain about the universe it is that it is governed by law, and if there is anything plain about law it is that it can never be anything but a manifestation of Will.

Not only had he challenged atheism, he had also found that certain of his sympathies were "with the fundamentalists." "Either Christianity is true or it is not true," he reasoned, "and if it is true then modernism is an absurdity." Another time he remarked in his miscellaneous notes on the "uneasy feeling" in the heart of the unbeliever that "he *may*, after all, awake post-mortem and find himself immortal. . . . This is the agnostic's Hell."

It is clear, then, that Mencken had a mind as open as it was possible for him to have when he turned to the writing of *Treatise on the Gods* in early 1927. He had considered the subject long and hard, and he had great hopes for his study. "I am trying to clear decks to write the damndest book ever heard of," he wrote in January 1927, and by February he was telling friends about his "work of Christian doctrine." But in 1927 he was so overwhelmed with other work that he made little progress. It was not until 1929, after the Smith-Hoover campaign, the trip to Havana, and numerous other interruptions, that he seriously got down to work on "God and his peculiarities."

Mencken later wrote that he made "more careful preparations" for *Treatise on the Gods* than for any other of his books, and his letters of 1929 support that judgment. He was "soaking himself in theology" as well as reading "endless books on religious psychology." He was "at it day and night." He continued sweating over the book all spring and summer: it was giving him, he wrote Boyd, "more trouble than any other [book] I have ever tackled." But it also came "closer to fundamental realities than I have ever got elsewhere." On Thanksgiving night, when Charlie, Mary, and Virginia were visiting from Pittsburgh, he finished his treatise.

His most ambitious book was indeed the reasoned discourse he had described, written from the point of view of the "amiable skeptic," one devoid of the religious impulse but with no "antipathy" to religion. In the beginning he stated his belief that all religions were "at bottom . . . pretty much alike," that all stemmed from the sense of man's "helplessness before the cosmic mysteries" and from attempts to combat that helplessness "by appealing to higher powers."

In five lengthy chapters, totaling 353 pages, he explored the origins of religion, assuming the role of anthropologist and mythologist as well as religious historian.

Not until the final two chapters of the book did he turn exclusively to Judaism and Christianity, and not until the final chapter do we find a hint of that archenemy of Christianity that Mencken had often appeared to be. And even here he contended that Judeo-Christianity was "vastly superior" to any other religion by virtue of its "lush and lovely poetry." Indeed, the Bible was "unquestionably the most beautiful book in the world." If religion were objectionable because it was sentimental by nature and practice, if it lacked a certain "hardness of the mind" possessed by science, it nonetheless appealed to something deep in human nature and thus would remain central in the lives of most people.

There, in 1929, Mencken let it stand. He typed the final page, waited for August and Gertrude and Charlie's family to return from their evening's activities, and then had a drink to celebrate. In November 1929 it would have seemed to many Americans that there was little reason to celebrate. But the attention of America's keenest social observer had been drawn this autumn much more to his work on the gods than to the consequences of the October stock market crash. He feared his book would be judged a "complete flop," he wrote Ernest Boyd in October 1929, but the returns would not be in until the following year.

For Mencken the next year, 1930, was to bring returns on many fronts.

# TAKING A WIFE

The marriage of a first-rate man, when it takes place at all, commonly takes place relatively late. He may succumb in the end, but he is almost always able to postpone the disaster a good deal longer than the average poor clodpate, or normal man.

*—H. L. Mencken, 1922*

"As long as you have a mother, you won't get yourself a wife," one of Mencken's German friends had written him in 1924, and any number of his close friends in Baltimore and New York would have agreed. Not only had Anna Mencken met many of his material and emotional needs, but Mencken had been a dutiful son, a man of obligation whose most deeply felt allegiance was to his parents. Just as he had not been released to chart his own course professionally until the death of his father, so he had not felt altogether free to take a wife until after Anna Mencken's death in 1925.

For all his public fulminations against marriage, his less-than-honorable retreat when once he had been forced to the brink (with Marion Bloom), for all his fame as the nation's most confirmed bachelor, Mencken had never fully ruled out marriage for himself. Indeed, after his mother's death some of his friends believed he had virtually ruled it *in* for some point in his future. It may be overstating the case to contend, as at least two of his close friends later did, that it was not so much a question of whether he would marry but whom and when. But it was true, as it was for no other period in his life, that in the last three years of the 1920s one of Mencken's primary concerns was romance. Professional success had become routine, fame was assured, Anna Mencken was no longer a factor, and, as Mencken himself had earlier suggested, in one's late forties the defense mechanisms begin to break down. The man who had once defined marriage as "the end of hope"—and had announced that he personally had "no gifts for marriage"—had also written, "A man of thirty-five or thirty-eight is almost woman-proof. . . . But by the time he is fifty he is quite as easy as a Yale sophomore." The anonymous psychiatrist who once analyzed him in the Baltimore *Sun* may not have been altogether wrong when he concluded, "He wants to marry"—and to marry into an eminently respectable family.

The process toward such an end had begun long before the late twenties, indeed before Anna Mencken's death. From the spring of 1923 on, after it was clear that no reconciliation with Marion was possible or desirable, Mencken had cast about for other candidates, certainly not at this point for marriage but for female companionship. As it turned out, he had met the prime candidate for such a role that very spring (although he hardly realized it at the time), barely two months before Marion's marriage and only one month after he had maintained in *The Smart Set*, "I have yet to meet any woman rascally enough to deserve the fate of being put to living with me."

As he had approached Goucher College on the evening of May 8, 1923—to lecture to the assembled "virgins," as he wrote Phil Goodman—there was no indication that the occasion would be at all remarkable. He was in the habit, once or twice a year, of traveling the three or four miles to the small, rather select college for women on St. Paul's Street and speaking to the students on various matters. He had made such an expedition the previous December with no memorable results. "I always advise them to marry early," he had written Goodman at that time, "as, after all, the most sanitary and economically secure way of life for a Christian girl." His message in 1923 was approximately the same. He put away his prepared talk on "The Trade of Letters" and launched into his familiar discussion of "How to Catch a Husband." He had discerned "27 appetizing cuties in the audience," he wrote Goodman the following day.

Sara Powell Haardt, a twenty-five-year-old English instructor from

Montgomery, Alabama, would hardly have described herself as a cutie. She possessed a certain bearing and in all respects was far too dignified to merit that description. But she was the woman who principally had caught Mencken's eye, and she was one of the small Goucher party who dined with him later that evening. He did not recall having accepted a four-line poem from her for *The Smart Set* in 1919, when she was a Goucher senior, nor was he aware that she had published in Emily Clark's *Reviewer*. When he discovered that she was a short-story writer, he asked to see her work. Two weeks later she wrote him, requesting a meeting to discuss her writing, and he responded immediately, suggesting that they talk over lunch.

Shortly after they got together, Sara Haardt left for Alabama for the summer. She had sent him two or three stories to consider for *The Smart Set;* although he rejected them, he continued to encourage her to write. "Montgomery must be alive with stories," he advised. "I think you have a good novel in your head." Not long afterward, he did accept a story that he used in the October *Smart Set*. The remainder of the summer they carried on a friendly correspondence, focused largely on her writing. It is obvious that Mencken was doing more for her than he would have for any other promising writer. He advised her on her novel in progress, "paved the way for it with Knopf," and encouraged her to contribute to the new *American Mercury*.

As they wrote throughout the summer, they became more familiar, but theirs was still largely a professional relationship: he addressed her as "Miss Haardt" and she him as "Mr. Mencken." She was, after all, some eighteen years younger than he, and she was still in awe of the Sage of Baltimore. But it is clear that Mencken, as he sometimes had before, was using his position to pursue a young woman who particularly interested him, and Sara—although she was serious about her writing—was also using her stories as a vehicle to become better acquainted. By August they were planning to meet to discuss her novel when Sara returned in late September. When she did come back to Baltimore, bringing with her the Alabama moonshine he had requested, they began to meet, often downtown at Marconi's for lunch. In his letters Mencken was wooing in his accustomed manner—with wit, cleverness, and irreverence—but proceeding even more slowly than he had with other women.

By the end of 1923 he was taking an even closer look at Sara

Haardt. She was a dark, statuesque beauty of exactly Mencken's own height—five feet, eight inches—and with soulful eyes. But he admired much else about her as well. She was a southerner with the requisite manner and soft accent, but she was also partly of German descent. Johannes Anton Haardt had come from the Rhein-Pfalz six years before Burkhardt Mencken had come from Saxony, and he too had been a man of learning and a freethinker. Further, Sara claimed that one of her ancestors, like Mencken's, had been a professor at Leipzig in the seventeenth century.

She too had inherited the iconoclastic bent of at least certain of her forebears, and she shared many of Mencken's own views about religion, literature, American culture, the booboisie, and the American South. Mencken admired that iconoclasm as well as Haardt's pluck and determination. Although her family was eminently respectable, it was hardly prosperous, and after Sara's sophomore year at Goucher—after the death of the grandmother who had been paying for her education—she had been forced to pay much of her own way, finding part-time jobs and living as frugally as possible. After Goucher she had returned to Montgomery briefly, had taught history in a private school, and had found herself at odds with her conventional family and the "Sweet Flowering South." She had then left Dixie for good—other than for return visits—and, like any number of other literary southerners of her generation, had resolved to seek her fortune in the Northeast. For the present, that meant teaching English at Goucher.

Although by 1923 Sara had left Alabama behind, she was still being hotly pursued by a wealthy suitor from Montgomery—"the Pride of the Confederacy," she called him—and she came close to marrying him that same fall and winter she was making Mencken's acquaintance. After her marriage plans went awry, she was faced with troubles of an even more serious nature. She had long struggled with her health, had weakened herself further by eating poorly and living in cold rooms in Baltimore, and just before Christmas of 1923 she had fallen ill with bronchitis. She had done herself further damage by venturing out on a windy, subfreezing day in early January to meet Mencken at a favorite outdoor spot. By mid-January, seeing that her condition had not improved, Mencken had arranged for her to see several doctors in Baltimore. A small lesion was found on a lung, and tuberculosis was suspected.

It is significant that the first letter in which Mencken addressed Haardt as "Sara"—and in which he added the affectionate "I kiss your hand"—was the letter of January 20, 1924, in which he told her of the medical arrangements he has made for her. He told her there was "no reason whatever for alarm" and assured her in another letter that his brother August had recovered from a similar lesion. But he was himself concerned. When he heard that the doctors recommended that she check into a sanitarium near Baltimore, he concurred absolutely and wired her from New York: "Six months will restore you completely."

In fact, Sara was to remain in the Maple Heights Sanitarium for nine or ten months, and while she was there Mencken's affection for her grew enormously. At first he was not allowed to see her, but he wrote frequently, adopting a reassuring, good-natured tone, and sent abundant reading material. By late February he was allowed to come out, and upon his return from his first visit he wrote his most affectionate letter yet. He was "mashed" on her, he suspected.

He continued to make the fifteen-mile trip to Maple Heights weekly, battling late-winter weather and climbing the long hill to the sanitarium, sometimes alone, sometimes with Sara's younger friend and former student from Montgomery, Sara Mayfield. He brought gifts, he encouraged Sara to write to ward off boredom, and he constantly inquired about her medical condition: "What is the news? Is any temperature left? And how is your weight?" There was more than a little of a Victorian bedside courtship in all this—the man of health and vigor writing, visiting, and caring for the infirm object of his affection—and both Mencken and Sara knew their parts. Writing every two or three days, Mencken was constantly cheerful and optimistic. She wrote frequently as well, although she worried at first that she could not produce the kind of letters he wanted. She sometimes entrusted to her Goucher colleague and friend Marjorie Nicolson the task of composing such letters.

Neither Mencken nor Sara could have adequately defined their relationship at this point. He was part suitor and wooer, assuring her in letters that she had never been lovelier and adding the gallant "Ich küss die Hand," but he was also the older, wiser friend, overseeing her case, consulting with her doctors, sometimes questioning their advice and making his own recommendations. He was, as well, literary adviser, reading her stories and bombarding her with recommendations on where to send them. At his suggestion she wrote an article, "Alabama," for *The American Mercury* and began a novel, "Career." She had become dependent on him in nearly every respect, particularly so because she was not in close touch with her family in Montgomery. He dispensed financial as well as literary and medical advice, and he counseled her as to where she might go when she left the sanitarium.

His care seemed nearly "parental," one of her close friends believed, and Haardt herself, in a letter to Sara Mayfield, referred to Mencken as an "old dear." For the most part, Mencken kept his own feelings as well as his activities to himself. Although he had earlier introduced Sara to some of his out-of-town friends, including the Hergesheimers and Knopfs, not even his closest Baltimore friends— including Hamilton Owens, whom he saw nearly every day when he was in town—knew that he was now making the long trip out to Maple Heights every week.

When Sara left the sanitarium in the fall of 1924, she returned to her mother's home in Montgomery. She had at first resisted the move, but Mencken had felt that sunny Alabama would be a better place to recuperate than Baltimore. She was to remain in Montgomery all of 1925, resting, reading, and writing, although not composing at the pace she had earlier attempted. She tried all year to place her novel "Career," while Mencken advised her where to send it and spoke to publishers on her behalf. In his letters of early 1925 he assured Sara that he missed her "horribly," "infernally," but those letters, which in time grew somewhat less frequent, usually turned to a discussion of health, hers and his, as well as to her writing. He kept her informed of his activities, writing several letters from Dayton, Tennessee, in July, and later in the year he wrote several times about his mother's suffering. A few hours after Anna Mencken's death on December 13, he announced to Sara, "It is the end of many things for me." "This is desolation indeed," he repeated three days later. "My father's death was nothing, but now I am in the depths." Sara must have viewed Anna's death with conflicting emotions: she had been certain that Mencken would not marry her while his mother lived. In fact, she had told Jim Cain she felt she could never even go out to Mencken's house because such a visit would have meant meeting Anna Mencken.

Sara gained strength during her year in Montgomery, and by late

# FOREBEARS

Johann Burkhard Mencke,
eighteenth-century patriarch
of the Mencken family,
an iconoclast
with whom H. L. Mencken
closely identified.

August Mencken, the master
of his own modest world, in
an 1895 photograph taken by
his son H. L. Mencken.

Anna Abhau Mencken in 1898: a benevolent despot "not to be trifled with," one Mencken descendant remarked.

## HAPPY DAYS

"The larva of the bourgeoisie": Henry Louis Mencken, 1880.

From left: Charles Mencken, Henry Louis Mencken, Gertrude Mencken, and August Mencken II, about 1890. Young Henry, the eldest son of an eldest son, certainly seems to be living up to that role in this photograph.

From left: Charles Mencken, Anna Abhau Mencken, Gertrude Mencken, August Mencken II, August Mencken, Sr., and Henry Louis Mencken at Mount Washington, the family's summer home, about 1892.

# YOUNG MENCKEN

Mencken at his desk at the *Baltimore Herald,* 1901: "the maddest, gladdest, damndest existence ever enjoyed by mortal youth."

A brooding young Mencken, about 1903.

From left: August, Henry Louis, and Charles Mencken clowning in the backyard at Hollins Street, about 1906.

The Saturday Night Club, 1913. Mencken is at the far left.

At last, the war correspondent: Mencken (at center) in Germany, 1917.

## CELEBRITY:
## THE TWENTIES

The twin terrors of Manhattan:
George Jean Nathan (left) and
Mencken, 1923. Their intense
friendship was already
on the wane.

Mencken (with an unidentified though predictably attractive companion) in Berlin, 1922.

Mencken (far right) with Paul Patterson, Sunpapers publisher and longtime friend (second from left), at a convention of fire chiefs, New Orleans, 1926.

The fruits of celebrity: Mencken in Hollywood, 1926. Mencken is standing at center, Joseph Hergesheimer is seated directly in front of him, Aileen Pringle (holding the bottle) is to Hergesheimer's immediate left, and Anita Loos is in the bassinet. Hollywood has always seemed to bring out the puckish in its visitors; even Mencken was not immune.

Mencken and Will Rogers at the Democratic National Convention, Houston, 1928. The two were not particularly close, though Mencken did appreciate Rogers's company on the few occasions they met.

At the piano: Hollins Street, 1928. Though Mencken was known both
to write and to play in his undershirt, this is the rare occasion on
which he allowed himself to be so photographed.

## IN DEFENSE OF WOMEN

"O lovely Marionne": Marion Bloom on the beach, in a photograph likely
taken in the 1920s.

"A new gal in Washington": Gretchen Hood in a photograph published in the *Washington Times* in 1927.

Mencken with Aileen Pringle, Hollywood, 1926: "the most sophisticated and charming actress in Hollywood," she was once called.

Sara Haardt, at age eighteen or so.

Sara (in the late 1920s) looking rather severe, her characteristic expression before the camera. She called herself a refugee from "the sweet, flowering South."

Mencken in February 1930, returning from the London Naval Conference. He and Sara had just become engaged, though the delight he felt is nowhere to be seen in this photograph.

The wedding of Mencken and Sara, August 1930.

# THE THIRTIES

Visions of *biergemütlichkeit*: Mencken (left) and Clarence Darrow in
Mencken's Cathedral Street apartment, 1930.

Mencken celebrating the end of Prohibition, 1933.

Mencken covering the Republican National Convention, Cleveland, 1936.

The inner circle: Mencken (at extreme left) with Sunpapermen (Paul Patterson has his arm around Mencken), in a photograph probably taken in the late 1930s.

Mencken aboard the *Columbus*, bound for Germany in June 1938. This would be his final trip to Europe.

## THE FORTIES

Mencken in September 1940: The death of many friends and the wartime gloom were taking their toll on him.

Reconciliation: Mencken and George Jean Nathan at the Stork Club, 1947.

## MENCKEN AT SEVENTY-FIVE

This Aubrey Bodine photograph of Mencken in his backyard at Hollins Street was taken four months before Mencken's death in January 1956.

summer she was considering coming north again. Late in 1925, however, she had a relapse, spent early 1926 recuperating from that, and did not return to Baltimore until early spring 1926. In the meantime she achieved a measure of professional success by publishing two stories in *The American Mercury*. She and Mencken now did not seem quite so close as they had before, although they still met frequently for lunch and dinner and he continued to write warm, flirtatious letters, recycling lines such as "Ah, that we two were Maying" that he had used on Marion Bloom ten years earlier. They grew even more distant in the fall of 1926, when Mencken took his trip to Hollywood. Although he wrote her from New Orleans that he had been delighted to meet her brother and sister in his stopover in Montgomery and assured her from California that "I yearn for a sight of you," she was not reassured. The news stories spoke of his adventures with Hollywood actresses, news photos captured his good times, and his own letters referred to many of the women he was meeting.

He tried to regain lost ground when he returned in late November, but Sara now chose to be distant. They met on occasion in 1927, had lunch at Marconi's and the Southern Hotel, got together with the Hergesheimers and, another time, with Scott and Zelda Fitzgerald, and they continued to write. But their correspondence now was usually professional. Mencken was paying Sara $100 a month to do research for his work in progress, "Homo Sapiens," and she was correcting the proof of *Prejudices VI* for him as well. She was also clipping and collecting newspaper and magazine epithets for his book of self-promotion through self-defamation, *Menckeniana: A Schimpflexikon*—an assignment Mencken must have known would further increase his stature in her eyes.

In the summer there was a brief thawing when he and Sara met at the Hergesheimers' for a long weekend. Sara approached the trip with great anticipation—she wrote to Sara Mayfield wanting to borrow enough "Arabian perfume to last three days"—and Mencken too saw a chance to recover his footing. When he returned to Baltimore, he responded to what must have been a suggestion by Dorothy Hergesheimer that he and Sara marry: "The idea is charming! Ah, that it could be executed. But I already have one foot in the crematory, and spies hint that she is mashed on a rich Babbitt in Birmingham, Alabama."

In any event, that idea could not have been executed in the summer of 1927 because a month after Mencken and Sara met at the Hergesheimers, she was off on her own Hollywood excursion. Earlier in 1927 Mencken had put her in touch with a producer, and she had accepted a screenwriting job at $250 a week, with a chance to make still more money. As she prepared to leave in September, Mencken wrote his Hollywood friend Jim Tully, announcing her arrival, advising that she was a "special case," and asking him to look out for her: "She was brought up in Montgomery, Alabama, and is still extremely shy. The life of Hollywood will probably shock her half to death." On September 28, armed with a letter of introduction to Tully, Sara left by train for California. The next day Mencken wrote her that if he had seemed "idiotic" when he saw her last, it was because it had "suddenly dawned" on him that he would not be seeing her again for some time.

While Sara was in Hollywood the autumn and early winter of 1927, Mencken was able to stand back and take stock. Despite the weekend in August and the affectionate send-off, in many ways they were not as close as they had been in 1924, during her year in the sanitarium, and now they were to be separated for another extended period of time. He had known her for more than four years now, and during that period she had gained a great deal of confidence both personally and professionally. She was not nearly as shy as he suggested to Tully, and she approached Hollywood with a degree of ambition and independence that Mencken could hardly have imagined in 1924. They had become very well acquainted during those four years, had progressed from the mentor-student stage of their first year to a romantic relationship, but one that was still far from being stable and was almost certainly nonsexual. Mencken knew that Sara cared a great deal for him, and at times he was overwhelmed with what he felt for her. But neither of them was ready for the exclusive company of the other, and both would have a great deal of thinking to do before they would be.

Sara had long been jealous of other women who set their sights on Mencken. She viewed warily even such rivals among the southern literati as Emily Clark and Frances Newman (with whom she had once tangled at a literary gathering), although in fact both Clark and Newman lacked Sara's looks and charm and neither had a chance with Mencken. With other women, however, Sara had good reason for suspicion, for during the entire time she had known Mencken, he had never focused his attention altogether on her, nor had he given her any indication that he intended to. If she had been pursued by those champions from the Sahara, "The Pride of the Confederacy" and a "Rich Babbitt from Birmingham," he had been involved with several women who were more substantial threats. Such had been the case nearly from the beginning of their acquaintance.

At the time he met Sara, Mencken had also just begun to see New York journalist and writer Beatrice Wilson, a witty, charming, and thoroughly independent woman. In the dozens of letters he had written Wilson, he had played his usual dual role of suitor and literary adviser, remarking on her stories but also teasing and flirting in his customary manner. He had cared a great deal about her for a short time but had soon cooled off and was not at all wounded when she married an engineer in late 1925.

He had often seen Wilson in the presence of Ernest Boyd and other friends in New York. Indeed, throughout the mid-1920s, if his letters are any indication, Boyd was arranging dinner companions for Mencken, mentioning a certain "fair creature" on one occasion, a "quite personable female" or "fair partner" or "fair lady" on others. At still other times Mencken sought his own drinking and dinner companions in New York and Hoboken. In 1926 and 1927 he wrote to Goodman and Hergesheimer about certain "attractive wenches" and "cuties" they might engage for the evening.

Late in 1926 he had found another interesting woman closer to home, in Washington, and by the time Sara left for Hollywood in September 1927 he was paying a great deal of attention to Gretchen Hood. A forty-year-old opera singer and a liberated spirit who doubled as a writer and editor, Hood had earlier written the New York *World* not only praising Mencken but also demonstrating a certain Menckenesque wit. He had written her remarking on the letter and had begun a correspondence that led to dinner in Washington in March and a number of other engagements later in the spring. "I have turned up a new gal in Washington," he had written Nathan in March, "and she looks very promising."

From the beginning their association was based on a shared "sense

303

of the ridiculous," as Hood later put it, as well as shared acquaintances in Washington, a mutual interest in politics, and a definite physical attraction. The daughter of a well-respected Washington journalist, Hood had grown up in Washington, had studied in Europe and lived in New York before returning to Washington, at the time of her father's death in 1923, to live with her mother. When Mencken came to Washington he sometimes had dinner with both Hood and her mother—whom he immediately charmed—and sometimes took Hood to the Madrillon, one of the few Washington restaurants of which he approved. Once he brought along his niece, Virginia, for lunch and a tour of Mount Vernon.

By mid-April reporters were calling Mencken to check the rumor—as Mencken expressed it in a letter to Hood—"that I was engaged to a lovely creature in Washington," and the rumors increased as Mencken traveled by train to New York with Hood and was seen with her there. Although he laughed off the reports, they disturbed Hood—as well as Sara Haardt, of whose existence, at this point and for a long time to come, Hood was unaware.

That summer Mencken wrote Hood every two or three days, showing a penchant for flattery and sexual innuendo. They also began to spend more time together, both in New York and in Washington. Just before and after his August weekend with Sara in West Chester were dates with Hood in Manhattan, lunches and dinners out and other lunches in his Algonquin suite. In mid-September both *The Washington Post* and the *New York Mirror* predicted Mencken's marriage to "a beautiful opera-singer." He again laughed off the rumors, but Hood found the business too serious for laughter and issued her denials. In fact, as she later revealed, by this point she indeed hoped to marry Mencken and as time went on she felt he gave her grounds for hope. Nearly from the beginning he had teased her about marriage, and he continued to assure her that he cared for her. "The more I gaped at you, the more I was wobbled," he wrote after seeing her in New York, just before traveling to West Chester to see Sara. But in fact he never seriously considered marrying Hood.

While Sara was in Hollywood, however, he continued to see her. The day or the day before Sara left, he had lunch with Hood at Marconi's, the Baltimore restaurant he and Sara often frequented. Previously he had introduced her to Hergesheimer, Nathan, and other friends in New York. Now she introduced him to her friends

Fiorello La Guardia, then a congressman from New York, and Nicholas Longworth, Speaker of the House of Representatives and the son-in-law of Theodore Roosevelt, whom they met for dinner on several occasions.

Hood and Mencken made a successful social team, and their letters suggest they were getting along well indeed the fall of 1927. If Gretchen was occasionally given to insecurity and jealousy—she still did not know of Sara, but she knew of other girlfriends past and present—most of the time she demonstrated an irreverence and lightness of spirit in which Mencken delighted. She found him a curious combination of traits and noted in particular his fascination with human frailty and bodily ills: "Was ever a man so beset by physical ailments? I wonder if he realized how he dwelt on them? Most people don't, who are hypochondriacs like him." She also found him, she later remarked, something less than a "romantic man," not someone to "jump in bed with"—and despite their sexual wordplay and occasional expressions of passion, she probably never did. But still she knew she wanted to marry him.

Gretchen Hood was hardly the only woman with such goals the summer and fall of 1927; in fact, she was far from Sara's stiffest competition. Sara had long been alarmed by the "movie gals" (as Mencken called them) with whom he was frequently linked in the newspapers, and never more than after his Hollywood trip in 1926. At various times he was rumored to be involved with Anita Loos, Aileen Pringle, and Lillian Gish, although two of the three were married and the third, Gish, was shortly to become involved with George Jean Nathan.

But Loos's marriage was a flexible Hollywood arrangement, allowing her a great deal of freedom. A small, dark, clever scriptwriter from an early California show-business family, Loos had idolized Mencken since the *Smart Set* days and had wanted to meet him when she first came to New York just before 1920. She had stayed in the Algonquin, had been impressed, she later wrote, by his "arresting masculinity" as well as by a "boyish appearance" which "aroused a girl's motherly instincts." But "the very excess of my adoration made me bashful," she later remarked, and she had not been bold enough to approach him at that point. Other women had no such reluctance, she recalled much later, and he was "too polite to turn them down."

When Loos had returned to New York in the early 1920s, she was married to film director John Emerson, but, she later wrote, if Mencken had acknowledged her sooner, "I would . . . have relegated John Emerson to second place." Even at this point, she nearly did that, making it a point to get to know Mencken, then seeing him frequently for dinner at Lüchow's or his favorite haunt in Union Hill, New Jersey. Often they dined with Hergesheimer, Boyd, or Nathan, other times with Dreiser, Sinclair Lewis, or Sherwood Anderson, but still other times they were alone. During this period, she later confessed, she was "in love with Henry Mencken," and when she visited Germany with Emerson in the mid-twenties her travels in Mencken's spiritual homeland made her think even "more romantically than ever" about him.

But she apparently never fully expressed these thoughts and feelings, and Mencken certainly was not forthcoming with such sentiments. He enjoyed her company greatly, felt a deep sympathy with her, and in his memoirs described her as "an extremely intelligent woman, . . . full of a kind of wit that was often malicious, and indeed downright cruel." He flirted in his accustomed manner, in person and in letters, wanting (as Loos later remarked) to keep "our romance very actively alive." But he was also, she felt strongly, a "man of honor," as well as her husband's friend, and so their "romance" in the end came to nothing. Its principal legacy was Loos's novel *Gentlemen Prefer Blondes* (1925), which had its origins in a particular occasion in New York when Mencken had seemed taken by a blond girlfriend of Nathan's. He "liked me very much indeed," Loos realized, "but in the matter of sex he preferred a witless blonde."

Sara Haardt had much less to fear from Lillian Gish than from Loos. Although Mencken was certainly fond of the slender, light-haired beauty, saw her in New York, sent her wine, flowers and copies of his books—and was rumored in newspaper reports in 1926 to be considering marriage to her—he never, in fact, viewed her as anything more than a good friend. She felt the same way, writing him affectionate letters, addressing him as "Beloved Menck" and sometimes signing "Much love"—but with Gish such expressions of affection were routine. In fact, Mencken sat back and observed with much amusement as his friends fell for Gish—first Hergesheimer, who was sent by the mischievous Mencken and Nathan to interview her for an *American Mercury* piece, and then, more seriously, Nathan himself.

Loos had earlier told Mencken that Gish was unintelligent, "next door to an idiot," but to the contrary, Mencken found her "shrewd, well-informed and amusing."

The only one of the Hollywood stars with whom Mencken was seriously involved—who in fact posed far more of a threat than Sara realized as she herself left for Hollywood in September 1927—was Pringle, the actress whom he had met at Hergesheimer's in June 1926, had seen again in West Chester in August, and who had entertained him in Hollywood two months later. None of the three encounters was as innocent as Mencken had suggested. Pringle had been enamored of him since their first visit to Hergesheimer's. Two hours after they met in the station in Wilmington, Delaware—"the most important day of my life," she wrote him—she was "in [his] arms," and later that day, as they retreated to Hergesheimer's library, "I knew I loved you." Immediately she was taken by Mencken's manner—he was "the most charming man I ever knew," she said a half century later—his iconoclastic wit, his down-to-earth quality, and even his looks, a certain "circumsized look about the ears . . ."

Mencken had been equally smitten—and with good reason. A brown-haired beauty in her early thirties whom one reporter labeled "the most sophisticated and charming actress in Hollywood" (and who even Anita Loos admitted was intelligent and "cultured"), Pringle came from a prominent San Francisco family which certainly met that standard of "respectability" Mencken required. As a child she had attended schools in London and Paris, she had traveled widely, and she had come to appreciate good writing—including Mencken's own since the *Smart Set* days. Married in her twenties but long estranged from her husband—who now lived in Jamaica—Pringle preferred the company of literati such as Mencken, Hergesheimer, and the Knopfs to that of most other film stars.

From the moment they left West Chester in late June 1926, Mencken and Pringle were making plans to meet again. Mencken found the "days dreary and dull without you," he had wired her in early July, and in the weeks that followed they had met several times, including the second visit to Hergesheimer's. As Aileen returned by train to California, reading the *Selected Prejudices* as she crossed Kansas, she had assured Mencken that he was "the most wonderful of all men . . . I'm not sure how I will be able to get along without you." She was overjoyed by his frequent expressions of love—and already she spoke of "loving [him] forever," of wanting him "forever beside me." For the short term, she had looked forward to seeing him in Hollywood in October.

Mencken's California trip of October and November 1926, then, far from being the aimless excursion he had described to several friends, had had among its primary goals being with Aileen as much as possible. Aside from mugging for photographers in Hollywood, they had spent a great deal of time together in private. With his customary regard for propriety, Mencken had declined her invitation to stay with her during his entire visit—although she could not understand his reluctance. After he left Los Angeles, she had joined him briefly in San Francisco, where Mencken met her mother—and then, after George Sterling's suicide hastened his departure, he had headed east, leaving Aileen "lonely and miserable." Mencken was uncharacteristically open in expressing his own feelings: "A dreadful day . . . Endless love," he had wired from New Mexico. And when he returned to New York, the city had seemed "dull and dismal . . . Something is missing. The whole East, in fact, is not what it used to be."

Thus was established a pattern that would define Mencken's relationship with Pringle for the next two years. They were nearly three thousand miles apart, and Aileen was "always wondering when next we will meet." In the months following she wrote daily, sometimes twice daily, filling her letters with expressions of love and devotion. Although we have only her letters to him during this period, as well as a number of postcards and telegrams from Mencken (the fate of his letters to her will later be apparent), it is clear that he wrote nearly as often, that he sent photographs and gifts, and that he signed even telegrams (as he never had before) "Love forever." By December 1926 Aileen had spoken openly of marriage, and from her letters it is clear that Mencken had as well. She had written of moving to New York, where she and Mencken could live most of the time in their "tiny little nest," but she realized that Mencken had responsibilities in Baltimore as well: "Our marriage isn't ever going to trespass on [our freedom]. . . . We will only really be separated for short intervals. . . . Nothing will be taken for granted except our love for each other. . . . How . . . happy we will be."

There is no doubt that, as Pringle said repeatedly, she loved

Mencken "with all my heart," found him "so perfectly the one thing I want in life" and would have divorced Charlie Pringle (she would, in time, anyway) and given up her career in Hollywood to come to New York to be with him. As for his feelings, for once the newspapers had it right: he had "fallen hard" for Aileen, had himself considered marriage, and, as he wired her, had become "enslaved" by his love for her, if not "forever," as he claimed, at least for late 1926 and early 1927. Unlike Gretchen Hood, Aileen was "rather overjoy[ed] seeing our names linked so intimately" in the newspapers, but by February and March 1927 she had already begun to fear that Mencken would "change [his] mind" about marriage. She wondered if he considered her merely "a souvenir brought home from the county fair during a fustian mood," and she feared that he wanted her "out of [his] life." Since Baltimore seemed "farther away than Mars" and since Mencken would not commit to another western trip, she had vowed to come East. First she suggested June but changed her mind when Mencken failed to express the requisite interest. In October—the month after Sara left for Hollywood—she felt she could wait no longer. She wired Mencken that she was coming later that month. He wired that he would be delighted to see her, and he met her at Grand Central Station in late October.

He and Aileen spent a great deal of time together in New York the following two weeks, and in mid-November they traveled to West Chester for another visit with the Hergesheimers. In at least three letters to Sara, Mencken mentioned that he would be going to West Chester, but never did he suggest that Pringle would also be there—just as, the year before, when he had written Sara from Hollywood, he had omitted Pringle's name from the list of luminaries he was seeing. As he prepared to leave for Pennsylvania, he assured Sara, "I am eager for a sight of you"; "I am crazy to see you again."

Mencken's stay at Dower House with Aileen in November 1927 was cut short by Dorothy Hergesheimer's sudden attack of appendicitis, and a few days later Pringle left for California. He had "shed a tear" at her departure, Mencken wrote Dorothy Hergesheimer, at the realization that he would "not see her again until June!" He "mourn[ed] for Aileen like a cow robbed of its calf," he wrote Joe Hergesheimer, and at least one friend of Sara's believed that he and Aileen might have moved toward marriage if their stay at West Chester had not been interrupted. The newspapers and magazines, as in 1926, certainly did nothing to discourage such rumors; *Photoplay* speculated that Pringle would seek a divorce from her absentee husband and marry Mencken. F. Scott Fitzgerald, among others, spread stories about that possibility. As for the newspaper reports, Mencken had written a friend kiddingly in October 1927, "My engagement to AP is off. Her husband made pedantic objections to it."

In fact, seeing Aileen in New York and Pennsylvania had a more powerful impact than Mencken had anticipated, and in private he could hardly dismiss what he felt. If he had seemed to retreat from further involvement with her in his letters during the spring and summer of 1927, now he seemed to leap at the prospect. "You are infinitely completely and perfectly dear," he wired her as she left New York—and, two days later, "You are grand, lovely, gorgeous, incomparable, peerless, perfect." Without her he was "unutterably low . . . completely desolate." Her letters make it clear that they were surely lovers now, if they had not been earlier, and Mencken missed her as never before. Again, he assured her of his love, again—upon her return—he showered her with gifts, and he proposed coming to California in January (just as Sara would be returning from California). Friends in New York and West Chester might have been right after all when they judged him closer than ever to taking Aileen up on her offer: "I am prepared to marry you and suffer the consequences." In any event, she wrote him in December, she had seen a lawyer and "I'm getting a divorce immediately."

But that—as had been the case with Marion Bloom—was as far as matters went. Mencken did not come in January, nor apparently did his ardor last more than a month or two after Aileen returned to Hollywood. Her letters were more direct than ever: she again spoke of coming to New York to marry and live with him, in one instance even spoke of moving to Baltimore, and her repeated assurances— "I'm desperately in love with you," "I'm yours for the asking . . . I want only to live by your side"—were far more than melodramatic utterances. She meant what she said: she was completely willing and fully prepared to give up her highly successful career and move east to live with Mencken wherever he wanted to live.

Despite his obvious attraction to her, he didn't take her up on it, and the reasons he did not are far harder to fathom than those for his earlier rejection of Marion Bloom. Pringle had her own explanation—"The thing that worries you is that I won't have enough money to meet my requirements"—but the matter went beyond Mencken's very real concerns about supporting Pringle if she gave up her career. Even more, he seems to have been threatened by the sheer intensity of her love for him and (although she often denied it) her possessiveness. "I shall actually perish if I don't have you all to myself forever," she wrote in December 1927. "Life without you would be unbearable." She took the initiative, she effaced herself absolutely: "How I adore and worship you"; "I am the most love sick individual to whom you have ever written a line"; "You're tired of my telling you how much I love you." Despite his own talk of marriage—despite his speculation about a home, even children—marriage was *her* idea, and at last he responded as he had when Marion Bloom had pushed too hard. He fled from the prospect. With Aileen, at least after their first six months in 1926, he was more pursued than pursuer. With Sara Haardt, he was indisputably in charge.

It was hardly a question, however, of Aileen or Sara—or even Gretchen Hood—the fall and winter of 1927–28. Astoundingly, as if seeing Pringle and Hood, and writing Sara in Hollywood, were not enough, Mencken was also thinking of rekindling the oldest flame of all, the now-divorced Marion Bloom. From Marion's point of view, that flame had never really been extinguished. Her marriage to Lou Maritzer had been a failure; he had abandoned her after twenty months, and she had been in Paris for more than a year seeking a divorce. She had come to realize, in fact, what had earlier been obvious to others—that her primary reason for marrying Maritzer had been to "get away from" Mencken, to "snap ties" with him. She was less melodramatic than truthful when she described herself to her sister Estelle as having been a "slave . . . to love, never free, never my real self."

Marion had gone to Paris not only for a divorce but also to discover that "real self," and for a long period of time she was successful in neither pursuit. After she had reestablished contact with Mencken, with her letter of condolence upon his mother's death in December 1925, they had fallen back into their habit of corresponding and quarreling. At issue this time had been the Paris trip itself: Marion had said she could more easily obtain a divorce there—and she had financial backing for the trip from Estelle and Estelle's husband—but Mencken had written in February 1926 that he felt it altogether foolish to go to France with such an aim in mind. After seeing her and speaking with her, he was still of that opinion. But as he had written Estelle, "I long ago gave up any hope of arguing with her successfully."

After Marion sailed, she and Mencken had been out of touch for a couple of months, although she had continued to write Estelle about him, complaining that he had "buried me alongside" his mother. By May 1926, however, Mencken was writing again, and by midsummer he was suggesting that he might come to Paris by the end of the year. Marion, as she had written Estelle, was "very scared" at the prospect of his "coming here catching me with my pants down": "I have no idea of going into such slavery again. . . . I'm going to fight like a tiger to keep clear of entanglements with [him]. . . . I just get sick at heart at the idea of [his] coming and me standing like a grinning servant girl . . ." Her Paris letters to Estelle, frequent and lengthy, reveal a Marion who by turns still wanted badly to marry Mencken and wanted to flee from him. At the same time, he had been writing to Estelle as well, referring to Marion as "the New Windsor vampire," "the female Nietzsche."

He had been quite serious about hoping to visit Paris by the end of 1926, although his primary purpose had been not to see Marion but to travel with Goodman. By late July, however, he had seemed less certain he would come, and by late August, after having met Pringle at Hergesheimer's, he had decided on Hollywood, not Paris. He had told Bloom that, while in California, he might "drop off in Los Angeles, to see the movie gals," but he had assured her he would come to Paris in the spring. When Marion had protested his Hollywood plans, he resorted to his old strategy of defusing objections with humor: "Can't a young fellow take a look at the gals without getting roasted? No less than two eminent female stars, known everywhere in the wide, wide world, have got mashed on me . . ." A month later he had written that he regretted not having been able to come to Paris: "I am homesick for a sight of you. . . . We used to quarrel too much. But you are very nice when indignant . . ." On a note attached to the envelope Bloom had written "A. Pringle."

Although Marion had kept busy with other matters—a business venture, her pursuit of the divorce, and now a succession of older suitors—Mencken had continued to dominate her thoughts. When he had written again in December 1926 that he was "homesick" for her and that he would "certainly be in Paris" within the next year, her spirits had lifted. When he had forgotten to write, especially at Christmas, or when he had seemed indecisive about the trip to Paris, she had been hurt. Marion had vowed to "take the offensive" to "snare him this time" if he indeed came to France: "he'll marry me and like it too." In his letters Mencken had given her what she took to be encouragement, assuring her in early 1927, "God knows I wish you were not so damned far off"; "if I came to Paris I would neck you so violently that the chastity of both of us would be in grave danger." But in a February letter after she had spoken of marriage—whether in general or in particular isn't certain—he had responded, "You are trying to drive me to suicide. If I ever marry, it will be on a sudden impulse, as a man shoots himself."

As 1927 wore on, Mencken had continued to delay his trip. His work, including the beginning of *Treatise on the Gods*, had been tying him up, and though he was "flirting wickedly" in his letters, Marion wrote Estelle, he would not be pinned down. In fact, alone in Paris, Marion was despairing of Mencken and many other things. Ill health, poverty, business failure, an increasing awareness of growing old—all had led her to write Estelle in March 1927, "I have been very close to suicide these last months . . ." She had resisted largely because it was "cowardly to involve others as [I] just gaily trip off . . ."

Her feelings toward Mencken were more ambivalent than ever. On the one hand she assured Estelle, who had visited her in April, that he did not mean so much to her anymore, that she would marry him if he asked but was no longer "dying for love of Henry at all." On the other hand, she often felt a "red rage" against him, particularly when she realized how dependent she still was. Her letters to Estelle, as well as diary entries that she sent to her sister, provide an indictment of Mencken rivaling the self-defamatory *Schimpflexikon* that Sara Haardt, at that moment, was putting together.

Marion complained of Mencken's "cold values of peoples [*sic*] and women," his "phase of flamboyancy these days," and she likened him to "a trapeze performer . . . who must show off but sometimes grows too old for his struts and wants rest . . ." She complained, in a remark Mencken would have found particularly ironic, of a loss of "a lot of his exclusive tone since Maryanne dropped out of his life." Yet when it still seemed probable that he would come to visit her in Paris, she wanted above all to please him. She thought "frantically" that she would borrow "a great pile of money" from Estelle's husband to buy better clothes, find a better hotel, and start "riding in taxis" a week before he arrived "to give myself a rich easy feeling." And even when she damned him, she expressed the belief, as late as August 1927, that he would mend his ways and "it will be me he will turn to."

Until the end of Marion's two-year stay in Paris, Mencken spoke of coming for a visit. "I'd die before he should see me now," Marion wrote her sister in late 1927, "my face chewed with ravages and my hair . . . streaked." She felt that he could not understand "the chain of events that has swirled me blindly about." As she prepared to leave Paris, she wrote Estelle that she was "very low in spirits." The winter of 1927–1928 was "a brilliant climax to Paris, hovering between suicide and America." "Don't herald my coming to Mencken," she wrote Estelle. She did not want his "cool pitying judgment."

<hr />

Sara Haardt, of course, heard nothing from Mencken of Marion Bloom when she was in Hollywood in the fall of 1927. Nor did he mention Aileen Pringle or Gretchen Hood (which was only fair, he might have said, since he did not mention Sara to them), although she could hardly have missed the numerous newspaper articles announcing his impending marriage to both. Since his return from California in November 1926 she had been disturbed by his sometimes public flirtation with Pringle, and back in Baltimore she had herself decided to seek the company of other men, at least in part to make him jealous.

Earlier she had seen Mencken's friend Jim Cain, who liked her a great deal and found her "quite easy to look at." Cain had stopped seeing her, he later wrote, only when he learned that she was Mencken's "special weakness." In 1926 and 1927 Sara had also been squired to dinner, the theater, and dances by R. P. Harriss, a dapper North Carolinian four years her junior who had just come to the Sunpapers. The romantic Harriss had been taken with her, speaking in a letter to a mutual friend of "that charm of manner which, in a less prosaic age, inspired men to go out on the field of honor and shoot each other full of holes." For Sara, the gallant Harriss served

a valuable purpose. "He fell for my pulchritude," she wrote her
Alabama friend Sara Mayfield. "God has delivered him into my
hands, and he is useful and not too moonish."

Given the relative coolness between Mencken and Sara since the
autumn of 1926, as well as Mencken's involvement with three other
women during that period, it seemed likely that her stay in California
during the fall and early winter of 1927 would make things even
worse. But, as was often the case with Mencken when distance was
involved, it worked quite the other way. At first his letters to her were
principally businesslike, full of professional counsel, even if he sometimes ended them with "Ah, that thou wert here." Sara was working
for Famous Players of Hollywood, and he was advising her on how
to deal with her employers, as well as cautioning her to take care of
her health.

It is clear that Sara, while taking some pride in making her own
way, was deeply grateful for his help, and by late fall that gratitude
had begun to take the form of renewed expressions of real affection.
She was "as loyal as hell to you," Jim Tully wrote him from California, and Mencken's letters to her grew warmer. Although he was
seeing Hood and Pringle, he had also written Sara more frequently
while she was in California than he ever had before, often every day
or two. By late December he could write, "The news that you are
coming back at last is glorious. I have missed you horribly." The
same day he had written Gretchen Hood, making a date and assuring
her, "Both your hands are kissed." But in his letter to Sara he
seemed to mean it more.

When Sara, after a stopover in Montgomery for Christmas, arrived
in Baltimore on December 31, Mencken met her at the station. She
had found Hollywood distasteful and felt she had been deceived and
exploited, but she had made a good deal of money, not only the $250
a week but a $1,500 advance on a film she was to write. On that
amount she would be able to live and write fiction for a year or two.
Mencken saw her frequently in early January before he left to cover
the Pan-American Conference in Havana—a city he explored in the
company of Will Rogers and found swarming with Yankees—and he
continued to see her frequently when he returned in late January. He
had not given up on Aileen Pringle during the early months of 1928.
Nor had he given up on Gretchen Hood, getting together with her
and her friends Longworth and La Guardia, and in his letters he kept

315

up his usual stream of mock-romantic banter. In fact, his letters to Hood were more frequent and more flattering than ever. But he saw Sara even more often.

He spent evenings at her Baltimore apartment drinking gin and ginger beer, although—still the cautious conventionalist, and never more so than in Baltimore—he invited Sara Mayfield over as a chaperone. He fell back into the habit of taking Haardt to Marconi's for lunch and to Schellhasse's for beer, and on occasion she helped him give dinner parties at the Rennert Hotel. Of one such occasion, he wrote Dorothy Hergesheimer, "Sara will be in charge of the blackamoors." He took her to the Hergesheimers for an occasional weekend and later to New York. On the New York trips, Mencken always kept in mind Sara's Alabama prejudices. When Carl Van Vechten invited them both for dinner, he exacted a promise that no blacks would be present. On at least one other occasion he turned down a party invitation in New York because Haardt would be along and James Weldon Johnson and his wife were to be present.

It was clear by mid-1928—though Aileen, Marion Bloom, and Gretchen Hood knew nothing of it—that Sara was the object of Mencken's greatest affection. Their three months apart in late 1927 had accomplished what their earlier time together had not; Mencken was committed to her as never before. She still saw other men on occasion, most frequently Harriss. Another time she was invited to dinner to meet John Owens, widower and editor of the morning *Sun*, who was, she wrote Mayfield, considered to be "very eligible." Sara's excessive vanity was never more evident than when she considered her other suitors. She wrote to Mayfield of certain "new admirers," and to another friend she continued to write of Harriss: "He has sent me volumes of roses and rides me in taxis to any place of my notion and wants to do any dirty work I will push off on him. . . . He hangs upon my words . . ." She was fond of Harriss and others and loved the attention they paid her. But they were still no competition for Mencken. "I'm devoted to him, as you probably know," she had written Sara Mayfield.

Life was pleasant for Mencken and Sara during the first three quarters of 1928, but in October, shortly after a weekend at Hergesheimer's, it grew more ominous. Sara, whose health had been reasonably good since her illness in 1924, began to experience what

Mencken could describe in letters only as "Female Weakness." When he learned of her suffering, he got in touch with his friend Dr. Louis Hamburger, who consulted with a gynecologist. They decided surgery was necessary.

The operation, which was delayed until Mencken was able to return from a scheduled campaign trip with Al Smith, was more involved than Sara had been led to believe. Finding a benign ovarian tumor, the surgeon (in the words of a close friend of Sara's) "scraped all that was left" of one ovary and removed the other completely. According to the same Goucher friend, Sara was angry when she awoke and discovered what had been done. If she had ever entertained hopes of having children, that possibility was now gone.

Since Mencken had the flu at the time of her surgery, he couldn't do his usual job of supervision. "Just what the operation was I still don't know," he wrote Dorothy Hergesheimer shortly afterward. Within a day or two he was able to consult with Hamburger as well as to visit Sara, who had had a rough two or three days. Within a week he was sweeping into her room with a suitcase full of beverages and a stack of Methodist and Baptist newspapers full of commentary on the Smith campaign. He wrote to their friends with his customary jauntiness: "Her first word, coming out of the anaesthesia, was 'Gettysburg.'"

Sara remained in the hospital several weeks and, according to another Goucher friend, after another two or three months still had never really "snapped back." She resumed most of her activities, continued to work on her novel, and spent a great deal of time with Mencken drinking beer at Schellhasse's and having dinner with friends. She went to New York with him and got together with Phil and Lily Goodman.

But in the winter and spring of 1929 Mencken was clearly concerned about her health. She was ill in late March and most of April, "a consequence of her operation last autumn," he wrote Jim Tully, and she spent much of May and June at Union Memorial Hospital, in considerable pain, as doctors attempted to diagnose her ailment. "She is bearing the thing very bravely," he added to Tully, "but it is beginning to wear her out." To Sara he wrote, "I can't bear to see you in pain. It must be stopped"—and, several days later, "the horrible examinations are over. You have been immensely

317

brave . . ." Mencken himself continued to consult frequently with Dr. Hamburger but told Sara nothing of the seriousness of her condition.

By early July doctors had confirmed a tubercular infection in Sara's left kidney, and for several days they debated not so much whether but when to operate. Writing to Sara Mayfield back in Alabama, Mencken expressed his fears and marveled at Sara's courage. He and the doctors still withheld the bad news from her, and Mencken was against telling her family of the gravity of the situation until the final decision to operate had been made.

On July 6 the surgeons removed Sara's left kidney. Mencken was on hand for the surgery, and he hovered about the hospital for the critical days afterward, witnessing a recovery that was even more difficult than before. Ten days after the surgery, he wrote a friend, she still had not been informed of the tubercular infection or even of the removal of the kidney. Indeed, for a time, Mencken wrote Jim Tully, the doctors thought Sara "was finished"; one of them had called him at Hollins Street and told him he believed she would die. Again, her great determination had pulled her through. "I've had a pretty dreadful time of it," she told a friend when she felt strong enough to write, "but it looks as if my time still isn't yet. God knows why."

Mencken realized, far more than Sara, the bleakness of her prospects. Although she had survived the surgery, her doctors had told him that she probably had but three years to live, and according to Sara Mayfield, at the time of the surgery he had vowed that he would marry Sara and make those years the happiest he possibly could. They had, in fact, been speaking of marriage before the tubercular condition flared up and had discussed plans for late 1929. If she pulled through, Mencken was determined, they would go through with these plans as soon as she was able.

As Sara endured a slow and painful recovery in the fall of 1929, there was a great deal of unfinished business for Mencken to take care of, ties to be severed or at least loosened. He had continued to see Gretchen Hood occasionally and to write her frequently in 1928 and early 1929, still calling her on occasion his "lady friend," reminding her "Your lovely paw is kissed," and continuing that combination of flattery, teasing, and occasional sexual punning his letters to her had always contained. But increasingly those letters (more than one hundred in 1928) turned to a description of his activities and a discussion of health—his, hers, her mother's and that of numerous acquaintances. Less frequently now was he the gallant suitor, and when she now turned the topic, even half humorously, to marriage, he insisted that celibacy might be the better course after all.

It was much more difficult to conclude matters with Aileen Pringle, who had still entertained—with some reason—very real hopes of marrying Mencken even after Sara returned to Baltimore in late December 1927. Aileen knew of Sara; in one letter she had referred to Sara's success as a writer in Hollywood, in another, in early January 1928, she had told Mencken that a Hollywood acquaintance of theirs "didn't think much of your girl." But she had little idea of the depth of Mencken's feelings for her rival. Aileen had continued to write almost daily the first few months of 1928, and for a while he had written and had sent telegrams nearly as often. But he kept postponing the date of their proposed summer rendezvous, and Aileen—who now sometimes signed "Hopelessly yours"—again realized that her chances were slipping away.

She had confronted Mencken directly in several letters, asking if she still fit into his plans, but he was still evasive. When he wrote, however, that he would not, after all, come to California in July after the Democratic convention in Houston, a plan he had earlier proposed, she responded, "The news . . . finishes me." She found hope in the fact that he still signed his telegrams "Much love" and "Love forever" and that he wired in December 1928, "It will never be a good Christmas so long as you are so far away." But she was skeptical when he wired in July 1929—by which time, just after Sara's second surgery, he had essentially made up his mind to marry Sara—suggesting to Aileen, "Fly with me to West Chester where we will bathe in ruin. Yours until death." By now Aileen knew better. And if he were kidding, she no longer appreciated his humor. She realized he would never come west to see her again and any chance they had to marry was past.

It was almost as difficult to settle things—for a final time that would indeed be final—with Marion Bloom. When she returned from Paris in the early spring of 1928, divorce in hand, it was with a renewed "horrible feeling of liking" for Mencken "creeping around me like a snake." "I wish to God," she wrote Estelle, "I'd hear he was married or dead." Mencken had heard nothing from her in months, but he had told Estelle that he would like to see her when she arrived. A week later they were making plans to meet, Mencken assuring her, "I refuse absolutely to do any preaching. . . . All I desire is to feast my eyes on you again." Immediately after they had lunch at Marconi's, Mencken wrote her, "I have never seen you look more handsomer" and reminded her that they would meet again the next week at the Algonquin.

At that second meeting Mencken said something at which Marion took great offense, and their letters that summer show that they were clearly at odds again. After lunch in late July, shortly after Marion's mother's death, Mencken wrote her sister that she seemed to him to be "plainly in a disturbed state of mind." His tone in another letter suggested that all between them lay in the past, and at one of their meetings Marion asked Mencken not to write again. But in mid-November (shortly after Sara's first serious surgery), he was not so sure they were finished. "I have a notion," he wrote Marion after having lunch in Baltimore, "that we called the coroner's inquest before the patient was actually dead. He is up today, walking around the room, smoking a cigar and singing like a bird. . . . We theorize and plan and then the band begins to play, and it is all off." "God roast me in hell," he concluded, "if you ain't getting better looking all the time."

But the patient, if not dead, was dying, and Mencken's few letters to Marion in 1929, though friendly, lacked the old passion. She already belonged so firmly to the past that when Gretchen Hood wrote in January 1929 inquiring about Bloom, he could reply: "I know of no gal who has lately lost her husband [through divorce]. . . . Nor do I recall any fair one who was a Christian Scientist."

Hood was asking, of course, about the wrong woman. By this time Mencken was not only preoccupied with Sara Haardt's medical condition but was also deeply in love with her—even if he still gave mixed signals, on occasion, to Hood and Pringle. After his discussion of marriage with Sara in early 1929, interrupted by her second surgery in July, the only thing that delayed their wedding was Sara's recovery and his professional obligations. She remained in Union Memorial Hospital during the late summer and early fall, largely to treat an infection in the surgical incision, and when she was released she continued to see doctors frequently. In mid-December Mencken still pronounced her "unfit for travel." He was spending more time with her than ever. By late 1929 they considered themselves engaged, although they told no one.

After a strenuous autumn of caring for Sara and completing *Treatise on the Gods,* he was ready in late December to make one last European trip before settling down. He had been hoping to make such a journey since early 1928, but Sara's health had kept him at home. Now her condition was stable, at least for the time being, and the Sunpapers wanted him to cover a European naval conference in London in late January. He would leave in late December, travel in Europe for much of January, and reach England in time for the conference.

He sailed from New York on December 27 on the *Columbus* and spent his time on board reading, drinking "colossal Pilsner," catching up on sleep—ten to fourteen hours a day, he wrote Hamilton Owens—and talking with Dudley Field Malone, one of the Scopes lawyers. He also found, as he had earlier with Marion, that sea voyages inspired him to write letters more loving than any he penned on dry land. Although he wrote "Dearest Aileen" in the old flirtatious manner, teasingly suggesting that she come to New York, it was to Sara that his truest sentiments were directed. "How lovely you are, and how I'll miss you," he wrote Sara the day he sailed. "You will never know how much I think of you, and depend on you, and love you." "I am horribly homesick for you," he wrote a few days later. "Next time you will be aboard, and everything will be perfect. I love you."

It was the best of situations for Mencken. He was in love, he would return to Sara, and for the time being he also had the kind of freedom he always relished in Europe. He landed at Cherbourg, immediately linked up with Phil Goodman in Paris, and saw the city more closely than he had ever before. He rejected an invitation to call on Gertrude Stein but had tea with Emma Goldman in a luxurious studio provided her by an admirer. From Paris he took the Orient Express to Vienna, where he visited Beethoven's grave in the Central Friedhof, and after a week he moved on to Budapest—"the most beautiful [city] that I have ever seen"—for a few days. All the while he was writing Sara the most devoted letters he had ever written: "I miss you dreadfully, and love you completely"; "I love you beyond everything, I am horribly homesick for you"; "You are infinitely dear . . . I'll love you forever."

Mencken arrived in England on January 23 for the naval conference, but that meeting, he wrote Sara, turned out to be "the usual tedious horror . . . so dull a show." The English, the French, and the Americans, it seemed to him, could agree on nothing, and he concluded in a *Sun* piece, "If anything is certain in this world it is that another war is coming"—although at this point he saw France and England as the adversaries. He remained in England for nearly three weeks, staying with Paul Patterson in the Savoy, attending (with Will Rogers) Dudley Malone's wedding, making the rounds of parties, and traveling briefly to Manchester and Chester. In London he dined with Arnold Bennett, the author of some "superb novels" he believed, but a man with "an eradicable air of the plebian about him . . ." He traveled to Oxford for a reunion with Robert Bridges, now eighty-six years of age and not far from death. But, he had written Estelle Bloom, he would not call on his old hero George Bernard Shaw: "He is a teetotaler and I detest them."

Mencken had never been so happy to return from a European trip as he was in February 1930. The remainder of that winter and spring he and Sara made plans for marriage, while Sara continued to recuperate. In April she traveled to Montgomery, both to visit her ailing mother and to tell her family of their plans, and she remained in Alabama some three weeks. Meanwhile, Mencken spent several days working in New York and visited Hergesheimer in West Chester and the Prince and Princess Troubetzkoy at Castle Hill—and waited for the appropriate moment to tell not only his friends but also his often prickly sister, Gertrude, of their plans to marry.

Although both he and Sara had qualms about Gertrude's reaction, in fact, he wrote Sara, she "greeted the news with cheers." She was "genuinely delighted," he reported, and Mencken was "immensely relieved . . . as happy as the boy who killed his father." She had had no idea they were "seriously thinking of marriage," Gertrude wrote Sara, and added that Mencken was "somewhat worried about leaving me here alone." But she assured Sara that their marriage was "the most wonderful thing that could happen." "No one could have made Henry as happy, or cared for him as devotedly as you," Sara responded, and she assured Mencken's sister that she would need her "counsel." She also hoped Gertrude and August would "be with us as much as possible."

Shortly after Sara returned to Baltimore in mid-May, she began to get into shape the third-floor apartment they had leased in an elegant brownstone at 704 Cathedral Street, overlooking Mount Vernon Place, just north of downtown. They still had not told friends why Sara was leaving 16 W. Read Street, so they had to invent excuses. Sara wrote Sara Mayfield that "the medical faculty say I have to have a lighter apartment." As spring moved into summer, her closest friend, Anne Duffy, helped her furnish their new quarters.

In early summer they finally began to tell close friends. Mencken broke the news to Goodman in late June and to Brödel and the Hergesheimers in July. Sara told Mayfield and Mary Parmenter in late July. Mencken's tone in letters announcing his intentions to some of his old friends was nearly apologetic: "You will be astounded (but I hope not horrified)," he wrote Brödel, and he assumed Goodman too would be "astounded." To Olga and Hamilton Owens he wrote a note asking them—kiddingly, they assumed—to pray for him. Other friends found out only when they saw an August 2 Baltimore *Sun* announcement or an Associated Press story announcing the engagement and the projected wedding date of September 3. The stories and editorials that followed that announcement filled four of Mencken's clippings scrapbooks. It was major news indeed that the nation's most famous bachelor—and most famous opponent of marriage—had announced he was taking a wife.

Nearly all of Mencken's and Sara's friends responded with delight. "You are doing exactly the right thing at the right time and with the right person," Hergesheimer wired. "As a war-scarred veteran," wrote the recently separated Ernest Boyd, "I welcome you . . . to the ranks." But the cries of astonishment that rose from old Baltimore friends who belonged to that part of his world that was exclusively masculine suggest the extent to which he had successfully compartmentalized his life. "The news seems to have surprised the [Saturday Night] club," Mencken wrote Brödel. "And the Sun brethren. All John Owens had to say was 'Well, I'll be goddam.' " To Brödel, who had never once met Sara—despite his residency in Baltimore and his close friendship with Mencken—and to whom Mencken in his letters had never mentioned Sara, he even had to identify his intended: "The bride is Sara Haardt, a lovely girl . . ." Brödel's response to Mencken should have been expected: "What will Sara do to the club!"

If he had anticipated surprise from the Saturday Night Club,

Mencken apparently had not realized the shock his news would create in other quarters. One of his first letters, even before those to Goodman and Hergesheimer, had been to Aileen Pringle, who had responded on June 19: "Wire me at once and tell me every word in your letter is nonsense, and did you time its arrival for the nineteenth [the date Mencken and Aileen had met four years earlier]? I thought somehow you would always be there . . . I'm having rather a rotten time of it." It is not clear whether it was at this point, or somewhat later, that Mencken also asked Aileen to return all his letters to her—a request she found especially heartless since his letters, she once wrote, were "all that I have." But she complied, withholding only postcards, telegrams, and one or two letters. Mencken consigned the returned letters to the fire—and then placed Aileen on the list to receive a wedding announcement.

For Gretchen Hood the shock was even greater. During the period that he and Sara considered themselves engaged, Mencken had continued to write Hood, on occasion in the old familiar manner: "I hear from private sources that you are more beautiful than ever" or "I shall give you a chance to lavish some of your money on a handsome man." He had meant nothing by such remarks, indeed had not written Hood at all since mid-May and had not seen her for a much longer time. But Gretchen, still very much taken with Mencken, had read a great deal into what she took to be continued expressions of favor. She was especially shocked when, in early August, she read of Mencken's engagement in the newspaper. He had never given her any indication that Sara Haardt meant anything to him. In fact, she had "never heard him mention . . . Sara Haardt's name," she later said, and in the two or three hundred letters he had written to Hood he had indeed mentioned it only once and then only in passing and with no suggestion that he cared for her at all. Worse, he had not written to warn her of the Associated Press announcement.

When he did write, five days later, it was in an all-too-jocular voice: "I suppose you have heard of my approaching marriage. The bride is a rich woman and promises to treat me tenderly." Hood felt she had no choice but to adopt his tone, and her response was only slightly barbed. "I only ask that I be permitted to sing 'You Promised Me' at your wedding," she replied, and then added, "I hope you will be the most militantly happy husband in captivity." In fact, as she later wrote, "This was the worst shock I ever had . . . I never got over it."

If Hood wondered why Mencken had decided to marry Sara Haardt, she was hardly alone. Marion Bloom, hypothesizing forty years later, concluded that he felt great pity for Sara: "I think one part of his fall for Sarah [sic] was that she was frail and could play the part." Others of his friends agreed to varying degrees. Knopf felt that he married Sara at least in part because he felt great concern about her health, and Hamilton and Olga Owens believed as well that Mencken's great desire was to take care of her, particularly after learning that she could not live long, and that he could best accomplish that end by marrying her.

There is much in Mencken's actions and in his letters, to Sara herself and to other friends, to suggest something of the sort. It was during her periods of serious illness—tuberculosis in 1924, the life-threatening surgeries of 1928 and 1929—that he was most attentive to her, and at those times, particularly in 1928 and 1929, he virtually took control of her life, arranging medical care, consulting with doctors, becoming one of that small group of older men who determined her fate. He had decided what information should be given her and what information withheld, had decided (in 1929) when her family should be told of her condition, had decided when she was well enough to travel. He indeed had a proprietary interest, had already become both husband and father.

But the reason for that proprietary interest went far beyond pity. He was concerned about Sara's condition because he deeply loved her, and the depth of that love is clear to anyone who reads the letters of this normally dispassionate man in the winter of 1930 when he was in Europe and that spring when she was in Montgomery. If illness played some part in that love—other than bringing to the surface a compassion in Mencken that was never far submerged when family and truly close friends were involved—it was that, in facing her illness, Sara showed a "magnificent" courage and determination that absolutely astounded him. She was, a friend of hers wrote, "the pluckiest person I know anything at all about," and Mencken found her valor irresistible.

But he had reasons to love Sara Haardt that went far beyond her precarious health and his admiration of the manner in which she faced it. Her Baltimore suitors Jim Cain and R. P. Harriss were hardly alone in testifying to her beauty and charm. Hergesheimer too saw in her "a delicacy of beauty and wit," and others agreed. Although that beauty had already begun to fade by 1930 because of the rigors of illness and the attempts of doctors to fight it, the charm remained in abundance. "In many ways she seemed a bit elegant for our family," Mencken's cousin William C. Abhau said later, and to that elegance she added a highly cultivated dramatic sense. "The Queen of Drama," as her friend Marjorie Nicolson called her, she was given to such flourishes as, upon learning she had tuberculosis, asking for a revolver.

There was more than a little that was southern in all this—all of which made Marion Bloom more insightful than she knew when, still pondering Mencken's marriage forty years later, she reasoned: "Sarah [sic] was southern and southern women are famous for grabbing their men." It was partly a determination to land Mencken that was at work, but it was more than that. In fact, he had always been susceptible to charm, elegance, a sense of drama, and the other qualities that he assigned to the right kind of southern woman. He himself spoke of Sara's possessing "a great deal of the traditional charm of the South," and beyond that he saw in her a refinement that he associated with southerners of high breeding. If her father's family was German, her mother was descended from the Powells and the Farrars of Virginia, "well-known Southern . . . families," Mencken later wrote, and no matter how she tried to flee from her southern heritage, it was that influence that was primary in her early years and most evident in her years in Baltimore.

It did not matter that Sara's immediate family was not, in fact, materially well off. Though her father and uncle had owned a respectable enough dry-goods store in Montgomery, it was Sara's grandmother with Virginia roots, Sarah Powell Farrar Hall, who had provided the funds to send her to Goucher. To Mencken, wealth was never so important as refinement as a measure of good family, a refinement manifesting itself in a certain manner, demeanor, and taste, and it was *that* in Sara Haardt that largely appealed to him. She was a writer, and that was important, but so was Marion Bloom a writer of sorts. She had wit and an independent spirit, but so did Marion Bloom. But what she had over Marion, put quite simply, was what Mencken perceived to be a certain *fineness*, a sense of self and a confidence stemming from good breeding that he finally felt Marion, for all her appeal, did not possess. And what she had over Aileen Pringle, for all *her* fineness, was a certain reticence and reserve, a demeanor that conformed to Mencken's belief that one's ideal woman should be the hunted, not the hunter.

Like Mencken, Sara was a Victorian, and indeed there was much in their attraction, as we have seen, that is reminiscent of the Victorian courtship between the strong, compassionate gentleman and his bedridden love. They were Victorian as well in their adherence to conventional behavior and propriety: one of Sara's closest friends felt they were not sexually intimate before they married, and she was probably right.

What they had, then, was a meeting of backgrounds, partly German and partly southern (for Mencken never relinquished the illusion that he was, in part, a southerner), as well as a similarity of temper—skeptical and freethinking—and a strong sense of decorum in personal behavior. Theirs was a meeting of minds, as well as the coming together of a young woman in need and an older man with a desire to nurture, but there is no doubt that it was a great deal more than that. It was, as Mencken was later to describe his own parents' marriage, a "love match."

The Baltimore wedding was an event of August 27, 1930, in the Episcopal Church of St. Stephen the Martyr. It should be no surprise that any number of editorialists reflected on the aptness of the church's name. Mencken had not cared to marry in a church at all, but since there was no civil marriage in Maryland, he had no choice. He did manage to snare an iconoclastic clergyman and old friend, Herbert Parrish of New Jersey, for the ceremony, and he managed as well to deceive and elude a curious national press. He and Sara had planned all along to marry a week before the announced date of September 3.

He approached the "solemn orgies" (as he wrote Brödel) with a combination of self-deprecating humor and immense satisfaction. "I begin to tremble," he had written Hamilton Owens a week earlier, and two weeks before that he had written Blanche Knopf that he was going to North Carolina "for a few days of celibate relaxation—my last on this earth." "The hour approaches," he wrote his old friend A. H. McDannald. "I can about hear the sheriff's stealthy step."

When the day arrived, however, he came to the altar not, as he had told Marion Bloom he would, "on a sudden impulse, as a man shoots himself," but rather with calm resolve and no second thoughts. He had made his preparations and had attended a final Saturday Night Club orgy in which he and his old friends had drunk the house dry. He had answered much of his even heavier than usual correspondence and had submitted to a prenuptial interview with the United Press. When *The New York Times* reported that he had applied for a marriage license on August 21 and was apparently planning to do the deed before the announced September 3 date, he and Sara denied it.

Thus the ceremony came off as smoothly as he could have wished. Mencken and August, his best man, reached the church shortly after 4:00 P.M., and Sara, accompanied by her mother, sister, brother, and nephew, drove up shortly afterward. Hamilton Owens assured Sara— who did not at first see Mencken and was concerned—that he had indeed arrived. Others in attendance included Gertrude, Charlie and his wife and daughter, and, according to the wedding book, Owens and Paul Patterson. After Parrish married Mencken and Sara, they posed for pictures (Sara, as usual, was unphotogenic), departed as the wedding guests threw rice, and were driven to Pennsylvania Station to catch a train. Three weeks short of his fiftieth birthday, Mencken was off for a honeymoon in Canada.

# Chapter 14

# A BEAUTIFUL EPISODE

> My days with her made a beautiful episode in my life, perhaps the only one that deserves to be called romantic.
>
> —*H. L. Mencken, Diary*

The train speeding north took Mencken and Sara through Montreal to Quebec. They had decided on Canada because the weather would be cool and because Mencken's hay fever, which was always severe in late August and early September, would be milder there. They had invitations for stops along the way. Robert Frost, whom Mencken had met but did not know well, had asked them to spend a night with him in Vermont. Max Brödel had written from Ontario, wanting Mencken and Sara to come to his summer house. But Sara preferred to decline most such invitations and travel directly to Quebec.

They stopped in Montreal long enough for Mencken to jot a note to Phil Goodman—"This is a swell town. Having a swell time. Everyone treating us swell."—and then pushed on to Quebec City. There they checked into the Château Frontenac and were entertained by a friend of Mencken's. But they also found the city crowded with Labor Day vacationers, and the weather, Mencken wrote a friend, "as hot as Arkansas." They decided to move on to Halifax, Nova Scotia, where the weather was much cooler and the streets less crowded. After a few days at the Lord Nelson Hotel and another comfortable stay in St. John's, New Brunswick, they were ready to come home. "I begin to feel like an old married man already," Mencken wrote a friend, and Sara's evaluation of the honeymoon was even more to the point. "I have the one perfect husband," she wrote a friend at Goucher.

After brief stops in Vermont to see Sinclair Lewis and Dorothy Thompson and in Boston and New York, Mencken and Sara arrived back in Baltimore. They came home to the elegant, spacious Cathedral Street apartment Sara had worked on most of the summer. She had given free rein to her tastes, bringing in Victorian mirrors, hangings, and furniture, and Mencken had contributed his piano, his small-scale brewery, a spittoon, a portrait of Kaiser Wilhelm, his picture of the Pabst brewery, and little else. Five years earlier he had written that he could "scarcely imagine living" in any house other than 1524 Hollins Street, but now he found he rather liked his first new residence in forty-seven years. Located some three or four miles northeast of Hollins Street, the apartment looked down on beautiful Mount Vernon Place. Mencken also noted that it was located between the Christian Science reading room and the Knights of Columbus building.

He and Sara plunged into a social life far busier than either had undertaken before. In Baltimore they dined with Hamilton and Olga Owens, with Sara's close friend Anne Duffy and her husband, Edmund, a Sunpapers cartoonist, and with Mencken's old friends Max Brödel, Willie Woollcott, and Theodor Hemberger and their wives. From out of town came the Hergesheimers and the Knopfs, as well as Clarence Darrow, Edgar Lee Masters, and their wives. On several occasions in the following year Mencken took Sara with him to West Chester to visit the Hergesheimers, to North Carolina to see his good friends Fred and Betty Hanes and their family, and to New York, where they frequently saw the Knopfs, Lily and Phil Goodman, and numerous other literary friends.

Less frequently in New York they saw, among other literary acquaintances, Ernest and Madeleine Boyd, George Nathan and Lillian Gish, Carl Van Vechten, and—at the Knopfs'—Willa Cather, Dashiell Hammett, Fannie Hurst, and Stephen Crane's biographer Thomas Beer. On another occasion they had dinner with Marion Bloom's sister Estelle, whom Sara found she liked a great deal. But Sara raised "frightful objections" to their going to Hoboken and Union Hill, as Mencken customarily had gone with both men and women. She preferred staying in Manhattan. In particular, she liked

Moneta's, an Italian restaurant that was also to become one of his favorites.

For periods in 1931 the Menckens had to curtail their social activities because of Sara's health. After a relatively sound 1930, in late January she came down with influenza, with her temperature running as high as 104 degrees, and the influenza resulted in pleurisy. In mid-February Mencken took her to Union Memorial Hospital. Later that month, when she seemed little better, he was clearly upset. In mid-March she came home after more than a month in the hospital, but her recovery continued to be slow. By mid-April, however, she felt strong enough to attend a dinner party at the home of her doctor, Louis Hamburger, and by May Mencken was planning to attend the Bach Festival at Bethlehem, Pennsylvania, while she traveled to Atlantic City for a "week's rest and sea air." By late May Mencken was able to pronounce in a letter to Dorothy Hergesheimer that "Sara seems to be completely recovered." But Sara knew better. She still went to the hospital for treatment, and she had a nurse in three times a week. "I don't expect to be rid of my miseries in my lifetime," she wrote Sara Mayfield in Alabama.

In the summer of 1931 she and Mencken managed a trip to Vermont with Phil and Lily Goodman to see Sinclair Lewis and Dorothy Thompson. Because of Lewis's bizarre behavior all that preceding spring, Mencken should have known better. Three months before, the novelist had shown up one night at Cathedral Street—Mencken wrote Phil Goodman—"with a bunged nose and blood all over his overcoat"; he had insisted on seeing Sara, who, because of her illness, had gone to bed early. Although Lewis said he had tripped and fallen in Washington, Mencken suspected he had been in a fight. A few days earlier, he admitted to Mencken, he had had a fight with Dreiser. After drinking too much, he had accused Dreiser of plagiarizing Dorothy Thompson's book on the Soviet Union, had called him a son of a bitch, and Dreiser had hit him. It had been only one of Lewis's drunken outbursts in the first half of 1931.

So Mencken should have suspected what he was letting both Sara and himself in for, but he accepted Lewis's invitation anyway and planned at first to stay nearly a week. The calamities began shortly after they arrived. First, as Lewis and Thompson drove their guests to a maple sugar camp up the mountain, they came so near to turning over and sliding down the slope that the Menckens and Goodmans refused to ride down. Two days later, after Lewis had started drinking heavily and Goodman had sprained an ankle, Mencken suggested they cut their visit short by a couple of days. Lewis objected vigorously, then, at 4:00 the following morning, clad in his dressing gown and "palpably drunk," he barged into the guesthouse where Mencken and Sara were sleeping, awakened them, and begged them not to go. When they did leave the following morning, with Lewis still drunk, Thompson had a wreck on the way to the train station, and they had to abandon her car.

The remainder of 1931 was less eventful, although both Mencken and Sara suffered from a series of physical maladies and Knopf for one was concerned about their health. By December they were planning to take an eighteen-day West Indian cruise, and in early January 1932 they set out on the steamship *Columbus* for Puerto Rico, Venezuela, Panama, Jamaica, Cuba, and Nassau. The cruise proved salubrious. "What between the sun and the Pilsner we are both cured," Mencken wrote Hamilton Owens after a week at sea. "I have been burned as red as an archbishop on Judgment Day. . . . The infections are gone." The highlight of the trip was a journey across the mountains of Jamaica, a journey Mencken had first made thirty-one years before, when he had also come to the Caribbean in search of good health.

Although Sara returned to a series of medical treatments in Baltimore, she was now in "good shape," Mencken wrote Goodman, and hard at work on several short stories. Again she felt well enough to accompany him to New York, where he combined his new, more refined nightlife with his old routine of drinking on the town. "Let us victual Sara," he wrote Goodman on one occasion, "and then park her somewhere and settle down for the evening." In the summer both he and Sara went on diets and he lost weight rapidly, down from the 192 pounds of the spring. (That much weight, he insisted to Dorothy Hergesheimer, "is surely too much for an aesthete.") Although Sara was in the hospital for ten days in September, he was quick to assure their friends that she was not truly ill this time but just suffering from heat exhaustion.

That September marked both Mencken's fifty-second birthday and his second wedding anniversary, and he had rarely been in better spirits. Not only did Sara surprise him on his birthday with twenty-seven separate gifts, ranging from a necktie to toothpicks, but his hay fever and its debilitating effects—we learn from his carefully detailed illness diary—was better than it had been in years. Most important, he had grown somewhat hopeful about Sara's health. He began to plan for the two of them, along with Phil and Lily Goodman, to "put in a couple of months wandering around Germany" the following summer. He was determined to show Sara "the only civilized country left in the world," as well as "the jails where so many Menckenii suffered in the past."

In short, Mencken was absolutely delighted with his marriage, and he had been from the beginning. After five months, he had written Dorothy Hergesheimer from New York, "I am lonely here without the Wife . . . I have come to this," and on his first anniversary he had reflected in a letter to Goodman: "I can scarcely remember the day when I was young and innocent. . . . Frankly, I expected to make rather heavy weather of the first year. I feared I'd be homesick for Hollins street. . . . Nothing of the sort ensued. I am far more comfortable than I was in Hollins street."

He frequently bought Sara presents—often, odd pieces of glass which he found in antique shops—and he wrote her loving letters when he was away, assuring her that he missed her "dreadfully," "too much to be endured." He even softened his long-held antipathy toward Christmas: they decorated the apartment and celebrated the holiday to the hilt. Such behavior would have shocked the millions who saw Mencken as the thoroughgoing rationalist and cynic, incapable of tender feelings—or those friends who believed he had married Sara primarily because he felt sorry for her. As Alfred Knopf wrote him just after he had visited Mencken and Sara in Baltimore, "In all the years I have known you I have never known you looking so thoroughly and completely happy and at home."

His marriage was working because, to an even greater extent than they had earlier realized, he and Sara were altogether suited for each other. They shared the same prejudices, the same essentially Victorian values, the same fascination with illness and disease (Mencken because he chose to, Sara because she was forced to), the same skeptical temper. "I have never known," Mencken wrote, "a more rational woman." Neither of them placed sexual passion at the center of married love. "I protest that frigging is much less important in marriage than you seem to make it out," he once wrote to Sinclair Lewis. "The main thing is simply talk." Talk they did, together and with others, although Mencken later acknowledged that, in groups, he himself perhaps talked too much. The result was that "poor Sara" too often felt compelled to remain silent.

Mencken certainly knew when they married that Sara could not have children, and yet, curiously, he seems at times not to have absolutely grasped that fact. Her "bad health . . . made motherhood impossible for her," he later wrote, but he added that "if she had recovered there might have been another story to tell." The truth was that after 1929 she could not have "recovered," could not have regained a reproductive capacity, but that fact was not as melancholy as it might seem. For Mencken pronounced himself "implacably against" having children, and it was a position, to this point, that he had always held. He was "too lazy to become a father," he had once written Marion Bloom, and on another occasion, after taking care of his young niece, Virginia, for a few days, he had written: "The rearing of children makes it impossible to carry on any other human activity." We need hardly to accept the testimony of his brother August that Mencken believed, for some unstated reason, that any children he had "would all have been idiots" to see why he objected to fatherhood. In fact, he seemed to sense even more than most people the sacrifices and burdens of being a parent. Although Sara indeed had a desire to have a child, for his temperamental reasons as much as her medical ones it was out of the question from the beginning.

In any case, Mencken seemed to feel that he and Sara were sufficient for each other, and she appeared to be of the same opinion. He believed their marriage gave to her "a kind of security" she had not known since her benefactress grandmother had died while she was a student at Goucher. With marriage she had no financial cares: an old-fashioned husband, Mencken preferred that she not hold a job, and thus she was free to write. Once married, she was hardly possessive. She trusted Mencken absolutely—a trust he now fully merited—and they agreed from the beginning that occasional separations would be good for them. Mencken held to the counsel he gave Phil Goodman's daughter: "Marriage is largely a matter of give and take. Each must respect the individuality of the other." And he held as well to the ideal of marriage he had described to an interviewer in the 1920s: that each party always act with dignity and do honor to the other, that each be worthy of trust, and that neither ever humiliate the other. Mencken abided by all these principles and more. If with Marion Bloom he had sometimes appeared to be at his worst, with Sara he was nearly always at his best.

At times it must not have been easy, for numerous friends and contemporaries suggest that, for all her grace and charm, Sara Haardt was not always pleasant to live with, and that the Menckens' marriage, although indeed happy, was not altogether as ideal as Mencken later depicted. According to acquaintances, Sara could be prickly and duplicitous, could "give a fierce face," and could be extraordinarily demanding of her husband. Although no one doubted her love for Mencken and her loyalty to him, it was clear— Phil Goodman's daughter later remarked—that "beneath her soft manner there lay some malice, much intelligence and a certain ferocity."

Sara's relationship with Mencken's family was also more complicated than it had appeared at first. August remained her devoted friend and supporter, no small accomplishment since Mencken's brother was already known as something of a misogynist. He appreciated Sara's intelligence and sense of humor ("good . . . for a woman" he later said), liked to come to Cathedral Street for dinner, and delighted in accompanying her on her rounds of antique shops. Her relations with Gertrude, though, were never as friendly as Gertrude's warm letter of April 1930 had suggested they might be. Mencken's sister considered Sara a bit spoiled and self-indulgent, as well as foolish in her judgments of her physicians and remedies for her ills. "That silly wife of his," she once called Sara in a letter to August, and on another occasion she insisted that Sara had come to fashion herself after Elizabeth Barrett Browning, rather willingly taking to her bed.

For the most part, however, Sara was most understanding of Mencken's continuing commitment to his family. At the same time as she was recuperating from her hospital stay in the spring of 1931, Gertrude underwent serious abdominal surgery to remove a benign tumor, and Mencken was greatly concerned about his sister's condition. He continued to look after the medical needs of Charlie's family as well, and Sara helped care for Mary Mencken—and in one instance Virginia—when they came to Baltimore for treatment. When Mencken sent Virginia to Sweet Briar College in Virginia, steering her to the socially correct southern women's college and then paying her tuition, he and Sara welcomed her to Baltimore for occasional weekend visits. He ordered books for Virginia, bought her a typewriter and other supplies, and took care of many other of her financial needs as well.

He and Sara also came to pay a great deal of attention to Mencken's younger first cousin, William C. Abhau, to whom Sara took a particular liking. When Abhau, in 1931, had a chance to go to West Point but wanted to attend the Naval Academy, Mencken advised him to hold out for an appointment to Annapolis—and then wrote to Maryland Senator Millard Tydings on his behalf. When Abhau received the appointment to Annapolis, he brought friends home on holidays and took them over to meet Mencken and Sara. Fully as much as Mencken (who sometimes, in correspondence, referred to Abhau as his "nephew"), Sara took a great interest in him, he later said, and helped him through an awkward age.

While Mencken lived in the Cathedral Street apartment, he always kept one eye on a Hollins Street that was growing shabbier by the year. He fell into the habit of going over once a week, usually Sunday mornings, and Sara sometimes went along for dinner. He was dismayed in 1931 when Gertrude proposed that she and August give up the house and take an apartment in the suburbs. His inclination was "to take over the house, lock it up, and keep it substantially as it is. I couldn't bear to think of strangers living in it." He was spared that necessity when Gertrude and August decided not to move after all.

If he had trouble relinquishing his old house, he absolutely refused to give up his old Baltimore friends. Most of his New York acquaintances, as well as well-heeled friends such as the Hergesheimers and the Haneses, Sara embraced, but certain of his older hometown companions—unliterary, in some cases unsophisticated, and sometimes, she felt, uncouth—she merely tolerated. Individually or in twos or threes, she could enjoy their company on occasion, but as a group the Saturday Night Club members—otherwise refined men who, when gathered together, were given to drink, merriment, and ribaldry—were too much for her more refined sensibilities. The club did meet at Cathedral Street on occasion, but Sara preferred that it not. Its discourse—on one occasion a discussion of the horrors of hemorrhoid surgery, on another a discussion of the optimum duration of sexual intercourse, on still another a discussion of a Japanese sex shop manual—were hardly suited to Sara's drawing room. But she did not mind Mencken's keeping his Saturday night engagement when the club met elsewhere. Nor did she mind, particularly when she was ill, if he went out after work on a weeknight for—as Mencken put it—"talk of men."

The man whose company he enjoyed most, who had long since become his closest Baltimore friend, was Raymond Pearl, a professor of biology and medical statistics at the Johns Hopkins whose tastes in food, drink, and music matched Mencken's own. Other friends he occasionally saw outside the club—Brödel, Heinrich Buchholz, Willie Woollcott, and, in a somewhat different realm, Maryland governor Albert Ritchie, who sometimes dropped by Cathedral Street for a late-night chat, greatly to Sara's displeasure. But Pearl, that rare true Yankee among Mencken's largely German Baltimore friends, was the nearest thing he had to a soul mate.

Like James Gibbons Huneker earlier and Phil Goodman in New York, Pearl had that quality of gusto that Mencken prized above all else. A large, handsome man, over six feet tall and weighing well over two hundred pounds, he exuded confidence and high spirits. He also shared with Mencken a fascination (Mencken later wrote) with "the congenital infirmities of the human race," an unswerving belief in the scientific method, and a deep religious skepticism. "A man of wider knowledge or greater intellectual daring and vigor," Mencken wrote, he had never met, but Sara preferred that he not spend as much time with Pearl as he would have liked—a preference shared by Mrs. Pearl, who considered her husband's friend not an altogether salutary influence. Although Mencken usually abided by Sara's wishes, he must have reflected on the turn his life had taken. The two worlds that he had always kept separate, moving from one to the other with ease—men and women, roughness and refinement, ribaldry and Victorian gentility—were harder to separate now.

---

Whether it was because he had recently married, because he had just turned fifty—or because he sensed the end of one era and the beginning of another for America and for himself—for whatever reason or reasons, in the fall of 1930 Mencken had begun to keep a diary, a record he was to maintain for the remainder of his active life. He had kept journals and records before for short periods and on specific occasions, such as his German trip in 1917, but never had he committed himself so completely to a record of activities and observations for a sustained period of time. Into his diary he did not pour hopes and fears and personal philosophy, as other men of mind from St. Augustine to Henry Adams had done in autobiographical writing before him. He rarely reflected on personal failures, doubts, or a declining reputation; he did not agonize over Sara's health. In fact, except for occasionally mentioning their activities and her periods of hospitalization, he rarely mentioned Sara at all. Rather, Mencken reported largely on his own activities, his writings, people he encountered. But in his largely straightforward reporting he revealed a great deal more of himself than he intended.

It is difficult to see how Mencken had the time to keep a diary, particularly one in which, as time went on, he often included rather lengthy entries. Professionally, in the early 1930s he was as busy as ever. Indeed, for all their comings and goings, their entertaining visitors "in clumps" ("some welcome and others merely welcomed," Mencken wrote Phil Goodman), for all their physical maladies and all their talk, the life that he and Sara Haardt shared was more than anything else a life devoted to work. Except for those periods when Mencken was in New York alone—or when he put in an appearance at the Sunpapers, for which he still wrote his Monday column—he and Sara usually stayed at home, working for three or four hours in the morning, stopping for lunch and a nap, then returning to work until late afternoon. After dinner they usually resumed their labors until 10:00 P.M. or so, when they would retire to the drawing room for a drink and conversation.

Sara, whose novel *The Making of a Lady* had appeared in 1931 to polite but generally unenthusiastic reviews, devoted herself to short stories and sketches, most of which, like her only novel, dealt with the South. Mencken held to the schedule he had earlier set for himself, but he now had the assistance of a secretary, Rosalind Lohrfinck, who was to become so important in his life that he could hardly envision work without her. In the morning he would read his mail and, with Lohrfinck's help, would answer it. In the afternoon he would take care of *American Mercury* business and perhaps do a little writing, but he still saved most of his writing for night. In spare moments he would write in his diary, a task he did not see as burdensome at all. For him such writing was nearly as natural as thinking; indeed, to think something was to write it down, to record it. As a result, virtually nothing was lost, nothing wasted or overlooked.

He had a number of longer projects under way or contemplated in 1931 and 1932, some new, some resuscitated from the 1920s. He was again considering a "psychological history of the American share in the World War," was thinking about a translation of Johann Burkhard Mencke's *De Charlataneria Eruditorum* as well as a final edition of *The American Language*. He was also tempted to return to "Homo Sapiens," the study he had put aside in the late twenties but for which he still had particularly high expectations. It would deal, he now decided, with the human race as scientists had recently "dealt with the ants." "My hope," he had written in 1930, "is to put all that I have to say about the human race in 'Homo Sapiens.' "

All these projects he pondered in the early 1930s, but the one on which he actually labored was a discussion of what he had come to call "realistic ethics," a book that in certain respects would serve as a sequel to *Treatise on the Gods*. The matter of "right and wrong" was a subject in which he had long been interested. Indeed, it had been a deeply personal concern ever since, early in his career, he had detected a great distinction between morality and honor. "I have never met a thoroughly moral man who was honorable," he had written in *Prejudices*, by which he had meant that fervently moral men would employ any means, including dishonorable ones, to achieve their ends. An honorable man he considered himself to be, but not a moral one, and an academic friend agreed that "the cardinal principle in the Mencken canon was a sense of honor." Such a principle, Mencken believed, led to his own position on any number of matters, including, he liked to think, his opposition to American conduct in World War I. The treatment of German Americans in particular had been "dishonourable," he maintained—and all the more despicable to him because it had been directed by that most "moral" of men, Woodrow Wilson.

*Treatise on Right and Wrong* would be a long time in the writing: Mencken found it as difficult to complete as any other book he ever undertook. But he had more immediate professional concerns in 1931 and 1932, primarily his difficulties with Alfred Knopf and *The American Mercury*. In 1931 he had notified Knopf that he had tired of the editorship and wanted to resign. When Knopf pleaded with him to stay, he reconsidered, but the following year he again tried to leave. This time the death of Knopf's father, the *Mercury* business manager, had left affairs in a confused state and made Mencken's departure impossible. But Mencken knew his leaving was only a matter of time.

Meanwhile, he was hardly restrained from speaking his mind about the *Mercury*. He found he disagreed with Knopf on a number of matters, and in late 1931 and 1932 he wrote his friend and publisher three lengthy and detailed letters setting forth his complaints. He felt the magazine's business and advertising departments were poorly managed and believed the advertising appealed to the wrong clientele. He felt, further, that the magazine needed more capital to operate; he suggested that Knopf bring in a well-heeled associate. But most of all, he was concerned that he and Knopf no longer wanted the same kind of magazine. He did not want—and he felt the *Mercury*'s readers did not want—"an imitation Atlantic or Harper's." He strongly believed the *Mercury* should remain "the voice of that eager and unconventional minority." If Knopf did not want that kind of magazine—or if the magazine "as you have told me half a dozen times . . . has become dull and largely unreadable," then "it plainly needs a new editor" or "a publisher who is in sympathy with it."

Knopf rejected Mencken's criticism outright. He rejected as well the suggestion that he and Mencken "spread the idea that we are rich." "Who would be fooled," Knopf responded, "except a lot of boobs who mean nothing to us anyway . . . ?" In fact, the *Mercury* was not financially as badly off as most other American magazines in 1932; because of its advertising proceeds it even continued to show a small profit. But Mencken and Knopf continued to argue in 1932 and 1933, although probably not so vigorously as Mencken's managing editor, Charles Angoff, later reported. Neither was Mencken's mood in these late years as *Mercury* editor quite so somber as Angoff later claimed. Lawrence Spivak, who had taken over as business manager and who joined Mencken in frequent forays to Lüchow's, was amazed to find him still so buoyant a man, full of enthusiasm and even a kind of childish humor.

By early 1933, however, it was not a question of whether Mencken would leave but when. In late January, while Knopf was visiting in Baltimore, Mencken said he could wait no longer, and he suggested Henry Hazlitt, then with *The Nation*, as his successor. He told Knopf he would be willing to continue contributing to the magazine. He also expressed his belief that the *Mercury* "should be far more literary than it has been, and far less political." It was precisely the reverse of the direction he had felt, ten years earlier, the magazine should take. But politics for Mencken, as we shall see, was less enjoyable now.

In late February he met with Hazlitt in New York and proposed the *Mercury* editorship to him. Later in the year, after negotiations with Knopf, Hazlitt accepted. By October 6 the New York press had learned of Mencken's resignation, and by mid-October he had traveled to New York to help Hazlitt with the transition. He was as generous as any departing editor could be, even going to the point of suggesting that Knopf and Hazlitt should not be reluctant "to say anything . . . which may seem to be a repudiation of the scheme followed [by the *Mercury*] in my time, or a criticism of me personally. . . . It is my firm belief that the magazine ought to take a new line."

Mencken's own final issue would be in December, and he was to bow out as controversially as he had entered. For once, however, he did not intend or anticipate the controversy. In the "Library" section he reviewed, among other books, Adolf Hitler's *Mein Kampf*, and although he labeled Hitler a "mob orator" of the William Jennings Bryan stripe, remarked on the absurdity of many of his ideas, and pointed to his anti-Semitism, he also made the mistake of contending that some of what Hitler had written about German expansionism was "sensible enough" and remarked that the presence of Jews in the German Communist party made his anti-Semitism appealing to many loyal Germans. In no way did he defend Hitler. But neither did he demonstrate the requisite alarm.

Knopf came across the essay review in October while looking over proof for the December number, and he immediately wrote Mencken about his concerns. Assuring him that his "personal feelings" were "not at stake," he went on to say that Mencken underestimated "the really terrific concern that many of our supporters have about Hitler." He feared the piece would leave in many minds "the idea that you are, yourself, at least lukewarm in your feelings about der schoene Adolph [sic]." Knopf objected in particular to the final paragraph in which Mencken suggested that Hitler had abandoned many of his "worst . . . notions" since writing *Mein Kampf*. In response, Mencken insisted that Knopf overestimated "the extent to which our customers are heated up over the Hitler business." But he would not object at all if Knopf eliminated the final paragraph.

When Knopf indeed excised the offending section, explaining "we can't see eye to eye on everything," Mencken did not seem particularly disturbed. His friendship with Knopf was more resilient than that with anyone else; it could absorb disagreements that his friendships with Dreiser and Nathan and others never could. As will become evident, Mencken's problems with Hitler—his intense dislike of Germany's new ruler but his disinclination to take him seriously—had just begun. For now, exactly ten years after he had begun the *Mercury*, he was very happy to be leaving it. For two decades, one each for the *Mercury* and *The Smart Set*, he had been tied down by monthly editorial duties, and now he longed to devote full time to his own writing and to Sara. "For the first time in twenty years," he wrote a friend, "I feel free."

The *Mercury* editor's departure was accompanied by numerous editorials, more than one of which was entitled "The Passing of Mencken." Literally hundreds of newspapers ran stories about the resignation: nearly all saw it as a great cultural watershed, the end of an era. In fact, the resignation was not so much the end of that era—the waning of Mencken's great influence—as the certification of a process that had begun in earnest three or four years earlier. Since 1930 editorialists and headline writers had been proclaiming "H. L. Mencken Is Dead" and "Mencken Is Passé." Their remarks now seemed to ring truer than such pronouncements had in the late 1920s.

Mencken found himself with no shortage of opportunities upon leaving the *Mercury*. He continued to write for the Sunpapers, although he declined Patterson's offer to "join the general staff in some responsible capacity—say as vice president in charge of all editorial matters, or as chief editor." He did consent to sit on the board of directors of the A. S. Abell Co., a post to which he was elected shortly after leaving the *Mercury* and one he would take seriously indeed. He took equally seriously his duties as board member of Alfred A. Knopf, Inc., a position to which he had been elected in 1932. Despite his resignation as editor, Mencken frequently consulted with Knopf about the *Mercury* as well. He observed with alarm both the rapid decline of Hazlitt, who lasted only four months as editor, and the brief editorship of Angoff, who took the magazine to the political left. He approved of its sale in 1934 to Lawrence Spivak, for whom he had a high regard.

Mencken also had offers in 1933 from several leading newspaper syndicates; he accepted only the New York *American*'s proposal to write a series on the American language and other subjects. He kept busy as well with magazine pieces not only for the *Mercury* but also for *The New Yorker, The Nation, Saturday Review, Vanity Fair, Harper's,* a number of literary quarterlies, and the NAACP journal, *The Crisis.* In 1933 he agreed to do a series of broadcasts for NBC— the first, in October 1933, on beer.

It was not that he was in dire need of money. Although his royalties had declined greatly in 1931 and 1932—"less than 10% of . . . two years ago," he wrote Goodman—his *Sun* salary and dividends were still between $7,000 and $8,000, his total earnings exceeded $15,000 annually, and his Baltimore bank seemed to be solvent. Besides, Sara was contributing a small amount to their income by selling stories. If "for the first time in [his] life," he began to "give serious thought to money," as he wrote Goodman, he certainly did not dwell on the subject. As always, there were certain things he would not do for money. He would, and did, write for the *Junior League Magazine* and even *The Rotarian,* but somewhat earlier he had drawn a line at a suggestion by Upton Sinclair that he write for and participate in a filmed debate on Prohibition that would have paid him $2,500 in addition to a share of profits from the film.

Primarily Mencken wanted to return to writing books. In 1932 he had put together *Making a President,* a potboiler consisting largely of his dispatches to the *Evening Sun* on the 1932 Democratic and Republican conventions. He had not wanted to undertake the book, but Knopf had urged him. The result, he felt, was a "dismal failure— in fact, the worst I have ever had." He had had no great interest in the election and had not followed the candidates as closely as he had in 1928. The Republican convention, filled with "country postmasters, Federal marshals and receivers in bankruptcy masquerading as the heirs of Lincoln," was "the stupidest and most boresome ever heard of," and Hoover, he wrote Ezra Pound, had been "unbearably offensive": "I hate to look at him or even think of him." Franklin Roosevelt had seemed a "weak sister" to him, but Mencken had no particular animosity against FDR—yet. Thus he had voted for Roosevelt. Hoover's defeat, he wrote a cousin, "gave me a great thrill."

In articles announcing Mencken's retirement from the *Mercury*, he had been quoted as saying that he wanted to work on his book "Advice to Young Men," but in fact the book he wanted to return to was his treatise on morals. He had at first hoped to have the book ready for Knopf by the end of 1931, but a larger amount of research and rewriting than he had expected, in addition to Sara's poor health and the troubles of *The American Mercury*, had delayed him. In 1932 and 1933 he ran into other problems. When his doctors ordered him to stop using tobacco, he found he was reduced for a time to "complete mental impotence." More important, he had come to suspect that there existed in him "a deep-lying conviction that ethics is a delusion . . . scarcely worth writing about." "Something within" him had worked against the book, he wrote Fielding Garrison, and in the summer of 1932 he had come as close to experiencing a writing block as he ever came. He felt "tremendously out of sorts and almost unable to work," although he knew the difficulty would pass. It was the kind of "crisis," he wrote Garrison, that he went through every seven years. "After a while the storm passes and I am back on an even keel."

After another year and a half of fits and starts, Mencken completed his *Treatise on Right and Wrong*. At last he felt good about it, and when Knopf saw the manuscript he called it "quite the best of your books." It was hardly that. A sound, nearly scholarly inquiry, lacking much of the old flair, it followed basically the pattern of *Treatise on the Gods*. Mencken explored first the nature and origins of morality, then its evolution and its contemporary manifestations. Aristotle and the Greeks, Marcus Aurelius and the Romans fared better than St. Paul and Christian law. Catholics fared better than Protestants and Jews better than either. But it was clear that the author preferred a code of ethics dissociated from a religious creed of any sort.

The reception given *Treatise on Right and Wrong* showed just how much the popular view of Mencken had altered since the 1920s, or even since 1930, when *Treatise on the Gods* had appeared. The reviews of the earlier book had been largely favorable (even if few reviewers shared Mencken's own view that it was his finest work), sales had been so good that he found himself in an unaccustomed position on the best-seller list, and the work had generated no small amount of controversy. Such was hardly the case with *Treatise on Right and Wrong*. Whether favorable or not—and the American reviews were generally favorable—reviewers remarked on how sober and restrained the book was. "Interesting but mild" was *The New Yorker*'s assessment, and reviews in *The New York Times, The Herald Tribune, The Washington Post,* and *The Nation* did not depart radically from that conclusion. The English reviews were almost unanimously unfavorable: the land that had played a great part in the rise of Mencken's reputation now seemed determined to play a great role in its decline. On neither side of the Atlantic, in fact, did his work now inspire great praise, outrage, or anything else. At the time, the early 1930s, of his greatest personal happiness, his reputation as writer and cultural force had fallen as low as it was ever to fall.

How long even that personal happiness would last seemed to depend largely on Sara's health. She had already lived beyond the three years her doctors had predicted for her in 1929, and Mencken was determined that they both would live as fully as possible while her health still allowed it. They continued to entertain out-of-town guests ranging from the Knopfs and Hergesheimers to the Virginia novelist Ellen Glasgow and the Prohibitionist Methodist Bishop James Cannon, with whom Mencken had struck up an unlikely friendship. In letters to friends Mencken spoke of taking Sara to Germany. He also spoke of looking for land in rural Howard County, of planning to take Sara to an Orioles baseball game, and other activities for which he earlier had had no time. He continued to get together with his Saturday Night Club friends—and in early April 1933 he celebrated the official end of Prohibition by drinking the first glass of legal beer to come over the bar at the Rennert Hotel. ("I am having two new esophagi drilled beside my old one," he wrote an old friend.) But most of all, he spent his time with Sara. After she accompanied him to New York in September 1933 to celebrate their anniversary, Mencken wrote their good friend Betty Hanes, "After three years of marriage I find myself completely contented. Sara is perfect, and I begin to believe that I have improved a bit myself."

The trips Mencken and Sara now made were often southward, for reasons of health as well as family and friends. After influenza floored them both in February 1933, they left for Sea Island, Georgia. "Sara and I are burned red, and feel much better," Mencken reported to Paul Patterson a week later. But Sea Island was "full of very old people at this season, and it scares me to see them wobbling about."

From Sea Island they traveled to Florida and then to Montgomery to visit Sara's family. On the way across south Georgia—country he had not seen since 1901, when he had gone south to report on the destruction of the great Jacksonville fire—he satisfied himself that all his earlier impressions of the backcountry South had indeed been on target. He still found an "almost incredibly dismal place, full of hideous Methodist and Baptist churches, but showing no sign whatsoever of civilization . . . the most desolate landscape I have ever seen—all gaunt pine woods . . . and the yokels looked like savages." It was a relief to reach Montgomery. Mencken liked Sara's family, and they seemed to like him. He was on his best behavior, *The Birmingham News* reported, at a Sunday afternoon tea given for the visiting celebrities.

The Menckens also traveled on occasion to the North Carolina mountains, particularly in hot weather, to visit their friends the Haneses. There, away from newspaper responsibilities in Baltimore and literary friends in New York, they were able to relax as they could in few other places. Moreover, Mencken approved of the Haneses altogether. Like many of his Baltimore friends, Fred Hanes was a medical man, educated at the Johns Hopkins. Like his Richmond friends, though somewhat less steeped in tradition, he and his wife were southerners of high birth and broad interests, that variety of ex-Confederate that always appealed to Mencken. They were exceedingly fond of Sara. And they had the wealth to support a graceful and charming way of life, a family fortune built largely on Winston-Salem textile interests. At Roaring Gap in the high Blue Ridge, he and Sara saw not only Fred and Betty Hanes but numerous other members of the genial Hanes clan as well as various other southern plutocrats, such as tobacco heir R. J. Reynolds, Jr., who came by for visits.

It appears, in fact, that Mencken was coming to prefer Roaring

Gap to West Chester—the Haneses to the Hergesheimers—for escape and relaxation. Despite his friendship with Hergesheimer, he had always found the novelist exceedingly vain and, on occasion, foolish. He still resented to some extent an incident in the late twenties when Hergesheimer had been tardy in paying Sara for historical research she had undertaken for his book *Swords and Roses*. He remembered, even further back, Hergesheimer's objections to Knopf's naming him, along with Nathan, to the *Mercury* editorship. He usually overlooked such offenses because both he and Sara genuinely enjoyed Hergesheimer's company and regarded Dorothy Hergesheimer, as he once wrote her, "the queen of all hostesses, American or European." But by 1933, after a visit to Dower House, he concluded that Hergesheimer's friends and visitors were not sufficiently stimulating: "Looking back over 15 years I can't recall ever meeting anyone of solid distinction under his roof."

Back in Baltimore, Scott and Zelda Fitzgerald—who had moved to Maryland in 1932 and were occasional guests of the Menckens—were, if anything, so stimulating that after a time both Mencken and Sara discouraged their friendship. At first, motivated partly by Sara and Zelda's shared Montgomery background, he and Sara had been hospitable. They felt, as well, a deep sympathy for Zelda, who was battling mental illness. Even before they had come to Baltimore, Fitzgerald had wired Mencken asking for "the name of the biggest psychiatrist at Johns Hopkins for nonorganic nervous troubles." Now in Baltimore and a patient at the Phipps Clinic, Zelda was still, Mencken believed, "plainly more or less off her base," with "a wild look in her eye."

He recorded in his diary the events of an evening in March 1933 when he and Sara accepted an invitation for dinner at the Fitzgeralds' rented home outside the city. "It was a somewhat weird evening," he noted, the "spookiness" of the setting in the woods being reinforced by "the fact that Zelda is palpably only half sane." The other dinner guests, aside from their twelve-year-old daughter, Scottie, were three of Zelda's doctors, but they were of little interest to Mencken. Rather, he closely observed Zelda, the way she constantly gritted her teeth as she talked to Sara of Montgomery days. Even her paintings on the wall were "full of grotesque exaggerations and fantastic ideas." According to August Mencken, Sara was so frightened by the evening that she resolved never to return. But they probably did get together with both Fitzgeralds on at least one other occasion, on which they found Scott drunk and Zelda as irrational as before, and they continued to see Scott, alone, more frequently than they wanted.

They saw him largely because he often dropped by Cathedral Street, occasionally as a lunch guest but more often uninvited, sometimes late at night, hoping to speak with Mencken. Fitzgerald remained somewhat in awe of the man whom he had seen as a virtual literary god when he himself had first begun to publish fiction in 1919. In certain respects he felt a curious bond with Mencken (a bond Mencken did not encourage) as a fellow refugee from the good times of the 1920s whose reputation had not survived the crash.

For all his poor judgment in many matters, Fitzgerald had always been a keen analyst of Mencken. As early as 1920, even before the *Smart Set* editor approached the height of his success, Fitzgerald had reflected on what might eventually come: "Will he find new gods to dethrone . . . Or will he strut among the ruins, a man beaten by his own success, as futile, in the end, as one of those Conrad characters that so tremendously enthrall him?" Now in the mid-thirties, with a chance to see Mencken at closer hand, the novelist found that same curious "aloneness" Mencken had earlier identified in himself, a "state of isolation neither sought for nor avoided." "I suppose if one creates a world so willfully, effectually and completely as you have," Fitzgerald wrote him, "there is nothing much to do except to live in it."

For his part, Mencken was still fascinated with Fitzgerald as another one of those many artists of his acquaintance who had been ruined by disorderly living, and several times in his diary he remarked on behavior he found every bit as bizarre as Zelda's. "A charming fellow . . . when sober . . . an excellent companion," he noted on one occasion after Fitzgerald had come for lunch, but "liquor sets him wild and he is apt, when drunk, to knock over a dinner table, or run his automobile into a bank building." On another occasion he noted that Fitzgerald was "boozing in a wild manner" and had "become a nuisance." He reported that Scott had shocked Sara's friend Anne Duffy "by his performance" when he appeared at her apartment one day, and then went on to relate an earlier occasion when, visiting Hergesheimer in West Chester, Fitzgerald had "caused a town sensation by arising at the dinner table and taking down his pantaloons, exposing his gospel-pipe." Hergesheimer had "refused to have anything to do with him since," and so—at least they decided at this point—would Mencken and especially Sara. When Fitzgerald called, "always plainly tight" and "usually proposing that Sara and I go automobiling with him," they declined. Although he and Sara were fond of him, they finally decided that he "had better be barred from the house thereafter."

Mencken and Sara did not make the long-anticipated trip to Germany in 1934, but the Mediterranean cruise they took instead ended up being even more taxing than Germany would have been. Mencken had intended the cruise, in February and March, to be another escape from Baltimore's winter, and when they sailed on the *Columbus* on February 10 it was "in the midst of the coldest weather for years." They were, in part, retracing the travels described by Mark Twain in *Innocents Abroad*, visiting Italy, North Africa, Palestine, Turkey, and Greece. Indeed, Mencken set out with Mark Twain's book in hand, planning to use it as a guide.

He was amazed at what he found when they landed in Naples, that city which, when he last encountered it in 1914, had been "a human swamp," "the dirtiest, smelliest, most disorderly town ever seen on earth." Now, under Mussolini's efficient hand, all was "orderly, precise, soldierly. No beggars. No streetwalkers. No pick pockets." Mencken was less impressed with Algeria, Morocco, and Egypt, although he did gaze with wonder upon the ruins of Carthage, astounded that a city once so substantial could so completely vanish from the earth.

Palestine, in particular, worked its charms upon him, as he noted in two pieces sent back to the *Evening Sun*. He had approached the Holy Land with modest expectations and a great deal of irreverence. "Jerusalem!—and then Gomorrah!" he wrote Henry Hyde, "I tremble with anticipation." But what he found overwhelmed him. Palestine was "indeed gaudy," he wrote Knopf. "I have never seen such scenery, not even in Switzerland."

It was not Jerusalem and Bethlehem that impressed him so: like Mark Twain before him, he believed the Church of the Holy Sepulchre and the Church of the Nativity were fakes. But the back reaches of northern Palestine had another effect altogether; he marveled not only at the beauty of the countryside but also at the energy and prosperity of the farmers. The Jews who had settled there after World War I had made the desert bloom, and Mencken made it clear that he greatly preferred them to the Arabs, whom he termed among the "dirtiest, orneriest and most shiftless people" anywhere. But what struck him "most forcibly" about northern Palestine, he wrote a friend, was the absence of any sign of orthodox Judaism in the colonies. All of the farmers were "skeptics of a somewhat extreme wing."

Mencken did not often mention Sara in his letters home, and for a reason. The trip was too strenuous for her, and during most of his overland expeditions, including the one into northern Palestine, she remained aboard ship or in their hotel. In his diary he referred to the trip as "perhaps our happiest time together," but he also became greatly concerned about her health. After four or five days in Cairo, during which she did not feel well enough to accompany him on a journey up the Nile, she developed a fever and was confined to bed by the ship's doctor. She returned to Baltimore having lost ten or fifteen pounds.

Sara continued to run a fever throughout the early spring, and in mid-May Mencken took her to Union Memorial Hospital. Doctors disagreed over precisely what was wrong: one believed she might have contracted some form of malaria in the Mediterranean, another believed—and Mencken agreed—that the tuberculosis infection was flaring up. She was not in pain, but the fever was stubborn and she remained in the hospital several weeks.

When she came home, her temperature had dropped but she still did not feel well. Part of the summer she spent at Gertrude's farm, lying in the sun daily until she developed a new pain in the area of her shoulder blades. Dr. Hamburger and Dr. Baker still disagreed on the diagnosis, and she herself accepted Baker's diagnosis of pleurisy. If Sara had come to see herself as Elizabeth Barrett, Gertrude believed that Baker was becoming her Browning, spending a great deal of time at her bedside.

Baltimore was experiencing, Mencken wrote in the *Evening Sun*, its "most hellish" summer on record, and Sara considered going north to escape the heat. Instead, in late summer she went south to Alabama to visit her mother, who was ill. Mencken remained in Baltimore, paying Gertrude a visit in the country and then returning to Cathedral Street to catch up on his writing. He was experiencing a rough summer himself, battling the heat and, for a time, the Catholic hierarchy of Baltimore. After a *Sun* foreign correspondent offended Archbishop Michael Curley by carelessly comparing Hitler to Ignatius Loyola, Curley had called for a boycott of the Sunpapers. Serving as emissary from the Sunpapers, Mencken had used his diplomatic skills, considerable when he chose to employ them, to reach a compromise with the Church.

He and Sara planned to meet in North Carolina in mid-September and travel to Roaring Gap to visit the Haneses. When she stepped off the train in Greensboro, however, he could tell at once that her condition had grown worse while she was in Alabama. She looked "pale and almost transparent," Mencken later wrote in his diary. Nevertheless, after "three terrible weeks" in Montgomery—which turned out to be Sara's final trip home—she wanted to cool off in the mountains, and she and Mencken spent nearly a week with the Haneses. While they were there, Walter Winchell, with absolutely nothing to go on, reported in his newspaper column a rumor that Sara was pregnant.

When she and Mencken returned to Baltimore in late September, Dr. Baker immediately put her into the hospital for another examination. Though her lungs were clear, he still felt she had a tubercular infection in an undetermined area. She was also "in a terrible shape . . . psychologically speaking," Mencken wrote Betty Hanes. After remaining in Union Memorial nearly a month, Sara came home in late October, but with orders to remain in bed. Mencken was hopeful at first: her fever was gone, the pleurisy had cleared up, and their primary concern was a possible relapse. She had "endured her imprisonment with great courage," Mencken wrote in his diary, and now she was able to return to work on her short stories and articles. Mencken remained in Baltimore most of the time, forgoing trips to New York and declining Knopf's invitation to take a week's auto trip through New England in October.

"If all goes well, she should emerge from the adventure in better health than she had been [*sic*] for ten years past," Mencken wrote Blanche Knopf in October. But just as Sara seemed somewhat improved, word came from Alabama that her mother had suffered one stroke, then another, which left her in "very perilous condition." In little more than a week, on December 24, Mrs. Haardt died. Since

351

Sara's health was still too precarious for her to travel, she and Mencken remained at Cathedral Street for Christmas Day. In letters to friends he reflected on the "usual gloomy Christmas": since his own mother and father had died during or near the holiday season, he wrote Knopf, he felt December was "always my unluckiest month." "May 1935 be bigger and better in every way," Knopf wrote him on New Year's Eve, and Mencken himself issued his customary New Year's greeting to friends: "Here's hoping that we are all lucky in 1935."

It was not to be, although at the beginning of the year Mencken had further hope. In January Sara was sitting up each day and writing, and in mid-February, he wrote Blanche Knopf, she was able to leave "her bed of pain." He himself was able, briefly, to return to something approaching a normal life. He got to New York in late January, had dinner with Edgar Lee Masters, and saw other friends. Back in Baltimore he and Sara had Louis Untermeyer for dinner, and on other occasions Albert Ritchie, who had just stepped down after fifteen years as governor of Maryland, and Henry W. Nice, the new governor, came by—separately—at night to talk. Despite all their troubles, Mencken still preferred his life with Sara to any other he could imagine. When his old friend Fanny Butcher remarried in February, he sent her a congratulatory note, adding "I have never regretted it a single moment."

In March Sara returned to the hospital, this time to the Johns Hopkins. What afflicted her now, at least at first, was a painful case of lumbago, which Mencken attributed to her attempt to walk after being in bed for so long. She went in principally for X rays, but her general condition baffled the doctors and she wound up staying more than a month. "The poor girl has had a horrible year," Mencken wrote Blanche Knopf. Indeed, it had been a full twelve months since Sara had returned, ill, from the Mediterranean cruise.

Mencken's illness file fairly bulges with entries for early 1935, and not all of them relate to Sara. In early April, while she was still at the Hopkins, he himself was floored for several days with bronchitis. It was the first time since his thirties that he had "been actually laid on [his] back." "I can't recall feeling worse for many years," he wrote Knopf. In other letters and notes he complained of a "violent laryngitis," a sinus infection, and an infection in the trachea. As he was suffering, Sara seemed to be recovering, and for the time being she was "in excellent spirits." In mid-April she came home from the hospital.

The doctors recommended that Sara go north for the summer, and throughout April and May Mencken made arrangements to take her to the Adirondacks. He had rented a cottage near Saranac and was planning to go up with her the first of June, then to come back through New York to see Knopf. There was no alarm in a letter of May 21 to Knopf, nor in other letters that same day to Gertrude and his cousin William Abhau. Sara had a cold, he told Gertrude, but she was lying in the sun daily and he believed that "a few months in the mountains" would "restore her completely." The "medical gents" could discover "nothing radically wrong with her." Speaking for herself, Sara was less optimistic. "I'm quite weary with my miseries," she wrote Sara Mayfield.

Two days later Mencken remarked in a letter to Knopf that Sara had come down with a "mild flu," but it did not seem to be serious. In a letter to Scott Fitzgerald that same day he mentioned the flu, but he seemed more concerned with discovering whether Fitzgerald, whom (despite his earlier resolve) he still saw on occasion, were still on the wagon: "If you ever slip off far enough to endulge [sic] yourself in a few rounds of beer, I hope you let me hear of it. I'd like very much to have a sitting."

Not until May 25, in a letter to Betty Hanes, did Mencken express any alarm. Sara had a "severe influenza" and he had taken her back to the Johns Hopkins Hospital. In a letter to Gertrude the same day, he seemed relatively unconcerned; he discussed at some length Gertrude's financial situation before adding, in the final paragraph, that he had taken Sara to the Johns Hopkins. But in a letter to Knopf, reporting a possible change in plans, he added, "I greatly fear that if [the illness] goes on much longer she'll begin to crack."

The next day, Sunday, May 26, it was clear to him that Sara was "desperately ill." The doctors suspected tubercular meningitis, and an examination of the spinal fluid confirmed that fear. With such a diagnosis, Mencken later wrote, he knew she was doomed. She suffered greatly the next two or three days, principally from a excruciating headache, and her mind became clouded, partly because of her condition, partly because of the morphine she was given. On Wednesday, May 29, Mencken saw her for the last time. For a few minutes she was both rational and cheerful, but immediately after that—he later reported in his diary—"she went downhill rapidly, and Baker advised me not to see her."

Mencken spent the next two days bracing himself for the inevitable. Despite Sara's uncertain health nearly from the time he had met her, despite her doctors' pessimistic assessment before their marriage, he was not prepared for her death. Regardless of all the evidence to the contrary, he wrote in his diary, it had always seemed to him that he would die first, "for I was her senior by 18 years, and had been badgered by all sort of illnesses for years." They had often spoken of death. Sara had stressed her own complete lack of "hope or belief in immortality" and had given instructions that she was to be cremated and her ashes buried in Baltimore, not Alabama. But principally, even now, Mencken preferred to think of her courage: "How gallantly she [had] faced the pains and terrors," especially of the last year. Only once in all her "cruel illness" had he ever seen her truly despair—on an occasion when she had been told by one of her physicians that the tuberculosis had returned, in the form of an infection in her eye.

As Sara lay dying, he was able to express these thoughts and feelings in letters to friends. On Thursday he reported to Betty Hanes that Sara was "much worse": "I fear I'll never hear her speak again." He had "dreaded" this moment "constantly," he wrote Max Brödel; it was "appalling to face." To the Knopfs, to Fitzgerald, to Hamilton and Olga Owens, to his old friends A. H. McDannald and Benjamin de Casseres, to Sara's Montgomery friends Grover Hall and Hilton Rice and Goucher friends such as Marjorie Nicolson, and, most of all, to her family in Montgomery, he gave the same message: all was "utterly hopeless." The letters and telegrams he received during those two or three days in some cases offered hope; most echoed his own despair.

So strong was Mencken's commitment to duty, order, and personal responsibility that even in those terrible days he continued to meet his obligations. He thought to write young William Abhau to explain that he would not be able, after all, to attend his commencement from the Naval Academy that weekend—and two days later, as Sara lay unconscious, he sent Abhau the issue of the *Congressional Record* that reported his nomination as an ensign in the navy. The same day he wrote the woman at Saranac from whom he had rented Sara's cottage, notifying her that Sara was critically ill and would not be able to come after all. He asked how much he owed her—"I sent you a small check last week, but it seems to me that you should have more"—and offered his "apologies for putting you to so much trouble to no end." The following day, May 31, he even carried on with professional correspondence, writing to an Icelandic scholar to acknowledge a letter he had just received.

Mencken was dealing with grief, even before the issue was finally resolved, in the manner he always had—working, writing, doing what he felt was necessary. Since he determined that it would serve no purpose to see Sara—she was now unconscious and to see her would only cause *him* great pain—he resolved not to visit her further. So he went home to Cathedral Street, passed part of the time with August, part with Sara's friend Anne Duffy, and waited for the call. He was told she had suffered little those last two days, though he had no way of knowing firsthand.

He was not with her, then, when she died on May 31 at 6:30 P.M., but once he was notified of her death he immediately did what had to be done. He wired Sara's family and various friends, he prepared to meet the Haardts at the station, he recalled Sara's strong resolve to be cremated and feared (needlessly) the objections to that resolve her sisters would raise when they arrived from Montgomery. At Cathedral Street he received friends, including Louis Cheslock and several other members of the Saturday Night Club—which planned to carry on, in its accustomed manner, with its weekend activities. Mencken was, as always, perfectly composed. "There was no sign of stress," Louis Cheslock wrote in his diary, "except around the eyes." But, Mencken later wrote in his own diary, "I did not look upon [Sara] in death. It was too dreadful a thing to face."

He confronted the moment as he had faced all other painful moments, without the consolation of religion or philosophy. "I can well understand why the more naive sort of people cling to the hope of a reunion after death," he later wrote of that late May day. "But I do not share it." If he pondered anything related to the gods or the fates during those cruel days, it was the fact—which he noted later—that Sara too had died on a Friday ("a generally unlucky day," he had written a friend only three months earlier), not on the 13th, but on the 31st.

The nation's newspapers the following day reported the death of Sara Haardt Mencken at age thirty-seven, and a story in the *Sun* the day after that reported that a private service with no flowers and no pallbearers would be held at a Baltimore funeral home. The day of the funeral, Monday, June 3, Mencken wrote an acquaintance, was "the most dreadful day I have ever gone through on this earth."

About forty people—family members and close friends—attended the service, conducted (despite Sara's "complete skeptic[ism]" Mencken wrote) by a young Episcopal minister. Cheslock and Hamilton Owens jotted down the names of those in attendance, including the Knopfs and the Hergesheimers, as well as Raymond Pearl, Brödel, and Governor Ritchie. After the service August, Charlie, and Sara's brother, John, took Sara's body to the crematory. "I did not go," Mencken reported in his diary. It would have done no good.

Sara's ashes were buried at the foot of his mother's grave.

# Chapter 15

# THE CONSOLATIONS
# OF AN AGNOSTIC

I was fifty-five years old before I ever envied anyone, and then
it was not so much for what others had as for what I had lost.

*—H. L. Mencken, "Autobiographical Notes"*

"There is a tremendous let-down today and I feel dreadful,"
Mencken wrote Hamilton Owens the day after Sara's funeral,
"but a lot of accumulated business must be tackled." As the executor
of Sara's will, he had to meet with lawyers to dispose of her small
estate: according to that will, dated May 17, 1932, he himself was to
receive a small amount of property, Sara's sisters were to receive
jewelry and other valuables, and Goucher College was to receive most
of her books. In the days after the funeral he had the melancholy task
of sorting through those books, preparing them for appraisal, and
packing away her clothes, many of which he sent to Alabama. In his
somber duties he was again helped by Sara's closest friend, Anne
Duffy, whose services he valued but with whom he had often felt a
certain rivalry.

He preferred to put the events of the preceding two weeks out of
his mind as much as possible: he wrote nothing in his diary about
Sara's death. Five days after her funeral he had the Saturday Night
Club over to Cathedral Street, but it was a somber evening. The
apartment, he found, still seemed "filled with Sara." In any case, he
had to read and acknowledge the hundreds of letters and notes of
condolence that had poured in from both sides of the Atlantic.

Many of the letters came from friends and professional associates—Nathan, Cabell, Fitzgerald, Sinclair Lewis, Edgar Lee Masters, Jim Cain, Ellen Glasgow, the Knopfs, and others. From Sara's sister as well as Marjorie Nicolson and Sara Mayfield came the assurance that he had given Sara the happiest years of her life. From other friends and relatives came only further bad news, that his cousin Felix Flugel and one of his oldest friends, Louis Michael, had died within a day or two of Sara. And from scores of readers Mencken had never met came a variety of messages. Many offered religious consolation, others expressed the hope that Sara had left him (as one correspondent expressed it) "the only visible evidence of immortality we have, one or two children," and still another mixed condolences with the hope that Mencken would read some of her work. If it had not been so painful, Mencken might have laughed at the crassness of some of his anonymous comforters.

To most of these, even some of the religious well-wishers, he responded almost immediately. To Nathan he described his brief marriage as "a lovely adventure," to Ellery Sedgwick as "a beautiful adventure." To a friend who had earlier experienced a similar loss, he exclaimed, "I am wondering whether [my house] will be endurable." But he would resign himself, he wrote another friend, to "such consolations as are available to an Agnostic."

In fact, Mencken's house was not altogether empty. August had come over from Hollins Street to stay with him during the final days of Sara's illness, and now he remained. It was at August's suggestion, in early June, that he decided to sail to England as the best way of clearing his mind. Despite his anti-British sentiments, he continued to believe London "the most interesting city in the world"; besides, Paul and Elsie Patterson would be there. Thus in mid-June he and August sailed on the *Bremen*, had a restful trip over—he slept most of the first three days and nights, he wrote Sara Mayfield—and met Patterson in London. By day he walked around the city, by night he and August went to the theater or to newsreel movies. On other days they took trips to Norwich and Oxford.

When they returned to New York in mid-July, Mencken had recovered much of his buoyancy. Upon landing he made headlines by proclaiming that the United States should have a king: he nominated Roosevelt, with Huey Long to be Prince of Wales. When he returned to Baltimore, August settled in with him at Cathedral Street, planning at first to stay until the end of the summer, and Mencken immediately got to work on the new edition of *The American Language*, which he had unsuccessfully attempted to write during Sara's illness. Indeed, as had been the case after Anna Mencken's death ten years before, he saw "hard work"—he wrote a friend the day after Sara's death—as the only "remedy" for grief. In London, three weeks after her death, he had written Hamilton Owens that at last he had begun "to feel like work," and within a day or two of returning to Baltimore he had written another friend: "I'll probably be blazing away twelve hours a day by next week." Hard work would help him "in the long run to plan out a method of living that is more or less bearable."

He had great hopes for his new edition of *The American Language*, a work far more ambitious than its predecessors. Since the third edition had appeared in 1923, he had made notes, collected data, and maintained a voluminous national and international correspondence with linguists and his own lay readers, and now he felt a certain sense of urgency. Earlier in the year, in order to concentrate on the volume, he had turned down an offer of $10,000 to write five magazine articles on contemporary American life. Having fallen even further behind schedule, his resolve to complete the work was even greater.

As before, he would discuss differences in American and English speech, would cite hundreds of disparities in spelling, meaning, and pronunciation, would discuss both American contributions to the English language and non-English contributions to the American language. He would remark on the British "war upon Americanisms": "For months there may be relative quiet on the linguistic Western front, and then some alarmed picket fires a gun . . ." He would again attack those American guardians of British English, teachers of literature: "There is no faculty so weak as the English faculty. It is the common catch-all for aspirants to the birch who are too lazy or too feeble in intelligence to acquire any sort of exact knowledge . . ." And he would ridicule those Americans "of fashionable pretensions" who

pronounce the words *path, secretary, melancholy* and *necessarily* in a manner that [is] an imitation of some American actor's imitation of an English actor's imitation of what was done in Mayfair—in brief, an imitation in the fourth degree. The American actor did his best to mimic the pronunciation and intonation of the English, but inasmuch as his name, before he became Gerald Cecil, was probably Rudolph Goetz or Terence Googan, he frequently ran upon laryngeal difficulties.

This time, however, rather than contending as he had before that British and American English were two divergent languages pulling increasingly apart, he would argue that, in the years since his 1923 edition, "the pull of American has become so powerful that it has begun to drag English with it, and in consequence some of the differences once visible have tended to disappear." The United States, formerly a cultural colony of England, was threatening to reverse the flow of influence. American English, it still seemed to Mencken, was vastly more vital and colorful than "the prissy fashionable dialect that passes as Standard English." Indeed, he would offer "evidence . . . that the American [language] of today is much more honestly English, in any sense that Shakespeare would have understood, than the so-called Standard English of England." The language of the United States showed "all the characters that marked the common tongue in the days of Elizabeth, and it continues to resist stoutly the policing that ironed out Standard English in the Seventeenth and Eighteenth Centuries."

Mencken knew, then, what he wanted to say, but there was the enormous task of getting it all onto paper. He put in "hard work . . . the hardest imaginable" in the late summer and fall of 1935. Despite the severe heat—some of Baltimore's worst in years—he was working "night and day," he wrote Gertrude. Though at times it was a "really dreadful job," he was generally satisfied with his progress.

He seemed to have time for little else that summer and fall. He no longer wrote in his diary: the only entry for the last seven months of 1935 reported his fears at occupying seat number 13 on a train from New York to Baltimore on Friday, September 13. He continued to write his Monday column, and at least briefly he considered a trip to Japan and the Far East on Sunpapers business. But nothing came of it. All he did, he wrote a friend, was put in "twelve hours a day on that infernal book." At times, however, he wondered, "To what end so [sic] labor so damnably." With Sara gone, he wrote Emily Clark, "all work seems somewhat futile."

Thoughts of Sara were never far away. He lived, he wrote Sara

Mayfield, in a "house . . . full of ghosts." "Every inch of the apartment," he had earlier written, "suggested [her]," and that was still the case. In late August, on their fifth wedding anniversary, he remarked to a friend, "Those five years were filled with dread and trouble, but nonetheless they were lovely." In late October, accompanied by Hergesheimer, he visited Goucher to present her books to the library, in a brief ceremony covered by the *Sun*. Shortly before that, when Sara Mayfield was back in Baltimore, he had taken her to the cemetery. In the cab, observing Mencken's set face, the unlit cigar between his teeth, Mayfield thought he could have served as a model for a Stoic. After a few silent moments at Sara's grave, he was ready for a drink.

August remained at Cathedral Street not only through the summer but until mid-November, and when at last he returned to Hollins Street to join Gertrude, Mencken became even lonelier. For the first time in his fifty-five years he would live by himself, and he viewed the prospect with alarm. His work schedule changed little, but with August gone he missed whatever nightly companionship he had enjoyed before. Soon he fell into the habit, every night about ten, of walking the four or five blocks to Schellhase's restaurant, where he would meet Heinie Buchholz for a few drinks. Sometimes August, as well as Raymond Pearl and Brödel, joined them. Aside from those attempts at the old *gemütlichkeit* and the weekly gathering of the Saturday Night Club—where, Louis Cheslock reported, he was more irritable than usual—Mencken lived a life as solitary as he had ever lived.

Christmas, an unhappy season in the best of times (save the first year or two with Sara), was especially bleak in 1935. He turned down invitations to the Knopfs' and the Hergesheimers' in order to stay in Baltimore and work. Except for Christmas dinner with August and Gertrude, he spent the day at his desk. To add to the sorrows of the holiday season, four of his oldest friends died between December 23 and January 1 and a fifth was seriously injured in an explosion. This was, Mencken wrote another old friend, "the most dreadful" of all the dreadful Christmases in his recollection. When less than two months later his friend Albert Ritchie died, Mencken could not even bring himself to attend the funeral. He concluded that he was "surrounded by nothing but death and destruction."

In late March he gave up and moved back to Hollins Street. He had completed the *American Language* manuscript—more than 325,000 words and weighing more than fifteen pounds—and with the book off his hands and the departure of August, the Cathedral Street apartment had become "a tomb . . . almost unendurable," so "gloomy that I can't stand it." Gertrude was planning to leave Hollins Street: she was tired of housekeeping, and she did not always get along well with August. Since she already lived on her farm nearly half the year, she would take a small apartment in Baltimore for the winter months. Mencken would pay her rent.

He felt it "a dreadful thing to break up the [Cathedral Street] house," Mencken wrote Dorothy Hergesheimer, but he saw no alternative. One of Sara's sisters came up from Alabama to arrange for the disposition of Sara's furniture: she and the other sisters would take most of it, Mencken would take some himself and give still other pieces to Gertrude. He found some comfort in the fact that Hester Denby, Sara's cook, would come with him to Hollins Street, along with Emma Ball, the maid he had hired shortly after Sara's death. Moving was burdensome, but by late April he had largely settled in, had set about making improvements on the old house, and had already set out flowers. The back garden—"the green grass under my feet and the chance to dig in the earth"—is what he had missed most in the five and a half years he had been away.

He welcomed the opportunity to live with August, the brother to whom he had grown especially close. Although his brother, now a consulting engineer, was considered dull by some of his New York friends and eccentric by others in both Baltimore and New York, Mencken prized not only his loyalty but also his sharp mind and cynical wit. In many respects he was like Henry, only more so. They not only looked somewhat alike, as Mencken himself once wrote, but August held most of his brother's prejudices, then added some of his own. He too was an author: in the years to come he was to publish books on subjects ranging from ship travel to hangings.

In leaving Cathedral Street for Hollins Street, Mencken was returning to a house over which a different ghost presided. What he had written in 1930, less than a month before his marriage, was still true to some extent: "I still miss my mother . . . every day. . . . It is a fact that I often catch myself planning to tell her this or that." To some of his friends such as Olga Owens who came to visit that spring and summer, it seemed in fact that Mencken had never left Hollins

Street. It was as if his five-year marriage, happy though it had been, was an uncharacteristic interlude, and now he was back where he truly belonged. "It's nice to see the old address," a friend wrote from New York. "I could never remember the other one offhand."

---

May 1936 marked both the first anniversary of Sara's death and the publication of the fourth edition of *The American Language*. In anticipation of that first occasion, Mencken wrote Sara Mayfield, asking her to send magnolia blossoms for Sara's grave up from Alabama. After he visited the cemetery and left the flowers, he wrote of how ghastly the day had been: "Sometimes I wish we could forget." It seemed "a downright imbecility."

But the reception of the book, more favorable than any he had ever received, could not help but break into his gloom. From the first, sales were impressive for a book of its kind, within four months topping eight thousand copies and continuing to climb, particularly after the Book-of-the-Month Club offered the book as a bonus for its subscribers. More important, American reviewers were nearly unanimous in their praise. In the week of publication glowing reviews appeared in both *The New Yorker* and *Saturday Review*, and not long afterward Edmund Wilson, writing in *The New Republic*, accorded Mencken the sort of praise he had largely withheld for several years. To both popular and critical audiences it seemed remarkable that a book on language, so full of lists and footnotes, could make such interesting reading. It could because Mencken was tying language to life, was writing social history, tracing patterns of migration and settlement, reflecting on questions of tradition and change, propriety and impropriety, dealing with the larger matter of culture.

Bolstered by the return to Hollins Street and the reception of *The American Language*—a reception that represented a first stage of his critical rehabilitation—Mencken felt revived by late spring 1936. His "troubles start[ed] fading," August noted, and after an eight-month hiatus he began again to write in his diary. He also turned with a new enthusiasm to a number of other tasks confronting him and considered still other projects he had earlier contemplated or actually begun but had not completed.

One work he had finished was a collection of Sara's short stories and sketches entitled *Southern Album*, and he pored over reviews of the book the spring and summer of 1936. He had put the book together and had written an introduction during the period he was completing *The American Language*. Uneven in quality, the stories were largely about the South; perhaps Sara's finest offering was a nonfiction piece, "Dear Life," a reflection on her love-hate relationship with the "cloying, sickish, decadent" South, its "sweetness tinged with the melancholy of death." Bearing a heavy emotional investment in the collection, Mencken was disappointed at the reviews, which offered only mild praise—at the same time as reviews of *The American Language* were extravagantly favorable.

Now that his book on American speech was out of the way, his own work took various directions. He spent a great deal of time during the remainder of 1936 working on his section of *The Sunpapers of Baltimore*, a book marking the newspapers' one-hundredth anniversary on which he collaborated with Gerald Johnson, Hamilton Owens, and political reporter Frank Kent. He also returned to Johann Burkhard Mencke's *De Charlataneria Eruditorum*, which he had had translated seven or eight years before and which he now prepared to publish with Knopf. With great enthusiasm and no little pride, he wrote an introduction for the English version of the treatise in which his eighteenth-century kinsman had excoriated scholars and pedants.

He considered—and rejected—still other projects. Earlier he had proposed to Knopf "Diary of a Plague Year," a work that would be "an accurate day-to-day diary of the events in one year under Roosevelt II." Although he wanted to "give a somewhat bawdy show, with plenty of personalities," Knopf was not enthusiastic about the idea, and Mencken had given it up. He also gave up, at least for the present, his earlier "Homo Sapiens." He had discovered that Raymond Pearl had a similar work going, and he believed Pearl, as a biologist with an inquiring mind, could do the job better.

One book he still entertained was his long-contemplated "Advice to Young Men." Such was the title he had given in 1922 to a brief essay in *Prejudices, Third Series*, and it was a topic that even then he had in mind for more extensive treatment—"a frank, realistic, unsentimental treatise on such things as politics, education, business, sex, etc., revolving around the idea that the most precious possession of man is *honor* [his italics]." It was to be Ben Franklin for the twentieth century, Franklin's counsel to youth without morality at its core, and Mencken had often referred to the project in letters to friends and acquaintances. In 1931, according to his diary, he had written the first words of his "Advice," but that is as far as he had gone.

Now, in May 1936, he announced in letters to both Blanche Knopf and Sara Mayfield that he would consult his "enormous pile of notes" and "fall upon" the writing of the manuscript. The same week, in an interview with the *Providence Bulletin,* he declared the same intention. Throughout the next two years he was to mention the book in letters to friends, and as much as five years later, having accumulated twenty or thirty pounds of notes, he still hoped to "put it through some day." It would indeed have been something new in the Mencken canon, an instruction manual in the tradition of the eighteenth century, part Franklin, part Lord Chesterfield, from this most confirmed of eighteenth-century men—but a guide tailored to the needs of the twentieth century. It was never to be written.

These undertakings, contemplated and in some cases completed, helped to fill the void left by Sara's death. So did numerous articles and essays written in 1935 and 1936 for the *Evening Sun, The American Mercury,* and other publications. With the move back to Hollins Street, Mencken was also able to assume more fully that role of family patriarch and caretaker that he had never really relinquished. Rarely had there existed a more conscientious and generous, and occasionally long-suffering, brother, uncle, and cousin.

Now that Gertrude was in the country for much of the year, he wrote to her constantly, advised her on investments, and sent her checks as well as trees, plants, specialty foods, and even a turtle for her yard. He went out to Choice Parcel as often as he could, usually on Sundays, and he helped her with repairs and yard work. With his brothers he was equally helpful, although among his siblings only August fully reciprocated that help.

Living with August ran as smoothly as he had thought it would. In March 1936 the two had agreed that they would trouble each other as little as possible—that if either were ill enough to be confined to bed, he would check himself into the hospital. Mencken did just that on several occasions, including Christmas 1936, when he came down with tracheitis and found that holidays in the Johns Hopkins were in most ways preferable to holidays outside. He and August also fell into the habit of going south, usually to Florida, for a week or two in the winter. They found the sun "baked the bacteria out of them." Besides, if he went in several miles from the Florida coast, Mencken had a chance to inspect the backwoods southerners—"only partially human," he wrote a friend—in whom he had always delighted.

His generosity continued to extend to Charlie's family as well, although with Charlie, as always, fewer of the rewards and more of the burdens of brotherhood presented themselves. Charlie was genuinely proud of his famous brother—although, he once announced in a newspaper interview, more for his beer-drinking capacity than for his writing—and he continued to call on Harry for assistance. Mencken still helped with Mary Mencken's medical care and, when Charlie was laid off his job as a railway engineer, sent him checks for subsistence.

The hopes he had earlier entertained for his niece, Virginia, had largely been dashed. After several months at Sweet Briar in 1933, she had grown homesick for Pennsylvania, and, following a long talk with Mencken and Sara over a weekend in Baltimore, she had transferred to a small college near her parents. Although Mencken disapproved of her decision, he continued to pay her college expenses. He continued as well to invite her to Baltimore, and he visited her in Pennsylvania on occasion. He could afford to take care of Virginia— his income in 1936 topped $20,000—and Charlie was indeed grateful for his generosity. But at the same time Mencken could not conceal his disappointment. Virginia was the only Mencken of her generation in his immediate family, as he sometimes lamented, and it was clear that she had neither the intellectual interests nor the sense of family responsibility that he had hoped she would demonstrate.

If he grew increasingly disappointed in his only niece, he took an increasing pride in his young cousin William Abhau. After Abhau completed his work at the Naval Academy in 1935, he and Mencken remained in close touch, meeting in Baltimore on occasion and writing often on subjects ranging from Abhau's career plans to his own interest in the American language. William Abhau's rise as a naval officer was further evidence to Mencken that the Abhaus had eclipsed the Menckens in the twentieth century. For additional proof, he had only to consider the sad case of his Uncle Henry Mencken, now living in Cleveland with a daughter. Mencken had never forgiven his father's brother for the financial mismanagement which had led to the closing of Aug. Mencken and Bro. in 1925, and he made little attempt to stay in contact. On a trip to Cleveland in 1936 he felt obligated to see his uncle, but not with pleasure. "It is a dreadful chore," he wrote Gertrude, "but I see no way of escaping it."

Relations with many of his old friends in the years immediately after Sara's death were equally troubled. From several of those friends, including Nathan and Ernest Boyd, he was now altogether alienated, and others, such as Sinclair Lewis, he also avoided whenever possible. He had rejected Boyd for the same reason he had judged many of his other friends unworthy: he was irresponsible, he didn't know when to stop drinking, and he had borrowed large amounts of money without repaying them. In brief, Mencken later wrote, his old friend had become a "nuisance." When Boyd wrote to him a number of times, asking how he had "offended" his friend, Mencken was noncommittal in his response. In his diary he was more forthcoming: Boyd not only borrowed money but he borrowed "as a result of [his] own indolence." He also disliked "listening to Boyd's troubles." Although the two men got together somewhat more often after Sara's death, they would never be reconciled.

Another way in which Boyd had "offended" Mencken, though hardly his primary offense, had been his part, along with Nathan, Dreiser, James Branch Cabell, and Eugene O'Neill, in establishing *The American Spectator* in November 1932. Founded as a monthly, the magazine saw itself as a competitor of *The American Mercury* (although not a serious one, as it turned out), and Nathan, who had not broken all ties with the *Mercury* until 1930, was chief instigator in a scheme that many saw as a betrayal of Mencken by his oldest friends.

In fact, he was probably less upset by Nathan's role in *The American Spectator* than he had been by another plan of Nathan's to put together a book of reminiscences, to be entitled "Friends of Mine," that would include a chapter on Mencken himself. When Mencken had seen a copy of the chapter—which in fact treated him rather sympathetically, although without the requisite dignity—he had written to Nathan, calling it a "trashy kind of humor." He had objected in particular to Nathan's reference to his church wedding—

which, he had always insisted, had been made necessary because the state of Maryland allowed for no civil ceremony. The author had seemed genuinely perplexed at Mencken's objections—he protested that Boyd and others considered the remarks innocuous—as well as Mencken's insinuation that Nathan was out to avenge his own earlier dismissal from the coeditorship of the *Mercury*. Only after Knopf, who was to publish the book, agreed that some of the material might be objectionable did Nathan agree to remove it. Indeed, Nathan pledged to Mencken that the book would not be published at all, "at least in its present form." But Mencken, whose relations with Nathan were already shaky at best, was not willing to make up. "Imagine falling into my arms after all the rancor of that chapter," he wrote Knopf. "I shall steer clear of that gentleman hereafter." He could "do his worst to be damned," he reiterated four days later. "I am through with him."

That earlier encounter with Nathan had reflected perhaps more harshly on Mencken than on Nathan. It had suggested a prickly side indeed, as well as a great fear of being made to appear ridiculous. It had even hinted, as Nathan suggested, at a certain lack of humor in the humorist himself. But when *The Intimate Notebooks of George Jean Nathan* had appeared in 1932, including a chapter on Mencken, the reference to Mencken's wedding was nowhere to be found. Nathan did make light of Mencken's frequent medical complaints—his hemorrhoids, "pain in the prostate," and "burning in the gospel pipe." Otherwise, the treatment was largely favorable.

But Mencken was not to forgive him for that, nor for an occasion two years later on which Nathan had cooperated with Burton Rascoe, who was editing a collection of writing from the old *Smart Set*. He had refused to let his *Smart Set* pieces be used, partly because he did not want to be linked with Nathan again. But he had been indignant when *The Smart Set Anthology* appeared with an introduction by Rascoe taking Nathan's side of their earlier break and portraying Mencken as a shrewd, hearty commoner to Nathan's "aristocrat." Nathan's "picture of himself as an aloof and haughty aristocrat and me as a peasant standing in awe of him is really too rich," he had written Knopf. He and Knopf had "made a great error in being merciful" to him. "We should have thrown him out on his backside and let him yell. It is foolish to be decent in dealing with a rat."

After those episodes in the early and mid-thirties, he and Nathan had been out of touch for some time; although they made feeble efforts to reestablish contact after 1935, it is clear that the two were no longer friends. But the conflict with Nathan and Rascoe in 1934 had served, in a way Mencken could hardly have anticipated, to reestablish contact with another old friend, Theodore Dreiser, after a silence of nearly nine years. They were brought back into touch by Rascoe's erroneous claim, in a pamphlet promoting *The Smart Set Anthology*, that their break in 1926 had come because Dreiser was called upon but refused to contribute to *The American Mercury*'s expenses in the "Hatrack" case. When he had read that, Dreiser had written Mencken immediately that he had told Rascoe no such thing and was writing to Rascoe with his objections. Mencken had responded with gratitude and something of his old humor. After another letter in which Dreiser had proposed to meet, "white flags in hand" in a "genial, if visibly armed neutrality," the two men had agreed to get together in New York.

Mencken had anticipated that their meeting would be an awkward one. Although out of contact with Dreiser, during the previous decade he had not hesitated to let various friends know what he thought of his old friend's socialist politics. Dreiser had been "succumbing to all sorts of exploiters, especially Greenwich Village Bolsheviks," he had written Fielding Garrison in 1931. "They are making a dreadful fool of him." In his diary he had remarked that he did not care to see Dreiser again. Encountering him, he had written Garrison, "would be like visiting an old friend who has gone insane."

Although he had indeed approached Dreiser rather warily when they met for dinner in New York in 1934, in fact he found his old friend "little changed." The two men had corresponded frequently over the following year—in January 1935 Dreiser had even proposed that Mencken join him for an auto trip to Alaska—but they would never recover the old closeness. By 1936 they rarely ran into each other and after 1938, when Dreiser returned to California, not at all.

Mencken had also given up on Sinclair Lewis shortly after the disastrous trip he and Sara had made to Vermont in 1931, although he still maintained a great curiosity about Lewis and in letters to mutual friends asked for news of his decline. The responsibility for that decline he placed not only on alcohol, a "very active inferiority complex," and the "stigma of Sauk Center [*sic*] [Minnesota]," but also on his "two poisonous wives," particularly Dorothy Thompson.

He resented the fact that Thompson had encouraged Lewis to accept the Nobel Prize in 1930—when Mencken wanted him to decline it—although in his Nobel acceptance speech Lewis wound up praising Mencken and saying about American literature what he himself had been saying for two decades.

By 1932 he had decided that Lewis was "hopeless," "completely sunk," a "sad mess." "It is highly improbable," he had written Phil Goodman in May, "that I'll ever see him again." But he carefully recorded in his diary what Goodman wrote him about Lewis's boorish behavior, his "decay." Mencken's own dubious contribution to Lewis's sobriety was an outfit for making beer that he sent Dorothy Thompson. If Lewis drank beer in moderation, he reasoned, he might not drink whiskey. In fact, he knew such an effort was hopeless: "He craves whiskey, and when he gets the chance he drinks it straight, drink after drink." Professionally, Mencken had advised Knopf not to take Lewis, who was interested in changing publishers, under any circumstances—and Knopf did not. Lewis was simply a "peasant"—the term Mencken used for Dreiser and feared that Nathan used for him—and "he must be dealt with as such." He applied to Lewis the same standard he had applied to numerous other friends. "Once a man becomes actively disgusting," he wrote Goodman, "it is hard to be polite to him."

In his mid-fifties Mencken had come to prefer less stimulating and more dependable company. "Life is too short," he wrote in his diary, "to be burdened with friends who demand too much." Men like Knopf and Edgar Lee Masters demanded less—although Masters and his wife, now separated, sometimes wrote to him with their complaints about each other. Since Joseph and Dorothy Hergesheimer demanded less still, Fred and Betty Hanes least of all, Mencken continued to travel to West Chester and Roaring Gap for well-deserved holidays. On one occasion, in 1937, he and Hergesheimer set out on a two-day tour of the Pennsylvania Dutch country, and Mencken, witnessing the farmers getting in their tobacco, was reminded that his father and grandfather, a half century before, had traveled through this very country every summer to buy tobacco in the field. In Roaring Gap he inhaled the clear mountain air, talked with the Haneses, walked the golf links with Fred Hanes, and read as much as he chose. He had still another reason for visiting the

Haneses. "The place is full of memories of Sara," he wrote in August 1937. She "was their special idol and hearing them talk of her did me good."

If memories of Sara Haardt were still vivid two years after her death, Mencken did not dwell on her to the exclusion of friendships with other women. In one respect, after 1935, he seemed to forge closer ties to women than he ever had before, a fortunate turn of events since he had lost a good many of his earlier male comrades. He renewed several friendships immediately after Sara's death; indeed, her death—and the letters of condolence it brought—provided an avenue for reestablishing contact with several women whom he had not seen or written since his marriage. From Aileen Pringle, Anita Loos, Lillian Gish, Bee Wilson, Gretchen Hood—nearly everyone but Marion Bloom—came notes of sympathy, and in his responses Mencken not only thanked them for their thoughts but, in nearly all cases, expressed a wish to get together.

The renewed correspondence provided a chance for him to make restitution for various wounds, large and small, that he had inflicted in the past. Pringle, who had been hurt by his request that she return his letters but who had nonetheless written occasionally in the early 1930s, now sent a deeply felt letter of regret, and he responded warmly. Gretchen Hood, still bitter over the manner in which she had learned of his impending marriage, wrote a letter less consoling than self-pitying: "Well, at least you have had five years of happiness and that is more than some of us get. . . . These past five years have been pure hell for me."

Mencken had nevertheless responded graciously to Hood's letter, remarking that he regretted to hear of her mother's illness, her own financial distress, and her other troubles. "I hope you let me see you," he added. "It seems a long, long while since our last meeting." When he returned from England in July, he had written again asking to see her, but she was wary. Even after five years, Hood noted later, "I was . . . never able to forgive him." She wrote on occasion, but she never took Mencken up on his suggestion that they meet. She did not respond to his final letter, or, rather, her unmailed response was jotted on his own letter. She may have been foolish, she noted, "not to have picked up the threads," but "I felt I couldn't ever believe in him or trust him again."

Mencken seems to have forgotten Hood quickly, but his tone in letters to other women during the summer and fall of 1935 belies his protest that he could find consolation only in work in the months immediately after Sara's death. "I can imagine nothing more pleasant than witnessing you again," he wrote Pringle in California. "I hear confidentially from reliable sources that you are more beautiful than ever." In other letters he asked when Aileen was coming east again, and he spoke of going west to see her. He also wanted to see Bee Wilson "the next time [he was] in Babylon." In October he was again able to report to Masters, in his old jocular voice, that he had "the damndest time resisting [the] voluptuous fascinations" of a woman who stopped off to see him in Baltimore and took "advantage of my lonely widow state." The next month Hergesheimer invited him to West Chester for a "small gay party" with "girls of the finest quality."

Whatever the impression he gave certain friends, Mencken was clearly not engaging in a lengthy period of mourning. For him, indulgence in grief hardly seemed the best route back from the deep sorrow he had felt at Sara's death. Refusing to mourn too long, he would have maintained, was hardly disrespect for Sara: it was rather that, in his eminently practical manner (that same manner that had driven him from Sara's hospital bed back to Cathedral Street once she had lapsed into unconsciousness), he must have decided that looking backward would only bring more pain. Having done all he could while she still lived, he could do no more now. Besides, his Baltimore friends later agreed, even if he had been interested in renewing old acquaintances, he had no deep romantic interest at all after Sara, neither in 1935 nor any time thereafter. It was as if, one said, he "retired" from romance in 1935. As another later remarked, something great went out of his life with Sara's death, and he was never quite the same again.

That may indeed have been the case as far as love was concerned. And yet, if we look at his letters carefully enough, we find that Mencken certainly continued to give the *impression* of romantic pursuit, the old game of teasing and flirtation, gallantry and mock formality—and never more so than in late 1935 and 1936, and principally with a woman unknown to most of his Baltimore friends.

The object of his attention was a woman in her early fifties named Jean Allen Balch, a contributor to *The Smart Set* in the early 1920s who had been a friend of Mencken, Dreiser, and Nathan as well as *Smart Set* publisher Eltinge Warner. In Mencken's memoir, released long after his death, he briefly mentioned Balch, identifying her as a free-verse poet, the daughter and wife of wealthy New Yorkers, and a woman who had become so desolate upon the death of her second husband that she had begun to drink heavily. He mentioned having seen her at "longish and irregular intervals" after the early twenties but gave no indication of the nature of their relationship during the period 1935–1937. He did not mention her at all in his diary, and as he customarily did with women to whom he was close, he destroyed her letters to him and kept only a few copies of the more than one hundred letters he wrote her. Those letters, saved by Balch, were given to the Enoch Pratt Free Library of Baltimore in 1987.

Mencken, it seems, had renewed his old acquaintance with Balch on a casual and friendly basis in April 1935, a little over a month before Sara's death. Until that time, he had not seen or written to her since late August 1930, when he had encountered her on his honeymoon in Montreal. At that point she was still recovering from the recent death of her husband. She and Mencken had then been out of touch until late March 1935, when Dreiser wrote that he saw Mencken's former "admirer" Balch occasionally in Mount Kisco, where they both lived, and suggested that the three of them get together for dinner when he was in New York. Mencken had responded that he would be delighted to see Balch. In early April he had written to her, suggesting that they meet in Baltimore, which she planned to visit in late April, and then take the train together to New York.

Such was, at this point, simply the renewal of an old friendship. Sara was in and out of the hospital, and Mencken was devoting most of his time to her. At Sara's death he had received a telegram of condolence from Balch, then a letter (which he later destroyed), and he had responded immediately: "How often I have thought in these dreadful days of our meeting in Montreal in 1930. You were alone then, and now I am alone too." In a couple of letters in early June before he sailed for England, he suggested they get together, and in one of the letters he seemed to have regained something of his jaunty spirit. He remained, his "chiropractors" told him, "a magnificent specimen of German manhood."

When he returned in July he immediately made contact: "Will you let me write to you again? I can imagine nothing more charming than seeing you." He wrote several other times in July, making plans to see Balch in early August in New York. Immediately after an afternoon together in Manhattan, he resorted to the kind of courtly banter that was as close to wooing language (save with Sara) as he usually came. He assured her that her "hand is kissed" and observed that she had looked "particularly good" when they met—but "my prejudices, as you know, run violently in your favor." "When do we meet again?" he wrote in late August. "I surely hope it will be soon."

He wrote to Balch frequently that late summer and early fall— more than a dozen times in August and September alone, another dozen in October and November—and they met in New York on several occasions. The tone of his letters remained the same: he "crave[d] the honor of seeing [her]"; or "it was grand to see you. . . . I am looking forward to waiting upon you at your country estate [Mount Kisco]"; or "My dear Jean: You're the grandest girl ever heard of . . ." Despite the somber note with which their correspondence had resumed in early June, with Mencken reflecting on loss and loneliness, he rarely came back to those subjects. Never in his many letters that summer and fall did he mention Sara, except once to note that department stores kept sending her circulars, despite his notification that "she is no longer here to read such stuff."

He saw Balch when he was in New York in the winter and spring of 1936, and they continued to write frequently. When she made plans to sail to the Barbadoes, she apparently asked him to join her, and Mencken at least pretended to consider that possibility: "On the one hand [because of a mild bronchitis] a trip to the tropics becomes even more attractive than it was before, and on the other hand I am so slowed down in work that I fear it will be impossible for me to cut loose." Although he assured Balch "I wish I had a ticket for the Barbadoes too," in fact he had little intention of joining her. "You are an angel," he wrote her, but his work as well as his Victorian propriety—the unseemly nature of taking a pleasure cruise with a woman only eight months after Sara's death—would keep him at home in Baltimore.

For another year he and Balch continued in this manner, writing frequently and seeing each other when they could. Mencken got to know her young daughter, who also favored him with occasional letters. In his letters to Balch he continued to be gallant and flirtatious, even indulging in the sort of mock-serious talk about marriage, or at least cohabitation, that he had carried on with Aileen Pringle, Gretchen Hood, and, more soberly, Marion Bloom. "Being kept is the right life for a literary man. . . . And of all the women on God's green footstool, I'd rather be kept by thou than by any other. . . . Get the house in England ready, and I'll move in at once. Or in Arkansaw. Or anywhere." He would meet her in New York so "we can . . . draw up our contract."

Yet their relationship went no further than this. As he always had before, except with Sara, at a certain point Mencken began to retreat from commitment, even from serious talk. When Balch ended things by marrying in 1937, he did not seem noticeably disappointed: he continued to write on occasion, usually sending regards to her "handsome husband." He had not so much tired of her by that point as he had realized that matters with her could go no further. She had served her purpose, and it had been a valuable one: providing him a focus of attention and affection, the illusion of romance if not the reality of it, in the painful months following Sara's death.

Other women, some former friends or romantic interests, some now married, served that role as well, if to a lesser degree. He got together on occasion with Bee Wilson, with journalists Margaret Chase Harriman and Gladys Baker, and once, in 1937, apparently even with Marion Bloom—although Marion's name is curiously absent from the letters he frequently exchanged with her sister Estelle. In 1938 or so his ill-considered early love, Jane O'Roarke—now out of prison—even got in touch again and asked to see him. He "declined politely."

His New York friends sometimes tried to arrange dinner and drinking companions for him as they had twenty years before, and Mencken himself spoke of "entertaining a female customer" in his room at the 1936 Townsend convention. Just how intimately he entertained her or other women during these years we cannot be altogether sure. He had a vasectomy in February 1937 and was to boast in later years that he had tested its success on a certain woman in New York. But the surgery may have been performed, at least in part, for reasons other than preventing pregnancy. He had long suffered intermittently from prostatitis as well as from occasional inflammation and irritation of the testicles and epididymides, and in the 1930s vasectomies were commonly performed to relieve just such afflictions as well as to bring about a general rejuvenation of the patient.

Whatever the case, Mencken's renewed contact with other old friends, his former Hollywood companions, was certainly both non-sexual and nonromantic. After Aileen Pringle's letter in the summer of 1935, he and Pringle wrote occasionally, but with little of that fervor that had earlier caused Mencken to request the return of his letters. To Anita Loos his letters were equally innocuous, although he did stop in 1936 to observe that it had been ten years since his memorable trip to Hollywood and he longed "to cast eyes" on her again. To Lillian Gish he wrote with greater regularity, and he and Gish got together in New York on several occasions—at least once at her apartment in 1938 with Sinclair Lewis and another time with Edgar Lee Masters. Gish was still charmed by Mencken, saw him every chance she had, and invited him to California to visit her. She had, by this time, broken with Nathan, and Mencken noted with some interest her animosity toward his former cohort.

If these and other friends helped to fill the void created by Sara's death, Mencken remained in touch with other women precisely be-cause they reminded him of Sara. In letters to Sara Mayfield in particular he continued to speak of Sara, and never more so than each May, when the anniversary of her death approached. "My chronology appears to have gone haywire," he wrote on one such occasion in 1938, after visiting her grave. "There are days when it seems that ten years have passed [since Sara's death], and others when I can hardly believe that as much as a year has gone by." "I hope you don't forget Sara," he wrote on another occasion, and there was hardly a chance of that. More than anyone else, Mayfield was devoted to both Sara and Mencken. Her regard for Mencken, her "old . . . affection" for him as a "deep and trusted friend," eventually gave way to a roman-tic infatuation that, she confessed in a letter to him, seized her late in 1936. It was an infatuation that went completely unreciprocated.

Increasingly, Mencken found that the relationships with women he prized most were those grounded in deep friendship and mutual interests and usually devoid—at least on his part—of romantic or sexual intent. Indeed, as he grew older, he seemed to spend more time with women and less with men. To two women, Blanche Knopf and Marcella du Pont, he had drawn particularly close. Both were married—Blanche to his good friend Alfred, Marcella to Alfred du Pont of the wealthy and powerful Delaware family—although neither was married altogether happily. Each was an independent woman of means and discrimination who naturally sought out a man such as Mencken, intellectually fascinating and forceful yet unfailingly thoughtful and courteous.

A stylish, painfully slender, intense woman, sometimes distinguished (Mencken wrote confidentially) by an "alarming lack of tact," Blanche Knopf valued Mencken as a confidant and adviser. She saw him as a friend aside from any professional association he had with her or with Alfred; since the 1920s she and Alfred had often led rather separate lives and each, independent of the other, had often invited him for social engagements. In the twenties Blanche had written frequently (sometimes as often as three or four times a week), openly and affectionately, and when he married she extended her affection to Sara as well, often inviting them both to New York. Both she and Alfred were fond of Sara and, throughout the early thirties, expressed great concern about her health.

After Sara's death the invitations continued. While Alfred wrote on two or three occasions asking Mencken to take holiday auto trips with him, Blanche sometimes invited him to visit her alone in summer retreats and weekend cottages. In July 1937 she asked him up to Cape Cod for a week: "It would be divine. We are going to alternate. Alfred is there next week, and I will . . . be there [the] next week. Why not come up [the] next week?" Later that summer she suggested again that he come to the Cape, where she would be alone, and another time she asked if he could meet her for a weekend in Stockbridge. On still other occasions she invited him to New York; she kept an apartment in the city, while more and more Knopf preferred to stay in their country home in Westchester County. Many other times she came alone to Baltimore to see her physicians—both the ophthalmologist who was treating her for a serious eye problem and Mencken's own doctor, Ben Baker. Usually she had lunch or dinner with Mencken, and often she stayed overnight at the Belvedere Hotel. The "real reason" she came to Baltimore, she wrote Mencken more than half seriously, was "seeing you."

The frequency, the tone, and the language of Blanche's letters—"Yours, with all my love," "With much, much love"—as well as the invitations they contained, might suggest that she had more in mind than a discussion of literary matters or medical ills. If this were the case—and she was no stranger to romantic encounters—such hopes almost certainly came to nothing. Even if she were interested in an affair, Mencken was not, and she knew that. She knew when she proposed Stockbridge or the Cape that he would not come. And he never did.

The truth is that, even if he had been romantically or sexually interested in Blanche Knopf, Mencken would never have let himself become involved with her. Alfred Knopf was not only his publisher but, more important, one of his oldest and closest friends—one of very few with whom he had not, at some point, broken. By Mencken's code, to become involved with his friend's wife would have been unthinkable. He still considered himself, above all, a man of honor.

Blanche Knopf was one very intimate friend, and so, particularly after Sara's death, was Marcella du Pont—although their closest association would not come until the 1940s. He and Sara had met Marcella, an attractive Smith graduate then in her late twenties, on their Caribbean cruise in 1932, and in the three years after that they had visited Marcella and Alfred in their home in Wilmington, Delaware. Marcella had also come down to Baltimore several times for lunch at Cathedral Street. Soon the du Ponts, the Menckens, and Joe and Dorothy Hergesheimer had become close friends.

After Sara's death, Mencken had continued to travel to Wilmington to see the du Ponts, his first visit coming on Sara's birthday in 1936. He and Marcella wrote frequently after that, and her letters were particularly affectionate. They visited back and forth, met occasionally in New York, and traveled to West Chester or Stone Harbor, New Jersey, to visit the Hergesheimers. Sometimes they were accompanied by Alfred, sometimes not. Mencken was obviously charmed by Marcella and delighted in talking with her about subjects from illness to religion, but he was also a friend of Alfred du Pont, and in his letters of the late thirties, when she and Alfred were still together, he never forgot she was married. Marion Bloom, looking back at Mencken after his death, suspected he had been in love with Marcella, but there was little to suggest it, at least in the late 1930s.

At this point—despite his close friendships with Marcella and Blanche, despite his wooing of Jean Balch and his occasional dalliances with women in New York—the truth was that Mencken still sorely missed Sara. "Her presence is still vivid in this house," he had written a friend a few months after he had moved back to Hollins Street, even "though this house is not the one she lived in." It seemed "completely incredible," he wrote another friend in 1937, that she had been dead two years. She was still "tremendously real" to him: "I simply can't think of her as vanished."

# Chapter 16

# TIME OUT OF JOINT

I f the 1920s had been Mencken's decade, a time of irreverence and exhilaration, the 1930s, grim and earnest, emphatically was not. He seemed out of step in everything—politics, economic and social philosophy, literature, international affairs—abandoned not only by the larger reading public (save for *The American Language*) but by most of his fellow intellectuals as well. Not that he cared greatly, it seemed at times, so wrapped up during the first half of the decade was he in private concerns, principally Sara's health and the completion of *The American Language*. But after her death he was able to look outward more than in the preceding years. He wanted "to devote most of 1936 to politics," he wrote a friend in November 1935.

One aspect of politics that already engaged him, an interest so strong that at times it seemed nearly as much personal as political, was his quarrel with Franklin D. Roosevelt. After his qualified support of Roosevelt's candidacy for president in 1932, an advocacy motivated more by his strong dislike of Hoover than any great fondness for FDR, he had turned against "Roosevelt II" and his New Deal. But the turnabout in 1933 had not come all at once. Although he disapproved from the beginning of Roosevelt's projected expansion of the federal government—and the "easy overconfidence of a man with ten drinks under his belt"—in March 1933 he still found Roosevelt a man "of courage and enterprise" as well as "a highly civilized fellow with a good deal of humor in him." Besides, as he wrote a *Sun* colleague who wanted him to write a critical "Open Letter" to Roosevelt, his own personal relations with the new president had been "very pleasant." In any event, he had concluded, "There is not much likelihood that he will run amuck as [Woodrow] Wilson did."

A year later Mencken had changed his mind, a reversal that was inevitable. For one thing, it appeared to him that the New Deal was progressing rapidly toward a socialism that he himself had always opposed and had publicly decried ever since the publication of his book *Men Versus the Man* in 1910. For another, he believed the New Deal was becoming a sort of "religion," "a despairing reaction from the Hoover religion," a new faith that was just as fraudulent as the old.

But at least as important, Mencken could not accept the New Deal because he could not fully accept the Great Depression. He had not been able to acknowledge it, at least publicly, in 1931 and 1932, even under the "transparent fraud" Hoover, and now under Roosevelt he still could not. Although privately he would concede on occasion, as he did in a letter to Phil Goodman in 1933, that "we go downhill very fast . . . the full impact of the Depression is just beginning to be felt," in his published remarks on the subject, and even more in newspaper interviews, he "refused"—as one newspaper put it—"to worry over the Depression." "The effects of depression are greatly exaggerated, mainly by the interested parties," he had contended in 1932. "Some of them are communistic sympathizers. . . . Others are charity mongers . . ." At various times in the thirties he referred to the "incompetent unemployed," of whom the hangman could "make a quick and durable job," and to "the anthropoids of the dust bowl." In 1932, as he and Sara were leaving New York for their Caribbean cruise, he gave an interview in which he blamed the crash and the Depression in part on women who "not only nagged their husbands into the idea that the way to get rich was to gamble, but . . . also went in for petty gambling and time-wasting on their own accounts." The following year, in a letter to Phil Goodman, he referred to the "late Depression."

He made such remarks although he could hardly fail to detect evidence to the contrary. At the Republican convention in Chicago in 1932 he had noted the "hundreds of homeless men" sleeping outside his hotel window every night. In New York he could not miss the panhandlers, although—according to so good a friend and great an admirer as Anita Loos—he was unsympathetic to their plight. Much closer to home, his brother Charlie, laid off his railroad job, was forced to go on the dole. "The W.P.A. is feeding me," he wrote his brother on more than one occasion. Still, Mencken professed to be opposed to such government handouts.

There is little wonder, then, that his critics were to speak of "the misanthropy of Mencken," although he himself would have claimed that he was simply holding to the Confucian ethic of his father— taking care of oneself and one's family—and being faithful to his early mentors Nietzsche and the Social Darwinist William Graham Sumner. It is true that he was, in some measure, taking care of *his* own family, helping to support Charlie and Charlie's daughter, Virginia, as well as making generous loans to various friends who he knew would not repay him. But that personal generosity in which Mencken prided himself hardly sufficed in a world that had grown infinitely more complex than the nineteenth-century Baltimore in which he had come of age.

Neither did his 1920s voice, mocking and gleeful, any longer suffice. "The only thing to be said in favor of the United States is that life here continues to be very amusing," he wrote a German friend in 1935, although in fact it was anything but amusing to most Americans. But he himself had fared well enough, had (on a tip) taken enough money out of the bank just before the 1933 moratorium to "last [him] a good while" if necessary, had sounded *his* note of alarm only when he detected the decline of decent beer in America. For all his compassion for family and close friends he lacked a larger compassion, one that embraced people whom he did not know or care for personally.

For these reasons and others, he had come by mid-1934 to declare himself strongly against Franklin Roosevelt and the New Deal. In no fewer than nine Monday columns during the summer and fall he had blasted "the New Deal psychology," the "imbecility of the New Deal." Roosevelt had read Mencken's attacks, had bided his time, waiting for a moment he could strike back. He would choose a time and place guaranteed to embarrass Mencken most.

That moment came in December 1934, at the semiannual dinner of the Gridiron Club, that gathering during which Washington journalists and politicians rib and ridicule one another, off the record, with skits, speeches, and generally barbed humor. As a notable critic of Roosevelt, Mencken had been invited to give the customary anti-administration speech, and he had agreed to deliver a brief address in the spirit of the evening. In remarks not nearly so damning as most of his Monday columns, he had not even mentioned the president by name—and thus was hardly prepared for the response in which Roosevelt, after acknowledging the words of his "old friend Henry Mencken," had bathed the assembled in what Mencken often called his "Christian Science smile" and had begun to deliver a harsh indictment of American journalism. Mencken realized immediately, and others more gradually, that the words he offered were in fact not his own but rather those of Mencken, taken from an editorial printed in *The American Mercury* in October 1924 in which he had spoken of "the stupidity, cowardice and Philistinism of working newspapermen." It was indeed a coup: Roosevelt had had his revenge.

It has long been assumed that Mencken was furious at Roosevelt's sly attack. "I'll get the son of a bitch," one of his early biographers has him muttering to Governor Albert Ritchie, who was sitting next to him. If that were indeed the case, Mencken concealed his anger from others. In a diary entry the next day and another two days later, in letters to various friends, in a note he included with his correspondence, in his posthumous memoir "Thirty-Five Years of Newspaper Work"—in none of these did he display any bitterness at all. He acknowledged that Roosevelt had probably held a grudge against him and had come prepared to do "some violent execution," and he reported that others told him Roosevelt had not played fair. But, as for himself, he later wrote privately, he believed the president's speech had been in "good humor," and he had told Roosevelt "fair shooting" as the president passed by for a handshake. In fact, according to a note Mencken included in his Gridiron correspondence, he had rather admired Roosevelt's technique in carrying off his ploy. And he added, in retrospect, that since the president had not seen his own speech in advance, he had probably assumed that Mencken was going to be much rougher than in fact he was. In any case, he concluded, Roosevelt's speech had been written for him by one of his aides and, in all likelihood, he had not fully read it over before he delivered it.

Whatever he felt at the moment, then, after the fact Mencken had been gracious and even generous in most of his remarks about the president's speech. He could well afford to be. For he himself, of course, was to have the last word, was to draw out his revenge over another decade. In the months following the Gridiron exchange, he had continued his assault on Roosevelt, but his words began to have a different ring. Formerly his columns, with one or two exceptions, had contained harsh criticism of the New Deal but not principally of FDR himself. Indeed, as late as January 1934 he was still praising Roosevelt for his "intelligence and courage" and declaring that "more than any President since Cleveland [Mencken's own standard of excellence], he is his own man." But after the Gridiron affair the personal criticism came more naturally: he did not hesitate to call the president a "quack" or, even more pointedly, "the Führer." In two particularly harsh pieces in *The American Mercury* in early 1936, he was unsparing in his indictment of Roosevelt's "Planned Economy" and his Brain Trust. The president's approach was "that of a snake-oil vendor": a "wizard," he employed "frauds" and "sorcerers" to help him hoodwink the American people.

In his March 1936 *Mercury* essay, "Three Years of Dr. Roosevelt," Mencken concluded by prophesying the president's defeat in November. "A Chinaman, or even a Republican" could beat him, he wrote, thus demonstrating that same ineptitude for prognostication he had shown in 1931, when he had predicted Hoover's reelection the following year. Later in 1936 he publicly endorsed a candidate, the Republican Alf Landon, and took a truly partisan part in a campaign for the first time ever. He covered the conventions as usual, not only the Republicans in Cleveland and the Democrats in Philadelphia but also the third-party Townsendites in Cleveland later in the summer—the "most magnificent" show, he wrote, "since the Scopes trial"—and, still later, the convention of Father Charles Coughlin's Union Party. Plunging again into the raucous world of campaign politics, he suffered through 114-degree heat in Kansas, then joined the Landon campaign train for an eastern tour. "The politicking," he wrote Gertrude, "will probably keep me jumping until election day."

By mid-September it was clear to him that Alf Landon was "sunk beyond help," and on election day he was proved right. He stuck with Landon until the end, however, announcing the day before the election that, as a "lifelong Democrat," he would vote for his first Republican presidential candidate since Harding in 1920. He supported Landon partly because of his genuine friendship for the Kansan: he would, in fact, entertain Landon in Baltimore the month after his landslide defeat, and the two men would remain friends for many years. But again his primary motivation for voting Republican was not his friendship with Landon but rather what had become a genuine animosity toward Roosevelt.

It was an animosity of which the nation had taken note throughout 1936. Dozens of newspapers had called attention to his attacks, many of them, including *The New York Times*, censoring him for going too far. Mencken had never been sparing, of course, in his remarks about presidents living or dead—not only Wilson, Harding, Coolidge, and Hoover but before them the first Roosevelt and even Lincoln, "a shifty politician," "the *beau ideal* of a rube." His criticism of Franklin Roosevelt, however, was of a different stripe altogether, going beyond even that of Wilson, his earlier *bête noire*. In his mind now, Roosevelt had indeed "run amuck as Wilson did."

Few editorialists asked *why*—beyond his opposition to the New Deal—Mencken objected so strenuously to Roosevelt, although the question would have been a fair one. Indeed, the answer went beyond practical politics, beyond social and economic philosophy, beyond even the unmistakable fact that Roosevelt was, finally, another of those authority figures against whom he had long rebelled. More immediately, it went beyond the Gridiron dinner, although that was part of it. With other leaders, Mencken's stated prejudices had accounted for his approval or disapproval. "Dr. Wilson" was a puritan. William Jennings Bryan, to him, was an ignorant, country-bred rube, with all the rube's vices and prejudices. And so on. But Roosevelt was an eastern patrician of precisely the type Mencken often embraced—a genial sort, moneyed, urban bred, an opponent of Prohibition, certainly neither puritan nor rube—and a good friend, to boot, of Mencken's friend and Sunpapers employer Harry Black.

Why, then, did he dislike Roosevelt so intensely? The answer lay in part in what Mencken believed to be class betrayal: he felt the president had turned against the people to whom he—and, Mencken would say, he himself—belonged. Such behavior was in stark contrast to that of the president's distant cousin Theodore Roosevelt, Jr., who struck up a friendship with Mencken, invited him to Oyster Bay, and delighted him with "denunciations of his cousin Franklin." But even more than a betrayer of his class, Mencken believed Roosevelt was a fraud masquerading as a messiah, a charlatan who had pulled something over on the American people. It was precisely that fraudulent variety of humanity, whether in the world of public affairs or letters, that he most abhorred.

It is possible, finally, that his attitude toward Roosevelt can be explained, at least to some extent, by envy—a feeling of which, Mencken insisted time and again, he was incapable. For the most part he was. At the same time, he could not help but notice, as he himself put it in his memoirs, that the "mounting woes and insoluble problems of the Depression threw the college boys and gals into the arms of Roosevelt II." "I was relieved to get rid of them," he quickly added, and to some extent he was. It was not, however, only "college boys" but an entire generation of educated Americans—who, as Walter Lippmann pointed out in the 1920s, were in *his* camp—who deserted him as well. If the twenties was Mencken's decade, the thirties was FDR's.

As important as why Mencken loathed Roosevelt was the effect of that loathing on Mencken himself. His preoccupation with his adversary threw him off balance intellectually, caused him to make questionable judgments, led him, in private, to attribute to the president qualities—"a touch of mental unsoundness," "an extremely vendictive [sic]" nature—that simply were not there, at least no more than they are present in any other mortal. His animus against the president led him as well to reject as worthless friends and colleagues who supported the New Deal, colleagues for whom he had previously had a high regard. Mencken himself had brought Gerald W. Johnson, a brilliant editorial writer, to the Sunpapers in 1926. But once "the New Deal fetched [Johnson] in 1933," Mencken later wrote, he "began to go to pieces." In fact, Johnson had not gone to pieces at all: he achieved his most notable success as a writer after 1933. But to Mencken he was a loss from that point on.

One's position on Franklin Roosevelt and the New Deal, then, became for Mencken nearly the same sort of touchstone of character and intelligence that World War I had earlier been. Those who did not agree with him were now found wanting, and certain former adversaries—such as the Prohibitionist Bishop James Cannon—now became strange bedfellows indeed. It would be overstating the situation to contend that Mencken developed the siege mentality he had demonstrated during the war, but something of the sort was close to the truth. He was forced onto the defensive, forced to make certain political allies on the far right that he might not otherwise have made. At the same time, he was cut off from many of those supporters of the 1920s who had not labeled him politically at all, left or right, but rather had embraced him as the courageous, iconoclastic spirit he had been.

Thus his vitriolic opposition to Roosevelt helped to distance him from an entire generation of intellectuals and writers with whom, in other circumstances, he might have been a kindred spirit. His intellectual compatriots and frequent correspondents were no longer Harold Stearns, Edmund Wilson, and Van Wyck Brooks, but rather fellow Roosevelt haters such as Albert Jay Nock, Roscoe Peacock, and Paul Palmer, whom even Mencken called "a genuine Fascist." As for younger writers, Mencken wrote a friend in 1935, "all . . . seem to be headed toward the left. . . . The left-wing movement . . . is bound to be transient, but while it lasts it has pretty well killed intelligent criticism in this country. Books are judged not by their worth as works of art, but by their political content . . ."

At the same time as he was making such pronouncements, Mencken's relations with intellectuals and writers on the left were somewhat more complicated than many of his detractors realized. Although he had decided long before that Marx "bored" him and that *Das Kapital* was "the worst book written on earth since St. Augustine's City of God," he had also written in the early thirties that if he "were young and on my own," he would "be sorely tempted, I suspect, to take a look at Russia. It is what the U.S. used to be: a great nation in a state of rapid change." Although most Communists were "laughable," communism was "at least an interesting idea . . . quite as sensible as 'democracy.' " In 1922, in fact, the New York consul of the Soviet government had offered to obtain for him an official invitation to visit Moscow. He had declined only because German friends warned him that travel in the Soviet Union was unusually arduous.

In the 1920s, because of his critique of capitalist society, he was often viewed by socialists as a kind of ally, and even in the 1930s he was able to find merit in certain leftist intellectuals. If he now dismissed Van Wyck Brooks, in large part because of his politics, he still thought highly of Edmund Wilson, who had not only veered sharply leftward but also, in the eyes of most observers, had succeeded Mencken himself as America's leading literary journalist. (Wilson, on the other hand, now faulted Mencken for his unswerving faith in *laissez-faire* and his ignorance of the nation's economic problems, although he still admired him as philologist and prose stylist.) Further left, he corresponded with and sometimes even praised Max Eastman as well as Michael Gold of *The New Masses*. Gold, who was very critical of Mencken in print but friendly in his letters, had even attempted to recruit him to communism—and in 1931 had asked him to travel with Dreiser and himself to Harlan County, Kentucky, to aid coal miners in their struggle against mine operators. Gold had known, in both cases, that he had no chance.

Of all the intellectuals on the left, Emma Goldman perhaps appealed most to Mencken personally. After their dinner in Paris in 1930, he had petitioned the U.S. government to grant her a visa to return to the United States for a visit—only to have his request denied and Goldman's 1919 deportation order upheld. At the same time he had written the attorney general's office in an attempt to help her recover missing papers that the Justice Department had seized in 1917. He had had no success in that endeavor either. "It seems dreadfully hard that it should be impossible to let the poor woman come home to visit her relatives," he had written in response to the earlier rejection, especially since she now seemed "to be out of politics." He and Goldman continued a friendly correspondence throughout the 1930s, and when, in 1940, she suffered a stroke and lay gravely ill in Toronto, he helped with her medical bills.

He maintained friendly relations as well with several novelists on the left, although he did not in most cases think highly of their fiction. Although he had earlier published the proletarian novelist Jack Conroy and continued a friendly correspondence with him, he showed little sustained interest in Conroy's work. Neither was he particularly interested in John Dos Passos, whom he later described, after meeting him, as an "extremely amiable fellow" but without much to say. "Who is Steinbeck?" he wrote, entirely seriously, to Estelle Bloom in 1937. "I know nothing of him or his books." Two years later, after reading *The Grapes of Wrath*, just out, he concluded that it was "well-written, but . . . full of the damndest political hoey [*sic*] ever heard." "I think Steinbeck," he wrote a friend, "is definitely a Red."

The only novelist on the left he genuinely admired—an independent thinker among the Marxists—was James T. Farrell. Indeed, Mencken probably thought more highly of Farrell and his stories of Chicago's Irish Catholic working class than he thought of any other American writer of any political stripe in the 1930s. Near the end of his reign at *The American Mercury*, he had accepted a Farrell story and, somewhat later, a short section of *The Young Manhood of Studs Lonigan*. Although he and Farrell did not meet until the summer of 1935 and after that saw each other infrequently, they kept up a lively correspondence in the mid- and late thirties. Despite their political differences, they had similar literary tastes.

Among the other writers Mencken valued in the thirties was Henry Miller, whose *Tropic of Cancer* he believed "a really excellent piece of work" (although "unquestionably obscene, at least in part") and whose *Tropic of Capricorn* he judged even better. But the truth was that very few writers, left or right, really interested him any longer. Even those novelists whom he had championed and helped bring to prominence, Dreiser and Lewis, appeared to him to be finished. Sherwood Anderson, he felt, had also declined greatly, and only in part because he too had turned politically leftward. The one story, in fact, that Anderson had sent him in his last year as *Mercury* editor he had rejected for reasons other than politics or aesthetic worth. "Though it is capital stuff," he had written Anderson, "[it] deals with the homosexual. I have long had a rule against stories about homos. . . . For some reason or other, such things jar me."

Although he rejected Dreiser, Lewis, and Anderson (largely for good reason), Mencken now regarded Ernest Hemingway perhaps more highly than he had in the 1920s. He continued to believe Hemingway demonstrated "poor judgment" and was out "to shock the old ladies of Oak Park, Illinois," but he also concluded that the novelist had "great talent," and in fact had placed *Death in the Afternoon* first on a list of the finest books he had read in 1932. Gertrude Stein he had also tried to read, largely at Scott Fitzgerald's urging. After finishing *Three Lives*, as he was nursing Sara through her final illness, he had conceded that Stein "wasn't as dismal" as he had thought. But he still held that, on balance, "her writing is bad."

He still wrote to Fitzgerald on occasion, although he had virtually given up on Fitzgerald as a creative artist. Mencken's longtime admirer, however, had hardly given up on him. Even in the mid- and late thirties Fitzgerald viewed him with a respect few others were willing to accord him, and on one occasion not long after Sara's death, finding the "urge to write irresistible," he had expressed even more openly than before the link he felt with Mencken, both because of their share in a period of literary history and because of a "mutual grief":

> We have both lived too deeply in our own generations to have much communication except with a mutual respect, but that you accepted me as an equal . . . settled something that had been haunting me about my relations with men ever since my tacit break with Ernest Hemmingway [sic]. I suppose like most people whose stuff is creative fiction there is a touch of the feminine in me (never in any sense tactile—I have always been woman crazy, God knows)—but there are times when it is nice to think that there are other wheelhorses pulling the whole load of human grief and despair. . . .

Not only had Mencken now largely abandoned Fitzgerald and the other writers he himself had championed in the 1920s, but he also virtually ignored two southern novelists, Thomas Wolfe and William Faulkner, who were now providing evidence of the southern literary renascence he himself had prophesied in the twenties. His relations in general with leading southern writers, excellent for a time in the early and mid-twenties, had in fact soured by the thirties: not only was he now rejected—nationally—by the literary left but, in the South, by the literary right, the Nashville Agrarians and the New Critics. Wolfe and Faulkner, largely apolitical writers, had no connection with the Agrarians; they were, in fact, writing the kind of fiction, portraying a benighted South of cultural backwardness and racial conflict, that Mencken himself had advocated throughout the twenties. Yet he paid little attention to either, and the reasons he did not are revealing.

With Wolfe in particular the inattention might appear surprising, both because the North Carolinian in his early work had been as devoted a Menckenite as the South could boast and also because Mencken himself had often heard Wolfe's praises sung by Sara and by various mutual friends. The novelist's early agent was Ernest Boyd's wife, Madeleine, a good friend of Mencken's up until the time she, like her estranged husband, had asked once too often for a large loan. Among those who also knew Wolfe was Mencken's friend Emily

Clark, who wrote to him on one occasion, proposing a private dinner for the two men. And in 1934 Mencken had been introduced to Wolfe's mistress, Aline Bernstein; after accompanying the Knopfs to dinner at her home, he had been favorably impressed. He had seen Bernstein—whom Blanche Knopf teasingly called "your girl friend"—infrequently after that, and what she told him of Wolfe must have depended on the state of their stormy affair at any given time.

At one point, shortly before the publication of *Look Homeward, Angel*, Mencken had asked Madeleine Boyd if he could see some of Wolfe's work (almost certainly parts of the novel), but what he saw he had rejected. Later, when Boyd had sent him several Wolfe short stories in an untidy manuscript, he is reported to have said, "Take them out! They're not even sanitary." In fact, Mencken was much more interested in Wolfe's personality than in his work. "An enormous fellow [with] the innocent appearance of a magnified baby," he described the novelist to one friend, and although he disapproved of the manner in which Wolfe conducted his life—at least as much as other writers of Mencken's acquaintance, he could not exercise moderation with women and alcohol—he was fond of Wolfe personally and saw him on occasion. When the novelist was brought to the Johns Hopkins Hospital, gravely ill, in September 1938, Mencken immediately checked with his sources at the Hopkins, anxious to do something to help. He learned only that Wolfe's situation was "hopeless," and the novelist died a few days later from tuberculosis of the brain. In a letter to a friend a month later, Mencken regretted that he had not seen "poor Wolfe" before he died. But, he remarked in a letter to another friend, he had never read his novels.

He had, at least briefly, a somewhat higher opinion of Faulkner's work. As editor of the *Mercury* in the early thirties, he had accepted four stories from the Mississippian, including the eventual classic "That Evening Sun," but in his letters, his diary, and his memoirs he never showed any particular enthusiasm for Faulkner's longer fiction and never reviewed any of his books. Although we can hardly take the word of Charles Angoff that it was he, not Mencken, who was responsible for Faulkner's *Mercury* stories—that in fact, Angoff charged, Mencken called "That Evening Sun" "gibberish"—it is clear that Mencken failed to recognize the emergence of that writer, bold, imaginative, and painfully honest in his portrait of the American South, for whom he himself had earlier called. When in the fall of 1929 both *The Sound and the Fury* and *Look Homeward, Angel* had appeared, Mencken had ignored both, had instead concerned himself in his *Mercury* review columns with discussions of Ambrose Bierce, Ellen Glasgow, and Ward Greene, as well as various works of history and biography.

In fact, when he remarked on Faulkner at all in letters, notes, and diary, it was to repeat his familiar complaints about the dissipated life of the artist. He remembered well a party at Knopf's in 1931 at which Faulkner had become so drunk that at 4:00 A.M., unable to stand on his own, he had to be helped to his hotel. Three weeks later Mencken had devoted another diary entry to Faulkner's six-week binge in Manhattan before his departure for Mississippi "leaving a powerful odor of alcohol behind him." He was offended not only by Faulkner's drunkenness "every night he was [in New York]" but by his "extraordinary boorishness" on one occasion at the expense of Alfred Knopf. Just before Faulkner left New York, Mencken had been notified that he would likely stop off in Baltimore on his way home: Mencken was "to persuade him to return home to Oxford . . . too many parties and too many people are not good for him." He was relieved when the novelist did not, in fact, stop in Baltimore after all but rather went straight "to Prohibition Mississippi with enough alcohol in his veins to last him a year."

Mencken's reports of Faulkner's behavior were accurate enough. But what is striking is that such conduct interested him in the 1930s far more than *The Sound and the Fury, Absalom, Absalom!*, or Faulkner's other great novels of that period. Again, it was evident that the man who was America's primary literary force in the late 1910s and the 1920s had lost almost all interest in belles lettres by the thirties. Although he had announced in an interview in 1933 that American literature was in the "doldrums," in fact he himself was in the literary doldrums, as he freely admitted on other occasions. With the advent of the New Deal and the "chance to batter the frauds political," "pure literature" suddenly seemed much less important. He had "never got back to it," he later wrote, simply because it seemed he had "said everything [he] wanted to say about it."

That would account for his interest in Faulkner and Wolfe as personalities, but not in their work. It would also account for his judgment, expressed in private, that James Joyce's *Ulysses* was "pornographic hooey," "hollow stuff," a "deliberately mystifying and mainly puerile" novel "concocted . . . as a kind of vengeful hoax" on those critics who had not sufficiently appreciated his earlier work. It would account as well for his belief, also expressed privately, that "no one would pay any attention" to either *Ulysses* or D. H. Lawrence's *Lady Chatterley's Lover* "if it were not for the frequent obscenities." It was responsible for his persistent judgment, expressed to Edgar Lee Masters, that T. S. Eliot seemed to him "the very worst type of literary quack." And it would account, finally, for his reaction, recorded in his diary, to his only meeting with Eliot, while the poet was lecturing at the Johns Hopkins in February 1933. After stopping off one night to see Eliot at the home of George Boas, one of Eliot's hosts in Baltimore, he had returned home and, the following day, written in his diary: "An amiable fellow, but with little to say. . . . We discussed magazine prices. . . . I drank a quart of home-brew beer, and Eliot got down two Scotches. A dull evening."

Mencken was doubtless right. No doubt Eliot took to him no more than he took to Eliot—although, as Mencken pointed out, Eliot had specifically asked to see him. But whatever his deficiencies in Mencken's mind, Eliot was nonetheless widely considered the leading Anglo-American poet-critic of the century, a figure whom, twenty years before, he would have been eager to engage. He would have engaged him in a discussion of the American language and its differences from the English of the British Isles. He would have engaged him in a discussion of Mark Twain, in whom Eliot, a native Missourian, also had a great interest. The Mencken of 1915 would have engaged him on a number of other topics. But in 1933 he noted briefly what Eliot said on two or three meaningless subjects, noted what he drank, and put it all down as a dull evening.

In part, Mencken could not appreciate Eliot—could not even try—because their worlds were so vastly different. Still largely the Victorian, he could not identify with Eliot the modernist, although in fact the poet had been born only eight years after he himself had been. Mencken's traditionalist sensibility—a sensibility that required linear order, a no-nonsense cast of mind that regarded free verse and stream of consciousness as gimmicks and hoaxes—*this* sensibility could never fathom the high-modernist world of Eliot and the later Joyce.

He could not fully understand Eliot and Joyce for those reasons, and for the same reasons he could not fully appreciate William Faulkner. He also could not appreciate Faulkner—just as, two years later, reading *Moby-Dick* for the first time, he could not appreciate Herman Melville—because, as before, he would not fully acknowledge that "power of blackness" of which Melville spoke and that was present, in abundance, in the work of his twentieth-century descendant Faulkner.

For all Mencken's powers of observation, his penetration into the heart and mind of a nation—indeed, for all his own personal suffering in 1935—there still existed in him that earlier disinclination to probe too deeply, to take cosmic matters too seriously. The Mencken who had left Sara's bedside once she lapsed into unconsciousness, who had then declined to look at her in death—in both cases because seeing her would be too painful to bear—that Mencken still veered away from the abyss and would for some time to come. In matters of pain and suffering, personal *or* cosmic, as well as matters of good and evil, those great strains in the American moral imagination running parallel from the Puritans onward, he was still, by choice as much as by temperament, nearly as innocent, as blind, as he sometimes felt the earlier Transcendentalists to be.

# Chapter 17

# GERMANY

I n the mid-1930s, as Mencken became less engaged by literature and more interested in politics and public affairs, he also began to play a more active role in the operations of the Sunpapers. In late 1935 he had accepted Paul Patterson's proposal that, beginning in January 1936, he would give *Sun* business "more regular attention" than he had given it in the preceding five or six years. He would go to the downtown offices five afternoons a week, not one or two as had been his custom, he would serve as a general adviser and trouble-shooter for the newspapers, and his salary would be increased from $5,000 to $12,000 a year. He accepted the offer in part because he was concerned about the direction of the newspapers. In 1925 he had called the *Evening Sun* "in many ways the most intelligent newspaper in America." Now he felt that both it and the morning *Sun* had descended to the rank of "fat and contented provincial papers."

His involvement with the Sunpapers for the next two and a half years was to be closer than it had been in more than a decade and closer than it would ever be again. Although he would soon cut his five afternoons a week to three, he represented the newspapers on a number of fronts. Not only did he devote a great deal of time to arguing management's position in labor negotiations with Sunpapers pressmen, he also consented to undertake various diplomatic missions. In 1936 and 1937 he made trips to New York to meet with William Randolph Hearst about the possible purchase of the Baltimore *News-Post,* which Patterson wanted to set up as a friendly competitor for the Sunpapers. On his first trip he had a pleasant but fruitless discussion with the seventy-three-year-old newspaper magnate. His second meeting, with William Randolph Hearst, Jr., was equally friendly and unproductive. He did not particularly care that Patterson's purchase plan did not work out: Patterson had wanted to install him as editor of the new paper, and he wanted no part of such an operation. Neither did he have any interest in a position as a daily columnist, at $1,000 a week, that the older Hearst was soon to offer him. Such an undertaking, he felt, would be "lunacy . . . at my age."

But he relished such high-stakes negotiations, as well as his role as Sunpapers confidant and counselor. He wrote frequent notes to Hamilton Owens, John Owens, and other *Sun* editors, remarking both favorably and unfavorably on current and prospective staff members and recommending promising outsiders who had expressed interest in the *Sun.* He endorsed Alistair Cooke, whom he had earlier befriended, for a position of "theatrical correspondent" and on several occasions recommended a young North Carolina editorial writer and *American Mercury* contributor, W. J. Cash. To Hamilton Owens he raved about Cash's "thunderous, but very effective style" and judged him "one of the best writers ever developed in the South." It was not his fault that the Sunpapers did not hire Cash but rather left him down in North Carolina to continue struggling with his eventual masterpiece, *The Mind of the South.* "That manuscript when published," Mencken wrote Blanche Knopf, again demonstrating his ineptitude at prophecy, would not "have much of a sale."

He also threw himself into writing for the Sunpapers with renewed enthusiasm. He indulged his great interest in illness and medicine by doing a twenty-part series on the Johns Hopkins Hospital. He did a long Monday column on the abdication of Edward VIII (an "idiot," he believed) to marry Wallis Warfield Simpson, a column he was not surprised to hear that Wally Simpson, a Baltimore native, found "very unfriendly." Of the greatest news story "since the resurrection," he wrote:

The blood-sweating bishops of England may be gloating today over the exile of Enzesfeld ["the Hoboken of Vienna" to which Edward had fled], but I doubt if anyone else is. [Edward] is a poor fish who has brought his life to complete disaster, and if, in his lonely despair, he now regrets his monumental folly it is certainly no wonder. It will be, indeed, no wonder if he shoots himself before La Simpson [who had another husband "out at pasture"] shakes off her shackles.

But most of all, he continued to write about Roosevelt and the New Deal. He was as hostile toward FDR as ever, although he recognized that others on the Sunpapers' editorial staff, particularly the *Evening Sun*, felt differently. On one occasion, after writing an especially harsh Monday column, he jotted Hamilton Owens a note suggesting that Gerald Johnson might want to write "a counterblast to my piece. . . . If so, I'm all for it."

Mencken's most complete immersion into the life of the Sunpapers came early in 1938, when he agreed to serve as *Evening Sun* editor for three months during a transition period in which Hamilton Owens was to move to the morning *Sun*. He prepared for the stint by accompanying August on a two-week cruise of the West Indies— including Jamaica, where he again looked up his mulatto McLelland relatives—and when he returned in early February he plunged into his work with a renewed energy. "I haven't sat at a newspaper desk for twenty-five years," he wrote Jean Balch. "Coming back is somewhat fatiguing but certainly very amusing." He had never pulled rank at the Sunpapers—during his period of greatest fame he was not above writing obituaries and performing other routine tasks in a pinch—and as editor he demonstrated the same capacity for hard work, from 9:00 A.M. to 4:00 P.M., and the same egalitarian spirit. He also created a stir with such feats as an editorial page, on one occasion, filled with six columns of small dots—each representing "a jobholder at the Federal trough"—and, on the fifth anniversary of Roosevelt's first inauguration, an editorial against the president that filled the entire editorial page.

Despite such stunts, he was not a particularly effective editor, and he left his position in the spring of 1938 with great relief. During his stint he had experienced respiratory trouble, and he checked into the Johns Hopkins Hospital for diagnosis and treatment. He feared heart trouble, a stomach ulcer, and any number of other afflictions. Over the past year or two, in fact, he felt his health in general had declined: he had battled flu, bronchitis, and tracheitis, had entered the hospital at least twice, and had had, aside from the vasectomy, two other minor operations, including an epididymectomy occasioned by a troublesome cyst.

He was sensitive to the manner in which his hospital stays in 1936 and 1937 had been received. According to Cheslock's diary, when he went in for the epididymectomy Cheslock and other Saturday Night Club members believed that, in fact, he had had a testicle removed—although Mencken went to great lengths to assure other friends, including Hergesheimer, that "my balls are absolutely intact. Let this be clearly understood." That same winter Cheslock and other Saturday Night Club members were given to understand that Mencken had suffered a "mild stroke," when in fact he had experienced respiratory problems.

Thus he was understandably concerned when he checked back into the Johns Hopkins in May 1938, concerned both with what his doctors might find and with how his condition might be perceived. Before, he had virtually boasted of his afflictions; now, he asked both Hamilton Owens and Blanche Knopf to "say nothing to anybody about my so-called illness." This time he need not have worried: Ben Baker found a spastic pylorus, irritating but not serious. Mencken's response to his most recent afflictions, however, revealed a great deal. He was indeed feeling old and discouraged, his "illness file" now seeming not so much a celebration of the variety of afflictions to which the human body was subject but rather a record of the greatest personal importance. When he walked out of the Sunpapers building at the end of April, his newspaper days, at least as he had known them, were over—although, in fact, not principally for reasons of health. And when he walked out of the Johns Hopkins Hospital a few weeks later, he was under doctors' orders to take a "complete rest."

---

The form that rest took in June 1938 was a trip Mencken had long planned and anticipated, surely not the least stressful he might have taken but one he felt he had to make while he was still able. When he left New York on June 11 on the *Columbus*, bound for Germany, he was already in much better spirits than he had been two weeks before. He hardly knew what to expect, however, on the other side of the Atlantic. It was his first trip to Germany in sixteen years, and, as he wrote a friend, "I am very eager to find out what is really going on. My guess is that the news dispatches are full of hooey."

For all his bravado, his great fear was that the dispatches about Hitler's Germany might be accurate after all. Twice before he had declined the *Sun*'s offer to go to Germany as a correspondent because of his "suspicion," he had written another friend, "that the situation there is really very bad and I hesitate to be the one to have to report it." Now he would indeed "look around" for the *Sun*, and he would carry with him a letter from Hamilton Owens certifying that he was a *Sun* employee. But he did not plan to send back dispatches. His reasons for going were more personal: "There are parts of Germany that I have not seen, and I am eager to take a look before the coroner calls for me."

Indeed, Mencken's feelings about Germany had become much more proprietary since his last trip in 1922. Since then he had explored his German roots, poring over genealogical records with all the fervor of some refugee from the United Daughters of the Confederacy, and he had begun to write to German relatives in Oldenburg, Wiesbaden, Leipzig, and other cities, as well as numerous German relatives in the United States. He had begun a long and affectionate correspondence with his older cousin, Anna Mencke, the matriarch of the Oldenburg branch of the family, and had visited with Tante Anna when she came to New Jersey in the early 1930s to visit her nephew. Both Mencken and Sara had liked her a great deal and had planned a return trip to Germany, a trip Mencken was still discussing with Anna up until the month before Sara's death.

Always writing in German, which Mencken read but could not write very well, Anna sent information on those family members remaining in Germany, sent German mementos (among them, books related to the family and a portrait of Bismarck), and gave him impressions of life in contemporary Germany. He wrote to her in some detail, and always in English, about the Mencken family in America, about his travels and Sara's health. To Anna he wrote much more frankly about the Depression and his own financial concerns than he had written to any American correspondent. But her primary importance to him is that she represented the Mencken family in its original seat. With her death in 1937, he wrote, "the Mencken family seems to be extinct in Oldenburg."

It was extinct in Oldenburg, but not altogether in the rest of Germany. Tante Anna had put Mencken in touch with a number of other cousins, whom he wrote with some frequency in the mid-1930s. From a Major Hermann Mencke in Koblenz, from Oskar Mencke, a clergyman in Wiesbaden, and from other relatives in Darmstadt and Frankfurt, Mencken learned of still other relations. He was told of a nineteen-year-old cousin studying languages at Heidelberg and her fourteen-year-old brother, who, he was told, "will be an officer in the German Army like his father and grandfather." To many of these kinsmen and others Mencken sent his edition of Johann Burkhard Mencke's *Charlatanry of the Learned* when it appeared in 1937.

Partly through Tante Anna and partly through his own digging, Mencken discovered and kept in touch with numerous distant cousins in America as well. He occasionally saw Tante Anna's nephews Eric and Walter Langemann in New York and New Jersey and became particularly close to Eric, a prosperous broker who had lost his wife at an early age in a manner that prefigured Mencken's own loss. He also corresponded about genealogy with a number of cousins in South Dakota, Ohio, and California. Although he discovered chapters of Mencken genealogy that "we had better not go into," as he wrote one cousin, he also found that certain cousins had followed the family tradition and become professors at Stanford and Berkeley. If Mencken could not approve of his closest Mencken cousins, Uncle Henry and his children, he absolutely embraced certain of these far-flung relatives. With one, Clarissa Flugel in California, he became particularly friendly, writing frequently, lending her money without expecting repayment, and frequently expressing concern about her well-being.

Extended family, then, became far more important in the 1930s, particularly just after Sara's death, than it had ever been before, and along with family Germany came to occupy, even more than before, a position at the center of his thoughts. He had already begun to send certain of his books, including his Ibsen collection, to the University of Leipzig; he had also made contributions to a hostel for needy students in Leipzig. In addition, he had asked Tante Anna if there were a museum in Oldenburg that would like his collection of Mencken books, portraits, and papers at his death. "Neither of my brothers has a son," he had explained, "and I seem to be destined to die childless myself."

At Sara's death he had made a new will, leaving Mencken materials to August and Charlie but suggesting that at their deaths (Virginia apparently having been disqualified both by gender and her own disinterest) the collection be sent to Oldenburg. His ties to Germany were thus closer than ever. He was entirely serious when he wrote Tante Anna that he often regretted that his grandfather had not stayed in Germany. Even more, he regretted the dying out of the line: "It seems appalling that the Mencke and Mencken family should be so near extinction."

It was not, of course, because of family alone that Germany was very much on Mencken's mind as he sailed in 1938. Both through news reports and through correspondence with German friends he had closely followed German political affairs. He heard from his old friend Willy Sohler, from Thomas Mann's son Klaus, from numbers of authors and scholars in Leipzig, Berlin, Heidelberg, and Munich, and from Nietzsche's octogenarian sister, who wrote principally about the Nietzsche archives.

Very few of these German friends and acquaintances spoke in favor of Hitler, but two or three German-American friends resident in Germany did. One had written in 1933, just after Hitler had been appointed chancellor, speaking enthusiastically of a "new spirit in this Hitler-controlled Germany" and reporting that "the spirit of class-conflict and brother-hatred" had "been swept out." Another friend, who had met Hitler and was "profoundly impressed by him," wrote asking Mencken to come see the "new Germany." Still another with ties to the Nazi government wrote praising "the strength and power of the entire [Nazi] movement" and adding that certain leading Nazi intellectuals would like to approach Mencken about lecturing in Germany.

Mencken had no interest at all in doing that. In fact, aside from the 1933 *Mercury* piece on Hitler to which Knopf had objected, he had had little interest in speaking or writing publicly about Germany at all. *Evening Sun* readers, accustomed to his candor on all subjects, remarked on his "silence upon the subject of Hitlerism." It was not an absolute silence: on occasion he did refer to Hitler's "obscene monkeyshines." But for the most part he preferred to take Franklin Roosevelt to task and leave Hitler alone.

On a couple of occasions, in private correspondence with readers, he had attempted to defend himself. To one he had responded, rather lamely, "It would be belaboring the obvious to denounce Hitlerism. Moreover, it is surely done sufficiently by other hands." To another who had challenged him more forcefully, he grew almost angry. "A man who has a gifted pen," the New York reader had charged, "and does not use it to fight the powers of darkness and savage barbarism is not a friend of humanity." He had added that Mencken was "more interested in alcoholic beverages than in the sufferings of agonizing humanity." "What makes you believe that I am 'a friend of humanity'?" Mencken had responded. "As a matter of fact, I believe that humanity will deserve to be blown to hell."

In any case, his virtual silence on Hitler's Germany, his well-known German sympathies in World War I, his German pride, and his continued association with Germans made Mencken suspect to any number of Americans in the late 1930s. It is no wonder that one of his early biographers, not to mention numbers of his more casual readers, assumed (as Edgar Kemler wrote) that he was "quietly flirting with the newfangled doctrines of Nazism and Fascism." Such a charge might find support in a statement made thirty years later, after Mencken's death, by his sister, Gertrude, in a letter to his brother August: "During Hitler's early days we [she and Henry] wrote of him in a friendly way. I think Henry destroyed such letters but maybe you had better go through the file to be sure."

If Mencken had indeed written the letters Gertrude mentioned, he and later August did a very effective job of destroying them—except, of course, for Gertrude's own damaging note. There exist, in fact, in the hundreds of extant letters in which Hitler is mentioned, virtually no statements in which he is "friendly" to Hitler. Gertrude herself may have been friendly for a time, and Mencken made no secret that he was (as he put it in 1934) "congenitally and incurably pro-German," but in fact his letters to friends at home and abroad from 1932 to 1938 are full of nothing but denunciations of Hitler. On that subject he was as effusive in private as he was reticent in public. Hitler was, in various letters, an "idiot," a "dreadful jackass," a "lunatic," a "maniac," a "preposterous mountebank," a "buffoon," and "a blatant . . . damned fool" whose "whole scheme seems to be insane." Most damning of all, he was "a Puritan of high amperage." Mencken offered such assessments in letters, and he repeated them to his Baltimore friends. "Conversation began with a denunciation of

Hitler by Mencken," wrote Louis Cheslock in 1934 in his Saturday Night Club diary. Mencken had held "Hitler to be a fool."

It was not only Hitler and his "thugs"—"hoodlums" with an allegiance to their leader that was "completely idiotic"—to whom Mencken objected. He cared for the German people, but he had also come to see them as "completely hopeless," unaware of "the veriest elements of politics." If they were indeed in "an exalted and happy mood," as all reports indicated, "it is the kind of euphoria that goes with acute infections."

He found German Americans, as he always had, even worse. They too were "quite hopeless," "mainly ignoramuses" who damaged Germany in their fervor to defend it. If Mencken went to a "Bierabend" at Baltimore's Germania Club on occasion, he still rejected such organizations in general. As he had earlier written Alfred Knopf, they consisted mainly of "a gang of professional Germans." When he himself was elected to membership in the America-based Friends of Germany in May 1933, four months after Hitler had become chancellor, he declined the invitation. "By talking and acting in a completely lunatic manner," he had written an organization spokesman, "Hitler and his associates have thrown away the German case and given the enemies of their country enough ammunition to last for years." He refused to be associated with Hitler's "gross and gorgeous imbecility."

There is no doubt, then (opinion early and late to the contrary), that Mencken was firmly and unequivocally against Hitler. But if so, the question Sunpapers readers had put to him between 1933 and 1938 was a valid one: why did he not speak out publicly? He did not, in part, because he refused to give his enemies the satisfaction of seeing him do so. He was deeply ashamed of what was happening in Germany—"the Hitler outfit has committed the almost inconceivable error of making Germany ridiculous," he wrote another German American—and he would not add his voice to the chorus of those who were pointing out just how ridiculous.

There had been other reasons for his silence as well. First, in the beginning he simply did not take Hitler seriously enough. Although he was an embarrassment to Germany, Mencken reasoned, he was hardly a threat to the world. Thus, particularly in the years 1932 to 1935, in numerous letters—and occasionally publicly—he spoke of

Hitler as a "joke," predicted in 1934 that he would "be bumped off very soon," then again in 1935 that he would "be an angel before this time next year." As he later confessed in his memoirs, he had no "conception of Hitler's stupendous cunning." Again Mencken had been undone by his inability, or disinclination, to see evil, that "power of blackness," even when it stared him in the face.

And there was a final reason why he did not speak out: his characteristic stubbornness in the face of pressure. If the letter writers to the *Sun* had left him alone, he later maintained, "I might have said in print . . . what I had already said in [private], but in the face of their attempt to browbeat me I could only refuse to write a line." Even at that, he confessed to a London friend in 1935, the entire Nazi scheme was so "insane" he might reverse his policy and "bust out" publicly "any moment."

Even if he had spoken out on the subject of Hitler's Germany, his readers would likely have judged as less than honorable his reasons for opposing Hitler. As a "life-long and incurable monarchist," he first opposed the Nazi leader in large part because he saw him as the inevitable product of democracy—"a demagogue of a very familiar democratic sort," "a politician of a type very familiar in America." The brand of ruffianism Hitler directed was "quite indistinguishable from the ruffianism of the Ku Klux Klan and the American Legion in the United States." It was Hitler's *style*, then, to which he objected as much as anything else. Before the Nazis came to power he had even agreed—in a letter uncharacteristic in its sentiment—with a Hitler sympathizer in Germany that "his ideas in the main are sound ones," but even at that point he could not abide Hitler's ranting, emotional manner. It reminded him of nothing so much as the rantings of politicians and evangelists in the American South whom he had been ridiculing for thirty years. As so often with Mencken, it was, among other things, a matter of class. Hitler, fully as much as Bilbo and Vardaman in Mississippi, he simply considered one of the unwashed. As one of the well-born himself, he vastly preferred the Hohenzollerns—who he expected, at any moment, would put Hitler to flight.

Even in his letters to friends, then, Mencken usually spoke of Hitler's offenses not so much as moral affronts but as "mistakes," "imprudent acts," and "errors"—miscalculations that had led the

Nazis to make "an apparent incredible mess of things." Their primary "mistakes," he had concluded by 1935, were the suppression of free speech, the burning of books, and, most damaging of all, "attacking the Jews, for they are extraordinarily influential in both England and America." "Turning thugs loose against the Jews," he wrote a German-American friend in 1935, "has immensely damaged German prestige and reputation."

Certainly Mencken's concern over the fate of German Jews, as will become apparent, was more than a problem in public relations, but given the past charges of anti-Semitism against him, particularly after the publication of *Treatise on the Gods* in 1930, some of his readers might well have thought that was the case. He had, in fact, received nearly as much attention for a single paragraph in *Treatise on the Gods* on the contribution of Jews to world history and literature as he had for the other 363 pages in that book. In his discussion of the Bible, "unquestionably the most beautiful book in the world," he had marveled that Jews—who "could be put down very plausibly as the most unpleasant race ever heard of"—had been largely responsible for such a work:

> As commonly encountered, they lack many of the qualities that mark the civilized man: courage, dignity, incorruptibility, ease, confidence. They have vanity without pride, voluptuousness without taste, and learning without wisdom. Their fortitude, such as it is, is wasted upon puerile objects, and their charity is mainly only a form of display.

Yet Mencken had added on the same page:

> These same Jews, from time immemorial, have been the chief dreamers of the human race, and beyond all comparison its greatest poets. It was Jews who wrote the magnificent poems called the Psalms, the Song of Solomon, and the Books of Job and Ruth; it was Jews who set platitudes to deathless music in Proverbs; and it was Jews who gave us the Beatitudes, the Sermon on the Mount, the incomparable ballad of the Christ Child, and the twelfth chapter of Romans. . . . No heritage of modern man is richer and none has made a more brilliant mark upon human thought, not even the legacy of the Greeks.

Mencken had hardly expected the outcry over those remarks that came from the Jewish press, the loudest of many charges of anti-Semitism to be directed his way over the following years. In fact, his book as a whole was anything but anti-Semitic, and even in the single paragraph that was so objectionable, he reasoned, he had deprecated the Jews only to make more dramatic his claim that they were the world's "greatest poets," the "brilliant" architects · of human thought. But that had mattered little to numerous Jewish editors who had considered Mencken, to this point in his career, their friend and who felt that he had betrayed them. In 1930 they had made, as one Jewish reporter observed, "a Dreyfus affair out of the episode."

Those same Jews, particularly in Baltimore, had been among the first to notice that Mencken was largely silent on the subject of Hitler, and they had been in the forefront of those who wrote to the Sunpapers in 1933 and 1934 asking why he did not speak out. They were also among those who called on him at Hollins Street to ask him the same question. What he had told them was precisely what he had told numerous non-Jewish friends: that it did little good to protest too loudly or too often, that, indeed, a leading cause of anti-Semitism in this country as well as in Europe was the "shrill" cries of anti-Semitism by Jews themselves. Vocal Jewish leaders with their frequent protests, he had written Dreiser and others, were making the world "Jew conscious at all times" and thus were paving the way for anti-Semitic demagogues. "Let the Jews shut down for two weeks running," he had written Benjamin de Casseres, himself a Jew, "and the Germans in America will be howling against Hitler loud enough."

In one respect, Mencken was being perfectly consistent with what he had always said. He greatly objected to rhetorical outbursts from patriots or zealots of any sort, whether from Jews, socialists, southerners, Prohibitionists, or professional Germans. Indeed, he had also told German-American friends that the surest way to stir up anti-German feeling in America was for German patriots, both in Germany and in the United States, to raise their voices. But such logic, when applied to anti-Semitism, understandably seemed dubious to his Jewish critics in Baltimore, some of whom had also been his friends. Was it really possible that this professional disturber of the peace felt such scorn for those who were themselves, for a better cause than his, also disturbers of the peace? They found it difficult to accept his reasoning. What he defended as the wise course they decried as an evasion of responsibility. Such participation in a conspiracy of silence had served from 1932 on to revive the old charges of anti-Semitism against him.

Mencken himself was sensitive to such charges in the 1930s. He continued to consider himself, in his personal relations as well as his professional conduct, anything but anti-Semitic. Indeed, he often identified and criticized anti-Semitism in others. When his friends— Edgar Lee Masters, Ezra Pound, Jim Tully, Roscoe Peacock, and others—burst out with accusations against Jews, he almost always refuted their charges. When a correspondent in New York wrote about a "Jewish conspiracy" in the United States, he responded that such an idea was nonsense; when a Baltimorean sent him an article that he considered anti-Semitic, he responded that the piece was "rather too hard on the Jews" and added that his own "acquaintance among Jews is very large and convinces me that the average Jew is a man of sound common sense . . ." And in particular to Masters, who filled his letters with anti-Semitic sentiments on more than one occasion, he responded: "I incline to believe that you are wrong about the Jews. As a matter of fact, they seem to be more intelligent than the Christian in literary matters and also more honest." He regretted the rise of an American anti-Semitic movement, "for my own adventures with Jews have been pleasant enough," and—"for a German" he added—"I am quite free of anti-Semitism."

Such an awareness of anti-Semitism was hardly isolated. When, during a session in 1935, Dreiser "broke out into an anti-Semitic tirade," Mencken recorded the fact in his diary. After a conversation with the evangelist and staunch anti-Communist Gerald L. K. Smith, Mencken reported that Smith was "preparing to get abroad [a] great anti-Semitic movement." He cautioned one correspondent that "a great amount of anti-Semitism exists in this country and . . . tends to grow," and to still another he wrote that when an anti-Semitic movement finds "a convenient opportunity" to "bust out," he would "mount the battlements and holler for the Chosen."

In his letters to Hamilton Owens at the *Sun*, he expressed concern that he would be accused of anti-Semitism, and he went so far as to change his wording in certain pieces to avoid offending Jewish critics. Indeed, earlier in the *Evening Sun* he had written, as one of "Nordic blood," that "taking one with another, it seems obvious to me that the Jews are enormously superior to the Nordic blonds," not only "vastly more civilized by nature, and hence better artists and thinkers" but "even greatly superior on the low planes where the typical Anglo-Saxon lives and has his being." "As between the Jews and the general run of Americans," he had remarked another time, "I am violently in favor of the Jews, if only because I have found them more civilized and more honest."

Thus, it was hardly for the embarrassment of Germany alone that Mencken objected strenuously, at least in private, to Hitler's treatment of the Jews. "It seems to me," he wrote a German friend in 1936, that "the gross brutality to harmless individuals must needs revolt every decent man." By the time he wrote that he had some idea, not only from news dispatches but also from Jewish acquaintances in Germany, of the nature of that brutality. As early in 1932 Emma Goldman had written that she feared for her safety if "the Hitler gang" assumed power: "Being a Jewess and an anarchist besides, it is reasonably certain that I would be the first to be turned into a pancake." Later letters from his fellow Nietzschean Oscar Levy, who had been forced to flee to France, informed him of Nazi atrocities. "God knows what the Nazis are up to," Mencken had written Dreiser in 1935. "They seem to be a gang of lunatics to me." He had heard that he himself was on their blacklist: "Whether they suspect me of being a Jew I don't know. Every now and then I am listed among Jews in some European paper." And when he argued with pro-Hitler German Americans, Mencken maintained, they "accuse me of taking Jewish money."

Such was indeed a curious picture of an anti-Semite, as Mencken was still labeled in many quarters, all the more curious since Knopf, Louis Cheslock, Lawrence Spivak, Abraham Cahan, and other Jewish friends continued to maintain that he was anything but anti-Semitic. Yet—as some of his accusers might also have said if they had been privy to all his correspondence—if he were indeed favorably disposed toward Jews, he often had a strange way of demonstrating it. Throughout his letters and his diary he sprinkled references to "kikes"—once a "dreadful kike," another time a "horrible kike"—as well as "Jewish scoundrels" and "characteristically Jewish mistakes." In other letters, both to reactionary friends such as Albert Jay Nock and to Jewish friends such as Benjamin de Casseres, he expressed the belief that "the Jews probably deserve their problems" and explained his opposition to anti-Semitism "not on the ground that it is without logical justification, but on the ground that it makes for trouble in the world and annoys me personally." Even his harsh criticism in the early thirties of Hitler's treatment of the Jews was qualified: "Though I believe thoroughly that many innocent Jews have been badly used, I am also convinced that there are plenty of Jews in Germany who deserve to be set down." Despite his disapproval of Hitler's tactics, he wrote Tante Anna, "I agree with him that [Jews] ought to be kept within bounds."

Many of these, to be sure, had been expressions of the early 1930s, not the late thirties, when it began to be evident, in general if not in particular, what Hitler had in mind for European Jews. But even in the early thirties certain of Mencken's Jewish friends—if not Knopf and Cheslock and Spivak—found his views too much for their friendship to bear. His attitude toward Germany and the Jews in letters to Phil Goodman was not the sole reason their friendship, once the closest Mencken had had, came to an end in 1933: Mencken's remarks about Roosevelt and the New Deal also played some part, as well as a $500 loan that Goodman did not repay. But their quarrel over Germany was by far the most important reason for that break and says a great deal, besides, about the relationship between friendship and intellectual compatibility as far as Mencken was concerned. In 1932 his letters to Goodman, who was in Europe for an extended stay, had been as frequent, as friendly, and as good-humored as they had ever been, and so were Goodman's to him. In July 1933 these letters ceased abruptly, and although Goodman returned to the United States that summer, Mencken never saw him again.

What had happened, Mencken later wrote Jim Cain, was that Goodman "began ranting like any other hysterical Jew and so I stopped seeing him." And what had led up to Goodman's "ranting" was the combination of his close observation of events in Germany and the letters he received from Mencken. In most of the several dozen letters he had written in 1932 and early 1933 there had been little mention of international affairs, and when Mencken had mentioned Hitler and German politics it had been in their customary lighthearted manner: "Certainly a man who wears a Charlie Chaplin moustache can't be altogether bad." He could hardly have been blamed for thinking that Goodman, despite an occasional note of alarm, still went along with his good humor. "Think what a dull world it would relapse into without Hitler," Goodman himself had written as late as June 1933. And after Mencken had remarked that Goodman remained "a shade too anti-Semitic for me," Goodman had replied, "I fear I shall die somewhat intolerant of the Jews."

Mencken, then, had apparently not at first fully recognized Goodman's deeper concerns, and when he himself began to discuss Germany seriously in his letters he had hardly thought his friend would be offended. Hitler seemed to him to be "a shabby ass," he had written Goodman in May 1933, "but I can well understand why so many Germans are supporting him in the present situation": Hitler was against "the idiotic internationalism that has kept Germany impotent since the war." As for his own situation, Mencken wrote Goodman, "I am beset by Jews who insist that I compose and print something about their sorrows. I have invited all of them to go to Hell."

When Goodman had finally spoken out against Germany in the spring of 1933, Mencken resented the change in his position. Three months earlier, he complained, Goodman had been praising Germany excessively; now he was saying it was unfit to live in, all because "a few Jews had their doki bombed." The same day he wrote that to Goodman, he also complained to Sinclair Lewis that Goodman had "turned 100% Jewish and [was] bombarding me with letters denouncing everything German."

Not long after that, Mencken later noted privately, he had suggested to Goodman that they suspend their correspondence—and with it their friendship. "The shattering impact of Hitler," he repeated, "made him turn Jewish on me . . ." Goodman had "announced that he was a Communist," had denounced "the Germans as fiends in human form," and, as Mencken wrote Sinclair Lewis three years later, referring to Goodman's apostasy as well as to his outstanding loan, he did not care to hear from him anymore. What had happened was not only that Goodman had turned against Germany—to which he, at least as much as Mencken, had long been devoted—but that he had also broken a tacit agreement between the old friends, had violated the spirit that had always governed their correspondence. He had grown serious.

Mencken should have learned something from Goodman's expressions of concern over events in Germany: if a Germanophile this fervent, and at much closer hand than Mencken himself, had so quickly grown bitter toward Germany, the situation must have become truly grave. But instead Mencken, when challenged, rejected both the message and the messenger and embraced Germany all the more. The break with Goodman, indeed the entire history of Mencken's uneasy relationship with the Jews before 1938, introduces more questions than it answers. How could a man who had expressed great concerns about anti-Semitism both in the United States and in Germany, who had written of Hitler's "gross brutality" against Jews, resist those charges so vigorously when they came from one of his best and oldest friends? How could he maintain that Jews were "vastly more civilized" and "more honest" than Nordics and at the same time, in his letters, refer to them as "kikes and kikesses," speak of a particular Baltimore neighborhood as being "infested by Jews," and insist that, in Germany, Jews should be "kept within bounds"?

The answers, as with so much else about Mencken, are various and complex. First, not only did the world of his fathers, as we have seen, hold a deep suspicion of Jews, but the world in which he existed as an adult, domestically and professionally, was full of anti-Semitism as well. Sara Haardt, in her letters from Hollywood in 1927, had complained time and again of "insufferable" Jews, and Mencken's sister's letters also contained frequent expressions of anti-Semitism. The Anglo-American republic of letters of which he was a part was at best mildly, sometimes deeply, anti-Semitic as well—his letters from Ezra Pound, Edgar Lee Masters, and Jim Tully are hardly needed to document that—as was the world of American journalism he inhabited. He himself pointed to anti-Semitism on the Sunpapers, and when Alfred Knopf remarked that Mencken was no more anti-Semitic than a good number of Jews, he might well have had in mind Walter Lippmann, who himself sometimes blamed Jews for anti-Semitism and was noticeably silent about the Nazi treatment of German Jews. In short, in a pre-Holocaust world in which a certain amount of anti-Semitism was nearly assumed among most non-Jewish Americans and Western Europeans, it may be somewhat remarkable that, to this point, Mencken was no more culpable than he was.

The world in which he moved accounts for part but hardly all of the answer. For he himself was alternately blessed and cursed, by nature he would say, both by a penchant for colorful and explosive language—hyperbole, slang, and epithets—and by a need to categorize and to abstract everything, including nations, regions, religions, and ethnic groups. Thus, rhetorically at least, he lived life more dramatically than most other mortals, attempted more, risked more, said more, and said it more colorfully on a wider range of subjects than perhaps any other writer of his generation. The result, depending on what he came out with at any given time, was that he appeared to be both the best friend and the worst enemy of Jews, blacks, and numerous other segments of the population.

The truth is that a hundred statements could be chosen to "prove" Mencken anti-Semitic and a hundred to "prove" he was not. As Whitman embraced multitudes, so Mencken vilified multitudes, Jews in fact less than many other groups. At various points in his career he called Poles "a gang of brutal ignoramuses," Norwegians "uncouth yokels," the Dutch "a money-grubbing and unimaginative people, with bad manners," and the "whole race" of Scots "vulgar and lowdown . . . near the bottom of the civilized races." Russians and Japanese and Chinese fared even worse. And, within the United States, southern poor whites—and Methodists of all stripes—were irremediably dismal.

But of all ethnic or religious groups Mencken seemed to be most fascinated by Jews. With numerous Jewish friends—Isaac Goldberg and Benjamin de Casseres, Louis Cheslock and Rabbi Morris S. Lazaron—he discussed Jewish culture, language, politics, and cuisine. With Goldberg and Cheslock he joked about both Christianity and Judaism, he discussed with Goldberg epithets for Jews, and he urged Goldberg to do a Yiddish dictionary. It is perhaps not so important that the qualities he assigned Jews were often in fact more positive than those he assigned non-Jews; what is important is that he nearly always *separated* Jews, divided them, categorized them. In his diary he could not resist—even when he intended no conscious censure or praise or judgment of any kind—identifying numerous people as Jews: "We were let into the room by a young Jewish fellow. . . . At 10 o'clock a young Jewish woman lawyer appeared." In particular, he was aware of the various national origins of Jews, greatly preferring the more established and conservative German Jews to Russian and Polish Jews. In the late thirties he wrote of "the hysteria prevailing among the [Baltimore] Polish Jews. . . . My belief is that it is impossible to write anything that will satisfy the Eastern Jews—saving, of course, gross and idiotic flattery." Indeed, any examination of Mencken's anti-Semitism must include the question: which European Jews did he have in mind?

Finally, any discussion of that topic must also consider particular periods of his life: in general, Mencken appeared to make harsher remarks about Jews in the 1930s than in the 1920s and, curiously, harsher ones in the late 1930s than in 1932 and 1933. The reasons were various, as much personal in origin as political. By 1938 he was looking back on the breakup of his close friendships with Nathan and Goodman, and he had also gradually become aware of his betrayal by Charles Angoff, his Jewish assistant on the *Mercury* whom he had earlier believed to be altogether loyal to him. Finally, in the mid- and late thirties, as spokesman for the Sunpapers' management, he had unpleasant relations with Jewish representatives of the Newspaper Guild, which he felt had been "gobbled" by "the New York Jews."

Certainly the whole direction of American life in the 1930s, as well as Mencken's interpretation of it, tended to feed his incipient anti-Semitism as well. The United States, he believed, was turning toward socialism, and—he later wrote with great exaggeration—"the great majority of American Jews, in 1933 . . . were violent partisans of the Bolsheviks." More accurately, and at least as offensive to him, the majority of Jews *were* supporters of the New Deal and of his archfoe Roosevelt. In letters and in his diary he referred to "Franklin's Jews," to excessive "seeking of public office by Jews" during the New Deal, to Knopf's praise of FDR, which "evidently echoed what he is hearing from the rich Jews he admires." And Mencken, who had earlier objected when a correspondent heaped blame on Jews—or praised Hitler—remained silent in the late thirties when Ezra Pound blasted "god damn Frankie Roosenstein" and added that "Adolf I figger is about 90% right in the present shindig." Roosevelt, and any Jews linked to him, seemed to be fair game under any circumstances.

It was not so much, then, that Mencken's feelings about Jews, occasionally critical but generally amiable before 1932 or 1933, had changed substantially. It was rather that now he could not abide certain old Jewish friends, could not abide Roosevelt and his New Dealers, could not abide those "professional defender[s] of [their] people" who, by shouting "shrilly," disturbed his peace, and, most of all, could not abide those who told the whole truth about Germany. Those offenders in the 1930s often happened to be Jewish. When his

413

Jewish friend Benjamin de Casseres wrote him in 1934, "Every German is a Peasant-Lout, and Hitler is . . . the greatest of them all"—and added that "the German situation is the only thing to my knowledge, that you have shirked from facing straight in the face"— he was placed on the defensive and retreated even more deeply into public silence.

What if England, not Germany, had burst forth in virulent anti-Semitism in the 1930s? Mencken would have led the public charge in defense of the Jews. But it was not England. It was Germany, still the land of his heart, the land he wished, in certain moments of both frustration and nostalgia, that his grandfather had never left, and finally he could not abide such attacks directed against it. He found it easier to blame the "hysterical" voices of American Jewish "propagandists" who were leading the charge against Germany. Not until much later did he admit—a rare admission for a man who, even after the fact, admitted little—"Better than the rest of us, they sensed what was ahead for their people."

———※———

It was with this intellectual and emotional baggage that Mencken set sail for Bremen on June 11, 1938. In a very real sense, it was not so much contemporary Germany, Hitler's Germany, he went to see as an older Germany, that earlier land of his fathers. When in 1934 he had pronounced himself "congenitally and incurably German," it was that earlier Germany he had in mind, an allegiance more to a nation of the spirit than to any existing political entity. He would "loaf down the Rhine for a couple of weeks." Then he would revisit Leipzig and Oldenburg and, for the first time, visit the village of Laas in Saxony, where his great-grandfather had owned a stock farm, and he would visit other towns and villages from which the Menckens were now gone forever. It was this—literally, the Fatherland, rather than political Germany—he wanted to see, almost certainly for the last time. "I hate the thought of Berlin," he wrote Sara Mayfield. Thus he would "keep away from Berlon [sic] as long as possible." And when he did reach Berlin, he wrote a German friend, he did not want it to be known he was there. "Above all, I don't want to meet any political personages." Indeed, he wrote Gertrude, "if Adolf is in eruption and travel is unpleasant, I'll probably shove off for England."

As it turned out, he visited Berlin much sooner than he had planned. After a smooth and restful voyage, a couple of days in Bremen, and a brief stop in Hamburg, he decided against the Rhine, traveled to the capital after all, and made his headquarters at the Bristol Hotel. Almost immediately, however, he left for other destinations—to Potsdam to see Mrs. Henry Wood, the kaiser's friend who had helped him arrange the interview with the crown prince in 1922, and to Leipzig and other sites in Saxony. In Leipzig he rented a car and kept his resolve to visit Laas, the village where his grandfather had been born more than a century before. No one in the village had ever heard of the Menckes or Menckens—the old woman who was reputed to be the village historian turned out, he wrote Gertrude, to be an "idiot"—but in the area he found a number of stock farms not significantly different from the one his great-grandfather had operated. He found the village "charming," the countryside "lovely."

A few days later, after a return to Berlin, he traveled by train through the Polish Corridor to East Prussia, made his headquarters at Marienburg, and traveled the short distance to Marienwerder. There he located a memorial to the earliest of the notable Menckens, Eilard, the archpresbyter of the cathedral and the benefactor of the ancient Mencken family stipend. On July 4, hiring a war veteran as a driver, he traveled by automobile to the World War I battlefield of Tannenberg on the Polish border and observed the war memorial to Hindenberg, the German soldiers on guard at his tomb, and the pilgrims who flocked to the shrine. The East Prussian countryside, which he had last seen in his brief stint as a war correspondent in 1917, was even more beautiful, he reported to Gertrude, than the area of Saxony around Laas.

In between his trips into the German countryside and his visits to provincial towns and cities, Mencken returned to Berlin. There, politics—a military buildup, demonstrations of Nazi power, harsh treatment of the Jews—could hardly be escaped. The countryside had only occasional reminders of the new, militant Germany— soldiers on country roads, airplanes in the sky, the remark by his chauffeur that Germans avoided a certain hotel in Leipzig because it was "a Jewish headquarters." But in Berlin his attention was fully drawn to such matters.

Shortly after he arrived he learned that "a gang of vigilantes" had just painted the windows of Jewish shops in the West End and that all West End shops were required to post the names of the proprietors. On another occasion he learned of "an anti-Jewish outbreak . . . one or two smashed windows"—a chilling preview of the terror that would, four months later, mark Kristallnacht. To Max Brödel he reported that "the situation of the Jews is very bad," and to Blanche Knopf he remarked that conditions were "somewhat less dreadful than refugees make [them] out, but nevertheless . . . sufficiently dreadful." To Paul Patterson he gave his impressions in somewhat more detail. Jews were "no longer roughed, but the pressure on them is terrific. All decent Germans seem to be ashamed of the business." But all Germans insisted "that the Jews must get out. Where they are to go is not mentioned. The American consulate is jammed every day."

For the most part, however, Mencken demonstrated a curious lack of alarm in his letters home. To Gertrude he also mentioned the crowds of Jews attempting to obtain visas, but he added that "there is no active sign of any persecution." If Jewish stores in the West End had to be marked, they also "seem[ed] to be doing business as usual." In a letter to a German-American cousin he joked, "Hitler invited me to a party but I had another engagement and couldn't go." To Marcella du Pont he remarked, "The Hitler New Deal seems to be working better than Franklin's. There is actually a shortage of labor. . . . In the evenings there is always a parade, and usually two, with bands playing." And to Paul Patterson he reported: "A good deal of the news emanating from Berlin seems to be bogus. The London Times has twice announced that its issues have been confiscated here, and yet I have bought it on the streets every day. The Moscow Pravda is openly for sale, and so are all the French papers."

Even in his memoirs, written several years later, when he was well aware, at least in broad outline, of the fate of German Jews, Mencken expressed a curious lack of concern in describing the Berlin summer of 1938. He recorded in passing the mob's attack on Jewish stores, but went on in the same paragraph to describe his pleasant dinner on the Kurfürstendamm—with good food, beer, and music—and his accustomed activities after dinner: "I commonly took a taxicab for the Schloss at the other end of downtown Berlin, where there were concerts in the courtyard . . . by the Berlin Philharmonic Orchestra." The courtyard in darkness "was very picturesque and romantic."

Although he insisted to Patterson that he "kept away from newspapermen and official persons," in Berlin he did talk a good deal with well-placed German friends, including Otto Julius Merkel, head of a large airship company, and two professors at the University of Berlin. One of the professors, a former Sunpapers correspondent, was now a Nazi. The other, not a Nazi, did not like Hitler's "methods and manners," Mencken wrote in his memoirs, but "had begun to see that the Hitlerian system was serving Germany well, and had come to be in favor of it, at least to that extent." If "the roughing of Jews upset" the second professor, he had also "come to the conclusion that [the Jews'] own gigantic folly was to blame for it." "Whatever [Hitler's] outrages," Mencken maintained in his private memoirs, he had "found a way to restore hope and self-respect to the country, and, what is more, confidence." His aggression—taking Austria into the Reich, making plans to acquire the Sudetenland—Mencken saw as "rectifications of the Treaty of Versailles."

Such matters were certainly of interest to him—he reported and commented on them as he did on other aspects of German life—but they were not the principal reason he was in Germany. As he had said in the beginning, he did not care to remain long in Berlin. As the time drew near for his return to America, he realized he had two other trips to make to complete his pilgrimage, trips that would indeed take him back into the Germany of the eighteenth century and before. The first was to Halle and Wittenberg, where Menckens had also been professors in the eighteenth century, and the second was to Oldenburg, the home of the earliest members of the family.

The countryside on the way to Wittenberg he found the most beautiful yet. As the train passed through the foothills of the Harz Mountains, he later wrote, "Never in this world [had] I seen more smiling fields or more charming villages." The other trip took him south and west from Berlin, to the Schwarzwald, then down the Rhine by steamer to Koblenz, to Cologne, and on by train to Oldenburg. There he hired a car for a trip through Frisia, the flat, marshy country in which (he wrote in his memoirs) "the Mencken clan seems to have originated." It was his first and last sight of the small towns "in which long-dead Menckenii had lived." Afterward, there remained only his futile search, in Oldenburg's St. Gertrud Cemetery, for the recent grave of Tante Anna, and the somewhat more successful search for the much older graves of previous generations of Menckens. And, after that, to reflect:

> I had now seen all of the places in Germany in which my people lived in the old days—Marienwerder, Potsdam, Leipzig, Halle, Wittenberg and the Oldenburg towns—and in nearly all had found memorials of them. I started for home feeling that a chapter had ended—that I'd probably never visit Germany again. I was already 58 years old, and my state of health was showing it: moreover, another great European war was certain, and it would be a long while before peaceful travel would again be possible.

The 1938 trip was indeed the end of a chapter: Mencken would never again cross the Atlantic. In his farewell to Germany he had traveled three thousand miles across and through the country, more than seven hundred by car, intent upon seeing—he wrote a friend—"all the backwoods that I had never visited." He had been overwhelmed by the beauty of the country, the bounty of the harvest, the energy of the people, the hold of the land on him. When he wrote friends, "My trip abroad was a great success," he had both this in mind and the recovery of his health from the "rocky state" of the previous spring. He was fully aware, of course, that all was not well. He had heard and seen evidence of the plight of Germany's Jews. But, as his letters suggest and as several friends observed when he reached home, he was strangely calm, even silent, about it all.

It is tempting to compare Mencken's farewell journey to Germany and his remarks on it to a similar farewell journey and remarks by another American writer, another German American and Germanophile—and one at least as anti-Semitic as Mencken—made only two years before. Thomas Wolfe had also returned to Germany, in part to evaluate the current state of affairs but also to renew his personal ties with the land to which he owed greater loyalty than to any other save his own. He too had marveled at the countryside, "so haunting and so beautiful," and the blooming gardens of Berlin, he too had observed the crowds sauntering on the Kurfürstendamm, had entered the lively cafés, had heard the "sound of music in the air." To him, too, Germany had seemed "enchanting."

But to Wolfe, for all the enchantment, there was a poison in the air, "a plague of the spirit—invisible, but as unmistakable as death," which "through all the golden singing of that summer" sank in on him. Encounters with Nazis, sights of Jewish persecution, the suppression of intellectual freedom: all had caused Wolfe—equally certain (as he wrote of his highly autobiographical protagonist) that he "would never again be able to return to this ancient land he loved"—to sail for America with a rage to explain what he had witnessed in Germany. And that had been in 1936, when matters were not nearly so grave as they had become in 1938.

For all his awareness of what was happening to Germany—keener, by far, than Wolfe's—for all his compassion for the plight of the German Jews, expressed earlier and, on occasion, later—despite all that, Mencken could not bring himself to speak out as Wolfe did. His trip had been a reminiscence, his nostalgic farewell to the Germany to which his family had belonged. Thus, with rare exceptions, in his letters and even in his diary and private memoirs he suspended that critical vision that usually served him so well and focused instead on the picturesque and romantic Germany of tradition.

There would be no equivalent to Wolfe's "I Have a Thing to Tell You." There would not even be—he noted in his memoirs—any "report on my observations in Germany to either [Paul] Patterson or John Owens" or to any other of his Sunpapers colleagues. Neither would he describe, in any detail, the situation in Germany for his Saturday Night Club friends. Mencken, Louis Cheslock reported in his diary that fall, "has been inordinately uncommunicative about the scene under Hitler." He preferred rather to speak "of the 'Christmas-card' prettiness of the Black Forest [and] the church where one of his ancestors was dignified with a [memorial] some centuries ago."

Or, as Mencken was reported as saying in an interview when he landed in New York, Germany "looked like a church to me, it was so quiet."

# Chapter 18

# LOOKING TWO WAYS

I f Mencken chose to turn his eyes from the true condition of Germany in the summer of 1938, he was hardly deluded into believing that war would not come, soon or late. For twenty years he had been prophesying German revenge, predicting even before the *First* World War was well under way that if Germany lost that war, "a crushed and humiliated [Fatherland] would harbor a hatred against England beside which the French thirst for revanche would seem a gentle and friendly passion." As early as 1915 he had spoken of the "next" war, in which Germany would "proceed to that unpleasant but necessary business which the law of natural selection has put into [its] hands"—defeating the English and the French. "German rache [revenge]," he had written in 1919, "will be doubly ferocious when the time comes, because it will not be tempered by the aristocratic ideas which qualified it in 1870."

As another conflict drew nearer in the early and mid-1930s, he had, in fact, been convinced that the "slaughter" to come would be "the bloodiest war in history." What he had been told in the summer of 1938 by informed sources in Germany further convinced him that war lay ahead. "Every German that I encountered," he wrote later, "looked upon another war as inevitable. All hands believed that the Polish cancer would have to be cut out . . . and that the operation would bring in France and England, and probably also Russia." The Poles "were hated in a bitter and all-out way."

In particular, information from his old friend the aircraft manufacturer Otto Julius Merkel persuaded him of the gravity of the situation in Europe. Merkel "had access to the highest army circles," Mencken wrote in his private memoirs, "and I gathered from him that the German General Staff regarded another great war as [certain.]" He learned that Merkel's own company was "engaged in the manufacture of airships on an immense scale, and from him I learned a great deal about the German preparations for the war then impending." Merkel had told him that the French would "be disposed of almost as quickly as in 1870." He had spoken freely, "for he knew that I would write nothing indiscreet; as a matter of fact, I wrote nothing at all."

Mencken knew all this when he returned from Germany in July 1938, yet in letters that summer and fall to Benjamin de Casseres, Aileen Pringle, and a number of other friends, both American and European, he had said he was convinced "there will be no war." He said the same thing in an interview with *The Washington Post*. What he had meant was that he was convinced there would be no war in the following year or two, and he believed he had that on good authority. Merkel had told him the German Army was not yet fully prepared and would not be until 1940. Then, Mencken believed, "Adolf will try it on the poor French—that is, if he is still alive himself. The chances seem to me to be at least even that he will be bumped off within the next year or two."

In many of his letters Mencken seemed eager for war. His longstanding dislike of the British grew more intense in 1938 and 1939 as he found American statesmen and journalists again falling under the sway of what he believed to be English propaganda. "Thousands of persons, apparently intelligent," he wrote Ezra Pound, "are swallowing the same stuff today that they swallowed twenty-three years ago," and Roosevelt, with his "violent anti-German campaign," was assuming the role Wilson had played in World War I. Mencken disliked the French nearly as much as the British. "I confess that it wouldn't displease me to see them knocked off," he had written a friend in 1934, and he still felt that way. More immediately, he seemed to sympathize with the German determination "to get rid of the Czech nonsense at any cost."

By 1938 he had already lapsed into the same attitude of detachment and scorn he had assumed in World War I. "I only hope to live long enough to see another general war," he wrote one friend that summer, and to another, an Englishman, he explained, "After all, war is a great Christian activity. The last one was a grand show and the next one may be even better." To a number of other friends— Dreiser, de Casseres, and Sunpapers colleagues—he expressed the same sentiment: the coming war would be "buffoonery on a colossal scale . . . a magnificent show"; "I only hope it comes before I am summoned to bliss eternal." And when news came in 1939 of the Stalin-Hitler pact, which not only made war almost certain but embarrassed American Communists as well, he was "seized by a fit of mirth."

But gleeful detachment was hardly Mencken's only response to the events in Europe in 1938 and 1939. All the while he was expressing a certain sympathy with German war aims, he was also engaged in an activity that would have puzzled his increasing number of critics: he was working quietly to help a number of Jews escape Hitler's terror. He had first volunteered his services in 1935 to fellow Nietzschean Oscar Levy, whose nephew, still in Germany, wanted to come to the United States. Mencken had sent immigration documents, had offered to "sign any affidavit or other document," and had written a number of letters on the young man's behalf. He had found out how difficult it was to come to America when Levy's nephew ran into trouble with immigration authorities and eventually emigrated to Brazil. But that did not prevent him from helping a second nephew of Levy's in 1939, nor from aiding a number of other Jewish refugees in 1938 and 1939. He received "dozens of letters" from Jews, he wrote a friend not long after returning from Germany, "asking me to sign immigration affidavits for them. In some way or another the news has got around among the German Jews that I am one of them."

In particular, he devoted a great deal of time and effort on behalf of various family members of his late friend Leon Kellner, a University of Vienna professor and early *American Mercury* contributor. He wrote numerous letters for Kellner's grandson, submitted affidavits to the U.S. State Department, petitioned the U.S. Consul in Australia (where the young man was temporarily interned), and pledged that he would personally "take care" of Stefan Benjamin "in case he [ran] into difficulties" in the United States. He wrote as well for Kellner's daughter and nephew and spent a great deal of time, in particular, helping Kellner's granddaughter, Hannah Arnold, a medical student who had recently escaped from Vienna only to be trapped in Zurich. He besieged the authorities in Washington with requests for papers, signed her affidavit, and agreed that he would "provide financial assistance" for her if necessary.

When Hannah Arnold at last obtained a U.S. visa and reached America, her grateful mother wrote from Palestine that Mencken had been "chiefly responsible for getting her to the States." Once she arrived, he continued his assistance, traveling to Washington to plead her case at the State Department, introducing her to his friends at the Johns Hopkins, writing to other hospitals on her behalf (she later became a neurosurgeon), serving as her financial adviser, and meeting with her on several occasions. Later he would consent to serve as a sponsor for five other members of her family, volunteering in a letter to the State Department to "take care of them in case they get into difficulties."

Again, one might ask, what manner of man was this: one who both excoriated "dreadful kikes" in letters to friends and also spent countless hours and assumed great financial risk in helping Jews to flee that country, Germany, that he professed to admire above all others; one who charged that "hysterical" Jews were responsible for many of their own woes but who nonetheless became, as Leon Kellner's daughter wrote him, the "embodiment of hope" for members of the "Disinherited and Exiled"? The answer lay, as always with Mencken, in the fact that in helping members of Leon Kellner's family he was simply helping friends. He had long liked and respected Kellner, and their friendship, even though Kellner was now dead, demanded no less.

Whatever the case, Mencken's relations with Jews, always curious, were particularly curious in 1938 and 1939. Not only was he working for their benefit behind the scenes, but in November 1938 he wrote an *Evening Sun* column, "Help for the Jews," that urged President Roosevelt to relax immigration quotas and admit more European Jews to America: "Why shouldn't the United States take in a couple of hundred thousand . . . or even all of them?" He was quick to add that he was "speaking, of course, of German Jews, and of German Jews only. They constitute an undoubtedly superior group." In so writing, he was both demonstrating his old prejudice against Eastern European Jews—who, he charged, tended toward "radicalism"— and taking advantage of a chance to show up his old enemy Roosevelt. The president, he wrote, "is sorry for the Jews, but unwilling to do anything . . . that might cause him political inconvenience at home." For once, Mencken was seizing the high moral ground.

The next month he devoted another column to the plight of European Jews—and in his diary noted the beginnings of a "violent anti-Semitic movement . . . in New York." But at the same time he could not be dissuaded from his earlier belief that "the more extreme types of kikes," with their "incessant clamor," were largely responsible for that anti-Semitism. Even his "friendly" pieces in the *Evening Sun*, he reported, had been met with protests that he was not friendly enough. "I wash my hands of them," he wrote a Sunpapers colleague. Or, as he wrote in his private memoirs, he "resolved to write nothing more about the Jews, no matter how poignant their sufferings." That resolve, to a great extent, he would keep.

Something else was undoubtedly at work during late 1938 and early 1939 in Mencken's charges of ingratitude by Jews, although he did not mention it at all in letters to friends or in his diary. In December 1938, within a month of his two columns, his former Jewish assistant Charles Angoff—rumors of whose disloyalty had reached him for the past two or three years—published in *The North American Review* a long piece, "Mencken Twilight," in which he maintained that Mencken's reputation, always inflated, was now altogether devalued. According to Angoff, Mencken was widely held in "disrespect," if he was considered at all.

Angoff devoted little time to what he believed to be Mencken's anti-Semitism—that would come later—although he did at one point accuse him of endorsing some of Hitler's attitudes toward Jews and referred to his "strange complacence toward the Nazis." For now Angoff was content to bring other charges that to Mencken must have seemed at least as grievous. Mencken, he maintained, was deficient as literary critic, social commentator, philologist, political theorist, and economist; he succeeded, Angoff added, only as a daily newspaperman. His attack was indeed harsh, but even more disturbing, it was written in a tone of condescension: Angoff professed regret that Mencken's powers had declined and that many of his old friends had stopped seeing him. After lamenting the condition of his old boss, Angoff had added, somewhat unctuously, that he still felt "friendly toward Mencken."

Angoff's feelings, of course, were anything but that. For years he had chafed under Mencken's control, had resented being described as "Mencken's slave," but for years he had held his fire. He had done such a good job of hiding his anger, at least through the mid-1930s, that Mencken in various letters to Knopf, Henry Hazlitt, Phil Goodman, and Joseph Wood Krutch of *The Nation* had praised him as "a really superb managing editor" and "intelligent" worker, and he had recommended Angoff "unreservedly" to his successor, Hazlitt: "He works hard [and] is completely loyal." Although he had felt Angoff lacked the "ideas" to be *Mercury* editor in chief and had disapproved of both his performance and his leftist politics when he had briefly risen to that position in 1934, he had continued to speak of Angoff's diligence and "loyalty" even after that time.

It is little wonder, then, that he was shocked by the *North American Review* essay. Although he had known since 1935 that his old assistant did not feel as warmly toward him and toward Knopf as he once had, he had no idea of the extent of Angoff's resentment until "Mencken Twilight" was published. When it did appear, to some fanfare, his friends—Knopf and Lawrence Spivak among them—leaped to Mencken's defense, pointing out Angoff's long-held jealousy, and Mencken himself tried to laugh off the attack. Angoff was "a poor fish consumed by gigantic ambitions," he wrote one friend, "a caboose with locomotive delusions," he wrote another. To still another he explained that Angoff had "developed a violent hate of both Alfred [Knopf] and me and howls against us all over New York." But the treachery by his once-faithful lieutenant, on top of the other charges of anti-Semitism and general benightedness brought against him during the past year or two, must have hurt more than he acknowledged. Worst of all, given his own doubts about his reputation in 1939, he might have wondered if Angoff might have written, with only slight exaggeration, what many others were thinking—that he was, indeed, finished.

———※———

In one particular in his essay, Angoff was certainly correct: Mencken was worrying excessively about his health in 1939, and to an even greater degree than in the preceding two years. Among other findings of Ben Baker during his 1938 hospital stay—entered into Baker's report of May 1938—had been "arteriosclerosis . . . questionable arteriosclerotic heart-disease." Although Mencken had returned from Germany feeling somewhat better, he had soon found himself feeling "rocky" again, "in the dumps," unable to do any sustained work through the autumn and early winter of 1938. His specific complaints often seemed to be relatively minor—a "severe belly-ache" at one point, a throat infection at another, the old indignity of hemorrhoids, which drove him to the Johns Hopkins for further surgery—and in letters to friends he managed to be philosophical about his sufferings. "The plain truth is that I live a very unhealthy life, with almost no exercise, and an enormous mass of hard desk work," he wrote Oscar Levy. Further, "My belief is that every man after fifty-five is always ill more or less."

He could not be as philosophical about an event the next summer. As he walked down Baltimore Street on a hot July day, he felt what he later described as a numbness at the back of his head, followed by a tingling on the left side of his face and in the fingertips of his left hand. When the tingling continued the following morning, he saw Baker, who immediately ordered him to the hospital. After a thorough examination Baker could find no evidence of a hemorrhage but nonetheless entered into his diagnosis the ominous words "cerebral arteriosclerosis . . . paresthesia of left face and left arm, due to thrombosis." It was a "spastic cerebral episode," Mencken recorded in his diary. He had suffered his first stroke.

He remained in the Johns Hopkins Hospital a little more than a week, soon feeling better but still finding himself very much alarmed. In letters to friends he announced his hospitalization, but in several cases he added, "Please say nothing about this. . . . I don't want the report to get out that I am seriously ill." To several friends he reported that he was just "laid up . . . for minor repairs," and with Gertrude he avoided the truth altogether: "My sinuses have been acting badly of late, and Baker has clapped me into the Johns Hopkins."

Shortly after he left the hospital, Mencken went to Roaring Gap to visit the Haneses and recuperate in the cool Carolina mountain air. He returned to Baltimore in mid-August feeling somewhat better but "still wobbly." For the first time ever he was "really disabled," he wrote a friend. "I believe that I'll have to look forward to being disabled more or less for the rest of my life." It was hardly that bad, but later, in his diary, Mencken always dated his physical decline from that minor stroke in July 1939. Not only had Baker diagnosed the "cerebral episode," but he had found some "heart symptoms" as well. He did not tell Mencken precisely what those symptoms were, but the patient assumed the worst: "This is an incurable condition, and I can only look forward to its gradual worsening. Thus my life-long feeling that I would probably not live much beyond sixty appears to have been well-grounded."

Fearing, then, that he was "deteriorating steadily," Mencken turned with renewed determination to a project that had already engaged him for two or three years. Within a year of Sara's death, in fact, he had begun the task of arranging and organizing his records, a task he undertook with such vigor that Henry Miller wrote him from Paris in December 1936 that he seemed "to be putting your things in order, as though preparing for the end."

He had always saved compulsively, everything from hotel receipts and menus to fingerprints, old driver's licenses, and scraps of hand-written notes; the same impulse that had driven him to record every-thing had driven him to preserve almost everything as well. He also had access to the thousands of articles sent him by his clipping service over the past thirty-five years, as well as a separate scrapbook made up of references to himself in books he had read between 1930 and 1936. In 1937 he had brought together these scrapbooks, had written prefaces for collected typescripts of his early fiction and early plays, had produced a lengthy account of the 1926 "Hatrack" case, and had begun numerous other endeavors. In that year alone his bills for mounting and binding his records had come to $2,700, and in 1938 he had sent eighty-nine bound volumes to the Enoch Pratt Free Library.

In particular, he had begun to organize family materials. He wrote to dozens of relatives, close and distant, intending to put together a record, as he wrote Mary Mencken, that would stand "as a perpetual memorial to a patriotic and Christian family" after he himself "be-came an angel." He cut the registry of births and deaths out of the old family Bible, put the registry into one of the volumes to be bound, and consigned the rest of the Bible to the flames; it had been in childhood, he wrote Gertrude, "a nuisance." Making his way through old bills and receipts, he located in one stack of old material the address of his birthplace on Lexington Street. After learning from city officials the present house number, he went in search of his first home. He found a "pleasant little three-story house, directly opposite a slum area that is being cleared off under the Federal housing scheme." The black owner, "a very intelligent and decent fellow," was working on the house.

The retrospective mood, heavy upon Mencken in 1938 and 1939, took forms other than the preparation of records for the Enoch Pratt. Shortly after Sara's death and as soon as *The American Language* was out of the way, he had begun to contemplate a book about his "early nonage" on Hollins Street. The subject, in fact, had interested him long before that—as early as the 1920s, when he had written Phil Goodman about old times on Hollins Street, had included a long section about boyhood and schooldays in his autobiographical notes, and had written columns for the *Evening Sun* on his early years.

In January 1936 he had sent to *The New Yorker* a light essay, "The Ordeal of a Philosopher," that recounted his happy encounters with the black inhabitants of the alley behind Hollins Street. When *The New Yorker,* which published the piece in April, wanted more, he had obliged with "Innocence in a Wicked World," a sketch of Aunt Sophie, an ancient black woman who specialized in attending funerals all over West Baltimore. In an autobiographical statement in 1936 he had expressed a desire to do an entire volume "about my early youth—say from the dawn of consciousness to adolescence," and in 1937 he had written numerous friends that he hoped to get to work soon on a book to be entitled *Happy Days.*

Although it was the book he wanted to do, it was not at first the book he believed he should do next. For a time, he wrote Jim Tully, he fully intended to turn to the long-delayed "Advice to Young Men." He had now accumulated "forty or fifty tons of notes" for that work, but he kept postponing its writing, first in 1937, then again in 1938, then—in 1939—for good. He was no longer in the mood for a book that, however light in tone, still sounded like a successor to Ben Franklin's *Autobiography* and *Essays to Do Good.* Reminiscing, in any case, was more in his line than advising, Mark Twain more to his taste than Franklin. Thus he put aside his "Advice," took up *Happy Days* as a "private pleasure," and plunged more happily into the writing of a book than he ever had before.

Mark Twain, indeed, was on his mind as he began his own *Tom Sawyer.* "It will be a pleasure to meet him in Hell," he had written a friend the year after Sara's death, and as he neared his sixties, seeing death and decay all around him and reflecting cynically on the vanity of human wishes, he must have again identified at some level with his old hero, who had experienced many of the same anxieties at the same point in *his* life. Thus, Mencken too would find release from the concerns of the moment by writing of childhood; he too would "mainly" tell the truth but throw in a few "stretchers"; he would depict a life even more innocent than Samuel Clemens' Hannibal days of the 1840s. *Happy Days*, he wrote, would be devoid of any "psychological, sociological or politico-economic significance," indeed "of any purpose save to entertain." He could have said, with Mark Twain in his "notice" at the beginning of *Huckleberry Finn*, that "persons attempting to find a moral in it will be banished."

It is no accident that Mencken had begun to write the sketches that would lead to *Happy Days* just at the moment in 1936 when he determined to return to Hollins Street or that his imagination was stimulated all the more once he actually came back. Coming home, in one respect, served the purpose that returning to the Mississippi had served for the middle-aged Samuel Clemens. It had brought back a flood of memories, in Mencken's case tied to house and garden and back alley and Union Square across the way. It is idle to speculate whether *Happy Days* would have been written at all if Mencken had remained at Cathedral Street. In fact, he had mentioned in a letter to a friend three months before Sara's death "a book of reminiscences," whether about childhood or not he did not say. But it is almost certain that the book would not have taken the shape it did, would not have been nearly so rich and full, if he had not come home early in 1936.

Even so, because of delays of various sorts he did not get down to writing in earnest until early 1939, just after he had recovered from his self-diagnosed "malaise" of 1938; and after a burst of writing during the first half of the year, he was again interrupted by the slight stroke in July. Despite his health concerns, he was able to finish the final chapters in August and September, working partly in Baltimore and partly at the Haneses' retreat at Roaring Gap.

He was happy indeed with what he had wrought in his impressions of his first eleven years. "I have made a reasonably honest effort to stick to the cardinal facts," he wrote in the preface to *Happy Days*, although no one was better aware than he of "the fallibility of human recollection." In his narrative, he insisted, he would depart from the "current fashion" of describing unhappy and disadvantaged childhoods; if, in fact, he had his life to live over again, he would not want any other birthplace, parents, or education. Thus he included in his book some twenty essays, totaling exactly 313 pages (the number "somewhat upset" him at first), on school, play, the "rural delights" of Ellicott City, the Hollins Street Gang, the pleasures of reading, his attempts at athletics, and his early interest in newspapers. Throughout the tone was affectionate, nostalgic, good-humored. Mencken was writing a particularly concrete form of social history and at the same time indulging himself in his memories of a past that seemed far better than the present.

He devoted one chapter of *Happy Days* to his father, whom he portrayed as a man who never borrowed a nickel, divided "all mankind . . . into two great races—those who paid their bills and those who didn't"—and rarely worked after lunch, preferring to attend Orioles baseball games, concoct "hoaxes and canards," or while away the afternoon in a saloon next to his office. In the pages of *Happy Days* he also brought to life a number of other memorable characters of his youth: his Grandfather Mencken, formally dressed, somewhat remote, his "bald head [rising] in a Shakespearean dome," exercising dictatorial control over the family; his German schoolmaster, "a virtuoso with the rattan, [choosing] his tool for a . . . caning with apparent care"; another teacher, "greatly given to scenting himself with *Kölnischewasser*"—a "powerful aroma [that] served admirably as a disinfectant"—and preaching the virtues of an eight-hour workday, much to the displeasure of August Mencken; and old Wesley, the alley metaphysician who had answers "to all the . . . great riddles of the universe." Mencken captured the Baltimore of his youth, a paradise on the "immense protein factory of Chesapeake Bay," which offered up hard crabs "at least eight inches in length . . . and with snow-white meat almost as firm as soap." And he described at length the "larval stage" of the reader and writer he was to become, the "domain of new and gorgeous wonders" to which *The Adventures of Huckleberry Finn* had introduced him.

If the reception given *The American Language* in 1936 began the resurrection of his reputation, *Happy Days* helped to complete the job. The reviews in early 1940 were almost unanimous in their praise, sales from the first five months totaled nearly 10,000 copies, and Mencken, urged by *The New Yorker* to undertake more sketches, immediately began work on a second volume of reminiscences, this one dealing with his days as a young newspaperman in Baltimore. After writing a few chapters of *Newspaper Days* in the early spring of 1940, he put the book aside for a time, returned to it early the next year, and, writing as much as three thousand words a day, finished it in June 1941.

Again, what he had written had been a labor of love, and he was pleased with the result. In reminiscing, he had relived those early days on the *Herald* as police and City Hall reporter, theater critic, and Sunday editor. He had recalled his heroic role in reporting the great Baltimore fire, had included accounts of his first voyage to Jamaica in 1900 and his trip to cover the aftermath of the 1901 Jacksonville fire, and had recounted (in his classic "A Girl from Red Lion, P.A.") his part in saving a fallen farm girl from a life of prostitution. The rosy-cheeked young woman, it seems, with her "air of blooming innocence, almost like that of a cavorting lamb," had shown up in Baltimore early one morning, had been taken to the "high-toned studio of Miss Nellie d'Alembert, at that time one of the leaders of her profession in Baltimore," and Miss Nellie had summoned Mencken to hear the girl's story. Having been deflowered by her beau back home, the farm girl "of four-square Pennsylvania Dutch stock" thought she had no option but to take to a life of shame. Mencken and a colleague convinced her otherwise, paid her passage back to Red Lion, and sent her on her way.

What Mencken captured, most of all, in *Newspaper Days* was the exciting life of the Baltimore streets—cops and whores and colorful characters—and, just as exciting, the lively inhabitants of the old *Herald* newsroom and composing room before reporters and printers came to take themselves too seriously. He wrote of what he called "The Days of the Giants," that time between 1900 and 1903 when men could drink more, eat more, and live more vigorously than at any time since, although in fact, as he himself realized in part, it had only *seemed* that way: "I was young, goatish and full of an innocent delight in the world," and life was "one continuous, unrelenting, almost delirious moment." If *Happy Days* had been Mencken's *Tom Sawyer*, *Newspaper Days* was his *Life on the Mississippi*, the story of his apprenticeship to more than a trade, an introduction to a world that, just as surely as Samuel Clemens' riverboats, was full of wise mentors, delightful frauds, and bogus nobility.

Mencken viewed the *Newspaper Days* page proofs, as he had those of *Happy Days,* with a combination of affection and alarm; again he discovered to his "consternation" that the last page was 313, "which reads 13 both ways." His "long-standing suspicion about 13" suggested that he "either cut the book to 312 pages or expand it to 314." In fact, he did neither, decided instead that it was truly "extraordinary" that he had made the books exactly the same length, and trusted that *Newspaper Days* would meet with the luck of its predecessor. He was not disappointed.

The familiar essays in the two *Days* books, covering large segments of his life from birth to his mid-twenties, were "strictly genre painting," as his colleague Gerald Johnson remarked, but genre painting with certain details omitted. It was obvious to Mencken's readers that *Happy Days* had concluded not long before his eleventh birthday and that *Newspaper Days* had picked up again when he was eighteen—and thus that he had omitted what he himself called in the preface to *Happy Days* "the terrible teens," a time when life began to grow much more complicated.

Just how much more complicated he did not explore, or even suggest, in the published *Days* books, but he gave some hint of a darker side of childhood in another record he compiled shortly afterward, put away, and ordered locked up until twenty-five years after his death. These "Additions" to the *Days* books were made up of both leftover material from the published volumes—innocent facts such as the names of all Baltimore breweries in the 1880s and a list of some three dozen shops near Hollins Street—and more sensitive information that would have seriously altered the tone of the two volumes. As mentioned earlier, the picture Mencken painted in *Happy Days* of his father as genial jokester was somewhat at variance with information he included in the "Additions"—of a father who had rigid expectations for his eldest son and enforced them in a dictatorial manner. We have also seen that, in the published *Days* books, he concealed both his deep resentment of his father's control and his own fleeting thoughts of suicide in his teens. There are, as well, other aspects of the "Additions" to *Happy Days* and *Newspaper Days* that broke in upon the idyllic past Mencken was intent upon recapturing and brought him back to a more demanding present.

Among other things, in the "Additions" Mencken revealed the

unhappy fate of many of the companions of his youth, particularly his five next-door cousins. Of Uncle Henry's three daughters, we learn, one moved to Cleveland and made a "dreadful mess" of her life; the second made an unfortunate marriage and had a hard life as well; and the third married a Catholic and became "a convert herself." Of his uncle's two sons, one—"stupid and indolent . . . full of curious eccentricities"—married a woman who became a Seventh-Day Adventist, and the other, Arthur, went west to learn mining and froze to death in a hunting accident in Idaho. When Uncle Henry deemed Arthur's widow unfit to bring up her two children, he "kidnapped" them and brought them into his home.

"I often wonder what my grandfather Mencken would have said if he could have been brought back from Hell," Mencken wrote in the "Additions" to *Happy Days:* one Catholic, one Seventh-Day Adventist, one Methodist, and the other two, in Mencken's estimation, fallen on hard times. He must have wondered as well what his grandfather Abhau would have thought if he too could have returned and seen those relatives whom he had taken young Henry Mencken to visit in 1891. Mencken had concluded *Happy Days* with his account of that visit to the prosperous farm of his Ohio cousins, the Almroths. He had marveled at their hospitality, their happiness, and the plenitude of their table—the "enormous country dinners and suppers, with their pyramids of fried chicken and their huge platters of white home-cured hog-meat." But now, nearly forty years later, he discovered that the Almroths had lost the family farm and that "the lovely Mary [Almroth] of 1891" had led a "hard and dismal life." What had happened, Mencken asked himself in his "Additions"?

> Was it the disabling of the wife and mother in 1912, followed by her death in 1915, that started the family downhill? Or did its fate simply offer one more example of the curious degeneration that has overtaken so many families of German immigrants in the United States? Certainly it would be impossible to imagine a sharper contrast than that between the competence, hopefulness and security that I saw in 1891 and the black despair visible in poor Mary [at present]. America, alas, is not always kind.

It was impossible, then, even in writing about his childhood, for Mencken to escape the darkness altogether, but at least he could

433

exercise over that earlier world a degree of control that was forbidden him as he viewed events in 1940 and 1941. Since September 1, 1939, when Hitler's army had invaded Poland, he had been forced to return to a version of that siege mentality that he had adopted during much of the First World War. At first, indeed, he had seen the situation in 1939 as nearly a reenactment of the early days of World War I. "We are going through the bogus neutrality of Wilson all over again," he had written a friend in Berlin. "The situation, indeed, is worse than it was in 1916."

At the beginning of the war he had been tempted, if only briefly, by several offers to go abroad as a correspondent. "If I were younger," he had written Ezra Pound in November 1939, "I'd be in Berlin even now." He had hesitated to go because of his health, he had told Pound—whom he had earlier proposed (unsuccessfully) as a *Sun* foreign correspondent. But the following month he had written Pound that he was "still hoping to see you in Italy before very long," whether as a correspondent or not he did not say.

He did not reach Europe in any capacity but rather stayed home, continued to write (for the time being) for the Sunpapers, and prepared himself, as he wrote several friends, for the grand spectacle to come. His letters during the weeks after the German invasion had echoed more loudly those sentiments he had expressed in 1938, that combination of comic detachment and outright callousness. "The war seems to me to be a great show," he had written Lillian Gish, "and I am hollering against the English as usual." "I enjoyed the last war," he had written his sister two weeks earlier, "and I'll probably enjoy this one even more." The war gave him "a great kick," he had written another friend; it promised to be "swell . . . I only hope that I live long enough to see the end of it." He simply could not "work up much indignation against the slaughter," he had explained to a priest with whom he was friendly. "To be sure, it is no fun to be wounded, but after all most wounds are not serious. The dead die happy and the living rejoice."

With the beginning of war and the prospect of another German contest with England, Mencken's view of Hitler had also changed somewhat—or rather, the focus of that view had shifted. Earlier he had judged Hitler altogether in a German context and had found him, in comparison to German alternatives, a ranting demagogue, a joke. As he had often said, he himself preferred a restoration of the monarchy. But now Germany was at war with Poland, then immediately afterward at war with England, and he felt he had no choice but to support Germany, Hitler or no Hitler. He had instructed his "chaplain . . . to pray for Hitler," he had written Marcella du Pont the week after the war began, and the same day, in a more serious vein, he had written another friend that "the preponderance of logic" was on Hitler's side in his invasion of Poland. He still believed Hitler to be "a demagogue of a peculiarly exaggerated and obnoxious sort" but also held that Germany's leader "should be free to police his own back alleys [Czechoslovakia and Poland] without any interference from the English." It would "delight" him, Mencken wrote a friend in Berlin, "to see Hitler bring the English hypocrites to their knees."

As the British stepped up their propaganda offensive—the "holy crusade against Hitler"—he grew increasingly sympathetic to the German cause. He joked in a letter to Lillian Gish that he hoped Hitler would soon "be marching his guns down Oxford Street," but he wrote more seriously to James T. Farrell, "It is my belief that if Hitler landed on the English coast tomorrow thousands of Englishmen would cheer him. . . . As a matter of fact, practically every civilized Englishman that I know is violently anti-democratic." He believed, he wrote Farrell on another occasion, that "Hitler's history will follow that of Bonaparte's—that is to say, he will be denounced violently as a moral leper while he lives but after his death judgment will be revised and he will come to be a sort of hero." There was another reason as well—his memories of World War I—for his support of Germany against England. "I can't get away from the fact that [Hitler] is giving the English a just and sufficient reward for their inhuman attitude in 1918," he was to write a friend once the battle between England and Germany was under way. "Every time a bomb falls on London I think of the German children who starved after the Armistice."

In the years after 1939, then, his hatred of England partially blinded Mencken to the reality of Hitler. He was blinded as well because of his continued abhorrence of Roosevelt, to whom he now objected on grounds of foreign as well as domestic policy. The week the European war began, he had written Marcella du Pont that "as long as Roosevelt and [Cordell] Hull [were] whooping against [Hitler] I must give him a hand." The next year he had concluded that Hitler, though still "a complete scoundrel," was not "appreciably

435

worse" than FDR and British Prime Minister Neville Chamberlain. The Führer, in fact, was "more intelligent" than Chamberlain, "more honest" than FDR.

From the beginning Mencken had been convinced that Roosevelt was a "violent Anglomaniac" who would "horn the United States into the war." He would do so to ensure a third term, if for no other reason, and it was to prevent such an eventuality that Mencken met in 1939 and early 1940 with leading Republicans—Wendell Willkie, Thomas Dewey, and Robert Taft—who were possible presidential challengers. He was not impressed with any of them: Taft lacked force; Dewey had energy but an inadequate grasp of the problems facing the nation; and Willkie, whom he met for dinner in New York, he found charming but something of a New Dealer and Anglophile himself. Mencken covered both conventions the summer of 1940 and traveled with Willkie's "funeral train" during the final campaign, but he knew from the beginning that the Republican candidate was doomed. Finally, he did not even seem to care. After all, Roosevelt, while a "fraud from snout to tail" and a man who would "wreck the country," would nonetheless put on a "magnificent show." As for the war, he wrote Ellen Glasgow, it too would be "a grand show."

If, in 1940, Mencken felt comfortable with his own position on the war, the Sunpapers certainly did not. As in 1915 and 1916, his anti-British sentiments disturbed numerous readers and caused problems for the newspapers. He himself was equally upset with the thinking of Paul Patterson and his Sunpapers colleagues. From 1937 on he had suspected that Patterson sided with John Owens and his "wholly pro-English view of the international situation," and in September 1939, after a long talk with Patterson, he was convinced of that. Throughout 1940 he stewed, and in November 1940 he devoted three pages in his diary to a denunciation of the newspaper and its "idiotic" editorials on the war. Patterson, he said, was "completely under the spell of the English," and nearly all the editorial writers as well were "Anglomaniacs." John Owens was "naive and prejudiced" and Gerald Johnson "notably stupid," with the mind of a "second-rate Southerner." Other writers were even worse.

In January 1941, finding that he could "no longer endure the nauseous atmosphere of the *Sunday Sun* editorial page," Mencken determined to resign his position. He met with Patterson, who protested his decision, then convinced him that if he must give up writing, he must at least remain on the newspaper's board of directors and must continue to serve the papers in labor negotiations and other areas. When he requested a cut in salary, Patterson initially protested, then at last agreed. As far as he stood with the Sunpapers, Mencken was now a businessman, not a writer or editor. His last contribution to the *Sunday Sun* editorial page came on February 2, 1941. It charged Roosevelt with doing all he could to bring the United States into the war.

"The [Sunpapers] brethren and I are still on the best of terms," he had written Lillian Gish just before his last column, but that was not altogether true. In fact, as in World War I—though perhaps not to the same extent—his relations with old friends were very much affected by his view of events in Europe. He was trapped by an anti-British and pro-German position he was too proud to abandon, and he could not fully respect other men, especially Gerald Johnson and the two Owenses, who did not share that position.

As he had in World War I, he preferred silence, and not only where the Sunpapers were concerned. Earlier he had declined Lawrence Spivak's offer to write an essay for *The American Mercury* "in defense of the German people"—he continued to dislike German "professional patriots" as much as American ones—and now he declined offers from several other magazines and newspapers as well. Despite everything, what institutional loyalty he had still belonged to the Sunpapers. He attended board meetings (on at least one occasion speaking up on behalf of women employees who he felt were receiving "starvation wages"), and, despite his public silence, he continued in private to denounce Patterson and his support of the "Roosevelt war."

Not only had Mencken lost all faith in his newspaper colleagues in 1940 and 1941, but it appeared to him that the rest of his world was little better. His literary reputation may have made a comeback with the reception given *Happy Days*, but on all other fronts he saw nothing but woe: his enemies were in the ascendancy, his friends and relatives ill and dying, and his own health none too good. The unexpected death at age sixty-one of his closest Baltimore friend, Raymond Pearl, was a great blow to him. There was no one, he wrote Dorothy Hergesheimer, that he "saw more of, or had more confidence in," no one who would take Pearl's place. He was shaken the same year by Phil Goodman's death at age fifty-five; although he and

Goodman had not spoken since their falling out over Germany in 1934, he had not forgotten that for several years Goodman had been his closest companion. Following on the heels of those deaths was that of his old friend Max Brödel. "I had sat beside Max every Saturday night for exactly thirty years," Mencken wrote a mutual friend, "and we were naturally on the most intimate terms." His death was a "stupendous blow."

His old newspaper friends seemed to be dropping off at an alarming rate as well—no fewer than four in the five months after Brödel's death—and Mencken's own family, with its multiplicity of troubles, was faring no better. Uncle Henry had died in late 1939 and had been brought back to Baltimore for burial near Mencken's parents in Loudon Park Cemetery. Shortly afterward, Mencken's sister-in-law, Mary, whom he had attended off and on for more than twenty years of medical trips to Baltimore, died of a heart attack in Pennsylvania. He noted the date of her death—October 13—reflected on the deaths on the thirteenth of his father and mother and Sara's death on Friday the thirty-first, and wrote Alfred Knopf, "The family tombstone begins to look bewitched."

Death, however, seemed to be a sweet release when he considered the woes of other family members. His uncle William, in whose home Gertrude lived for a time and whom he himself visited with some regularity, was "virtually . . . a vegetable" after five or six cerebral hemorrhages. Uncle Charlie, crippled his entire life and now in a wheelchair "tranquilly awaiting death," he also visited in the Baltimore Home for Incurables. From other Abhau cousins came equally bad news, reports of illness and hard times.

When Mencken considered the example of the older Abhaus, for once he cursed his luck. As a family they tended to live long and die slowly, enduring years of disability, and he wondered if the same fate were in store for him. In his diary he despaired over his own health, and in letters to certain friends, particularly Hergesheimer, he seemed nearly obsessed with the subject: about all he could hope for was an "easy finish." He complained of a general "wretchedness" and a "malaise" so disabling it seemed "hard to believe it is the effect of arteriosclerosis." He had other complaints—severe throat infections, stomach disorders, sciatica, a sacroiliac sprain, conjunctivitis, and, as always, disabling hay fever, which made him in 1940 and 1941 "more uncomfortable" than he had been for years. In April 1941 the malaise became so severe that he was sent back to the Johns Hopkins Hospital for a lengthy and thorough examination. The diagnosis was the same as before: arteriosclerosis and possible heart disease. He was ordered to Havana for a vacation; there his spirits lifted and he felt, he wrote Patterson, "fairly good again."

It was his inability to write for extended periods that concerned him most. Throughout 1940 and 1941 he was not only completing *Newspaper Days* but also wrapping up an ambitious dictionary of quotations for Knopf. At times, particularly in the winter of 1940–1941, work was almost impossible. Other times he found he was able to work nearly as hard as ever. He was aware of the amount of writing he still wanted to do—in June 1940 he spoke of "definite plans" for "at least a dozen" more books—and increasingly he saw his writing as a battle with time. When he answered dinner invitations with notes such as "I'll be on hand if I am alive," he was at least half serious. In September 1940 he had celebrated his sixtieth birthday "trying to forget it" (as he wrote Gertrude), and as he told Lillian Gish the following year during a particularly bad period, "I feel as if I were 250 years old."

Even those areas of life that might have offered a refuge for other men seemed to bring him more trouble. In May 1941 he staged and paid for his niece, Virginia's, wedding in Baltimore, but he seemed to take little joy in the proceedings. It was not that he disapproved of Virginia's bridegroom—in fact, he rather liked David Morrison, an amiable engineer from a "well-to-do" Pennsylvania family of "substantial" undertakers—but rather that Virginia herself continued to be a disappointment. She was unreliable, often unresponsive to letters, and certainly she lacked the professional ambition that Mencken had once hoped she would have; after considering a department store job, she had gone to work for the telephone company. He would not have gone so far in his displeasure with Virginia as his sister Gertrude did: "I really think I am going to enjoy this wedding. It will be such a relief to see Virginia handed over to another family." But, as he wrote a friend the day after the wedding, "I find as I grow older that I get less and less pleasure out of the society of the young. They simply bore me to death."

He found little more consolation in old friends—those who remained—than he did in family. Hergesheimer, whom he still saw on occasion, he found in a "wretched" condition from arteriosclerosis and diabetes. Edgar Lee Masters, whom he saw in New York in 1941, he found "in a low state mentally and physically." That fall he found Sinclair Lewis "almost ghastly. His face is the dead white of a scar, and he is thin and wizened. . . . He is in a state of mental collapse, not to mention physical decay." And Sara Mayfield, once Sara's close friend and Mencken's great admirer, had been institutionalized in the Sheppard Pratt outside Baltimore—"undoubtedly insane," Mencken feared. When Mayfield wrote him from the Sheppard Pratt asking his assistance in obtaining her release, he declined on the grounds that she needed to remain in the hospital "to be studied." He consented to come out for a visit, although, he wrote a hospital official, it would be "painful" to see her.

He was glad, he wrote Jim Tully, "my own Sara is not here to suffer through" Mayfield's affliction. But he still missed Sara Haardt "constantly," he wrote another friend, and he still marked the anniversary of her death in letters to their friends. On May 31, 1940, the fifth anniversary of that occasion, he even broke his long silence in his diary and reflected at length on her life and death and their marriage. "It is amazing what a deep mark she left upon my life," he observed. "It is a literal fact that I still think of [her] every day of my life, and almost every hour of the day. . . . I can recall no single moment during our years together when I ever had the slightest doubt of our marriage, or wished that it had never been."

At the conclusion of an uncharacteristically personal passage, he reflected further:

> Her ashes are buried at the foot of the grave of my mother, and beside her there is room for mine. Thinking of her, I can well understand the great human yearning that makes for a belief in immortality, but I do not believe in it, and neither did she. We have parted forever, though my ashes will soon be mingling with hers. I'll have her in mind until thought and memory adjourn, but that is all . . . We were happy together, but all beautiful things must end.

Such was the cast of Mencken's mind as he looked backward in the bleak years of 1940 and 1941. He was well aware of the world around him, but he saw little in it or in the future to offer consolation. His 1941 New Year's greeting to numerous friends had been even gloomier than usual: "I predict formally that 1941 will be the worst year the human race has seen since the Black Death." He still professed to have no concerns over the war; "I don't care [who wins]," he wrote an old friend, "as long as it is not England." His greatest fear, he wrote Marcella du Pont, was that if America jumped in "Lüchow's will be closed." Otherwise, he professed to Sinclair Lewis, "I am in the happy position of not caring a damn what happens."

When news came on December 7, 1941, of the Japanese attack on Pearl Harbor—and, the next day, of the American declaration of war—he did not even record the facts in his diary. He had his own run of bad news to record. He duly noted that in December he attended two more funerals of old friends, one of which required his first visit since Sara's death to the funeral home in which her services had been held. He also made note of August's poor health and a "tingling" in his own left hand and foot—"obviously, the first warning of a cerebral episode" that would "finish" him. On Christmas morning he and August went out to Loudon Park Cemetery and laid a wreath on the family tombstone:

> It was the forty-first Christmas since my father's death, the seventeenth since my mother's, the seventh since Sara's, and the second since my sister-in-law Mary's. My mother has begun to recede into the shadows, but Sara is still clearly before me. . . . Nevertheless, I am half glad that she is dead, for the future looks dismal, and 1942 is certain to be the worst year I have ever seen.

Back at Hollins Street he wrote a friend, "I sit quietly in my cell watching the show roar by."

# Chapter 19

# WARTIME

M encken was not surprised by America's entry into World War II; in private, he blamed the Japanese bombing of Pearl Harbor on Roosevelt and "that long series of gross violations of neutrality and other deliberate provocations which finally drove the Japs to . . . attack." As early as his Berlin diary of 1917, in fact, he had foreseen an eventual German-Japanese alliance, a "love affair that Washington had better watch." Ten years later he had also predicted that if "war ever came with Japan," Japanese Americans on the West Coast would suffer greatly: "It will be a felony to so much as hint that the Japs are civilized, or even that they are human." He was uncharacteristically prophetic.

He himself affected disinterest in the war. He had cousins fighting on both sides, those Menckes of Koblenz and Darmstadt with whom he had become acquainted during the 1930s and, closer to home, his favorite American cousin, William C. Abhau. But he continued to view the proceedings from afar as a "grand show." At dinner at the home of Hamilton and Olga Owens he shocked his hosts, who had a son missing in the Pacific, by proclaiming that war, after all, was a great benefit to mankind. He could not remain completely uninvolved, however: he advised Gertrude to take out an insurance policy against war damage in case hostilities should reach the Maryland shores. And he himself was briefly investigated by the FBI, although he may not have known it. After receiving several complaints against

442

him, including a typescript of a newspaper column that may well have been sent to authorities by a Sunpapers colleague, the FBI sent agents to talk to several of his friends and associates, including his physician, Ben Baker. But his earlier acquaintance with J. Edgar Hoover may have helped forestall any further investigation. This time, unlike in World War I, he was not harassed.

Mencken's everyday activities, in fact, were changed little by the American declaration of war. He certainly did not, as an early biographer contended, "[bury] himself in Hollins street with such finality that it seemed doubtful that he would or could ever come out again." In fact, his letters and personal records show that he continued to take an active part in Sunpapers board and stockholders' meetings, continued to represent newspaper management in labor negotiations, traveled to Washington and New York on *Sun* business, and still railed against Patterson about the Sunpapers' position on the war. He was as active as ever in the Saturday Night Club, which still numbered among its members two Jews and a Czech as well as a number of German Americans—although early in the war all of them had agreed that discussion of events in Europe was taboo. Only occasionally did the members slip, and then, according to Louis Cheslock's diary, the transgressors were usually Henry and August Mencken.

All things considered, Mencken wrote Dreiser in 1942, "on the East coast the war seems enormously far away." He was overwhelmed, in any case, with other matters. More friends were dying: he attended at least five funerals, mostly for newspaper friends but one for a member of the old Hollins Street Gang, during the first half of 1942. Such services, he wrote Gertrude, were "coming fast and close together." He himself felt none too well. In April he entered the Johns Hopkins Hospital with a painful throat infection and remained two weeks. Shortly afterward he checked into the Hopkins again, this time for surgery to remove infected throat tissue. His spirits were hardly lifted when, in the fall of 1942, a journalist representing *Reader's Digest* called Hollins Street to inquire as to the date of H. L. Mencken's death. "When I told him that I was still alive," Mencken wrote a friend, "he seemed to be genuinely astonished."

If readers needed proof that he was alive, the appearance in 1942 and 1943 of two more books provided it. His 1,300-page *New Dictionary of Quotations*, a prodigious undertaking of more than 800,000 words and 40,000 separate quotations, was published by Knopf in early 1942. A life's work for any other writer but nearly an after-thought for Mencken, the *Dictionary* received numerous and favorable reviews.

*Heathen Days*, the third and final book in his autobiographical series, appeared early the next year. A collection of twenty personal essays covering a period from 1890 to 1936 and subjects ranging from YMCA memories to the Scopes trial, the work employed the reminiscent and irreverent tone of the earlier *Days* books. Some of Mencken's best travel writing appeared here—descriptions of his 1914 Italian holiday, his 1917 winter voyage to Europe, the 1922 trip to the remote Dutch island where he had interviewed the German crown prince, and his 1934 excursion to the ruins of Carthage and Jerusalem—and much of it was written with the exuberant spirit of Mark Twain's *Innocents Abroad*.

In "A Roman Holiday" he described with great relish the manner in which he and his Baltimore friends Edwin Moffett and A. H. McDannald had managed their audience with the pope: they had ducked into a select group of "pious pilgrims" just off the train from Vienna—"I could well believe it by their smell"—and after a brief course in Vatican etiquette ("Küsst den Ring . . . Nicht die Hand") they had made their way to a modest room where they knelt before Pius X and received his blessing. In "Winter Voyage," his account of his 1917 voyage to Germany, he described with even greater delight the stupendous appetite of "the Walrus," the haughty Russian general whose ability to put away food—at one sitting a leg of veal, at another an entire ham—astounded Mencken. At one breakfast, a rather modest repast by comparison:

> He began with three oranges *au naturel*, followed them with a large plate of oatmeal swimming in cream, topped it with a double order of ham and eggs, and then proceeded to run through all the Danish delicacies on the table—six or eight kinds of smoked fish, as many of sausage, a bowl of pickled pigs' ears, another of spiced lambs' tongues, a large slab of Gjedser cheese, and five or six slices of toasted rye-bread spread with red caviare. . . . When he finished at last a couple of waiters rushed up to help him to his feet, but he shook them off, arose with the dignity of Neptune emerging from the sea, and stalked away in his best parade-ground manner.

In other essays Mencken created or memorialized characters reminiscent of Mark Twain's, primary among them Hoggie Unglebower, who lived in a Baltimore stable, resisting cleanliness and any "effort to denaturize him"—a "magnificent specimen of Natural Man, somehow surviving unscathed every corruption of an effete and pusillanimous civilization"; A. Toxen Worm, "the undisputed king of theatrical press-agents . . . a Dane of circular cross-section, immense appetite, and low humor"; and Abraham Lincoln Herford, boxing promoter, manager of lightweight champion Joe Gans, and announcer of unmatched eloquence and protean humor.

*Heathen Days* lacked the chronological and thematic unity of its predecessors; it was, Mencken wrote in his preface, "simply a series of random reminiscences." Indeed, he had not intended to write the book at all, but since he had several chapters left over from *Newspaper Days* and since Harold Ross of *The New Yorker* had urged him to continue, he had added essays in 1941 and 1942 to complete the work. Although *Heathen Days*, like its predecessors, was well received and sold reasonably well—nearly 10,000 copies in the first few months—Mencken vowed he would write no more books in this vein. He was at work on reminiscence of another sort now.

What had taken up much of his time over the past two years was a work not intended for publication at all, at least not in his lifetime. He had begun "Thirty-Five Years of Newspaper Work" in July 1941 in order to give his version of his activities and observations as a journalist from 1906 to 1941, to name names and assign blame and occasionally to give credit as he could not in *Newspaper Days* or the earlier *Sunpapers of Baltimore*. He had wound up with 1,648 pages of typescript (including appendices) when he completed the job in May 1942. In these pages he included not only a detailed account of his activities in Baltimore as reporter, columnist, editor, and board member of the Sunpapers but also extended accounts of his trips to Germany in 1922 and 1938, his European trip of 1930, his excursion to Tennessee for the Scopes trial, and his coverage of national political conventions from 1912 to 1940.

In his preface he spoke with some justification of "Thirty-Five Years" as a "contribution toward the general history of the country." He had written of adventures that had been to him "a great romance," including the attempt "to make a great newspaper of the

*Sun*." That the attempt, in his opinion, had failed was "no argument," he insisted, "against the men who . . . were responsible for that failure." But in fact he was less than kind in many of his remarks about old friends and colleagues who had declined to heed his counsel and who had departed from the course he himself had set for the newspapers in 1920.

He felt, in 1941, that he had arrived at the point at which he could at last indulge in painful truth telling, or at least in his own version of the truth, because he believed his newspaper career was essentially over. "Once a principal actor in the exhilarating but far from profound or important drama" of the Sunpapers and American journalism in general, he had now "retired to a stage-box, and [become] a spectator of the show which no longer really engrossed" him. He found "little to regret" in his thirty-five years with the Sunpapers: the "game" had been "brisk and amusing while it lasted," but now it was "nearing its foredoomed end" and he would get in his word for posterity. No one would be hurt by his record, he reasoned. The manuscript was destined for the vault of the Enoch Pratt Free Library, not to be opened until 1980 or thirty-five years after his death, whichever date came later. (The release, in fact, would not come until 1991.) "When time has released all confidences and the grave has closed over all tender feelings," he wrote, "my narrative may be useful and even instructive to persons coming after."

Much of his time, in fact, was now occupied by similar projects for subsequent generations. As soon as he completed his newspaper record, he began a detailed record of his career as magazine editor, planning to include an account of his days with *The Smart Set* and *The American Mercury* as well as his experiences as an author. As he turned to "My Life as Author and Editor" he felt a certain sense of urgency. "The time remaining to me is not likely to be long, and so I'll probably never get to the business," he had written in February 1942, and his pessimism over the literary record had grown even more pronounced after he checked into the Johns Hopkins Hospital in May. "Dr. [Charles W.] Wainwright's warning . . . was plain enough," he wrote in his diary. "I may have a stroke at any minute, or the coronary occlusion may fetch me." Thus for the time being he was giving "what energy [he could] muster" to the business of arranging his books and papers. He now doubted whether he would "ever be fit again for so severe a labor" as the private record of his magazine days, but he would make the attempt. He was working under a deadline like none before.

"My Life as Author and Editor" was an even more ambitious undertaking than his newspaper narrative, not in the projected length of the manuscript (in fact, he felt at first that it would be much shorter) but in what he hoped to accomplish. If he lived to finish the work, he was to write in his diary, it would be "the most detailed and heavily documented record that any American writer has ever left behind him." He would tell his own story, but he also planned to paint intimate portraits of Dreiser, Fitzgerald, Hergesheimer, Sinclair Lewis, James Branch Cabell, and numerous other figures whom he had known well. In it he would be, for a change, not only Johnson but Boswell.

When he had first envisioned such a book of reminiscences as early as 1932, he had written a friend that "four-fifths" of the literati with whom he would deal were "insane," by which he meant that, by his own standards, they were self-indulgent and undisciplined. In other letters to Marcella du Pont and James T. Farrell he remarked that he was dealing "very frankly with various geniuses," was including "some rather intimate accounts." He would draw the line at a certain point—"there will be very little about my private life, and next to nothing about women"—but in most regards, he wrote in the preface to the manuscript, he would "deal . . . freely" with close friends and confidants, "depicting them precisely as I saw them. . . . Inevitably there must come a time when confidences no longer run." Indeed, writers, like candidates for public office, "offered themselves for public inspection and invited public approval." This fact "materially conditions the ordinary right to privacy."

Mencken's plan was to begin "My Life as Author and Editor" with his own earliest attempts at verse in 1896 and carry on through the *Smart Set* and *American Mercury* days, and he was able to make greater progress than he had anticipated in the late summer and fall of 1942. Beginning in August, by January 1943 he had written three hundred pages, plus another 250 pages of appendices on Percival Pollard, Frank Harris, and other acquaintances. He would work on his record until July 1943, when he would move on to other projects, not to return to his "Life" until the summer of 1945. He had written enough in 1942 and 1943, however, to convince himself that his magazine record would probably be even longer than his newspaper history—and that, as he had thought in the beginning, it too could not be printed or even seen in his lifetime "or the lifetimes of the persons principally dealt with." It too would be put under lock and key until thirty-five years after his death.

Although Mencken's "Life" and "Thirty-Five Years" took up much of his time in 1942 and 1943, they were hardly his only secret works in progress. His other most revealing manuscript of the early and mid-forties he did not consider a literary work at all, although it was to prove, fifty years later, to be precisely that. The diary he had begun in 1930, then had largely neglected for the three or four years after Sara's death, he returned to during the war with renewed energy and purpose. Devoting large amounts of time to the diary, on certain days he turned out entries of ten to twenty pages—partly, no doubt, as another way to keep busy but even more as another means of ordering existence. Into the diary he now poured nearly everything—his hopes for future books, his deep concern over his health, his dismay at what he perceived to be the decaying state of the nation, the city of Baltimore, his Hollins Street neighborhood, the Mencken family itself. Into his diary, that is, he now entered nearly everything except remarks about the war (save infrequently) and, as will be evident, one or two other subjects he deemed too sensitive to trust to the eyes of his readers even a half century hence.

Into the diary he also packed gossip, rumor, and trivia—that Al Capone was a patient in Baltimore's Union Memorial Hospital, suffering from syphilis and paresis; that Capone's wife felt his table manners had deteriorated in Alcatraz; that Gertrude Stein, while in medical school—he learned from a former Johns Hopkins classmate of hers—was called the Battle-ax; that Dwight Eisenhower—he learned from another well-placed friend—was thought to be having an affair with his driver, Kay Summersby. Into it he entered criticism of wartime beer, censorship, modern literature, modern art—virtually everything *except* himself. As before, he was anything but self-questioning (except about his health) and self-analytical, was very rarely given to the confessional mode, was still as far from such earlier self-doubters as Henry Adams as he could possibly be. Intending to reveal virtually nothing of himself, he nonetheless, in ways he hardly suspected—in his reactions to events, in the often harsh verdicts he passed on others, in prejudices too deep to have been voiced even in those volumes called *Prejudices*—revealed a great deal about himself.

Much of the diary in 1941 and 1942 amounted to a virtual death-watch, particularly after Mencken's stay in the Johns Hopkins Hospital in May 1942. In June he reported rising blood pressure and "signs of further damage to my coronary arteries"; he tired quickly and had been awakened several times by "heart distress." In other entries that summer he reported his general discomfort, and in September he noted the probable "beginning of serious heart trouble." In December, again noting "heart difficulty," rising blood pressure, several sleepless nights, occasional headaches, and tingling on the left side of his face, he concluded, "I begin to deteriorate." His "deterioration continu[ing] apace" the following month, he complained in several entries of the same numbness on his face, pains down his left arm, and occasional spells of dizziness and exhaustion, as well as further "discomfort in the heart region." By late January 1943 he was lamenting that he could work "only under the burden of great discomfort," and in late March he reported that "anything resembling sustained work is now impossible." He felt "unutterly miserable."

He had also begun to have confused and alarming dreams for the first time in his life. "The dreams that wake me," he wrote, "always involve some sort of irrational and futile effort. When I come to consciousness I feel warm and my bed-clothes seem over-heavy . . ." In another entry he reported being awakened on three consecutive nights by "irrational dreams, all full of struggle against fantastic obstacles." He realized that those dreams of struggle and pursuit—such as missing a train (an almost unknown occurrence for him in reality) and running after it frantically—suggested a fear of losing control, even a fear of being neglected and forgotten. The dreams themselves, however, concerned him less than the heart discomfort that accompanied them and that may have been more responsible for his waking than the dreams themselves. "More than once," he reported in March 1943, "I began to believe that my end had come."

It was hardly the deterioration of his health alone of which Mencken complained in his wartime diary; nearly as disturbing was the deterioration of his street, his neighborhood, and his city, the world he observed and in which he moved. In 1936 he had written, with great exaggeration, to Marcella du Pont, "My house is in the heart of the slums." By late 1941 he was able to write with more conviction:

> The Hollins street neighborhood is slowly going downhill, and in the course of time it is bound to be a slum. Filthy poor whites from Appalachia and the Southern tidewater are already living in the 1600 and 1700 blocks, and their foul children and dogs swarm in Union Square. When I was a boy the square was very well kept, and no child thought of trampling the lawns, but now the brats of the Okeys dig them up and pull the shrubs to pieces. When the last Mencken clears out of 1524 the house will have to be sold, and in a little while all the fittings that we have put in during the past thirty years will be ruined—the mahogany doors, the parquette floors, the tiled baths . . .

As the movement into the Hollins Street neighborhood of poor southern whites, drawn to Baltimore in search of jobs, continued during the war years, he grew more and more distressed. The southern and Appalachian whites he saw as a nearly foreign species, as alien as Swift's yahoos, and in his diary as well as in letters to friends he held forth with Swiftian disdain on the specifics of their degradation. They were "anthropoids," "vermin," "true savages," and the "fantastic specimens" of "oakies, lintheads [and] hill-billies . . . swarmed into Baltimore" like so many locusts. The women were "squatty and hideous creatures . . . filthy, slatternly," the men "shabby, ill-fed," "thin and evil-looking," the children equally hideous and filthy, "covered with head and body lice." None, he charged, had any regard for order or beauty: "Some instinct forces them to destroy every green thing." The men were given to alcohol and crime, the women to "carousing" and sloth, and "only a rare linthead girl remains a virgin after the age of twelve. Her deflowering, in fact, is usually performed by her brothers . . . [or] father." In sum, Mencken believed his new neighbors in and around Union Square "live[d] like animals, and [were] next-door to animals in their habits and ideas."

Thus he railed with a savage eloquence, all the more impassioned because these were the "pure Anglo-Saxons" of whom the South had always boasted and whom he himself had ridiculed and excoriated in the 1920s. He no longer publicly denounced them, at least not often; for that matter he now rarely denounced, in public, any group at length. But those readers were greatly mistaken who assumed that the absence of a public fury, along with the publication of the nostalgic *Days* books and the *New Yorker* essays, meant that Mencken had mellowed. He had only gone underground.

He was not much kinder, only less colorful, in the diary entries devoted to other neighbors he had known for much longer. On two or three occasions he held forth at length on his next-door neighbors, the Fortenbaughs, their barking dog, and their general degeneration. "Morons," "poor simpletons" of "very low mentality"—despite the fact that they had once been "wealthy Germans"—they had lived beside the Menckens for nearly fifty years, leading "hollow" lives, "without intelligence, information or taste." "The total amount of intelligence" in the family, he added, "would be hardly enough to outfit a street-car conductor." Their yard was "gradually falling into decay," their house had seen no improvements in years: "It would be impossible to find three people more completely incompetent and useless. They haven't even the virtue of being vicious. They are simply vacuums." The elderly maiden sister, Mencken noted at her death, had lived a life almost as "insignificant . . . as the life of her dog."

Such dismissals were hardly unusual. In his diary Mencken often moved from general observation into brief biographies of totally obscure but representative families whose lives fell short of even quiet desperation. He pondered the insignificance of such lives and their decline, finally, into anonymity. Such outbursts, given his low regard for the mass of humanity, were hardly surprising. More dismaying but hardly surprising either, given his dismissal of many of his Sunpapers associates in "Thirty-Five Years of Newspaper Work," were his judgments on those old newspaper friends.

Much of the diary, indeed, was devoted to the Sunpapers, entries describing their operation, their editorial policy, and his own role— now that he was no longer a writer—as board member, stockholder, labor negotiator, and adviser to Paul Patterson. Mencken's impressions of his colleagues recorded in his diary were, if anything, even more severe than those expressed in the secret "Thirty-Five

Years"—impressions that, at the very least, would have shocked those associates with whom, to all appearances, he carried on friendly relations.

His closest friend on the newspaper was Paul Patterson, but in the diary he charged the head of the Sunpapers with a lack of courage and vision, a deep suspicion "of men of ideas," and primary responsibility for what he believed to be the newspapers' decline into mediocrity. With Hamilton Owens, editor of the morning *Sun*, he also seemed on the best of terms, seeing Owens socially, even extending to him a "standing pass" to the Saturday Night Club. Yet in the diary he described Owens, altogether unfairly, as "a time-server with no more principle in him than a privy-rat." John Owens, editor in chief of the Sunpapers, was even worse, "a country evangelist" who wrote "idiotic" editorials. Even as Owens lay ill in September 1942 with what Mencken believed at the time was a fatal brain tumor, he maintained in his diary, "I have seldom had close contact with a more ignorant man, or a more bigoted."

If Mencken's remarks on those colleagues were harsh, his references in the diary to Gerald Johnson—the best known nationally, save Mencken, of the *Sun* writers and soon to become renowned as the other sage of Baltimore—were even harsher and equally surprising. Mencken had been responsible for Johnson's coming to the Sunpapers from North Carolina in 1926; "the best editorial writer in the south," he had called him, and he had continued to extol Johnson throughout the 1920s. Even in the 1940s he had seemed to remain friendly, almost always attending Johnson's small Christmas parties on Bolton Street and generally seeming to enjoy his company. The two men were "always good friends," August Mencken noted long after his brother's death, and Johnson, in numerous letters, interviews, and essays, assumed the same thing. Yet in his diary, after the late 1930s, Mencken was severely critical of Johnson. Several times he spoke of his colleague's "deteriorating skills" as a writer and described him as having been "practically useless" from the mid-1930s on. In 1943, after he received the "exhilarating news" that Johnson had resigned to undertake more profitable writing projects, Mencken noted in his diary: "He has become more and more the Southern cracker—dogmatic, unreliable, and incapable of learning anything new."

What Johnson had become, in fact, was a fervent New Dealer. And what had happened in the cases of Patterson and the Owenses was similar. Hamilton Owens had supported the New Deal; John Owens had declared himself fervently for England and against Germany; and Patterson "succumbed to Roosevelt's war-mongering," refused to "do anything to embarrass Roosevelt," and finally, Mencken insisted, would "believe anything" the English say. Johnson's "deterioration" he dated from 1933, exactly the beginning of the New Deal, and Patterson's from the moment "he began to let the English take him into camp." A. S. Abell board chairman Harry Black, of whom he had once been exceedingly fond, had also grown increasingly "banal" as he grew "more and more English." Mencken's position was clear: to be politically incorrect by his standards, particularly during these days in which he felt himself on the defensive, was to be personally deficient.

Although he would have shocked his friends with such harsh pronouncements, his diary entries on other subjects, particularly Jews, would hardly have surprised those critics who had already labeled him as generally misanthropic and, in particular, anti-Semitic. During the war years his remarks, rather than softening as the fate of European Jews, at least in its broad outlines, began to be known, in fact became more rigid. The man who in the mid-thirties had spoken with real compassion of the plight of European Jews, who had denounced anti-Semitism in others and had himself given a good deal of time and effort working for the immigration of a number of Jews, now lapsed into what by all appearances was indeed anti-Semitism.

There were perhaps two primary reasons for such a development. The first was the war itself; even more German in allegiance than before, Mencken responded to reports of Nazi atrocities not so much with disbelief as with a *suspension* of belief. He became increasingly irritated by those messengers, usually Jewish, who were telling the awful truth. Further, as a representative of the Sunpapers in labor negotiations, he often found himself across the table from Jewish labor leaders, government officials, and union lawyers. One of the Baltimore "radicals," he wrote, was "a Jew . . . an extremely unpleasant fellow." Most of the labor leaders with whom Knopf dealt were also, in Mencken's opinion, "Jewish communists."

But his wartime complaints about Jews and Jewishness, both in his diary and in letters to friends, went far beyond objection to the tactics of labor negotiators and what he perceived to be the "constant bellowing" of American Jews about the war. He now complained, as he had never before, of excessive Jewish influence in journalism, publishing, and the arts. *Esquire* was "run by a gang of kikes who are most unpleasant," he wrote Marcella du Pont; the Annenbergs of *The Philadelphia Inquirer* were "low-grade Jews," he observed in his diary; and J. David Stern, publisher of the *Philadelphia Record*, was a "most unpleasant Jew." Even Alfred Knopf, he wrote a friend, was beginning "to turn Jewish" because of "the impact of Hitler."

He complained about Walter Winchell and another Jew whom he charged with inaccurate reporting: "It is certainly not pleasant to reflect that such irresponsible kikes are now the most successful of all American journalists." He railed against Jews in other realms as well, complaining about the "so-called modern paintings" fashionable in New York "especially among the rich Jews"; of the decline of Pabst beer, "now brewed by Jews [and] unspeakable"; of what he believed to be the "decline" of the Johns Hopkins University, partly because, by 1930, "fully a third of the undergraduates were Jews, and most of them . . . Jews of the kike moiety." And he wrote of a ceremonial dinner he had attended in Washington: "I was put at the table with Isidore Lublin and several other Jewish stars of the Administration. Their society, of course, was not attractive . . ."

It was clear, then, in the diary and in a number of letters that what before the war might have been passed off as an occasional and genteel anti-Semitism had, during the war years, become much harsher, at least rhetorically. Even to his Jewish friend Oscar Levy, now exiled to England, he complained several times of "professional Jews." And to Edgar Lee Masters, whom he had earlier taken to task for his anti-Semitism, he now sent one of the most damning letters he ever wrote on the subject:

I believe that [Jews] are the most imprudent, and in fact, idiotic people ever seen on earth. Give them half a chance and they'll inevitably walk into trouble. Certainly they are doing so in the United States at the present moment. . . . What they are doing here now is precisely what they did [in Germany] in the days of the Weimar Republic. It was simply impossible for the Germans to escape them. They were all over the place and nine-tenths of them were advocating means and measures that most Germans regarded as dangerous to the state. That is precisely what is going on here now.

Such was the reception Jews met in Mencken's wartime diary and correspondence, a reception harsher by far than that accorded another group he is widely accused of slandering, black Americans. From the 1920s on, in fact, following his support for black writers, he had continued to demonstrate a far greater sensitivity to black needs and concerns than most other white Americans of his time. In the Sunpapers he had condemned racial violence on the Eastern Shore of Maryland, at some financial risk to the newspapers, and had argued for the admission of a black student to the University of Maryland law school. He had also testified before a U.S. Senate subcommittee on behalf of the Costigan-Wagner antilynching bill, had protested the arrest of a black artist (who had earlier painted his portrait) for attempting to dine in a New York restaurant, and had condemned racial injustice in many other forms. "So few men are really worth knowing," he had written, "that it seems a shameful waste to let an anthropoid prejudice stand in the way of free association with one who is."

One man who he felt was particularly worth knowing—more deserving of his friendship, he believed, than most of his white associates in the early 1940s—was George Schuyler, the black journalist whose essays he had published in *The American Mercury* and with whom he still stayed in touch. Not only was Schuyler "the most competent Negro journalist ever heard of" but, he wrote in the 1940s, "the best columnist, of any race, now in practice in the United States"—and, he noted in his diary, "enormous[ly] superior" to the "dunderheads now roaring on the *Sun*." Such praise might be qualified in part by the fact that Schuyler shared nearly all of Mencken's own prejudices and expressed them in a similar manner; indeed, Schuyler was one of the few intellectuals who he felt had not abandoned him in the 1930s. But his respect and friendship went beyond that. The two men corresponded at length on race, politics, and numerous other subjects, and on several occasions Mencken, the self-proclaimed southerner, violated one of the most sacred of southern racial taboos by having Schuyler into his home for dinner. Such social interaction was hardly an isolated instance for Mencken, at least when Sara was not around. From the 1920s on he had dined on occasion with blacks, and at a time very few white Americans, and virtually no southerners, socialized in such a manner.

Far more revealing, however, than his diary entries on black leaders such as Schuyler and Walter F. White are his comments on the black women—his cook, Hester Denby, and maid, Emma Ball—who kept his household running. If on rare occasions he was dismissive in his remarks—suggesting once that black women were resistant to "judgment" and "all essentially child-like"—most of the time he spoke of his cook and maid with great respect and always treated them with the greatest courtesy. Emma Ball was "intelligent," "extraordinarily good" in her work: both she and Hester Denby were efficient, industrious, and dependable. In the same entry in which he referred to Emma's "child-like" quality, he went on to reflect on his dependence on the two women: "If they quit tomorrow August and I would be in a really desperate state." Mencken paid his domestic help much more than the going rate in Baltimore—and on several occasions in his diary reminded himself just how well. Not only did he pay them generously, he let it be known, but he and August also gave them liberal time off, paid their medical bills, and took care of many of their other financial needs.

Such was indeed paternalism, but it was paternalism of a more humane sort than that practiced in most of the rest of the United States in the 1940s, particularly south of the Mason-Dixon Line. Mencken's essential respect for black Americans can be seen in a number of other diary entries, from his remarks on the intelligence and economic astuteness of the Haneses' chauffeur in North Carolina to his sympathetic portrait of the black man whom he had encountered renovating the house on West Lexington Street in which he himself had been born. Never in his discussion of individuals or of racial relations in Baltimore did he apply to blacks the kind of invective he heaped on poor whites. When he spoke of himself as "living in Hollins street, surrounded by gorillas," or of his neighborhood as being "taken over by baboons . . . and lesser anthropoids," he made it clear that he was referring not to the nearby blacks but to the recent white arrivals from the Appalachians and the Carolina mill towns. He expressed a belief on at least one occasion that too many blacks were coming up from the South, but even at his worst he did not bear toward blacks the personal animus he felt toward poor whites. "The Negroes," he noted in his diary, "are much more civilized."

Just what, besides personal observations, motivated Mencken's judgments on blacks, Jews, and poor southern whites is curious indeed. Why should he, on most occasions, have shown great compassion for the plight of black Americans—and, after 1940 at least, have expressed very little for the plight of European Jews or the position of their American cousins? It was more than the matter of being German American and thus refusing to criticize Germany. It was also a question of control. With blacks, and decidedly not with Jews, he always felt himself in charge—never threatened, never challenged. It was easy to be magnanimous in such a circumstance; he was merely operating within the old southern tradition of *noblesse oblige*. And why, beyond feeling encroached upon in Hollins Street, was he utterly devoid of compassion when it came to poor whites? There too he was in a notable tradition. Had not genteel southerners, those very Virginians and Marylanders in whose tradition he often placed himself, also detested poor whites above all others?

The Mencken of the diary (nearly demonized after the posthumous publication of large chunks of that manuscript) was a man of deep prejudices, but he was clearly no misanthrope. It is being too charitable to attribute his anti-Semitic remarks in the 1940s (as some have) to his medical condition, particularly the small stroke or two he had suffered, but other forces were certainly at work. Primarily, he felt a deep sense of hurt at seeing his enemies in control, his own side (Germany) on its way to disgrace, and his own advice ignored at the Sunpapers and elsewhere.

He was, even during these days, capable of great compassion, but only selectively, only when he felt himself in a commanding position. In the wartime diary he could write a touching tribute to a lonely friend dead at sixty-eight, could lament the sufferings of a plumber of his acquaintance, "an excellent workman and an honest man," could even, on at least two occasions, express pity for those "anthropoid" poor white children who gathered in Union Square to play marbles. They had "uprooted" the lawn, he observed from his study window, but "on the whole I do not begrudge them their sport. It must be a dreadful ordeal for such youngsters to live in a big city." Indeed, "it is . . . pleasant to watch them at play, and I often do so.

The boys have brought back games that had begun to be forgotten in Baltimore . . ."

There is a deep sadness at work in many of the diary entries from the early and mid-1940s, a longing for the lost days when Mencken himself had been the boy shooting marbles in Union Square, a longing for lost friends, lost health, not only for youth but also for those other happy days with Sara only ten or fifteen years before. At times Mencken reminded himself how well off he was compared to many of his old friends, noting his comfortable income ($24,450 in 1941, $23,500 in 1942), his net worth (in 1943, $185,000 plus life insurance, book rights, and stock in Alfred A. Knopf, Inc.), and his advantageous professional and domestic position:

> "I am in an almost ideal situation for an aging man. I do precisely what I want to do. . . . I drop in at the *Sun* office to gossip. . . . I write what I please. . . . My . . . situation [at home] is very comfortable. . . . August and I have two good servants. . . . The best lunches I ever get in Baltimore are in my own house . . ."

All that was true, yet he could not help but observe the disaster and gloom around him, could not fail to see his well-ordered world falling apart, could not (despite his earlier resistance to such temptations) help reflecting upon it in his diary. Whenever he stopped by the *Sun* offices during the last half of 1942, he heard further gloomy details of what seemed to be the "hopeless" case of John Owens, thought to be fatally ill. Several months later he was called on to arrange the funeral of his old friend and Sunpapers associate Edwin Murphy. When he reported the death of such a friend, he often lapsed into a reflection on the brevity and inconsequence of human life.

After one funeral, "depressing indeed," of another member of the Hollins Street Gang, he considered the example of that "extraordinarily showy fellow" and his "gaudy and prancing" family: their "collapse . . . is a tragedy of a familiar sort. . . . All of the boys of the family, save [one], turned out badly. They were, however, less vicious than stupid." The case of another old friend, a hapless bank teller, was even more moving:

There is something tragic to me about the life of so charming and yet so futile a fellow. Everyone who knew him liked him, and yet everyone was conscious of something feeble about him. His days were spent in dull drudgery and he got only transient satisfactions out of his leisure. He never had any projects or ambitions. . . . Now he is dead, and in a little while nearly all of his old associates will be dead too, and nothing whatsoever will remain of him, not even a name.

With such chilling reminders of mortality and oblivion (the words "tragic" and "tragedy" at last creeping into his vocabulary), Mencken could hardly refrain from somber reflections in the diary, and the somberest of all were those rare entries in which he allowed himself to ponder his own fate and that of his family. In a particularly bleak entry in late December 1942, written just after "the gloomiest of all the gloomy" Christmases he could recall, he noted his various holiday activities. Just before Christmas he and August, as they often did, had visited their uncle Charles Abhau at the Home for Incurables: "He shows mental confusion and looks like a corpse." On Christmas morning they went to Loudon Park Cemetery and found the family gravestone "dingy with greasy grime." From there they proceeded to Gertrude's apartment for dinner: "Downstairs was our Uncle William [Abhau], lying helpless upon his bed and unable to speak." He had now been in bed eight years, "suffering stroke after stroke but never dying."

Four months before that entry, on the twelfth anniversary of his marriage to Sara, Mencken had been equally bleak: "When she died I was still in full vigor, but a year later I began to break up. . . . Now I face some hard years, even supposing that I live at all." He moved from one melancholy observation to another:

In a few years the Mencken family will be at an end in America. . . . I am rather glad of it. My grandfather . . . was an unhappy man himself and his descendants have had many troubles. I believe, in truth, that immigration is always unwise—that is, when it is not enforced. I believe my chances in Germany would have been at least as good as they have been in America, and maybe a good deal better. I was born here and so were my father and mother, and I

459

have spent all of my 62 years here, but I still find it impossible to fit myself into the accepted patterns of American life and thought. After all these years, I remain a foreigner.

---

Such was a great part but not the entirety of Mencken's life during the war years. He was, in some measure, like one of those Henry James characters, living two lives, one on the surface, active and sociable, the other nearly hidden, deeply pessimistic, looking backward, fearful that he might "have a stroke at any minute." While privately he sat in his Hollins Street study, pouring into his diary his fears and doubts and harsh judgments of friends, publicly he continued to make appearances, to meet obligations, and in most instances to exhibit that exuberant self-confidence and complete self-control he had always demonstrated. As he himself noted, despite all his troubles, "outwardly, I look quite well." He "manage[d] to get about," and he assumed "that people who meet me notice nothing amiss."

He got about, indeed, nearly as much as he had before the war, visiting the Haneses in Roaring Gap and the Hergesheimers in West Chester and Stone Harbor, New Jersey, and going with Alfred Knopf to the Bach Festival in Pennsylvania. Hergesheimer he also saw in Baltimore when his old friend came for medical treatment. Hergesheimer's situation made Mencken's, by contrast, appear cheerful: not only was he suffering from diabetes and arteriosclerosis but he could no longer write productively, and he complained of financial worries. By 1943, severely depressed, he told August that he would commit suicide if it were not for the effect on his wife. Mencken was a great source of strength for Dorothy Hergesheimer during this period. She wrote to him frequently with her concerns, and she too came to Baltimore on occasion to talk with him.

Although he insisted in 1943 and 1944 that he now got to New York "very seldom," in fact Mencken still traveled there at least every month or two, usually occupying a suite at the Algonquin. On those occasions his social calendar was as full as ever, consisting of dinners and other engagements with a wide assortment of friends and acquaintances from all shades of the literary, journalistic, and political spectrums. Among those he saw were Harold Ross of *The New*

*Yorker* ("superficially . . . a very uncouth Scotsman" but "I marvel at his skill and success as an editor") and Frederick Lewis Allen of *Harper's,* as well as Oswald Garrison Villard, Grantland Rice, Fannie Hurst, Lawrence Spivak, Maxwell Geismar, Paul Palmer, Max Eastman, and his old friend the theatrical producer Edgar Selwyn. Among other friends he entertained as they passed through Baltimore were Alf Landon, Edward Weeks of the *Atlantic Monthly,* and Dr. Francis E. Townsend, the old-age pension advocate and 1936 third-party presidential candidate.

Most often, in New York, he still saw Alfred and Blanche Knopf, now almost always separately. After Knopf board meetings he frequently went out to Alfred's home at Purchase for the night. They discussed business—Mencken continued to advise Knopf on the suitability of particular writers and manuscripts—but just as often they discussed Knopf's personal problems: Blanche would no longer live at Purchase, and Alfred was growing increasingly lonely. Mencken himself did not seem so close to Blanche as he had before. She still wrote frequently and affectionately, and he still met her for lunch and dinner in New York as well as for "sessions" in Baltimore when she came for medical treatment. But in her letters she no longer suggested holiday rendezvous as she had before.

In New York, Mencken still looked up Edgar Lee Masters, another old friend whose life made his own appear pleasant by contrast. He continued to find Masters an engaging dinner companion, an amusing and bawdy storyteller, and a correspondent in Mencken's own mock-epic vein. When in 1942 he discovered that the poet had fallen on hard times and was living alone in a dilapidated hotel, he provided financial help. Not only was Masters impoverished and ill—at times in the hospital, at other times in a bleak convalescent home in the Bronx—he was also at the center of a jealous dispute between his estranged wife and his mistress. Both claimants sought Mencken's support in their contest, in more letters than he cared to acknowledge, and he soon tired of them both.

Of all the old friends—Masters, Sinclair Lewis, and others—that Mencken encountered in New York in the war years, George Jean Nathan had come to resume his old position as closest companion. After a number of years apart, they had met again in 1939 and had not so much patched up old differences as decided to forget them. By 1941 they were again seeing each other frequently, seeming in some manner to be reliving the days a quarter century earlier when they had been *Smart Set* editors and twin terrors of Manhattan. It was "most strange to sit at dinner with you and G.J.N. again," Blanche Knopf wrote Mencken, and she was hardly alone in expressing surprise at the apparent reconciliation. Mencken and Nathan went to Lüchow's and other old haunts, they delighted in teasing Harold Ross, Red Lewis, and other dinner companions, and they reverted to their old practice of squiring charming women around town—often the same women whose company they had kept a quarter century earlier. They got together with Claire Burke, whom Mencken had known as Willard Wright's girlfriend in 1915; they saw Zoë Akins and Anita Loos, who came east from Hollywood, and "enjoyed [their] communion with the two ladies immensely." Loos looked "very good" after all the years and was, as always, "amusing."

Mencken seemed to enjoy the company of women, especially those good friends from better days, as much as he ever had. He carried on a warm correspondence with both Loos and Akins, as well as with Lillian Gish. On several occasions he saw both Lillian and her sister, Dorothy—in Chicago once, in New York several other times, in Baltimore when Lillian came to appear in a play—and it is clear that he and Lillian were even closer than they had been earlier. But she, like Loos and Akins, lived in California, and when he did not accept her several invitations to visit—"I see so little of you during these years that race by so swiftly"—they began to write less frequently.

Although he had also resumed a correspondence with Aileen Pringle, the tone of most of their letters was hardly romantic. Pringle wrote reminding him of the day they had met at Hergesheimer's long before—"I've always been glad there was the 19th day of June 1926"—but she was as aware as he of the passage of time: "Would that I were Circe and could lure you to these parts but unhappily that day has gone." Pringle herself had come east for a time in 1939 and 1940, and she and Mencken had seen each other frequently in New York. It is clear that at some point, probably about 1940, she again wanted to discuss marriage. Although Mencken destroyed one unmistakably pointed letter she wrote on that subject—as he did most of her letters after 1930—his undated response to that letter, which found its way into Pringle's own collection at Yale, offers poignant evidence of Mencken's sad assessment of himself as man and writer at age sixty:

My dear,

Your lovely letter hangs me on the hooks of a dilemma. . . . I am too immensely fond of you to even think of hail and farewell. But there always remains the uneasy feeling that you have deceived yourself—that the whole thing is simply an illusion. . . . Every shred of common sense is against it. You are still young, and beautiful, and still eager for life, and the best of it is ahead of you. But I am beginning to crack, and in a few years I'll be a sad sight indeed. The country will soon tire of me. . . . What is ahead for me? I see a few more books (if, in fact, I can actually pump up the energy to write them), and then a long dullness. I have practised a trade that uses men up, and leaves them empty. It looks easy now when I have (at least transiently) an audience, but getting that audience was a violent and exhausting business, and now I have no respect for it. . . . Maybe there is something left and maybe there isn't. But it would distress me horribly to see you sharing that chance. You are infinitely charming even to think of it.

You have invented a fellow who doesn't exist, and maybe never could exist. . . . I only wish he were real, and that all the rest of it were about to begin. . . . [As it is] I am tied here by the leg and can't get near you. And you are fastened too. Let us at least admire the irony of it.

To "admire the irony of it"—Mencken's equivalent of Hemingway's "Isn't it pretty to think so?"—was all he could envision as he took stock of himself and looked ahead. As for Aileen, although he still assured her "I think you are lovely," he felt he could serve her now only as friend and confidant, responding to her queries about other affairs of the heart. When his old friend Jim Cain met Aileen in 1944, reported to him "She is still single and still stuck on you," and seemed to suggest that Mencken again pursue her, he did not respond. When Cain himself wooed Pringle so successfully that they decided to marry in July 1944, Mencken seemed genuinely happy. When Cain canceled at the last minute (one of his four "good-byes," Pringle wrote Mencken) he offered consolation; and when they indeed went through with the ceremony later in 1944, again he congratulated them both. As Mencken might have predicted, their marriage ended in divorce not long afterward, largely because of Cain's alcoholism. "I had a sort of crush on him," Pringle wrote

Mencken of Cain, "mainly because we talked of you and [he] had a bawdy humor that was reminiscent of you."

Despite these warm friendships with women, Mencken gave the impression that he no longer had any romantic interests at all, and certainly his gloomy letter to Aileen would suggest that. "I haven't looked at a gal for years," he wrote Harry Elmer Barnes in 1942. In letters he occasionally dropped lines such as "I'll probably be [at Lüchow's] in the company of a very endurable gal . . ." But as for any serious involvement with women, his friends—and particularly those in Baltimore—still felt that romance, fully as much as marbles in Union Square, belonged altogether to the past.

Such was not altogether the case. Even in his diary, that chronicle of woe in which he expressed a fear of death at any moment, it is clear that he was sometimes alert to possibilities. At a birthday dinner in New York for Oswald Garrison Villard during an otherwise "dismal week," his eye "fell upon a really beautiful woman . . . dark and slim, and [apparently] a Latin. I asked who she was, but nobody near me recognized her. When the dinner was over I made efforts to identify her, but . . . she was lost in the shuffle." More to the point, Mencken's personal correspondence, even that which escaped the fires to which he consigned many of his romantic letters, tells a somewhat different story. Although most of the time he insisted that he had lost all romantic interest in women, at other times he certainly gave the impression of being interested, and, even more, he encouraged a reciprocal attention.

After his interest in Jean Balch in the mid-1930s, he played the role of pursued more often than that of pursuer, but he still enjoyed the game. When Ruth Alexander, an attractive brunette in her mid-forties, met and was charmed by him and began to write loving, flattering and devoted letters (she thought of him "almost constantly" and found him "too utterly fascinating to live so far away"), he was quick to respond. When Doris Fleeson, a divorcée and prominent newspaperwoman—"not without good looks," he acknowledged—wrote letters, also filled with genuine affection and sexual playfulness, he reciprocated as well. But Alexander, a Chicago-based economist and popular lecturer billed as "The Brilliant New Star of the Lecture Platform," was at least as busy as he was, and although he sent her gifts (including a picture of himself) and, for a time, strove mightily to see her, they could rarely get together. Fleeson, a former president of the Women's National Press Club, was too public a presence and besides—a lusty, good-humored, tough-talking woman with a "healthy Kansas appetite"—too much one of the boys. Although he enjoyed seeing her in New York, when she invited him for a weekend at a friend's farmhouse outside Philadelphia, he preferred to remain in the safer precincts of Baltimore. And when another old acquaintance, Virginia Alvarez, a fiery Venezuelan in her mid-forties, wrote from Philadelphia in 1942 insisting that she had loved him for twenty years and would make a perfect "companion" for him, Mencken resolutely fled her clutches. A physician as well as a writer, "a slim panther-like woman with coal-black eyes," she had her charms. But certain that he needed no "companion" except perhaps August, Mencken dampened her enthusiasm by responding that she had "over-estimated" him both "as a writer and as man."

Clare Leighton, for a time, seemed to be different. A young Englishwoman in her late thirties, she had come to Baltimore in 1939 and, armed with letters of introduction from mutual friends, had quickly made Mencken's acquaintance. At first Leighton found him "unexpectedly tough looking"; he reminded her of "an English pork butcher or an old-time barber." But she soon was convinced that he was "the most sentimental of creatures." They quickly fell into the habit of meeting at frequent intervals for lunch or dinner.

Much later Leighton spoke of their acquaintance as a "warm constant friendship," and so it was. But her letters to him, and some of Mencken's to her, suggest that they were very much taken with each other. "The fact is that I am exceedingly fond of you," she wrote after they had known each other two months. In her letters she took the offensive, sending her "wild, rebellious love," inviting him to her Jefferson Hotel room "one of these days—or evenings," and remarking on shared "sins of the flesh." But Mencken was, in his courtly manner, equally fervent. He "crave[d]" the chance to see her and wrote her frequently suggesting times they could meet in Baltimore and in New York. He assured her that he found her company "charming," remarked on how "handsome, buxom and intelligent" she was, and frequently reminded her, "I kiss your hand."

Leighton was a writer and artist, much younger than he, and it was almost as if he were assuming the same role he had played with many earlier apprentice writers, including Marion Bloom and Sara. He took

Leighton to the familiar haunts, including Marconi's and the Belvedere, and he bought her gifts. When she was in the Johns Hopkins Hospital for a tonsillectomy, he visited every day, bringing presents and playing pranks. She "gloried," she later said, "in his oblique protectiveness."

But he was "resentful and sad," Leighton felt, when she left Baltimore in the early 1940s to move to North Carolina, then to Virginia. Despite her assurances that she greatly missed him, despite her expressions of love and her hope that "you still love me"— despite, finally, her wish that when she returned to Baltimore they could "resume where we left off—and some into the bargain"—they rarely got together after that. Mencken was at least as much to blame as she was. As always, he had, on some level, retreated into his private self. In all the time she knew him, he never invited her to his home, never introduced her to August, never mentioned the name of Sara Haardt. Some things were not to be shared.

Feeling himself older than was in fact the case—in his memorable phrase, he was but the "sad wreck of a once magnificent mammal"— Mencken was gratified by the attention of attractive younger women such as Leighton, Alexander, and Alvarez, not to mention the continued devotion of Aileen. No doubt he was also amused by Alvarez's assessment that he was not old at all, "just ripe and mature like good wine." But the truth was that he now fled from anything approaching involvement, even an involvement with Clare Leighton, whom he had initially encouraged.

The most appealing younger woman in his life, safe in his eyes because she was married but also accessible enough since her marriage allowed her a great deal of independence, was his longtime friend Marcella du Pont. Throughout the early 1940s he and Marcella met in Baltimore and New York, at her home in Delaware, in Washington, where she lived for most of the war, and especially at Hergesheimer's homes, first in West Chester, then at Stone Harbor. Sometimes, as before the war, Marcella's husband, Alfred, accompanied her. Usually he did not.

Often Marcella drove up from Washington and picked up Mencken for the long drive to the Hergesheimers'; other times he took the train to Wilmington and met her there, and they traveled together to Stone Harbor. Her Baltimore visits, like those of so many of his friends, were partly for medical counsel and treatment, partly to see him. Playing his usual role as medical broker, he had put her into touch with doctors of his acquaintance. And when she came to Baltimore for surgery, he was nearly as attentive to her as he was to Clare Leighton. He visited her daily, dispensing gifts and good humor.

When they were apart, Mencken and Marcella wrote frequently, with the easy familiarity of longtime intimates, she assuring him "how I miss you . . . and how eager I am to see you." According to Marcella, she later destroyed a great number of his letters to her—at his request—but the letters that survive suggest how close they had become. After one of her visits she spoke of the "joy" of being with him and the "regret of being away" from him. In expressing herself in letters she felt her writing hand "tied down to my side" because there were certain things that she could not easily say in letters. And even in talking, "so much [was] left unsaid."

Marcella was often cryptic in her written remarks, at times seeming to refer to her faltering marriage, at times to other concerns. "Be patient a little while longer," she wrote on one occasion just before meeting Mencken for an evening in New York, "and I will work this out with myself." On other occasions she was teasing and flirtatious. The thought of "using the Mann Act on you," she wrote after one visit, "presented luscious pictures to my mind." But whatever his high regard for Marcella and the obvious delight he took in her, Mencken apparently did not want her to leave Alfred du Pont—as she later would, in fact. He rather preferred things as they were in 1943 and 1944. She was pretty, she was charming, she adored him— and she did not demand too much.

As the war wore on, Mencken's primary observation concerning it in letters and in his diary was how very little he was touched by it. In July 1943 he had remarked that its "effects upon my . . . life have been curiously slight," and that October he had noted that "no one that I knew has been killed, or even wounded." A year later, in November 1944, he made a similar claim. Although that was shortly to change when he learned of the death of Sinclair Lewis's son, he was still "astonish[ed] how little the war impinge[d]" upon him. Other than gasoline shortages and the difficulty of getting "a decent meal" out, his life went on as usual. He even continued to write to friends in England. Although he read their accounts of German bombing, sent sympathy for the "dreadful" days they were enduring, and in at least one instance mailed copies of his own books to a friend who had lost his in the bombing, the sufferings of the English, after all, were far away and, according to Mencken, largely self-inflicted. In general, he still affected the role of disengaged and occasionally delighted spectator. "The times are full of magnificent events," he wrote Lillian Gish in April 1944. "I have a swell time watching the show."

Many of his diary entries, as before, focused on his health. After the "horrible malaise" of 1942 and early 1943, he had been surprised to discover in the summer of 1943 that (he feared to admit it) he felt much better. He had much less heart discomfort, fewer spells of "quick breathing" at night, fewer disturbing dreams. His fears that the good health could not last were well founded. By April 1944 he was again complaining of pain in the area of the heart, "severe malaise," a sensation of pressure in his head, numbness in his right hand, and occasional feelings of faintness. The complaints continued throughout the summer and fall. No matter how vigorous he might still appear in public, in his diary the deathwatch had resumed.

He continued to drop by the Sunpapers, although he still found their editorial policy "absurd almost beyond endurance." He declined Patterson's offer to attend the 1944 national conventions, to write if he wanted, to observe if he did not. These would be the first conventions he had missed in twenty-eight years, but he felt he could not rely on Patterson's assurance that the editors would not change what he wrote. "Either I must Tell All," he wrote Lillian Gish, "or I must subside altogether." He was astounded when the Sunpapers endorsed Dewey: he had bet Patterson that the papers would support Roosevelt. But in fact he believed Dewey "an even weaker reed than Willkie," and although he now believed Americans were "living in a totalitarian state without knowing it," he himself would end up voting for FDR. "The country richly deserves him," he wrote Sara Mayfield.

After Roosevelt's reelection and the "dismal Christmas" of 1944, he settled back to watch the war wind down. He was long past reacting to entreaties such as that in March 1945 from an old friend: "You haven't written anything about . . . nazi devilishness. . . . Have you lost your guts?" He noted Roosevelt's death on April 12 with a mixture of disgust—over the *Sun*'s praise for him—and envy: "Roosevelt's unparalleled luck held out to the end. He dies an easy death, and he did so just in time to escape burying his own dead horse."

In his diary he acknowledged that Roosevelt would likely "take a high place in American popular history—maybe even alongside Washington and Lincoln. . . . He had every quality that morons esteem in their heroes." Three days after the president's death he also noted in his diary that his old adversary, even in death, had foiled him. "All the saloons and major restaurants of Baltimore were closed last night as a mark of respect to the dead Roosevelt, whose body passed through the city at midnight. It was silly. . . . As a result, the Saturday Night Club missed its usual post-music beer-party for the first time in forty years."

In the weeks and months that followed, Mencken seemed little concerned with politics or with events in Europe and in the Pacific. In his diary he gleefully reported that midwestern newspapers were "almost unconcealed" in their "rejoicing over Roosevelt's death," concluded that Roosevelt's successor, Harry Truman, was "a third-rate . . . politician on the order of Harding," and made brief mention of the celebration of VE Day in Baltimore. On August 3, three days before the bombing of Hiroshima, he seemed eerily prophetic: "I begin to believe seriously that the end of the world may be at hand." As usual, he was kidding. When the bomb was dropped on August 6, he made no note at all of it in his diary. He waited two weeks, in a letter to a friend, to pronounce his bitter verdict: "The atomic bomb crowns our Christian civilization. . . . It appears that the firing of Japanese women and children was specifically ordained by our Redeemer . . ."

When the end of the war was announced on the night of August 14, Mencken was working in his second-floor study at Hollins Street. He listened to the ringing bells and factory whistles, but as he looked over Union Square he had other thoughts. The war itself might not have touched him, but its conclusion, just as its beginning, had coincided with the deaths of several friends whom he would mourn instead. Two days after Hiroshima he had received news of the death of Adolph Torovsky, Saturday Night Club member ("the favorite of all the members without exception," Mencken wrote), friend of forty years, and traveling companion for part of his 1922 European trip.

A few days later came word of the death of his "most intimate friend in . . . later boyhood"—and, the next week, the deaths of three other friends.

Mortality was very much on Mencken's mind that summer. On May 30 he had marked the tenth anniversary of Sara's death by paying a visit to Loudon Park Cemetery, laying white carnations on her grave, and reflecting on their life together and her death. Rain had created a puddle on the family tombstone, in the carving on the family coat of arms. Dirt—"how foul Baltimore has become," he wrote in his diary—had turned the rain to mud. "The names carved on the stone already show darkly," he concluded in his diary, "but the white surface is still clean and bright. . . . There is room left for all the rest of us. My own name will be there soon enough."

# Chapter 20

# AN ANCHOR AGAINST OBLIVION

I have delivered myself from anonymity.

—*H. L. Mencken, "Minority Report" notes*

The First World War had been a creative experience for Mencken, a period of marshaling resources, defining enemies, identifying shams and frauds, and preparing himself to burst onto an unsuspecting world after Versailles. World War II had worked altogether differently: it had closed his mind, intensified his prejudices, contributed not to eloquent truth speaking but, in some areas, to an avoidance of the truth. He could never admit that a victory by Hitler's Germany would have meant, in Europe, an end to that individual liberty and freedom of expression he prized above all else. Even at the end of the war, he maintained that American participation had been "wholly dishonorable and ignominious." And the man who as far back as 1922 had feared "a colossal massacre of Jews" in Germany turned his eyes from that massacre when at last it occurred.

For Mencken himself, the end of the war meant few changes. Although he had complained earlier in 1945 that "I'll never see any freedom again. . . . It is highly improbable that even the rudiments of free speech will be restored in my time," in late 1945 he silenced himself. Earlier in the year he had declined a request by Paul Patterson that he go to San Francisco to cover the Allied conference on the grounds that if he could not write freely he would not write at all, and even after the war he declined to write for the Sunpapers. In November he asked that Patterson again reduce his salary, in part so he would feel free to write for other newspapers if he should choose.

471

What now principally engaged him—other than, he wrote a friend, "the spectacle of democracy committing suicide," a series of international crises that he was "malicious enough to enjoy"—was a series of writing projects, some contemplated and others in progress, that he feared he would not live to complete. Death itself, he insisted on several occasions, he did not fear—even during one nighttime attack when he "was half-convinced that [he] was dying" he had no fear—but what he did regret was the "cutting off of my work before it was done." The very act of writing had become a race against time.

In 1945 his health had been more dismal than ever. Not only did he complain of the usual afflictions—high blood pressure, pain around the heart, dizziness, shortness of breath, more "nightmarish dreams," and, at times, a "striking loss of memory"—but now those afflictions often made work impossible for long stretches. He spoke in one diary entry of feeling so "completely miserable" while walking one day that it "wouldn't have surprised me if I had fallen to the sidewalk"; another day he felt that he might "be floored at any moment by a cerebral hemorrhage." As he was to write shortly afterward, it was a contest "between my deteriorating coronary arteries and my general arterio-sclerosis."

He had either in mind or under way another eight or ten books he wanted to complete if he lived long enough. In his diary and in letters to friends he spoke of a volume of his own miscellaneous thoughts and notes as well as a work to be entitled "Thoughts in War Time." He also mentioned "a little book setting forth my conclusions about human existence" and a "sort of Mencken encyclopedia, made up of extracts from my writings over the years," as well as his own medical history (since no layman had "ever attempted anything of the sort"), a revision of *Treatise on the Gods,* and a supplement or supplements to *The American Language.* He wanted to complete the record of his magazine days, a good chunk of which he had already written, and he spoke of further writings for *The New Yorker* based on early Baltimore experiences and even a resurrection of those long-abandoned projects "Advice to Young Men" and "Homo Sapiens." Indeed, during the early 1940s he had written that if he had the "time and energy" he could "fill up at least 25 [more] volumes." His existing books, he had maintained, were "all bad." Nonetheless, during the war years he had published five books, and "all of them," he wrote Sinclair Lewis, "have sold better than those 20 years ago."

By late 1945 he had given up several of his ideas—including, for a final time, "Homo Sapiens" and "Advice to Young Men"—and others he had either completed or made substantial progress on. During the war he had begun an ambitious supplement to *The American Language* on which he had worked throughout late 1943 and 1944. Despite his poor health as well as a delay because of the serious illness of his indispensable secretary, Rosalind Lohrfinck, he had completed most of the first half of the supplement late in 1944 and had seen it published in a separate volume in August 1945. More than 700 pages in print and 350,000 words, the first supplement included new material he had accumulated since 1936 on the beginnings, development, and continued distinctiveness of the American language. It equaled the monumental 1936 edition in scholarship, stylistic flair, and inclusiveness, and both glowing reviews (by Edmund Wilson, among others) and sales figures announced his achievement. Within two months Knopf had sold more than 17,000 copies, and at the end of 1945 Mencken received, principally from *The American Language* supplement, his largest half-year royalty check ever, $14,547.

By the fall of 1945 he was hard at work on a second supplement, a volume drawing on some thirty boxes of accumulated notes that would grow to 900 pages and would include new material on American pronunciation, slang, and proper names. By this point it was obvious that, despite the fame of his early polemical volumes, *The American Language* had become not only the work that had interested him longest but also, by far, his most substantial work—some 3,800 pages, counting the three early editions, the 1936 volume, and the two supplements—as well as his most favorably received, save perhaps the *Days* books. It would also be, he sometimes suspected, his most enduring work.

He must have realized at some point over three decades of writing about the American language that, except for his love of a frontier vitality in speech, he had been a rather unlikely champion of American English. Not only did he feel a distaste for most things American, particularly those belonging to the American masses, but he also believed, as he once wrote a friend, that philology was "a dreadful subject." From the beginning, and still in the 1940s, he himself often favored not American but British usage. Although as early as 1910 he had called attention to the British preference for "in" rather than "on" a street—and the standard Baltimore usage of his childhood, if we judge by Baltimore *Sun* style in the 1890s, was usually "on"—he persisted till the end of his days in using "in Hollins Street" and "in hospital." He also persisted in British spellings such as "theatre," "meagre," "centre," "practise," and "programme," this at a time when the vast majority of his countrymen had departed from the British spelling altogether. By the 1940s only he, confirmed American Anglophiles, and a few of the tradition-bound professors he vilified took refuge in such British usage and spelling.

If he recognized such contradictions in himself, he never remarked on them. Rather, in late 1945 he plunged into the second supplement of *The American Language* with all the determination, if not the enthusiasm, with which he had approached the first, rising resolutely each day and hanging on grimly. Before he got to work in earnest on that volume, however, he returned, between July and December 1945, to the other ambitious project of the mid-forties, the record of his *Smart Set* and *American Mercury* days that he had begun in 1942 and halted in the summer of 1943 after writing several hundred pages.

He made rapid progress on "My Life as Author and Editor"; by mid-September 1945 he had written 850 pages and had added some twenty-eight appendices, numbering another 550 pages. By mid-November, just before he interrupted the work to return to *The American Language*, he had reached 1922 and had dealt fully with his early days as book reviewer as well as his own early books, his acquaintance with numerous writers, and his editorship of *The Smart Set*. He had tried, as he wrote in the preface, "to maintain a reasonable objectivity," but, he felt, "without any great success. After all, the story I have to tell is my story." Possessing "strong likes and dislikes," he had "made no attempt to conceal them."

Some of the most intimate portraits in his "Life" he placed in the body of the narrative, some in the appendices. The woes of Scott Fitzgerald—alcohol, Zelda, the general shambles of his life after 1930—he enumerated, and he remarked more briefly on the vanity and bellicosity of Hemingway and the querulousness and ingratitude of Sherwood Anderson. Dreiser, Sinclair Lewis, and Edgar Lee Masters he saved for more detailed treatment. "Wrecked [by] drink and two bad wives," Lewis was now "on his way to the boneyard on the water wagon, with an even worse wife [Marcella Powers] preparing to climb up beside him." Masters, too, was love-stricken and undependable, and battling poverty besides; drawing on the diary of Masters' mistress Alice Davis, Mencken painted another picture of a life out of control.

He included as well the seventy-nine-page portion of Dreiser's private diary, given to him by Estelle Bloom in 1925, which recorded Dreiser's sexual exploits during a ten-month period in 1917 and 1918. Apparently his earlier vow to include "next to nothing about women" and "very little" about "private life" applied only to his own women and private life, not Dreiser's. He also devoted lengthy appendices to the disorderly lives of Ernest Boyd and numerous other figures. Mencken's own position was clear: he was the solid rock among many talent-squandering alcoholics, womanizers, and egomaniacs.

Some of the finest portraits in "My Life as Author and Editor" were those not of celebrated writers but of figures now nearly forgotten—of Paul Armstrong, the popular playwright acquaintance of Mencken's early manhood who, filled with gusto if not always with good judgment, represented a gaudy version of the literary good life; of the critic Percival Pollard, Germanophile and fellow rebel against the Genteel Tradition; of James Gibbons Huneker, beer drinker supreme and the great literary influence of Mencken's twenties; of E. W. Howe, Frank Harris, Ludwig Lewisohn, Ben Hecht, and the Greenwich Village tramp poet Harry Kemp, many of whom had played a more significant role in American literary and cultural life than, fifty years later, would have seemed possible. The series of appendices was a modern version (sometimes a Grub Street one) of Johnson's *Lives of the Poets*, brief biographical portraits, often of soon-forgotten men, giving life to figures many of whom would otherwise find none beyond the grave.

One of the problems with "My Life as Author and Editor" was precisely that: Mencken treated as vastly more important than they were figures such as Armstrong, Hendrik Van Loon, and Paul de Kruif, who cut no great figures even in their own time, while giving far less attention to certain more notable writers with whom he was also acquainted. The manuscript also bore its share of prejudices that were sure to draw the fire of readers when a large portion of the "Life" would see light, some fifty years later, in a far more politically and semantically sensitive age. Not only did Mencken again appear anti-Semitic (though perhaps less so than in the diary), he added homophobia to his recorded catalogue of prejudices—particularly in his remarks on his trip to London in 1922, when he had encountered Hugh Walpole and Aleister Crowley. More to his discredit—by his own standards—his rejection of homosexuals, this "loathing for homos," he delivered in the indignant tones of a moralist.

Although "My Life as Author and Editor" was perhaps not to be the "most detailed and heavily documented record" of any American writer, as Mencken had hoped it would be (partly because he would be unable to complete it), it was indeed a significant work, among other reasons because here, as rarely before, he was not hesitant to sing his own praises. In many respects, popular opinion to the contrary, he had long been an authentically modest man: when he remarked to Paul Patterson in 1935 that there were "in point of fact, no 'world-famous' Baltimoreans," he genuinely meant it. In his other memoirs, both published and left to posterity, he had rarely departed from that modesty. But here, in his final account of many of the crucial events of his time, he was less reluctant to acknowledge his own importance in American cultural life of the 1910s and 1920s.

Most of "My Life as Author and Editor" was completed by early 1946, but not all. Mencken again set it aside, planning to return to it later, still certain that it could not be published in his lifetime or for a long time thereafter. Another work that engaged him, however, he did intend for publication, although he was not precisely sure when—a work that did not require nearly the same expense of time as the "Life," since it was a yoking together of miscellaneous thoughts rather than a sustained narrative.

"A small book of very short essays à la Bacon and Montaigne," as Mencken had described the work in his diary, it would consist of insights, preferences, and prejudices he had noted for many years and to which he had continued to add during the early and midforties. The *pensées* were on many subjects—the New Deal, England, democracy, political liberalism, communism, Methodism, and the American South, among them—although many would be excised before publication. This volume, too, could easily have been entitled "Prejudices" for it perhaps deserved that description even more than its predecessors. In fact, the titles Mencken considered varied from "Studies for Unwritten Books" to the one on which he finally settled, "Minority Report."

The reason many of the notes would be deleted from *Minority Report* when it was later published (in fact, would remain unpublished to this day in the Mencken Room of the Enoch Pratt Free Library) is that they were, even by Mencken's standards, vituperative indeed. Particularly explosive were those dealing with his old enemy Roosevelt and, predictably for the Mencken of the 1940s, with Jews. He was harsher here than he had been even in the secrecy of the diary, and what was remarkable was not only the rancorous tone of his remarks against Jews but their sheer volume. As well as repeating his old accusations that Jews "howl[ed] too much," "succumb[ed] to all sorts of hooey," "incline[d] toward communism," and possessed an "extraordinary lack of tact," he added new charges. Jews were "the most intolerant people on earth," had "never been fully civilized," and held to a "sharp, unyielding separateness . . . based on their assertive racial egoism." Jews asked others "to believe that Jahweh chose them above all other peoples [and] to believe He passed over a long series of enormously superior people and concentrated all his favor upon a petty tribe of desert Bedouins." And finally he charged, "The rage of the Jews against anti-Semitism is often only a thin veneer of anti-Goyism. They both hate and disdain the Goy."

These were the observations of the post-1939 Mencken, made mainly in the mid-1940s, and again they represented the private, not the public, Mencken of the war years. Even while he was writing such invective, he was maintaining his close friendship with Knopf, seeing other Jewish friends such as Abraham Cahan, and getting along better with George Jean Nathan than he had in two decades. He was also increasingly sensitive to the charge of anti-Semitism leveled against him, and he attempted in some small measure to combat it. When in 1945 and 1946 he revised his *Treatise on the Gods* for a new edition, he carefully eliminated his 1930 statement "The Jews could be put down very plausibly as the most unpleasant race ever heard of." Although he had gone on in the earlier edition to praise Jewish poets and thinkers, that single sentence had been used too often against him.

The anti-Semitism of the *Minority Report* notes hardly stood in isolation. Thoughts on many other subjects that Mencken had made and filed away reflected an attitude as close to misanthropy as he had ever come or was to come. If before he had resembled Samuel Clemens in numerous other ways, now he resembled him in the dark

477

meditations on mankind of his late years, similar to those in Mark Twain's *The Mysterious Stranger, What Is Man?,* and *Letters from the Earth,* works not to be published until long after *his* death.

Neither man nor God escaped Mencken's wrath in those notes that, for the time being, went unpublished. "The lower animals," he declared, sounding very much like the bitter old Mark, "not having man's power of formulating ideas, at least escape the disaster of cherishing bad ones. The ants never made the mistakes that man makes." Or, "Man, in truth, is the prince of killers, not only of animals, but also of his own kind. No other wages war. . . . Others kill only when hungry; man in sheer wantonness." He included other remarks: "If all the farmers in the Dust Bowl were shot tomorrow, and all the sharecroppers in the South burned at the stake, every decent American would be better off . . ." And "Man undoubtedly runs the world badly, but does he run it any worse than God?" As for Jesus: "His stupendous ignorance must be obvious even to Christians and His false reasonings are gross and innumerable. He was probably dirty in person, and he was clearly superstitious, for he believed in devils." As regards subsequent Christian civilization, he announced not in his private notes but in a letter to an old friend in September 1945, "I am still convinced that the invention of the atomic bomb is the greatest triumph of Christianity since Martin Luther was hanged [*sic*]."

Such were the views of God and man emanating from the second-floor study of Hollins Street in the days during and just after the war. But the remarkable fact, as before, was that while Mencken was pronouncing such dire estimates in private, in 1945 and 1946 he was also plunging into life nearly as vigorously as he ever had, although in a somewhat different manner. Now less frequently playing the role of *public* immoralist, the heaver of dead cats into the sanctuaries of America, he had become, to all appearances, the sober and responsible man of affairs his father, fifty years before, would have wished him to be. He took seriously indeed his membership on the board of directors of Alfred A. Knopf and the A. S. Abell Company, even presiding on occasion at Sunpapers board meetings in the absence of

Harry Black. Taking management's side in battles with the Baltimore Typographical Union and the "boss-haters" of the Newspaper Guild, making frequent diary entries on business transactions of the Sunpapers, the iconoclast of the twenties appeared to have settled down. "It is strange," Mencken's brother later remarked, "but of all his accomplishments he took the greatest pride in being a director of the A. S. Abell Company."

It was not strange at all, given the forces that had shaped the younger Henry Mencken. Nor was it strange that he now served as a consultant to the American Medical Association in its fight against government restrictions or to the Associated Press, which was battling similar restrictions. It was perfectly consistent with what he had always been that, in his capacity as Knopf board member, he raised strenuous objections to what he considered to be an overly generous pension plan for Knopf employees and said, in an earlier diary entry, "When authors quarrel with their publishers I usually sympathize with the publishers."

In all these respects, again, he was reflecting the probusiness, antiunion views of his father; he had become, like the first August Mencken, a shrewd, prosperous businessman, the burgher of Hollins Street. He owned stock "in 58 different corporations," he announced in his diary, "all of it . . . paying dividends," and he took great pride in his ability to manage his finances. And if he chose at times in Sunpapers board meetings to bestow his beneficence on *Sun* employees, suggesting not only that the lowest-paid employees, principally women, be compensated more generously but that any dependent of an employee killed in the service of the Sunpapers be given ten years' salary, that too was in keeping with August Mencken's paternalism.

Once he had become a director of the A. S. Abell Company, Mencken also found himself on new social terms with members of the Baltimore business elite. Earlier he had declined all suggestions that he join the Maryland Club, the University Club, the Baltimore Club, or certain other bastions of the Baltimore establishment. The University Club, to which Raymond Pearl had extended an invitation, was "full of fourth rate pedagogues and drunken lawyers," he had written in 1931. "I'd be as unhappy in such a gang as I'd be in the Klan." He had continued to be isolated as well from the Baltimore cultural and literary community. In all his life he had met only once, in 1931, that most celebrated of Baltimore poets, Lizette Woodworth Reese, although he thought highly of some of Reese's verse and wound up serving as a pallbearer at her funeral.

Lizette Reese's Baltimore, of course, was the Anglo-Saxon Baltimore to which he had never really belonged. But when he became a director of the Sunpapers, he became part of that world—which may be one of the reasons (his brother's surprise notwithstanding) that the directorship meant so much to him. The other directors were members of the Maryland Club, perhaps the most venerable of all the Baltimore clubs, and after he became a director and found himself alone after Sara's death, he too had become a member.

By the 1940s, then, his social life, at least during the week and when he was in Baltimore, differed little from that of any other prominent Baltimore businessman or professional. He frequently lunched and dined at the Maryland Club with doctors, lawyers, and bankers, particularly with such good friends as Judge Eugene O'Dunne of the Supreme Bench of Baltimore. He also entertained numerous out-of-town guests at the Maryland Club and other Baltimore establishments, friends such as Justice Felix Frankfurter, Alf Landon, John Gunther, and James T. Farrell. He continued to travel to Washington for Gridiron Club dinners and other elaborate affairs. At one Gridiron dinner he found himself at the head table, two places away from President Truman and three from the Duke of Windsor. On another occasion he met General Dwight D. Eisenhower, who struck him as "a hollow fellow—all smiles and back slapping."

Mencken contended that he did not enjoy such public affairs, but his diary entries suggest that he often delighted in them. Other entries show that he also enjoyed the company of men who, thirty years before, he had helped to make his reputation by debunking—university professors. He had never, in fact, been as hostile toward individual professors as his readers might have thought. All the while he had characterized "Professor-Doktors" as "hollow and preposterous asses," he had also carried on a friendly correspondence with such luminaries of the American academy as William Lyon Phelps, Howard Mumford Jones, Charles Beard, James Truslow Adams, Samuel Eliot Morison, Harry Elmer Barnes, Fred Lewis Pattee, and Howard W. Odum, as well as Sara's friends Ola Winslow and Marjorie Nicolson and, of course, his own good friend, Fred Hanes of Duke.

After the publication of the first three editions of *The American Language*, he had added to that group a large number of prominent philologists and linguists, including Louise Pound, editor of *American Speech*. Although his objections to professors as a species remained, he was gratified when many of them recognized the merits of his own work in American speech. "However much an editor may pretend to scorn [professors]," he once wrote A. G. Keller of Yale, "he is always flattered when one of them shows him any attention."

Other than genuine friendship in certain cases, the reason Mencken struck up an acquaintance with a large number of academics was professional self-interest, and such was particularly the case in the 1940s. Louise Pound helped him enormously with *The American Language;* as he remarked several times, he could not have written the volumes without her spadework. By 1945 he was also aware of self-interest of another sort: the professors of literature and history he had decried—along with those other representatives of the Genteel Tradition, librarians—would be the guardians of his manuscripts as well as his own reputation when he could no longer speak for himself. One of his closest acquaintances of the 1940s was Julian P. Boyd, the Princeton University librarian who undertook to collect, copy, and edit a massive number of his letters. He became not only a professional associate but a close friend of Boyd, whom he entertained in Baltimore and visited in Princeton on several occasions. "It is easy to understand the charm of life in a college town," Mencken reflected after one such weekend stay, "at all events, for the man who likes quiet." But he himself was a "cockney, and could not be contented save in a large city."

He spent more time on university campuses, particularly in the 1940s, than he acknowledged publicly—certainly at Johns Hopkins and Princeton but on numerous other campuses as well. Although he contended in his memoirs, in a passage from the mid-1940s, that he had spoken to "college boys" but once in his life—at Harvard, in 1926, after the "Hatrack" triumph—his correspondence tells a different story. In fact, he spoke to students on at least a half-dozen other occasions, at Columbia, Yale, Johns Hopkins, Union College, and Harvard. He now belonged as well to such eminently respectable groups as the Modern Language Association and the Linguistic Society of America—although, as he explained in a letter to Julian Boyd, he felt he was forced to "for trade reasons," and when the MLA asked him to speak to its members at their annual convention he declined. He was correct in contending that, even in the 1940s, he was not altogether comfortable in the presence of "the learned." When he was working in the Johns Hopkins library on *The American Language*, Marjorie Nicolson observed, he was often "somewhat ill at ease." And to the end he agreed to speak on university campuses only with the understanding that he would never be offered an honorary degree: "I have avoided such things deliberately all my life."

Mencken's exchange with professors was only one direction his correspondence took in the 1940s. The extent of that correspondence had always been astounding, ranging from preachers to prisoners, and it was continued testimony to his gregarious nature as well as to his deep personal and professional curiosity that he nearly always indulged any man of the cloth or man behind bars who wrote to him. He had always been a soft touch for prisoners who wrote with hard-luck stories and a shred of literary talent or an interest in the American language. In the 1940s he wrote numerous letters to and on behalf of convicts in New York, New Jersey, Pennsylvania, Virginia, and California, sent them books, and in some cases helped them with publication.

Saints continued to interest him fully as much as sinners. Earlier he had developed a warm friendship with his prohibitionist adversary, Bishop James Cannon of the Methodist church, and at least a friendly acquaintance with the rabble-rousing evangelist and demagogue Gerald L. K. Smith. He had written to Cannon frequently, had visited with him in Baltimore and Washington, had arranged medical treatment for him at the Johns Hopkins Hospital, and on at least one occasion had invited Cannon and his wife to lunch with him and Sara at Cathedral Street. He had also begun an extensive and friendly correspondence with Roman Catholic bishop Francis Clement Kelley, with whom he had spent a great deal of time on his Mediterranean cruise in 1934, and with Sister Miriam Gallagher, an English professor and Huneker scholar whose attempts to convert him did not in the least diminish his warm regard for her. But his favorite cleric was Kelley's assistant, Monsignor J. B. Dudek, whose correspondence with Mencken in the 1940s was as detailed and as extensive as anyone's save perhaps Alfred Knopf's. Dudek flooded him with material for *The American Language*, but, more important to their friendship, he and Mencken shared a tone—irreverence—and a number of prejudices, against Roosevelt, against Southern Protestants, against teetotalers.

In his diary Mencken spoke of these friends and many others, but none of them could replace Raymond Pearl, Max Brödel, and other Saturday Night Club members who had died in recent years. By 1946, in fact, he was the lone surviving member of that original group of ombibulous music lovers who had first gathered more than forty years before. Although the club was now "a mere shadow of itself," as one of its members observed, Mencken still approached Saturday nights with enthusiasm and threw himself into the sessions. Louis Cheslock, who now sat at the keyboard with him, painted in his own diary a portrait of a man in baggy pants and colorful suspenders, cigar in mouth, sitting at the piano and playing as vigorously as ever, sweating profusely, occasionally spitting on the floor or in the fireplace, and uttering a lusty "Shit!" if a piece didn't come off as planned. His consumption of beer had dropped from seven to three or four seidels a night, and now he usually left at 11:30 P.M., not 1:00 A.M., but he continued to take the club seriously indeed. Sometimes, now, he exercised an almost dictatorial control over its affairs, proposing the banishment of certain members, the reinstatement of others.

He traveled to New York less frequently now, but he still took the train to Wilmington to see Marcella and Alfred du Pont and, on other occasions, to ride with Marcella to Stone Harbor to visit the Hergesheimers. Marcella and her husband were at last contemplating divorce, and Mencken was certainly more aware of "Marcella's troubles" than he claimed to friends. At Stone Harbor they found time for walking alone on the beach, and Mencken still enjoyed her company. He declined her invitation in August 1946, however, to join her at a cottage on Cape Cod. And even she did not always fare well in his diary. "A considerable gossip," he judged her on one occasion, "far from reliable." Another time, when he was especially tired and wanted to be alone with the Hergesheimers at Stone Harbor, he was irritated that Marcella, "very talkative and energetic," had also been invited.

Hergesheimer himself still looked "wretched," Mencken observed—he continued to harbor a "death wish, and suicidal moods [were] on him often"—but he was virtually the only old literary friend save Nathan whom he himself still saw with any regularity. He had written to Sinclair Lewis for the final time in October 1945, expressing regret that they no longer got together and concluding, "Maybe we will meet in Heaven. I surely hope not." Shortly afterward, in June 1946, he had seen Edgar Lee Masters—"not long for this world"—for what may have been the last time. That same spring he saw Ezra Pound once or twice, traveling to Washington, where Pound—charged with treason because of his World War II activities and found insane—was confined to St. Elizabeth's Hospital. He sent money, books, and magazines to the hospital for Pound's use.

Although he was sorrowful as he reflected on the condition of close friends, as well as others like Pound who had never been close but had been lively correspondents, he experienced the greatest blow of all in the death of Theodore Dreiser in December 1945. His old friend's death, he wrote Helen Dreiser, left him "feeling as if my whole world had blown up. . . . There was a time when he was my captain in a war that will never end." If he exaggerated somewhat for the widow's benefit (it was Mencken himself who had been captain), he did feel keenly the death of the man who had once been his staunchest ally but from whom he had distanced himself. Although they had continued to correspond in the early and mid-1940s, the two men had never become close again. They had disagreed about too much. Mencken had "no use for the common man," Dreiser had charged in a letter of 1943, "but I have. . . . I was born poor." And Mencken had little desire to resume contact because of what he saw as Dreiser's "increasing imbecility."

In his last years Dreiser had made more of an effort than Mencken—had written letters in the old familiar manner, expressing both his debt to Mencken and his deep affection—but Mencken had not responded in kind. When, in 1944, Dreiser had been awarded the Award of Merit medal by the American Academy of Arts and Letters, Mencken had written deploring "the fact that you are having any truck with that gang of quacks." Dreiser had proposed seeing Mencken when he came east to receive the medal. It would be his last trip east, he predicted, and he asked his old friend to attend the dinner in New York during which he would be honored. "Unless I can have your aid and support . . . I am going to feel . . . forlorn, deluded. . . . What a pleasure it would provide [me] if you were to go with me."

Mencken had responded that, even thirty years later, he could not forgive the American Academy, that "some of the chief members of that preposterous organization" had "made brave efforts to stab you in the back in 1916." Thus he could not attend the dinner. Neither did he choose to visit Dreiser during the remainder of his three-week stay in New York, despite Dreiser's earlier wish that they meet one last time and have "one dinner at least" to "settle the affairs of this world." Mencken gave "tedious business" and a "somewhat shaky state physically" as reasons he could not come, but he was not convincing. Whatever his true reasons—his inability to forgive the American Academy and Dreiser for accepting its award, his utter rejection of the novelist's ideas, his disapproval of Dreiser on many other grounds, or simply his wish to avoid a moment so painful as a final meeting with his old friend—whatever the reasons, Dreiser had been hurt by Mencken's disinclination to meet, and he had written less frequently after that.

When Mencken had received the telegram announcing Dreiser's death from Helen Dreiser the following year and had responded with great courtesy to the widow, he had also written a couple of other responses. To Nathan and Masters, with whom he had often joked about Dreiser, he assumed his usual jocular tone, noting that the novelist was being "deposited in one of the movie cemeteries [Forest Lawn]": "I am sending a gang of grave robbers out to Hollywood to rescue [his] carcass" and bring it east to be "buried at Arlington next door to the grave of [William Jennings] Bryan . . ." But his diary entry was closer to the tone of his letter to Helen. Despite the distance, he wrote, Dreiser's death "depress[ed]" him: "It recalls to me the long-ago days when hope hoped high in both of us, and we had a grand time. I can hardly imagine grand times hereafter."

In some ways, however, the entries in Mencken's dairy between 1946 and 1948 were less pessimistic and bleak than they had been during the war years. He rejoiced that many of the poor whites in his Hollins Street neighborhood seemed to be going home after the war (although many remained), and at even closer hand he took an unprecedented pleasure in the natural beauty of his own backyard. In dozens of entries he noted the early appearance of daffodils, the endurance of "extraordinarily beautiful" morning glories into early November, the beauty of petunias, coleus, and scarlet sage. In detail worthy of Thoreau, he described the winter work he and August did to prepare the garden for spring, then the planting and tending of flowers as the year went on. Other entries remarked on the beauty of the pear tree and dogwood and maple in the backyard. He preferred the light green of spring to the dark rich green of summer, and he was particularly sensitive to the fading and dying of plants and flowers in the autumn. Although he recorded with delight the appearance of an "almost perfect Indian Summer" day, he was aware that the yard's "bleak and dismal Winter aspect" would soon follow.

Despite the cultivation and appreciation of his own garden—it had "never looked more lovely," he wrote in the spring of 1946—he could not be diverted for long from what had at last become the truly perilous state of his health. On the morning of July 30, 1947, he had another small stroke, awakening in "a considerable state of confusion," and he found, over the following week, some difficulty in speaking, typing, and writing by hand. Only three days before the "cerebral accident"—as Dr. Baker termed it—he had remarked in his diary that "what I most fear is that I may become disabled," and the day after the stroke he was able to write, with some difficulty, "I fear I am in for it." It was a "dreadful experience," he noted the next month, when he had improved. "It is hard for a man as active as I am to be disabled."

In 1946 and 1947 he noted the deaths of other old friends, among them Jim Tully, Frank Hazlehurst of the Saturday Night Club, Fred Hanes in North Carolina, and Ernest Boyd, impoverished and alone in New York. At Boyd's death he felt relief. He had long since decided the Irishman was a "dead-beat," "drunk most of the time," and unable to work, but he had still been "beset by the feeling that I ought to look him up," as he had written Nathan. At Fred Hanes's death, however, he felt only deep sorrow, and as much for himself as for Hanes. "Now that is done for," he wrote of his treasured visits to Roaring Gap, "as so many other pleasant things are done for."

Such was Mencken's tone about many matters in 1946 and 1947: a retrospective mood, an air of finality, was upon him. After returning from the 1946 Bach festival with Knopf, he wrote Hergesheimer, "I'll probably never go back again." After attending a Gridiron Club dinner, he noted, "I'll probably never go to another . . ." After going to the circus with August, he noted that it was "probably our last time on this earth." He'd probably "never open" another novel, he wrote his cousin William Abhau (no great sacrifice since he had read only one in the preceding four years), and to Betty Hanes he wrote that he believed his "travel days" were "over." In his diary he expressed disapproval of those friends who did not go gentle into old age. Patterson's flying and Knopf's skiing and tennis, be believed, were risky and foolish.

Increasingly, Mencken looked backward, measuring and evaluating his life. Although he professed to be largely satisfied with what he saw, he wondered on occasion how it might have been different. What would have happened if, in 1904, he had taken Ellery Sedgwick's offer and had gone to New York? What if Sara had lived? What if, after all, he had had children?

Most of the time he still said he was happy he had not. He had seen the hard times many of his friends had with their own sons and daughters—unmet expectations, medical and psychological problems, accidental death, in one instance suicide—and he concluded: "Such are the troubles of people with children. I have never known a father who escaped them." He could "imagine nothing more distressing . . . than the thoughts of a man with a family growing up. The boys stand a good chance of being butchered in their young manhood, and boys and girls together face a world that will be enormously more uncomfortable than the one my generation has known."

For that reason, as he and August sat around their fire at night, they congratulated themselves on their childless state. And yet at other times, as he once wrote half kiddingly to Benjamin de Casseres, children "would have been a considerable consolation in my old age," and a child, in addition, would have satisfied a dynastic impulse, a sense of Mencken family continuity. He may not have been altogether serious with de Casseres, but he had been when he wrote Jean Balch, shortly after Sara's death, "I envy you the children. My own house will be empty . . . ." When he visited Sara's good friend Anne Duffy and encountered her young daughter, named for Sara and born the year before her death, he must have reflected on such matters. When, on another occasion, he returned from a December weekend with Julian Boyd in Princeton, he sat down and wrote, "What a lovely home you have, and what a charming family: I frankly envy you. When I got back to Baltimore at the end of a gloomy Winter afternoon this house took on the appearance of a concentration camp." He was attentive to the children of friends, writing notes and sending gifts to Paul Patterson's granddaughter Tina, visiting R. P. Harriss's wife and baby daughter in the hospital, and, as "Uncle Henry," giving in marriage his late friend Albert Hildebrandt's daughter. He especially delighted in the visits of his niece, Virginia's, son, David Mencken Morrison, born in 1943 and "the first baby in the family for twenty-six years." He laid in a supply of toys, cake, and ice cream, and he observed Virginia's son for hours. "Young Davy is an extraordinarily lively and bright fellow," he reported in May 1946. He was "very orderly," he behaved "beautifully," and even at age three he used "excellent English."

But entertaining his grandnephew, as well as writing letters and giving presents to the sons and daughters of numerous friends, was vastly different from having his own child, and the family with which Mencken still felt most comfortable consisted of August and Gertrude. His devotion to August was well known to his friends, but not so his attachment to Gertrude. Many of them believed he merely tolerated her, although his hundreds of letters to her, particularly in the mid- and late 1940s, tell a different story. He was genuinely warm and attentive as well as good-humored; indeed, his letters to Gertrude in the late forties show little of the pessimism and despair that he was entering into his diary much of the time. He still loved to visit her farm in Carroll County, and he worried that she worked too hard maintaining it.

His brother Charlie he never saw now—they had gone three or four years between visits—and when Charlie wrote he spoke of his continued woes and thanked Mencken for the checks Henry periodically sent. He continued to lead a lonely life with the railroad, living in hotels in Ohio, West Virginia, and Pennsylvania, always hoping for something better and never finding it. But Mencken's greatest disappointment continued to be Virginia, who was redeemed only by having contributed Davy to the family. Despite all he had done for her, she had wound up, he now determined, a complete failure. She read nothing, had "no conversation," no "range of interest" beyond "cards, shopping and idle gossip," was "completely devoid of tact"—and had no interest at all in Mencken himself. He was shocked to discover that she had destroyed all the letters he had written to her since childhood, including those "diligent efforts" to help her become a writer. Indeed, despite his fondness for Davy, he had concluded that even her child belonged "to his father's family, not ours." His grandnephew seemed "so remote" that he and August did "not speculate or worry about his fate."

For a final time, then, he counted the failures of the Menckens during their hundred years in America. The Abhaus still showed some promise, largely in the person of William Abhau, now risen to commander in the U.S. Navy, but the Menckens as a family were about played out. Even more than before, he reflected on their unremarkable lives, mediocrities at best, he judged, utter failures at worst. His cousin Pauline, he learned, had at last disappeared into the anonymity of Cleveland; when Charlie had attempted to look her up at her last known address, he had found only a burned-out house in "a hell of a neighborhood . . . cheap—dirty—tenements." Not all his cousins had fared quite so badly, but their collective woes led Mencken again to consider the marginal status of so many in his grandfather's family. No Mencken in America, he noted, had ever held public office, none—at least of his branch—had served in the armed services, none—except Virginia, on whom he felt it was wasted—had ever gone through college.

Such musings reinforced his earlier ideas about the deterioration of German families in the United States. He had had in mind another German family in Baltimore when he wrote in his diary, "The first settlers commonly did well, and some of them left substantial estates. In the second generation . . . there was usually a decline, and in the third there was collapse." But he had added that he could recite at least twenty other such German-American histories in Baltimore, and now he realized to his dismay that the family of Burkhardt Mencken—Henry Mencken excluded—was among them.

It was more a circumstance of history, however, than such reflections on Germans in America that led Mencken, between 1946 and 1948, to look back to Germany perhaps more than he had ever before. He had not been able to provide aid and comfort to the German people during the war, but after the war he would help in every way he could. Although the death of Tante Anna in 1937 had severed his closest personal German connection, he nonetheless knew of distant relatives who were suffering deprivation of food and clothing, and he himself—never a do-gooder but a firm believer in taking care of one's own—could provide abundant relief in that line.

Thus he sent packages of sugar, coffee, tea, meal, and chocolate, as well as shoes, clothes, woolen products, and soap to relatives in Leipzig, Munich, Berlin, Wiesbaden, Darmstadt, and other locations. He also mailed packages and books to old friends in Berlin and other cities, and similar materials to complete strangers who wrote asking for help.

In all, he gave aid to literally dozens of Germans in the three years after the war, and he received numerous and lavish expressions of gratitude; one cousin insisted that her survival in 1946 and 1947 was altogether attributable to his kindness. In the course of his correspondence with another cousin in Wiesbaden he discovered the fate of still other German Menckens and Menckes during the war. According to her count, no fewer than eleven family members had died, including one of her daughters, killed in the bombardment of Berlin in April 1945. He found in his correspondents a varying degree of sympathy with the late Nazis. One had been relatively sympathetic to their aims, another had been adamantly against them, still another reported having been persecuted by the Nazis. From all he heard tales of loss and displacement—and from a cousin in Wiesbaden, nearly his own age, an anguished cry as to why the British and Americans had not sided with Germany against the Bolsheviks. From still another cousin he learned of the captivity of Burkhard Mencke, a young German soldier who bore the name of his own grandfather. Mencken began to send packages and letters to him as well.

That he intended no explicit political statement in his aid to the German people (he had, after all, helped one or two English friends as well) is not to say that he did not still entertain strong feelings about the war. Privately he continued to express the belief that the United States had "backed the wrong horse." He declined, even in private correspondence, to mention Nazi concentration camps and gas chambers, and he particularly believed that letting the Soviet "barbarians into Western Europe" was "the worse error made by Western statesmen since the Middle Ages." But when he looked to Germany in 1947 he looked primarily backward, for what he learned after the war confirmed his earlier belief that the Mencken family there was dying out just as surely as in America. He took small comfort in learning that the Mencken portraits in the law school of the University of Leipzig had survived the war.

It was, then, without even the consolation of enduring family prominence, not to mention the consolation of religion or philosophy or wife or children, that Mencken entered the phase of his life when he felt he must surely set his affairs in order. Whatever immortality he himself was to achieve, he realized, would be achieved not through offspring or through conventional religious means—since he had no belief in the afterlife—but rather through his own words, published or to be published postmortem, and through people who had enough interest in those words to ensure that they would be preserved.

He had, of course, begun to sink his anchor against oblivion as far back as the late 1930s, after Sara's death, when he had begun to collect, preserve, and make notes on family records, and he had been at it ever since. It sometimes seemed from that time on, despite many other interests and achievements, that his primary business in living had been getting ready to die—and, he might have added, with William Faulkner, "to stay dead" a long time. That is precisely what he had intended to accomplish in his "Thirty-Five Years of Newspaper Work," in "My Life as Author and Editor," in his "Additions" to the *Days* books and in other confidential manuscripts that would not be released until twenty-five—in some cases thirty-five—years after his death.

That is also what he had had in mind as he sorted through letters to give to the New York Public Library, through "almost interminable notes" and autobiographical statements, photograph albums and clippings scrapbooks to give to the Enoch Pratt Free Library in Baltimore. That is what he had done as he corresponded with and sent items to various collectors of Menckeniana, as he listened to suggestions (although he rejected them) of a "Mencken Academy" for the study of the American language, as he urged Louis Cheslock to resume his Saturday Night Club diary, and particularly as he aided Julian Boyd in Boyd's massive project of collecting, copying, and editing thousands of letters he had written. "God knows," he had written Boyd in 1942, "I hope you don't abandon this book."

He knew on one level, of course, that it was all in vain: "It is a folly to try to beat death. One second after my heart stops thumping I shall not know or care what becomes of all my books and articles." But he found it "psychologically impossible" to approach the end in any other way. "I know very well that oblivion will engulf me soon or late, and probably very soon," he had written at some point in the 1940s, "but I simply can't resist trying to push it back by a few inches. . . . I'll know nothing of it when it happens, but it caresses my ego today to think of men reading me half a century after I am gone."

For many years now he had taken the long view. "A hundred years after you are dead and in hell," he had written Marion Bloom in 1926, "your letters will be dug up and published and all the literati will marvel." He had been joking, but only in part, and now that he felt he might be fatally stricken "any moment," it was surely no laughing matter. That man is ultimately forgotten, absolutely and irrevocably, unless he wills himself otherwise, had been one of the recurring themes in his confidential scribblings during his last years. In his "Additions" to *Newspaper Days* he had recalled the glories of numerous "Prominent Baltimoreans" of the turn of the century, all now "as dead as Rameses" and forgotten. He feared that, for all his own prominence, he too could be forgotten. So great was his fear that he determined to send copies of his diary as well as "Thirty-Five Years" and "My Life as Author and Editor" not to a single library but to several libraries. "There is the risk," he wrote, "that some or all of them may be destroyed in some future war or in a revolution. . . . If there is ever any raid on American libraries by radicals my papers will be among the first destroyed." The prospects were bleak even if such a calamity did not occur. His papers were "bound to be neglected as I pass out of memory, and some of them, in all probability, will be forgotten altogether."

He was not always quite so pessimistic. From time to time he observed that "the nascent Ph.D.'s of the future—if libraries survive in the bright new post-war world" would mine "My Life as Author and Editor" for material they could find nowhere else and would be "snuffling my bones" for various other historical facts. He had "tried hard to tell the truth," and now he believed there was "probably no trace in history of a writer who left more careful accounts of himself and his contemporaries." He had indeed been careful, on occasion forgetting or conveniently omitting certain facts but otherwise being as inclusive as possible. Overcoming for the moment his fear of oblivion, he concluded, "I have delivered myself from anonymity." For a man who had no children, no belief in God or an afterlife, that indeed was a form of immortality.

By 1947 it was clear that, in addition to Julian Boyd's preservation of letters and the efforts of several collectors of Menckeniana, he would have help in his deliverance. Newspapers reported a "renewal of interest" in his work, partly because of the publication of the 1945 supplement and, the next year, the popular *Christmas Story*, Mencken's humorous account of a low-life Baltimore holiday feast. Beyond that, as one reporter noted, "There is something in the air of this second post-war period . . . which has renewed the appeal of the Sage of Baltimore." *Life* did a cover story on him in August 1946, and although his remarks in the *Life* interview were as acerbic as ever, nearly all the mail he received was favorable.

Biographers and other chroniclers seemed to be lining up. Considering an edition of letters to be but "the first step" in his plan to preserve Mencken for posterity, Boyd had already requested "the honor of being your Boswell." So had, indirectly, Louis Cheslock and even, in his vengeful manner, Charles Angoff. Others, less personally close to Mencken, had undertaken ambitious book-length studies of his life that would supplant Goldberg's 1925 work. If biography to Mencken, as to Oscar Wilde, added "to death a new terror," that terror paled beside the terror of anonymity. He would rather take his chances with misinterpretation.

Never, then, had there been a more cooperative subject when two aspiring biographers approached him in the late 1940s. Edgar Kemler, a political scientist by trade, he had known for some time, and the fact that he and Kemler did not agree politically—Kemler, a New Dealer, was a "young Harvard pink"—seemed to him, he wrote Kemler, "to be an advantage rather than the reverse." He went far beyond mere courtesy in helping Kemler with his biography; he nearly collaborated, not only making his records available, answering written questions, and meeting with him on numerous occasions, but also approving Kemler's outline for the biography and reading chapters as soon as they were completed. In their correspondence it was Mencken himself who often suggested their "sessions," and he suggested further what about his life should be stressed and what deemphasized. Although he did not attempt, at least directly, to influence Kemler's interpretation of his life and work, he helped in nearly every other way.

To Kemler he expressed great delight in the course of the book, although privately he had some doubts. By the time Kemler was well along with his writing, Mencken had come to believe he might be better served by another aspiring biographer, William Manchester, who had first written to him in 1947 about a journalism thesis he was writing at the University of Missouri on Mencken's *Smart Set* criticism. Shortly afterward, he had come to Baltimore to meet his subject. With Mencken's encouragement, Manchester soon moved to Baltimore, took a job with the Sunpapers, and began work on his own biography, receiving the same generous assistance Kemler had been accorded. In fact, Mencken saw Manchester as more of a kindred spirit than Kemler, not only a fellow newspaperman but a man ideologically more compatible.

***

By the beginning of 1948, then, with most of his memoirs finished (except for "My Life as Author and Editor") and with Kemler and Manchester at work, Mencken felt his task of summing up to be nearly complete. In January he occupied himself with destroying the voluminous notes he had accumulated for his long-since-abandoned "Homo Sapiens"—"a somewhat melancholy business, interring the remains of a book on which I once set such high hopes"—but he was "too old now to tackle anything so laborious." In truth, though, he felt better than he had for some time. His second supplement of *The American Language* was about to appear, he had found the energy to write another piece for *The New Yorker,* and as he noted in his diary, "My psychical state reflects itself in a feeling of physical well-being." "This, of course," he added, "won't last."

It did last for a while. In late February he and August left for two weeks in Florida, where he spent his time "loafing beautifully," reading and writing nothing, and watching the St. Louis Cardinals twice daily in spring training. Shortly after his return his spirits were lifted further by the reception given his final *American Language* supplement. Joseph Wood Krutch in *The New York Times,* Carl Van Doren in the *Herald Tribune,* and numerous other reviewers were lavish in their praise; the entire *American Language* series, the *Time* reviewer contended, was "surely one of the great curiosities of literature." In early April Mencken appeared on the covers of *Saturday Review* and *Newsweek*, both of which included features on him and his work. And from Oxford, Mississippi, came a letter from William Faulkner, saying how much he looked forward to getting into the new supplement: "It's good reading, like Swift or Sterne."

After the second *American Language* supplement, Mencken wrote Betty Hanes, "I'll never think of philology again." He did have other projects in mind—further work on his "Life as Author and Editor," now completed up to 1922, as well as a few more pieces for *The New Yorker* and a collection of his earlier work to be published, in a single volume, by Knopf—but none of these would be particularly taxing. That was fortunate since his period of "physical well-being," as he had predicted, did not last long. By spring he was again complaining of heart discomfort, numbness, fatigue, and more "nightmarish dreams," and again he found work difficult.

He experienced another series of shocks in the spring and summer of 1948. Paul Patterson was laid up in the Johns Hopkins Hospital with hepatitis, perhaps worse, and Mencken was pessimistic about his chances for recovery. In addition, his old friend Henry Hyde had suffered a stroke, and Hergesheimer's condition had grown even worse. In March he also learned of the death of Zelda Fitzgerald in a hospital fire in Asheville, North Carolina. In his diary he remarked on the end of the Fitzgeralds' "tortured saga" and sat down to write to Zelda's mother in Alabama and Scott and Zelda's daughter, Scottie, whom he had earlier befriended.

The greatest shock of all came in May, when, early one morning, his longtime housekeeper, Hester Denby, was stabbed and killed by her daughter—who then made her way to Mencken's house muttering that she also wanted to kill him. Mencken and August escaped harm when the police apprehended her at their doorstep, but Mencken was both shaken and moved by Hester's death. He immediately stepped in to take care of her affairs, locating her relatives, paying her funeral expenses, offering to pay the legal expenses of the daughter, who seemed to him "completely insane," and lending money to at least one member of Hester's family. In his diary Mencken expressed the immense gratitude he felt to Hester, not only for her many years of service but also for her selflessness. After she was stabbed in the chest, she had run into the street and told neighbors to alert the police to her daughter's threat against Mencken: "Poor Hester's last thought was to protect me against the assault that was ending her own life."

The other diary entries occasioned by Hester's death show as clearly as anything he ever wrote the mixture of feelings—compassion, gratitude, respect, puzzlement—Mencken had when he considered the plight of most black Americans. He was startled to discover that he knew "really . . . nothing about" Hester Denby, what kind of life she had lived at home, whether she had in fact been married, whether her murderer was actually her daughter. He discovered that she had been in debt and had gone to loan sharks. "I would have lent her the money gladly, and without interest," he insisted, but "poor Hester lied to me to keep up her own courage and save her own pride." "Dead," she remained "almost as mysterious as she was alive." Thus blacks, at least "in the servant class," he concluded, were "a mysterious people, and no white man ever penetrates them." In reflecting on the difficult life and violent death of this "very superior colored woman," Mencken revealed both his humanity and the limits of his understanding.

It seemed almost as if, in his diary entries of late May, he focused on Hester's misfortunes in part to keep from thinking about his own. The other woes he pondered hit closer to home—not only the illnesses of Patterson, Hergesheimer, and Hyde but the unrelievedly sad spectacle of his uncle Charlie, now "completely cuckoo," whom he helped financially and continued to visit at the Home for Incurables. The reason Uncle Charlie "depress[ed] him horribly" was, quite simply, that he wondered if he were witnessing a preview of what could be his own sad end: "I fear the dreadful tenacity of life of the Abhau family may fetch me too, and make me a nuisance to August and Gertrude. I only hope to die quickly."

It is little wonder that his letters during 1948 were full of gallows humor; "I have been reprieved . . . and hope to live a little while longer," he wrote in September. In fact, as he trudged to the funerals of friends, he found he could often view the whole spectacle with a certain detachment. Serving as an honorary pallbearer on one such occasion, he even observed "a good-looking young woman present, and I entertained myself during the pastor's harangue by admiring her. . . . Her name was Miss Sarah Powell [curiously, Sara's two given names]. . . . In all probability I'll never see her again on this earth."

He wrote Aileen Pringle in April 1948 that he was "simply sit[ting] here patiently waiting for the holy angels to collar me." But such was not altogether the case. In fact, for a period in 1948, as if sensing that his own end was near and that he must take advantage of what time he had, he threw himself into his activities more vigorously perhaps than at any other time over the past decade. He started to visit the Sunpapers more often, he accepted several speaking engagements in Baltimore and Philadelphia, he went to the April Gridiron Club dinner (after having announced three years before that he had attended his last), and the following month he went with Knopf to the Bach Festival in Bethlehem (which he also, two years earlier, had announced would be his last). He got together in New York with Nathan, Harold Ross, Grantland Rice, and the Knopfs, went to the theater for the first time in years, and saw Marcella du Pont both in Baltimore and at her home in Delaware as well as at Hergesheimer's at Stone Harbor.

In many ways, in 1948 he seemed closer than ever to Marcella, and certainly as she moved closer to divorce from Alfred du Pont she felt closer than ever to him. For the past year her letters had revealed how greatly she depended on him and how much she hated to part after they were together. In early February, after he and the Hergesheimers spent a weekend with her in Delaware, she had written asking him to return alone in the spring. She would have on hand a "third person" who "could stay here . . . and pursue her own routine but provide the necessary 'chaperonage' for us." With his eye, as always, on propriety, he responded that it would be unwise for her to have "any unmarried man to stay the night at Calmar," even with a chaperone, "while your [divorce] negotiations are under way," and that he would have to see her elsewhere. They continued to meet off and on during the following months, although presumably not at her home. In her letters Marcella was full of gratitude for the "courage" she gained, "somehow, by being with you."

Not only did Mencken find himself with a full social calendar in the spring and summer of 1948, he was also busier as a working journalist than he had been in years. When Patterson's son Maclean had asked him well in advance to cover the national political conventions in the summer of 1948, he had accepted for what he felt would surely be his last hurrah. As the time drew near, he had his doubts he would be "physically able" to cover the conventions, but he vowed to go if Paul Patterson, still in the hospital, recovered enough to go with him.

With Patterson by his side, he took off in mid-June for the Republican convention in Philadelphia. The Sunpapers had assured him that he was not required to write anything if he did not want to, but he took his typewriter along because he knew it would be "psychologically impossible" for him not to write, and within an hour of reaching Philadelphia he was hard at work. After three days of sending dispatches to the Sunpapers, he came down with tracheitis from sleeping in an air-conditioned room, had to return to Baltimore, and thus missed the nomination of Governor Thomas Dewey. After a quick recovery in the humidity of Hollins Street, he was eager to return to Philadelphia for the Democratic convention: the events swirling around the nomination of Truman would be "a magnificent show," he predicted to his sister, Gertrude. The fight between the national Democrats and the Dixiecrats indeed turned out to be a spectacle "of almost incredible obscenity," he wrote in his diary, and Mencken felt fit as he plunged in, staying up one night until 6:00 A.M., another night attending a dinner party outside Philadelphia with Dorothy Thompson and Rebecca West.

He was not through with conventions yet. For some time Paul Patterson had wanted him to cover the Progressive party convention, also in Philadelphia, at which Henry Wallace would be nominated, and this was the show—featuring, he felt, "all the worst idiots in the United States"—he had looked forward to most of all. He was pleased to find that he could still write quickly and with flair in the face of a rapidly changing story, but most of all he delighted in the hijinks of a convention for what he felt must surely be the final time. According to his fellow journalists Alistair Cooke and Bradford Jacobs, he was in characteristically gruff good spirits, staying up late, entertaining Wallace supporters in the Sunpapers suite, spouting wisecracks, and leading the singing of "The Star-Spangled Banner" and "God Save the King." He also assumed his old role as gadfly, Mencken noted in his diary: not only did he vigorously challenge Wallace at a press conference, but the Maryland delegation introduced a resolution denouncing him for racism and anti-Semitism. The presiding officer refused to entertain the motion.

Forgetting for a time the precarious state of his health, Mencken had covered two national conventions and part of a third in a little more than a month, and he approached the 1948 campaign with a similar relish. As usual, he disapproved of both of the major candidates. Truman, whom he had observed closely at two Gridiron dinners, seemed "a small town haberdasher . . . a quite honest man and . . . not altogether stupid," but overwhelmed by his office. By the fall of 1948 his estimate was harsher—"a fifth-rate man" whom the country "will be well rid of"—but he thought no better of Truman's Republican challenger. Ever since dining with Dewey in 1939, he had believed the New York governor to be essentially mediocre, and what he saw now convinced him that Dewey, he wrote in private, was "a vain and hollow fellow," "shifty and somewhat slimy," "one of the most transparent frauds of all time." The candidate he preferred was South Carolina Dixiecrat Strom Thurmond, the very sort of race-baiting southern reactionary he had made his reputation by ridiculing.

Although early in the summer of 1948, in a speech to a group of Baltimore lawyers, Mencken had predicted Truman's victory, as the summer and fall wore on he too had become convinced that Dewey would win. Since Thurmond was not on the Maryland ballot, he reluctantly voted for the Republican challenger, went to the Sunpapers office to observe the returns, and then went home assuming like everyone else that Dewey had won. When he learned the next day of Truman's victory, he wrote what would be his final piece on national politics; the country, he contended, deserved Truman. Two days later he wrote the last story he would ever write for the *Evening Sun*. He might have preferred the archsegregationist Thurmond for president, but when it came to Maryland, as always, he was strongly for civil rights. In a piece protesting the segregation of tennis courts in Baltimore's Druid Hill Park, he concluded, "It is high time that all such relics of Ku Kluxry be wiped out in Maryland."

In October he made note of his customary ailments—pain in the area of the heart, shortness of breath, and an occasional loss of memory—but with no greater urgency than before. In his correspondence he did seem to worry somewhat more than usual about whether he would be able to keep commitments he had made. For the past year he had often adopted just such a position, telling Julian Boyd on one occasion that he would come to Princeton to speak in a few months "if I am still alive," on another occasion declining a Baltimore physician's invitation to address the American Gynecological Society because "I become disabled now and then and there is no telling when such a spell will strike me."

In October and early November, however, such warnings became more frequent. He hesitated to accept an invitation to speak to a Baltimore club in early 1949 because he feared he might find himself "disabled at the last minute." To Knopf he wrote that he would accept an invitation to speak to the Grolier Club in New York "if I am still alive January 27." "I predict formally," he wrote a week later, "that on the night of the Grolier dinner I'll be laid up at the Johns Hopkins."

In mid-November his letters were full of the usual forebodings— "the heavens are full of gloomy portents," he wrote Felix Frankfurter—and he must also have noted the uncharacteristically ominous tone of a letter from Charlie: "I too am approaching the day when I will have to lay aside the tools and wait for the reaper." But such forecasts hardly curtailed his activities. On November 4 he traveled to Philadelphia to speak before the American Philosophical Society. Addressing a nearly full house, including Julian Boyd and the Knopfs, he shocked some of the members with his cynicism about presidential politics. Two weeks later he accepted an invitation from the Princeton History Club to address the members at some future date, and several days after that, on November 20, at the Saturday Night Club Louis Cheslock remarked on his "very jovial spirits." Earlier in the week he had been afflicted with an intestinal virus so violent that "while it lasted . . . I began to smell the angels," but he had fully recovered and now boasted a "florid complexion and a high good humor."

He was making plans for the weeks ahead—getting together with August and Gertrude for Thanksgiving and Christmas, traveling to New York in December for a Knopf board meeting and dinner with Nathan and with Blanche Knopf, as well as getting together with Anita Loos and Marcella du Pont in the near future. When Marcella had last seen him a few weeks before, she had found him looking better than in some time, "hale and full of hell." The time they spent together in October, she wrote, was "the most successful, in some ways, we have ever had."

There was little immediate warning, then—other than August's impression that he looked less well than usual—of the events of

Wednesday, November 23, 1948. The previous day Mencken had dictated to Rosalind Lohrfinck a series of letters to Julian Boyd, publisher Roscoe Peacock, and Harry Elmer Barnes, in which he said he was looking forward to four years of civil rights controversy and "really exciting stuff" under Truman. He had completed and mailed a tribute he had written for a *festschrift* in honor of Johns Hopkins linguist Kemp Malone. He had written an Australian friend, C. R. Bradish, that he was ready for a holiday. And he had made plans to meet William Manchester and the English novelist Evelyn Waugh for lunch at the Maryland Club the next day.

In the early evening of November 23 he left Hollins Street for Rosalind Lohrfinck's apartment to check on a manuscript she had been typing. As he was discussing matters with her, he suddenly began to speak incoherently, then continued to talk and act irrationally. Lohrfinck immediately called Dr. Baker, who arrived within a few minutes and at once saw the gravity of the situation. Mencken had at last suffered the major stroke he had long anticipated, either a cerebral hemorrhage or a cerebral thrombosis, and Baker quickly got him into his car to take him to the Johns Hopkins Hospital.

August Mencken reported later that Baker told him that night that Mencken was "practically dead on arrival" at the hospital and that he could not "conceivably live until morning," but both Baker and Mencken's later physician Philip Wagley said afterward that such was not the case. In fact, he was in no great immediate danger of dying, as Alfred Knopf discovered the next day when he phoned Baker to check on the patient's condition. "Mr. Mencken has suffered a stroke," reported Baker, "and I am sorry to say he is recovering from it."

It proved to be, Knopf later remarked, a "wise comment."

# Chapter 21

# REQUIEM IN HOLLINS
# STREET

M encken later referred to 1948 as the year he "died," and for very good reason. The massive stroke of November 23 had taken away his ability to read and write and, in every respect, had ended his literary and journalistic career. Like so much else, the timing of the stroke conformed to that curious historical symmetry that had always marked his life, coming almost exactly fifty years after his career had begun, fifty years after his father's death, and one hundred years, to the month, after the arrival of his grandfather Mencken in the United States. In November 1948, for all practical purposes, the Mencken century in America was over.

For a good many months, however, most of the world—including many of his close friends—was unaware of the severity of the stroke, or even, in the beginning, that he had suffered a stroke at all. As he lay in the Johns Hopkins Hospital those late November days, severely stunned if not actually near death, his secretary, Rosalind Lohrfinck, wrote several of his friends, including George Nathan and Julian Boyd, that his illness was "slight," "trivial," or "not serious." She told still others that he had "gone to the hospital for a check-up," and informed several professional acquaintances that he was simply "absent from the office" for a time. Whether August Mencken instructed her to avoid the truth (as was probably the case), whether Mencken's doctors did, or whether Mencken himself, intent upon keeping up appearances, had the capacity to issue such orders, we cannot be sure. But it is clear that, aside from Knopf, Mencken's immediate family, and a very few Baltimore friends, almost no one at first knew the extent of the damage done to him.

They did not know even after an Associated Press dispatch of November 30—a full week later—reported that Mencken had suffered a "small stroke" and was a patient in the Johns Hopkins Hospital, or after a similar announcement the following day on national radio news. Another widely circulated AP story on December 1 reported that his condition was "improving," the same news Lohrfinck now gave to several other friends. His friends outside Baltimore did not seem particularly alarmed. Aileen Pringle wrote with no awareness of the gravity of the situation, and one of Marcella du Pont's primary concerns was that they would probably "have to abandon any idea of a house party" she had planned before Christmas. A friend in Massachusetts teased Mencken about having experienced only a "small shock," whereas "FDR [had] managed to have a massive shock, and I always thought you the better man." A distant cousin remarked, with unintended irony, that she assumed he was "enjoying" himself, "getting caught up on your reading, etc." An acquaintance who couldn't reach Mencken assumed he had gone on vacation, and even his good friend Harold Ross wrote from New York that he had heard from August that Mencken was "away for a couple of days."

Only those very close to him, then, knew the truth—that the stroke (as Louis Cheslock noted in his diary for November 24) had "impaired Henry's speech," that doctors were not at all optimistic about the prognosis, and that August, for one, was "dubious about the [possibility] of his mental recovery." According to August, for the first few days of his hospitalization he thought he was in Philadelphia (where he had briefly fallen ill the previous summer), and most of his doctors could not understand him at all. Within a week, however, he was alert enough to inquire, after a fashion, about the mailing of manuscripts and the cancellation of lunch engagements, and in the following weeks he improved, at least physically, to the point that he was walking without assistance and was anxious to get home. At this point, August's account and that of at least one of Mencken's physicians differ. According to Mencken's brother, he was told that Mencken was so irrational that he needed to be institutionalized and that arrangements had been made for him to enter a hospital

in Catonsville, outside Baltimore. August himself then wrote to Paul
Patterson, who recommended a nurse to care for Mencken at Hollins
Street, and the doctors reluctantly agreed to let him go home.

In any case, Mencken was released from the hospital on January
6, 1949, "considerably improved," the newspapers reported, but
again the reports were misleading. According to a physician's report
of January 6, he "was considerably dismayed over his predicament,
and at the same time threatened suicide as a procedure of choice in
his particular situation." Although Mencken derived "considerable
benefit from repeated attempts at reassurance," he remained depressed. His despair was to grow worse in the following months.

For a short time, however, coming back to Hollins Street was
enough to raise his spirits. On his second night at home August
invited Louis Cheslock over, and Mencken amazed Cheslock by
greeting him "standing and beaming and saying how glad he was to
see me. . . . I was surprised at how much he could make clear . . ."
The entry in Cheslock's diary captured Mencken's condition in some
detail.

> His first few sentences were among his best. His speech at times
> became quite confused and irrelevant. At times quite good. There
> were flashes of his old penetrating wit and also lapses into vagaries.
> Almost always he called days, weeks or months "years"—being
> gently corrected by August. His chief complaint was about his
> eyes—not being able to read—but frequently referred to his eyes
> as his "ears"—window was "wind," alien words & stray fragmen-
> tary phrases kept cropping up despite his intense effort to steer a
> straight course in his thinking & speech.

At first Mencken did not let such handicaps deter him. He immediately summoned Rosalind Lohrfinck and had some success in dictating several dozen letters—to Nathan, the Knopfs, Joe Hergesheimer,
Harold Ross, Aileen Pringle, Betty Hanes, Julian Boyd, and other
friends—over the next two or three weeks. Several other brief notes
he may even have typed himself, with only a few mistakes. In the
dictated letters he was to some degree able to discuss business with
Knopf, Ross, and Nathan. He signed all the letters—the one act of
writing he could perform with no problem.

To Knopf he reported—in a letter he dictated to Lohrfinck—that "reading is still difficult and even almost impossible," but he added, in a statement more wishful than truthful, that his mind was "perfectly clear . . . I can understand anything that is read to me without the slightest difficulty." To Bradford Swan in Rhode Island he remarked upon his "excellent progress" and added that "by the end of the month I may be really quite well again." He dictated a letter to the Sunpapers management thanking them for paying his hospital bills and adding that he would now reimburse them. (The bill, $2,176, he paid the following week.) He told Edgar Kemler in late January that he would be "delighted" to see him in two or three weeks to discuss Kemler's biography. He confided to Blanche Knopf his hopes of getting to New York in a couple of months. And he received several friends at Hollins Street, among them Hergesheimer, Knopf, and, more frequently, Louis Cheslock.

From his correspondence and the reports of his admittedly limited activities, one might have thought Mencken had made at least a partial recovery. But such was hardly the case. He only *hoped* he was getting better: he had improved physically in December and early January, and he still had limitless faith in his doctors, so he assumed the reading and writing would soon come along as well. He blamed his inability to read and write on his eyes, and he had been assured by his friend Alan Woods, a Johns Hopkins ophthalmologist, that that problem could be corrected "in a short time."

Soon, however, reality began to set in. The letters he dictated may have looked approximately as they had before the stroke, but in fact he was having a great deal of trouble dictating. Rosalind Lohrfinck often had to supply words when he himself could not think of them. His friends Knopf and Hergesheimer and Cheslock may have told him that he seemed better, but in fact they were alarmed at the lack of improvement. He himself realized that his speech was so bad that, as he wrote Hergesheimer, "I'd not care to meet anyone at the [Maryland] club." His ability to recall names was woefully diminished.

He realized in particular the shape he was in when, in mid-January, he was faced with the task of reading proofs for the selection of his early writing, *A Mencken Chrestomathy*, that he had prepared for Knopf the previous fall, as well as proofs for an essay he had earlier written for *The New Yorker*. In mid-January he had told both Knopf and Harold Ross that he would be able to go over the works, but soon he realized he would have to turn the task over to Mrs. Lohrfinck. Although he himself expressed no great sense of alarm in notes to Knopf and Ross, in early February Lohrfinck wrote Knopf that Mencken was again "very much upset and unhappy about his condition."

In an attempt to break out of his depression—and against the advice of at least some of his doctors—he made plans with August for a Florida trip in early March. He attached a great deal of importance to the trip; he felt the warm sunshine would revive him as it had so often before, and he dictated letters to several friends in which he said he would be able to write to them at some length "after I return from Florida." The week or so in Florida was indeed a turning point, but not in the way he had anticipated. The weather was cold, both he and August came down with sinus infections, and he was discouraged (he told Cheslock) at the sight of "the great hordes of sour old folk." He returned to Baltimore with the realization that his condition had not improved at all.

After his return he seemed to lose hope. Except on very rare occasions, he no longer attempted to dictate letters but rather insisted that Lohrfinck answer all letters herself. She wrote Nathan that it would be unwise for him to come to Baltimore for a visit after all, and she was more honest than before about Mencken's condition. "His illness has been much more serious than most people know," she wrote, although she added that he still asked Nathan to "keep this to yourself." To Betty Hanes she revealed how "discouraged and unhappy" Mencken was, how "lonely," how "terribly . . . distress[ed] . . . not to be able to write to you."

For the next few months Mencken saw a number of doctors, each trying to determine whether anything could be done. For a time he continued to believe that his primary trouble was with his eyes, that if he could improve his close vision he would be able to read. In fact, his eyes had not been significantly affected by the stroke; the problem was the reading itself, the brain's incapacity to transform written images into meaning. Not only that, another physician reported the week after he returned from Florida, his "abilities to comprehend auditory messages" were "severely impaired." He continued to be able to communicate with August and with close friends, although, August noted, not only did he forget names but he often used words incorrectly—"bound" for "clown," "corn" for "horn," "snooze" for "sneeze."

August had now become the chronicler of his brother's health that Mencken himself had earlier been. He kept an extensive medical diary in which he recorded Mencken's symptoms and moods as well as August's own estimate of his condition and what might be done for him. He noted his brother's frustration with his condition and his impatience with doctors, and he called on a number of physicians and listened to proposals for what might be tried. He entertained one suggestion that Mencken be sent to the Mayo Clinic, another that he travel to California to work with a doctor there. "Something [had] to be done," August believed, "if [Mencken] was not to go insane."

Mencken could not speak for himself now, at least not on paper, but he must have been aware that what had happened to him was precisely what he had anticipated for some ten or fifteen years. It was what he had dreaded from the time he had first remarked on "the Abhau curse"—that "dreadful tenacity of life" that ensured that the afflicted, though cruelly disabled, would linger helplessly for years before dying. In his diary he had remarked often on the dismal condition of his uncle William, and finally his uncle Charlie as well, and he had noticed that same quality of doleful endurance in others outside his family. Throughout the 1940s he had been especially interested in the condition of his friend Bishop Kelley, who, after suffering a massive stroke, could no longer read and speak with any facility and was severely depressed. "It must be a dreadful thing to die by inches," Mencken had written his friend and Kelley's assistant, J. B. Dudek. He had observed the "mental confusion [and] severe depression" of another friend felled by a stroke, and he had remarked on how "tragic" it was that still another acquaintance, "once so hearty and prosperous," had been "reduced to such a pass" that Mencken "hate[d] to think of visiting him." It was perhaps fortunate, in that respect only, that Mencken could no longer read the eerily prophetic words that he himself, forty years earlier, had written about the last years of his own mentor Nietzsche: "There he would sit day after day, receiving old friends but saying little. His mind never became clear enough for him to resume work, or even to read. He had to grope for words, slowly and painfully, and he retained only a cloudy memory of his own books. His chief delight was

507

in music . . ." There was "something poignantly pathetic in the picture of this valiant fighter," Mencken had written, "this foe of men, gods and devils—being nursed and coddled like a little child."

Despite his fear of the Abhau curse, Mencken had hoped that he himself might escape such a fate. His father had died quickly, after all, and his mother, though an Abhau, had not suffered long. He himself had once rejoiced, in his autobiographical notes, that he belonged to "the pycnic type of man, with a short neck and a comfortable pouch," and such a creature "usually [makes] a quicker business of dying" than tall, slender sorts. He had hoped, then, "to be bumped off with reasonable dispatch"—he had envied friends like Phil Goodman as well as enemies like Roosevelt their swift and tidy ends—but in more realistic moments he felt that his oft-proclaimed luck, always with him through his mid-fifties, would desert him in the end and he would "[come] down with some drawn out illness, full of misery." "Unless I am humanely and briskly finished by an automobile or the public executioner," he had written even before he suffered the first in his series of small strokes in the late 1930s, "my exitus from this world, I greatly fear, will be terribly prolonged. . . . When I come down at last [doctors] will strive magnificently to keep the breath of life in me, and so I'll probably linger on and on, a dreadful spectacle . . ."

Now that it seemed to be happening as he had feared, now that he was embarking upon that seemingly endless ordeal that he had earlier described for Nietzsche, he considered his own bleak options as best he could. In the hospital, of course, he had spoken of suicide, and he still did not rule that out, at least not at first. His writings of thirty years, public and private, had commended those who took it upon themselves to end their own misery. The death in 1926 of his friend George Sterling, ill and hopeless, had been "almost the ideal finish. . . . He had come to his time and he knew it." The suicide of another friend "in a hopeless situation," he wrote Dorothy Hergesheimer, "was very courageous and, what is more, very sensible." In *Prejudices, Sixth Series* he had defended suicide as "logical" and "rational" under certain circumstances, and in a manuscript note he defended it as justified when one made up one's mind that "life [is] no longer worth living." He had spoken even more to the point in a newspaper interview in 1926. "Before the day closes in which I have no work to do," he had told a reporter, "I shall end my life."

"Curiosity," he had written Gretchen Hood about the same time, was "enough to keep us going," enough to keep him from "cut[ting] [his] throat." But without curiosity and the wit to satisfy it, he would be in perilous shape. He feared the boredom above all else.

But now that the moment had come when he had "no work" he was able to do, that moment in which boredom was indeed his fate, did he actually consider suicide—as a real possibility, that is, not just a vagrant thought? In the winter and early spring he certainly made threats: "My life is so hideous. . . . I believe I'd commit suicide if it weren't for my brother," or "I don't have any children. Why should I be kept alive?" To Cheslock and other friends he expressed the wish that he were dead. But after some months warm weather came, he could work in his garden, he could eat and drink most of what he wanted. He would tough it out, at least for now.

In May and June he resumed some semblance of an active life. He sometimes went to the Saturday Night Club, now as a listener rather than a pianist, and he went out to dinner with Louis and Elise Cheslock. After his initial resistance, he also began seeing friends at the Maryland Club for lunch, he attended a luncheon at the Sunpapers for members of a Gridiron Club committee, and he consented to visits from the Knopfs, the Hergesheimers, George Nathan, James T. Farrell, and Huntington Cairns.

But other friends, particularly women, he still resisted seeing. Lillian Gish wrote assuring him, "I miss you [and] love you," but he sent word that he did not feel up to seeing her, at least not yet. Betty Hanes wrote from North Carolina that she would be passing through Baltimore and wanted to come by, but Lohrfinck wrote that because of Mencken's "difficulty in talking . . . I think it would be unwise for you to stop off . . . ." Other women he had known well—Aileen Pringle, Bee Wilson Macdonald, Doris Fleeson, Ruth Alexander—wrote or were to write asking to see him. August and Lohrfinck did not encourage them either.

Feeling most keenly the virtual ban on women visitors (other than wives of friends) was Marcella du Pont. Once she had learned of the severity of the stroke she had written frequently, greatly upset at Mencken's condition. "It is awfully hard to be so near and not see him," she wrote Lohrfinck. She wanted to "come at once," but Mencken, with strong support from August, would not let her. "May we meet again, as in old times," she finally wrote, but this time

August jotted on her letter, "No reply." Despite appearances that Rosalind Lohrfinck and August were screening Mencken's visitors—that August had become, quite literally, his brother's keeper—it was principally Mencken himself who resisted seeing women, particularly younger women or those in whom he had once shown some romantic interest. One explanation in particular offers itself. Mencken was a man, an old friend once remarked, whom he had never seen "at a social disadvantage." Now he was at a cruel disadvantage in every way.

August noted that Mencken's speech improved somewhat during the summer of 1949, although Lohrfinck questioned that assessment. He was "having a really terrible time of it" and was "unhappy indeed," she wrote Hergesheimer, and August himself later acknowledged that at times the situation was "horrible . . . dreadful." But Mencken had indeed adjusted, in some measure, to life on a new scale. He had detested movies all his life, their "idiotic and irritating technic," he had written in 1927, "a maddening chaos of discrete fragments," and he had stayed away from them as much as possible. Now he and August went to movies on a regular basis—more than three dozen in the late winter and spring of 1949, according to his secretary, sometimes "two and three . . . in one night," according to August. He had found some of them, to his surprise, "really superb entertainment." Nor was he always depressed, his doctors later stressed; at times he could flash his old sense of humor, and even in the letters he instructed his secretary to write for him he was not above adding jokes about religion, politics, and occasionally even his own condition. He had "engaged thirty head of clergymen" to pray for him, he asked Lohrfinck to tell his cousin Walter Lagemann.

As summer moved into fall, he and August explored new treatments that might enable him to read; both still assumed there was someone who could help him. August sometimes suspected that he did still have some capacity for reading on a limited basis: one day the previous spring he had come upon his brother down on the floor of his study sorting his clippings, and Mrs. Lohrfinck later told August that they were sorted properly. But whatever abilities the sorting required did not carry over to the reading Mencken longed to do. He could, in fact, barely make out newspaper headlines. According to the director of the Speech and Hearing Center at the Johns Hopkins, who evaluated him in late August, his "attention span [was] short and his verbal confusions many," although he had made some progress in "phrase and sentence recognition, in both reading and writing." Another reading specialist who had examined him earlier concurred that he was "confused," although the earlier specialist held out some hope that "he eventually would be able to read some."

For a time Mencken went to the Hopkins two or three times a week, and he was instructed to practice such activities at home as copying on the typewriter the names of the forty-eight states so that he might learn or relearn certain procedures. His doctors also recommended new glasses (though those in fact made little difference) and talking books (though Mencken usually resisted listening to them). Some of his doctors reported progress, but Mencken knew better. By late fall, again profoundly discouraged, he stopped making the trips to the Hopkins. He now seemed "rather hopeless," Lohrfinck reported to Nathan in late November. In spirit he had returned to the state of profound dejection that his old friend Siegfried Weisberger had described in a letter to another friend several months before:

> Henry Mencken is no good. . . . A different man . . . Depressed and blue: uneasy, restless with a noticeable vail [sic] over his eyes, he no longer cares about anything around him. He could not spell my name. . . . No word of my own writing [Mencken said] do I recognize. . . . I [don't] give a damn is the end of each of his sentences. . . . Alone is HM in his house. With his face against the window he gazes to Hollins Square watching old man [sic] sitting on the benches and laughs to himself when he sees children comming [sic] from school. What a sad finaly [sic]. . . . Had I lost both of my legs [Mencken said] I would have been happy to be in a wheel chair. I could write and have a lot of fun. Now I am through and I don't give a damn.

The year 1950 was to prove little better than 1949—indeed, before it was over, even worse. To all appearances, Mencken now managed to carry on in some fashion, often to the extent that much of his reading public assumed he was recovering. His *Chrestomathy*, the 600-page collection of many of his out-of-print articles, had been published in mid-1949, and it had been received favorably, in certain quarters enthusiastically. Virtually none of the reviewers mentioned, if they knew, that the career of the author was over. That fall he had pieces in *The New Yorker* and *Esquire*, although both had been written, of course, before the stroke; the *Esquire* piece, in fact, was a reprint of a story he had published a half century before. Later in 1949 Walter Winchell noted on his nightly broadcast that Mencken was "on the mend," and in April 1950 Jim Cain reported in *The New York Times* that he was now "liv[ing] happily with his brother August" in Baltimore.

To be sure, Mencken was inviting friends in more frequently than before and sometimes getting out himself. Late in 1949 he had attended a ceremony marking the laying of the cornerstone of the new Sunpapers building on Calvert Street, and in February 1950 he attended his last board meeting of the A. S. Abell Company—during which, true to form, he voted against a motion to contribute to the Community Fund. Although he had submitted his resignation from the Sunpapers' board the previous month (he would receive an annual pension of $7,500), he continued to see newspaper associates on occasion at the Maryland Club. He now had dinner out occasionally, went to concerts with August, and frequently attended the Saturday Night Club, still as a listener. He and August made plans for another trip to Florida in March, then a more ambitious trip to Guatemala later in the year, although both trips eventually were canceled.

In fact, his plans and his frequent public outings were deceptive. After the Sunpapers cornerstone ceremony he was despondent because he had experienced a great deal of trouble speaking with old colleagues. After a lunch at the Sunpapers on another occasion a former colleague observed that he now seemed a shell of his former self—ruddy in appearance, with "all the old manner, but none of the substance." After a time, Mencken vowed he would no longer visit the Maryland Club for lunch because casual friends and acquaintances, seeing him looking physically more vigorous, approached him and asked questions he could not answer, even if the questions dealt with his own books. Visits from friends such as Knopf did not always turn out satisfactorily. And even the Saturday Night Club was no longer the refuge it had been. Mencken was "very insecure in expressing his thoughts, his speech filled with unrelated words and desperate groping for names," Louis Cheslock reported in his diary.

When once he tried to play the piano he soon "lost confidence, and quit."

Aside from August, he still seemed to feel most comfortable with Louis and Elise Cheslock. He and August now saw Cheslock almost weekly, inviting him to Hollins Street, going to his home for German beer and sandwiches, venturing out on picnics in warm weather and occasionally to festivals and carnivals. Cheslock, who had become Mencken's latest (and last) Boswell and whose diary (along with August's medical notes) provides the most detailed account of his life during this period, now had little hope his friend would ever improve. He tired quickly, and "mentally he [could not express] the thoughts which possess him." The doctors' primary job, Cheslock believed, was simply to see that Mencken's "hope is kept alive in order to prevent his doing anything radical." But at other times he observed the delight Mencken still took in everyday things, in good food and drink, in the flowers in the Cheslocks' backyard, in children at play. "He is fascinated by [children]," Cheslock noted; ". . . if [he and Sara] had had a child. What a comfort this would be to him now."

In the summer and early fall of 1950 Mencken was also able to visit Gertrude more frequently on her farm. His sister insisted that he was happier there than in Baltimore, and she may have been right. He could work in the yard or set out with her by automobile to Harper's Ferry, Gettysburg, and other destinations close enough for day trips. Like August, Gertrude kept looking for signs of progress. On one occasion she noted that he took the map and traced the route to Harper's Ferry, another time that he actually came down the stairs singing one morning.

Mencken had not seen his other brother, Charlie, for more than a year when Charlie finally arrived for a visit in September 1950. The reason he had been out of touch so long, he explained in a letter to August, was that he had remarried the previous year and he had thought the news might upset Henry. When he came at last, August gave him very explicit instructions about how he should deal with his older brother. Charlie was not to say anything that might lead to an argument, was not to mention his own high blood pressure or other medical problems (since Mencken would want to send him to the Johns Hopkins Hospital), was to expect a discouraging account of Mencken's own condition, and was not to be surprised if Mencken forgot Charlie's name at first. Most of all, he was not to mention his brother's stroke. Mencken still did "not have a very clear idea as to what hit him."

Although Charlie's visit went better than expected—Mencken had good days and bad, and that was a good one—August had greater concerns. With the onset of autumn and winter his brother would be forced to spend more time indoors, and it was during such periods that he became particularly discouraged. Along with Knopf and Hamilton Owens, August had attempted for some time to find a way to keep him occupied, to make him feel that he was not altogether— as he had described himself to Owens—"a vegetable." Since his memories of certain past events were sometimes surprisingly good, August and Knopf thought Owens might be able to induce him to cooperate in some "as told to" pieces for the Sunpapers. Although Owens agreed to try, Mencken was not interested. Knopf had another idea: some young writer in Baltimore might work with Mencken in making a book out of material lying around the house. Nothing came of that either, nor of another proposal by August that he buy a small press and let his brother return to his earliest days of setting type, operating a press, and turning out booklets.

August had still another idea that for a time appeared more promising. As he had explained it several months before to the doctors at the Johns Hopkins Speech and Hearing Center, "if [Mencken] could be convinced that he was being used in part as a guinea pig and that the information derived from the work you are doing with him was of interest and value to the medical profession . . . he would look at things in a different light." Since his "great ambition" had "always been to be of some help to medicine," he might cooperate if he felt a "medical history" would result from his ordeal. Shortly afterward August had asked his friend Dr. Arnold Rich to suggest a physician at the Johns Hopkins who might be interested in working on such a project. Some activity at that point was especially important, August felt, because Mencken had almost completed the project on which he had worked, with at least limited success, for much of the past year—sorting out, with his secretary's help, the rest of his material to be given to the Enoch Pratt and other libraries.

Rich had suggested Dr. Philip Wagley, a young Hopkins physician who met Mencken and took a great interest in his case. Up until this point he had been examined by a battery of physicians—internists, neurologists, ophthalmologists, and reading specialists, as well as a psychiatrist—but "as a man with strange and unusual pregedices [*sic*], strong likes and dislikes" (as August described his brother), he had rejected much of what he had been told. The truth was that the damage from the stroke was so severe that none of the doctors could do anything of real value; nor could they have, in all probability, even forty years later. Besides, Mencken was not the easiest patient to work with.

But he wanted to feel that he had some part in determining his own medical fate. As August explained in a long letter in the spring of 1950, he had now improved to the point that he could no longer tolerate a steady diet of movies and the radio—"and television, of course, is banned from the house." Yet he lacked the confidence, as well as the interest, to undertake many of the projects proposed for him. He had not cooperated with Hamilton Owens in the Sunpapers scheme because he felt he was unable to do the job. He had to be convinced, August wrote, that he was capable of undertaking limited work, and again he had to be interested in the subject. The "medical history" would interest him most.

Wagley was not, in fact, able to make great headway on the medical history August had envisioned, but, more important, he became a close companion to Mencken. In September 1950 he put his patient into the Hopkins for another round of examinations by a number of doctors, and although the examinations turned up nothing significantly new, Mencken's spirits were lifted—as they often were at the Hopkins—by the week of medical attention. By the autumn of 1950 he had adopted, at least at times, a somewhat different view of his own condition—"no longer gloomy," Hamilton Owens wrote Knopf, "but quite philosophical." Owens found "none of that self-pity or self-condemnation" which had "formerly obsessed him." Dr. Baker concurred. Mencken still talked at times of being "dead" or "half-dead," but now he did so without the earlier tone of desperation.

Such is hardly to suggest that at times he was no longer severely depressed. On the day before his seventieth birthday Louis and Elise Cheslock came by and found him sitting in his backyard, "very low in spirits," and although he brightened up briefly as they sang "Happy Birthday" to him, he soon excused himself ("for the first time I have ever known him," Cheslock wrote) and went up to bed. But he was cheered the next day by a birthday luncheon given for him in the Sunpapers' boardroom, and he continued to enjoy frequent visits from old newspaper friends. As he turned seventy he was further gratified by the recent publication of Edgar Kemler's biography—although Kemler's portrait was not altogether flattering—and, even more, by the knowledge that William Manchester's biography would be out later in the year. Kemler's book, focusing on Mencken as satirist and skeptic, was unreliable in places: Mencken had never really "flirt[ed] with . . . Nazism," as Kemler charged. Manchester's, written with greater flair, was also the more reliable and more inclusive of the two. Both biographies were warmly received, although Manchester's more so; Edmund Wilson's review of Kemler's book gave him the opportunity to pronounce his judgment that Mencken had been "without question, since Poe, our greatest practicing literary journalist." The subject himself, of course, could read neither biographies nor reviews, nor would he allow the books to be read to him. "At that stage," August said, "he detested people reading to him."

One embarrassing result of what seemed to be a new public interest—but that also emphasized Mencken's inability to fully understand the nature of honors and praise coming his way—was his acceptance in May 1950 of the Gold Medal for Essays and Criticism of the American Academy of Arts and Letters. He had not wanted the medal at all; in fact, it was the very sort of honor he had always rejected, the kind he had criticized Dreiser for accepting in 1944. But he had not understood what was being offered when Lohrfinck had read him a letter notifying him of the award. She had responded to the academy that Mencken "received the news of the award with great pleasure," but when the recipient realized what he had accepted—after Knopf, seeing a newspaper story, alerted August—he was "greatly disturbed and upset," according to Knopf, and wanted the medal to be "withdrawn." It had been too late, however, to renege without offending friends such as Louis Untermeyer and Carl Van Doren, so Mencken accepted the honor, in absentia, with good graces. With Van Doren's presentation speech, he was at last ushered into that realm of institutional respectability he had fought all his life to avoid.

During the summer of 1950 Mencken insisted that he did not expect to live more than another six months, at most a year, but when he was discharged from the Johns Hopkins Hospital on October 4 after a thorough physical examination, both he and August felt somewhat better about his general health, if not his ability to read and write. Because he was pronounced in "good physical shape," considering his age and infirmities, August was not particularly concerned when the next week, on October 12, he complained of a pain just below his breastbone. Nor was he overly alarmed when Mencken suffered severe vomiting and diarrhea and Wagley came out to take him to the hospital. The problem seemed to August to be a severe gastric upset.

Thus he was surprised by a call from the Hopkins about 10:30 that night informing him that his brother was suffering a "severe" heart attack and might not make it until morning. Mencken had been "in near extremis" upon arrival and had immediately been placed in an oxygen tent and administered morphine and other opiates. The next twenty-four hours—as Mencken might have scripted it, it was Friday the thirteenth—would be critical. He pulled through, but the call had been close. He had dodged the date on which he had often predicted he would die.

For the next few days, however, he remained in critical condition—"near death," according to an Associated Press dispatch. The AP story was essentially correct not only in that assessment but also in the report that some of the Johns Hopkins doctors had almost "abandoned hope that [he] will live." Soon he was battling not only the heart condition but also pneumonia and a temperature that rose to 104 degrees. Each day he survived, Wagley felt, gave him a better chance, and by the end of the week he seemed to be out of grave danger, at least for the present. But he took little satisfaction in having pulled through. He was "depressed," August reported, and told his brother "he wanted to die and get it over with."

After a scare in early November and another just after Thanksgiving—in which he experienced increased congestion in his lungs, developed a possible blood clot, and again appeared to be slipping toward death—Mencken again rallied, and by early December his condition had stabilized. Realizing that his state of mind was as important as his physical condition, his doctors began to accede to his wishes on several fronts. First he was allowed to take beer in limited quantities, then he was permitted to eat pig's feet and then

517

Emma's sauerbraten and lamb stew, both of which August brought from Hollins Street. By December his interest in the world around him seemed to return: he was able to discuss Paul Patterson's retirement from the Sunpapers and the "horrible shape" of the country, and he took pleasure in listening to opera on the radio. On Christmas Day he saw a production of *Hansel and Gretel* on television, and even "enjoyed it immensely," August reported.

Neither Mencken nor his doctors wanted him to see visitors for most of his first ten weeks in the hospital. Gertrude did not come for nearly two months and Charlie not until early January. Soon Patterson, Hamilton Owens, Louis Cheslock, and other Baltimore friends were visiting, as well as an official from the Mercantile–Safe Deposit and Trust Company (in which Mencken and August had deposited funds to cover just such medical expenses as these) to assure Mencken that his long period of hospitalization had not damaged him financially to any degree. These and other visitors came, but in late February, when Marcella du Pont asked to stop by, August said no—that Mencken "did not like women visitors." A few days later Mencken relented, and when Marcella arrived the last day of February she found him in relatively good spirits and reasonably fluent in speech, except when he tried to think of names. When she came to the bed to kiss him good-bye, she told him, "Your biographers don't know anything about *me*. Someday, it's going to make us look awfully bad!" Only then did she get the "prolonged belly laugh" she had hoped for.

From November on doctors had spoken of discharging Mencken when he regained strength, but various setbacks—the two critical periods in November as well as another blood clot in late January— kept him in the Hopkins. In early December they had raised the possibility of sending him to the Baltimore Home for Incurables, but August, remembering his uncle Charlie's languishing at that institution for ten years, knew that such a move "would be fatal" for his brother. So Hollins Street it would be, and the only question was when. Mencken's physical condition was more perilous than it had been after the stroke two years earlier—examinations now indicated that he had an enlarged heart—although both Wagley and August liked to think that, if anything, his speech was somewhat better than before the heart attack. After a visit in late December, Cheslock agreed with that assessment.

For all his complaints about being hospitalized, in many ways Mencken liked being in the hospital more than he liked being out. He received constant attention, he was fond of his nurse, he could speak with doctors and other medical personnel without the fear of being embarrassed by his speech, and now that his condition had improved he enjoyed frequent nightly sessions of beer and conversation with August and Philip Wagley. By early March he was making the rounds and talking to patients on the hall, asking Wagley about their condition, and demonstrating to Wagley a flash of his humor: when they passed the portrait of the benefactor of the Brady Urological Clinic he stopped, knelt, and crossed himself. By mid-March he was certainly ready to leave, and on March 20, 1951, August, Wagley, and William Manchester drove him home to Hollins Street. A photograph of his arrival shows a frail man, much thinner and appearing much older, than the one who had entered the Hopkins more than five months earlier.

When he returned home, Mencken resumed his old routine, but with a difference. Since he was much weaker physically than before, he had brought with him his Hopkins nurse, Lois Gentry. For the first two or three months at home he rarely ventured out, and when he did it was to a movie or to the Cheslocks' for supper on Saturday night. As spring turned to summer Dr. Wagley allowed him to visit the Hollins Street market, sometimes with Wagley accompanying him. Not until early autumn was he allowed to make the fifty-mile trip to Gertrude's farm in Carroll County. It was not so much now a matter of his weakness—for by early summer he had gained weight and strength and was able to walk half a mile—as the distance from emergency aid if he should have another heart attack.

To add to his problems, for a time in the autumn Mencken feared he was going blind. An examination now showed that his vision was lost "to the right side of whatever he looked at," but, again, that was not what kept him from reading and writing. In the summer of 1951 he resumed reading lessons, and, although his instructor discovered he could often manage short, simple sentences, that was as far as he could go. He worked on his speech as well, but with no appreciable improvement. Sometimes in social situations, at least away from home, he made little attempt to speak. At dinner at the Cheslocks' in late October—an occasion on which the Cheslocks' son had set up a tape recorder—there is evident no flaw in his speech, only silences and a very few brief, simple utterances: "Where the hell is August?"; or, in response to the declarations of others, "Yah, yah, yah." Once the autocrat of the dinner table, he was now nearly mute, forced to let others hold forth.

He now saw friends even less frequently than he had in 1949 and 1950, turning down virtually all lunch and dinner invitations except the Cheslocks' and for long periods of time falling out of touch even with such old companions as Knopf and Hergesheimer—although Nathan still phoned faithfully every other Sunday morning. He now rejected all invitations to Stone Harbor, fearing the travel, a possible medical emergency, and the social awkwardness that might result. He still received visits from a few Sunpapers friends, he enjoyed seeing his young cousin William C. Abhau and his family when they came to call, and he delighted in the company of Dr. Wagley. Otherwise he withdrew further into himself, becoming for a time, his cousin later recalled, nearly a recluse. Even the Saturday Night Club belonged to the past: it had perished in December 1950 while Mencken was in the hospital, with the members (including Mencken, in absentia) voting to disband. That boisterous group had lasted half a century, but now most of its members were dead or dying.

Even more than before, Mencken now discouraged visitors from beyond his Baltimore circle. Lillian Gish, again wanting to see him, was turned down, and so were Aileen Pringle and Clare Leighton. William Randolph Hearst, Jr., was turned away at the door, and when William Manchester suggested a visit from John Dos Passos, Mencken was not interested. Jim Cain, fearing he had "upset [Mencken] badly" on a previous visit, came no more. Another visitor had earlier come away with Mencken's bitter self-assessment ringing in his ears: "It's a hell of a state of things when the only thing a man can read or write is his name." Finally, Lohrfinck was instructed to discourage most correspondents. As she had told a distant cousin of Mencken's to whom he had earlier enjoyed writing, "He suggests that it would probably be better if you don't write to him until he has recovered sufficiently to read letters sent to him." Now she was able to tell people that that time might never come.

Devastating as the results of Mencken's stroke were, they were probably made even worse by the manner in which he received them. Not only might another patient have adjusted better to the inability to read and write—one whose entire life had not been devoted to those pursuits—but another patient, one of Mencken's doctors later suggested, probably would have accepted with better grace the inability to speak with facility. Among other things, Mencken was a victim of that great pride, as well as an aversion to social embarrassment, that he had always possessed. From his youth he had been orderly, precise, competent in all he undertook—above all, *in control*—and if he could not now do things well, he sometimes refused to do them at all.

Despite his condition, he could have continued to dictate letters, letting Rosalind Lohrfinck or August supply a missing word or name here and there. In fact, as Lohrfinck wrote George Nathan in February 1952, on good days he could now dictate perfectly. Neither did his condition prevent him, with some degree of competence, from playing the piano; as he passed the piano at the Cheslocks' he occasionally played a few bars, and not badly, Cheslock observed. Nor did it prevent him from venturing out more often to the Maryland Club. And certainly it did not prevent him from allowing others to read to him or from listening to the radio or to phonograph records—all of which he had resisted for a time.

August and Gertrude, as well as Knopf, even believed he could read and write somewhat more than he claimed. On a visit to a cemetery near her farm, Gertrude found him correctly reading names on tombstones, and August sometimes found him in his study, typing a note to himself: "Order cigags" [*sic*] or, after a medical appointment, "Saw Ben Baker at his office today at 3:00 P.M. Blood and unrin tests and electrocardagraf. He said he would call me in about a week." Wagley found him capable of discussing, on some level, politics and current events, and a Huneker scholar whom Mencken allowed into Hollins Street in late 1951 found that, to some extent, he could still discuss ideas and authors—Huneker, Shaw, Percival Pollard. But he could not discuss politics or ideas with anything approaching the facility he had once possessed, and he had too much pride even to try in public, as well as too much integrity to dictate letters and claim them as his own when in fact his secretary had supplied an occasional word. Another patient's standards might not have been so high. But no other patient at the Hopkins had used words as effectively as he had, and he found it difficult to compromise now.

Three years after his stroke, then, Mencken felt he had made very little progress, and now he was virtually convinced that there would never be any improvement. Like Tithonus, the legendary Greek figure doomed to live forever, he wanted to die—he still expressed that wish to numerous friends—but after his narrow escape with the heart attack in 1950 he had grown somewhat stronger, and now he realized that death might be far away. He was indeed living out the Abhau curse, assuming the role of his poor uncle, mentally incapacitated and "suffering" (Mencken had written in 1942) "but never dying." Now *he* had become the family invalid, and he began to settle in for the long haul.

He never really stopped working, however, on his speech and his reading—as Dr. Wagley later remarked, at times he worked on it very hard—and as a result there may have been a very slight improvement in those areas in 1952 and 1953. Some of his self-defeating pride diminished as well; as time went on he no longer minded listening to the radio or even occasionally looking at television, and he no longer refused to have others read to him. Sometimes, now, he again dictated letters to old friends, including a greeting to Nathan on his seventieth birthday: "God knows that you and I have had a great time in this world." In the few letters he dictated and in others he asked Lohrfinck to write for him, he was now able to view his own condition both realistically and with a certain irreverence. He instructed his secretary to tell one friend that he was "in a hell of a mess and . . . cursing God," and he himself wrote Nathan that "God may decide to grab me up to Heaven in the near future." Although he asked numerous out-of-town friends and relatives to stop sending him gifts at Christmas because he couldn't reciprocate, from close Baltimore friends he graciously accepted gifts of cigars, wine, Scotch, bourbon, and rye. His doctors, seeing little to risk now, let him drink and smoke nearly as much as he wanted.

Around the house he required the services of a retinue of women—his nurse, his secretary, his cook, sometimes a cleaning woman, at other times a speech therapist or reading teacher—as well as his male orderly and, of course, August. All of them worked constantly both to make him comfortable and to keep him entertained. Often he was "alarmingly low" in spirits, according to Cheslock (who also pointed out that he was never one "to suffer in silence"), but Cheslock's diary also captures another side of Mencken's life in these last years. At certain times he was "in really good spirits," "excellent spirits," "looking really well." The diary catches Mencken, on one occasion, lustily singing German folk songs, on another occasion during the holidays joining in singing Christmas carols. Cheslock reports another time when Mencken was "cultivating a mustache," partly for comic effect, and looked "all the world like a Disney cartoon of an old German grandpa type." Cheslock speaks of numerous evenings in the backyard at Hollins Street, of one in particular, drinking Manhattans, listening to Mencken ponder the cosmos, and watching the moonlight play over the Beethoven mask in the garden.

There was a certain symmetry in all this—in all the time Mencken now spent in his own backyard, occupying the same ground he had occupied as a child, his consciousness now waning in the very place where, seventy years before, it had first been awakened. It seems that in any number of ways in these last years he had come full circle: again accompanied by a younger brother, he spent warm days in the backyard leading an altogether unliterary life, dreaming up activities to keep busy, only rarely leaving the Hollins Street premises and then usually to wander the back alleys of his youth or to venture to Union Square across the way. The brother now was not Charlie but August, and Mencken himself was no longer the brother in command. But in other ways it was very much the same, a world seemingly without women but nonetheless controlled by women who took care of the house and met his daily needs. And what else were Mencken's nurse, his cook, his housekeeper, and his reading teacher but what Anna Mencken, assuming all those roles, had been seventy years before?

Except for that, it sometimes again seemed a boy's world (the nurse was with "the boys in the yard," Cheslock wrote of Mencken and August), and August often had to occupy Mencken's time with boys' pursuits—picking up firewood in the alley, sawing small sticks, sifting out twigs from the mulch, going with him to the neighborhood candy store. It seemed a boy's world, and it is no accident that two of the best neighborhood friends Mencken made in these last years were young Butch next door and Alvin from down the street. They and the other neighborhood children—the recipients of the candy Mencken bought—might even be said to have constituted a sort of latter-day Hollins Street Gang. On one level it all appears to have been carefree, idyllic. The problem, of course, was that a richer, fuller, more challenging life had come in between, and the old man could not, with any contentment, return to the simpler pleasures of the boy.

The Mencken brothers, now more than ever, must have seemed a strange pair—Henry with his obvious infirmities, but August as well, with his "sensitive, nervous disposition," Cheslock observed, his "strange whistling habit—a kind of puffing, tuneless, indefinite emission of sound," his hand constantly pounding a table or chair. August was more eccentric than ever, still the misogynist ("I am sick of these women around the house") but, as Cheslock also noted, altogether devoted to his brother: he had given up his job as an engineer to spend all his time with Henry. Perhaps he thought it only fitting since in his early years, when he was tubercular, weak, and lacking in confidence, Mencken had looked after him, had spoken on his behalf, had supervised his recovery. Now August had assumed his older brother's role as spokesman, caretaker, family arbiter, and correspondent, "Without [him] I'd be lost indeed," Mencken had written even before the stroke. Now that was immeasurably true.

But finally that was not enough. Nor were the visits to Gertrude's farm, nor to the Cheslocks' for dinner, nor even the compassionate care and friendship of Philip Wagley. At bottom Mencken was still desperately unhappy at having to face (as August wrote Gertrude) the "dreadful monotony of [a] life" without reading and writing, the terrible frustration—for this man who had always expressed himself so clearly—of muddled thought and less-than-intelligible speech. He still had physical complaints, largely chest pains and poor vision, and he was placed in the Hopkins on several other occasions for examinations and at least once for minor surgery that, because of the condition of his heart, became serious. But the "dreadful monotony" was still the primary problem. More forthcoming than ever, Lohrfinck now spoke in letters to his friends of "dark bleak days," and in the spring of 1953 August wrote more than once of "the horrors of the past winter." At times, when Mencken was feeling "especially miserable," he "would [lie] on his bed and groan." Other times, "cooped up in the house with nothing to do," he was "driven to the point," August felt, "where he was going insane." Even in the summers August faced the problem, as he wrote Gertrude, of "let[ting] Henry do enough work to keep him from going [mad] and at the same time to hold it to a point where it does him no injury."

One by one Mencken saw his remaining friends die—Gustav Strube and Heinie Buchholz of the Saturday Night Club, Charles Abell and James Fenhagen of the Sunpapers board, Paul Patterson, and finally Hergesheimer (his "closest friend," Lohrfinck wrote Dorothy)—and he was fully capable of appreciating the irony of it all. Most of them, still mentally alert, had been struck down quickly, and he, wishing for death, had outlived them all—and for no purpose. He both marveled at and decried a medical science that could keep him alive but could do nothing to make him better. In desperation he himself now suggested possibilities—once he demanded brain surgery, which would have been altogether futile—but in fact, as August later remarked, he finally relinquished his belief in doctors as the possessors of near-magical powers, and that in itself was a great cause of his distress. As his brother noted, to Mencken physicians had always been "sacred cows"—"his attitude toward doctors would be roughly parallel to a Catholic's attitude toward priests . . . he thought they could do miracles"—and his letters to friends, urging them to come to Baltimore for a cure, had always shown this unwavering faith. But they could not perform miracles. His experiences with Sara should have taught him that but had not, and now he was learning in the most painful way possible.

Only once during his last seven years did Mencken speak, at length and for the record, about his own condition, and that was when his doctors asked him to dictate to his secretary, over a period of some four months, his exact feelings about himself. The results, in his own struggling, repetitive language taken down verbatim by Lohrfinck, suggest more poignantly than anything else both the inadequacy of his expression and the frustration he ultimately felt:

My talking is now so difficult that it is extremely difficult for me to give a reasoning of my method of working. (Throw it away. See, it is no good.)

It is more difficult for me to give an account than it used to be, and the result is that it is more difficult than ever for me to give an account. (Throw it away.) See, I can't talk and that's all there is to it. . . . It is possible that I may be better as I go on [in this account], but on that I am not so sure. I simply can't give an account of what I am doing. Things are more difficult than it was formerly and I can't go to the matter at all. (See, this is terrible.) My opinion is that in a little while I'll be unable to talk at all and that I'll have to devote myself to a few words now and then and nothing else. Things are very unpleasant as things are now. (Don't change it. Always print it as I said it. They want to see what I have said.) . . .

My description is now so bad that it is completely impossible for me to talk. When I start on a subject I lose it very quickly and in a little while it is gone altogether. It is not general to most people that I am so difficult. They imagine that I can understand what everybody says, but actually I see very little and it doesn't last any time. My whole time is half dead. I am like a man who is half awake. I don't wake up sometimes for an hour. When I am working on stuff here I do nothing whatever and think of nothing whatsoever. My mind is completely dead. . . .

My hope is that I'll go very quickly, because this thing is something awful. I feel all the time rotten. If anyone talks to me I am pretty well done. Oh, well, what the hell! I don't give a damn. I can't see anything at all, you see. Everything is bad. I am going to hell. I'll never finish this job. I can't talk about my illness and I can't think of it in detail. It just doesn't come to my mind. I don't know what I am talking about. It is really an outrage to be sick like this. I should die and get done with it.

At times in his lengthy dictation Mencken speaks of escaping the horrors of a locked-in mind—once he describes a "perfectly superb evening" in the backyard with August and Philip Wagley, another time a pleasant stay at Gertrude's farm—and at times he speaks in a concrete, nearly lyrical language that Hemingway might have appreciated: "I am going down in the yard to do some painting on the new stuff that August made. It will be very gaudy. We will paint it red and it will be a gaudy affair." Or "My brother and I spent yesterday evening in the yard. It was extraordinarily lovely, cool and yet somewhat warmish and very bright." But most of the time he could not escape the anguish:

My mind won't follow. It won't come in and I don't know what to say for it. . . . I can't see anything. I always seem in danger of falling down and may fall on myself sometime soon. I don't give a good goddamn. It's the hardest thing to imagine—to be not caring what is happening to me. It is really comic. It is a dreadful thing.

---

Having for five years expressed a wish to die, but at last seeing he was neither going to die anytime soon nor get well, in 1954 and 1955 Mencken did a surprising thing. If only in a very limited way, he reemerged into the public eye. First he began to grant occasional interviews, initially to William Manchester for the Baltimore *Sun*, then to R. P. Harriss for Harriss's Baltimore magazine, *Gardens, Houses and People*, and finally to another reporter for the Associated Press.

In Manchester's widely circulated piece Mencken publicly expressed political opinions for the first time in more than five years, and he was more charitable than he had formerly been. Eisenhower was doing a "better-than-average" job as president, he believed, and even Truman had done "some good work." Manchester reported that Mencken was pessimistic about his own condition—"I wish it were all over" he again said—but in other parts of the interview he sounded somewhat more sanguine. Harriss also found his subject more cheerful than he had expected, believed his memory had improved somewhat since their last visit, and even caught a glimpse of Mencken's old gusto. The AP article captured a man gracious but obviously sorrowful, now referring to himself in the past tense: "The trouble is I didn't live long enough to write all I wanted."

For whatever reason, while his physical condition deteriorated in 1954 and 1955, his speech improved. He more frequently welcomed out-of-town visitors now, including Felix Frankfurter, Alistair Cooke, Phil Goodman's daughter Ruth, and Sara's sister Philippa and her daughter, now a student at Goucher. He even had Lohrfinck instruct Aileen Pringle that, if she were in Baltimore, she should call; if he felt well enough, he would like to see her.

In addition to his close circle of Baltimore friends, he invited old acquaintances who were never really intimates, men he had not seen since his stroke, and he also saw more recent friends such as Manchester, who often came over in the evening for drinks and conversation beside the fire. He even consented to have Manchester read to him each morning, first the newspaper, then his old favorites Twain and Conrad. When Manchester left Baltimore in the spring of 1955, August engaged Robert Allen Durr, a Hopkins graduate student, to continue the reading. August even devised another scheme to "teach" Mencken to read: he felt it would be easier, for rather complicated reasons he explained to Wagley, if Mencken could learn to read aloud to himself. Although that plan, like so many others of August's well-intentioned schemes, came to nothing, Mencken's willingness to listen to others read, as well as his new pair of yellow-tinted lenses, which took care of many of his complaints about his vision, made life at Hollins Street somewhat more bearable.

Equally indicative of his somewhat improved spirits was his renewed interest in what was being written about him. Not all of it was favorable. In September 1954 his nemesis Charles Angoff had presented him with a dubious seventy-fourth birthday gift, a piece in *The New Republic* again claiming that Mencken had been an inferior critic, philologist, and thinker—but, Angoff still insisted, a good editor and an old friend. Other publicity was more favorable. When Nathan married, at age seventy-two, in October 1954, editors fondly recalled "The Age of Mencken," the days when the *Smart Set* editors had flourished. Shortly afterward Knopf made plans to bring out *The Vintage Mencken*, a collection of some of his finest shorter work with an introduction by Alistair Cooke. At the same time as Mencken was preparing to submit his formal resignation from the board of directors of Knopf, a step he finally took in April 1955, he was gratified to see that his old friend was again publishing his work.

His plans did not stop there. Since the time of the stroke he had had on hand a body of material he had earlier produced or that had been halted abruptly in November 1948. Some of it—such as the diary, "My Life as Author and Editor" (which had reached only 1923), and "Thirty-Five Years of Newspaper Work"—he still did not intend for publication in his lifetime. But other material he thought might be published. In 1952 he had instructed Lohrfinck to send Knopf eight autobiographical essays, half of them unpublished, which he thought might make a fourth volume of the *Days* series, but at that time he had agreed with Knopf's assessment that "it would be a great mistake to publish such a little volume." Now, in 1955, Lohrfinck came across still more unpublished material in the basement in which Knopf would surely be interested.

It was the collection of "brief paragraphs—sometimes mere sentences" that Mencken had mentioned in his diary in the 1940s, and just before his stroke had begun to prepare for publication. When he had first written a preface for it, in July 1943, he had decided the book had "a hex riding it" because he "had done the preface before [he] noticed that the day was the 13th." For that reason, he had written in his diary, he was "not too sure that it will ever be finished," and indeed his plans to publish it in 1949 had been thwarted by the stroke. At that point he had forgotten about the manuscript. When his secretary unearthed it, he spent several months going over the material with her deciding which items to use, which to excise.

About the time he began to work on that volume, *The Vintage Mencken* appeared to great acclaim. The volume was part of a general outpouring of tributes in September 1955, the occasion of his seventy-fifth birthday. Cooke and Manchester both had pieces in *Saturday Review* (which placed Mencken's picture on the cover), Gerald Johnson wrote an encomium for the Baltimore *Sun* and Edgar Kemler for *The New York Times*. More than a thousand letters and hundreds of telegrams also poured into Hollins Street to commemorate the occasion.

Mencken was genuinely moved by the tributes. Shortly before he had complained to his reader, Bob Durr, that five or six years after his death "nobody will remember my name." About the same time he had heard from a Japanese correspondent that a visiting American was spreading the news that he had already "passed on." But now he was convinced that, after all, he was not forgotten. He was particularly pleased with *The Vintage Mencken*, copies of which reached him the day after his birthday, and with the tributes by Manchester and Johnson. He might have taken issue, however, with Kemler's overly optimistic assessment that he had become "reconciled to the 1948 stroke" and "enjoys life again": "By his willingness now to limp along where he once soared, he has found himself . . ." And the satisfaction he felt in being remembered was tempered by sorrow. Among the letters he received was one from Hedda Hopper recalling the hilarious time he had enjoyed in Hollywood thirty years before with Hergesheimer, Aileen Pringle, and Jim Tully. "It makes him very sad," Lohrfinck responded, "to think that those days and those wonderful times are gone forever."

Not long after his birthday Mencken encountered further physical problems. His hay fever, always a nuisance at the time of his birthday, was worse than it had ever been, and he also suffered from an arm and shoulder injury he had sustained rolling out of bed. Already August dreaded "the return of winter because it is a time of horror here." However, the remainder of the fall passed more smoothly than August had anticipated. With a burst of sociability not seen since his stroke, Mencken had Lohrfinck invite even more friends, mostly from the Sunpapers, to stop by. He and August continued to see the Cheslocks on Saturday evenings for beer, snacks, and music. And even when he checked into the hospital in October to have his arm treated, he found that experience far from unpleasant. Dr. Wagley had left Baltimore earlier in the year for military duty, and Mencken, needing one of his periodic examinations, had decided to abandon the Hopkins, which both he and August had come to find rather cold and impersonal, and turn instead to the Bon Secours Hospital, a much smaller institution within walking distance of 1524 Hollins. With Wagley no longer available, August had engaged Dr. Joseph Muse, the son of an old neighbor of theirs, as his brother's primary physician. Mencken had been "greatly pleased" with his spring visit to the Bon Secours. When he returned in October for treatment on his arm, he found the same hospitality.

In nearly every respect he was coming home—to the Hollins Street house and garden to which he was now largely confined; to the neighborhood hospital and doctor after all his years of allegiance to the Johns Hopkins. From his room in the Bon Secours he even had the same reassuring sight of nuns in their garden below that he had had as a boy looking from the upper floors of the Hollins Street house into the "vast, mysterious compound" of the House of the Good Shepherd. His memories of his early years must have been stirred further by a letter he received earlier in the year from a domestic, now confined to the Baltimore City Hospital, who had worked for the Menckens long before. She had just come across *Happy Days* and had reflected, in a letter eloquent in its utter artlessness, on what Mencken had written in that book: "You've often spoken of the little alley in the Back of your home. And just to think that is where my residence was during My Childhood Days." She recalled the "powerful preaching" and the singing in the alley, and other sights and sounds of a Hollins Street long gone. "You and Mr. Charlie sure had some happy Days together, while you'all were children." She signed, "Sincerely yours with Remembrance."

As late fall moved into winter, Mencken was growing weaker—in December his secretary had to cancel or postpone several visits—but he still had the one bit of unfinished business. He and Lohrfinck worked through November and December on the volume of aphorisms and brief essays he now considered calling "H. L. Mencken's Notebook" but which was to become *Minority Report*. By mid-December his secretary had finished typing most of the manuscript. When Alfred Knopf came to Baltimore in December to discuss the work, he was pleased with what he found. Both he and Mencken excised certain items—some relating to archaic political matters, some (Knopf wrote) because "you could not reply to criticism" of them—but much remained, including remarks on the New Deal, the South, and Christianity. Mencken knew he had put together another contentious book and dictated a letter to Knopf saying as much: "I suppose I'll be denounced violently by various people, but always remember that there are other people who will like it very much."

As 1956 dawned he occupied himself with routine tasks. He mailed out several copies of *The Vintage Mencken*, he obliged a collector of Menckeniana who requested one of his half-smoked Uncle Willies, he had Lohrfinck write to Nathan expressing concern over Nathan's poor health, and he dictated a letter—which was to be his last—thanking a twelve-year-old girl, a neighbor of Gertrude's, for candy she had sent him. He got together for at least one more Saturday night in mid-January with Cheslock, and on January 12 he felt well enough to receive a French visitor.

But principally he looked forward to the publication of *Minority Report*. It was now with the printer, Knopf announced in a January release, and would be out soon. Mencken, he explained, wanted "to see it . . . before the angels see him." The volume received further publicity in late January when an Associated Press reporter interviewed Mencken and wrote a feature that was distributed nationally. "It will be nice being denounced again," the author remarked, as he had earlier to Knopf, and he went on to explain that the book would be "controversial." The AP story described Mencken sitting in an easy chair and smoking a cigar; it referred to his stroke of 1948 but made little mention of his current physical condition. "It is heartening to infer from the newspapers that Mr. Mencken's health has recently improved," Mark Schorer wrote Lohrfinck. Indeed, to all appearances, this was the most alive he had been in the more than seven years since his stroke.

The day after Schorer wrote, a Saturday, Mencken spent as he had many other Saturdays—resting, listening to the Metropolitan Opera on the radio (Wagner's *Die Meistersinger,* an appropriate offering), and preparing for Cheslock's visit that evening. When his guest arrived about 7:30 (as Cheslock recorded, in detail, in his diary), he first encountered August, who told him that Henry had felt ill and was resting upstairs. A few minutes later Mencken appeared on the stairs "looking disheveled" and told Cheslock, "Louis, this is the last you'll see me." Both August and Cheslock, believing he had an inconsequential virus, dismissed such a notion, and a short time later, after he vomited, he felt much better. They all had martinis and discussed music, movies, television announcers, and Mencken's forthcoming book. At 9:00 P.M., again feeling ill, Mencken excused himself, once more telling Cheslock he would not see him again. Cheslock left shortly afterward, pondering Mencken's statement. He had never said that before.

Death did not come as Mencken, twenty years before, had jokingly predicted it would: "The bells will toll, the fire engines will go rushing through the streets, the cops will yell and shoot off their pistols, and you will hear the news that I have been translated into an angel." It came instead as sleet was falling in the depths of a silent midwinter night, one not unlike that January night fifty-seven years before when his own father had died in the same house. Mencken was found about 8:30 the next morning in his third-floor bedroom by his orderly, and August immediately called both Dr. Muse and Cheslock. Dr. Muse arrived before 10:00 A.M., went upstairs, and shortly afterward came down to report that Mencken had died in his sleep between 3:00 and 4:00 A.M. August then called Gertrude, Knopf, and the Sunpapers, tried unsuccessfully to reach Charlie in Pittsburgh, and waited for attendants to come to deliver Mencken's body to the Johns Hopkins Hospital for an autopsy. The death certificate, issued two days later, would list, under cause of death, "coronary."

In preparing for death, as in life, Mencken had taken no chances. He had left instructions that the Sunpapers should "print only a brief announcement of [his death], with no attempt at a biographical sketch, no portrait, and no editorial." If those instructions seem curious for a man who feared more than anything else that he would be forgotten, the other directions were not puzzling at all. He wanted no funeral, and he wanted to be cremated. Once he had announced that a "crying need" existed in "this incomparable Republic" for "a suitable Burial Service for the admittedly damned," but he had never got around to writing it. Another time he had proposed the first movement of Beethoven's Third Symphony for his "own obsequies." But finally his primary concern was that his sister, Gertrude, a faithful Episcopalian, might try to give him a Christian burial, although she had earlier vowed she would not.

Mencken's first request met with little success. The Monday *Sun* printed both a lengthy story, with a large picture and biographical sketch, and a second piece by Hamilton Owens as well as an editorial. Newspapers across the country announced his death with headlines and stories. He was more successful in his second request: August carried out his instructions to the letter. No clergyman appeared on Tuesday, January 31, at the Witzke Funeral Home on Hollins Street (save a penitentiary chaplain who was an old friend, and he appeared in no official capacity), just Mencken's family and a small group of friends, including Knopf and Jim Cain and a contingent of Sunpapermen. Some friends, including Nathan, were prevented from coming because of illness. Shortly after 1:00 P.M. Hamilton Owens said a few words, explaining what all those assembled already knew—that Mencken wanted no formal service. There followed a minute or two of silence, after which August nodded to the undertaker to remove the simple, closed black casket. The proceedings were over in less than fifteen minutes.

After that there remained only for August and Charlie to accompany Mencken's body to the Loudon Park Cemetery, where it would be cremated and the ashes placed in the family grave. Loudon Park was familiar ground—unlike, Mencken would have said, the alien territory of Dreiser's Forest Lawn. Barely three miles from his birthplace, it was the cemetery that his grandfather Mencken had helped to create nearly a century before; that he himself, in a brief foray into advertising at age twenty-one, had promoted as "a beautiful and convenient spot for the burial of the dead"; and, most of all, it was the ground in which his father and mother and Sara lay.

There was, to the end, that same order and harmony, a remarkable symmetry, to Mencken's life.

# CODA

# THE POSTHUMOUS LIFE OF
# H. L. MENCKEN

Although it is true of almost any writer of note that his story hardly ends with his death—that posthumous publication of manuscripts, changes in critical tastes and political sensibilities, and any number of other factors affect the fluctuations of his stock in the literary market—such a condition is particularly the case with H. L. Mencken. By his own reckoning he was, or was to be, the man who died twice, once with the stroke of 1948, when his writing was terminated, and again, as it turned out, in 1956, when at last his ashes were deposited in the Loudon Park Cemetery. But what he had not anticipated was that, as a writer, he would lead a third life more productive and certainly more vigorous than the death-in-life he had endured between 1948 and 1956, as active as certain parts of that life before 1948. Or perhaps—it becomes increasingly evident—he anticipated the third life after all, indeed in some measure orchestrated it by delaying the release of his voluminous literary correspondence until fifteen years after his death, the opening of his diary for twenty-five years, and the release—and certain publication—of the two autobiographical manuscripts, "My Life as Author and Editor" and "Thirty-Five Years of Newspaper Work," for a full thirty-five years. In any event, if we are to measure literary success by original manuscripts published, impassioned reviews inspired, and controversy sparked (not the only measures of that success, to be sure), not since

Mark Twain, perhaps, has an American writer had a more notable, some would say notorious, posthumous career.

Hardly had August and Charlie committed him to the grave than that career began. The author of "Bryan," that scathing editorial obituary of the Great Commoner, could hardly have expected to escape the same treatment himself, and thus editorials bearing such titles as "The Scoffer Withereth Away" (although in the minority) would not have surprised him at all. Neither would the five votes cast in the Maryland State Senate opposing a resolution expressing "sorrow . . . over the passing of Henry Louis Mencken," nor even the knowledge that the FBI, postmortem, was adding to its files on him. Placed in his dossier and stamped February 3, five days after his death, was a clipping of the *Sun* story reporting his last interview, three days before his death.

It was almost as if he had timed the publication of *Minority Report* to answer just such foes who assumed that at last he was silenced (even if still dangerous, as the FBI entry suggests). Speaking from the grave in the spring of 1956, he was fully as combative, if not always as eloquent, as he had been in his heyday of the 1920s. Despite the absence of the more offensive passages that he and Knopf had removed in the months before his death, enough remained on politics, religion, and American culture to remind the reader that the author of *Prejudices* was, in a polemical sense, still stirring. Although now he largely spared Jews and Englishmen, with only two or three thrusts at each, a sampling of his maxims would suggest that he was as uncompromising toward religious belief in general and Christianity in particular as he had ever been:

> God is the immemorial refuge of the incompetent, the helpless, the miserable.
>
> The idea at the bottom of the Christian eucharist is precisely the idea at the bottom of cannibalism.
>
> The time must come inevitably when mankind shall surmount the imbecility of religion, as it has surmounted the imbecility of religion's ally, magic.

"Out of the past [Mencken's voice] comes, and as vibrant, penetrating and provocative as ever I have heard it," wrote a reviewer somewhat too effusively in *The Atlantic,* and other reviews, if not always favorable, were lengthy and numerous. Knopf sold over 20,000 copies of *Minority Report* in a few months, the book appeared on the *New York Times* best-seller list in June and July, and the ghost of Mencken had only begun its long and contentious life. Readers "will refuse to believe," Julian Boyd wrote in a protracted discussion in the *Times*, "that the vast bin from which these thoughts were culled has become empty."

That bin was to be raided for still another book a few months later—*A Carnival of Buncombe* (edited by Malcolm Moos), a collection of Mencken's writing on American politics from 1920 to 1936. In the following two years, as three more collections of his work appeared, newspapers were speaking of a "Mencken revival." But the voice in the Mencken chorus that was to reverberate most loudly during that period was not the author's own or those of his champions but rather that of his longtime detractor Charles Angoff. Only a month after *Minority Report* appeared, less than five months after Mencken's death, Angoff produced—in ghoulish fashion, it seemed to the subject's friends—the book that Mencken had known was coming: it was that full measure of revenge that his *Mercury* "slave" had been waiting twenty years to exact. *H. L. Mencken: A Portrait from Memory* repeated the charges Angoff had earlier brought—that Mencken was an inferior thinker, critic, and philologist—and it added a great many more besides. While Mencken lived, Angoff had hesitated to accuse him of anti-Semitism. Now he not only leveled that charge but accused him as well of pettiness, mean-spiritedness, betrayal of friends, and general misanthropy: "Mencken most often despised people." Claiming to have known his boss better "than almost anyone else" between 1925 and 1935, he painted a picture of a man despicable in nearly every aspect.

Mencken's friends, Knopf in particular, were furious. Angoff was an "unbelievable swine," he wrote Arthur Schlesinger, and he had written an "obscene" book. Even those reviewers who were not friends or supporters of Mencken recognized the animosity of Angoff's "mean . . . book," his "posthumous biting . . . of the hand that fed him." It was not that Angoff was wrong in all particulars, although his gossippy tone and feeble attempts, twenty-five years later, to quote Mencken verbatim compromised his credibility. It was rather that the purpose of his writing was so obviously vengeance. He had always taken Mencken literally, had missed altogether, or preferred to ignore, the teaser, the practical joker, that Mencken by all accounts had been in his heyday. He himself had been the butt of much of that humor, as well as the object of Mencken's criticism once the *Mercury* editor stepped down and Angoff himself had his brief attempt at running the magazine. As Knopf later said, "Slaves have a way of turning ultimately on their masters."

Angoff was to devote much of the remainder of his career to the business of debunking the debunker. More immediately, as soon as his book appeared in the summer of 1956 he pressed his case in other forums, in July excoriating Mencken on an hour-long NBC radio "Biography in Sound" and, the following year, denouncing him in *The New Republic* as a racist and Nazi sympathizer. At the same time, Knopf was emerging as Mencken's primary defender, writing to Robert Sarnoff of NBC to express his objections to the radio biography and letting numerous writers and publishers know how strongly he objected to Angoff's book. He was joined in his initial defense by Schlesinger, Gerald Johnson, and William Manchester.

Mencken's other staunchest defender—as steadfast a protector of Mencken's reputation in death as he had been of his well-being in life—was his brother August. The Mencken family had not fared well since Henry's death. First, Charlie and Charlie's wife, impoverished as always, had been displeased with the terms of Mencken's will—which provided for August and Gertrude for life, left $10,000 to Rosalind Lohrfinck and more modest sums to Charlie, Virginia, and Mencken's housekeeper, Emma Ball, and stipulated that three quarters of the remainder of the $300,000 estate go to the Enoch Pratt Free Library and one quarter to the Johns Hopkins Hospital. Before they could take legal action, Charlie died of heart disease barely two months after Henry's death. August and Gertrude disapproved so greatly of his widow, Ruth, and of Virginia that they declined to attend the funeral in Pennsylvania—and five months later still did not know exactly where their other brother was buried.

In the spring of 1956, while August and Gertrude were fighting off threats from Ruth Mencken to overturn Mencken's will, they were also resisting what they saw as attempts by television producers and filmmakers to exploit their brother in death. In May August rejected a proposal for a "motion picture, television or stage play" on Mencken's life, and although he initially approved the idea of the NBC radio biography in July, to be narrated by Chet Huntley, he later felt the radio program had been "altered for [Angoff's] benefit" when "the radio people got news of [his] forthcoming book." Gertrude was even fiercer than August in her suspicion of those who might tarnish her brother's reputation, and in her opposition to Angoff and to radio and motion-picture "ghouls" she demonstrated an anti-Semitism far harsher than any Mencken himself had ever shown. She suspected the "horrible Jews" in broadcasting and film of a conspiracy: "I think [they] have discovered, probably through Angoff, something I have always known. That is, while Henry was fond of individual Jews [such as Knopf] he scorned them as a race and they are out to discredit him." She wrote Knopf, asking him to discourage plans for a motion picture in particular. Even if the filmmakers were not out to expose Mencken, "I can see no honor for my brother in putting him in a class with ex-ballplayers—blues singers—rock and roll musicians—and such."

Filmmakers and broadcasters were hardly the only threats to the memory of their brother that August and Gertrude wanted to preserve. Mencken himself had expected, indeed desired, the exhuming of his literary and intellectual remains: he would have approved enthusiastically of the job Carl Bode, William H. Nolte, and several other "professor-doktors" heterodox for their species were performing on the corpus. Certainly he would have welcomed the posthumous tribute from Van Wyck Brooks, who called Mencken "the rude forefather of us all." But what he had not envisioned was the extent to which his emotional remains would also be dragged out, examined, and displayed. He thought he had taken care of that possibility when he broke contact with those women with whom he had been close, destroyed most of their letters, and asked that many of his own be destroyed. He could not have anticipated that those women (save Sara) with whom he had been closest—Marion Bloom, Aileen Pringle, Gretchen Hood, Marcella du Pont—would, after his death, possess their own rage to explain, if only in private (at least initially) and, in several cases, often to an audience of one.

That audience was Betty Adler, a librarian at the Enoch Pratt and a woman, crippled with polio, who gave much of the last two decades of her life to finding out as much as possible about Mencken and bringing as much additional material as possible to the Pratt. Within a decade of his death, she had established close contact with Bloom, Hood, and du Pont and provided them with the sympathetic ear they required if they were ever to discuss Henry Mencken. In the Pratt today one finds dozens of letters to Adler from the three women, testifying to the fact that Bloom and Hood in particular, even after forty or fifty years, had never stopped thinking about him, had never ceased to blame him at some level, had never stopped considering what life with him might have been like. Both now eighty years old and battling the ravages of age and ill health, both living in Washington, even seeing each other on occasion and exchanging stories about Mencken, Bloom and Hood seemed at times real-life embodiments of certain old Faulknerian spinsters, each telling her story partly because she wanted to come to terms with it but even more because she wanted it heard, wanted it known that she had once been part of the life of a man so vital and so celebrated.

As far as the official record is concerned, Mencken had virtually erased Marion Bloom from his life after 1929. He had seen her sister Estelle sometimes and had even heard from Marion herself in the late 1940s concerning a professional matter. But in his memoirs, as we have seen, he had ignored her altogether, and when correspondents chanced to mention Marion, he usually professed little knowledge of her. He had apparently retained some private interest: when Estelle sent him her own letters from Marion, in which he himself had played a leading part, he went over the letters carefully, made notes in the margins, and in a rare unguarded moment included the letters in his own correspondence to be given to the New York Public Library.

But Marion was hardly aware of that fact when she began to write to Betty Adler—Estelle's correspondence was still sealed in New York—and in her letters to Adler it seemed most important that she make clear that she had been, along with Sara, "one of the two most important women in his life." She was critical of Mencken at times, not only for what she considered to be his unfair treatment of her but also for what she believed was a lack of constancy in his male friendships—but she still viewed him with great affection. Her position remained what she had expressed to Estelle much earlier: Mencken had "given me more happiness than anyone, and more unhappiness." Now aging, impoverished, afflicted with emphysema and failing eyesight, she wanted their story told in all its complexity. She feared August would be "against" her writing a book about her liaison with Mencken, but that is precisely what she first had in mind. Finally, in 1971, when Adler declined to help her with the book, she was content to sell her Mencken letters to the Pratt for $5,000. When she died in 1975 at age eighty-three, her obituary in *The Washington Post* identified her as "an Army nurse during World War I [and] a friend and aide to H. L. Mencken." She was not, as the obituary also claimed she was, the "author of several books," although she had always wanted to be.

Hood was also eager to write a book about Mencken, or rather to publish his letters to her, and she too wrote to Adler of her plans. Both Macmillan and Knopf were interested, she said (although neither ever published them), and although she too cited money as a reason for publication, it was clear that, like Bloom, she primarily wanted certification as part of Mencken's life. "What a pity I couldn't have him!" she exclaimed to Adler, but her tone was no longer as resentful as it had been forty years before. With time even Hood, the most embittered of all of Mencken's rejected women, could be philosophical. Eventually she too was to sell his letters, complete with her own annotations, to Emory University. Several years later Aileen Pringle—who may have loved Mencken most of all, or at least had expressed that love most openly—took a similar course. She had determined that her Mencken letters—which included those letters she had written him between 1926 and 1929 (returned to her by Mencken) in which she had openly expressed her love—should be preserved. Shortly after her death in 1989, her letters were given to Yale University. She too had wanted the world to know.

It is curious the interest these women, especially Bloom and Hood, took in each other, forty years after they had known Mencken. Bloom approved of Hood altogether—"a charming woman to look at," she decided after meeting her at the National Press Club—but was acquainted with Marcella du Pont, now a poet and Washington hostess, only by reputation and wanted to know more. "I am so very curious," she wrote Adler, "to know if the duPont and Henry were in love." In her own letters to Adler in the 1960s and early 1970s, du Pont would admit only to being a dear friend who still missed Mencken sorely. But she too had plans, at least had entertained such plans in the early sixties, to publish her correspondence with Mencken, and had enlisted the help of a mutual friend to convince August that the letters should be in print. She should have known in advance what August's reaction would be. The letters were never published.

In September 1980, the centenary of Mencken's birth, several hundred friends, journalists, scholars, and fans, including the governor and attorney general of Maryland, gathered in Baltimore's Belvedere Hotel and Pratt Library to celebrate that auspicious occasion. Among the assembled were Alfred Knopf, now eighty-eight and the unquestioned patriarch of the Mencken brotherhood, as well as Alistair Cooke, William Manchester, and others who had contributed to a centennial volume Knopf had brought out. Knopf himself had the last word in that volume, an affectionate memoir similar in tone and spirit to his earlier tribute, "For Henry with Love."

No member of the Mencken family was present, except for Mencken's younger cousin Admiral William C. Abhau. August had died in May 1967, having lived at Hollins Street until his death. The years after Henry's death had not been altogether easy ones for him. The quarrel over Mencken's estate had continued for a time after Charlie's death, with his wife hiring a lawyer and threatening to sue to overturn Mencken's will on the grounds of mental incapacity. August had also worried about the fate of the Hollins Street house. After having been concerned earlier that it would fall into his niece, Virginia's, hands, he came to fear that it would succumb to the blight that was overtaking Union Square and be "wrecked." From the time of Mencken's illness he had hoped it might become a "museum" to honor his brother, and indeed in his own last years it had already become something of a shrine. August's friends reported that he often still set a place for Henry on those rare occasions when he had dinner guests and that he kept his brother's room exactly as it had been before his death. Gertrude's form of tribute, since she had not been able to give Mencken a Christian burial, was to present a gold chalice to her church in his memory.

The significance of September 1980 for the Mencken family went far beyond the festivities in the Belvedere Hotel and the Pratt Library. For in keeping with that remarkable coincidence of events that had marked Mencken's own life, the month of his centenary also saw the deaths, on consecutive days, of the only remaining Menckens he would have claimed as members of his family. Two weeks after the celebration in Baltimore, his sister, Gertrude, died at ninety-three near her farm in Carroll County and his niece, Virginia, died at sixty-five in Pennsylvania. It was not precisely true, as one report had it, that with their deaths "the Mencken family line comes to an end." Although Virginia's son David Mencken Morrison, the "Davy" of whom Mencken had been extremely fond in his early years, had died in a plane crash in 1974, a younger son survived. But Mencken had never seen him, and as far as he had been concerned, Virginia and David were indeed the end of the line.

The events of September 1980 and shortly thereafter marked a transition in the posthumous life of Mencken the writer as well. They signaled the end of a period during which he had nearly settled into the role Walter Lippmann, fifty years earlier, had prophesied for him—"one of the grand old men, one of the beloved patriarchs of his time." He had approached that lofty status because many later readers had nearly forgotten him as the combative polemicist of the 1920s and instead remembered him as the author of *The American Language*, the best selling of his works, and, close behind it in sales, the *Days* volumes. Neither of these works showed the author at his feistiest. As Charles Fecher had written in *Mencken: A Study of His Thought* only two years before the centenary, the author of the *Days* books, with their "smiling and amiable tolerance of human foibles," was the Mencken that "readers of later generations" would know.

In Baltimore he had also assumed the role of favorite son. The city celebrated his birthday not just in 1980 but each year, a Mencken Society was now flourishing, and a journal, *Menckeniana* (begun by Betty Adler in 1962), appeared quarterly. The home on Hollins Street, after serving for a time in the unlikely capacity of office space for the University of Maryland School of Social Work and as a residence for VISTA volunteers, had at last become the "museum" August had envisioned. Mencken had indeed become a sort of "grand old man" in Baltimore, a civic treasure surpassed only by Babe Ruth and the newly constructed Inner Harbor.

The release of the diary from its twenty-five-year time lock on January 29, 1981, just four months after the centenary, was not to negate that celebrity in Baltimore, but it was to alter (particularly outside Baltimore) the image of the man being celebrated. Or, rather, it was to return to center stage the sharp-tongued commentator of the 1920s and 1930s and to diminish the 1940s chronicler of childhood. The diary—at times bitter and despairing, as we have seen, at times

543

mean-spirited toward friends, associates, and literary acquaintances—was to create controversy throughout the 1980s, even before
it was published at the end of the decade. The initial phase of the
controversy revolved around the question of whether it should be
published at all. When Mencken had determined that the diary
should go to the Enoch Pratt Free Library, he had stipulated not only
that it be sealed for a quarter century after his death but also that,
even when it was released, it be made available "only to students
engaged in critical or historical investigation." But he had also
seemed to suggest in occasional letters to friends that (as he expressed it in 1934 to Fielding Garrison) such confidential reflections
might be "printed properly" at some point "long after my transition
to the fields of bliss," when the subjects of his entries would also be
dead. It was a case for the lawyers, and in October 1985 the Maryland
attorney general ruled that the diary might indeed be published.

Not only had Mencken's diary created a stir even before its publication—partly because of the legal dispute but also because news of
its contents and tone had already leaked out—but various other
manuscript materials, both published and unpublished, had brought
their author back into the national spotlight. The publication in the
mid-eighties of his letters to Dreiser, as well as volumes of letters to
Sara and to Gretchen Hood, resulted in essays such as Alfred Kazin's
"Mencken and the Great American Boob" in *The New York Review
of Books* in February 1987. Kazin's portrait of the "Voltairean
Mencken," his recollection of the "guilty delight" with which he had
read Mencken in the 1930s, his utter disapproval of the author's
politics but the great attraction to the earlier Mencken as hedonist,
freethinker, and skeptic—"above all . . . the always *happy* man"—
was one of several pieces that prepared the way for the 1989 edition
of the diary.

The impassioned response given to the diary itself was equaled
only by the receptions given the *Prejudices* volumes in the 1920s or,
perhaps, *Treatise on the Gods* in 1930. The diary's editor, Charles
Fecher, who in his earlier study of Mencken's thought had defended
him against anti-Semitism, now declared in his introduction "clearly
and unequivocally" that Mencken had been an anti-Semite. It was
charges such as that, as well as what seemed to be the corroborating
evidence of the diary itself, that inspired the great Mencken debate
of 1989 and 1990, thrust the author into the middle of the growing

American dialogue on political correctness, and made Mencken "live" more fully than he had for forty years. The Sunpapers themselves led the charge against their "tarnished" hero, Garry Wills chimed in with a scathing attack in *The New Republic*, and numerous other reviewers of the diary, in some cases unfamiliar with Mencken's earlier works, were zealous in their condemnation of what one called his "virulent anti-Semitism, racism and pro-Nazi sympathies."

But the widespread criticism, as well as such reactions as the attempt to rename the H. L. Mencken Library of the National Press Club, also had the effect of unleashing a counterreaction at least as powerful as the original condemnation. Even before the worst of the onslaught, Jonathan Yardley and Russell Baker had urged the diary's readers to assess Mencken as "a man of his times" rather than judging him altogether by the standards of a later age. Shortly afterward William Manchester in *The New York Times Book Review* (also decrying "generational chauvinism") and a number of writers in a letter to *The New York Review of Books* leapt to Mencken's defense as well. Pointing to his "warm friendships" and cordial professional relations with Jews and his encouragement of black writers as well as his penchant for hyperbole, the writers in *The New York Review* reminded readers that the "harshest" remarks in the diary were directed not toward Jews and blacks but rather toward poor southern whites. Among the signers of the *New York Review* letter were Jewish writers Arthur Miller and Norman Mailer and one of the nation's most distinguished black novelists, Ralph Ellison.

The debate continued over the following year. Joseph Epstein, in a lengthy essay in the Jewish journal *Commentary*, also concluded that Mencken "was no anti-Semite," Gore Vidal used a discussion of Mencken's work as an occasion to launch an attack on political correctness, and numerous other writers added their voices. Now thirty-five years in the grave, Mencken would have delighted in the spectacle—reviewers, critics, and scholars battling over a "book" that had been written a half century before and had reached the reading public only because of a ruling by the highest legal authority in Maryland. And there would be more manuscript material to fuel the controversy—the release in January 1991 of "My Life as Author and Editor" and "Thirty-Five Years of Newspaper Work," the former edited by Yardley and published early in 1993, the latter brought out by the Johns Hopkins University Press in 1994. Although neither work brought forth the barrage of criticism the diary had generated, each was widely reviewed and its author, at least occasionally, vilified. Furthermore, the two books brought to life for the late twentieth century Mencken and his colorful, turbulent world of early-century journalism and publishing, of "Roosevelt Major," "Roosevelt Minor," and "The Archangel Woodrow," of Sinclair Lewis and Fitzgerald and the "Hoosier Lothario," Dreiser.

With the publication of his three late manuscripts, Mencken had dropped still other anchors against oblivion. But they were to be his last. After 1991 no more manuscript material was forthcoming from the locked cages of the Enoch Pratt and the New York Public Library, no more revelations to disturb the sensibilities of a more finely tuned age. After that, he would have to stand on the merits of what he had written and published before. By the final decade of the century it was clear that his reputation as a potent American literary and cultural force was secure, although just what the nature of his reputation as a literary *figure* was to be was still in the balance. Whatever else Mencken was, he was a journalist, and although such eighteenth-century English literary journalists as Addison and Steele and Samuel Johnson qualify fully as "literary figures," twentieth-century American ones such as Mencken and Edmund Wilson are not always accorded that honor. Journalism, even literary journalism, it seems, should be a century or two in the past and across the ocean before it fully qualifies as *belles lettres*.

Because of the prominence of the *Days* books, the diary, and the recently published memoirs, as well as the autobiographical cast of much of Mencken's other work, it is entirely possible that he is one of those writers, like Dr. Johnson or Thomas Carlyle or Henry Adams, whose *life*, both as fact and as metaphor, will always inspire as much interest as his work. That life, as we have seen, was both at one with and the same time often at variance with the work. "Human life is basically a comedy," he maintained until the end (in the 1956 *Minority Report*), yet in any number of ways, of course, it was anything but that for him. His close friend Clare Leighton spoke of the "tragic, lonely dignity" in the older Mencken, and whatever the books tell us, especially the books published before 1930, she was right in the end. His was not the more familiar variety of American literary tragedy, the story, say, of Scott Fitzgerald, the writer spoiled by fame and glitter and ruined by riches. Those rewards had little attraction for him. Rather, his story, at its conclusion, presents us with an even more compelling version of tragedy, one nearly Greek in its implications: the immensely gifted and self-sufficient man who denied the gods and rose to the loftiest of positions through the power of words, only to be felled by a blow that robbed him of the ability to use words meaningfully but left him alive another seven years. Only a man with an immense measure of pride, that first and most universal of tragic flaws, could have suffered as he did. But only gods with a peculiar sense of justice and irony could have contrived so cruel an end.

But that, after all, was the older Mencken whose world had already begun to fall apart in the mid-1930s—with Sara's death, Germany's movement toward national suicide, and, in his eyes, America's Rooseveltian apostasy—before that world shattered altogether in 1948. Because of the diary, because of our knowledge of the even greater unhappiness in the years after the diary, it is all too tempting now to see that later man as the quintessential Mencken, the Mencken of our primary consideration. And the dark qualities, including the deep skepticism that went beyond a distrust of American institutions to a skepticism about human nature itself, were indeed firmly in place from the beginning. But that is not the reason we read Mencken, is not the essential Mencken any more than Samuel Clemens after 1895 was the essential Mark Twain. What was essential, rather, and what made Mencken *sui generis*, was an exuberance, a boldness, a courage to challenge old and established ways of thinking—in short, the confidence to be a free man. The early work in the *Book of Prefaces*, the *Prejudices*, and the other essays of the 1920s, all the while denying the transcendent importance and the intrinsic worth of human life, issued that denial with all the energy and joy of an affirmation by any other man. "Here I stand, unshaken and undespairing, a loyal and devoted Americano," Mencken wrote in the early 1920s. "Here am I, a bachelor of easy means, forty-two years old, unhampered by debts or issue, able to go wherever I please and to stay as long as I please—here am I, contentedly and even smugly basking beneath the Stars and Stripes . . ."

The rhythms and cadences were unmistakably Whitman's, the boldness and sassiness of this earlier Mencken. His writing of the early twenties was his own "Song of Myself," chanted not long after he had burst fully onto the national scene, just at the moment he was celebrating the nation's imbecilities and miseries—the sins of the South and the pruderies of New England, the fakeries of California and the provincialism of the hinterlands in between—with all the vigor and gusto with which that earlier rude and vulgar fellow had sung the nation's triumphs and glories. For all his European antecedents and, in an American context, his parallels to Samuel Clemens, Mencken bore at his indomitable peak a remarkable resemblance— if, sometimes, as in a distorted mirror—to that other exuberant nineteenth-century American voice. He was our nay-saying Whitman, and whatever his manifold inadequacies of heart and conscience, he sounded his own barbaric yawp over the roofs of the timid and the fearful, the contented and the smug.

# ACKNOWLEDGMENTS

Dozens of institutions and individuals—libraries and librarians, Mencken acquaintances, countless scholars, family and friends—contributed to the making of this book in ways too various to enumerate. My greatest institutional debts are to the National Humanities Center, whose fellowship in 1991–1992 provided a year for writing; the National Endowment for the Humanities, which also provided support during the 1991–1992 fellowship year; the University of North Carolina at Chapel Hill, particularly the Department of English and the Institute for the Arts and Humanities, which provided a research fellowship for spring 1991; the New York Public Library, which houses most of Mencken's literary correspondence; and the Enoch Pratt Free Library of Baltimore, the home of much Mencken correspondence and an astounding amount of memorabilia. I am also grateful to the Pratt Library, particularly Averil J. Kadis, for permission to quote from the mass of unpublished and published Mencken material I employ in the biography.

Institutional debts, in reality, are more than institutional. In addition to Averil Kadis, I wish to thank a number of staff members, current and emeritus, of the Enoch Pratt Library, many of whom became not only professional associates but also valued friends: Neil R. Jordahl, John Sondheim, Wesley Wilson, William S. Forshaw, Richard Hart, Wilbur McGill, Thomas Himmel, Faye Houston, Charlotte Gettes, Ralph Clayton, Shirley Viviano, Mark Sober, Robert Burke, and, particularly, Vince Fitzpatrick, authentic son of Baltimore, guide not only to Mencken treasures but to Chesapeake culinary delights. I would also like to acknowledge the valuable assistance of several members of what I might call the greater Baltimore Mencken community, particularly Charles Fecher, Marion Rodgers, Arthur and Wheezie Gutman, Shawn and Cynthia Cunningham, and Carol Fitzpatrick.

Besides the Pratt, I owe a debt to the following libraries, which shared with me the numerous Mencken letters and manuscripts in their collections: Columbia University, Cornell University, Emory University, Goucher College, Princeton University, Tulane University, Yale University, the Universities of Alabama, North Carolina at Chapel Hill, Pennsylvania and Texas, and the University of Denver.

Personal debts are legion. First, I am grateful to those friends, professional associates and acquaintances of Mencken himself (not a great many left since the Sage would now be 114 years old) who sat for interviews and helped in innumerable other ways. Among those are Dr. Benjamin M. Baker, Mrs. Louis (Elise) Cheslock, Ruth Goodman Goetz, R. P. and Margery Harriss, Richard Hart, Bradford Jacobs, Gerald and Kathryn Johnson, Gwinn Owens, Mrs. Hamilton (Olga) Owens, Mrs. Maclean (Betti Anne) Patterson, Lawrence E. Spivak, Dr. Philip F. Wagley, Philip Wagner, and, particularly, Mencken's younger and closest cousin, Admiral William C. Abhau. I would also like to acknowledge the generosity of the late Carl Bode, who made available to me his extensive collection of Mencken-related interview tapes, notes, letters, and other materials in the Enoch Pratt Free Library.

Others to whom I owe debts too various to specify are Patricia Angelin, Philippa Bainbridge, Ralph Bogardus, Dr. John Boswell, James Bready, Vincent P. Brennan, S.M., Karen Carroll, Jiwei Ci, Bruce Clayton, Alistair Cooke, Frances Coombs, Caroline Davis, William R. Day, Carl Dolmetsch, Peter Dowell, David Ellis, Weston Fenhagen, Joseph Flora, Catherine Fry, Donald C. Gallup, Elliott Gorn, Cynthia Graff, Caroline M. Hickman, Jane Hobson (I and II), Linda Whitney Hobson, I. B. Holley, Roy Hoopes, Hunter James, Dr. Eric W. Jensen, Alfred Kazin, Bruce Kellner, William E. King, Joyce Lamont, Theo Lippman, Townsend Ludington, Malcolm M. MacDonald, Nancy Magnuson, William Manchester, Arthur Marks, Edward A. Martin, Linda Matthews, Linda Morgan, Nancy E. Met-ger, Dorothy Moore, Frank and Catherine Murphy, William Nolte, Priscilla B. Pearson, Marsha Poliakoff, Joseph Prescott, Peter S. Prescott, Thomas P. Riggio, Lyn Robey, Joseph Solomon, Terry Teachout, Thomas Underwood, Nina Wallace, Richard L. Watson, I. A. Werner, James L. W. West, Jane and Fred White, Jim and Patty Williams, Lola Williams, Patricia C. Willis, and Ed Wortech.

I am especially grateful to my parents, who helped with this book, as with others, in ways that go beyond documentation; to my daughter Jane, traveling companion for research in western archives; to Molly and Sarah, who also learned to live with the sounds of an ancient manual typewriter clattering through the night; to Ann Henley, wordsmith extraordinaire and authority on Sara Haardt Mencken; to Louis D. Rubin and Lewis P. Simpson, whose counsel and encouragement over the years can hardly be overstated; to my editor at Random House, Robert D. Loomis, for his strong commitment to this book as well as his sure feel for what it needed at any given moment; to Benjamin Dreyer and Lynn Anderson, also of Random House; to the staff of the Johns Hopkins University Press, particularly Douglas Armato; and, finally, to my distant cousin and good friend Burke Davis, who inspired by example and gave better advice than he knew when he uttered those words, "Rise early and hang on grimly."

# NOTES

Abbreviations

|  |  |
|---|---|
| AAK | Alfred A. Knopf. |
| *A&E* | H. L. Mencken, *My Life as Author and Editor* (ed. Jonathan Yardley), Alfred A. Knopf, 1993. |
| "A&E" | Mencken, "My Life as Author and Editor" (ms.), Enoch Pratt Free Library, Baltimore. |
| *AL* | Mencken, *The American Language: A Preliminary Inquiry into the Development of English in the United States.* Alfred A. Knopf, 1919. Revised editions, 1921, 1923, and 1936. Supplements I and II, 1945 and 1948. |
| AM | August Mencken. |
| *AM* | The American Mercury. |
| "AN, 1925" (EPFL) | Mencken, "Autobiographical Notes, 1925," Enoch Pratt Free Library. |
| "AN, 1925" (NYPL) | Mencken, "Autobiographical Notes, 1925," New York Public Library. Shorter version. |
| "AN, 1941–" | Mencken, "Autobiographical Notes, 1941–," Enoch Pratt Free Library. |
| AP | Aileen Pringle. |
| *BES* | Baltimore *Evening Sun.* |
| BH | Elizabeth (Betty) Hanes. |
| BK | Blanche Wolf Knopf. |
| *BS* | Baltimore *Sun.* |
| CM | Charles Mencken. |
| DH | Dorothy Hergesheimer. |
| *Diary* | [Mencken], *The Diary of H. L. Mencken* (ed. Charles A. Fecher), Alfred A. Knopf, 1989. |
| "Diary" | Mencken, diary (ms.), Enoch Pratt Free Library. |
| *D–M Letters* | *Dreiser–Mencken Letters: The Correspondence of* |

|  | *Theodore Dreiser and H. L. Mencken, 1907–1945.* Two volumes (ed. Thomas P. Riggio), University of Pennsylvania Press, 1986. |
|---|---|
| EB | Estelle Bloom. |
| ELM | Edgar Lee Masters. |
| EPFL | Enoch Pratt Free Library, Baltimore. |
| EU | Woodruff Library, Emory University. |
| FHG | Fielding H. Garrison. |
| FSF | F. Scott Fitzgerald. |
| GC | Julia Rogers Library, Goucher College. |
| GH | Gretchen Hood. |
| GJN | George Jean Nathan. |
| GM | Gertrude Mencken. |
| *HD* | Mencken, *Happy Days, 1880–1892*, Alfred A. Knopf, 1940. |
| "*HD:* Additions" | Mencken, "*Happy Days:* Additions, Corrections and Explanatory Notes" (ms.), Enoch Pratt Free Library. |
| *Heathen Days* | Mencken, *Heathen Days, 1890–1936*, Alfred A. Knopf, 1943. |
| "*Heathen Days:* Additions" | Mencken, "*Heathen Days:* Additions, Corrections and Explanatory Notes" (ms.), Enoch Pratt Free Library. |
| HLM | Henry Louis Mencken. |
| *In Defense* | Mencken, *In Defense of Women*, Philip Goodman, 1918; Alfred A. Knopf (revised), 1922. |
| JB | Julian Boyd. |
| JH | Joseph Hergesheimer. |
| LC | Louis Cheslock. |
| *M&S* | *Mencken and Sara: A Life in Letters* (ed. Marion Elizabeth Rodgers), McGraw-Hill, 1987. |
| MB | Marion Bloom. |
| MD | Marcella du Pont. |
| *MR* | Mencken, *Minority Report: H. L. Mencken's Note-books*, Alfred A. Knopf, 1956. |
| *NPD* | Mencken, *Newspaper Days, 1899–1906*, Alfred A. Knopf, 1941. |
| "*NPD:* Additions" | Mencken, "*Newspaper Days:* Additions, Corrections and Explanatory Notes" (ms.), Enoch Pratt Free Library. |
| NYPL | New York Public Library. Most of the letters *from* HLM in the NYPL are copies, and are so numerous they are not designated as such individually in these notes. |
| PG | Philip Goodman. |
| *Prefaces* | Mencken, *A Book of Prefaces*, Alfred A. Knopf, 1917. |
| *Prejudices* | Mencken, *Prejudices* (First through Sixth Series), Alfred A. Knopf, 1919–27. |
| PU | Firestone Library, Princeton University. |
| "Reminiscences" | August Mencken, "Reminiscences" (ms.), Oral History Collection, Columbia University Library. |

| | |
|---|---|
| SH | Sara Haardt. |
| SHM | Sara Haardt Mencken. |
| SL | Sinclair Lewis. |
| SM | Sara Mayfield. |
| SNC diary | Louis Cheslock, Saturday Night Club diary, Enoch Pratt Free Library. |
| *SS* | *The Smart Set.* |
| TD | Theodore Dreiser. |
| "Thirty-Five Years" | Mencken, "Thirty-Five Years of Newspaper Work" (ms.), Enoch Pratt Free Library. |
| *T on Gods* | Mencken, *Treatise on the Gods*, Alfred A. Knopf, 1930. |
| UA | Gorgas Library, University of Alabama. |
| UD | University of Denver Library. |
| UNC | Wilson Library, University of North Carolina at Chapel Hill. |
| UP | Van Pelt Library, University of Pennsylvania. |
| UT | Ransom Research Center, University of Texas. |
| UVa | Barrett Library, University of Virginia. |
| YU | Bienecke Library, Yale University. |

## Prelude: The Elusive Mencken

p. ix.   "Called by Walter Lippmann": Lippmann, "H. L. Mencken," *Saturday Review*, 11 December 1926, p. 413.

"by the mid-1930s": Elrick B. Davis, Cleveland *Press*, 20 July 1935, in HLM clippings scrapbook, EPFL.

"he suffered in": HLM, quoted by Alistair Cooke, in "H. L. Mencken," *Six Men* (Alfred A. Knopf, 1977), p. 117.

p. x.   "The most important": HLM, "Diary," 18 August 1945.

"Although Mencken could": HLM to DH, 16 March 1942, NYPL.

p. xi.   "He was also": Joseph Wood Krutch, quoted by William H. Nolte, "The Literary Critic," *On Mencken*, ed. John Dorsey (Alfred A. Knopf, 1980), p. 197.

" 'If Mencken had' ": Alfred Kazin, *On Native Grounds* (Reynal & Hitchcock, 1942), p. 198.

"But to other": *Palm Beach News*, [March 1928], HLM clippings scrapbook, EPFL.

"It is no": Isaac Goldberg, *The Man Mencken* (Simon & Schuster, 1925); William Manchester, *Disturber of the Peace: The Life of H. L. Mencken* (Harper, 1950); Carl Bode, *Mencken* (Southern Illinois University Press, 1969).

p. xii.   " 'There is, indeed' ": HLM, *Diary*, 12 September 1945, p. 382.

"and Charles Fecher": Fecher, "Researching a Book on Mencken," *Menckeniana*, Winter 1978, p. 9.

p. xiii.   "As Fecher remarks": *Ibid.*, p. 9.

" 'I have tried' ": HLM, *Diary*, 12 September 1945, p. 382.

" 'I have always' ": HLM, *A&E*, p. xx.

p. xiv.   "The author concluded": HLM, *HD*, p. viii.

"Bode tells us": Carl Bode, *Mencken*, p. 24.

p. xv.   "As Louis D. Rubin, Jr.": Rubin, "If Only Mencken Were Alive," in Rubin, ed., *The Comic Imagination in American Literature* (Rutgers University Press, 1973), pp. 229–30.

p. xvi.  "Yet, at age": HLM, *Diary*, 29 January 1945, p. 351.

p. xvii.  "No biographer has": Alistair Cooke, "Mencken and the English Language," *On Mencken*, ed. John Dorsey, p. 93.

"A biographer is": HLM, *A Little Book in C Major* (John Lane, 1916), p. 52.

p. xviii.  "as Alistair Cooke": Cooke, in proceedings of HLM centennial banquet, 12 September 1980, *Menckeniana*, Spring 1981, p. 6.

## Chapter 1: The Fathers

p. 3.  " 'People of my' ": HLM, "AN, 1941–."

" 'I often regret' ": HLM to Anna Mencke, 2 December 1932, EPFL.

p. 4.  "Thus it was": HLM, "*HD:* Additions," p. 169.

p. 5.  " 'How did I' ": HLM, as told to Ruth Crawford, in "How I Got That Way," United Features Syndicate, [1926], HLM scrapbook 15, EPFL.

"But no member": HLM, "AN, 1925" (NYPL), p. 2.

p. 6.  "The owner of": HLM, "Menckeniana: Documents, Portraits . . . ," EPFL.

"Lüder traveled to": HLM, introduction to "Lüder Mencken: Sundry Documents" (1938), EPFL.

"For it was": HLM, "AN, 1925" (NYPL), p. 2.

"The most notable": HLM, Preface to *The Charlatanry of the Learned* (Alfred A. Knopf, 1937), p. 9.

p. 7.  "He traveled to": HLM, *ibid.*

"Johann Burkhard had": HLM, "AN, 1925" (NYPL), p. 6.

"In reading that": HLM, Preface to *Charlatanry*, p. 44.

"When he first": HLM to FHG, 21 August 1919, NYPL.

"Johann Burkhard Mencke had": HLM, Preface to *Charlatanry*, pp. 47, 49.

"He had remarked": Johann Burkhard Mencke, *Charlatanry*, p. 175.

"The task, he": HLM, Preface to *Charlatanry*, p. 45.

p. 8.  "H. L. Mencken did": HLM to FHG, 21 August 1919, NYPL.

"The late seventeenth": HLM, "AN, 1941–."

"At least thirteen": HLM, "A&E," p. 8.

"It is little": HLM, quoted in Charles Fecher, "Mencken and Goethe," *Menckeniana*, Fall 1980, p. 43.

p. 9.  "Indeed, he later": HLM, "AN, 1941–."

"That century, Mencken": HLM, "The New Architecture," *AM*, February 1931, p. 164.

"One line, to": HLM to Clarissa Flugel, 8 April 1937, EPFL.

"The decline of": HLM, Introduction to scrapbook "Johann Christian August Mencken . . . ," EPFL.

p. 10.  "After the Napoleonic": HLM, "A&E," p. 8.

"Both because of" and "It was common": HLM, "AN, 1925," p. 23.

" 'It will be' ": HLM, "AN, 1925" (NYPL), p. 23, Mencken says one hundred thalers in scrapbook F31 but five hundred thalers in "AN, 1925."

p. 11.  "He was, his": HLM, *HD*, p. 91.

"On his naturalization": HLM, Introduction to scrapbook F31 Folio, EPFL.

"But he continued": HLM, "Thirty-Five Years," p. 175.

"He refused to": HLM, "A&E," p. 478n, and HLM, "Thirty-Five Years," p. 175.

"There was, to": HLM, "A&E," p. 478.

p. 12.  "Thus, the language": HLM, "A&E," p. 478.

"If the Menckens": HLM, scrapbook F31, EPFL; and HLM, "*HD:* Additions,"
pp. 10, 95.

p. 13.  "H. L. Mencken *knew*": HLM to Charles Abhau, 29 October 1938, EPFL.

p. 14.  " 'I am myself' ": HLM to TD, 27 March [1921], *D–M Letters*, II, p. 436.

"With his teenaged": The date August Mencken established his factory is
uncertain. In "*HD:* Additions," p. 248, HLM gives the year as 1873 and
writes that his father was not yet twenty. In other manuscripts—his autobiographical notes, written in 1925, as well as the introductory note to the
scrapbook "Johann Christian August Mencken . . ." HLM gives the date as
1875 and gives his father's age as twenty-one.

p. 15.  "August, too, was": HLM to Edgar Kemler, [1948], EPFL; and HLM, "A&E,"
p. 478.

"In 1867 he" and "As H. L. Mencken later": HLM, "*HD:* Additions," p. 169.

"He looked, his": HLM, "AN, 1925" (NYPL), p. 33.

"He also enjoyed": HLM to William Manchester, 13 August 1948, EPFL.

"She laughed, but": HLM, "*HD:* Additions," p. vii.

## Chapter 2: Happy Days

p. 17.  "He was born": HLM, *Heathen Days*, pp. 55, 202.

"He entered the": HLM, "Maryland," *BES*, 13 June 1921.

"Henry Mencken was": HLM to Charles Fleischer, 22 April 1940, NYPL.

p. 18.  "Henry was delivered": HLM, "*HD:* Additions," p. 7; and HLM, scrapbook
F178, EPFL.

"As for young": HLM, *HD*, p. vii.

"The Menckens remained": HLM, *Diary*, 27 July 1941, p. 157; and HLM to
Edgar Kemler, [1948], EPFL. In "*HD:* Additions" (p. 5) HLM puts the
figure at $2,800.

"What he saw": HLM to Ruth Thomson, 21 January 1935, NYPL.

p. 19.  "Anna ran the": AM, "Reminiscences," p. 34; and HLM to William Manchester, 13 August 1948, EPFL.

"She emerges as": HLM, "AN, 1941–."

"Given to propriety": HLM, "*HD:* Additions," p. 28. Other information in this
paragraph taken from *HD*, p. 28; "*HD:* Additions," p. 18; and "AN,
1941–."

"Anna was the": HLM, *HD*, p. 8; and HLM, "*HD:* Additions," p. 11.

p. 20.  "in their early"; HLM to ELM, 20 June 1939, NYPL.

"They also enjoyed": HLM, "*HD:* Additions," p. 27.

" 'My first recollection' ": HLM, "*HD:* Additions," p. 157; and HLM, "Borzoi
Battledore," pamphlet collection, EPFL.

"All in all": HLM, "AN, 1941–"; "AN, 1925," (EPFL), p. 30; "*HD:* Additions," p. 107; and HLM to ELM, 27 December 1935, NYPL.

p. 21.  "If there was": HLM to Miriam Gallagher, 8 March 1913, NYPL; HLM, transcript of radio interview with Vesta Eales, 1940, scrapbook H122, EPFL;
and HLM, "*HD:* Additions," pp. 54, 110.

"Even his next-door": HLM, "*HD:* Additions," p. 247. The Menckens' address
at first was 352 Hollins Street, but a later renumbering of houses made it
1524—the number Mencken would use even when he wrote of his earliest
years.

"Dislike for a": HLM, "AN, 1941–."

p. 22.  " 'There was never' ": HLM, *HD*, p. vii.

"August Mencken, in": HLM, "AN, 1941–"; "AN, 1925," (NYPL) p. 33; *HD*, p. vii; "*HD:* Additions," pp. 28, 96; and HLM to William Manchester, 13 August 1948, EPFL.

"August appears to": AM, "Reminiscences," p. 33; HLM, "*HD:* Additions," p. 103; HLM, "Havana Revisited" (ms.), scrapbook A119, EPFL; HLM, "AN, 1941–"; and HLM to FHG, [1930], NYPL.

p. 23.　"But August was": HLM to Edward Scanlon, 11 August 1934, NYPL; HLM to Adrian Hamersley, 6 April 1936, NYPL: HLM, *HD*, p. 301; and "*HD:* Additions," p. 35.

"Much of his": HLM, *HD*, p. 11.

p. 24.　"At about age": HLM, "Forty Years of Baltimore," *BES*, 11 October 1926.

"This 'enclosure in' ": HLM, "AN, 1941–."

"When he looked": HLM, *HD*, pp. 277–300; and HLM, "*HD:* Additions," pp. 277, 279.

p. 25.　"It was, H. L.": HLM, "The American Tragedy" (ms.), scrapbook A113, EPFL. In the year 1870 more than one fifth of Baltimore's population was foreign born, and nearly two thirds of those immigrants were German (H. George Hahn, "Twilight Reflections," *Maryland Historian*, Spring 1980, p. 35; and Charles Hirschfield, *Baltimore 1870–1900: Studies in Social History* [Johns Hopkins University Press, 1941], pp. 23–24).

"It was also": HLM, "*HD:* Additions," p. 147.

p. 26.　"His own grandfather": HLM to Louise Pound, 5 April [1920], NYPL.

" 'At 1403 W. Baltimore' ": HLM, "*HD:* Additions," p. 122.

" 'the 'flood of' ": HLM, "The American Tragedy" (ms.), scrapbook A113, EPFL.

p. 27.　"The latter group": HLM, *HD*, p. 26; and HLM to Louis Adamic, 28 July 1939, NYPL.

"Knapp, who was": HLM, "Musing in the Twilight" (ms.), "Répétition Générale" scrapbook, EPFL; and HLM, "Fifty Years of Baltimore," *BES*, 19 March 1923.

p. 28.　"Yet Harry Mencken": HLM, "*HD:* Additions," p. 54; HLM, "AN, 1925" (NYPL), p. 46; and HLM, "A&E," p. 13.

"From the beginning": HLM, scrapbooks and composition books, EPFL; and HLM, "A&E," p. 13.

"But Harry Mencken": HLM, composition books, EPFL; HLM to Isaac Goldberg, 31 October 1936, NYPL; and HLM, *HD*, pp. 24–25.

p. 29.　"In the summer": HLM, *HD*, pp. 203, 160.

"By the time": HLM, *HD*, pp. 161, 163.

"Indeed, the young": HLM, *HD*, p. 162.

p. 30.　"And like the": HLM to William Manchester, 13 August 1948, EPFL; and HLM, "*HD:* Additions," pp. 133ff.

"Mencken later recalled": HLM, "Forty Years of Baltimore," *BES*, 19 March 1923.

"Such was life": HLM, "*HD:* Additions," pp. 14, 53, 172; HLM, *HD*, p. 293; Eugene Newbold to HLM, 25 July 1939, EPFL; and HLM to Raymond Tompkins, 4 August 1937, EPFL.

p. 31.　" 'I believe I' "; HLM, "The Age of Horses," *BES*, 1 February 1926.

"They visited much": HLM, "West Baltimore" (ms.), scrapbook A131, EPFL.

p. 32.　"As August and": HLM to P. H. Callahan, 16 October 1934.

" 'My dear Parents' ": HLM, "Souvenirs of Childhood and Schooldays, 1880–1896" (scrapbook F178), EPFL.

"As the Menckens": HLM to Fulton Oursler, 7 February 1940, NYPL; HLM,

"Ellicott City Fifty Years Ago" (ms.), 1940, scrapbook A122, EPFL; and HLM, "*HD:* Additions," p. 82.

p. 33.  "His education in": HLM, "AN, 1925" (NYPL), p. 44.

p. 34.  "They soon dismissed": HLM, "*HD:* Additions," p. 229.

"By his early": HLM, "Forty Years of Baltimore," *BES,* 11 October 1926.

"Although Harry Mencken": HLM, "*HD:* Additions," pp. 19, 244.

"At Mount Washington": HLM, "*HD:* Additions," pp. 88, 229, 230.

p. 35.  "In 1891, the": In *HD* (p. 303) Mencken gives 1891 as the date of the Ohio trip, but in several other autobiographical accounts he gives 1892 as the year. Some of his notes on the trip are dated as late as 1894. The fact that his grandfather Mencken died in February 1891, just before Mencken's return from the trip, would seem to set 1891 as the date. Some confusion also exists as to whether the trip was made in February or April, although (again because of the date of his grandfather's death) February has much the better claim.

" 'The City of' ": HLM to J.R.D. Mason, 20 April 1892, in composition notebook, scrapbook F250, EPFL.

"What we see": HLM, entries of 9 May 1894 and October 1894 in scrapbook F250, EPFL; and HLM, "AN, 1925" (NYPL), p. 46.

p. 36.  "The 'wicked thought' ": HLM, *HD,* p. 313.

"Burkhardt's death was": HLM, introduction to "Aug. Mencken and Bro. Letter Book, 1894–1895," scrapbook F15, EPFL.

" 'I was then' ": HLM, *HD,* p. viii.

p. 37.  " 'Those were the' ": HLM to Philip Perlman, 28 December 1944, EPFL.


## Chapter 3: The Education of Henry Mencken

p. 38.  "He was given": HLM, "Travail," *BES,* 8 October 1928.

"In his particular": HLM to TD, 22 December 1939, UP, in *D–M Letters,* p. 656.

" 'The teens are' ": HLM, "*Heathen Days:* Additions," p. v.

p. 39.  "Still, for a": HLM to Edward Hungerford, 5 February 1940, NYPL; and HLM to Fulton Oursler, 7 February 1940, NYPL.

"In those days": HLM, "*Heathen Days:* Additions," p. 37; and Wilmer Leech to HLM, 9 May 1955, NYPL.

"So why Henry": HLM, "AN, 1941–"; and HLM, *HD,* p. vii.

"Although Mencken later": "AN, 1925" (NYPL), p. 55; HLM, "*HD:* Additions," p. 249; and HLM, scrapbook F250, EPFL.

p. 40.  "Despite Mencken's verdict": HLM, "*Heathen Days:* Additions," p. 39.

"But a more": HLM, "A&E," pp. 22–23.

"As a result": HLM to Ralph Cannon, 23 October 1937, NYPL; and HLM, "A&E," p. 21.

p. 41.  "He had subscribed": HLM, "*HD:* Additions," p. 216; and HLM, "A&E," p. 18.

"But the arts": HLM, "*HD:* Additions," p. 197; and HLM, "Earliest Attempts at Verse and Prose, 1895–1901" (scrapbook A51), EPFL.

"But he was": In *HD* Mencken writes that he read *Huckleberry Finn* at age seven, but in "*HD:* Additions," he changes the age to eight.

"Later, at eleven": HLM, *HD,* p. 216.

p. 42.  "The furious writing": HLM, "AN, 1925" (NYPL), p. 61; HLM, "*Heathen Days:* Additions," pp. 36; HLM, "*HD:* Additions," p. 174; HLM, *Heathen Days,* p. 40; and HLM, "A&E," p. 46.

"What Mencken read": HLM, "AN, 1925" (NYPL), pp. 59–61; and HLM, "The Artist," *BES*, 7 April 1924.

p. 43.  "In his early": HLM to A. G. Keller, 11 October 1943, EPFL.

" 'The greatest Englishman' ": HLM, "Thomas Henry Huxley, 1825–1925," *BES*, 4 May 1925. Also, HLM to Lew Sarett, 23 August 1943, NYPL; HLM to Edward B. Garside, 10 June 1939, NYPL; and HLM to D. G. Munroe, 29 February 1936, NYPL.

"He felt a": HLM to TD, 8 April 1939, UP, in *D–M Letters*, p. 639; and HLM to A. G. Keller, 6 January 1947, EPFL.

p. 44.  "Such an omission": Stressing Mencken's German-American background are Van Wyck Brooks, *The Confident Years: 1835–1915* (E. P. Dutton and Co., 1952), p. 473; and Gerald W. Johnson, "Re-consideration—H. L. Mencken," *Menckeniana*, Winter 1975, p. 2.

" 'The most massive' ": HLM, "Free Lance," *BES*, 29 September 1914.

"He was, as": HLM, "What Is This Talk about Utopia?" (ms., 1927, for *The Nation*), scrapbook A113, EPFL.

"Even when, just": HLM, *A&E*, p. 171.

"In fact, the": HLM, "*A&E*," p. 277; HLM, "The German Americans" (ms.), 1928, scrapbook A113, EPFL; HLM to Edgar Kemler, 24 October 1946, NYPL; HLM, *A&E*, p. 171.

p. 45.  "As it was": HLM to Edgar Kemler, [1948?], EPFL.

"If there was": HLM, "The South Begins to Mutter," *SS*, August 1921, p. 138; HLM, "Si Mutare Potest Aethiops Pellum Suam . . . ," *SS*, September 1917, p. 138; HLM, "Fortunata," *BES*, 11 April 1911; and HLM, "Conversations," *SS*, April 1921, p. 92.

p. 46.  "In 1895 three quarters": Douglas Stenerson, *H. L. Mencken: Iconoclast from Baltimore* (University of Chicago Press, 1971), p. 40.

"To begin with": HLM, "800,000," *BES*, 21 July 1930; HLM to Gerald W. Johnson, 25 February 1936, EPFL; and HLM to Mary L. Franklin, 19 August 1936, NYPL.

p. 47.  "In an essay": HLM, "Maryland, Apex of Normalcy," *The Nation*, 3 May 1922, p. 518.

p. 48.  "The young Mencken": HLM, "AN, 1941–"; HLM to Louis Adamic, 28 July 1939, NYPL; Gerald W. Johnson, "Re-consideration—H. L. Mencken," p. 2; and HLM, *A&E*, p. 173.

p. 49.  "Later he wrote": HLM, "*Heathen Days:* Additions," p. v.

"Mencken was a": David S. Thayer, "HLM and the Baltimore Polytechnic Institute," *Menckeniana*, Fall 1973, pp. 12–13; HLM, *NPD*, p. 77; and HLM, "AN, 1925" (NYPL), p. 12.

"Only twice in": HLM to ELM, 2 June 1939, NYPL; and HLM, *Diary*, 3 November 1945, p. 392.

p. 50.  " 'This highly virtuous' ": HLM, "AN, 1925" (NYPL), p. 44.

"Mencken had at": HLM, "*HD:* Additions," p. 231; and HLM, "AN, 1925" (NYPL), p. 46.

"By this time": HLM to Lee Hartman, 13 February 1936, NYPL.

" 'The scene is' ": HLM, "*HD:* Additions," p. 231.

"But that, after": HLM, *Heathen Days*, p. 28; HLM, note of 22 April 1939, miscellaneous notes, envelope A100.8, EPFL; and HLM, "AN, 1941–."

p. 51.  "Seeing that his": HLM, *Heathen Days*, pp. 27, 33–35.

"The reaction of": HLM to Miriam Gallagher, 11 October 1939, NYPL; HLM to GM, 28 July 1937, EPFL; HLM to A. G. Keller, 15 December 1939, NYPL; and AM, "Reminiscences," pp. 33–37.

p. 52.   "As Mencken's brother": AM, "Reminiscences," pp. 34–35.

"He had taken": HLM, introduction to "Souvenirs of Childhood and School-days" (scrapbook F178), EPFL; and HLM, "AN, 1925" (NYPL), p. 61.

"the universe was": HLM: "Sabbath Meditation" (ms.), for *AM*, May 1924, EPFL.

p. 53.   " 'It gives me' ": HLM, "AN, 1941–," [1945].

"H. L. Mencken": HLM, "AN, 1925" (NYPL), p. 49; HLM, "Souvenirs of Childhood and Schooldays" (scrapbook F178), EPFL; HLM, *Heathen Days:* Additions," p. 56; and John W. Saville to James B. Scott, quoted in *BS*, 24 January 1960, HLM clippings scrapbook, EPFL.

"Nonetheless, Mencken was": HLM, "A&E," p. 30; newspaper accounts of graduation in Baltimore *American*, 24 June 1896, and other newspapers (in "Souvenirs of Childhood and Schooldays," EPFL); Mencken graduation speech in "Souvenirs of Childhood and Schooldays," EPFL; and HLM to A. G. Keller, 8 June 1946, NYPL.

p. 54.   "But August Mencken": HLM to Anne Smith, 25 June 1937, NYPL; and HLM, "On Breaking into Type," 1929, HLM pamphlet collection, EPFL.

"As he had": HLM, "AN, 1941–"; HLM, "*NPD:* Additions," p. 4; and HLM to A. G. Keller, 9 February 1943, NYPL.

p. 55.   "When his father": HLM, "AN, 1925" (NYPL), p. 60.

"Selling cigars was": HLM, "AN, 1925" (NYPL), p. 60; HLM, introduction to and pp. 240–244 of salesman's commission books (scrapbook F16); and HLM to William Manchester, [July 1948], EPFL.

"After having been": HLM, "AN, 1925" (NYPL), p. 49.

p. 56.   "He was 'fully' ": HLM, "*NPD:* Additions," p. 4.

"He expressed his": HLM to Edgar Kemler, [1948], EPFL; HLM, "*NPD:* Additions," p. 4; HLM, "Under the Elms," *A Mencken Chrestomathy* (Alfred A. Knopf, 1949), p. 133; HLM, "AN, 1941–"; HLM, "AN, 1925" (EPFL), p. 81.

"For a time": HLM, "A&E," pp. 31–32.

p. 57.   "He was struck": HLM, quoted by Douglas C. Stenerson, in "Short-Story Writing," *Menckeniana*, Summer 1969, p. 13.

"Reading was not": HLM, "On Breaking into Type," 1929, HLM pamphlet collection, EPFL; and HLM, "Earliest Attempts at Verse and Prose, 1895–1903" (scrapbook A51), EPFL.

"So fanatical an": HLM, "A&E," p. 11.

p. 58.   "It was a": HLM, preface to "Typescripts of Early Fiction," EPFL.

"his correspondence school": HLM's instructor's remarks in "Earliest Attempts at Verse and Prose, 1895–1903" (scrapbook A51), EPFL.

"Under 'Occupation' he": HLM, "Souvenirs of Childhood and Schooldays" (scrapbook F178), EPFL; and HLM, "AN, 1941–."

"As Mencken later": HLM, "AN, 1941–."

" 'It was understood' ": HLM, "*NPD:* Additions," p. 4.

p. 59.   "That moment never": HLM, "*NPD:* Additions," p. 1; and HLM, "*HD:* Additions," p. 108.

"Thus began a": HLM, "*NPD:* Additions," pp. 1–3; and HLM to William Manchester, 13 August 1948, EPFL.

"August Mencken was": HLM, "*HD:* Additions," p. 99; HLM, "*NPD:* Additions," p. 1; and HLM to Mary Mullen, 9 April 1936, NYPL.

p. 60.   "But the death": HLM to Edgar Kemler, [1948], EPFL.

"his father, he": HLM, "AN, 1925" (NYPL), p. 69.

"He 'made no' ": HLM, "*NPD:* Additions," p. 1.

" 'If he had' ": HLM to ELM, 15 January 1940, NYPL.

"But sooner or": HLM to ELM, 15 January 1940, NYPL; HLM, *"NPD:* Additions," p. 4; and HLM, "Thirty-Five Years," p. 469.

p. 61.    "He once compared": HLM, quoted by Harry Lang in ms. "H. L. Mencken" for *Jewish Daily Forward,* 29 January 1928, HLM scrapbook "Miscellaneous Articles and Lampoons on HLM," EPFL.

" 'The main elements' ": HLM to Harry Lydenberg, 26 August 1942, NYPL; and HLM, *HD,* p. 253.

p. 62.    "He did refer": HLM, *"NPD:* Additions," p. 1.

" 'No really intelligent' ": HLM to ELM, 15 January 1940, NYPL.


## Chapter 4: His Yale College and His Harvard

p. 63.    "In his autobiographical": In *NPD* Mencken gives the time as the Monday evening after his father was buried on Sunday (p. 3), but in "AN, 1925" (NYPL) he writes that the period was two weeks (p. 69).

"It was 'the' ": HLM to Lionel White, 1 November 1934, NYPL.

"This much is": HLM, "AN, 1941–"; and HLM, *NPD,* p. 59.

p. 64.    "We cannot be": HLM, "A Third of a Century," ms. for *BES,* scrapbook A135, EPFL.

" 'A horse, a' ": HLM, *NPD,* p. 7.

"On July 2": In *NPD* and *"NPD:* Additions" Mencken puts the salary at $7. In his introduction to his scrapbook "Early Newspaper and Magazine Days" (EPFL) he writes $8.

"Thus began at": HLM, "Reminiscences," *BES,* 10 January 1927.

"It was 'the' ": HLM, *NPD,* pp. ix–x.

p. 65.    "Max Ways assumed": HLM, "Max Ways," ms. for *BES,* 6 June 1923, scrapbook A118, EPFL; HLM, *"NPD:* Additions," pp. 24–25.

"Mencken later said": HLM, *NPD,* pp. 37, vii; and HLM, *"NPD:* Additions," p. 25.

p. 66.    " 'Some day [Mark Twain's]' ": HLM, "Rhyme & Reason," Baltimore *Morning Herald,* 4 November 1900.

"He reveled in": HLM, *NPD,* p. 240; and HLM, "Night Club," *BES,* 3 September 1934.

"At first Anna": HLM, *"HD:* Additions," p. 13; HLM, *NPD,* pp. 55, 71–72; HLM to Jack Hart, 13 December 1939, NYPL; and HLM, "Loudon Park Cemetery" (pamphlet), 1902, EPFL.

p. 67.    "But there was": HLM, "AN, 1925" (NYPL), p. 73; HLM, ms. "How Have You Been?" (1925), Isaac Goldberg notes, EPFL; HLM to George Schuyler, 19 June 1931, YU; Carl Bode, "Mencken's Health," in Bode collection, EPFL; and Bode, interview with Dr. Manfred Guttmacher, in Bode, "Mencken's Health," Bode collection, EPFL. I am indebted to Professor Bode for sharing these materials with me.

" 'I was probably' ": HLM, "How Have You Been?" Isaac Goldberg notes, EPFL.

p. 68.    "The illness subsided": HLM to William McFee, 7 July [1926], NYPL; HLM to Leland Lovette, 4 March 1935, NYPL; and HLM to Harry Leon Wilson, 25 October [1911], NYPL.

"He listened to": Charles Angoff, *H. L. Mencken: A Portrait from Memory* (Yoseloff, 1956), p. 21. Mencken often spoofed Angoff, and Angoff took him seriously.

"The beauty of": HLM, "Where Orchids Are Called Weeds," Baltimore *Morning Herald*, 2 September 1900; HLM, "At the Edge of the Spanish Main," Baltimore *Morning Herald*, 26 August 1900; and HLM to GM, 11 July 1900, EPFL.

"What he discovered": HLM to GM, 11 July 1900, EPFL; HLM to Bishop Francis Kelley, 29 September 1944, NYPL; HLM to Benjamin de Casseres, 6 February 1938, NYPL; and HLM, *NPD*, p. 87.

p. 69.   "Mencken added, 'A' ": HLM to GM, 11 July 1900, EPFL.

"In later years": HLM to George Schuyler, 6 February 1938, YU.

"The trip to": HLM, *NPD*, pp. 94–105; HLM, introduction to "Early Newspaper and Magazine Days", EPFL; and HLM, stories in Baltimore *Morning Herald*, 11, 12, and 13 May 1901, HLM clippings scrapbook.

"When he returned": HLM, "AN, 1925" (NYPL), p. 71; HLM to A. N. Ward, 19 July 1934, EPFL; and HLM, *NPD*, pp. 105–08.

p. 70.   "In scenes supposedly": HLM, "Untold Tales," Baltimore *Morning Herald*, 29 May 1901–2 February 1902, *Herald* scrapbook, EPFL.

"In two other": HLM, articles of 2 and 8 March 1902, Baltimore *Morning Herald*, *Herald* scrapbook, EPFL.

"Mencken soon had": HLM, *NPD*, pp. 135–41.

"He worked in": HLM to William Manchester, [July 1945], EPFL.

"*Short Stories* had": HLM, "Early Newspaper and Magazine Days," EPFL; and Douglas C. Stenerson, "Short-Story Writing," *Menckeniana*, Summer 1969, p. 8. Mencken later wrote that he sold some twenty-five stories during this period, but fifteen or twenty is more accurate, and $15 to $35 per story was more typical than $50.

p. 71.   "Sedgwick first accepted": Ellery Sedgwick to HLM, 20 April, 11 September, 19 October, and 13 November 1901 and 5 August 1904, NYPL.

p. 72.   "At about the": Richard Badger to HLM, 6 and 21 September 1901, 16 January 1903, and 21 January 1902, NYPL; and HLM, *A&E*, pp. 8–9.

"Shortly after Mencken": HLM, introduction to "Earliest Attempts at Verse and Prose, 1896–1901" (scrapbook A51), EPFL; *The Bookman* to HLM, 4 December 1899, NYPL; and HLM, "On Breaking into Type," HLM pamphlet collection, EPFL.

p. 73.   "Mencken began *Ventures*": HLM, *Ventures into Verse* (1903), pp. 5, 6.

p. 74.   "While Mencken was": HLM, "On Breaking into Type"; and the following reviews in HLM clippings scrapbook: Brooklyn *Eagle*, 18 August 1903; Chicago *Record-Herald*, 17 August 1903; *Cleveland Blade*, 19 July 1903; New York *Telegraph*, [1903?]; *Deutsch-Amerikanes*, 7 November 1903; *The Nation*, 12 November 1903.

" 'I received Harry's' ": CM to GM, 16 July 1903, EPFL.

p. 76.   "As he later": HLM to Marion Bloom, [1914], EPFL.

" 'old women of' ": Gerald W. Johnson, "The Horrible South," *The Virginia Quarterly Review*, April 1935, p. 203.

"As he sat": HLM, *NPD*, pp. 21–75, 109–45, 172–248. On the subject of Mencken and masculinity, see also Edward A. Martin, *H. L. Mencken and the Debunkers* (University of Georgia Press, 1984), p. 50.

"As Mencken later": HLM, *NPD*, p. ix.

" 'The Mauve Decade' ": HLM, "Reminiscences," *BES*, 10 January 1927.

p. 77.   "About 1900 he": HLM, "AN, 1925" (NYPL), pp. 90–91.

"The Stevedores were": HLM, "Thirty-Five Years," p. 55.

"His autobiographical sketch": HLM, sketch, in "Autobiographies and Sketch [*sic*] of the Vagabonds," 1906, G file, EPFL.

"If the Vagabonds": HLM, "Thirty-Five Years," pp. 55–59; HLM to Carl
    Anthon, 15 December 1944, NYPL; and HLM to Julian Boyd, 29 July 1942,
    NYPL.

p. 78.  "From its beginnings": HLM, "AN, 1925" (NYPL); HLM, "AN, 1941–";
    HLM, *HD: Additions,*" p. 195; and HLM to Isaac Goldberg, quoted in
    Goldberg, *The Man Mencken,* p. 183.

"Through Joseph Callahan": HLM, "Thirty-Five Years," p. 56.

p. 79.  "When Gottlieb and": HLM, *Heathen Days: Additions,*" p. 88.

"Socially, then, in": HLM, "The Test," "Répétition Générale" scrapbook,
    EPFL; HLM, *HD: Additions,*" p. 5; HLM, *NPD: Additions,*" pp. 4, 154;
    and HLM, "A&E," p. 52.

"As he wrote": HLM to Tom Smith, 30 July 1935, NYPL.

p. 80.  "It is no": HLM to JB, 10 March 1941, NYPL.

"In 1904, just": HLM, "A&E," pp. 69–70.

p. 81.  " 'The wind had' ": HLM, *NPD,* p. 279. For a fuller account of the fire, see
    *NPD,* pp. 276–300. For a discussion of Mencken's exaggeration, see Harold
    A. Williams, "HLM and the Great Fire," *Menckeniana,* Summer 1987, pp.
    2–6. See also Williams, *The Baltimore Sun, 1837–1987,* p. 108.

"In his account": HLM, *NPD,* pp. 280, 277–78; and HLM, "Reminiscences,"
    *BES,* 10 January 1927.

p. 82.  "but he was": Joseph Conrad, "Youth," in *Youth and Two Other Stories*
    (Doubleday, Doran, 1933), pp. 36–37.

" 'The whole matter' ": Ellery Sedgwick to HLM, 9 February 1904, NYPL.

"Mencken seriously considered": Ellery Sedgwick to HLM, 17 and 23 February
    and 1 March 1904; and HLM to Sedgwick, 1 November 1941, NYPL.

"After rejecting the *Leslie's*": Ellery Sedgwick to HLM, 1 March 1904, NYPL;
    and HLM, "Hon. Henry G. Davis for Vice-President," Baltimore *Morning
    Herald,* 10 July 1904.

p. 83.  "When Mencken returned": HLM, "The Russian Masses," Baltimore *Morning
    Herald,* 8 July 1905, and "The Passing of the Hill," Baltimore *Morning
    Herald,* 15 March 1905.

"Mencken continued to": HLM, *NPD,* p. 274; and Ellery Sedgwick to HLM,
    20 March 1906, NYPL.

p. 84.  "*The New York Times*": C. V. Van Anda to HLM, 30 October 1906, NYPL.

"it was 'in' ": HLM, quoted in Charles Fecher, *Mencken: A Study of His
    Thought* (Alfred A. Knopf, 1978), p. 315.

" 'It is more' ": HLM, "Why Men Are Afraid to Get Married," *BS,* 20 Decem-
    ber 1906.

"Mencken greatly enjoyed": HLM, "Thirty-Five Years," *BES,* 15 April 1935;
    HLM to Joseph Katz, 25 July 1925, EPFL; Trumbull White to HLM, 7 and
    23 December 1904, 13 June 1905, and 6 April 1906, NYPL; Karl Harriman
    to HLM, 5 May 1906, NYPL; and HLM, *NPD,* p. 72.

p. 85.  "Well connected in": HLM, *A&E,* p. 7. In *The Irreverent Mr. Mencken* (Little,
    Brown, 1950) Edgar Kemler contends that the young Mencken once stood
    shyly in the background at a *Sun* reception for Mark Twain (p. 116), but
    in "AN, 1941–" Mencken wrote that on no occasion did he meet or even
    see Mark Twain.

" 'Through Shaw,' Mencken": HLM, *NPD,* p. 73.

"He had been": HLM, *NPD,* p. 122; Harrison Hale Schaff to HLM, 14 and 21
    March, 9 and 15 May, 11 and 17 July, 26 and 28 September, and 4 and 10
    October 1905, NYPL; and HLM to Miriam Gallagher, 20 January 1938,
    NYPL.

p. 86.   " 'Darwin made this' ": HLM, *George Bernard Shaw: His Plays* (Luce, 1905), p. xvi.

"What we get": Reviews in *New York Post*, 30 December 1905, and *The Nation*, 1 February 1906, both in HLM clippings scrapbook; HLM, prefatory note to "Typescripts of Early Fiction" (scrapbook A52), EPFL; HLM to George Bernard Shaw, quoted by Stanley Weintraub, "Mencken and Shaw," *Menckeniana*, Summer 1968, pp. 9–10; Harry Gershenowitz, "Mencken's Misinterpretation of Shaw's Position on Evolution," *Menckeniana*, Spring 1985, pp. 7–10; and HLM, "A&E," p. 89.

p. 87.   "Shortly after he": Harrison Hale Schaff to Isaac Goldberg, quoted in Goldberg, *The Man Mencken*, p. 372; Schaff to HLM, 19 December 1906, NYPL; and HLM, "A&E," p. 82.

"Schaff wanted Mencken": Harrison Hale Schaff to HLM, 19 December 1906, NYPL; and HLM to D. Fraser, 3 April 1935, NYPL. See also Charles Fecher, *Mencken*, p. 91n; Douglas C. Stenerson, *H. L. Mencken: Iconoclast from Baltimore*, pp. 15–16, 117–23; and HLM to Huntington Cairns, quoted by Carl Bode, "Mencken in Letters," in *On Mencken*, p. 244.

p. 88.   "Germany had taken": HLM, "The New Bugaloo," Baltimore *Morning Herald*, 25 June 1905.

"In August 1906": HLM, "Kaiser Wilhelm," Baltimore *Herald*, 26 August 1906; and HLM, "The Germans," Baltimore *Morning Herald*, 24 January 1908.

"He also proposed": Ellery Sedgwick to HLM, 20 March 1906, NYPL.

"First he prepared": HLM, "A&E," p. 478; and HLM, "AN, 1925" (NYPL), p. 62.

p. 89.   "He stressed the": HLM, *The Philosophy of Friedrich Nietzsche* (Luce, 1908), p. viii.

"Mencken was obviously": HLM, *Nietzsche*, pp. vii–ix, 303, 268–69, 146.

"For more than": HLM, *Nietzsche*, pp. 270, 291, 292.

p. 90.   *"The Philosophy of"*: *The New York Times*, quoted in "Book Notes," *The Broadside* (Luce and Co.), March 1908, HLM clippings scrapbook; and Nicholas Murray Butler, quoted in HLM, "A&E," p. 101.

p. 91.   "For the philosopher": HLM, *Nietzsche*, p. 29.

" 'In my own' ": HLM to Edward Stone, 1 March 1937, UVa, in Guy J. Forgue, ed., *Letters of H. L. Mencken* (Alfred A. Knopf, 1961), p. 414.

"The ideas he": HLM to FHG, 9 August 1919, NYPL.

p. 92.   " 'Like Nietzsche,' he": HLM, "AN, 1941–."


## Chapter 5: Stirring Up the Animals

p. 93.   "and was also": *Philadelphia Item*, 21 March 1908, HLM clippings scrapbook, EPFL.

"The highlight of": HLM, "A&E," p. 478.

p. 94.   "His prestige there": HLM, "A&E," p. 93.

"He was prepared": HLM, "Dr. Wilson's Candidacy," BES, [July 1910], and "Dr. Wilson's Campaign," BES, [1912], in HLM, BES scrapbook, 1910–1912, EPFL; Edward A. Martin, *H. L. Mencken and the Debunkers*, pp. 60–75; Martin, "On Reading Mencken," *Menckeniana*, Fall 1984, pp. 1–10; and HLM, "Thirty-Five Years," p. 90.

p. 95.   " 'Why print such' ": HLM, "The Expurgators," BES, 13 October 1910.

" 'What would become' ": HLM, "On Alcohol," BES, 6 May 1911.

p. 96.   "The column 'launched' ": HLM to Tom R. Smith, 30 July 1935, NYPL.

"Was that motivation": HLM, "Thirty-Five Years," p. 6.

"Or did the": HLM to Willard H. Wright, 25 April 1910, NYPL.

"Though now a": HLM, "AN, 1941–."

"*Hedda Gabler* was": HLM, introductory note to translations scrapbook, EPFL.

p. 97.   "Although the volume": HLM to Willard H. Wright, 6 March [1910], NYPL.

" 'The connection promises' ": HLM to Willard H. Wright, 24 January [1910], NYPL.

" 'I believe [socialism]' ": HLM, in HLM and Rives La Monte, *Men Versus the Man* (Holt, 1910), pp. 68–69.

p. 98.   " 'Work is a' ": HLM to TD, 2 February [1912], UP, *D–M Letters*, I, p. 90.

"He was often": HLM to Charles Abhau, 29 February 1936, EPFL; HLM, *A&E*, p. xix; and HLM, "AN, 1941–."

"In any case": HLM to Lillian Gish, 25 October 1939, NYPL; AM, "Reminiscences," p. 16; HLM, *A&E*, p. xx; and HLM, as told to Ruth Crawford, in "How I Got That Way," United Features Syndicate, [1926], HLM clippings scrapbook.

p. 99.   " 'a fundamentally believing' ": HLM, "A&E," p. 366.

" 'there appeared in' ": TD, "Henry L. Mencken and Myself," in Isaac Goldberg, *The Man Mencken*, p. 379. Information on the early stages of the Mencken-Dreiser friendship also taken from HLM, *A&E*, pp. 26–30; and HLM–TD letters, UP and NYPL, *D–M Letters*, I, pp. 9–52; also HLM, "AN, 1925" (NYPL); and Thomas P. Riggio, "Of the 'Black Horse Cavalry of Humor': Mencken's Contributions to *The Delineator*," *Menckeniana*, Summer 1984, pp. 1–3. See also Richard Lingeman, *Theodore Dreiser: An American Journey* (John Wiley & Sons, Inc., 1993), pp. 244 ff.

p. 100.  "Splint had heard": Fred Splint to HLM, 2 September 1939, NYPL. Mencken himself, on several later occasions, contended that Dreiser had suggested him (see, e.g., HLM, scrapbook A33, EPFL).

p. 101.  "After that piece": HLM, *A&E*, p. 11.

"As Mencken later": HLM, introduction to *Essays by James Gibbons Huneker* (Charles Scribner's Sons, 1929), p. xxiii.

"With these iconoclastic": HLM to C. C. Snyder, 28 November 1936, EPFL; HLM to A. G. Keller, 15 December 1939, NYPL; HLM, "The Burden of Humor," *SS*, February 1913, pp. 152, 153–54; HLM, "A Maker of Toccata" (ms.), "Répétition Générale" scrapbook, EPFL; and HLM to Harry Leon Wilson, 4 September [1911], NYPL.

p. 102.  "Mencken gained a": HLM, "The New Poetry" (ms.), *SS* notebook (scrapbook A118), EPFL; and HLM, "The Meredith of Tomorrow," *SS*, April 1911, p. 167. On Conrad, see, e.g., HLM, "Conrad's Self-Portrait," *SS*, October 1912.

"Conrad appealed to": HLM, "Synge and Others," *SS*, October 1912, p. 150.

"When, several years": Joseph Conrad to HLM, 11 November 1917, NYPL; and Conrad to George T. Keating, 12 December 1922, quoted in HLM, "A&E," Appendix XVIII, pp. 4–6.

p. 103.  " 'I had been' ": HLM, *A&E*, pp. 127–28.

" 'What I needed' ": HLM, *A&E*, p. 129.

p. 104.  "Mencken found him": HLM, *A&E*, pp. 129–32; HLM, "The Novel Today," *BES*, 22 March 1911; HLM to TD, 22 March [1911], UP, *D–M Letters*, I, p. 66; HLM to Harry Leon Wilson, 25 October 1911, NYPL; and HLM, "A Novel of the First Rank," *SS*, November 1911, p. 153.

"By this point": HLM, "A&E," p. 179.

"The *Smart Set*": "Henry L. Mencken," *Los Angeles Times*, 11 December 1910.

p. 105. "Neither would the": untitled article, Los Angeles *Examiner*, 3 November 1913, HLM clippings scrapbook, EPFL.

"According to a": Alfred A. Knopf, quoted by Sara Mayfield, *The Constant Circle* (Delacorte, 1968), pp. 50–51; Edward A. Martin, "In Defense of Marion," unpublished ms., forthcoming from the University of Georgia Press; and Louis Untermeyer, *From Another World* (Harcourt, Brace, 1939), p. 190.

"Some ten years": HLM, "A&E," pp. 59, 61.

p. 106. "But that was": HLM, "A&E," Appendix II, especially pp. 35–41; and HLM–Paul Armstrong correspondence, NYPL, 1905–1915.

" 'I want to' ": HLM to TD, 7 March [1909], UP, *D–M Letters*, I, p. 22.

"At times Mencken": HLM, *A&E*, p. 135.

"Dreiser's sexual adventures": HLM, "A&E," pp. 388, 395.

p. 107. "For his part": HLM, *A&E*, pp. 136–37.

p. 108. " '[I]t was unhappily' ": HLM, *A&E*, p. 136.

" 'I dismissed her' ": HLM, *A&E*, p. 137.

p. 109. "When Dreiser had": HLM to TD, 3 March [1911], UP, *D–M Letters*, I, p. 64; HLM to TD, 15 and 20 September [1911], UP, in *D–M Letters*, I, pp. 76–77.

"When Dreiser wrote"; TD to HLM, 12 November 1912, NYPL; and HLM to TD, 12 November [1912], UP; both in *D–M Letters*, I, pp. 107–08.

"Mencken was not": HLM, "Dreiser's Novel the Story of a Financier Who Loved Beauty," *The New York Times Book Review*, 10 November 1912, p. 654.

"Dreiser came to": HLM to TD, 23 and 27 March [1914], UP, *D–M Letters*, I, pp. 135, 138.

"Although the novel": HLM, "Adventures among the New Novels," *SS*, August 1914, p. 154.

"Not only did": HLM to TD, [November 1913], UP; TD to HLM, 10 August 1914, NYPL; and TD to HLM, 25 March 1914, NYPL; all in *D–M Letters*, I, pp. 123, 148–49, 137.

p. 110. "It would not": Burton Rascoe, introduction to *The Smart Set Anthology* (Reynal & Hitchcock, 1934), p. 34.

"Mencken encountered numerous": HLM correspondence with ELM, Louis Untermeyer, Ben Hecht, and Herbert Bayard Swope, all NYPL; Untermeyer, *From Another World*, p. 190; Hecht, *Letters from Bohemia* (Doubleday, 1964), pp. 72, 75; and Hecht, *A Child of the Century* (Simon & Schuster, 1954), pp. 175, 177, 356.

p. 111. "Although Percival Pollard": HLM–Percival Pollard correspondence, NYPL; and HLM, "Books to Read and Books to Avoid," *SS*, February 1910, p. 157.

"Mencken had long": HLM, "A&E," pp. 480–83 and Appendix III, pp. 424–90; and HLM, "The New Dramatic Literature," *SS*, August 1911, pp. 154–55.

p. 112. "Pollard's death at": HLM, "A&E," Appendix III, pp. 424–90; HLM to Willard H. Wright, 18 and 20 December 1911, NYPL; and Ben Hecht, *Letters from Bohemia*, pp. 77–79.

"It was a story": HLM, "A&E," Appendix III, p. 443; Ambrose Bierce to HLM, 25 April 1913, NYPL; and HLM, "Ambrose Bierce," *Prejudices*, *VI*, pp. 261–62.

p. 113.  " 'The thirties are' ": HLM to MB, [1914], EPFL.

" 'I was ill' ": HLM, *Diary,* 12 September 1945, p. 381.

p. 114.  "From those letters": HLM to TD, 7 March [1909] and 25 January [1912], UP, *D–M Letters,* I, pp. 22, 89; HLM to Willard H. Wright, 26 April and 28 November 1913, NYPL; and HLM to FHG, 15 August 1919, NYPL.

"On one particular": William Manchester, *Disturber of the Peace,* p. 52.

"It would be": Author's interviews with Dr. Philip Wagley, 29 July 1988, and Dr. Benjamin Baker, 14 June 1991.

"As Mencken himself ": HLM to A. H. McDannald, 28 March 1933, NYPL; AM, "Reminiscences," p. 47; and HLM to Oscar Levy, 21 April 1939, NYPL.

p. 115.  "At times his": HLM to TD, 9 March [1914], UP, *D–M Letters,* I, p. 133.

" 'I owed to' ": HLM, "Thirty-Five Years," p. 469.

"A number of ": Author's interview with W. C. Abhau, 27 July 1988; James Cain to SM, 19 August 1968, UA; HLM, "AN, 1941–"; and HLM to Edgar Kemler, 8 December 1946, EPFL.

"If Mencken enjoyed": HLM to TD, 1 April 1943, UP, *D–M Letters,* II, p. 693; HLM, "*HD:* Additions," p. 88; and HLM, *Diary,* 3 June 1945, p. 371.

p. 116.  "For a time": Author's interview with W. C. Abhau.

"He was met": HLM, "*Heathen Days:* Additions," p. 55.

"Mencken devoted": Author's interview with W. C. Abhau; HLM, "AN, 1925" (NYPL), p. 56; William J. Sabo, "An Interview with Rear Admiral William C. Abhau," *Menckeniana,* Summer 1977, p. 8; and CM to Anna Mencken, 7 October 1908, EPFL.

p. 117.  "Even closer than": HLM, "*HD:* Additions," p. 59; HLM, "The End of a Life," *BES,* 21 November 1932; HLM, "AN, 1941–"; and HLM, "*Heathen Days:* Additions," p. 92.

p. 118.  "Organized in 1910": HLM, "*Heathen Days:* Additions," pp. 77, 89; and HLM, "Thirty-Five Years," p. 58.

"Mencken, in a": HLM to GM, [April 1912], EPFL.

p. 119.  "The weather, the": HLM to TD, 27 April [1912], UP, *D–M Letters,* I, p. 94; and HLM to GM, 26 April [1912] and [May 1912], EPFL.

"Mencken had embarked": HLM, *Heathen Days,* pp. 107–17.

"The aspiring candidate": HLM, *Heathen Days,* p. 115.

p. 120.  "When Thayer approached": HLM to Willard H. Wright, 28 October 1909, NYPL; "Henry Mencken," *Los Angeles Times,* 11 December 1910; HLM to Wright, 28 October 1909, 19 November [1911], and 20 December 1911, NYPL.

" 'To me Wright' ": TD to HLM, 9 August 1913, NYPL, *D–M Letters,* I, p. 123.

" 'Once you are' ": HLM to Willard H. Wright, 18 January 1912, NYPL.

"In certain ways": William H. Nolte, introduction to *H. L. Mencken's Smart Set Criticism* (Cornell University Press, 1968), pp. xv–xvi; HLM to Willard H. Wright, 17, 25, 27, and 30 April, 2 May, and 4 July 1913, NYPL.

p. 121.  "But at the": HLM, "A&E," pp. 555, 176.

" 'From [Thayer's] talk' ": HLM to Willard H. Wright, 14 and 15 December [1913], NYPL; and HLM to Edgar Kemler, 27 November 1946, EPFL.

p. 122.  "He and two": HLM to Anna Mencken, 21 April [1914], EPFL; HLM to GM, 26 April and 7 May [1914], EPFL; HLM, *Heathen Days,* pp. 128–49; and HLM, "*Heathen Days:* Additions," pp. 130, 145.

"Nathan wrote essays": HLM to Edgar Kemler, 6 January 1947, EPFL.

p. 123. " 'I am by' ": HLM, "The Beeriad," *SS*, April 1913, in Carl Bode, ed., *The Young Mencken* (Dial Press, 1973), p. 253.

"Munich beer, then": HLM, "The Beeriad," pp. 254, 252, 265–66.

" 'Thayer is wholly' ": HLM to Harry Leon Wilson, 8 February [1914], NYPL.

p. 124. " 'John Adams Thayer' ": HLM to Ellery Sedgwick, 25 August 1914, NYPL.

"Mencken was also": HLM to TD, 11 and 17 August [1914], UP, *D–M Letters*, I, pp. 149, 151.

p. 125. "He had—he": HLM, "A&E," p. 342.

## Chapter 6: Love and War

p. 126. " 'I may visit' ": HLM to MB, 24 February [1914], 19 June 1914, and July–August 1914, *passim*, EPFL; MB note on HLM letter of 21 October 1914, EPFL; and MB to EB, 26 October 1921, NYPL. Concerning Marion Bloom's age, Betty Adler, in her *HLM: Man of Letters*, lists 1888 as Bloom's birthdate, but other evidence, including the Marion–Estelle Bloom correspondence, suggests June 1891. I am also grateful to Edward A. Martin, who shared with me his ms. "In Defense of Marion," forthcoming from the University of Georgia Press.

p. 127. "Just what sort": EB, autobiographical ms. in HLM–EB correspondence, NYPL.

p. 128. " 'I kiss your' ": HLM to MB, 23 August and 27 November 1914 and [1914], EPFL.

"He kept Marion": HLM to MB, 23 August, 4 and 15 September, and 11 and 12 November 1914, EPFL.

"You are 80": HLM to MB, [24 November?] 1914, EPFL.

"As always, Mencken": HLM to MB, [1914] and 3 February, 16 April, and 2 and 3 June 1915, EPFL.

p. 129. "On one letter": MB, noted on HLM letter, [1915]; MB to EB, 7 May 1927, NYPL; HLM to MB, 10 June 1915, EPFL.

"So great was"; TD, *American Diaries 1902–1926*, ed. Thomas P. Riggio (University of Pennsylvania Press, 1982), p. 169.

"He was not": MB to HLM, 29 July 1915; and HLM to TD, 23 December 1916, UP; both in *D–M Letters*, I, p. 290.

p. 130. "As he and": HLM to MB, [April 1915], [1915], and 11 February 1915, EPFL.

" 'Henry has been' ": MB to EB, [Summer 1916], NYPL.

"He frequently advised": MB to Betty Adler, 12 June 1966, EPFL.

p. 131. "She wrote on": MB to HLM, 1 November 1916 (copy), EPFL; and HLM to MB, 27 October 1916, EPFL.

" 'You infuriate me' ": MB to HLM, 1 November 1916, EPFL.

"Such a letter": MB to HLM, 1 November 1916, EPFL; and HLM to MB, 9, 15, and 18 December 1916, EPFL.

"An especially fine": HLM to Miriam Taylor, [1916], EPFL; HLM to MB, 18 December 1916, EPFL; and HLM to EB, 15 August 1927, NYPL.

p. 132. " 'God's benison upon' ": HLM to TD, UP, *D–M Letters*, I, p. 151.

"In several editorials": HLM, "The Motive of Germany," *BES*, [1911]; "The German Volcano," *BES*, [July 1910]; "The German Insurgents," *BES*, [August 1910]; and "In Germany," *BES*, 2 August 1910, all in Baltimore *Sun* editorials scrapbook (A58), EPFL.

p. 133. "He was not": Author's interview with W. C. Abhau; HLM to George Sterling, 15 May [1922], NYPL; and HLM, "AN, 1941–," EPFL.

"As for the": HLM, note in "The American: Clippings from *The Smart Set* and the *Atlantic Monthly*, 1913–1914" (scrapbook), EPFL.

"As his fellow": Oscar Levy to HLM, 16 October 1914, NYPL.

"But, as Mencken": *A&E*, pp. 173–74.

p. 134. " 'I am for' ": HLM to TD, 8 November 1914, UP; TD to HLM, 10 November 1914, NYPL; and HLM to TD, 12 November 1914, UP; all in *D–M Letters*, I, pp. 164–65.

" 'On to London' ": HLM to TD, 11 and 15 December [1914], UP, *D–M Letters*, I, pp. 169–70.

"If in his": HLM, "Free Lance," *BES*, 14 March and 25 June 1913.

p. 135. "It was the": HLM, "Free Lance," *BES*, 13 June 1914.

" 'More than any' ": HLM, "Free Lance," *BES*, 4 August 1914.

p. 136. "Soon, in 'The' ": HLM, "Free Lance," *BES*, 6 and 27 August 1914.

"He continued to": HLM, "Free Lance," *BES*, 10, 11, 12, 15, 17, 18, 19, 21, 22, and 23 September 1914; "Free Lance," 20 and 7 September 1914.

p. 137. "He insisted at": HLM, "Free Lance," *BES*, 29 September 1914.

"Autocracy and democracy": HLM, "Free Lance," *BES*, 19 November 1914 and [December 1914].

p. 138. "The letters continued": HLM, "Thirty-Five Years," p. 175.

"In May he": HLM, "Free Lance," *BES*, 8 May 1915; also "Free Lance," 31 May, 3 March, 2 June, and 6 October 1915.

"In fact, as": HLM, "Thirty-Five Years," p. 172; HLM to TD, 2 November [1915], UP, *D–M Letters*, I, p. 205; HLM, "Are the Germans Immoral? Of Course," *BES*, 11 November 1915; and HLM, "More Proofs of German Immorality," *BES*, 22 November 1915.

p. 139. "In less direct": HLM, "Oh Henry, How You Talk," *BES*, 5 October 1916; and HLM, "Variations in G Minor," *BES*, 11 May 1916.

"Whatever Mencken later": HLM, "Thirty-Five Years," p. 172.

"In August 1914": Ellery Sedgwick to HLM, 31 August 1914, NYPL; HLM to Sedgwick, 1 September 1914, NYPL; and Sedgwick to HLM, 10 September 1914, NYPL.

" 'The Mailed Fist' ": HLM, "The Mailed Fist and Its Prophet," *Atlantic Monthly*, November 1914, pp. 603, 607.

p. 140. "Moreover, Mencken was": HLM to Ellery Sedgwick, 10 October 1914, NYPL; Sedgwick to HLM, 13 October 1914 and 2 April 1915, NYPL.

"Mencken and Sedgwick": Ellery Sedgwick to HLM, 18 May 1915, NYPL; HLM to Sedgwick, 11 and 22 May 1915, NYPL; and Sedgwick to HLM, 24 June 1915, NYPL.

"Mencken and Sedgwick": Ellery Sedgwick to HLM, 24 November 1915, NYPL; and HLM to Sedgwick, 29 December [1915], NYPL.

p. 141. "As he had": HLM to Ellery Sedgwick, 1 September 1914, NYPL.

"If anybody was": HLM, *A&E*, p. 49.

"Financially, at first": HLM, *A&E*, pp. 49–55.

p. 142. "Mencken always insisted": HLM to Edgar Kemler, 13 August 1948, EPFL; and HLM, "A Note for Authors," in "A&E," Appendix XX, pp. 1–2.

"Mencken filled nearly": HLM, *A&E*, p. 52; and HLM to Edgar Kemler, 12 December 1946, EPFL.

p. 143. " 'The old town' ": HLM, "Good Old Baltimore," *SS*, May 1913, p. 85.

" 'that sub-brachycephalous and' ": HLM, "The American," *SS*, June 1913, p. 89.

p. 144. "He became acquainted": Eugene O'Neill to HLM, 26 May 1917, NYPL. For a full account of Mencken as *SS* editor, see Carl R. Dolmetsch, *The Smart*

Set: A History and Anthology (Dial, 1966); William H. Nolte, *H. L. Mencken: Literary Critic* (Wesleyan, 1966); and Nolte, ed., *H. L. Mencken's Smart Set Criticism.*

"It would not": Sherwood Anderson, *Sherwood Anderson's Memoirs: A Critical Edition* (1942; North Carolina, 1969), pp. 349, 369; Anderson to HLM, 4 January 1916, NYPL; and HLM, *A&E,* pp. 117, 238.

"Mencken's correspondence with": HLM–Ezra Pound correspondence, NYPL, especially 15 and 17 April 1915; HLM to ELM, 2 August 1943, NYPL; and HLM, *A&E,* pp. 61–66.

p. 145. "From the beginning": Ezra Pound to HLM, 20 January and 23 March 1915, NYPL.

"Joyce was grateful": James Joyce to HLM, 23 March and 7 July 1915, NYPL; and HLM, *A&E,* pp. 58–61.

"When Mencken met": HLM, *A&E,* pp. 101–10.

p. 146. "Some poems by": Carl R. Dolmetsch, *The Smart Set,* p. 79; HLM to Newton D. Baker, 21 January 1919, NYPL; and Maxwell Bodenheim to HLM, 26 July [1926], NYPL.

"As he wrote": HLM to Edgar Kemler, 13 August 1948, EPFL.

"In fact, Mencken": HLM–Thyra Samter Winslow and HLM–Lilith Benda correspondence, 1914–1920, NYPL; HLM, *A&E,* pp. 67–68, 251–54, 110–13; and HLM, "A&E," p. 299.

p. 147. "After he landed": HLM to Mrs. A. D. McNeil, 29 May 1945, NYPL; HLM to G. K. Spencer, 19 May 1937, NYPL; HLM to Ellery Sedgwick, 26 November [1916], NYPL; HLM to Ernest Boyd, 14 and 18 October and 14 November 1916, NYPL; HLM, "A&E," pp. 243–56, 288.

"Two of their": HLM, *A&E,* pp. 82–85, 200–03.

p. 148. "The first signs": HLM to TD, 6 and 14 October 1914, UP; and TD to HLM, 13 and 15 October 1914, NYPL; all in *D–M Letters,* I, pp. 159–63.

p. 149. "In 1915 and": HLM to TD, 15 October and 6 and 25 December 1915, UP, *D–M Letters,* I, pp. 203, 210–13; and HLM, "A Literary Behemoth," *SS,* December 1915, pp. 150–56.

"Despite such a": HLM to Ellery Sedgwick, 2 November [1914], NYPL; HLM to TD, 25 December [1915], 26 June 1916, and 5 July [1916], UP, *D–M Letters,* I, pp. 213, 239–42; and HLM, "The Creed of a Novelist," October 1916, pp. 138–43.

" 'Under you and' ": TD to HLM, 20 April 1915, NYPL; and HLM to TD, 22 April 1915, UP; both in *D–M Letters,* I, pp. 193–97.

p. 150. "For a time": HLM, *A&E,* pp. 139–42, 152–53; and HLM, "A&E," pp. 430–31.

"I sometimes think": TD to HLM, 26 April 1915, NYPL; and HLM to TD, 29 April 1915, UP; both in *D–M Letters,* I, pp. 197–99.

p. 151. "Nonetheless, when the": TD to HLM, 27 July 1916, NYPL; and HLM to TD, 28 July 1916 (and other letters), UP; all in *D–M Letters,* I, pp. 244ff; HLM, "Dreiser Protest" folder, EPFL; and HLM to TD, 4 August 1916, UP, *D–M Letters,* I, p. 248.

"Mencken had some": HLM, *A&E,* pp. 158–69.

"Dreiser should have": TD to HLM, 31 July 1916, NYPL; and HLM to TD, 5 September and [6 October 1915], UP; all in *D–M Letters,* I, pp. 247, 261, 266.

p. 152. "Dreiser resented these": TD to HLM, 9 October 1916, NYPL; and HLM to TD [10 October 1916], UP; both in *D–M Letters,* I, pp. 266–69.

"For the present": HLM to Ernest Boyd, 6 September 1916, NYPL; HLM to

TD, [20 December 1916], UP, *D–M Letters*, I, pp. 284–85; HLM to Ben Huebsch, 16 March 1918, Library of Congress, in Carl Bode, ed. *The New Mencken Letters* (Dial, 1977), p. 83; and HLM to TD, [16 December 1916], UP, *D–M Letters*, I, pp. 281–83.

p. 153. "Mencken knew quite": HLM to TD, [16 December 1916], 23 December 1916, [20 December 1916], and 26 December 1916, UP; and TD to HLM, 25 December 1916, NYPL; all in *D–M Letters*, I, pp. 281–93.

"It was an": HLM to Ellery Sedgwick, 19 October [1916], NYPL; HLM to U.S. State Department, 5 December [1916], State Department decimal file 841.-111/137; HLM, "A&E," p. 474; and HLM to MB, 28 December 1916, EPFL. I am grateful to Shawn Cunningham for sharing with me materials from the U.S. State Department files.

"Mencken was being": "Mencken to Germany," *BS*, 14 January 1917, HLM clippings scrapbook; and HLM, "A&E," p. 344.

p. 154. "He sailed three": HLM to MB, 28 December 1916, EPFL.

"The adventures at": HLM, *Heathen Days*, pp. 150–55.

"On New Year's": HLM to Anna Mencken, 31 December 1916 and 2, 7, 13, and 16 January 1917, all in HLM, "Germany 1917" (scrapbook A48A), EPFL; HLM to J. M. Bradbury, 30 July 1948, NYPL; HLM to Arthur H. Samuels, 16 August 1934, NYPL; HLM to Holger Koppel, [January 1917], NYPL; HLM to Willard H. Wright [January 1917], NYPL; and HLM, *Heathen Days*, p. 151.

p. 155. "It appeared, he": HLM to Anna Mencken, [January 1917], EPFL; and HLM, "Thirty-Five Years," pp. 196–97.

"Mencken spent only": HLM, "AN, 1941–"; HLM, "Mencken Gives Glimpses of Trench Warfare," *BS*, 13 March 1917; HLM, "Reminiscences," *BES*, 21 June 1937; and HLM, "Thirty-Five Years," p. 197.

"Life at the front": HLM, dispatches in *BS*, March 1917, in "Germany 1917," scrapbook, EPFL; and HLM, "Reminiscences," *BES*, 21 June 1937.

p. 156. "Mencken returned to": HLM, "Berlin Diary," 1, 2 and 4 February 1917, EPFL.

"What was chiefly": HLM, "Berlin Diary," 3, 6, and 7 February 1917, EPFL.

"In his diary": HLM, "Berlin Diary," 7, 9, 6, and 10 February 1917, EPFL.

p. 157. "He was ready": HLM, "Berlin Diary," 9 and 11 February 1917, EPFL.

"Mencken crossed into": HLM, "Berlin Diary," 12, 14, and 16 February 1917, EPFL.

"He was happy": HLM, "Berlin Diary," 16 February and 22 February–3 March 1917, EPFL; HLM to Ernest Boyd, 19 February [1917], NYPL; and HLM to Anna Mencken, 6 March 1917, EPFL.

p. 158. " 'The retreat from' ": HLM, "Berlin Diary," 5 March 1917, EPFL.

"For the next": HLM, *Heathen Days*, pp. 161–75; HLM to Anna Mencken, 6, 8, and 10 March 1917, "Germany 1917" scrapbook, EPFL; and HLM, "Berlin Diary," 8, 13, and 14 March 1917, EPFL.

## Chapter 7: Under Siege

p. 159. " 'I had the' ": HLM to JH, [March 1917], NYPL; HLM to Ernest Boyd, 19 February and 20 March [1917], NYPL; and HLM to Anna Mencken, 6 March 1917, "Germany 1917" scrapbook, EPFL.

"For the first": HLM, "Berlin Diary," 11 and 12 March 1917, EPFL.

p. 160.  " 'Mobs are already' ": HLM to TD, [March 1917] and 9 April 1917, UP, in
*D–M Letters*, I, pp. 295–97.

"He had planned": HLM to JH, [March 1917], NYPL; and HLM, preface,
"Berlin Diary," EPFL.

"He had been": HLM to TD, 20 February [1915], UP, *D–M Letters*, I, p. 188;
and HLM, "Thirty-Five Years," pp. 205–06.

"He was suspect": Paul Koenig to HLM, 3 November 1916, NYPL; HLM,
"Thirty-Five Years," pp. 177–78, 181; and HLM, "A&E," pp. 273–75.

p. 161.  "Thus he expected": HLM to Edgar Kemler, [1948], EPFL; and HLM,
"A&E," pp. 273–75.

"As he wrote": HLM, "AN, 1941–."

"When Sohler was": Letter of military intelligence officer of the War Department to Bruce Bielaski of Bureau of Investigation, Department of Justice,
and Billups Harris, report 73992, both in Justice Department file M1085-
0G73992. I thank Shawn Cunningham for sharing these materials with me.

p. 162.  " 'It might be' ": Colonel R. H. Van Deman to Bruce Bielaski, 28 November
1917, *ibid.*; and Billups Harris, report, 22 December 1917, *ibid.*

"Other allegations about": Justice Department file, *ibid.*; HLM to Edgar
Kemler, [1948], EPFL; HLM to TD, 11 October [1920], UP, *D–M Letters*,
II, p. 401; and HLM, miscellaneous notes, envelope A100.8, EPFL.

"He accepted honorary": HLM, "*HD:* Additions," p. 99; HLM to Edgar
Kemler, [1948], EPFL; HLM, "Thirty-Five Years," pp. 175–77.

p. 163.  "Mencken was aware": FHG to HLM, 19 August 1918, and HLM to FHG, 30
August 1918, in HLM, "A&E," pp. 654–55; and memorandum of conversa-
tion with FHG, 8 August 1918, Military Intelligence File 10720-70-7, War
Department.

p. 164.  "Far more disturbing": HLM, *A&E*, pp. 212–16.

"Mencken broke off": HLM to Ernest Boyd, [1917], NYPL; HLM to Stanton
Leeds, 9 April 1943 and 2 June [1919], NYPL; and HLM, *A&E*, pp.
214–16.

p. 165.  " 'I have never' ": Clare Leighton, "Cynical Fantasies," *Menckeniana*, Fall
1970, p. 2.

" 'A man of' ": HLM, "Types of Men," *Prejudices, III*, p. 276.

" 'I had to' ": HLM, "A&E," p. 343.

"The war was": HLM, "A&E," p. 344.

p. 166.  "He had not": HLM to BH, 27 October 1938, UNC; HLM to Anita Loos, 31
August 1935, NYPL; HLM, miscellaneous notes, 1933, scrapbook A117,
EPFL; and HLM, *A&E*, pp. 306, 199–201.

"Mencken made the": HLM–James Gibbons Huneker correspondence, 1905–
1921, NYPL; HLM, *A&E*, pp. 14–23; and HLM, introduction to *Essays by
James Gibbons Huneker*.

p. 167.  "Another such figure": HLM, *A&E*, pp. 205, 226–29.

"A failure as": HLM, miscellaneous notes, 1941–, in scrapbook A122, EPFL;
HLM, introductory note to "Letters to Philip Goodman," scrapbook,
EPFL; and author's interview with Ruth Goodman Goetz, 1 August 1988.

p. 168.  "Indeed, in 1914": HLM to TD, 27 March [1914], UP, *D–M Letters*, I, pp.
137–38; and HLM, *A&E*, p. 179.

"And, Mencken later": HLM, *A&E*, p. 178; and HLM, "A&E," Appendix
VIII, p. 12.

"It would be": HLM, "*HD:* Additions," p. 35; HLM, "A Jewish African State,"
Baltimore *Herald*, 26 September 1905; and HLM, "Free Lance," *BES*, 23

August 1912. Sara Mayfield was among those who assumed Marion Bloom was Jewish (*Constant Circle*, p. 152). Bloom herself recognized that she was often "spoken of as a Jewess, because I am small and dark" (MB to Betty Adler, 14 February 1973, EPFL).

p. 169.   "All this Mencken": Alfred A. Knopf, memoir (copy), Bode collection, EPFL; HLM, "AN, 1941–"; HLM to Louis Pound, 5 April [1920], NYPL; HLM, *A&E*, pp. 179, 200; and HLM, "A&E," p. 551.

"Regardless of whether": HLM, "A&E," p. 621; HLM, "Menckeniana: Documents . . ." scrapbook, p. 12, EPFL; and AM, draft of letter to Huntington Cairns, [n.d.—1960s?], EPFL.

p. 170.   "Mencken's suspicions about": In his *Smart Set Anthology* Burton Rascoe contended that Mencken had jumped to Goodman in 1918 because of a break in friendship with Knopf, but Knopf denied such a break. Goodman was simply "a closer friend of Mencken's in those days than I was," Knopf explained in 1963, and thus it was logical that Mencken would briefly publish with Goodman. Knopf to Alan Wycherley, 1 April 1963, EPFL; also, Knopf to Betty Adler, 18 March 1964, EPFL.

"Mencken had first": HLM, "Thirty-Five Years," p. 126; and Van Wyck Brooks, *Days of the Phoenix* (E. P. Dutton, 1957), p. 69.

p. 171.   "In the long": HLM note included with HLM–Boyd correspondence, NYPL.

" 'You matter, and' ": JH to HLM, 20 November 1914, NYPL. If we are to trust the dates on Hergesheimer's letters, there is one earlier letter, dated 4 December 1910, in which Hergesheimer asks Mencken for his advice on a novel and asks Mencken to "come over here for a night" to "hear a draft of the first part of a novel." In fact, the letter is likely misdated. It is unlikely that Hergesheimer would have been so familiar with Mencken in 1910.

"Mencken liked Hergesheimer's": HLM, "A&E," p. 207; and HLM, "AN, 1941–."

"To Boyd in": HLM to Ernest Boyd, [1916 or 1917], NYPL; and other undated letters from HLM to Boyd, almost certainly in 1916 and 1917, NYPL.

"What Mencken continued": TD, diary, included in HLM, "A&E," Appendix XIV.

p. 172.   "Mencken did not": *Ibid.*, pp. 8, 72.

"In fact, Mencken": HLM to EB, [1918], 9 March [1918], and 20 April [1918], NYPL; and HLM, "A&E," Appendix XIX, p. 3.

p. 173.   "He too—at": HLM, *A&E*, p. 222.

"But his friend's": HLM to EB, 12 March [1918], 23 January 1918, 17 April 1917, and various other letters, 1918–1920, NYPL.

"rather, he remained": TD, diary, in HLM, "A&E," Appendix XIV, p. 16.

p. 174.   "Mencken had written": HLM to MB, 7 and 11 January 1917 and [March 1917], EPFL; and MB to EB, [Spring 1917], NYPL.

" 'I had a' ": HLM to EB, 28 May [1918], NYPL.

"He made several": HLM to MB, [August 1918] and 20 September 1918, EPFL; and MB to Betty Adler, [August 1970], EPFL.

"He wrote several": HLM to MB, 21, 23, and 24 September 1918, EPFL.

p. 175.   "According to letters": MB to EB, [August 1923] and other letters, NYPL; MB to Betty Adler, 20 and 27 June 1971, EPFL. I am grateful to Carl Bode for sharing with me the transcript of his taped interview with Marion Bloom, 18 August 1965, in which she gives some of the same information she gave to Adler and remarks as well that she was to have met Mencken's mother when she returned from France (Bode transcript, pp. 26–27).

"Just how seriously": Information in this paragraph taken from HLM, *The Philosophy of Friedrich Nietzsche*, p. 58; HLM to EB, 2 February [1919?], NYPL; and HLM to MB, letters of March, April, July, August, and September 1919, EPFL.

p. 176. "In letters to": HLM to EB, 25 and 31 May [1919], NYPL.

"As far back": HLM, *Nietzsche*, p. 101; and MB to Betty Adler, 27 June [1971] and 15 November 1972, EPFL.

" 'What is this' ": HLM to MB, 10 September [1919], EPFL; MB to Betty Adler, 20 June 1971, EPFL; and HLM to EB, 12 May [1921], NYPL.

p. 177. "Marion later insisted": MB to Betty Adler, 20 and 27 June 1971, EPFL; and MB to EB, 26 February 1920, NYPL.

"It was probably": MB to EB, 22 March 1920, NYPL.

"She recalled, at": MB to EB, [1927] and [1923?], NYPL.

p. 178. " 'To one ineradicable' ": HLM, "Répétition Générale," *SS*, March 1920, p. 48. In his miscellaneous notes in the EPFL Mencken left these words: "I noted this almost universal respect for wealth early in life, and have put it to profitable use ever since. That is, I have always pretended to be a great deal better heeled than I am in fact. It has got me deference in quarters where, otherwise, I might have been scorned, and materially eased my days" (Envelope A100.8).

p. 179. "It was one": MB to EB, [1920s], NYPL.

"That may also": HLM, "A&E," Appendix XXVI, p. 10n; HLM to Bradford Swan, 18 March 1948, Bode collection, EPFL; and AAK to Betty Adler, 19 July 1971, EPFL.

"In a four-paragraph": MB, "Reflection," *SS*, March 1917, p. 31.

p. 180. "She was hurt": MB to EB, 22 March 1920, NYPL.

"Despite his disapproval": MB to EB, [1920s] and 14 February 1928, NYPL.

## Chapter 8: Marking Time

p. 181. "In September 1918": HLM to Ernest Boyd, 4 and 13 September, 9 August, and 21 January 1918, NYPL; HLM to George Sterling, 7 October [1918], NYPL; HLM to Boyd, 8 October [1919] and 16 October 1919, NYPL.

p. 182. "As before, he": statements (concerning August) by Anna Mencken, August's physician, and August's employer, Mencken family papers, EPFL; news account, 25 November 1917, unidentified newspaper in scrapbook F173.7, EPFL; and HLM to FHG, 17 September 1919, NYPL.

"Although his own": HLM to MB, 18 March [1919], EPFL; HLM to TD, 5 February 1916 and 3 January [1919], UP, *D–M Letters*, I, p. 218, and II, p. 330; HLM to Ellery Sedgwick, 20 May 1916, NYPL; and HLM, "How Have You Been?" (1925), EPFL.

p. 183. "His principal Baltimore": HLM to Ernest Boyd, 20 September [1918] and 3 February [1919], NYPL; HLM, "AN, 1925" (NYPL), p. 93; and HLM–Max Brödel correspondence, 1916–1919, NYPL.

"Mencken's old friend": HLM, "*Heathen Days*: Additions," p. 77; and HLM, *A&E*, p. 234.

"Financially, he suffered": HLM to Ernest Boyd, 1 August [1918], NYPL; HLM to Edgar Kemler, [1948], EPFL; HLM, "Thirty-Five Years," p. 19; HLM to Boyd, 8 January [1918], NYPL; and HLM, "A&E," p. 257.

p. 184. "Just before and": HLM to TD, 11 November [1912], UP, *D–M Letters*, I, p. 106; HLM to Willard H. Wright, 12 November [1913], UP; and HLM, *NPD*, p. vii.

"'I can recall'": HLM to Gordon Behrens, 8 April 1948, NYPL; and HLM, "AN, 1941–."

"If he took": HLM, "A&E," pp. 482, 344; HLM to Ernest Boyd, 20 April [1918] and [1916], NYPL.

p. 185. "In the former": HLM, "The Sahara of the Bozart," New York *Evening Mail*, 13 November 1917.

p. 186. "'On December 20'": HLM, "A Neglected Anniversary," New York *Evening Mail*, 28 December 1917.

"For Mark Twain": HLM, "Mark Twain's Americanism," New York *Evening Mail*, 1 November 1917.

"Occasionally he could": HLM, "Why Free Speech Is Impossible During War" (ms.), scrapbook A115, EPFL.

p. 187. "As far back": HLM, "A&E," p. 133; and HLM to Ernest Boyd, 20 October 1916, NYPL.

"*Heliogabalus*, she wrote": MB to Betty Adler, 12 June 1966, EPFL. In his introduction to the typescript of the play in his *Heliogabalus* scrapbook Mencken contended that producer Will A. Page later offered $10,000, plus royalties, for the play, but Mencken maintained that he and Nathan declined on the grounds that American audiences were "too little civilized" to see it.

p. 188. "There can be": HLM, "The Goat" (ms.), HLM scrapbooks, EPFL; and HLM, introductory note to "Attempts at Plays," EPFL.

"Several reviewers, rather": Reviews in Baltimore *News*, *Philadelphia Press*, *San Francisco Chronicle*, and *Boston Transcript*, in HLM clippings scrapbook, EPFL.

"'Love is the'": HLM, *A Little Book in C Major*, pp. 9, 19, 63, 9.

p. 189. "'Granting the existence'": HLM, *Damn!* (Philip Goodman, 1918), p. 88; Benjamin de Casseres, "H. L. Mencken and the Second Fall of Man," New York *Sun*, 20 October 1918, and review in *BES*, 15 June 1918, both in HLM clippings scrapbook, EPFL.

"'All my work'": HLM to Burton Rascoe, [Summer 1920], in Guy J. Forgue, ed., *Letters of H. L. Mencken*, p. 187.

p. 190. "it was 'the'": HLM, "Clinical Notes," *AM*, January 1925, p. 59.

"He had attacked": HLM to Willard H. Wright, letters of 1913, NYPL; HLM, "Free Lance," *BES*, 31 December 1914; and HLM to TD, 28 July 1916, UP, *D–M Letters*, I, p. 246.

"By mid-1914 he": HLM, "Free Lance," 8 and 10 July 1914; and HLM, "The War in Its Last Phases," *BES*, 8 November 1915.

p. 191. "All the while": HLM to Willard H. Wright, 12 November [1912], NYPL; HLM to Harry Leon Wilson, 25 October [1911], NYPL; HLM to TD, 6 June 1916, UP, *D–M Letters*, I, p. 235; and HLM, "A&E," p. 161.

"But he did": HLM, *A&E*, pp. 183–84, 186; and HLM, "A&E," pp. 467, 482–83, 498. *A Book of Prefaces* was first scheduled for publication by the American branch of the English publisher John Lane, but Mencken preferred Knopf and included in the manuscript a derogatory passage about Lane's principal author to which he knew Lane would object. Lane rejected the manuscript, as HLM knew he would, and he was free to publish with Knopf.

p. 192. "*A Book of Prefaces*": HLM, *A&E*, p. 177; and HLM, *Prefaces*, pp. 216, 199–200, 202, 232, 259, 225, 227, 230–32.

"Mencken's book was": Burton Rascoe review, *Chicago Tribune*, HLM clippings scrapbook, EPFL; Randolph Bourne, "H. L. Mencken," *The New*

*Republic,* 24 November 1917, pp. 102–03; and Los Angeles *Continent* [1918], HLM clippings scrapbook, EPFL.

"But the most": Stuart Sherman, "The Naturalism of Mr. Dreiser," *The Nation,* 2 December 1915, pp. 648–50; HLM to TD, 8 December [1915], UP, *D–M Letters,* I, p. 211; and HLM, *Prefaces,* p. 138.

p. 193.   "His review in": Stuart Sherman, "Beautifying American Letters," *The Nation,* 29 November 1917, pp. 593–94; Sherman, "Mr. H. L. Mencken and the Jeune Fille," *The New York Times Book Review,* 7 December 1919, reprinted in Sherman, *Americans* (Charles Scribner's Sons, 1922), p. 5.

p. 194.   "He 'seemed to' ": HLM to Ernest Boyd, 1 October 1936, NYPL; and HLM, *A&E,* p. 185.

"'The curse of' ": HLM, "Critics Wild and Tame," *SS,* December 1917, p. 138; and HLM, "A&E," p. 513. On HLM's war with the professors and New Humanists, see William H. Nolte, *H. L. Mencken: Literary Critic,* especially pp. 148–89.

"Depending on the": Article on HLM's speech to Baltimore Women's City Club, *BS,* 24 December 1910, HLM clippings scrapbook, EPFL.

p. 195.   "As early as": HLM to Ernest Boyd, [1916], 14 February 1918, and [March 1918], NYPL. See also, in *SS,* "The Infernal Feminine," April 1917, pp. 266–72.

"Women were superior": HLM, *In Defense* (Goodman), pp. 130–31, 28, 133, 5; and HLM to MB, 10 June 1915, EPFL.

p. 196.   "As a bachelor": HLM, *In Defense* (Goodman), p. 86; and HLM, *Diary,* 1 May 1939, p. 124.

"All this was": Vincent Fitzpatrick, "Wink Your Eye at Some Homely Girl," *Menckeniana,* Winter 1977, p. 6; HLM to Willard H. Wright, [June 1913], NYPL; HLM to EB, 19 October 1926, NYPL; HLM, quoted by John O'Donnell, "Mencken Says America Can Change Only from Imbecility to Worse," *Kansas City Post,* 8 July 1922; and HLM to TD, 14 April [1925], UP, *D–M Letters,* II, p. 532,

p. 197.   "Mencken would hardly": Friedrich Nietzsche, quoted by HLM in *The Gist of Nietzsche,* ed. HLM (J. W. Luce, 1910), pp. 22–23; HLM to SL, 15 October 1945, NYPL; HLM to SM, [1937], quoted by Mayfield in "HLM's Advice to Young Girls" (unpublished ms.), p. 12, UA.

" 'the lives of' ": HLM, *Prejudices, V,* p. 100.

p. 198.   "Indeed, in the": Author's interview with Dr. Benjamin M. Baker; HLM to EB, 12 May [1921], NYPL; and HLM, *In Defense* (Goodman), p. 44.

"Mencken believed, as": HLM to MB, 13 August 1914, EPFL; HLM, "Rattling the Subconscious," *SS,* September 1918, pp. 138–40; HLM, "A&E," p. 634; HLM to the Rev. Joseph J. Ayd, 28 January 1939, EPFL; HLM, *MR,* p. 273; and HLM, "A Visit to a Short Story Factory," *SS,* December 1912, pp. 153–54.

" 'It is the' ": HLM, *In Defense* (Knopf), pp. 207–08.

p. 199.   "Marion always thought": Carl Bode, *Mencken* (Southern Illinois University Press, 1969), p. 154; and HLM, "A&E," p. 264.

"But curiously, as": HLM, "A&E," p. 610. See, e.g., Adriana Yalta, "Mere Man to the Rescue," *Fashion Art,* February 1919, HLM clippings scrapbook.

p. 200.   " 'The allurement that' ": HLM, "The Incomparable Buzz-Saw," *SS,* May 1919, p. 54.

"His fascination with": HLM to R. C. Brown, 15 February 1937, NYPL.

"In any case": HLM, "Baltimore and the Rest of the World," Baltimore

*Herald*, 9 February 1902; HLM, "The Two Englishes," *BES*, 10 October 1910; "England's English," *BES*, 14 October 1910; and *BES* columns of 19, 20, and 25 October 1910.

p. 201.  "Reviewers in the": HLM, "A&E," p. 102.

"'I am . . . neither' ": HLM, *AL* (1919), p. vii.

p. 202.  "Not only did": Frederic J. Haskins, "Here at Last Is a Professor of Americanese," Minneapolis *Tribune*, 24 August 1919.

"In his introduction": HLM, *AL* (1919), p. vii; and Stuart Sherman, *Americans*, p. 10.

"By the time": HLM, "AN, 1925" (EPFL); HLM to FHG, 17 November 1919, NYPL; HLM, "AN, 1941–"; and HLM to Ellery Sedgwick [1916], NYPL.

p. 203.  "The year 1919": HLM, *A&E*, p. 299; HLM to Ernest Boyd, 18 January [1919?] and 19 January 1919, NYPL; and HLM to TD, 4 and 11 February [1919], UP, *D–M Letters*, II, pp. 337–39.

"The 'slaughterhouse' was": HLM, *A&E*, p. 299; HLM to FHG, [July 1919], NYPL; and HLM to Ernest Boyd, 5 June [1919], NYPL.

p. 204.  "On Veblen and": HLM, *Prejudices*, I, pp. 78, 53, 54, 58.

"In his *Prejudices*": HLM, *Prejudices*, I, pp. 90, 99, 181–90.

p. 205.  "In fact, *Prejudices*": HLM to FHG, 6 September 1919, NYPL.

"Focusing on the": HLM to Ernest Boyd, 26 September, 6 December, and 20 May [1919], NYPL.

"For a time": HLM to TD, [January 1914], 1 February [1919], and 2 February [1920], UP, *D–M Letters*, II, pp. 335, 369; and HLM to Ernest Boyd, 18 January, 13 March, and 16 July [1919], NYPL.

"If 'active contact' ": HLM to TD, 1 February [1919], UP, *D–M Letters*, II, p. 335; and HLM to Ernest Boyd, 25 February [1919], NYPL.

p. 206.  "Thus Mencken approached": HLM, "A&E," p. 778; HLM to Mrs. H. B. Smith, 7 December 1919, EPFL; HLM to Ernest Boyd, [December 1919], NYPL; and HLM to FHG, 24 December 1919, NYPL.

"Wait until 'after' ": HLM to Stanton Leeds, 25 November 1917, NYPL; and HLM to FHG, 17 November 1919, in HLM, "A&E," Appendix XXV, p. 14.

## Chapter 9: "A Sort of Heathen Missionary"

p. 207.  "On January 1": HLM, *A&E*, p. 308; HLM to Ernest Boyd, 17 January [1920], NYPL; HLM, "A&E," pp. 123, 361–62; and HLM, "On Being an American," *BES*, 11 October 1920.

"In fact, Mencken": HLM, "Thirty-Five Years," pp. 172–73, 221; HLM, *Diary*, 24 October 1945, pp. 387–90; and HLM, "Diary," 5 September 1942, EPFL.

p. 208.  "Mencken did not": HLM, "Diary," 5 September 1942; HLM, *Diary*, 30 August 1937, p. 107; and HLM to Ernest Boyd, 17 June [1920], NYPL.

"The Democratic convention": HLM, *Heathen Days*, pp. 176–87; and HLM, "Thirty-Five Years," p. 282.

"All other American": HLM, "San Francisco: A Memory," *BES*, 21 July 1920.

p. 209.  " 'Yesterday's session was' ": HLM, "Mencken Describes Session," *BES*, 3 July 1920.

"As always, Mencken": HLM–George Sterling correspondence, especially 1918–21, NYPL; HLM to FHG, 11 July 1920, NYPL; HLM to ELM, 19 February 1935, NYPL; HLM to TD, 20 November 1920, UP, *D–M Letters*, II, pp. 408–09; HLM, "Thirty-Five Years," p. 273; and HLM to George Sterling (copy), [1923], Bode collection, EPFL.

p. 210.  "A strike by": HLM to Ernest Boyd, 9 October [1919], NYPL; HLM to FHG, 28 January and, 6 and 31 December 1920, NYPL.

"Even more serious": HLM to Carl Van Doren, 1 March [1921], NYPL; HLM to FHG, 7 December 1920, NYPL; James Gibbons Huneker to HLM, 28 September [1920], NYPL; HLM to GJN, 19 October [1924], NYPL; and HLM to TD, 1 October [1920], UP, *D–M Letters*, II, pp. 396–98.

"Earlier that year": HLM, quoted by Edgar Kemler, *The Irreverent Mr. Mencken*, pp. 130–31.

"Nor was his": HLM to Ernest Boyd, 1 and 19 July [1919], NYPL; HLM to GJN, 19 October [1924], NYPL; HLM, *A&E*, pp. 367–75.

p. 211.  "He turned a": HLM, "Variations on a Familiar Theme," *SS*, December 1921, p. 144; and HLM, "The Home of the Brave," *SS*, October 1920, p. 42. As concerns the Midwest, it was Kansas, not the South, that Mencken had first compared to the Sahara Desert ("In Defense of Kansas," 1910, *BES* scrapbook, 1910–1912, EPFL).

"The ancestral home": HLM, "On New England," *SS*, October 1920, pp. 39–41.

p. 212.  The fragments that": HLM, *A&E*, pp. 395–97; HLM Harold Stearns correspondence, 1920–22, NYPL; HLM to TD, 15 March [1921], UP, *D–M Letters*, II, p. 432; HLM to FHG, [December 1920], NYPL; HLM to Ernest Boyd, 12 May [1921], NYPL; HLM to Louise Pound, 11 May 1921, NYPL; and HLM–AAK correspondence, 1921, NYPL.

"Despite such obstacles": HLM to FHG, 13 March 1920 and [November 1920], NYPL.

p. 213.  "As usual, he": HLM to TD, 11 November 1924, UP, *D–M Letters*, II, p. 526.

" 'Nearly the whole' ": HLM, "The Sahara of the Bozart," *Prejudices, II*, pp. 136–37, 143, 142, 139–40, 141.

p. 214.  "American literature was": HLM, "The National Letters," *Prejudices, II*, pp. 15, 65, 101, 82.

p. 215.  "the American people": HLM, "On Being an American," *Prejudices, III*, pp. 10–11, 12, 23–24, 63, 64.

"The 'show,' he": HLM, "On Being an American," *BES*, 11 October 1920.

p. 216.  "He covered the": HLM, "Brief Battle Was Hopeless," *BES*, 2 July 1921.

" 'Rank by rank' ": HLM, "Star-Spangled Men," *The New Republic*, 29 September 1920, in Alistair Cooke, ed., *The Vintage Mencken* (Vintage Books, 1955), pp. 110–11.

"But most of ": HLM, "The Late Master-Mind," *SS*, January 1921, pp. 142–43; HLM, "Bayard vs. Lionheart," *BES*, 26 July 1920; HLM, "Gamalielese," *BES*, 7 March 1921.

p. 217.  "Presidents past as": HLM, *Damn!*, p. 13; HLM, "More Notes from a Diary," *SS*, May 1920, pp. 140–42; and in Cooke, *The Vintage Mencken*, pp. 78–79. HLM, "The Library," *AM*, January 1933, p. 126; and HLM, "What Is Going On in the World," *AM*, April 1933, p. 390.

p. 218.  "With the *Prejudices*": Joseph Wood Krutch, "Antichrist and the Five Apostles," *The Nation*, 21 December 1921, p. 733; Edmund Wilson, "H. L. Mencken," *The New Republic*, 1 June 1921, pp. 10–13; Wilson, "From Maupassant to Mencken," *Vanity Fair*, December 1922, p. 25; and FSF, "The Baltimore Anti-Christ," *The Bookman*, March 1921, p. 81.

"Writing in *The*": Walter Lippmann, "The New Machiavelli," *The New Republic*, 31 May 1922, pp. 12–14.

p. 219.  "At first Mencken": HLM, "A&E," pp. 945, 819, 833–34; and articles in *The*

*Des Moines Register-Leader*, 26 February 1922, and *The Double Dealer*, March 1922, both in HLM clippings scrapbook, EPFL.

"He noted the": "Intrepid Herald Staff Man Beards Mencken in His Den," Washington *Herald*, 28 August 1921; "The Omnivorous Mencken," *BES*, 18 July 1921; "Roasting the South," *Little Rock Daily News*, 10 August 1921; "Menace of Herr Mencken," *Little Rock Trade Record*, 3 August 1921; "To Ask Congress," *Arkansas Democrat*, 3 August 1921, all in HLM clippings scrapbook, EPFL; and HLM to FHG, 31 December 1920, NYPL.

"In the early": Information in this paragraph taken from "Mencken's Fame Growing Apace," *Cincinnati Times-Star*, 13 July 1921, HLM clippings scrapbook, EPFL; HLM to TD, 2 September [1920], UP, *D–M Letters*, II, p. 386; Aldous Huxley, quoted by HLM in "A&E," p. 776.

p. 220.   "It was in": HLM, "Thirty-Five Years," p. 335; HLM to JH, 17 July, 26 May, and 12 June [1922], NYPL.

"He had met": HLM, "Thirty-Five Years," pp. 318–19; and AAK to HLM, 14 March 1921, EPFL.

p. 221.   "Or, as he": HLM, "A&E," p. 984.

"He had felt": HLM, "A&E," Appendix VIII, p. 15; HLM, "A&E," Appendix VII, p. 7; HLM, "A&E," pp. 646, 777, 984; and HLM, *A&E*, pp. 107–09, 367–68.

" 'Come over here' ": Hugh Walpole to HLM, 27 April 1920 and 7 June 1922, NYPL; and HLM, "A&E," p. 984.

p. 222.   " 'He refuse[d] to' ": HLM, "A&E," pp. 984, 777.

"He let it": HLM, quoted in New York *American*, 20 August 1922, HLM clippings scrapbook, EPFL; HLM, "Thirty-Five Years," p. 336; and *English Review*, August 1922, HLM clippings scrapbook, EPFL.

p. 223.   "In contrast to": HLM, "A&E," p. 948; HLM to MB, 4 September 1922, EPFL; and HLM, "Thirty-Five Years," p. 339.

"When he arrived": HLM, "Thirty-Five Years," pp. 340–41; HLM to H. W. Seaman, 8 November 1937, NYPL; and HLM to Robert Brown, 21 October [1931?], NYPL.

"From Munich he": HLM, "Thirty-Five Years," pp. 344, 350; and HLM to Edgar Kemler, [1948], EPFL.

p. 224.   "He had arranged": HLM, "Thirty-Five Years," pp. 350–51.

"He was ready": HLM, "Thirty-Five Years," p. 352; and HLM to Paul Patterson, 9 September 1922, Sunpapers documents, EPFL.

"Mencken had begun": Oscar Levy to HLM, 7 July 1919, NYPL; HLM to FHG, 15 January 1920, NYPL; pamphlet included with letter from Paul Koenig to HLM, 23 March 1921, NYPL; and HLM to FHG, 4 November 1920 and 7 March 1921, NYPL.

p. 225.   "Thus his trip": HLM to Harry Rickel, 30 September [1922], NYPL; HLM to JH, 30 September [1922], NYPL; HLM to Paul Patterson, 20 September 1922, EPFL; and HLM, "Thirty-Five Years," p. 341.

"Earlier, after reading": HLM to FHG, 15 January 1920, NYPL; and HLM, "Thirty-Five Years," pp. 349, 354.

p. 226.   "He later listed": HLM, *A&E*, pp. 241–42; and Allen Tate to Donald Davidson, 8 December [1924], Davidson papers, VU.

"Other writers Mencken": HLM to Upton Sinclair, 2 May 1936 (and other letters, 1920s–1930s), NYPL; HLM to Fanny Butcher, 9 May [1912], NYPL; HLM to FHG, 4 November 1921, NYPL; HLM to ELM, 23 October 1942, NYPL; HLM, *Diary*, 15 August 1931, pp. 32–35.

p. 227.   "His relations with": HLM correspondence with Joseph Wood Krutch, Ludwig

Lewisohn, Walter Lippmann, and Edmund Wilson, early 1920s, NYPL; Louis Untermeyer to HLM, 17 December 1913, NYPL. In letters, HLM was often critical of Lippmann; see, e.g., HLM to Burton Rascoe, [October 1917?], in Carl Bode, ed., *The New Mencken Letters*, p. 77.

"Wilson, as a": HLM letters to Edmund Wilson, early 1920s, YU (copies, Bode collection, EPFL); Wilson letters to HLM, NYPL; Wilson, *The Devils and Canon Barham* (Farrar, Straus and Giroux), pp. 92–104. Mencken and Nathan did accept for *The Smart Set* parts of *The Undertaker's Garland*, by Wilson and John Peale Bishop.

"Mencken's first impression": HLM, *A&E*, pp. 256–66; and FSF, inscription in *This Side of Paradise*, Mencken Room, EPFL.

p. 228. "Mencken disapproved of": HLM to Edgar Kemler, 24 October 1946, EPFL; and HLM to James Branch Cabell, 21 March [1922] (copy), Bode collection, EPFL.

"By Philadelphia he": HLM, "A&E," p. 855; HLM, *A&E*, pp. 327–49; HLM to SL, 27 October [1920], YU, in Guy J. Forgue, ed., *Letters of H. L. Mencken*, p. 206, and HLM, "Consolation," *SS*, January 1921, pp. 138–40.

" 'In drink,' Mencken": HLM, *A&E*, p. 329; HLM, "A&E," Appendix XXX, p. 66; and SL to HLM, 4 December 1921, NYPL.

p. 229. "Lewis's next novel": SL to HLM, 21 June 1922, NYPL; and HLM, "A&E," Appendix XXX, p. 42.

"In other letters": HLM to TD, 22 December, 25 March, and 14 April [1921], UP, *D–M Letters*, II, pp. 456, 435–36, 442.

p. 230. "Dreiser wrote him": HLM, "A&E," p. 952.

"Mencken was equally": TD to HLM, 2 January [1921], NYPL, *D–M Letters*, II, p. 418.

"Mencken recognized that": HLM to TD, 9 January [1921], UP, *D–M Letters*, II, pp. 418–19; and HLM, "A&E," pp. 867–68.

p. 231. "He notified Dreiser": HLM to TD, 6 and 22 May, 1 June, and 28 October [1922], UP; and TD to HLM, 8 June 1922, NYPL; all in *D–M Letters*, II, pp. 471–75, 479; and HLM, *A&E*, pp. 389–94.

"He often visited": HLM–JH correspondence, 1920–23, especially HLM to JH, 12 April 1923, NYPL; HLM to AAK, 20 May [1923], NYPL; and HLM to EB, 28 [May] 1923, NYPL.

"But the 'most' ": JH to HLM, 24 October 1921, NYPL; and HLM, *A&E*, pp. 356–57.

"Cabell, the author": HLM, "The Sahara of the Bozart," *Prejudices, II*, p. 138.

p. 232. "Thus he was": HLM, *A&E*, pp. 356–58.

"Fitzgerald had written": FSF to HLM, 6 September 1920, NYPL.

"For Cabell, as": HLM, unpublished preface to collection of American short stories to be translated into German, 1923, EPFL.

p. 233. "It is remarkable": See, e.g., HLM to Max Brödel, 24 December 1921 and 27 December 1923, NYPL; HLM Harry Rickel correspondence, 1919–20, NYPL; and HLM, *A&E*, p. 327.

p. 234. "He prized Lily": Author's interview with Ruth Goodman Goetz, 1 August 1988; and Goetz, "The Faces of Enlightenment," *Menckeniana*, Winter 1988, p. 2.

"Much of the": HLM to PG, 1920–25, *passim*, "Letters to Philip Goodman" scrapbook, EPFL; Paul de Kruif to HLM, [1920], NYPL; Ernest Boyd to HLM, 9 January 1924 and 1922–1924, *passim*, NYPL; and HLM to A. H. McDannald, 2 April [1920], NYPL.

"In his social": AAK to Walt McCaslin, 20 August 1956, "About Mencken" file, EPFL; HLM to PG, 2 February [1929], EPFL; and Sara Mayfield, *The Constant Circle*, pp. 61, 161.

p. 235. "He 'genuinely fell' ": HLM to George Sterling, [1923] (copy), Bode collection, EPFL; HLM to JH, 7 August [1920], NYPL; and HLM, *"Heathen Days: Additions,"* p. 187.

"For a time": HLM–Fanny Butcher correspondence, 1920–21, NYPL; and Butcher, *Many Lives, One Life* (Harper and Row, 1972), pp. 403–05.

"Through Hergesheimer, Mencken": HLM–Caroline Baird correspondence, 1922–23, NYPL; HLM to JH, 2 September 1923, NYPL; HLM–Bernice Lesbia Kenyon correspondence, 1921–23, NYPL; Ernest Boyd to HLM, 6 October 1923, NYPL; HLM to JH, 15 April [1921], NYPL; HLM to Fanny Butcher, 11 April [1921], NYPL; and HLM to Louis Untermeyer, 26 July 1920, NYPL.

p. 236. "He was 'full' ": HLM to EB, 18, 20, and 23 February 1920, NYPL.

"By May Mencken": HLM to MB, 31 May 1920 and 19 July [1920?], EPFL; MB to EB, 29 March 1920, NYPL; and HLM to EB, 19 June 1920, NYPL.

p. 237. "Thus began another": HLM to MB, 24 March [1920?], EB correspondence, NYPL; MB, note entitled "Marriage," 2 August 1923, Bloom diary, EB correspondence, NYPL; and MB to EB, 16 December 1920, NYPL.

"He did not": MB to EB, 23 August 1921, NYPL; HLM to MB, [9?] May 1921, EPFL; HLM to EB, letters of 1921 and 1922, NYPL; and MB to EB, 13 May and 14 March 1921, NYPL.

"At times—when": MB to EB, letters of 1921–22, especially 9 December 1921, NYPL; HLM to Paul Patterson, 9 December 1921, EPFL; and HLM to MB, 9 January 1922, EPFL.

p. 238. "She still loved": MB to EB, 16 October, 8 November, 20 March, and 26 October 1921, NYPL.

" 'I fell in' ": MB to EB, [August 1923], NYPL; and HLM to MB, 4, 17, and 21 September 1922, EPFL.

" 'Good cooking is' ": HLM to MB, 21 September 1922, EPFL; and MB to EB, [August 1923], NYPL.

p. 239. "One reason for": HLM to EB, 11 May and 7 June 1921, NYPL; MB to TD, 6 May 1921, NYPL; MB to EB, 13 May 1921, NYPL; HLM to MB, 4 November 1922, EPFL; and MB to EB, 28 November 1922, NYPL.

" 'He has merit' ": HLM to EB, 3 February 1923, NYPL; MB to EB, [August 1923], NYPL; and MB to TD, 6 May 1921, EB correspondence, NYPL.

"She felt pressure": MB to EB, [Summer 1923], NYPL; MB to Betty Adler, 27 June 1971 and 3 July 1966, EPFL; and HLM to MB, [August 1923], EPFL.

p. 240. " 'Well, such is' ": HLM to EB, 10 August 1923, in MB–Betty Adler correspondence, EPFL.


## Chapter 10: ''The Nearest Thing to Voltaire''

p. 241. "In August 1923": Information in this paragraph taken from HLM to William Manchester, 16 June 1947, EPFL; AAK to M. K. Singleton, 28 July 1959, "About Mencken" file, EPFL; HLM and GJN, statement to *SS* subscribers, 10 October 1923, D pamphlet collection, EPFL; and Carl Dolmetsch, *The Smart Set*, pp. 86–87.

"Only three days": HLM to Max Brödel, [30 July 1923], NYPL; and HLM and GJN, statement to *SS* subscribers.

p. 242. "In fact, he": HLM to Willard H. Wright, 28 October 1909, in HLM, "A&E," p. 542; AAK to E. A. Townley [n.d.], Betty Adler papers, EPFL; and HLM to Max Brödel, 30 July 1923, NYPL.

"To Dreiser he": HLM to TD, 28 July and 10 August [1923], UP, *D–M Letters*, II, pp. 496–97, 499; HLM to Joseph Katz, 17 August [1923], EPFL; HLM to Carl Van Doren, 20 August [1923], NYPL; and HLM to James Branch Cabell, 18 August [1923], UVa, in Carl Bode, ed., *The New Mencken Letters*, p. 174.

p. 243. "According to Mencken's": HLM, notes for Goldberg biography, in HLM–Goldberg correspondence, NYPL; AAK, "H. L. Mencken" (ms.), UT.

"Not only would": [HLM and GJN] Editorial, *AM*, January 1924, pp. 27–28.

p. 244. "Mencken was swamped": HLM, "Thirty-Five Years," pp. 390, 407; HLM to GJN, 15 October 1924, NYPL; and Goldberg notes.

"Several days later": HLM to GJN, 19 and 15 October 1923, NYPL; and AAK, "The Mencken-Nathan Breakup," *BES*, 22–25 June 1981.

"He complained to": GJN to HLM, [1924], NYPL; AAK to M. K. Singleton, 18 February 1959, EPFL; and AAK, "The Mencken-Nathan Breakup."

p. 245. "In October 1924": Charles Angoff to HLM, 14 October 1924, NYPL; and HLM, "Thirty-Five Years," p. 407.

"He intended to": HLM to Edgar Kemler, [1948], EPFL.

p. 246. "It was clear": HLM, "A&E," p. 812.

"He continued to": Ezra Pound to HLM, 18 January 1927, NYPL; HLM, "A&E," pp. 814, 564; Pound to HLM, 3 February 1915, NYPL; HLM to Dora Kellner, 21 April 1933, NYPL; and HLM, "A&E," Appendix VI, p. 1.

"In the fall": Michael Reynolds, *Hemingway: The Paris Years* (Basil Blackwell, 1989), p. 236; AM, "Reminiscences," p. 43; HLM, "A&E," p. 355; and HLM to James Cain, 18 November 1932, NYPL.

p. 247. "In fact, despite": HLM, "A&E," p. 355; HLM to James Cain, 18 November 1932, NYPL; and HLM, "A&E," p. 160.

"In particular, he": HLM correspondence with W.E.B. Du Bois (NYPL), James Weldon Johnson (YU), Walter F. White (Library of Congress, NYPL), and George Schuyler (YU, NYPL). For valuable discussions of HLM's relations with black writers in the 1920s, see Charles Scruggs, *The Sage in Harlem: H. L. Mencken and the Black Writers of the 1920s* (Johns Hopkins University Press, 1984), and Fenwick Anderson, "Black Perspectives in Mencken's *Mercury*," *Menckeniana*, Summer 1979, pp. 2–6.

" 'I am . . . almost' ": HLM, "AN, 1925" (NYPL), p. 36; HLM, "*Happy Days: Additions*," p. 27; and HLM, school composition notebook, 1894, scrapbook F250, EPFL.

p. 248. "He was still": HLM, "Free Lance," *BES*, 28 June 1911; HLM and Rives La Monte, *Men Versus the Man* (Holt, 1910), p. 116; and HLM, "The Aframerican: New Style," *AM*, February 1926, p. 255.

"If in his": HLM to Ellery Sedgwick, 6 December 1906, NYPL; and HLM, "Negro Spokesman Arises," New York *Evening Mail*, 19 September 1917.

p. 249. "With Schuyler he": HLM–George Schuyler correspondence, 1920s, YU and NYPL; and Walter F. White to HLM, 17 and 26 October and 17 December 1923, NYPL.

"The two had": James Weldon Johnson, *Along This Way* (Viking, 1940), pp. 305–06; and HLM to AAK, 27 November [1924], EPFL.

"His racial concerns": HLM, "Thirty-Five Years," p. 467; and HLM to Hamilton Owens, 25 April 1926, EPFL.

p. 250. "The man who": HLM to Gretchen Hood, [23 March 1928], EU, in Peter W. Dowell, ed., *Ich Küss die Hand: The Letters of H. L. Mencken to Gretchen Hood* (University of Alabama Press, 1986), p. 100.

"As he was": Richard Wright, *Black Boy* (Harper & Row, 1945), pp. 270–72.

"Wright dated his": Wright, quoted by Edward Aswell to HLM, 30 August 1939, NYPL.

p. 251. "If Mencken had": Walter Lippmann, "H. L. Mencken," *Saturday Review*, 11 December 1926, p. 413.

"His celebrity went": "Swimmerton and H. L. Mencken," *BS*, 29 September 1926; articles in *Vanity Fair* (January 1925), *Wooden Horse* (Winter 1925), and *Collegian* (March 1926), all in HLM clippings scrapbooks, EPFL; Klaus Mann, *The Turning Point* (L. B. Fischer, 1942), p. 137; and Sherwood Anderson to HLM, 29 December 1925, NYPL.

"Mencken was indeed": Burton Rascoe to HLM, 8 September 1926, NYPL; "The Menace of Menckenism," *Christian Index*, 15 April 1926; Walter Lippmann, "H. L. Mencken," *Saturday Review*, 11 December 1926, p. 414; "What's the Matter with Mencken?" *BS*, 7 August 1922; and "Roasting the South," *Little Rock Daily News*, 10 August 1921.

p. 252. "Mencken-watching had become": Ernest Boyd, *H. L. Mencken* (Robert McBride, 1925); Goldberg, *The Man Mencken*; Boyd to HLM, 27 and 29 May 1924, NYPL; and HLM to Boyd, 3 August [1925], NYPL.

"In 1924 Goldberg": HLM, "A&E," pp. 1016–20; HLM to Isaac Goldberg, [25 February 1925] and 17 March [1925], NYPL; and Goldberg to HLM, 27 January and 14 February 1924 and 4 April 1925, NYPL.

"Their correspondence in": Isaac Goldberg to HLM, 4 and 6 April, 12 May, 13 June, and other letters of 1925, NYPL; and Goldberg to Max Schuster, 13 June 1925, HLM correspondence, NYPL.

p. 253. "Goldberg's book proved": Goldberg, *The Man Mencken*, pp. 265–66; and Philip Strong, review in New York *World*, 29 November 1925, in HLM clippings scrapbook, EPFL.

"It would have": Goldberg to HLM, 1 July 1925, NYPL; and HLM, "Thirty-Five Years," pp. 406–07.

p. 254. "In several events": HLM, "Thirty-Five Years," pp. 390–403; HLM, "*Heathen Days:* Additions," p. 208; and HLM to Max Brödel, 20 June 1924, NYPL.

" 'There is something' ": HLM, "Post-Mortem," *BES*, 14 July 1924.

p. 255. " 'The Klansmen plodded' ": HLM, "Parade Unlike Anything Since Days of Roosevelt," *BES*, 9 August 1925.

" 'Of a thousand' ": HLM, "The Golden Age of Pedagogy," *BES*, 6 June 1927.

p. 256. " 'In a way' ": John Thomas Scopes in Scopes and James Presley, *Center of the Storm* (Holt, Rinehart, 1967), p. 93.

"Mencken had been": HLM, "*Heathen Days:* Additions," p. 219; HLM, "Thirty-Five Years," pp. 420–24; and Scopes and Presley, *Center of the Storm*, p. 66.

"The events in": Paul Patterson to HLM, 15 January 1925, EPFL; HLM, *MR*, p. 257; and HLM to George Schuyler, 5 January 1937, YU.

p. 257. " 'On to Dayton' ": HLM to Howard W. Odum, [June 1925], Odum papers, UNC; and HLM to FHG, 6 July 1925, NYPL.

"After a couple": HLM to Hamilton Owens, 14 December 1925, EPFL.

"At first, in": HLM, "Mencken Finds Daytonians . . . ," *BES*, 9 July 1925; HLM, "Impossibility of Obtaining Fair Jury . . . ," *BES*, 10 July 1925; and HLM, "Yearning Mountaineers' Souls . . . ," *BES*, 13 July 1925. Many of Mencken's articles on the Scopes trial, as well as some of the text of his other newspaper pieces, are collected in Marion Elizabeth Rodgers, ed., *The Impossible H. L. Mencken* (Doubleday, 1991).

p. 258. "He delighted in": HLM, "Mencken Likens Trial to Religious Orgy," 11 July 1925; and HLM, "Yearning Mountaineers' Souls . . . ," *BES*, 13 July 1925.

p. 259. "The entire scene": HLM, "The Tennessee Circus," *BES*, 15 June 1925; and HLM to SH, 8 July 1925, in *M&S*, p. 217.

"The trial itself": HLM, "Darrow's Eloquent Appeal," *BES*, 14 July 1925; HLM, "*Heathen Days:* Additions," pp. 230, 228; HLM to Harley K. Croessmann, 24 July 1925, NYPL; and HLM, "Thirty-Five Years," pp. 428–44.

p. 260. "Despite widespread stories": HLM, "Thirty-Five Years," p. 428; HLM, "*Heathen Days:* Additions," p. 218; and HLM to SH, 8 July 1925, *M&S*, p. 217. The Scopes verdict was later overturned, and the *Sun* was refunded its $100.

"It was evident": HLM, "Bryan," *BES*, 27 July 1925.

"Mencken should hardly": HLM to FHG, 27 July 1925, NYPL; HLM to JH, 27 July [1925], NYPL; and HLM to Louis E. Shecter, 30 July [1925], NYPL.

p. 261. "He had some": HLM to BK, 9 June 1923, NYPL; and HLM, "Thirty-Five Years," p. 468.

p. 262. "Anna Mencken's condition": HLM, "Thirty-Five Years," pp. 468–69; HLM to Harry Rickel, 31 December [1925], NYPL; Ernest Boyd to HLM, 12 October 1925, NYPL; HLM to AAK, 10 and 12 December 1925, NYPL; and HLM to BK, 12 December 1925, NYPL.

"His mother had": HLM to PG, 13 December 1925, EPFL; and HLM, "Thirty-Five Years," p. 469.

"Mencken immediately notified": HLM to MB, 14 December 1925, EPFL; HLM to Ernest Boyd, [13 December 1925], NYPL; HLM to FHG, 14 December 1925, NYPL; and HLM, *Diary*, 30 May 1945, p. 368.

"Anna Mencken's will": notice in *BS*, 18 December 1925, in HLM clippings scrapbook; HLM to PG, 17 December 1925, NYPL; HLM to DH, 10 January [1926], NYPL.

p. 263. "But 1524 Hollins": HLM to Harry Rickel, 31 December [1925], NYPL; HLM to Harley K. Croessmann, 2 January 1926, NYPL; HLM to MB, 15 December 1925; HLM, "Thirty-Five Years," p. 469; and HLM to TD, 5 February [1926], UP, *D–M Letters*, II, p. 552.

## Chapter 11: A Tory in a Democratic World

p. 264. "Hard work, as": HLM, "Thirty-Five Years," p. 469; HLM to JH, 10 June and 27 July [1926], NYPL.

"*Notes on Democracy*": HLM, *Heathen Days*, p. 53; HLM, "Thirty-Five Years," pp. 246–47; HLM, "The Last Round," *BES*, 4 October 1920; and HLM to PG, 31 July 1923, EPFL.

p. 265. "He had begun": HLM, *A&E*, pp. 43, 354, 376; HLM, inscription to AAK on typescript of *Notes on Democracy*, EP; HLM, *Notes on Democracy*, pp. 24–25, 64, 206–07, 208, 211.

"Mencken knew he": HLM to Norman Foerster, 28 October 1933, NYPL; HLM, "Thirty-Five Years," p. 471; HLM, introduction to ms. A161, EPFL; Walter Lippmann, "H. L. Mencken," *Saturday Review*, 11 December 1926, p. 413; Edmund Wilson, "Mencken's Democratic Man," *The New*

*Republic*, 15 December 1926, pp. 93, 95–96; and HLM, "The Hatrack Case," "Hatrack" scrapbook, p. 151, EPFL.

p. 266.　"a sixth *Prejudices*": HLM to FHG, 7 April 1926, NYPL; and HLM to Harley K. Croessmann, 25 March [1920s], NYPL.

" 'If you find' ": HLM, *Prejudices, V*, p. 304.

"If hard work": HLM, preface to "Hatrack" scrapbook, EPFL.

p. 267.　"Thus Chase was": HLM, "Hatrack" scrapbook, pp. 1–15. For an excellent treatment of the "Hatrack" controversy, see also Carl Bode, *The Editor, The Bluenose and The Prostitute* (Roberts, Rinehart, Inc., 1988).

" 'If my mother' ": HLM, "Thirty-Five Years," p. 471; and HLM to AAK, [April 1926?], NYPL.

"The encounter with": Information in this and the following paragraphs taken from HLM, "Hatrack" scrapbook, especially pp. 1–36, 102; HLM, "Diary," 25 June 1937; HLM to FHG, 11 April 1926, NYPL; HLM to Ernest Boyd, 24 April 1926, NYPL; HLM to JH, 13 May [1926], NYPL; and Herbert Asbury to HLM, 1926, *passim*, NYPL.

p. 269.　"He had been": HLM to Ernest Boyd, 24 April 1926, NYPL; HLM to JH, 13 May [1926], NYPL; HLM to George Sterling, 10 August 1926, NYPL; HLM, "The Sahara of the Bozart," *Prejudices, II*, p. 136; and HLM to Max Brödel, 8 September 1926, NYPL.

"He numbered among": HLM, "The South Rebels Again," *Chicago Tribune*, 7 December 1924; Emily Clark to HLM, 29 November 1925, NYPL; and HLM to F. A. Bridges, 2 December 1933, NYPL.

p. 270.　"After a weekend": HLM to JH, HLM typescript collection, PU; HLM, "Thirty-Five Years," pp. 475–81; and HLM to BK, 23 October 1926, NYPL.

" 'These ghastly wilds' ": HLM to MB, 25 October 1926, EPFL.

"Although still highly": HLM to Beatrice Wilson, 11 June [1925], NYPL; and HLM to FHG, 5 August 1926, NYPL.

p. 271.　"Through Pringle that": HLM to Ernest Boyd, 26 July [1926], NYPL; AM, "Reminiscences," p. 60; and HLM, "Appendix for Moronia," *Prejudices, VI*, pp. 305–11.

"She employed the": HLM, "Sister Aimee," *BES*, 13 December 1926.

p. 272.　"In nearly all": HLM to PG, [November 1926], EPFL; HLM to Raymond Pearl, [November 1926], American Philosophical Society, in Carl Bode, ed., *The New Mencken Letters*, p. 205; HLM, interview with New York *World*, 27 February 1927, HLM clippings scrapbook, EPFL; HLM, *Diary*, 3 November 1941, p. 170; and HLM to Harry Elmer Barnes, 17 March 1941, NYPL.

"In early August": HLM to George Sterling, 10 August 1926, NYPL; and Sterling to HLM, 28 August, 1 and 15 September, 27 October, and 10 November 1926, NYPL.

"Mencken was disturbed": HLM to SH, 16 November 1926, *M&S*, p. 271; HLM to Henry Dumont, 3 and 20 February 1935, NYPL; Thomas Lennon to HLM, 11 September 1951, NYPL; Charles Norris to Julian Boyd, 5 August 1942, HLM collection, NYPL; and news report in San Francisco *Examiner*, 21 November 1926, HLM clippings scrapbook, EPFL.

p. 273.　"Mencken could hardly": HLM to Henry Dumont, 20 February 1935, NYPL; HLM to MB, 13 January 1927, EPFL; and Dalton Gross, "H. L. Mencken and George Sterling," *Menckeniana*, Summer 1976, p. 6.

"Mencken was 'badly' ": SM, *The Constant Circle*, p. 109; and HLM to JH, 27 November 1926, NYPL.

"That opinion was": HLM, "Thirty-Five Years," pp. 515–34; and HLM to Hamilton Owens, [June 1928], EPFL.

"Mencken did not": HLM, "Thirty-Five Years," pp. 538, 533.

p. 274. "Although the conventions": HLM, note in HLM–Al Smith correspondence, NYPL; HLM, "Thirty-Five Years," p. 549; HLM, "Al and the Pastors" (6 August), "Onward Christian Soldiers" (24 August), "Civil War in the Confederacy" (28 July), and "Analysis Fails Mencken" (17 October) 1928, all *BES*.

p. 275. "Marion Bloom, now": MB to EB, [1927], NYPL; articles in *Greensboro News*, 10 November 1929; *The North American Review*, January 1928, p. 25; *The Bookman*, June 1927; *San Francisco News*, 6 March 1928, all HLM clippings scrapbook, EPFL; and John Aswell, review of *Notes on Democracy*, *The Richmond News-Leader*, 22 November 1926.

"He had become": "Was a Prominent Writer," Harvard *Crimson*, 2 February 1928.

p. 276. "The youngest of": Edmund Wilson, "The All-Star Literary Vaudeville" (*American Criticism*, 1926), reprinted in Wilson, *The Shores of Light* (Farrar, Straus, 1952), p. 236; and Rebecca West, "Mencken Feminine," *BS*, 8 December 1926.

"In the same": St. John Ervine, "America and the Nobel Prize," *The Philadelphia Enquirer-Sun*, 16 December 1928.

"Nor was it": HLM, *Diary*, 6 November 1930, p. 5.

" 'I'd rather have' ": FSF to HLM, 4 May 1925, [Autumn 1925], [March 1926], and 20 March 1927, NYPL.

p. 277. "He took these": HLM, "Thirty-Five Years," pp. 487–88, 406, 502; HLM to BK, 17 April 1927, illness file, EPFL; and author's interview with Elise Cheslock, 22 July 1988.

"But most draining": HLM to AM, 28 January 1920, illness file, EPFL; HLM to Ernest Boyd, 11 May 1920, EPFL; HLM to Ernest Boyd, 21 February [1920], NYPL; HLM to FHG, 18 March 1921, NYPL; and HLM notes of 12 May and 13 August 1921, illness file, EPFL.

p. 278. "On a third": HLM to Ernest Boyd, 4 and 15 June 1927, NYPL; HLM to SH, 15 June, 3 July, and 6 October 1927, illness file, EPFL; HLM to MB, 18 June and 29 July 1927, EPFL; HLM to BK, 2 June 1927, illness file, EPFL; HLM to JH, 25 November [1927], NYPL; HLM, note of 12 May 1921, illness file, EPFL; HLM to FHG, 11 February 1921, NYPL; and HLM, *A&E*, p. 356.

"Charlie's home in": HLM to Ernest Boyd, 20 December [1926], NYPL; HLM to PG, 22 December 1926, EPFL; HLM to FHG, 13 August 1926 and 30 July [1929?], NYPL; HLM to Max Brödel, 24 August 1927 and 30 July 1923, NYPL; HLM, note of 28 July 1923, illness file, EPFL.

"His preference for": HLM, "*HD*: Additions," p. 247.

p. 279. "He knew 'how' ": HLM, "*HD*: Additions," p. 247; and HLM, "Thirty-Five Years," p. 470.

" 'Of the men' ": HLM, *Prejudices, V*, p. 242; and HLM, *Diary*, 9 June 1940, p. 147.

"Since casting out": AAK, "The Mencken-Nathan Breakup," I, II, III, IV, *BES*, 23, 24, 25, and 26 June 1923; HLM to Arthur Samuels, 13 November 1934, NYPL; and HLM, "Thirty-Five Years," p. 390.

p. 280. "First, Dreiser, who": TD to HLM, [November 1925] and 28 November and 3 December 1925, NYPL; and HLM to TD, 14, 21, and 28 November 1925,

UP, *D–M Letters*, II, pp. 544–49; and HLM, *Diary*, 18 April 1931, pp. 21–22.

p. 280. "That matter had": HLM, *Diary*, 18 April 1931, pp. 21–22.

" 'This episode caused' ": HLM, *Diary*, 18 April 1931, p. 22

"He may indeed": Helen Richardson to HLM, 1 February 1946, NYPL; HLM to Richardson, 30 January [1946], UP; Richardson, *My Life With Dreiser* (World Publishing Co., 1951), pp. 114–18; TD to HLM, 2 February [1926] and 14 January 1926, NYPL; HLM to TD, 5 February [1926], UP, *D–M Letters*, II, pp. 550–54.

p. 281. "But in that": HLM to TD, 5 February and 28 January [1926], UP, *D–M Letters*, II, pp. 551–53; and HLM, "Dreiser in 840 Pages," *AM*, March 1926, pp. 379–81.

" 'Who reads you?' ": TD to HLM, 8 February 1926, NYPL, *D–M Letters*, II, p. 554.

## Chapter 12: A Loneliness at the Core

p. 282. "Despite the southern": HLM, "Thirty-Five Years," p. 488; HLM to Irita Van Doren, 10 September 1926; and HLM to GJN, [Autumn 1926?], in Edgar Kemler, *The Irreverent Mr. Mencken*, pp. 219, 231–32.

"In his twenties": HLM to TD, 22 December 1939, UP, *D–M Letters*, II, p. 656; HLM to Jim Tully, 4 May [1928], NYPL; and HLM, "Off the Grand Banks," *BES*, 7 September 1925.

p. 283. "The next year": HLM, "On Suicide," *Prejudices, VI*, pp. 86, 89–90, 91.

" 'I have had' ": HLM to Clarissa Flugel, 1 August 1935, EPFL; HLM to TD, quoted by Thomas Riggio, *D–M Letters*, II, p. 324; HLM, *Heathen Days*, p. vii; and Philip Wagner, "Mencken Remembered," *American Scholar*, Spring 1963, pp. 264–65.

" 'The only modern' ": HLM, typescript of interview with Roger Butterfield for *Life*, scrapbook 121, EPFL; and HLM, "A Boon to Bores," *BES*, 9 January 1922.

p. 284. " 'The Lindbergh business' ": HLM to MB, 18 June 1927, EPFL.

" 'The writing profession' ": HLM, quoted by Harry Lang in ms. "H. L. Mencken" for the *Jewish Daily Forward*, 29 January 1928, HLM scrapbook "Miscellaneous Articles and Lampoons on HLM," EPFL.

" 'What a life!' ": HLM to GH, 20 January [1929], EU; HLM to DH, 13 June 1940, NYPL; and HLM, *MR*, p. 19.

p. 285. " 'I probably belong' ": HLM to Isaac Goldberg, quoted in Goldberg, *The Man Mencken*, p. 256.

" 'It's a mania' ": Edmund Wilson, *The Twenties*, ed. Leon Edel (Farrar, Straus and Giroux, 1975), p. 67; and HLM, "Diary," 10 October 1943.

"He desired order": Vincent Fitzpatrick, "Wink Your Eye at Some Homely Girl," *Menckeniana*, Winter 1977, p. 6; HLM, quoted by MB to EB [mid-1920s], NYPL; and Clare Leighton, "Cynical Fantasy," *Menckeniana*, Fall 1970, p. 2.

"The folder groans": HLM, 1921, 1923, 1924, 1926, 1927, 1928, and 1929, illness file, EPFL, including HLM notes and copies of letters to PG, SH, JH, TD, FHG, Ernest Boyd, Hamilton Owens, Max Brödel, Harry Rickel, Ellery Sedgwick, Stanton Leeds, and Raymond Pearl; and HLM, "Thirty-Five Years," pp. 554–55.

p. 286. "It was nearly": HLM, illness file and hay fever diary, 1920s *passim.*, EPFL.

"It would not": HLM to SH, 6 October 1927, illness file, EPFL; HLM to Ernest
Boyd, 31 March 1926, NYPL; HLM to EB, 7 September 1928, NYPL; and
HLM to Boyd, 28 May [1924], NYPL.

p. 287.  "Indeed, he said": HLM, preface to "Hatrack" scrapbook, p. 130, EPFL.
"There is, in": L. Pratt, "Astrological Reading of Mencken," HLM scrapbook
"Miscellaneous Articles and Lampoons on HLM," EPFL; also, reading by
Myra Kingsley, 18 November 1945, pamphlet collection 1942–1947, EPFL.
" 'One of my' ": HLM, preface, "Hatrack" scrapbook, p. 130, EPFL; HLM to
Charles Shaw, 2 December [1927], NYPL; and HLM, quoted by Harry Lang
in ms. "H. L. Mencken."

p. 288.  "His response to": HLM, notes for *MR*, EPFL; HLM, preface to "Hatrack"
scrapbook; Isaac Goldberg, *The Man Mencken*, p. 294; Carl Van Doren,
"Calls Mencken All-American Institution," *BES*, 25 February 1923; and
HLM to H. M. Parshley, 14 February 1946, NYPL.
"In an entry": HLM, *A&E*, pp. 358–59.

p. 289.  "He was even": HLM correspondence with Ernest Booth, especially 1927,
NYPL; with Robert Blake, 1928 and 1929, NYPL; and with Texas governor
Dan Moody, January 1929, NYPL.

p. 290.  "At the same": HLM to Charles Shaw, 2 December [1927], NYPL.
"The first was": HLM, "Thirty-Five Years," p. 503; and HLM to Carroll Frey,
[1924?], NYPL.

p. 291.  "As it turned": HLM, "Thirty-Five Years," p. 503; and HLM, "A&E," p. 527.
" 'I have spent' ": HLM to Hamilton Owens, 12 September [1928], 24 October
1935, and 10 March 1937, EPFL; HLM to Edgar Kemler, 26 January 1948,
EPFL.

p. 292.  " 'I do hope' ": Howard A. Kelly to HLM, 14 March and 22 February 1916,
EPFL; see also D. G. Hart, "Mencken and Fundamentalism," *Menck-
eniana*, Fall 1988, pp. 2–3.
"In a series": HLM to MB, 9 May 1921 and 11 December [1920?], EPFL.
"Mencken's disapproval of": HLM, "On Suicide," *Prejudices, VI*, p. 89; HLM,
"Clinical Notes," *AM*, May 1924, p. 60; HLM to Harley Croessmann, 24
May 1933, NYPL; and HLM, miscellaneous notes, envelope A100.8, EPFL.

p. 293.  " 'I am trying' ": HLM to MB, 13 and 29 January and 27 February 1927, EPFL.
"Mencken later wrote": HLM, "AN, 1941–," EPFL; HLM to FHG, 9 April
1929, NYPL; HLM to MB, 2 February 1929, EPFL; HLM to Ernest Boyd,
5 October 1929, NYPL; HLM to PG, October and November 1929, EPFL;
and HLM, introductory note to ms. of *T on Gods* (scrapbook A176), EPFL.
"His most ambitious": HLM, *T on Gods*, pp. vi–vii.

p. 294.  "And even here": HLM, *T on Gods*, p. 345.
"He feared his": HLM to Ernest Boyd, 5 October 1929, NYPL.


## Chapter 13: Taking a Wife

p. 295.  " 'The marriage of' ": HLM, *In Defense* (Knopf), p. 100.
" 'As long as' ": Herman George Scheffauer to HLM, 5 May 1924, NYPL; and
Kyra Markham to HLM, 7 July 1945, NYPL.
"For all his": author's interviews with Olga Owens and W. C. Abhau; HLM,
*A Little Book in C Major*, p. 63; HLM, "On the Human Kind" (note of
August 1921), "Répétition Générale" scrapbook, EPFL; and "What's the
Matter with Mencken?," *BES*, 7 August 1922.

p. 296.  " 'I have yet' ": HLM ms. of "Connubial Bliss," April 1923, "Répétition
Générale" scrapbook, EPFL.

"As he had": HLM to PG, 3 December 1922 and 9 May [1923], EPFL.

p. 297.  "He did not": HLM, "A&E," p. 810; SH to HLM, 20 and 26 May 1923, GC, *M&S*, p. 77.

" 'Montgomery must be' ": HLM to SH, 5 June, 10 and 26 July, and 17 August 1923, GC, *M&S*, pp. 80–88.

"As they wrote": HLM to SH, 24 August, 17, 18, and 24 September and 8 October 1923; and SH to HLM, 9 October 1923; all in GC, *A&E*, pp. 90, 94–99.

p. 298.  "Johannes Anton Haardt": HLM, preface to Sara Haardt, *Southern Album* (Doubleday, Doran, 1956), p. xxi.

"She too had": For information about Sara Haardt's early life I draw largely on SH scrapbook, EPFL; Marion Elizabeth Rodgers's introduction to *M&S*; Sara Mayfield's *The Constant Circle*; and Ann Henley's "Sara Haardt and the Sweet Flowering South," forthcoming in *Alabama Heritage*. Although Mayfield is not always correct in her facts and interpretations, she was well acquainted with both Mencken and, especially, Sara.

"she was still": SM, "HLM on 'How to Catch a Husband' " (unpublished ms.), pp. 7–8, Mayfield papers, UA.

p. 299.  "It is significant": HLM to SH, 20 January 1924, GC, *M&S*, pp. 112–13; and HLM, telegram to SH, 23 January 1924, GC.

"He was 'mashed' ": HLM to SH, 23 February 1924, GC, *M&S*, p. 118.

" 'What is the' ": HLM to SH, 17 March 1924, *M&S*, p. 124; and Marjorie Nicolson to SM, 1 August 1971, UA.

p. 300.  "His care seemed": "HLM on 'How to Catch a Husband,' " pp. 7–8, UA; SH to SM, 5 May 1924, UA; and author's interview with Olga Owens.

"When Sara left": HLM to SH, 6 January and 1 April 1923, GC, *M&S*, pp. 185, 202–203; HLM to SH, 5 and 26 October and 13 December 1925, GC, *M&S*, pp. 228–30; author's interview with Ruth Goodman Goetz, 1 August 1988; Goetz, "The Faces of Enlightenment," *Menckeniana*, Winter 1988, p. 5; and James Cain to SM, 19 August 1968, UA.

p. 301.  "She and Mencken": HLM to SH, 27 January, 22 October, and 11 November 1926, GC, *M&S*, pp. 241, 265–66, 270.

"He tried to": HLM to SH, 20 December 1926 and 1 April 1927, GC, *M&S*, pp. 272–73, 280; HLM to SH, 10 February and 7 March [1927], GC; and Marion Elizabeth Rodgers, *M&S*, p. 280n.

"In the summer": JH to HLM, 20 July and 9 August 1927, NYPL: HLM to JH, 29 July [1927], NYPL; HLM to SH, 22 and 27 July 1927, GC; SH to SM, 5 August [1927], UA; and HLM to Dorothy Hergesheimer, 27 August [1927], NYPL.

p. 302.  "As she prepared": HLM to Jim Tully, 26 and 30 September 1927, NYPL; and HLM to SH, 29 September 1927, GC, *M&S*, p. 287.

"She viewed warily": HLM to James Branch Cabell, 29 January [1927] (copy), Mayfield papers, UA.

p. 303.  "At the time": HLM to Beatrice Wilson, 14 and 26 November 1923, and 1924 and 1925 correspondence with Wilson, *passim*, EPFL; and Carl Bode, "Notes on an Interview" with Mrs. C. S. MacDonald, 26 July 1964, Bode collection, EPFL.

"He had often": Ernest Boyd to HLM, 2 December 1925, 20 January and 26 July [1926], and 23 August [1927], NYPL; HLM to Boyd, 25 and 29 March [1927], NYPL; HLM to JH, 11 January and 12 October [1927], NYPL; JH to HLM, 12 May 1926, NYPL; HLM to PG, 3 June [1927], NYPL; and Ralph Barton to HLM, 12 January 1926, NYPL.

"Late in 1926": HLM to GH, 6 December 1926, 23 February [1927], 2 March [1927], [10 March 1927], and [14 March 1927]; GH to HLM, 11 March 1927, EU, *Ich Küss die Hand*, pp. 33–40; and HLM to GJN, 2 March [1927] (copy), Bode collection, EPFL.

"From the beginning": GH, notes in HLM letters (especially 14 March 1927), EU; GH, quoted in Donald P. Baker, "Oh, So Sincerely, H. L. Mencken," *The Washington Post*, 8 July 1973; and Peter W. Dowell, introduction, *Ich Küss die Hand*, pp. 1–27.

p. 304. "By mid-April": HLM to GH, 20 April [1927], EU, *Ich Küss die Hand*, p. 45; and GH, note on HLM letter of 20 April 1927, EU.

"That summer Mencken": HLM to GH, summer 1927, *passim*, especially 8 July, 13 August, and 18 September, EU, *Ich Küss die Hand*, pp. 49–63; GH note of 18 September [1927], EU; and articles in *The Washington Post* and New York *Mirror* (17 September 1927), HLM clippings scrapbook, EPFL.

"While Sara was": HLM to GH, 1, 8, 10, 23, 26, and 30 December [1927] and 2 and 4 January [1928], EU, *Ich Küss die Hand*, pp. 80–86; and Dowell, *Ich Küss die Hand*, p. 63n.

p. 305. " 'Was ever a' ": GH, note on HLM letter of 24 September [1927], EU, *Ich Küss die Hand*, p. 62; and GH, quoted in Donald P. Baker, "Oh, So Sincerely, H. L. Mencken."

"She had stayed": Anita Loos, *A Girl Like I* (Viking, 1966), p. 146.

p. 306. "When Loos had": Loos, *A Girl Like I*, pp. 163, 217, 248.

"He enjoyed her": HLM, *A&E*, p. 271; and Loos, *A Girl Like I*, pp. 218, 265.

"Sara Haardt had": HLM–Lillian Gish correspondence, 1920s *passim*, NYPL; and HLM, "A&E," p. 705.

p. 307. "The only one": AP to HLM, 18 December [1926] and 19 June and 27 December 1927, YU; and AP, quoted by Larry Cantrell, interview with AP, *Rocky Mountain News*, 5 October 1975, HLM clippings scrapbook.

"Mencken had been": "Miss Hollywood: Miss Pringle Stands Alone in Filmland," *Toledo Times* [n.d.], AP papers, YU; and Anita Loos, *A Girl Like I*, p. 120.

"From the moment": HLM to AP (telegram), 6 July 1926, YU; and AP to HLM, [August 1926] and [September 1926], YU.

p. 308. "Mencken's California trip": AP to HLM, [October 1926] and [November 1926], YU; and HLM to AP (telegram), 21 November and 1 December 1926, YU. Pringle's [November] letter has the date October 6 written on it—long after the fact—but because the letter refers to AP's seeing HLM in California, it could not have been written in October.

"Thus was established": AP to HLM, 22 November [1926] and December 1926–January 1927 *passim*; and HLM to AP (telegram), 26 November 1926, YU.

"There is no": AP to HLM, 5 December [1926], 9 December [1926], [December 1926?], 8 January 1927, February–March 1927, *passim*, [May 1927], 7 June 1927, and [October 1927], YU; HLM to AP (telegram), 24 December 1926, YU; and untitled article, Albany *Times-Union*, 31 December 1926, AP papers, YU.

p. 309. "He and Aileen": AP to HLM, [November 1927], YU; and HLM to SH, 12, 13, and 18 November 1927, GC, *M&S*, pp. 332–35, 338.

"Mencken's stay at": HLM to JH, 25 November and 6 December [1927], NYPL; HLM to DH, 23 November 1927, NYPL; SM, *The Constant Circle*, pp. 123–24, 96; articles in *Photoplay* (October 1927), *Albany Times-Union*

(31 December 1926), and *Philadelphia News* (31 December 1926), HLM clippings scrapbook; and HLM to GH, 17 October [1927], EU, *Ich Küss die Hand*, p. 70.

p. 310.  "In fact, seeing": HLM to AP (telegram), 23, 25, and 26 November 1927, YU; and AP to HLM, [November 1927] and [December 1927], YU.

"But that—as": AP to HLM, 22 December 1927 and 10 January 1928, YU.

"Despite his obvious": AP to HLM, [December 1927], 22 December 1927, [December 1927], 30 April and 29 January 1928, and [October 1927], YU.

p. 311.  "It was hardly": MB to Betty Adler, 15 December 1968, 20 June 1971, and 2 June 1966, EPFL; and MB to EB, 1 August 1926 and 18 June 1927, NYPL.

"but Mencken had": HLM to MB, 19 February 1926, EPFL; and HLM to EB, 23 February [1926], NYPL.

p. 312.  "After Marion sailed": MB to EB, 20 June, 13 July, and 1 August 1926, NYPL; and HLM to EB, 1926, *passim*, NYPL.

"He had been": HLM to MB, 26 June, 28 August, 20 September, and 25 October 1926, EPFL; and MB note on 25 October envelope, EPFL.

"When he had": HLM to MB, 19 December 1926, 29 January, and 18 and 27 February 1927, EPFL; MB to EB, 26 December 1926, 21 January 1927, and 6 November 1926, NYPL.

p. 313.  "His work, including": HLM to MB, 13 and 29 January, 15 and 27 February, and 20 April 1927, EPFL; MB to EB, 4 July and 13 March 1927, NYPL.

"On the one": MB to EB, 20 April, 1 and 7 May, and 8 June 1927, NYPL.

"Marion complained of": MB, diary [1927?], EPFL; and MB to EB, 15 August 1927 and [n.d.—1927], NYPL, and 26 July 1927, EPFL.

p. 314.  " 'I'd die before' ": MB to EB, 12 November and 26 December 1927 and 24 March 1928, NYPL.

"Earlier she had": James Cain to SM, 19 August 1968, UA; author's interviews with Olga Owens and R. P. Harriss, 27 July 1987; Harriss to SM, 25 January [1929], UA; and SH to SM, 9 June [1926], UA.

p. 315.  "At first his": HLM–SH correspondence, Autumn 1927, *passim*, GC, *M&S*, pp. 289–375.

"She was 'as' ": Jim Tully to HLM, 17 October 1927, NYPL; HLM to SH, 23 December 1927, GC, *M&S*, pp. 372–73; and HLM to GH, [23 December 1927], EU, *Ich Küss die Hand*, pp. 82–83.

"When Sara, after": HLM to JH, 3 January [1928], NYPL; HLM to SH, 17 January 1928, GC, *M&S*, pp. 377–78; and HLM to GH, 2, 7, 11, 14, 20, 27, and 31 January 1928 and 6, 9, 10, 15, and 18 February 1928, EU, *Ich Küss die Hand*, pp. 85–96.

p. 316.  "He spent evenings"; HLM to SM, 6 and 24 July and 24 August 1928, UA; HLM to DH, 15 April, 28 August, 26 September, and 1 October 1928, NYPL; SH to SM, 21 July and 8 October 1928, UA; HLM, *A&E*, p. 311; and SH to SM, 1 February [1929?], UA.

"It was clear": BK to HLM, 28 January 1928, EPFL; DH to HLM, [1928], NYPL; SH to SM, 2 and 10 August [1928], 10 and 16 March [1929], UA; SH to Mary Parmenter, 2 July 1928, EPFL; and SH to SM, 4 December [1927], UA.

"Sara, whose health": HLM to DH, 24 October 1928, NYPL; HLM to SH, 5, 8, and 12 October 1928, GC, *M&S*, pp. 395–96; and HLM to SM, 10 October 1928, UA.

p. 317.  "Finding a benign": Marjorie Nicolson to SM, 1 November 1928, UA; Mary Parmenter to SM, 29 October 1928, UA.

"Just what the": HLM to DH, 26 October 1928, NYPL; HLM to Jim Tully, 27 October 1928, NYPL; and HLM to SM, 20 November 1928, UA.

"Sara remained in": SH to SM, 20 November [1928], UA; Mary Parmenter to SM, 2 February 1929, UA; and HLM to PG, 19 January [1929], EPFL.

"She was ill": HLM to Jim Tully, 17 April and 4 May [1929], NYPL; HLM to Tully, 19 May and 15 June [1929] (copies), Mayfield papers, UA; and HLM to SH, 28 June and 2 July 1929, GC, *M&S*, p. 411.

p. 318. "Writing to Sara": HLM to SM, 25 and 29 June and 1, 3, and 5 July [1929], UA.

"On July 6": HLM to SM, 5 July 1929, UA; HLM to DH, 16 July 1929, NYPL; HLM to Jim Tully, [1929], NYPL; HLM, "Thirty-Five Years," p. 578; and SH to Marjorie Nicolson [July 1929] (copy), Mayfield papers, UA.

"Although she had": SM, *The Constant Circle*, pp. 136–37, 157–58; Marion Elizabeth Rodgers, *M&S*, p. 412; and SM, "HLM on 'How to Catch a Husband,'" UA.

"He had continued": HLM to GH, 6 and 10 February, 1 June, and 26 July [1928], EU, *Ich Küss die Hand*, pp. 93–95, 109–110, 117–118; HLM to GH, 7 February and 18 June [1928], EU.

p. 319. "It was much": AP to HLM, [December 1927] and 9 January 1928, YU.

"She had confronted": AP to HLM, January–April 1928 *passim* and 2 June 1928 (telegram); and HLM to AP (telegram), 10 and 29 June 1928, [December 1928], and 23 July 1929, YU.

"It was almost": MB to EB, 14 February 1928, NYPL; HLM to EB, 4 April 1928, NYPL; and HLM to MB, 11, 14, and 17 April [1928], EPFL.

p. 320. "At that second": HLM to MB, 29 June, 25 July, and 20 November [1928], EPFL; HLM to EB, 26 July [1928], NYPL; and MB to Betty Adler, 3 November 1968, EPFL.

"But the patient": HLM to MB, February, March, and Spring 1929, *passim*, EPFL; and HLM to GH, 31 January [1929], *Ich Küss die Hand*, p. 129.

"After his discussion": SH to SM, Autumn 1929, *passim*, UA; and HLM, "Thirty-Five Years," pp. 580–81.

p. 321. "After a strenuous": HLM–SH correspondence, Autumn–Winter 1929, *passim*, GC, *M&S*, pp. 413–17; and HLM, "Thirty-Five Years," p. 590ff.

"He sailed from": HLM to Hamilton Owens, 2 January [1930], EPFL; HLM to AP, 10 and 30 January 1930, YU; and HLM to SH, 27 December 1929 and 1 January 1930, GC, *M&S*, pp. 416, 421–23.

"It was the": HLM to Robert C. Brown, 5 January [1930], NYPL; HLM to Hamilton Owens, 10 January [1930], EPFL; HLM to BK, 1 January 1930, EPFL; HLM, "Thirty-Five Years," pp. 582–85; and HLM to SH, 5, 10, and 19 January 1930 and *passim*, GC, *M&S*, pp. 421–32.

p. 322. "Mencken arrived in": HLM to SH, 25 January and 6 February 1930, GC, *M&S*, pp. 432, 434–35; HLM to PG, January 1930, *passim*, EPFL; HLM, "Hands across the Sea," ms. in scrapbook "International Conferences," EPFL; HLM note on Arnold Bennett, 14 June 1940, in HLM–Bennett correspondence, NYPL; HLM to EB, 18 December 1929, NYPL; and HLM, "Thirty-Five Years," pp. 592–600.

"Although both he": HLM to SH, 25 April 1930, GC, *M&S*, p. 443; GM to SH, 26 April 1930, in SH scrapbook, EPFL; and SH to GM, 29 April 1930, EPFL.

"Shortly after Sara": SH to SM, 24 April [1930], UA; and author's interview with Olga Owens.

p. 323. "In early summer": HLM to PG, 27 June [1930], EPFL; HLM to Max Brödel, 28 July 1930, NYPL; HLM to Dorothy Hergesheimer, 28 July 1930, NYPL; SH to SM, 27 July 1930, UA; SH to Mary Parmenter, 27 July 1930, EPFL; author's interview with Olga Owens; and HLM clippings scrapbook, August 1930, EPFL.

"Nearly all of": JH to HLM, 30 July 1930, NYPL; Ernest Boyd to HLM, 4 August 1930, NYPL; HLM to Max Brödel, 28 July and 4 August 1930, NYPL; and Brödel to HLM, 4 August 1930, NYPL.

p. 324. " 'Wire me at' ": AP to HLM (telegram), 19 June 1930 and [November 1928], and wedding announcement (Mrs. John Anton Haardt to AP), [August 1930], YU.

" 'I hear from' ": HLM to GH, 26 March [1930] and 14 December 1929, EU, *Ich Küss die Hand*, pp. 137–38; GH, note in HLM letters, EU; and HLM to GH, [24 October 1928], EU, *Ich Küss die Hand*, p. 123.

" 'I suppose you' ": HLM to GH, 7 August 1930; and GH note attached to HLM letter, EU, *Ich Küss die Hand*, p. 139.

p. 325. "If Hood wondered": MB to Betty Adler, 27 June [1971?], EPFL; author's interviews with Olga Owens and W. C. Abhau; and AAK to Betty Adler, 19 July 1971, EPFL.

"If illness played": HLM to Jim Tully, [1919], NYPL; and Elinor Pancoast to SM, 3 December 1928, UA.

"But he had": Author's interviews with W. C. Abhau and R. P. Harriss; JH to HLM, 30 June 1947, NYPL; Abhau, quoted by William J. Sabo, "Interview with Rear Admiral William C. Abhau," *Menckeniana*, Summer 1977, p. 10; Marjorie Nicolson to SM, 1 August 1971, UA.

p. 326. "There was more": MB to Betty Adler, 27 June [1971], EPFL; HLM to Oscar Levy, 18 July 1935, NYPL; and HLM, preface, *Southern Album*, p. xxi.

p. 327. "one of Sara's": SM, in Carl Bode interview with SM, ms., Mayfield papers, UA.

"It was, as": HLM, *HD*, p. vii.

"He approached the": HLM to Max Brödel, 20 August 1930, NYPL; HLM to Hamilton Owens, 18 August 1930, EPFL; HLM to JH, 31 July 1930, NYPL; HLM to BK, 2 August [1920], EPFL; and HLM to A. H. McDannald, 16 August 1930, NYPL.

p. 328. "When the day": HLM to MB, 27 February [1927], EPFL; and HLM to Max Brödel, 20 August 1930, NYPL.

"Mencken and August": Author's interview with Olga Owens; and "Form of Solemnization of Matrimony," AM papers, EPFL.

## Chapter 14: A Beautiful Episode

p. 329. " 'My days with' ": HLM, *Diary*, 30 May 1945, p. 368.

"Robert Frost, whom": Robert Frost to HLM, 22 August 1930, NYPL; and Max Brödel to HLM, 14 August 1930 and *passim*, NYPL.

"They stopped in": HLM to PG, 30 August 1930, EPFL; HLM, note of 6 September 1940, HLM–E.L.M. Burns correspondence, NYPL; HLM to A. H. McDannald, 5 September [1939], NYPL; HLM to Hamilton Owens, 7 September 1930, EPFL; HLM to Theodor Hemberger, 4 September 1930, NYPL; and SH to Elsa G. Hoyden, [September 1930], in SHM condolence letters, GC.

p. 330. "After brief stops": HLM to SM, 14 August [1930], UA; AM, "Reminiscences," pp. 76–77; HLM to Max Brödel, 20 August 1930, NYPL; and HLM to J. B. Dudek, 30 December [1925], NYPL.

"He and Sara": HLM to Max Brödel, 3 November 1930, NYPL; HLM, *Diary*, 17 November and 31 December 1930 and 1931, *passim*, pp. 6ff.; HLM correspondence with JH, BH, and AAK, 1930–31, *passim*, NYPL; HLM–PG correspondence, 1930–31, *passim*, EPFL.

"Less frequently in": HLM, *Diary*, 1931, *passim*, especially 27 November 1931, pp. 40–41; HLM to EB, 9 and 24 November 1931, NYPL; HLM to PG, 10 October 1930, EPFL; and HLM to C. A. Moneta, 19 November 1932, NYPL.

p. 331.   "For periods in": HLM letters to Jim Tully, AAK, PG, BK, DH, and JH, 1931, NYPL; HLM to Hamilton Owens, 1931, EPFL; HLM, *Diary*, 16 April 1931, p. 20; and SH to SM, 27 May [1931], UA.

"Three months before": HLM to PG, 25 March [1931], EPFL; and HLM, *Diary*, 24 March 1931, pp. 18–20.

"The calamities began": HLM, *Diary*, 12 July 1931, pp. 26–30.

p. 332.   "The remainder of": AAK to HLM, 30 December 1931, NYPL; HLM, letters to JH and AAK, December 1931 and January 1932, NYPL; and HLM to PG and Hamilton Owens, December 1931 and January 1932, EPFL.

" 'Let us victual' ": HLM to PG, 16 March [1932], EPFL; HLM to DH, 13 October 1933, NYPL; HLM to AAK, 24 September 1932, EPFL; and HLM to GM, 9 and 28 September 1932, EPFL.

p. 333.   "He began to": HLM to EB, 8 July 1932, NYPL; HLM to Henry Nixdorf, 15 October 1932, EPFL; and HLM to SM [14 August 1930], UA.

"After five months": HLM to DH, 20 January 1931, NYPL; and HLM to PG, 26 August 1931, EPFL.

"and he wrote": HLM to SH, June 1932, *passim*, GC, *M&S*, pp. 470–87; and AAK to HLM, 18 November 1930, NYPL.

" 'I have never' ": HLM, *Diary*, 31 May 1940, p. 142; HLM to SL, 15 October 1945, NYPL; and HLM, *Diary*, 1 May 1939, p. 142.

p. 334.   "Her 'bad health' ": HLM, *Diary*, 30 May 1945, p. 367; HLM to MB, 18 July 1919, EPFL; AM, "Reminiscences," p. 77; and author's interviews with W. C. Abhau, Olga Owens, and Gwinn Owens.

"In any case": HLM, *Diary*, 31 May 1940 and 30 May 1945, pp. 142, 367–68; HLM to PG, 8 October [1931], EPFL; and HLM to "Miss Stein," [1920s], in miscellaneous HLM correspondence, NYPL.

p. 335.   "At times it": Author's interviews with Ruth Goodman Goetz and Olga Owens; and Goetz, "The Faces of Enlightenment," *Menckeniana*, Winter 1988, p. 4.

"Sara's relationship with": AM, "Reminiscences," pp. 10, 70, 75; GM to SH, 26 April 1930, SH scrapbook, EPFL; and GM to AM [1934?] and 8 February 1950, EPFL.

"For the most": HLM to Ernest Boyd, 7 April 1931, NYPL; HLM to AAK, 5 and 9 April 1931, EPFL; SH to HLM, 24 June 1932, GC, *M&S*, pp. 479–80; and Virginia Mencken Morrison, undated typescript, Bode collection, EPFL.

p. 336.   "He and Sara": Author's interview with W. C. Abhau; and Millard Tydings to HLM, 27 February 1931, EPFL.

"His inclination was": HLM, *Diary*, 18 January 1931, p. 12.

"If he had": author's interview with Olga Owens; HLM to Max Brödel, 30 September 1930, NYPL; LC, SNC diary, 21 April and 1 September 1934 and 2 February 1942, EPFL; and HLM, *Diary*, 31 May 1930, p. 143.

p. 337.   "The man whose": HLM, "Thirty-Five Years," pp. 367–68, 631–32.

"He also shared": HLM, "Thirty-Five Years," p. 368; and undated note in HLM–Raymond Pearl correspondence, NYPL.

p. 338. "Indeed, for all": HLM to PG, 14 November [1930], EPFL.

p. 339. "He was again": HLM, *Diary*, 25 April 1931, p. 23; and HLM to AAK, quoted by AAK in news release, 12 April 1930, HLM miscellaneous scrapbook, EPFL.

"All these projects": HLM to FHG, 27 March 1930, NYPL; HLM, "On the Nature of Man," *Prejudices, IV*, p. 200; and JB to HLM, 7 August 1942, NYPL.

"When Knopf pleaded": HLM, "Thirty-Five Years," p. 644.

p. 340. "He found he": HLM to AAK, 29 December 1931 and 7 and 8 November 1932, EPFL; and AAK to HLM, [2 December 1931], 24 December 1931, and 9 November 1932, EPFL.

"Knopf rejected Mencken's": AAK to HLM, 9 November and 22 December 1932, NYPL; HLM to PG, 5 May and 29 December 1932, EPFL; Charles Angoff, *H. L. Mencken: A Portrait from Memory* (Yoseloff, 1956), pp. 208, 217; and author's interview with Lawrence Spivak, 23 July 1992.

p. 341. "He also expressed": HLM, *Diary*, 31 January 1933, p. 54.

"In late February": HLM–Henry Hazlitt correspondence, 1933, NYPL, especially HLM to Hazlitt, 24 February, 30 September, and 3 and 12 October 1933, and Hazlitt to HLM, 2 and 23 October 1933; "Mencken Retires as Mercury Editor," *The New York Times*, 6 October 1933; "Mencken Quits as Mercury Editor," New York *Evening Post*, 6 October 1933; and HLM to AAK, 17 December [1935], EPFL.

"In the 'Library'": HLM, "Hitlerismus," *AM*, December 1933, pp. 506–10, and HLM, ms. of Hitler review, *AM* ms. scrapbook, EPFL.

"Knopf came across": AAK to HLM, 24 and 27 October [1933], EPFL; HLM to AAK, 26 October [1933], EPFL; and HLM to James N. Rosenberg, 5 December 1933, NYPL.

p. 342. "When Knopf indeed": AAK to HLM, 27 October [1933], EPFL; HLM to Nicholas Alter, 21 October 1933, NYPL; and AM, "Reminiscences," pp. 19–20.

"The *Mercury* editor's": HLM clippings scrapbook, 1933, especially Ted Shane, "H. L. Mencken Is Dead," New York *Journal*, January 1933; and Lee Taylor Gray, "By Way of Observation," *Rocky Mountain News*, 22 October 1931.

"Mencken found himself": HLM, "Thirty-Five Years," p. 667; HLM, *Diary*, 3 December 1934 and 29 January 1935, pp. 70–72, 90–92; HLM to JH, [January 1935], NYPL; HLM–Lawrence Spivak correspondence, 1934–35, NYPL; Spivak to SM, 13 March 1969, UA; and author's interview with Spivak.

p. 343. "Mencken also had": HLM, "Thirty-Five Years," pp. 772–73, 774–75; and HLM to BH, 12 October 1933, UNC.

"It was not": HLM to PG, 1 February 1932 and 15 January [1933], EPFL; HLM, "Sun Income to January 1946," in Sunpapers documents, EPFL; Upton Sinclair to HLM, 30 August 1930, NYPL; and HLM to Sinclair (telegram), 15 September 1930, NYPL.

"Primarily Mencken wanted": HLM, "Thirty-Five Years," p. 659; HLM to Ezra Pound, 26 November 1932, NYPL; HLM to PG, 7 November 1932, EPFL; and HLM to Eric Langemann, 12 November 1932, NYPL.

p. 344. "In articles announcing": HLM to AAK, 23 February and 31 December 1931, NYPL; HLM to Isaac Goldberg, 22 August 1933, NYPL; HLM to FHG, 12

September and 3 October 1932, NYPL; and HLM, *Diary*, 6 September 1931, pp. 37–38.

"At last he": AAK to HLM, 21 February 1934, EPFL.

p. 345. "Whether favorable or": Reviews in HLM clippings scrapbook, 1934, EPFL.

"How long even": HLM to Anna Mencke, 29 October 1933, EPFL; HLM to Frank Kent, 3 August 1933, EPFL; HLM to Joel Sayre, 14 July 1933, NYPL; HLM to Folger McKinsey, 18 June 1933, EPFL; and HLM to BH, 1 September 1933, UNC.

p. 346. " 'Sara and I' ": HLM to Paul Patterson, 1, 4, 7, and 8 March 1933, EPFL.

"From Sea Island": HLM, "*Heathen Days:* Additions," p. 189; and "H. L. Mencken Refutes Cynical Self," *Birmingham News*, 6 March 1933.

"The Menckens also": HLM–BH correspondence, 1930s, *passim*, UNC; and HLM, "Diary," 19 September 1934.

"It appears, in": James Cain to SM, 19 August 1968, UA; AM, "Medical Notes after 1928," September 1950, EPFL; HLM to DH, 1 May 1930, NYPL; and HLM, "Diary," 14 August 1933.

p. 347. "Even before they": FSF to HLM, 15 February 1931 (telegram) and [4 March 1931], NYPL; and HLM, *Diary*, 27 April 1932, pp. 44–45.

"He recorded in": HLM, *Diary*, 18 March 1933, pp. 56–57, AM, "Reminiscences," p. 43; and HLM, *A&E*, pp. 262–64.

p. 348. " 'Will he find' ": FSF, ms. of review of *Prejudices, Second Series* for *The Bookman*, in FSF to HLM, 30 December 1920, NYPL; FSF, "The Baltimore Anti-Christ," *The Bookman*, March 1921, pp. 79–81; and FSF to HLM, 29 April 1935, NYPL.

"For his part": HLM, *Diary*, 27 April 1932 and 12 June 1934, pp. 44–45, 62–63; and HLM, *A&E*, p. 264. Although Mencken found Fitzgerald's visits too frequent, he later did invite him over on occasion (HLM to FSF, 14 April 1934, NYPL).

p. 349. "Mencken and Sara": HLM, "Thirty-Five Years," p. 696; and HLM to ELM, 7 January 1937, NYPL.

"He was amazed": HLM, "Metamorphosis," *BES*, 23 April 1934; HLM to Emily Clark, 23 June 1937, NYPL; LC, SNC diary, 7 April 1934; HLM to Hamilton Owens, 6 March [1934], EPFL; HLM to AAK, 27 February [1934], EPFL; HLM, *Heathen Days*, pp. 239–55; and HLM, "The Ruins of Carthage" (26 March) and "The Land of the Moors" (19 March) 1934, *BES*.

" 'Jerusalem!—and then' ": HLM to Henry Hyde, [March 1934], EPFL; and HLM to AAK, 9 March [1934], EPFL.

"It was not": HLM, *Heathen Days*, pp. 267–70; HLM to Gilbert Freyre, 9 April 1934, NYPL; HLM to Paula Arnold, 8 January 1935, NYPL; and HLM to James Rosenberg, 24 April 1934, in HLM–AAK correspondence, NYPL.

p. 350. "Mencken did not": HLM to Hamilton Owens, 17 February 1934, EPFL; HLM to AAK, 9 March [1934], EPFL; HLM, *Diary*, 31 May 1940, pp. 140–41.

"Sara continued to": HLM to GM, 7 May 1934, EPFL; HLM to JH, 22 May 1934, NYPL; LC, SNC diary, 12 and 27 May 1934; and HLM, *Diary*, 31 May 1940, p. 141.

"When she came": GM to AM, 8 February 1950, EPFL; HLM to GM, 7 May 1934, EPFL; and HLM, *Diary*, 31 May 1940, p. 141.

"Baltimore was experiencing": HLM, "The Weather," *BES*, 6 August 1934; HLM to JH, 31 July 1934, NYPL; HLM to SHM, 2, [3], [5], and 10 September, GC, *M&S*, pp. 497–506; HLM, *Diary*, 21 July 1934, pp. 66–69; HLM to Henry Hyde, 7 August 1934, EPFL; and HLM, "Thirty-Five Years," pp. 701–66.

p. 351.  "He and Sara": HLM, "Thirty-Five Years," pp. 792–93; HLM to BH, 28 and 29 September 1934, UNC; HLM, *Diary*, 31 May 1940, p. 141; HLM to AAK, 10 September 1934, illness file, EPFL; HLM to GM, 13 September 1934, EPFL; and LC, SNC diary [September 1934].

"When she and": AAK to HLM, 10 September 1934, EPFL; HLM to AAK, 11 and 29 September 1934, EPFL; HLM to BH, 20 September 1934, UNC; and LC, SNC diary, 27 October 1934.

" 'If all goes' ": HLM to BK, 23 October 1934, NYPL; HLM to AAK, 11 and 15 December 1934, illness file, EPFL; HLM to Benjamin de Casseres, 24 December 1934, NYPL; AAK to HLM, 31 December 1934, EPFL; HLM to FHG, 26 December 1934, NYPL; and HLM to Henry Hyde, 24 December 1934, EPFL.

p. 352.  "It was not": HLM to BH, 18 January 1935, UNC; HLM to BK, 13 and 16 February 1935, illness file, EPFL; HLM, *Diary*, 10 January and 6 March 1935, pp. 83–84; HLM, "Diary," 24 January, 16 February, and 6 March 1935; and HLM to Fanny Butcher, 26 and 28 February 1935, NYPL.

"In March Sara": HLM to ELM, 7 March 1935, NYPL; HLM to BK, March 1935, *passim*, illness file, EPFL; HLM to BH, 20 March 1935, UNC. In "Thirty-Five Years" HLM writes that Dr. Baker sent Sara to Union Memorial Hospital in March, but Mencken's diary and his letters to friends say the Johns Hopkins. In "Thirty-Five Years" HLM made several similar mistakes, e.g., misdating the time of Sara's summer 1934 visit to Montgomery.

"Mencken's illness file": HLM to TD, 9 April 1935, *D–M Letters*, II, p. 585; HLM to AAK, 3 April 1935, EPFL; HLM, note of 13 January 1935, illness file, EPFL; HLM to BK, 5 and 9 April 1935, illness file, EPFL: and HLM to AAK, 17 April 1935, illness file, EPFL.

p. 353.  "The doctors recommended": HLM to AAK, 18 and 21 May 1935, illness file, EPFL; HLM to GM, 21 May 1935, EPFL; HLM to William C. Abhau, 21 May 1935, EPFL; HLM to J.A.M. Sanchez, 21 May 1935, NYPL; and SHM to SM [May 1935], UA.

"Two days later": HLM to AAK, 23 May 1935, illness file, EPFL; and HLM to FSF, 23 May 1935, NYPL.

"Not until May 25": HLM to BH, 25 May 1935, UNC; HLM to GM, 25 May 1935, EPFL; HLM to Bernice Lesbia Kenyon, 25 May 1935, NYPL; and HLM to AAK, 25 May 1935, EPFL.

"The next day": HLM, "Thirty-Five Years," p. 794; and HLM, *Diary*, 31 May 1940, p. 141. In a diary entry for 30 May 1945 (p. 368), HLM writes that he last saw Sara on 28 May 1935, but all other sources suggest 29 May.

p. 354.  "Mencken spent the": HLM, *Diary*, 31 May 1940 and 21 January 1942, pp. 143, 182; HLM to Mary L. Franklin, 19 August 1936, NYPL; HLM, "*HD: Additions*," p. 99; and HLM to BH, 30 May 1935, UNC.

"As Sara lay": HLM to BH, 30 May 1935, UNC: HLM to Max Brödel, 29 May 1935, NYPL; HLM to BK (telegram), 29 May 1935, NYPL; HLM to FSF, 30 May 1935; NYPL; HLM to Hamilton and Olga Owens, 30 May 1935, EPFL; HLM to A. H. McDannald, 30 May 1935, NYPL; HLM to Marjorie Nicolson, 30 May 1935, NYPL; and letters and notes to Mencken from BK, McDannald, Ida Haardt, and others (NYPL and GC). FSF's note—"I hope for the best"—was dated 1 June, the day after Sara's death.

"So strong was": HLM to William C. Abhau, 28 and 30 May 1935, EPFL; HLM to Harriet D. Jones, 30 May 1935, NYPL; and HLM to Vihljahmer Stefensson, 31 May 1935, NYPL. Mencken had originally planned to attend

Abhau's commencement (HLM to WCA, 16 May) but had apparently
forgotten that he had already written on 21 May to tell his cousin that his
plans to take Sara to Saranac would prevent his going to Annapolis.

p. 355.   "Mencken was dealing": HLM, *Diary*, 30 May 1945, p. 368.

"He was not": HLM to John Haardt (telegram), 1 June 1935, EPFL; HLM to
BH (telegram), 31 May 1935, UNC; HLM, *Diary*, 31 May 1940 and 30 May
1945, pp. 143, 368; and LC, SNC diary, 1 and 2 June 1935.

"He confronted the": HLM, *Diary*, 30 May 1945, p. 368; HLM to Helen
Hunter, 2 March 1935, NYPL; and HLM to AAK, 16 October 1940, EPFL.

"The nation's newspapers": HLM clippings scrapbook, June 1935; and HLM
to Mae Allison Osborne, 8 June 1935, NYPL.

p. 356.   "About forty people": HLM, *Diary*, 31 May 1940, p. 143; LC, SNC diary, 3
June 1935; and Hamilton Owens to HLM, 3 June 1935, GC.


## Chapter 15: The Consolations of an Agnostic

p. 357.   " 'I was fifty-five' ": HLM, "AN, 1941–."

" 'There is a' ": HLM to Hamilton Owens, June 1935, EPFL; HLM to SM, 8
June 1935, UA; SHM will, SHM scrapbook (F-46), EPFL; and HM to
William A. Maloy, 11 June 1935, EPFL.

"The apartment, he": HLM to SM, 5 June [1935], UA.

"Many of the": Ida Haardt to HLM, [June 1935], GC; Marjorie Nicolson to
HLM, 31 May and 7 June 1935, GC; SM to HLM, [June 1935], GC; Emil
Heimberger to HLM, 3 June 1935, GC; HLM to Clarissa Flugel, 7 June
1935, EPFL; HLM to Anna Mencke, 27 July 1935, EPFL; HLM to Mrs.
Louis Michel, 6 June 1935, EPFL; Harry Corry to HLM, 1 June 1935, GC;
and J. M. Cleveland to HLM, 24 June 1935, GC. Also, letters from GJN,
FSF, SL, Cabell, ELM, Glasgow, the Knopfs, and others, in condolence file,
GC.

p. 358.   "To most of": HLM to GJN, 4 June [1935], Cornell University; HLM to Ellery
Sedgwick, 7 June [1935], NYPL; HLM to Jean Balch, [12 June 1935],
EPFL; HLM to Josiah Combs, 6 June 1935, NYPL.

"In fact, Mencken's": AM, "Reminiscences," pp. 11–12; HLM to Ralph Wallace [1930s?], NYPL; HLM to EB, 10 October [1924], NYPL; HLM to SM
[June 1935], UA; HLM to BK, 18 June 1935, EPFL; HLM to SM, 17 July
[1935], UA: and HLM to Oscar Levy, 18 July 1935, NYPL.

"When they returned": HLM to Anna Mencke, 18 June 1935, EPFL; HLM to
Dean D. Lewis, 1 June 1935, GC; HLM to Hamilton Owens, 23 June [1935],
EPFL; HLM to SM, 17 July [1935], UA; and HLM to Oscar Levy, 18 July
1935, NYPL.

p. 359.   "He had great": HLM, "Diary," 29 January 1935 (II).

"He would remark": HLM, *AL* (1936), pp. 30–31, 60, 267.

p. 360.   "This time, however": HLM, *AL* (1936), pp. vi, 608.

"Mencken knew, then": HLM to Maud Pearl, 20 November [1940], EPFL;
HLM to GM, 22 August 1935, EPFL; and HLM to Max Brödel, 3 August
1935, NYPL.

"He seemed to": HLM, *Diary*, 14 September 1935, p. 93; HLM to Leland
Lovette, 21 September 1935, NYPL; HLM to SM, 23 November 1935, UA;
HLM to ELM, 5 November 1935, NYPL; and HLM to Emily Clark, 7
September 1935, NYPL.

"Thoughts of Sara": HLM to SM, 17 July 1935, UA; HLM to Grace Oursler,

8 June 1935, NYPL; HLM to J.A.M. Sanchez, 29 August 1935, NYPL; *BS* article, 1 November 1935, HLM clippings scrapbook, EPFL; and SM, draft of unpublished article "HLM: Advice to Young Girls," p. 6, Mayfield collection, UA.

p. 361. "August remained at": HLM to Anna Mencke, 14 November 1935, EPFL; HLM to J.A.M. Sanchez, 23 November 1935, NYPL; HLM, "Thirty-Five Years," p. 797; AM, "Reminiscences," pp. 12–13; and LC, SNC diary, 14 and 21 December 1935.

"Christmas, an unhappy": BK to HLM, 18 and 20 November 1935, EPFL; JH to HLM, 4 December 1935 (telegram), NYPL; HLM to BH, 27 December 1935, UNC; HLM letters to TD, AAK, Jim Tully, Jean Balch, Anna Mencke, and others, January 1936, UP, NYPL, and EPFL; HLM to A. H. McDannald, 2 January 1936, NYPL; and HLM to Charles Abhau, 29 February 1936, EPFL.

"In late March": HLM to GM, 30 November 1935, EPFL; HLM to Mrs. F. B. Grubb, 7 March 1936, NYPL; HLM to Julia Harris, 27 February 1936, NYPL; HLM, "Thirty-Five Years," p. 876; and HLM letters to DH, BH, MD, and others, 1936, EPFL and NYPL.

p. 362. "He felt it": HLM to DH, 10 March 1936, NYPL; HLM to Anna Mencke, 22 April 1936, EPFL; and HLM letters to William C. Abhau, Harry Black, Hamilton Owens, and GM, 1936, EPFL.

"He welcomed the": Author's interview with William C. Abhau; AM, "Reminiscences," pp. 115–30; and HLM, "*HD:* Additions," p. 95.

"In leaving Cathedral": HLM to DH, 28 July 1930, NYPL; author's interview with Olga Owens; and Ernest Boyd to HLM, 14 April 1936, NYPL.

p. 363. " 'Sometimes I wish' ": HLM to Otto Glauning, 28 May 1936, NYPL.

"But the reception": Reviews in *The New Yorker* and *Saturday Review*, HLM clippings scrapbook, EPFL; and Edmund Wilson, "Talking United States," *The New Republic*, 15 July 1936, pp. 299–300.

"His 'troubles start[ed]' ": AM, "Reminiscences," pp. 12–13.

"One work he": HLM, letters to GM, SM, DH, Charles Abhau, Mrs. Meredith Janvier, and others, 1936, EPFL, NYPL, and UA; SHM, "Dear Life," *Southern Album*, pp. 273, 277; and reviews of *Southern Album* in HLM clippings scrapbook, EPFL.

p. 364. "Now that his": HLM, "Thirty-Five Years," pp. 820–50; and HLM letters to Henry Hyde, Gerald W. Johnson, Eric Langemann, Francis A. Litz, and Hazleton Spencer, 1936, EPFL.

"One book he": HLM to Percy Marks, 2 December [1922?], NYPL; HLM to Nelson Perkins, 19 October 1936, NYPL; HLM, "Diary," 28 June 1937; and HLM to Gerald W. Johnson, 20 November 1934, EPFL.

p. 365. "Now, in May": HLM to BK, 9 May 1936, EPFL; HLM to SM, 2 May and 19 August 1936, UA; Selig Greenberg, "Tells of Plans to Write Guide for Young Men," *Providence Bulletin*, 9 May 1936; and HLM to JB, 29 July 1942, NYPL.

"Now that Gertrude": HLM to GM, 1936–37, *passim*, EPFL; and HLM to Hamilton Owens, 11 April 1938, EPFL.

"Living with August": HLM, "AN, 1941–"; HLM to Hamilton Owens, [January 1937], EPFL; HLM to George Schuyler, 23 January 1937, YU; and HLM letters to GM, Henry Hyde, and Olga Ross, December 1936–January 1937 EPFL.

p. 366. "His generosity continued": CM, quoted in "Brother Proud of Mencken's Beer-Drinking," Baltimore *Post*, 15 August 1932; and HLM to CM, 6

December 1933, 16 January 1934, 9 August 1937, and 26 July 1938, and 1939, *passim*, EPFL.

"The hopes he": CM to HLM, 21 November and 6 December 1933 and 16 January 1934, EPFL; HLM to GM, 7 August 1934, EPFL; HLM, "AN, 1941–": HLM to Julia Murphy, 24 December 1937, EPFL; and Virginia Mencken to HLM, 1933–37, *passim*, EPFL.

"If he grew": HLM to W. C. Abhau, 19 November 1935 and 1936–37, *passim*, EPFL; HLM, "*HD:* Additions," p. 247; and HLM to GM, 1 June 1936, EPFL.

p. 367.   "Relations with many": Ernest Boyd to HLM, 19 and 23 February 1932 and 1 and 15 May 1933, NYPL; HLM to Boyd, 5 and 22 May 1933, NYPL; HLM to Edgar Kemler, 16 August 1948, EPFL; and HLM, *Diary*, 30 July 1931, pp. 31–32.

"Another way in": "Mencken's Partner Planning New Mag," Holyoke *Transcript-Telegram*, 6 August 1932, and other reports, HLM clippings scrapbook, EPFL.

"In fact, he": HLM to GJN, 22 October and 7 and 25 November [1931], NYPL; GJN to HLM, 23 October and 6 November [1931], NYPL; HLM to AAK, 7 November [1931], EPFL; AAK to HLM, 9 November 1931, NYPL; and HLM, memo to AAK, 11 November 1931, NYPL.

p. 368.   "Nathan did make": GJN, *The Intimate Notebooks of George Jean Nathan* (Alfred A. Knopf, 1932), pp. 94–121, especially pp. 96–97.

"But Mencken was": Burton Rascoe, introduction to *The Smart Set Anthology*, p. xliii; HLM to AAK, 13 November 1934, EPFL; and HLM to Willard H. Wright, 22 November 1934, NYPL.

p. 369.   "They were brought": Burton Rascoe, "*Smart Set* History," HLM pamphlet collection, EPFL; HLM to TD, 21 November [1934], UP; and TD to HLM, 24 November 1934, NYPL, *D–M Letters*, II, pp. 564–65.

"Mencken had anticipated": HLM to FHG, 12 November 1931, NYPL; HLM, *Diary*, 18 April 1931, pp. 21–22; and HLM to MB, 16 April 1929, EPFL.

"Although he had": HLM, *Diary*, 5 December 1934 and 25 January 1935, pp. 73–74, 86–89; HLM to Ernest Boyd, 9 and 18 November 1936, NYPL; and HLM to ELM, 1936–38, *passim*, NYPL.

"Mencken had also": HLM, *Diary*, 3 February 1931, p. 14; HLM to PG, 5 May [1932], EPFL; and HLM, *A&E*, pp. 334–35, 348.

p. 370.   "By 1932 he": HLM to PG, 5 March and 5, 12, and 16 May [1932], NYPL and EPFL; HLM, *Diary*, 12 July, 3 February, and 10 March 1931, pp. 26–30, 13–16; HLM, "Diary," 17 December 1931; and HLM to AAK, 4 and 5 March 1931, EPFL.

"In his mid-fifties": HLM, *Diary*, 30 July 1931 and 6 September 1937, pp. 32, 108–10; HLM, "Diary," 16 August and 13 September 1937; HLM–ELM correspondence, 1930s, NYPL; HLM–BH correspondence, 1935–40, UNC; and HLM to SM, 9 August 1937, UA.

p. 371.   "From Aileen Pringle": Letters in SHM condolence file, GC.

"The renewed correspondence": James Cain to HLM, 19 June 1946, NYPL; HLM to AP, 1933 *passim*, YU, and 21 June 1935, NYPL; HLM to Beatrice Wilson, 11 September 1935, EPFL; Anita Loos to HLM, 25 August 1935, GC; HLM to Loos, 31 August 1935, NYPL; and GH to HLM, 10 June 1935, GC, *Ich Küss die Hand*, p. 141.

"Mencken had nevertheless": HLM to GH, 11 June, 30 July, and 21 December 1935 and 12 March 1937, EU, *Ich Küss die Hand*, pp. 140, 142–44; and GH, notes on HLM letters of 30 July 1935 and 12 March 1937, EU.

p. 372. "Mencken seems to": HLM to AP, 22 October 1935, NYPL, autumn 1935, *passim*, and 2 and 5 June [1936], YU; HLM to Beatrice Wilson, 11 September 1935, EPFL; HLM to ELM, 19 October 1935, NYPL; and JH to HLM, 18 November 1935, NYPL.

"Besides, his Baltimore": Author's interviews with Olga Owens, R. P. Harriss, Ruth Goodman Goetz, and Philip Wagner, 26 July 1988.

p. 373. "In Mencken's memoir": HLM, "A&E," pp. 814–15.

"Mencken, it seems": TD to HLM, 28 March 1935, NYPL, *D–M Letters*, II, p. 583; and HLM to Jean Balch, 13, 23, and 24 April 1935, EPFL.

"Such was, at": HLM to Jean Balch, 5 and 12 June [1935], EPFL.

p. 374. "When he returned": HLM to Jean Balch, 17, 23, 27, and 31 July and 20 and 27 August 1935, EPFL.

"He wrote to": HLM to Jean Balch, August–November 1935, *passim*, especially 29 August, 17 October, 1 November, and [November?] 1935, EPFL.

"He saw Balch": HLM to Jean Balch, December 1935–May 1936, *passim*, especially 15 and 29 January and 13 February 1936, EPFL.

p. 375. "For another year": HLM to Jean Balch, 14 May 1936 and June–October 1936, *passim*, especially 29 August 1936 and [November 1936?], EPFL.

"he continued to": HLM to Jean Balch, 31 May 1937, EPFL.

"Other women, some": HLM–Margaret Chase Harriman correspondence, 1937–41, NYPL; HLM–Gladys Baker correspondence, 1935–37, NYPL; HLM to EB, 1935–38, especially 8 April 1937, NYPL; and HLM, "Thirty-Five Years," p. 274.

"His New York": Ernest Boyd to HLM, 28 December 1935, NYPL; HLM, "Thirty-Five Years," p. 899; William Manchester, *Disturber of the Peace: The Life of H. L. Mencken* (1950; 1986 edition, University of Massachusetts Press), p. 322; HLM, Johns Hopkins medical records, 1936–37, EPFL; Willard Quennell to HLM, 29 September 1941, EPFL; HLM to JH, 18 February 1937, NYPL; HLM to Ernest Boyd, 17 February [1937]; author's interviews with Dr. Philip Wagley and Dr. Eric W. Jensen, January 1992, and Dr. John R. Boswell, February 1992.

p. 376. "Whatever the case": HLM to Aileen Pringle, 22 October 1935, 2 and 29 June 1936, and 22 September 1938, NYPL; HLM to Charles Norris, 1 October 1937, NYPL; HLM to Anita Loos, 22 May 1936, NYPL; and HLM–Lillian Gish correspondence, 1937–38, *passim*, especially Gish to HLM, 17 July and 21 October 1937, 9 November 1937 (telegram), and 29 September 1938, NYPL; HLM to ELM, 7 December 1938, NYPL; and HLM, "Diary," 26 October and 1 December 1938.

"In letters to": HLM to SM, 6 June 1938 and 10 September 1937, UA; SM to HLM, [1939?], NYPL; and HLM to SM, [1939?], NYPL.

p. 377. "A stylish, painfully": HLM, *A&E*, p. 376; and HLM correspondence with AAK and BK, 1933–35, EPFL and NYPL.

"After Sara's death": AAK to HLM, 20 October 1936 and 6 May 1937, EPFL; and BK to HLM, 6 and 19 July 1937 and 29 and 27 July and 19 November 1936, 11 June and 22 November 1937, and 1 June 1938, NYPL and EPFL; and author's interview with Dr. Benjamin Baker. I am also grateful to Peter S. Prescott, who is currently writing a biography of AAK, for sharing with me information about the relationship between Mencken and the Knopfs.

p. 378. "The frequency, the": BK to HLM, 1936–38, *passim*, e.g., 5 August 1937, NYPL.

"Blanche Knopf was": HLM, "Diary," 23 October 1938; HLM to DH, 27

February 1936, NYPL; and MD, "Heroic Days and Hours with Henry Mencken," *Menckeniana*, Summer 1966, pp. 5–9.

"After Sara's death": HLM, *Diary*, 20 June 1937, p. 101; MD to Betty Adler, 3 July 1966 and 25 November 1969, EPFL; and MD, "Heroic Days and Hours with Henry Mencken," pp. 7–8.

p. 379.   " 'Her presence is' ": HLM to Harrison H. Schaff, 1 July 1936, NYPL; HLM to Mary Parmenter, 5 March 1937, NYPL; and HLM to SM, 10 September 1937, UA.


## Chapter 16: Time Out of Joint

p. 380.   "He wanted 'to' ": HLM to Leland Lovette, 19 November 1935, NYPL.

"One aspect of ": HLM to PG, 5 and 7 November 1932, EPFL; HLM to J. Fred Essary, 7 September 1932, EPFL; HLM to J. Edwin Murphy, 14 September 1932, EPFL; HLM, "A Time to Be Wary," *BES*, 13 March 1933; HLM, "Thirty-Five Years," p. 677; HLM to Henry Hyde, 5 June 1933, EPFL; HLM to Miles Wolff, 26 November 1932, EPFL; Franklin D. Roosevelt to HLM, 28 November 1928, NYPL; and Roosevelt to AAK, 16 August 1932, NYPL.

p. 381.   "For another, he": HLM, "Diary," undated entry [1932?].

"But at least": HLM to PG, 5 November 1932 and 15 January [1933], EPFL; HLM to PG, 22 June 1933, NYPL; *Detroit News*, 25 May 1932, HLM clippings scrapbook, EPFL; HLM, quoted in "This Here Depression," N. Holyoke *Transcript-Telegram*, 27 May 1932; "Mencken Says Call In Hangman for Incompetents," *Chicago Tribune*, 14 June 1934; HLM, quoted in " 'Clowning' a Tragedy," *Fort Worth Star-Telegram*, 2 June 1939; and HLM, quoted in "Give Up Bridge . . . ," *The Buffalo News*, 14 January 1932.

"He made such": HLM, "Thirty-Five Years," p. 646; Anita Loos, *A Girl Like I*, p. 222; and CM to HLM, 26 July 1938 and 23 May 1939, EPFL.

p. 382.   "There is little": Leonard Kriegel, *Edmund Wilson* (Southern Illinois University Press, 1971), p. 26.

"Neither did his": HLM to Oscar Levy, 3 October 1935 and 1 November 1937, NYPL; HLM to Henry Hazlitt, 14 March 1933, NYPL; and HLM to PG, 8 December 1932, EPFL.

"In no fewer": HLM, *BES* columns of 21 May, 25 June, 2 July, 20 and 27 August, 24 September, and 1, 8, and 22 October 1934.

"That moment came": HLM, Editorial, *AM*, October 1924, pp. 155–59; and (on Gridiron remarks) HLM to James Wright, 27 November 1934, EPFL; Wright to HLM, 12 December 1934, NYPL; HLM, note in Wright correspondence, 9 December 1934, NYPL; HLM to B. A. Bergman, 12 December 1934, NYPL; HLM to Jean Balch, 2 November [1936], EPFL; HLM, *Diary*, 9 and 11 December 1934, pp. 75–77; and HLM, "Thirty-Five Years," pp. 776–80.

p. 383.   "It has long": Edgar Kemler, *The Irreverent Mr. Mencken*, p. 271; HLM, Gridiron correspondence, *ibid.*; HLM, note in James Wright correspondence, November–December 1934, NYPL.

"Whatever he felt": Author's interview with Lawrence Spivak; HLM, "Roosevelt," *BES*, 2 January 1934; HLM, "Three Years of Dr. Roosevelt," *AM*, March 1936, pp. 257–65; and HLM, "The New Deal Mentality," *AM*, May 1936, pp. 1–11.

p. 384. "In his March": HLM, "Three Years of Dr. Roosevelt," p. 265; HLM to ELM, 9 March 1931, PU; HLM to Henry Hyde, 28 July 1936, EPFL; HLM to GM, 11 August 1936, EPFL; HLM to Philip Wagner, Paul Patterson, and Jean Balch, Summer–Fall 1936, EPFL; and HLM to Ralph Wallace and BH, Summer–Fall 1936, NYPL. Francis E. Townsend asked Mencken to write campaign speeches for him, but Mencken declined the honor (Townsend to HLM, 30 September 1936; and HLM to Townsend, 1 October 1936, NYPL).

"By mid-September": HLM to Henry Hyde, 17 September 1936, EPFL; HLM, "The Choice Tomorrow," *BES*, 2 November 1936; and HLM to John Owens, 14 and 18 December 1936, EPFL.

p. 385. "It was an": *The New York Times* and other newspaper attacks, 1937, HLM clippings scrapbook, EPFL; HLM, "The Common Enemy," *BES*, 20 December 1937, and "Down with Boils," *BES*, 26 April 1937.

"Why, then, did": HLM, "Diary," 16 September 1937; HLM–Theodore Roosevelt, Jr., correspondence, 1930s, especially Roosevelt to HLM, 3 and 19 April 1935, NYPL; and HLM to Henry Hyde, 6 November 1936, EPFL.

p. 386. "At the same": HLM, *A&E*, pp. xviii, 386.

"As important as": HLM, "*Heathen Days*: Additions," p. 281; HLM to Paul Patterson, 3 August 1935, EPFL; and HLM, "Thirty-Five Years," p. 414.

p. 387. "Thus his vitriolic": HLM correspondence with Albert Jay Nock, Roscoe Peacock, and Paul Palmer, 1930s, NYPL; HLM, note in Palmer correspondence, 12 June 1946, NYPL; and HLM to E. L. Ingelson, 22 October 1935, NYPL.

"At the same": HLM to C. R. Bradish, 13 August 1940, NYPL; HLM, "The End of an Era," *BES*, 14 September 1931, and "The Communists," *BES*, 31 December 1931; and HLM, "A&E," p. 737.

"In the 1920s": HLM, undated note in HLM–Van Wyck Brooks correspondence, NYPL; HLM to James T. Farrell, 30 May 1941, NYPL; Edmund Wilson, "Brokers and Pioneers," *The New Republic*, 23 March 1932, pp. 142, 144; HLM to Harold Ross, 26 November 1943, NYPL; HLM–Michael Gold correspondence, 1930s and 1940s, NYPL; HLM to Ben Abramson, 25 June 1937, NYPL; and HLM to Frank Pease, 23 June 1937, NYPL.

p. 388. "Of all the": Emma Goldman to HLM, 9 January 1930, NYPL; HLM to Harry E. Hull of U.S. Department of Labor, 27 March and 20 April 1930, NYPL; HLM to O. R. Luhring, 11 March 1930, NYPL; Luhring to HLM, 24 April 1930, NYPL; and Millie Dessen to HLM, 8 April 1940, NYPL.

"He maintained friendly": HLM–Jack Conroy correspondence, 1930s, NYPL; HLM, note of 16 March 1946 in HLM–John Dos Passos correspondence, NYPL; HLM to EB, 5 October 1937, NYPL; HLM to Mark Watson, 12 June 1939, EPFL; and HLM to David W. Ryder, 16 June 1939, NYPL.

"The only novelist": HLM–James T. Farrell correspondence, 1930s, NYPL; HLM to J. H. Gipson, 26 September 1938, NYPL; HLM to Jean Balch, 27 August 1935, EPFL; and Farrell, "Notes Addressed to a Man Among the Angels," *Menckeniana*, Summer 1966, pp. 1–2.

p. 389. "Among the other": HLM–Henry Miller correspondence, mid- and late 1930s, NYPL; HLM to Hamilton Owens, 26 December 1935, EPFL; and HLM to Sherwood Anderson, 5 May 1933, NYPL.

"Although he rejected": HLM to Lionel White, 1 November 1934, NYPL; HLM to Miriam Gallagher, 29 November 1937, NYPL; HLM to Irita Van

Doren, 23 November 1932, NYPL; FSF to HLM, 29 April 1935, NYPL; and HLM to FSF, 23 May 1935, NYPL. In 1932 Mencken volunteered to review Hemingway's *Death in the Afternoon* for *The Nation*, but Henry Hazlitt turned him down because he planned to review it himself (HH to HLM, 20 December 1932, NYPL).

p. 390.   "on one occasion": FSF to HLM, [1935?], NYPL.

"With Wolfe in": HLM to Edward Stone, 26 September 1938, UVa; HLM to Madeleine Boyd, 29 September 1937, NYPL; HLM to Emily Clark, 1 April 1936, NYPL; Clark to HLM, 17 March and 12 December 1937, NYPL; AAK to HLM, 20 July 1934, EPFL; HLM to Aline Bernstein, 26 July 1934, NYPL; and BK to HLM, 24 November 1934, EPFL.

p. 391.   "At one point": SM, *The Constant Circle*, pp. 183–84; HLM to J. B. Dudek, 20 July 1939, NYPL; HLM to James Stevens, 14 September [1938], NYPL; HLM to Perry Molstad, 21 October 1938, NYPL; and HLM to Fred Highland, 7 May 1936, NYPL. See also David Donald, *Look Homeward: A Life of Thomas Wolfe* (Little, Brown, 1987), pp. 78–79, 90, 92.

"He had, at": HLM to William Faulkner, 7 November 1930, NYPL; and Charles Angoff, *H. L. Mencken*, p. 107.

p. 392.   "In fact, when": HLM, *Diary*, 27 November and 16 December 1931, pp. 40–42; Harrison Smith to HLM, 9 December 1931, NYPL; and HLM to PG, 23 November [1931], EPFL.

"Although he had": HLM, quoted in Miles H. Wolff, "America Still in Literary Doldrums," *BS* (AP), 8 September 1933; HLM to Edgar Kemler, 24 October 1946, EPFL; and HLM to Mrs. J. H. Gipson, 26 September 1938, NYPL.

"That would account": HLM to Lionel White, 6 November 1934, NYPL; HLM, *A&E*, p. 61; HLM to ELM, 1 October 1937, NYPL; and HLM, *Diary*, 2 February 1933, p. 55. In 1939 Eugene Lyons, who had become editor of *The American Mercury*, asked Mencken to review Joyce's *Finnegans Wake*, and Mencken—who would have been altogether unsympathetic to what Joyce had attempted—replied that he did not have time to undertake the review (May 12, NYPL). As for Eliot: in the miscellaneous notes left at his death, Mencken included the poet among those "pinks" who later embraced religion (note, 1 October 1937, EPFL). In fact, Eliot never leaned to the left politically.

## Chapter 17:  Germany

p. 395.   "In the mid-1930s": HLM, "AN, 1925" (NYPL), p. 83; and HLM, "Thirty-Five Years," pp. 452–53.

"His involvement with": HLM, *Diary*, 20 August 1936 and 17 March 1937, pp. 94–97; HLM, "Diary," 25 June and 18 September 1937; HLM, "Thirty-Five Years," pp. 916–22; and HLM to William Feather, 1 October 1937, NYPL.

p. 396.   "But he relished": HLM to Hamilton Owens, John Owens, and others, especially HLM to Hamilton Owens, 22 August and 11 November 1933 and 19 January [1934], Sunpapers documents, EPFL; HLM to Mark Watson, 17 September [1930s?], EPFL; HLM to John Owens, 12 December [1930s?], EPFL; and HLM to BK, 4 March 1936, NYPL.

"He also threw": HLM, *Diary*, 28 July 1937, pp. 104–05; HLM, quoted in "All Baltimore Awaits Climax," *Brooklyn Citizen*, 4 December 1936; HLM,

"The Exile of Enzesfeld," *BES*, 21 December 1936; and HLM to Hamilton Owens, 2 September 1937, EPFL.

p. 397. "Mencken's most complete": HLM to Jean Balch, 11 February 1938, EPFL; HLM, "Thirty-Five Years," p. 1015; and author's interview with Philip Wagner. Concerning the Jamaica trip, HLM letters to MD and Benjamin de Casseres, January–February 1938, NYPL; HLM to Jean Balch and GM, January–February 1938, EPFL; and HLM to BH, 15 January 1938, UNC.

"Despite such stunts": Author's interview with Philip Wagner; HLM, "Thirty-Five Years," p. 1027; and HLM letters to John Owens, Rosalind Lohrfinck, JH, GM, and EB, Spring 1938, EPFL and NYPL.

p. 398. "He was sensitive": LC, SNC diary, miscellaneous notes [n.d.]; HLM to JH, 18 February 1937, NYPL; and LC, "Some Personal Memories of HLM," *Menckeniana*, Spring 1974, p. 7.

"Thus he was": HLM to Hamilton Owens, 18 May 1938, EPFL; HLM to BK, 18 May 1938, EPFL; HLM, "Thirty-Five Years," p. 1028; numerous other sources on HLM's health, 1936–38, largely in Mencken's illness file or medical notes, Union Memorial Hospital and Johns Hopkins Hospital medical records, EPFL; HLM to Jean Balch and Henry Hyde, EPFL; HLM to JH, BK, and Karl Bickel, NYPL; HLM to TD (PU); LC, SNC diary; and author's interviews with Drs. Benjamin M. Baker, Philip Wagley, Eric W. Jensen, and John Boswell.

p. 399. " 'I am very' ": HLM to SM, 21 April 1938, UA.

"For all his": HLM to George A. Kubler, 14 May 1936, NYPL; HLM to Oscar Levy, 3 June 1938, NYPL; HLM to Hamilton Owens, 16 May 1938, EPFL; HLM to Stanton Leeds, 24 June 1938, NYPL; and HLM, "Thirty-Five Years," p. 1036.

"Always writing in": HLM–Anna Mencke correspondence, 1930s, EPFL; and HLM to D. Mencke, 9 October 1937, EPFL.

p. 400. "From a Major": Major Hermann Mencke to HLM, 26 September and 6 October 1937, EPFL; and Colonel Carl Mencke to HLM, 6 April 1938, EPFL.

"Partly through Tante": HLM to Anna Mencke, 11 January 1935, EPFL; and HLM correspondence with Eric Langemann, 1932–55, with Walter Langemann, 1946–55, with Sue Ashley, 1937–52 (especially 13 October 1937), and with Clarissa Flugel, 1933–39, all EPFL.

"Extended family, then": HLM to Frederick P. Keppel, 25 June 1930, EPFL; HLM to Arred Zoravitch, 16 September 1933, EPFL; HLM to Anna Mencke, 2 November 1933, EPFL.

p. 401. "At Sara's death": HLM to Eric Langemann, 11 June 1935, EPFL; HLM to Anna Mencke, 2 December 1932 and 27 July 1935, EPFL.

"He heard from": HLM correspondence, 1930s, with Willy Sohler, Klaus Mann, Elisabeth Forster-Nietzsche, Heinrich Spies, Walter von Molo, Stephen von Studonitz, and Friedrich Freska, all NYPL, and Camillo von Klenze, EPFL.

"Very few of": Ferdinand Hansen to HLM, 24 May 1933, NYPL; George Sylvester Viereck to HLM, 25 October 1933, NYPL; HLM to Viereck, 23 October 1933, NYPL; and Henry Nixdorf to HLM, 26 June 1935, GC.

"Mencken had no": Edwin C. White to *BES*, 24 July 1933, HLM clippings scrapbook; and HLM, "Some Objections to Monarchy," *BES*, 8 May 1933.

"On a couple": David Kemper to HLM, [June 1933], and HLM to Kemper, 7 July [1933], in private collection of Arthur J. Gutman; William J. Robinson to HLM, 30 August and 6 September 1933, NYPL; and HLM to Robinson, 1 and 9 September 1933, NYPL.

p. 402. "In any case": Edgar Kemler, *The Irreverent Mr. Mencken*, p. 280; and GM to AM, 20 October 1964, EPFL.

"If Mencken had": HLM to George A. Kubler, 10 November 1934, NYPL; HLM to Benjamin de Casseres, 25 July 1935, NYPL; HLM to F. J. Zeisburg, 28 November 1933, NYPL; HLM to TD, 15 January [1935], UP, *D–M Letters*, II, p. 574; HLM to PG, 26 April 1933, NYPL; HLM to R. D. Stevens, 9 August 1935, NYPL; HLM to David Kemper, 7 July [1933], Gutman collection; HLM to Elisabeth Forster-Nietzsche, 3 July 1933, NYPL; HLM to Edwin Emerson, 12 May 1933, NYPL; HLM to Gladys Baker, 15 August 1935, NYPL; HLM to Emanuel Haldeman-Julius, 24 June 1941, NYPL; HLM, "Thirty-Five Years," p. 673; and LC, SNC diary, 7 and 14 July 1934.

p. 403. "It was not": HLM to Edwin Emerson, 5 June 1933, NYPL; HLM to George Sylvester Viereck, 23 October 1933, NYPL; HLM to David Kemper, 7 July 1933, Gutman collection; HLM to A. J. Lynch, 27 July 1933, NYPL; and William Manchester, "The Diary of H. L. Mencken," *The New York Times Book Review*, 4 February 1990, p. 33.

"He found German": HLM to Gertrude Urban, 16 December 1935, NYPL; HLM to Paul Patterson, 23 November 1935, in "Thirty-Five Years," p. 809; HLM to George A. Kubler, 15 November 1934, NYPL; HLM to AAK, 23 November 1927, NYPL; and HLM to Edwin Emerson, 11 May and 5 June 1933, NYPL.

" 'the Hitler outfit' ": HLM to Edwin Emerson, 10 June 1933, NYPL.

"There had been": HLM, quoted in "Nazis Won't Burn Books," *Pittsburgh Sun-Telegraph*, 17 June 1933; HLM to Richard J. Beamish, 7 July 1934, NYPL; and HLM, "Thirty-Five Years," p. 675.

p. 404. "And there was": HLM, "Thirty-Five Years," p. 675; and HLM to Gladys Baker, 15 August 1935, NYPL.

"Even if he": HLM to Henry Nixdorf, 15 August 1932, NYPL; HLM to Edwin Emerson, 5 June 1933, NYPL; HLM to Anna Mencke, 13 April 1933, EPFL; HLM, "Thirty-Five Years," p. 673; HLM to PG, 6 April 1933, NYPL; and HLM to Abraham Flexner, 21 November 1935, NYPL.

"Even in his": HLM to Ferdinand Hansen, 24 May 1933 and 10 March 1936, NYPL; HLM to Anna Mencke, 13 April 1933, EPFL; HLM to Edwin Emerson, 10 June 1933, NYPL; and HLM to Kal F. Geiser, 7 January 1937, EPFL.

p. 405. "In his discussion": HLM, *T on Gods*, pp. 345–46.

p. 406. "In 1930 they": Meyer Weisgel, "Jews Down on Mencken," *Brooklyn Eagle*, 20 April 1930.

"Those same Jews": Simon E. Sobeloff to Armand Kemper, 19 December 1969, HLM correspondence file, EPFL; HLM to TD, 6 October [1936], UP, *D–M Letters*, II, p. 612; and HLM to Benjamin de Casseres, 30 July and 28 October [1936], NYPL.

p. 407. "Mencken himself was": HLM to N. W. Rogers, 26 November 1937, NYPL; HLM to Eric Goldman, 13 September 1934, NYPL; HLM to ELM, 15 October 1932 and 18 July 1933, NYPL.

"Such an awareness": HLM, *Diary*, 25 January 1935 and 19 June 1937, pp. 87, 101; HLM to B. H. Foreman, 28 June 1939, NYPL; and HLM to Benjamin de Casseres, 25 July 1935, NYPL.

"In his letters": HLM to Hamilton Owens, 24 July 1931, EPFL; HLM to William E. Moon, 16 October 1936, EPFL; HLM, "Why Not Tell the

Truth?" *BES*, 29 November 1922; and HLM, "The Invisible Empire," *BES*, December 1922.

p. 408. "Thus, it was": HLM to H. Ewald Netzer, 6 January 1936, NYPL; Emma Goldman to HLM, 3 March 1932, NYPL; Oscar Levy to HLM, 1932–40, *passim*, NYPL; William J. Robinson to HLM, 25 September 1933, NYPL; HLM to TD, 15 January 1935, UP, *D–M Letters*, II, p. 574; and HLM to S. Miles Bouton, 12 December 1933, EPFL.

"Such was indeed": AAK to Betty Adler, 30 March 1964, EPFL; AAK to Alan Wycherly, 1 April 1963, "About Mencken" file, EPFL; HLM, *A&E*, p. 247; author's interview with Lawrence Spivak; HLM, "Diary," 25 June 1937 and 12 August 1938; HLM to J. Edwin Murphy, 13 and 24 January and 1 and 8 February 1939, EPFL; HLM to SM, 4 November 1927, UA; HLM to George A. Kubler, 10 November 1934, NYPL; HLM to Benjamin de Casseres, 3 August 1935, NYPL; HLM to George Sylvester Viereck, 23 October 1933, NYPL; HLM to Anna Mencke, 13 April 1935, EPFL.

p. 409. "His attitude toward": HLM to PG, 10 June 1933, NYPL; HLM, "A&E," p. 522; HLM to BK, 28 November 1941, NYPL; author's interview with Ruth Goodman Goetz; HLM, introduction to scrapbook "Letters to Philip Goodman," EPFL; and HLM, "Thirty-Five Years," p. 678.

"What had happened": HLM to James Cain, 19 August 1940, NYPL; HLM–PG correspondence, 1932–33, EPFL, especially HLM to PG, 3 February and 22 May [1933], and PG to HLM, 2 and 4 June 1933, NYPL.

p. 410. "Mencken, then, had": HLM to PG, 13 May 1933, NYPL.

"When Goodman had": HLM to PG, 7 June 1933, NYPL; and HLM to SL, 7 June 1933, NYPL.

"Not long after": HLM, miscellaneous notes, 1941, in scrapbook A122, EPFL; HLM, *A&E*, p. 205; HLM, "Thirty-Five Years," p. 678; and HLM to SL, 28 May 1936, NYPL.

p. 411. "How could he": HLM to Tom R. Hutter, 20 August 1937, NYPL; and HLM to Anna Mencke, 13 April 1935, EPFL.

"The answers, as": SH to HLM, October–December 1927, GC; *M&S*, pp. 301–66; GM to HLM and AM, 1930s, 1940s, and (to AM) 10 November 1955, EPFL; HLM, "Thirty-Five Years," p. 677; and Ronald Steel, "Living with Walter Lippmann," in *Extraordinary Lives: The Art and Craft of American Biography*, ed. William Zinsser (American Heritage, 1986), p. 144.

p. 412. "At various points": HLM to A. G. Keller, 9 October 1938, NYPL: and HLM, "AN, 1941–."

"But of all": HLM correspondence with Isaac Goldberg (especially 7 November 1935) and Benjamin de Casseres, 1930s, NYPL; LC, SNC diary, 1935–48, *passim;* HLM, "Diary," 24 November 1937; and HLM to John Owens, 12 July 1938, EPFL.

p. 413. "Finally, in the": HLM, "Thirty-Five Years," p. 1117.

"Certainly the whole": HLM, "A&E," p. 662; HLM to J. Fred Essary, 24 June 1933, EPFL; HLM to Paul Patterson, 12 November [1935], EPFL; HLM, "Diary," 10 August 1933; and Ezra Pound to HLM, 27 and 31 October [1939?], NYPL.

"It was not": HLM to Tom R. Hutter, 20 August 1937, NYPL; and Benjamin de Casseres to HLM, 7 October 1934, NYPL.

p. 414. " 'Better than the' ": HLM, "Thirty-Five Years," p. 677.

"It was with": HLM to SM, 6 June 1938, UA; HLM to Theodore Findhal, 2 June

1938, NYPL; HLM to Friedrich Schönemann, 24 May 1938, NYPL; HLM
to BH, 26 May 1938, UNC; and HLM to GM, 9 June 1938, EPFL.

p. 415. "As it turned": HLM to GM, 17, 25, and 30 June 1938, EPFL; HLM to Jean
Balch, 17 June 1938, EPFL; HLM to Hamilton Owens, 17 June [1938],
EPFL; HLM to Sue Ashley, 28 July 1938, EPFL; and HLM, "Thirty-Five
Years," pp. 1044–45.

"A few days": HLM, "Thirty-Five Years," pp. 1040–41; and HLM to GM, 5
July 1938, EPFL. In his "Thirty-Five Years," written in the early 1940s,
Mencken reports that he visited Tannenberg and East Prussia *before* Leip-
zig and Laas. His letters to Gertrude prove that the order was reversed.

"In between his": HLM, "Thirty-Five Years," pp. 1039–45.

p. 416. "Shortly after he": HLM to GM, 25 June [1938], EPFL; HLM, "Thirty-Five
Years," p. 1046; HLM to Max Brödel, 1 July 1938, NYPL; HLM to BK, 7
July 1938, NYPL; and HLM to Paul Patterson, 7 July 1938, EPFL.

"For the most": HLM to GM, 30 June 1938, EPFL; HLM to Clarissa Flugel,
27 July 1938, EPFL; HLM to MD, 1 July [1938], NYPL; and HLM to Paul
Patterson, 7 July 1938, EPFL.

"Even in his": HLM, "Thirty-Five Years," p. 1046.

p. 417. "Although he insisted": HLM to Paul Patterson, 7 July 1938, EPFL; and HLM,
"Thirty-Five Years," pp. 1047–48.

"Such matters were": HLM, "Thirty-Five Years," pp. 1049–51; and HLM to
GM, 24 July 1938, EPFL.

p. 418. "The 1938 trip": HLM to Daniel Henry, 8 August 1938, EPFL; HLM to Harry
Maule, 27 July 1938, NYPL; HLM to DH, 18 August 1938, NYPL; HLM
to Henry Hyde, 1 August 1938, EPFL; HLM to J. Edwin Murphy, 3 August
1938, EPFL; and LC, SNC diary, 13 November 1938.

"It is tempting": Thomas Wolfe, *You Can't Go Home Again* (Harper and
Brothers, 1940), pp. 666, 622.

p. 419. "But to Wolfe": Wolfe, *You Can't Go Home Again*, pp. 633, 634.

"There would be": Wolfe, "I Have a Thing to Tell You," *The New Republic*,
10, 17, and 24 March 1937, pp. 132–36, 159–64, 202–07; HLM, "Thirty-
Five Years," p. 1051; and LC, SNC diary, 13 November 1938.

"Or, as Mencken": "H. L. Mencken Returns from European Trip," *BS*, 26 July
[1938].

## Chapter 18: Looking Two Ways

p. 420. "If Mencken chose": HLM to Grover Hall, 22 August 1938, NYPL; HLM,
"Free Lance," *BES*, 3 October 1914 and 19 April 1915; and HLM, miscellaneous notes in envelope A100.8, EPFL.

"As another conflict": HLM to Oscar Levy, 16 December 1933, NYPL; "U.S.
a Sucker for Next War, Says Mencken," *Washington Herald*, 18 January
1937; HLM to Maclean Patterson, 26 October 1933, EPFL; and HLM,
"Thirty-Five Years," pp. 1039–40.

p. 421. "In particular, information": HLM, "Thirty-Five Years," pp. 352–53, 1037.

"Mencken knew all": HLM, letters of August–October 1938 to F. L. Tietsch,
George A. Kubler, and Grover Hall, NYPL, and Anne Froehlich, EPFL;
HLM, "There'll Be No War, Mencken Asserts . . . ," *The Washington Post*,
21 April 1939; HLM, "Thirty-Five Years," pp. 1037, 353; and HLM to
Benjamin de Casseres, 4 October 1938, NYPL. However, to at least one

friend, J. B. Dudek, HLM wrote on August 5 that he was convinced another war was "almost certain" (NYPL).

"In many of ": HLM to John Pentz, 12 May 1939, EPFL; HLM to Ezra Pound, 20 November 1939, NYPL; HLM to Otto Julius Merkel, 26 August and 7 November 1938 and 27 December 1939, NYPL; HLM to Albert T. Lynch, 11 January 1934, EPFL; and HLM to Lorraine Yerkes, 19 September 1938, NYPL.

"By 1938 he": HLM to Theodore Findhal, 2 June 1938, NYPL; HLM to H. W. Seaman, 18 August 1938, NYPL; HLM to Benjamin de Casseres, 14 April 1939, NYPL; HLM to Miles Bouton, 5 August 1938, NYPL; HLM to Raymond Pearl, 25 August 1939, NYPL; and HLM to ELM, 25 August 1939, NYPL.

p. 422. "Mencken had sent": HLM to Oscar Levy, 10 December 1935 and 10 July and 8 August 1936, NYPL; Levy to HLM, 12 January and 25 August 1936 and 20 January 1939, NYPL; and HLM to Harry Rickel, 9 September [1938], NYPL.

"In particular, he": HLM to Albert M. Doyle, 18 April 1941, NYPL; HLM–Dora Sophie Kellner correspondence, 1939–41, *passim*, NYPL; HLM to C. R. Bradish, 23 October 1930, NYPL; HLM–Anna Kellner correspondence, 1939, *passim*, NYPL.

p. 423. "When Hannah Arnold": HLM–Paula Arnold correspondence, 1938–43, *passim*, NYPL; HLM–Hannah Arnold correspondence, 1939–43, *passim*, NYPL; HLM to H. K. Travers of U.S. State Department, 10 August 1942, Arnold correspondence, NYPL; HLM, note of 10 March 1943, Arnold correspondence, NYPL; and HLM, "Diary," 26 August 1941.

"Again, one might": HLM to J. Edwin Murphy, 6, 13, and 24 January and 1 and 8 February 1939, EPFL; HLM to Phil Ward, 1 May 1939, EPFL; HLM to Henry Hyde, 2 November 1938, EPFL; and Dora Sophie Kellner [Morser] to HLM, 12 September 1941, NYPL.

"Whatever the case": HLM, "Help for the Jews," *BES*, 27 November 1938; and HLM to Oscar Levy, 5 December 1938, NYPL.

p. 424. "The next month": HLM, "The Problem of the Refugee," *BES*, 1 January 1939; HLM, "Diary," 26 October 1938; HLM to J. Edwin Murphy, 1 February 1939, EPFL; HLM to Henry Hyde, 2 November 1938, EPFL; and HLM, "Thirty-Five Years," p. 1199.

"Angoff devoted little": Charles Angoff, "Mencken Twilight: Another Forgotten Man," *North American Review*, Winter 1938–39, pp. 226, 228.

p. 425. "He had done": HLM to Joseph Wood Krutch, 2 March 1935, NYPL; HLM to Henry Hazlitt, 30 September [1933], NYPL; HLM–PG correspondence, 1930–31, *passim*, EPFL; HLM–AAK correspondence, 1930–35, *passim*, especially 24 March [1935], NYPL; and HLM, *Diary*, 29 January 1935, pp. 90–92.

"Angoff was 'a' ": HLM to Andrew Molles, 26 January 1939, NYPL; HLM to J. B. Dudek, 6 February 1939, NYPL; HLM to Benjamin Stern, 28 September 1939, EPFL.

"In one particular": Dr. Benjamin M. Baker, medical report, May 1939, HLM illness file, EPFL; HLM to SM, 13 January 1939, UA; HLM to JH, [April 1939], NYPL; HLM to Oscar Levy, 16 September and 12 October 1938, EPFL; and other HLM letters on his health to J. Edwin Murphy, BH, TD, JH, and SM, 1938–Winter 1939, EPFL, UNC, UP, NYPL, and UA.

p. 426. "He could not": HLM, "Thirty-Five Years," pp. 1157–58; HLM, *Diary*, 9 June

1940, pp. 144–45; and Dr. Benjamin M. Baker, medical report, HLM illness file.

"He remained in": HLM to JH, 26 July 1939, NYPL; HLM to J. Edwin Murphy, 26 July 1939, EPFL; and HLM to GM, 26 July 1939, EPFL.

"Shortly after he": HLM to GM, 21 August 1939, EPFL; HLM to Philip Wagner, 21 August 1939, EPFL; HLM to George Radcliffe, 22 August 1939, EPFL; HLM to Oscar Levy, 23 August 1939, NYPL; and HLM, *Diary*, 9 June 1940 and 6 August 1945, pp. 145, 377.

p. 427.   "Fearing, then, that": HLM, *Diary*, 6 August 1945, p. 377; and Henry Miller to HLM, 29 December 1936, NYPL.

"He had always": HLM, "References to H. L. Mencken in Books, 1930–1936," EPFL; HLM to Herbert Asbury, 11 October 1937, NYPL; and HLM, "Thirty-Five Years," p. 1000.

"In particular, he": HLM to Mary Mencken, 26 July 1937, EPFL; HLM to GM, 28 July and 4 August 1937, EPFL; and HLM, *Diary*, 15 April 1939, pp. 119–20.

p. 428.   "The subject, in": HLM–PG correspondence, 1920s, *passim*, EPFL.

"In an autobiographical": HLM, autobiographical sketch in *Portraits and Self-Portraits*, ed. Georges Schreiber (Houghton-Mifflin, 1936), p. 107; HLM to Benjamin de Casseres, 23 and 26 February 1937, NYPL; and HLM to Wheeler Sammons, 23 February 1937, NYPL.

"Although it was": HLM to Jim Tully, 3 April 1939, NYPL; HLM to SM, 15 January 1938, UA: and HLM to Harrison H. Schaff, 5 February 1941, NYPL.

"Mark Twain, indeed": HLM to Gladys Baker, 13 February 1936; HLM, *HD*, p. vii; HLM, *Heathen Days*, p. ix; and Mark Twain, "Notice," *The Adventures of Huckleberry Finn* (1884; reprint, Holt, Rinehart, 1948), p. xix.

p. 429.   "In fact, he": HLM to Harley Croessmann, 2 March 1935, NYPL.

"Even so, because": HLM, *Diary*, 18 September 1939, pp. 127–28; HLM, "Diary," 16 September 1939; HLM to MD, 1 March 1939, NYPL; and HLM–BH correspondence, 1939, especially 16 June 1939, UNC.

"He was happy": HLM, *HD*, pp. v, viii, ix; and HLM, "*HD:* Additions," p. 313.

p. 430.   "He devoted one": HLM, *HD*, pp. 247–62, 22, 29, 31, 91, 93, 282, 55, 157, 160, 167.

"If the reception": HLM, "Diary," 13 May 1940; HLM to BH, 8 January 1941, UNC; and HLM, *Heathen Days*, pp. vi–viii.

p. 431.   "The rosy-cheeked young": HLM, *NPD*, pp. 229–30, 235.

"What Mencken captured": HLM, *NPD*, pp. 178, v, vi.

p. 432.   "Mencken viewed the": HLM, *Diary*, 11 July and 22 August 1941, pp. 155, 157–58; and reviews in HLM clippings scrapbook, Autumn 1941.

"The familiar essays": Gerald W. Johnson, introduction to William Manchester, *Disturber of the Peace* (1950 ed.), p. xiii.

"Among other things": HLM, "*HD:* Additions," pp. 7, 11, 19; HLM, "*NPD:* Additions," pp. 70, 71; and HLM, "Diary," 30 August 1945.

p. 433.   " 'I often wonder' ": HLM, "*HD:* Additions," pp. 19, 307; HLM, *HD*, p. 309; and HLM to Mary Almroth Hellwig, 12 February 1940, EPFL.

p. 434.   " 'We are going' ": HLM to Friedrich Schönemann, 1 August and 13 November 1939, NYPL.

"At the beginning": HLM to Ezra Pound, 13 November, 4 October, and 13 December 1939, NYPL.

"He did not": HLM to GM, 11 and 29 September 1939, EPFL; HLM to Gladys

Baker, 11 September 1939, NYPL; HLM to BH, 11 September 1939, UNC; and HLM to J. B. Dudek, 6 September 1939, NYPL.

"With the beginning": HLM to MD, 8 September 1939, NYPL; HLM to David W. Ryder, 8 September 1939, NYPL; HLM to J. B. Dudek, 27 September 1939, NYPL; HLM to James Cannon, 3 November 1939; and HLM to Heinrich Spies, 29 September 1939, NYPL.

p. 435. "As the British": HLM to Theodore Findhal, 3 January 1940, NYPL; HLM to Lillian Gish, 13 March 1940, NYPL; HLM to James T. Farrell, 28 March and 1 April 1941, NYPL; and HLM to George Seibel, 18 April 1941, NYPL.

"In the years": HLM to MD, 8 September 1939, NYPL; HLM to A. G. Keller, 12 April 1940, NYPL.

p. 436. "From the beginning": HLM to K. O. Bertling, 30 October 1939, EPFL; HLM to Ellen Glasgow, 24 July 1940, NYPL; HLM, "Diary," 10 January 1940; HLM, "Thirty-Five Years," pp. 1229–31, 1244–55; HLM, "Diary," 24 May 1939; HLM to BH, 16 September 1940, UNC; HLM to ELM, 29 March 1940, NYPL; HLM to Ellen Glasgow, 24 July 1940, NYPL; and HLM to Lillian Gish, 5 September 1940, NYPL.

"If, in 1940": HLM, "Thirty-Five Years," p. 1008; HLM, Diary, 6 October 1939 and 13 November 1940, pp. 130–31, 149–51.

"In January 1941": HLM, "Thirty-Five Years," pp. 1279–80, 1283; and HLM, "Progress of the Great Crusade," BS, 2 February 1941.

p. 437. "The [Sunpapers] brethren": HLM to Lillian Gish, 20 January 1941, NYPL.

"As he had": Lawrence Spivak to HLM, 2 May 1940, NYPL; HLM to Spivak, 24 May 1940, NYPL; HLM, "Thirty-Five Years," pp. 1299–1304; HLM to Paul Palmer, 18 September 1941, NYPL; HLM, Diary, 17 July and 18 September 1941, pp. 155–56, 160–62; HLM, "Diary," 24 November 1941; and HLM, note of 17 June 1941 in Sunpapers documents, EPFL.

"Not only had": HLM to A. H. McDannald, 20 November 1940 and 27 October 1941, NYPL; HLM to DH, [1940], NYPL; HLM, "Thirty-Five Years," p. 368; HLM to Lily Goodman, 7 August 1940, NYPL; HLM to Daniel Henry, 29 October 1941, EPFL; and HLM, Diary, 29 October 1941, pp. 165–69. Mencken had received two notes from Goodman in June 1935 after Sara's death, but that was the extent of their correspondence.

p. 438. "His old newspaper"; HLM, Diary, 14 March 1942, pp. 199–201; HLM, "Diary," 6 and 30 December 1941; Pauline Mencken to HLM, 28 November and 16 December 1939 and 6, 10, and 14 May 1940, EPFL; and HLM to AAK, 16 October 1940, NYPL.

"Death, however, seemed": HLM, Diary, 22 October and 8 November 1941, pp. 164–654, 171–73; HLM to GM, 6 October 1938, EPFL; and Mary A. Hellwig to HLM, 28 February, 15 March, and 1 April 1940, EPFL.

"When Mencken considered": HLM to JH, 23 October 1940 and 29 April 1941, NYPL; HLM, Diary, 1941–42, passim; HLM, "Thirty-Five Years," pp. 1160, 1299–1300; Johns Hopkins Hospital admissions record, 9–11 April 1941, HLM illness file, EPFL; and HLM to MD, GM, BK, and Paul Patterson, 1941, passim, NYPL and EPFL.

p. 439. "It was his": HLM, "Diary," 1940–41, passim; HLM to James T. Farrell, 30 May 1941, NYPL; HLM to George Debnam, 9 December 1940, EPFL; HLM to GM, 5 September 1940, EPFL; and HLM to Lillian Gish, 3 April 1941, NYPL.

"Even those areas": HLM to GM, 4 October 1939 and Spring 1941, passim, EPFL; HLM to W. C. Abhau, 20 May 1941, EPFL; CM to HLM, 15 May and 8 June 1941, EPFL; HLM to BH, 27 June 1939, UNC; HLM to J. B.

Dudek, 30 May 1941, NYPL. Virginia Mencken had originally scheduled the wedding for May 31, the anniversary of Sara's death, but Mencken had persuaded her to change the date.

"He found little": HLM, *Diary*, 16 October and 17 November 1941, pp. 162–63, 174–75; HLM, "Diary," 18 July and 21 October 1941; HLM to Jim Tully, 31 January 1941, NYPL; SM to HLM, [1940] and 5 September 1940, UA; HLM to Elizabeth Greene, 3 August 1940, NYPL; HLM to Reginald Baldwin, 4 and 14 September 1940, NYPL.

p. 440. "He was glad": HLM to Jim Tully, 31 January 1941, NYPL; HLM to N. W. Rogers, 31 January 1940, NYPL; HLM, *Diary*, 31 May 1940, pp. 139–40.

"At the conclusion": HLM, *Diary*, 31 May 1940, p. 143.

"Such was the": HLM to Benjamin de Casseres, 19 and 23 December 1940, NYPL; HLM to Julius Hofmann, 27 December 1940, EPFL; HLM to Cal Tinney, 5 February 1941, NYPL; HLM to MD, [1941], NYPL; and HLM to SL, 17 March 1941, NYPL.

p. 441. "When news came": HLM, "Diary," 6 and 30 December 1941; HLM, *Diary*, 29 December 1941, pp. 177–78; and HLM to Henry Hyde, 23 December 1941, EPFL.

## Chapter 19: Wartime

p. 442. "Mencken was not": HLM, "Thirty-Five Years," p. 1201; HLM, "Berlin Diary" (ms.), 2 March 1917, scrapbook A32, EPFL; and HLM, review of Hector C. Bywater, *The Great Pacific War*, quoted in Bernard De Voto, "The Easy Chair," *Harper's*, September 1943, p. 338. In at least one letter Mencken had retreated from his earlier prediction. The chance of a war between Japan and the United States, he wrote Leland Lovette in 1935, seemed to him "to be rather remote" (4 March 1935, NYPL).

"He himself affected": Author's interviews with Gwinn Owens and Dr. Benjamin M. Baker; HLM to GM, 12 June 1942, EPFL; and letter from unidentified citizen to Justice Department, as well as FBI notes and correspondence, 1940–41, in FBI file 61-1286.

p. 443. "Mencken's everyday activities": Edgar Kemler, *The Irreverent Mr. Mencken*, p. 285; HLM, "Diary," 1942, *passim*, especially 5 February 1942; and "Diary," 16 October 1943.

"All things considered": HLM to TD, 11 April 1942, UP, *D–M Letters*, II, p. 673; HLM, *Diary* and "Diary," Spring–Summer 1942, *passim*; HLM to GM, 29 April and 13 and 23 May 1942, EPFL; HLM to A. G. Keller, 23 October 1942, NYPL; and other letters to TD, JH, SM, and Gustav Strube, Spring and Summer 1942, UP, UA, EPFL, and NYPL.

p. 444. "A life's work": Reviews, 1942, in HLM clippings scrapbook, EPFL.

"In 'A Roman' ": HLM, *Heathen Days*, pp. 143–44, 152, 6, 71, 96–106.

p. 445. "*Heathen Days* lacked": HLM, *Heathen Days*, p. vii; and HLM, *Diary*, 18 June, 10 September, and 8 October 1942 and 15 June 1943, pp. 208–09, 215, 217, 258; and HLM, "Diary," 17 May 1943.

"In his preface": HLM, "Thirty-Five Years," pp. 3, 4.

p. 446. "He felt, in": HLM, "Thirty-Five Years," pp. 1390, 1391–3.

"Much of his": HLM, *Diary*, 5 February and 1 June 1942, pp. 190–91, 205.

" 'My Life as' ": HLM, *Diary*, 7 November 1942 and 31 March 1943, pp. 224–44; and HLM, "Diary," 13 April 1944.

p. 447. "When he had": HLM to PG, 12 September 1932, NYPL; HLM to MD, 28

April 1948, NYPL; HLM to James T. Farrell, 17 August 1945, NYPL; HLM, *Diary*, 5 February 1942, p. 191; and HLM, *A&E*, p. xviii.

"Mencken's plan was": HLM, *Diary*, 7 November 1942 and 1 January 1943, pp. 224, 229–30.

p. 448.  "Although Mencken's 'Life' ": HLM, *Diary*, 1942–43, *passim*, pp. 179–291.

"Into the diary": HLM, *Diary*, 25 November 1938, 29 November 1939, and 10 February 1941, pp. 115, 131–33, 152–53; and HLM, "Diary," 1 November 1943 and 18 March 1945.

p. 449.  "Much of the": HLM, *Diary*, 10 September 1942 and 1 February and 31 March 1943, pp. 215–16, 237, 243–44; and HLM, "Diary," 1 June and 31 December 1942 and 9 and 24 January 1943.

"He had also": HLM, *Diary*, 31 March 1943, p. 243; and HLM, "Diary," 31 December 1942 and 3 May and 25 October 1943.

"It was hardly": HLM to MD, 9 December 1936; and HLM, *Diary*, 27 July 1941, p. 157.

p. 450.  "As the movement": HLM, *Diary* and "Diary," 1944–45, *passim*; and HLM to ELM, 21 June 1943, NYPL.

p. 451.  "He was not": HLM, *Diary*, 30 April 1945, pp. 361–62; and HLM, "Diary," 4 July 1942.

p. 452.  "His closest friend": HLM, *Diary*, 30 July 1942, 29 April 1943, and 24 October 1945, pp. 209–10, 249–51, 388; and HLM, "Diary," 1 July 1941, 7 January and 5 September 1942, and 12 May and 30 June 1943.

"If Mencken's remarks": HLM to Emily Clark, quoted in Clark, *Innocence Abroad* (Alfred A. Knopf, 1931), p. 121; AM, "Reminiscences," pp. 17–18; author's interview with Gerald W. Johnson, 26 February 1970; Johnson, "Reconsideration—H.L. Mencken," *Menckeniana*, Winter 1975, pp. 1–3; HLM, *Diary*, 31 December 1943, p. 291; and HLM, "Diary," 12 and 19 October 1943.

"What Johnson had": HLM, *Diary*, 30 July and 12 October 1942 and 12 July and 31 December 1943, pp. 211, 219, 264, 291; and HLM, "Diary," 25 February 1942.

p. 453.  "Further, as a": HLM, "Diary," 27 April, 10 June, 8 July (II), 3 August, and 20 December 1943.

"But his wartime": HLM to Lou Wylie, 26 April 1943, NYPL; HLM to MD, 20 September 1940, NYPL; HLM, *Diary*, 29 October 1943, p. 277; HLM, "Diary," 18 September 1944; and HLM to Harry Elmer Barnes, 15 March 1943, NYPL.

p. 454.  "He complained about": HLM, "Diary," 1 October 1943, 18 March and 26 May 1945; and HLM, "Thirty-Five Years," p. 117.

"It was clear": HLM–Oscar Levy correspondence, 1940–45, *passim*, especially HLM to Levy, 12 June 1942, NYPL; and HLM to ELM, 14 November 1941, NYPL.

p. 455.  "In the Sunpapers": HLM, stories on Eastern Shore, *BES*, 7 and 14 December 1931; HLM, "The Mummy Case," 23 September 1935; Associated Press story, 21 February 1931; and *New York Post*, 20 February 1935, all HLM clippings scrapbook, EPFL; HLM, "Diary," 15 February 1935; and HLM, "The Library," *AM*, May 1931, p. 125.

"One man who": HLM correspondence with George Schuyler, 1930s and 1940s, YU; HLM, *Diary*, 24 September 1945, pp. 382–83; HLM to *Pittsburgh Courier*, [January 1947], in HLM–Schuyler correspondence, YU; and HLM to Fulton Oursler, 17 April [1948], NYPL. Arnold Rampersad writes that

Mencken did not have black guests in his home ("Mencken, Race, and America," *Menckeniana*, Fall 1990, p. 7), but several Mencken letters suggest that he did (HLM to Schuyler, 23 October 1937 and 6 November 1939, NYPL; Schuyler to HLM, 23 April and 26 September 1937 NYPL; HLM to Raymond Pearl, 20 May 1939, NYPL; HLM to Hamilton Owens, 1 November 1939, EPFL; also, HLM, note of 14 October [1941?], in HLM–Schuyler correspondence; YU; and Owens to *Times Literary Supplement*, 20 July 1959).

p. 456.  "Far more revealing": HLM, *Diary*, 15 January and 23 September 1943 and 2 June 1948, pp. 234, 272–74, 451–52; and HLM, "Diary," 23 February and 6 August 1943.

"Such was indeed": HLM, *Diary*, 15 April and 1 May 1939, 8 June 1942, and 19 July 1944, pp. 120, 124–25, 207–8, 326; HLM, "Diary," 15 July 1943; HLM to Charles Crowell, 3 December 1943, NYPL; and HLM to ELM, 21 June 1943, NYPL.

p. 457.  "He was, even": HLM, *Diary*, 17 January 1943, pp. 235–36; and HLM, "Diary," 25 March, 8 April, and 10 May 1945.

p. 458.  "There is a": HLM, *Diary*, 30 January 1942 and 4 February, 8 April, and 12 July 1943, pp. 185, 238, 244–45, 265–66; and HLM, "Diary," 4 August 1943.

"After one funeral": HLM, *Diary*, 17 January 1943, p. 236; and HLM, "Diary," 10 March 1942.

p. 459.  "In a particularly": HLM, *Diary*, 27 December 1942, pp. 227–28.

" 'When she died' ": HLM, *Diary*, 27 August 1942, pp. 214–15.

p. 460.  "Such was a": HLM, *Diary*, 23 January and 1 June 1942 and 1 February 1943, pp. 183, 205, 237.

"He got about": HLM, *Diary* and "Diary," 1942–45, *passim*; and HLM–JH correspondence, 1943–45, NYPL.

"Although he insisted": HLM, *Diary* and "Diary," 1942–45, *passim*, especially 10 August and 1 November 1943; HLM to DH, 10 March 1942, NYPL; HLM to BK, 3 April 1940, EPFL; and HLM to Hamilton Owens, 7 May 1943, EPFL.

p. 461.  "Most often, in": HLM, *Diary* and "Diary," 1941–45, *passim*; and HLM–AAK correspondence, 1941–45 *passim*, NYPL and EPFL.

"In New York": HLM, *Diary*, 9 August 1943 and 13 April, 12 June, and 25 October 1944; HLM–ELM correspondence, 1941–45, *passim*, NYPL; HLM correspondence with Alice Elizabeth Davis and Ellen Masters, 1940–43, *passim*, NYPL.

"Of all the": HLM, *Diary*, 23 May 1939, pp. 125–26; HLM, "Diary," 17 December 1942 and 6 October, 1 November, and 20 December 1943; HLM, *A&E*, p. 210; HLM–GJN correspondence, 1941–45, *passim*, NYPL; and BK to HLM, 25 February 1941, EPFL.

p. 462.  "Mencken seemed to": HLM correspondence with Zoë Akins, Anita Loos, Lillian Gish, and Dorothy Gish, 1940–45, NYPL, especially Lillian Gish to HLM, 25 February and 27 March 1945; ELM to HLM, 24 April 1943, NYPL; and HLM, "Thirty-Five Years," p. 1244.

"Although he had": HLM–AP correspondence, 1939–46, *passim*, especially HLM to AP, 18 February and 15 October [1941], YU, and 16 June 1942, NYPL; and HLM to AP, [1940], YU.

p. 463.  " 'Isn't it pretty' ": Ernest Hemingway, *The Sun Also Rises* (Charles Scribner's Sons, 1926), p. 247; HLM to AP, summer 1944 and summer

1945, *passim*, especially 12 August 1944 and 24 September 1945, YU and NYPL; James Cain to HLM, 9 March 1944, and HLM to Cain, 25 July 1944, NYPL.

p. 464. "Despite these warm": HLM to Harry Elmer Barnes, 21 July 1942, NYPL; HLM to ELM, 1 April 1940, NYPL.

"Such was not": HLM, *Diary*, 14 March 1942, p. 202.

"After his interest": HLM–Ruth Alexander correspondence, 1938–39, *passim*, especially Alexander to HLM, 21 February, 24 April, 19 May, and 9 October 1938 and 6 January and 18 May 1939, NYPL; HLM–Doris Fleeson correspondence, 1942–44, *passim*, NYPL; HLM, "Thirty-Five Years," p. 1245; HLM to AAK, 21 November 1946; HLM, "Diary," 25 October 1944; HLM–Virginia Alvarez correspondence, 1940–43, especially Alvarez to HLM, 4 August 1942 and [September 1942], NYPL; HLM to Alvarez, 6 August 1942, NYPL; and HLM, "A&E," pp. 321–24.

p. 465. "Clare Leighton, for": HLM–Clare Leighton correspondence, 13, 23, and 28 February 1939 and Spring and Summer 1939, *passim*, NYPL; and Leighton, "Cynical Fantasy," *Menckeniana*, Fall 1970, pp. 1, 2.

"Much later Leighton": Clare Leighton to HLM, 27 March and 7 May [1939], NYPL; HLM to Leighton, 2 February, 25 March, 7 May, and 22 October [1939], NYPL.

"Leighton was a": Clare Leighton, "Cynical Fantasy," pp. 2, 3.

p. 466. "But he was": Clare Leighton, "Cynical Fantasy," pp. 2, 3; and Leighton to HLM, 7 July 1940, 21 October 1941, and 23 August 1942, NYPL.

"Feeling himself older": HLM to BH, 4 August 1937, UNC; and Virginia Alvarez to HLM, [1942?], NYPL.

"The most appealing": HLM–MD correspondence, 1940–45, *passim*, NYPL; HLM to DH, 22 January 1942, NYPL; HLM to JH, 27 August 1940, NYPL; JH to HLM, 14 December 1942 and 22 January 1943, NYPL; and HLM, "Diary," 6 January and 21 April 1943 and 1 July 1944.

"Often Marcella drove": HLM–MD correspondence, *ibid.*; HLM to ELM, 1942–43, *passim*, NYPL; Alfred du Pont to HLM, 21 January 1941, NYPL; and MD, "Heroic Days and Hours with Henry Mencken," *Menckeniana*, Summer 1966, pp. 5–7.

p. 467. "When they were": MD to HLM, 8 January 1943, 2 March 1945, and 29 May 1946, NYPL; and AM to Huntington Cairns, 24 April 1961, AM file, EPFL.

"Marcella was often": MD to HLM, 15 July 1943 and 24 February 1944 (copies), Bode collection, EPFL.

"As the war": HLM, *Diary*, 12 July 1943 and 2 November 1944, pp. 263, 334–35; HLM, "Diary," 31 October 1943; HLM to SL, 28 November 1944, NYPL; HLM to Henry Hyde, 25 May 1943, EPFL; HLM correspondence with P. E. Cleator, Cecilia M. Fox, and James Whitaker, 1941–45, NYPL; and HLM to Lillian Gish, 15 April 1944, NYPL. See *Letters from Baltimore: The Mencken–Cleator Correspondence*, ed. P. E. Cleator (Fairleigh Dickinson, 1982).

p. 468. "Many of his": HLM, *Diary* and "Diary," 1943–44, *passim*.

"He continued to": HLM, *Diary* and "Diary," February–August 1944, *passim*; HLM to Lillian Gish, 22 May 1944, NYPL; and HLM to SM, 14 November 1944, UA.

"After Roosevelt's reelection": Harry Green to HLM, 14 March 1945, NYPL; and HLM, *Diary*, 13 April 1945, p. 358.

p. 469. "In his diary": HLM, *Diary*, 13 and 15 April 1945, pp. 358–60.

"In the weeks": HLM, *Diary*, 13 April 1945, p. 358; HLM, "Diary," 4 and 9

May 1945; HLM to Dr. Arnold Rich, 3 August 1945, EPFL; and HLM to
A. G. Keller, 24 and 31 August 1945, NYPL.

"When the end": HLM, *Diary*, 15 August 1945, p. 379; HLM, "Diary," 11 and
23 August 1945; and HLM to Vivienne Torovsky, 21 August 1945, EPFL.

p. 470. "Mortality was very": HLM, *Diary*, 30 May 1945, pp. 367–68.

## Chapter 20: An Anchor Against Oblivion

p. 471. " 'I have delivered' ": HLM, *MR* notes, EPFL.

"Even at the": HLM, "Diary," 4 March 1945; and HLM to Harrison H. Schaff,
27 October 1945, NYPL.

"For Mencken himself": HLM, *Diary*, 1 April (II) and 21 November 1945, pp.
357, 393–95; HLM to Lillian Gish, 5 March 1945, NYPL.

p. 472. "What now principally": HLM to L. M. Birkhead, 5 June 1945, NYPL; HLM
to Zoë Akins, 21 August 1946, NYPL; HLM, *Diary*, 20 March 1945; and
HLM, "*MR*: Second Series," *Menckeniana*, Spring 1970, p. 1.

"In 1945 his": HLM, *Diary*, 3 June 1945 and 29 April 1946, pp. 370, 415; and
HLM, "Diary," 5 March (II), 17 October, 9 November, and 4 December
1945.

"He had either": HLM, *Diary* and "Diary," 1943–45, *passim*; HLM to Eugene
O'Dunne, 15 September 1941, EPFL; HLM, "AN, 1941–"; HLM, "*MR*:
Second Series," p. 3; and HLM to SL, 15 October 1945, NYPL.

p. 473. "By late 1945": HLM, *Diary* and "Diary," 1943–46, *passim*; Edmund Wilson,
"The Progress of the American Language," *The New Yorker*, 25 August
1945, pp. 57–58; and reviews by Carl Van Doren, Robert Spiller, and
others, HLM clippings scrapbook, EPFL.

"By the fall": HLM, *Diary*, 3 December 1945, p. 396; and HLM, "Diary," 1
September 1944 and 2 and 13 December 1945.

"He must have": HLM to Henry Hazlitt, 8 December 1946, NYPL; HLM,
"England's English," *BES*, 14 October 1910; HLM to GM, 28 July 1937,
EPFL; HLM to Jean Balch, 2 September 1936, EPFL. The only instance in
all his letters when I found Mencken use "on" a street, not "in," was in a
letter to Max Brödel, 15 July 1927, NYPL.

p. 474. "He made rapid": HLM, *Diary*, 12 September 1945, pp. 380–81; HLM, *A&E*,
xvii–xviii; and Jonathan Yardley, introduction to *A&E*, p. vi.

" 'Wrecked [by] drink' ": HLM, *A&E*, pp. 347–48. Jonathan Yardley incorpo-
rates into the text the material on Lewis and other figures that Mencken
included in lengthy appendices.

p. 475. "Apparently his earlier": HLM, *Diary*, 5 February 1942, p. 191.

"Some of the": HLM, "A&E," appendices; and HLM, *A&E*, pp. 14–23, 101–
10, 94–98.

"The manuscript also": HLM, *A&E*, pp. 107–08, 119, 364; HLM, "A&E," p.
984; and (on "more politically and semantically sensitive age"), Jonathan
Yardley, introduction to *A&E*, pp. xii–xiii.

p. 476. "Although 'My Life' ": HLM, "Diary," 13 April 1944; and HLM to Paul
Patterson, 23 March 1935, EPFL.

" 'A small book' ": HLM, *Diary*, 18 June 1942 and 14 July 1943, pp. 209, 267.

p. 477. "The reason many": HLM, *MR* notes (envelope A100.8), EPFL.

"When in 1945": HLM–AAK correspondence, Autumn 1945, NYPL. See also
Mary Miller Vass and James L. W. West, III, "The Composition and
Revision of Mencken's *Treatise on the Gods*," *Menckeniana*, Winter 1983,
pp. 9–16.

p. 478. "Neither man nor": HLM, *MR* notes; HLM, miscellaneous notes in file A100.8, EPFL; and HLM to JB, 25 September 1945, NYPL.

p. 479. "Taking management's side": HLM, *Diary*, 13 February 1946, pp. 407–09; HLM, "Diary," 12 and 31 January and 5 June 1942; and AM, "Diary of HLM's Hospitalization," 9 January 1951, EPFL.

"Nor was it": HLM, "Diary," 15 October and 14 December 1942 and 24 April 1943; and HLM, *Diary*, 10 March 1931, p. 15.

"In all these": HLM, *Diary*, 6 September 1944, p. 332; and HLM, "Diary," 16 July 1945.

"Once he had": HLM, *Diary*, 14 March 1931, p. 18; and HLM, "Diary," 9 April 1932.

p. 480. "At one Gridiron": HLM, *Diary*, 15 December 1946, pp. 426–27; and HLM, "Diary," 16 December 1945.

"Other entries show": HLM, *Diary* and "Diary," 1940–48, *passim*, and NYPL correspondence; HLM, *Prejudices*, *VI*, p. 95. For further discussion of Mencken and professors, see Nolte, *H. L. Mencken: Literary Critic*, pp. 148–79.

p. 481. " 'However much an' ": HLM to A. G. Keller, 18 October 1943, NYPL.

"Other than genuine": HLM–Louis Pound correspondence, 1920s–1940s, NYPL; HLM–JB correspondence, 1940s, NYPL; and HLM, *Diary*, 29 November 1942 and 19 January and 14 June 1943, pp. 225–27, 236–37, 254–57; HLM, "Diary," 5 March 1942, 17 June 1943, and 8 June 1946.

"He spent more": HLM, *A&E*, p. 317; HLM to GM, 13 October 1937, EPFL; HLM to BH, 29 November 1937 and 15 January 1938, UNC; HLM to J. B. Dudek, 10 November 1937, NYPL; HLM to Werner Janssen, 18 January 1939, NYPL; Stephen Fitzgerald to HLM, 23 February 1938, NYPL; HLM to Ernest Boyd, 3 January 1940, NYPL; HLM to Jim Tully, 10 February 1941, NYPL; HLM, "Diary," 13 November 1940; HLM to JB, 13 January 1944 and 28 May 1948, NYPL; Harold Allen to HLM, 21 February 1940, NYPL; John Frederick to HLM, 7 October 1936, NYPL; James Hulbert to HLM, 18 October 1945, NYPL; and Marjorie Nicolson to SM, 1 August 1971, UA.

p. 482. "In the 1940s": HLM correspondence with Frank O'Leary, John F. King, Ernest DeBaum, Clinton A. Sanders, J. P. Watson, and Robert Tasker, 1920s–1940s, NYPL.

"Saints continued to": HLM correspondence with James Cannon, Gerald L. K. Smith, Francis Clement Kelley, Miriam Gallagher, and J. B. Dudek, 1930s–1940s, NYPL; HLM, *Diary*, 9 October 1931, 16 June and 12 October 1934, and 28 August 1941, pp. 39–40, 63–64, 69–70, 158–59; HLM, "Diary," 5 October 1939; HLM, "Thirty-Five Years," p. 637; and HLM, "*Heathen Days:* Additions," p. 239.

p. 483. "In his diary": HLM to Edgar Kemler, 8 December 1946, NYPL; LC, SNC diary, 1944–47, *passim*, especially 1 November 1947; and James Cain to SM, 19 August 1968, UA.

"He traveled to": HLM, *Diary* and "Diary," 1945–47, *passim*, especially 11 October 1945; HLM, "Diary," 28 October 1943; HLM–MD correspondence, 1945–47, especially MD to HLM, 6 August 1946, NYPL; and MD, "Heroic Days and Hours with Henry Mencken," p. 5.

"Hergesheimer himself still": *Diary* and "Diary," 1945–47, *passim*; HLM to SL, 15 October 1945, NYPL; HLM to Ezra Pound, 19 November 1945 and 6 May 1946, NYPL; Pound to HLM, 28 April [1946], NYPL; and HLM to Dr. Winifred Overholser, 15 April 1946, NYPL.

p. 484. "Although he was": HLM to Helen Dreiser, 30 December 1945, NYPL; TD to HLM, 27 March 1943, NYPL, *D–M Letters*, II, p. 689; and HLM to Edgar Kemler, 16 August 1948, EPFL.

"In his last": TD to HLM, 27 March 1943 and 9 March, 22 April and 3 and 14 May (telegram) 1944, NYPL; and HLM to TD, 1 April 1943 and 27 March, 27 April and 5, 9, and 15 May 1944, UP; all in *D–M Letters*, II, pp. 688–93, 708–13.

"Mencken had responded": HLM to TD, 9 and 15 May 1944, UP; and TD to HLM, 9 March 1944, NYPL; all in *D–M Letters*, II, pp. 707, 709–10.

p. 485. "When Mencken had": HLM to GJN, 3 and 14, January 1946, NYPL; HLM to ELM, 14 January 1946, NYPL; and HLM, "Diary," 31 December 1945.

"In some ways": HLM, *Diary* and "Diary," 1945–48, *passim;* and HLM to Walter Winchell, 20 September 1945, NYPL.

p. 486. "Despite the cultivation": HLM, *Diary* and "Diary," January–November 1946, *passim;* HLM, *Diary*, 27 and 30 July and 13 and 23 August 1947, pp. 436–38; and Dr. Benjamin M. Baker, entry of 6 August 1947, HLM medical file, Bode collection, EPFL.

"In 1946 and": HLM, *Diary*, 29 March and 24 June 1946, pp. 410, 417–19; HLM to GJN, 9 October 1945 and 3 January 1947, NYPL; HLM, note of 15 October 1945, HLM–Ernest Boyd correspondence, NYPL.

"Such was Mencken's": HLM, "Diary," 15 June and 16 December 1945; HLM to W. C. Abhau, 20 April 1945, EPFL; HLM to BH, 17 June 1946, UNC.

p. 487. "Increasingly, Mencken looked": HLM to A. G. Keller, 19 and 22 January 1943, NYPL; and HLM to Ellery Sedgwick, 3 November 1942, NYPL.

"He had always": HLM, *Diary* and "Diary," 1942–48, *passim,* especially 27 August 1942, 23 November 1944, and 31 August 1945; and HLM to Mrs. Julian Boyd, 20 December 1943, NYPL.

"For that reason": HLM, *Diary*, 10 March 1943 and 23 November 1944, pp. 240, 344; HLM to Benjamin de Casseres, 11 December 1938, NYPL; HLM to Jean Balch, 12 June 1935, EPFL; HLM to JB, 1 December 1942, NYPL; HLM to Bettina Patterson, 3 July 1940 and 28 December 1947, EPFL; HLM to Mrs. Albert Hildebrandt, 30 April 1936, EPFL; Carolyn Hildebrandt to HLM, June [1935], GC; author's interview with R. P. Harriss; HLM to Sue Ashley, 30 March 1943, NYPL; HLM to GM, 7 and 10 August 1945, 31 May 1946, and 19 May 1947, EPFL; and HLM, "*HD:* Additions," p. 8.

p. 488. "But entertaining his": Author's interviews with Gwinn Owens and R. P. Harriss; HLM–GM correspondence, 1940–48, especially HLM to GM, 18 October 1943, 1 November 1944, and 8 December 1947, EPFL; and HLM, *Diary*, 13 November 1946, p. 425.

"His brother Charlie": HLM–CM correspondence, 1943–48, EPFL; HLM, *Diary*, 23 November 1944 and 8 August 1945, pp. 345, 277–79; HLM to GM, 24 July 1947, EPFL; and HLM, *A&E*, p. xxi.

p. 489. "For a final": HLM–W. C. Abhau correspondence, 1942–48, *passim*, EPFL; HLM, "Diary," 11 December 1945 and 26 October 1947; HLM to GM, 21 May 1943; CM to HLM, [1940s?], EPFL; HLM, "Diary," 30 August 1945; and HLM, "AN, 1941–."

"Such musings reinforced": HLM, "Diary," 10 March 1942 and 30 August 1945.

"It was more": HLM correspondence with Rosi-Lotti Sturm-Pfeiffer, Hortense Thüm, Burkhard Mencke, Helen Schwartz, Agnes Susemihl, Hedwig Hanstein, Agnes Hermine Hermes, Heinrich Spies, Hugo Fischer, Erica Lullier,

Werner Spielberg, Luise Wegner, Otto Julius Merkel, Marianne Dieke, and Willy Sohler, 1946–48, *passim,* EPFL (primarily) and NYPL.

p. 490. "In all, he": HLM, letters from Hedwig Hanstein, Agnes Hermine Hermes, Agnes Susemihl, Burkhard Mencke, and O. Mencke, 1946–48, EPFL.

"That he intended": HLM to Heinrich Spies, 26 March 1948, NYPL; HLM to Sanki Ichikawa, 3 August 1948, NYPL; Clara Schroeder Mencke to HLM, 9 September 1951, EPFL; Agnes Susemihl to HLM, 4 November 1948, EPFL; and HLM, *Diary,* 28 April 1948, pp. 446–47.

p. 491. " 'to stay dead' ": William Faulkner, *As I Lay Dying* (1930; Vintage ed., 1964), p. 167.

"That is also": HLM, *Diary* and "Diary," 1943–46, *passim;* HLM–Bradford Swan correspondence, 1940–48, *passim,* NYPL; HLM–Hamilton Reeves correspondence, 1942, *passim,* NYPL; LC, SNC diary, 17 June 1944; and HLM–JB correspondence, 1942–43, especially 7, 14, and 28 July 1942, NYPL.

"He knew on": HLM, *MR,* p. 238.

p. 492. "For many years": HLM to MB, 28 July 1926, EPFL; HLM, "*NPD:* Additions," p. 49; and HLM, *Diary,* 15 July 1945, pp. 375–76.

"He was not": HLM to Bradford Swan, 24 October 1946, NYPL; HLM, *Diary,* 12 September 1945, pp. 382–83; and HLM, "*MR:* Second Series," p. 3.

p. 493. "By 1947 it": James Daniel, "Whatever Became of Mencken?" *The Pittsburgh Press,* 14 February 1948; HLM to GJN, 7 August 1946, NYPL; HLM to GM, 7 August 1946, EPFL; and Roger Butterfield, "Mr. Mencken Sounds Off," *Life,* 5 August 1946, pp. 45–52.

"Biographers and other": JB to HLM, 9 November 1942, NYPL; and Oscar Wilde, quoted by Ronald Steel in "Living with Walter Lippmann," p. 129.

"Never, then, had": HLM, *Diary,* 21 March 1945, pp. 444–45; HLM–Edgar Kemler correspondence, 1946–48, *passim,* especially HLM to Kemler, 8 February 1946, EPFL.

p. 494. "To Kemler he": HLM to Edgar Kemler, 14 and 30 November 1947 and 21 February 1948, EPFL; HLM–William Manchester correspondence, 1947–48, *passim,* especially HLM to Manchester, 21 July and 5 August 1947 and 27 September 1948, EPFL.

"By the beginning": HLM, *Diary,* 19 and 25 January 1948, pp. 442–43; and HLM, "Diary," 19 May 1948.

"It did last": HLM, *Diary,* 22 February and 12 March 1948, pp. 443–44; HLM to DH, 12 March 1948, NYPL; HLM to BH, 21 February 1948, UNC; *Time, Saturday Review,* and *Newsweek* reviews, April 1948, in HLM clippings scrapbook, EPFL; and William Faulkner to HLM, [Winter 1948], NYPL.

p. 495. "After the second": HLM to BH, 29 November 1947, UNC; HLM, "Diary," 14 and 27 March and 19 and 26 April 1948.

"He experienced another": HLM to BH, 10 and 29 March 1948, UNC; HLM, note in Sunpapers documents, EPFL; HLM, *Diary* and "Diary," March–October 1948, *passim;* HLM to Dr. Benjamin M. Baker, 14 October 1948; HLM to Scottie Fitzgerald Lanahan, 26 March 1948, NYPL; and Lanahan to HLM, 3 April [1948], NYPL.

"The greatest shock": HLM, *Diary,* 25 and 29 May 1948, pp. 449–51; and HLM, "Diary," 26, 27, 28, and 31 May 1948.

p. 496. "The other diary": HLM, "Diary," 28 and 31 May 1948; and HLM to BH, 24 May 1948, UNC.

"It seemed almost": HLM to BH, 29 March 1948, UNC; HLM to GM, 21

February 1948, EPFL; HLM, "Diary," 21 February 1948; and HLM to W. C. Abhau, 19 February 1948, EPFL.

"It is little": HLM to Perry Molstad, 14 September 1948, NYPL; and HLM, "Diary," 11 June 1948.

p. 497. "He wrote Aileen": HLM to AP, 12 April 1948, NYPL; William Manchester, introduction to *Disturber of the Peace* (1986 ed.), p. xv; HLM, *Diary* and "Diary," March–November 1948, *passim*; HLM to Henry Hyde, 21 April 1948, EPFL; and HLM–MD correspondence, 1948, *passim*, NYPL.

"In many ways": MD to HLM, 2 July, 15 October, and 31 December 1947 and 4 and 11 February, 21 April, and 28 October 1948, NYPL; and HLM to MD, 23 April 1948, NYPL.

"Not only did": Maclean Patterson to HLM, 1 and 4 November 1948, EPFL; and HLM to Patterson, 14 April 1948, EPFL.

p. 498. "With Patterson by": HLM, "Diary," 25 June and 16 July 1948; HLM, note of 26 June 1948, Sunpapers documents; HLM to GM, 29 June 1948, EPFL.

"He was not": Maclean Patterson to HLM, 12 April 1948, EPFL; HLM, *Diary*, 26 July 1948, pp. 454–55; author's interview with Bradford Jacobs, 22 July 1987; and Alistair Cooke, *Six Men*, pp. 111–16.

"Forgetting for a": HLM to S. K. Ratliff, 16 May 1946, NYPL; HLM to Edgar Kemler, [November 1948], EPFL; HLM, "Diary," 24 May 1939 and 25 June 1948; HLM to GJN, 8 November 1948, NYPL; HLM to Henry Hyde, 22 July and 7 October 1948, EPFL.

p. 499. "Although early in": HLM to Joseph Sherbow, 9 November 1948, EPFL; HLM, "Truman's Election," *BS*, 7 November 1948; HLM, "Mencken Calls Tennis Order Silly, Nefarious," *BES*, 9 November 1948.

"In October he": HLM, *Diary*, 9 October 1949, p. 458; HLM, "Diary," 28 May and 13 October 1948; and HLM to Dr. Emil Novak, 28 November 1927, EPFL.

"In October and": HLM to Herman Liebert, 21 October 1948, NYPL; HLM to AAK, 27 October and 3 November 1948, EPFL.

p. 500. "In mid-November his": HLM to Felix Frankfurter, 17 November 1948, NYPL; CM to HLM, 10 November 1948, EPFL; HLM, *Diary*, 5 November 1948, pp. 461–63; HLM, "Diary," 5 October 1948; HLM to JB, 8 and 11 November 1948, NYPL; Harold Bender to HLM, 17 and 20 November 1948, NYPL; HLM to A. G. Keller, 17 November 1948, NYPL; LC, SNC diary, 20 November 1948; and HLM to Howard F. Barker, 19 November 1948, NYPL.

"He was making": HLM to GM, 1 and 8 November 1948, EPFL; BK to HLM, 22 November 1948, NYPL; HLM to Anita Loos, 10 September 1948, NYPL; and MD to HLM, 28 October and 1 December 1948, NYPL.

"There was little": HLM to JB, 22 November 1948, NYPL; HLM to Roscoe Peacock, 22 November 1948, NYPL; HLM to Harry Elmer Barnes, 22 November 1948, NYPL; HLM to Thomas Kirby, 22 November 1948, NYPL; HLM to C. R. Bradish, 22 November 1948, NYPL; and William Manchester, *Disturber of the Peace*, p. 311.

p. 501. "In the early": LC, SNC diary, 24 November 1948; and author's interviews with Dr. Benjamin M. Baker and Dr. Philip Wagley.

"August Mencken reported": AM, "Reminiscences," p. 80; author's interviews with Drs. Baker and Wagley; AAK, "H. L. Mencken, A Memoir," *On Mencken*, p. 311.

"It proved to": AAK, *ibid.*

## Chapter 21: Requiem in Hollins Street

p. 502. "Mencken later referred": HLM, quoted by Alistair Cooke, *Six Men*, p. 117. Mencken's "death" had come at precisely the moment he had predicted it would. "The insurance companies," he had written in the autumn of 1923, "say that my expectation of live [*sic*] is exactly twenty-five years . . ." (HLM, "Fifteen Years," ms. for *SS*, scrapbook A118, EPFL).

"For a good": Rosalind Lohrfinck, letters to GJN, JB, A. H. McDannald, Westbrook Pegler, Robert J. Baumann, J. M. Bradbury, Raven McDavid, Clarissa Flugel, Wilmer Leech, and William Haley, 27–29 November 1948, NYPL and EPFL.

p. 503. "They did not": AP reports of 30 November and 1 December 1948, HLM clippings scrapbook, EPFL; Kyra Markham to HLM, 1 December 1948, NYPL; Rosalind Lohrfinck to Edgar Kemler, 30 November 1948, EPFL; AP to HLM, 1 December 1948, NYPL; MD to HLM, 1 December 1948, NYPL; William Heath to HLM, 3 December 1948, NYPL; Sue Ashley to HLM, [December 1948], EPFL; Wilmer Leech to HLM, 29 November 1948, NYPL; and Harold Ross to HLM, 29 November 1948, NYPL.

"Only those very": LC, SNC diary, 24 and 27 November and 10 December 1948; AM, "Reminiscences," pp. 80, 81–83, 86–89; and AM, medical diary, December 1948–January 1949, EPFL.

p. 504. "In any case": AP report of 7 January 1949, HLM clippings scrapbook, EPFL; and Dr. Benjamin M. Baker, medical entry of 6 January 1949, quoted in Bode, "Dr. Ben Baker" (notes), p. 9, Bode collection, EPFL.

"For a short": LC, SNC diary, 7 January 1949; HLM to GJN, 7, 14, 18, and 25 January and 7 and 15 February 1949, NYPL; HLM to BK, 24 January and 14 February 1949, EPFL; HLM to JH, 7, 11, 14, 18, and 26 January and 3 February 1949, NYPL; HLM to BH, 7 and 18 January 1949, UNC; HLM to AP, 17 January 1949, YU; HLM to JB, 7 and 13 January 1949; and HLM to Harold Ross, 17 and 31 January 1949, NYPL. Mencken may have even typed one letter himself, to Helen Dreiser (14 January 1949, NYPL), although it is difficult to be certain the typing is his.

"To Knopf he": HLM to AAK, 11 January 1949, EPFL; HLM to Bradford Swan, 14 January 1949, NYPL; HLM to E. P. Flaherty, 3 February 1949, EPFL; Rosalind Lohrfinck to the A. S. Abell Co., 14 February 1949, EPFL; Lohrfinck to Edgar Kemler, 21 February 1949, EPFL; HLM to BK, [January 1949], EPFL; HLM (concerning visits) to JH, BK, AAK, January–February 1949, *passim*, NYPL; and HLM to Kemler, 24 January 1949, EPFL. Mencken apparently did not see Kemler before his Florida trip, however.

p. 505. "From his correspondence": HLM to JH, 11 January 1949, NYPL; and HLM to AAK, 11 January, NYPL.

"Soon, however, reality": Rosalind Lohrfinck to Fred Lewis Pattee, 16 February 1949, NYPL; Lohrfinck to BH, [January–February 1949], UNC; HLM to JH, 18 January 1949, NYPL; and LC, SNC diary, 7 January 1949.

"He realized in": HLM to GJN, 14 October 1948, NYPL; HLM, *Diary*, 12 August and 14 September 1948, p. 456; HLM to AAK, 17 and 24 January and 3 February 1949, NYPL; HLM to Harold Ross, 17 and 31 January 1949, NYPL; AAK to HLM, 19 January 1949, NYPL; and Rosalind Lohrfinck to AAK, 7 February 1949, EPFL.

p. 506. "In an attempt": HLM to BK, 14 February 1949, NYPL; HLM to GJN, 7 February 1949, NYPL; LC, SNC diary, [March 1949]; Rosalind Lohrfinck to GJN, 15 March 1949, NYPL; Lohrfinck to BH, 21 March 1949, UNC.

August felt the trip was somewhat beneficial ("Reminiscences," p. 92), but all other evidence, including correspondence, suggests the contrary.

"After his return": Rosalind Lohrfinck letters to AAK (24 May 1949, EPFL), GJN (15 March 1949, NYPL), and BH (21 March and 4 April 1949, UNC).

"For the next": Author's interview with Dr. Philip Wagley; D. Theodore Lidz to Dr. Benjamin M. Baker, 22 March 1949, Bode folder, "Mencken's Health," p. 11, Bode collection, EPFL; and AM, note, [n.d.], medical notes, EPFL.

p. 507. "August had now": AM, medical notes, 12 April and 10, 25, and 30 May 1949; and Walter Myers to HLM, 18 August 1949, NYPL.

"Mencken could not": HLM, note in family correspondence, 23 November 1945, EPFL; HLM, *Diary*, 23 November 1944, p. 344; HLM to J. B. Dudek, 5 January and 26 September 1946 and 11 September 1947, NYPL; HLM to Charles Gallagher, 13 January 1944, NYPL; HLM to A. H. McDannald, 9 May 1936, NYPL; and HLM, *The Philosophy of Friedrich Nietzsche* (1913 ed.), p. 49.

p. 508. "Despite his fear": HLM, "AN, 1941–"; HLM to A. G. Keller, 13 November 1947, NYPL; HLM to A. H. McDannald, 29 November 1939, NYPL; and HLM, ms. of "The Last Scene," February 1924, "Clinical Notes" scrapbook, EPFL.

"Now that it": HLM, quoted in "Poet's Death Ideal, Says H. L. Mencken," *San Francisco Examiner*, 18 November 1926; HLM to DH, 21 April 1933, NYPL; HLM, *Prejudices, VI*, pp. 85–91; HLM, note from 1940s, later published in *MR*, p. 109; HLM, quoted by Ruth Crawford in "How I Got That Way," United Features Syndicate article, 1926, in HLM clippings scrapbook, EPFL; and HLM to GH, [9 May 1928], *Ich Küss die Hand*, p. 106.

p. 509. "But now that": Author's interviews with Dr. Benjamin M. Baker, Dr. Philip Wagley, and Philip Wagner; HLM, quoted by AM, "Reminiscences," p. 96; and LC, SNC diary, 1948–55, *passim*.

"In May and": LC, SNC diary, Spring 1949, *passim*; Rosalind Lohrfinck to Paul Patterson, 18 May 1949, EPFL; Lohrfinck correspondence with Huntington Cairns, James T. Farrell, JH, JB, DH, and GJN, Spring 1949, NYPL; and JH to HLM, 22 April 1949, NYPL.

"But other friends": Lillian Gish to HLM, 18 March 1949, NYPL; Rosalind Lohrfinck to BH, 12 September 1949, UNC; and Lohrfinck to AP, Beatrice Wilson Macdonald, Doris Fleeson, and Ruth Alexander, 1949–55, NYPL and EPFL.

"Feeling most keenly": MD to Rosalind Lohrfinck, 22 March 1949, Bode collection, EPFL; MD to HLM, 25 January 1949, NYPL; Lohrfinck to MD, 26 January 1949, NYPL; and author's interview with R. P. Harriss.

p. 510. "August noted that": Rosalind Lohrfinck to JH, 16 August 1941, NYPL; AM, "Reminiscences," pp. 73–75; HLM, *Prejudices, VI*, p. 291; Lohrfinck, quoted in Bob Thomas, "The Movie World," *Providence Journal*, 12 May 1950; author's interviews with Dr. Benjamin M. Baker and Dr. Philip Wagley; Lohrfinck to GJN, 30 September 1949, NYPL; and Lohrfinck to Walter Lagemann, 17 June 1949, EPFL.

"As summer moved": Rosalind Lohrfinck to AAK, 8 August 1949, EPFL; AM, "Reminiscences," p. 73; Dr. William G. Hardy to AM, 27 August 1949, in HLM illness file, EPFL; and report of Dr. Kathryn Dice, 30 May 1949, in AM, medical notes, EPFL.

p. 511. "For a time": HLM, illness file, 12 September 1949; AM, medical notes, 4 and

20 August, 9 September, and 30 October 1949, EPFL; AM, "Reminiscences," p. 73; Rosalind Lohrfinck to GJN, 29 November 1949, NYPL; and Siegfried Weisberger to Joseph Katz, 2 May 1949, HLM correspondence, EPFL.

"The year 1950": Reviews of *Chrestomathy*, Spring–Summer 1949, HLM clippings scrapbook, EPFL; HLM note of 21 October 1949 (dictated to Lohrfinck) in HLM–AAK correspondence, NYPL; HLM, "The Crime of McSwane," *Esquire*, October 1949, pp. 74, 132; HLM, "Postscripts to *The American Language*," *The New Yorker*, 1 October 1949, pp. 56–61; Walter Winchell, quoted by Edward Rosenheim to HLM, 17 October 1949, EPFL; and James Cain, "Mr. Mencken and the Multitude," *The New York Times Book Review*, 15 April 1950.

p. 512. "To be sure": Paul Patterson to HLM, 18 October 1949, EPFL; Rosalind Lohrfinck to Patterson, 10 October 1949, EPFL; "Cornerstone of the New Plant for Sunpapers Formally Laid," *BES*, 27 October 1949; Lohrfinck correspondence with William Abell, Philip Wagner, John Dewey, and JB, 1950, EPFL and NYPL; AM to GJN, 9 February 1950, EPFL; AM to Dr. Arnold Rich, 7 August 1950, EPFL; and LC, SNC diary, 25 February, [March], and 6 June 1950.

"In fact, his": Author's interviews with Bradford Jacobs and R. P. Harriss; Philip Wagner, "Mencken Remembered," *American Scholar*, Spring 1963, p. 274; AM to GJN, 9 February 1950, EPFL; and LC, SNC diary, 16 July 1949.

p. 513. "Aside from August": LC, SNC diary, 1949–50, *passim*, especially 1 October and 31 December 1949 and 21 August 1950; and AM, medical notes, 6 June 1950, EPFL.

"In the summer": GM to AM, 13 August and 10 September 1949, EPFL.

"Mencken had not": CM to AM, 1 June 1950, EPFL; AM to CM, 27 August 1950, EPFL.

p. 514. "Although Charlie's visit": CM to AM, 19 September 1950, EPFL; Louis M. Starr, interview with Hamilton Owens, Bode collection, EPFL; AM, medical notes, 22 March and 16 August 1950; AAK to Hamilton Owens, 22 May 1950, EPFL; and Owens to AAK, 10 July 1950, both in "About Mencken" file, EPFL.

"August had still": AM to Dr. William Hands, 5 January 1940, EPFL; and AM, medical notes, 19 May 1950, EPFL.

"Rich had suggested": AM, medical notes, 19 May 1950, EPFL; AM to Dr. Benjamin M. Baker, 14 April 1950, EPFL; and author's interview with Dr. Philip Wagley.

p. 515. "But he wanted": AM, draft copy of letter to Dr. Benjamin M. Baker, 14 April 1950, medical notes, EPFL.

"Wagley was not": AM, medical notes, [September 1950], EPFL; LC, SNC diary, [September 1950]; Rosalind Lohrfinck to Dr. Philip Wagley, 5 October 1950, EPFL; Hamilton Owens to AAK, 10 July 1950, "About Mencken" file, EPFL; and Dr. Benjamin M. Baker, report of 24 August 1950, in Bode folder, "Mencken's Health," Bode collection, EPFL.

"Such is hardly": LC, SNC diary, 11 September 1950; Edgar Kemler, *The Irreverent Mr. Mencken*, p. 280; Edmund Wilson, "Mencken Through the Wrong End of the Telescope," *The New Yorker*, 6 May 1950, p. 112; and AM, "Reminiscences," p. 72.

p. 516. "One embarrassing result": Rosalind Lohrfinck to Douglas Moore, 17 June 1950, NYPL; AAK to Moore, 25 April 1950, NYPL; AM, "Reminiscences,"

p. 30; Lohrfinck to Carl Van Doren, 6 June 1950, NYPL; and news stories in *BS* and *The New York Times,* 17 February and 25 May 1950, HLM clippings scrapbook, EPFL.

p. 517. "During the summer": Hamilton Owens to AAK, 10 July 1950, "About Mencken" file, EPFL; AM, medical notes, 12 October 1950, EPFL.

"Thus he was": AM, diary of HLM's hospitalization, 12 October 1950, EPFL; and LC, SNC diary, [October 1950].

"For the next": AP report, 17 October 1950, Mayfield collection, UA; AM hospitalization diary, 20, 21, and 22 October and 6 November 1950, EPFL; and LC, SNC diary, [October 1950].

"After a scare": AM, hospitalization diary, November–December 1950, *passim.*

p. 518. "Neither Mencken nor": AM, hospitalization diary, 7 December 1950 and 6 January and 8, 15, and 27 February 1951; and MD, "Heroic Days and Hours with Henry Mencken," pp. 8–9.

"From November on": AM, hospitalization diary, 4 December 1950, EPFL; and LC, SNC diary, 28 December 1950.

p. 519. "For all his": LC, SNC diary, 28 December 1950; AM, hospitalization diary, 14 February 1951, EPFL; author's interview with Dr. Philip Wagley; William Manchester, *Disturber of the Peace,* p. 318; and photograph in *BS,* HLM clippings scrapbook, EPFL.

"When he returned": LC, SNC diary, 26 June, 21 July, and 8 August 1951; AM to GM, 13 June, 10 August, and 5 October 1951, EPFL; AM to CM, 16 June, 10 October, and [October] 1951, EPFL.

"To add to": AM to CM, 10 October 1951, EPFL; Dr. Henry B. Wilson, "Recalls HLM as Patient," *Menckeniana,* Summer 1975, p. 10; AM to GM, 14 August 1951, EPFL; LC, SNC diary, 29 December 1951; and LC tape recording, October 1951, EPFL.

p. 520. "He now saw": LC, SNC diary, 12 January and July 1951; AM, "Reminiscences," pp. 108–09; HLM correspondence with DH, JH, and AAK, 1950–55, *passim,* NYPL; W. C. Abhau to HLM, 22 November 1951, EPFL; and author's interview with W. C. Abhau.

"Even more than": Rosalind Lohrfinck to Lillian Gish, 21 December 1952, NYPL; Lohrfinck to AP, 27 December 1951, YU; Clare Leighton, "Cynical Fantasy," p. 2; William Manchester, *Disturber of the Peace,* p. 322; James Cain to AM, 31 January 1956, AM file, EPFL; Dr. Manfred Guttmacher, note of 8 January 1951 in daybook, in Arthur J. Gutman, ed., "Guttmacher/ Mencken," *Menckeniana,* Winter 1979, p. 10; and Lohrfinck to Clarissa Flugel, 21 January 1952, EPFL.

"Devastating as the": Author's interviews with Dr. Philip Wagley and W. C. Abhau.

p. 521. "Despite his condition": Rosalind Lohrfinck to GJN, 2 February 1952, NYPL; and LC, SNC diary, 8 August 1951.

"August and Gertrude": GM to AM, 6 October 1950, EPFL; AAK to R. P. Harriss, 14 August 1956, in "About Mencken" file, EPFL; AM, medical notes, 29 June 1950, EPFL; HLM, note of 21 April 1950 in AM, medical notes, EPFL; author's interview with Dr. Philip Wagley; and Ronald T. Schwab, "H. L. Mencken and James Gibbons Huneker," *Menckeniana,* Fall 1964, pp. 10–11.

p. 522. "Three years after": LC, SNC diary, 21 July 1951; James T. Farrell to Betty Adler, [n.d.], EPFL; HLM to GJN, 4 December 1952, NYPL; author's interview with Philip Wagner; HLM, *Diary,* 27 December 1942, p. 227.

"He never really": Author's interview with Dr. Philip Wagley; HLM to GJN, 30 January 1952, NYPL; Rosalind Lohrfinck to Herbert Bayard Swope, 22 September 1953, NYPL; AM to John Haardt, 27 November 1953, EPFL.

"Around the house": LC, SNC diary, 16 July 1952, 9 May 1953, 30 January, 1 May, and 4 and 18 December 1954, and [n.d.].

p. 523. "Except for that": LC, SNC diary, 6 August 1952 and miscellaneous notes.

p. 524. "The Mencken brothers": LC, SNC diary, miscellaneous notes; AM to GM, 14 June 1954, EPFL; and HLM, *Diary*, 31 December 1943, p. 290.

"But finally that": AM to GM, 16 October 1952 and 1953, *passim*, especially 14 May and 22 June 1953, EPFL; AM to CM, 16 October 1952, EPFL; Rosalind Lohrfinck to Hamilton Owens, 19 November 1954, EPFL.

p. 525. "One by one": Rosalind Lohrfinck to DH, 27 April 1954, NYPL; AM to Dr. Philip Wagley, 19 and 22 March 1952, EPFL; AM, "Reminiscences," p. 48; and HLM to DH, 13 October 1933 and 2 and 7 January 1940, NYPL.

"Only once during": Typed notes labeled "Dictated by H. L. Mencken," 25 February and 9 May 1952, scrapbook A108, pp. 84ff, EPFL.

p. 526. "At times in": *Ibid.*, 16, 23, 26, and 30 May and 4 June 1952.

p. 527. "First he began": William Manchester, "Mencken, 73, Mellows," *BS*, 11 January 1954; R. P. Harriss, "H. L. Mencken at Seventy-Five," *Garden, Homes and People*, August 1955; and Robert McHugh, "H. L. Mencken at 74," 10 July 1955, in HLM clippings scrapbook, EPFL.

"In Manchester's widely": Manchester, "Mencken, 73, Mellows"; Harriss, "H. L. Mencken"; McHugh, "H. L. Mencken"; and Harris, "Scotus/Germanicus," *Menckeniana*, Winter 1980, p. 11.

"For whatever reason": AM, "Reminiscences," pp. 31, 44; and Rosalind Lohrfinck to AP, 9 April 1955, YU.

"In addition to": William Manchester, *Disturber of the Peace*, p. 321; LC, SNC diary, 25, 26, and 27 May 1955; and AM to Dr. Philip Wagley, 29 April 1954, EPFL.

p. 528. "Equally indicative of": Charles Angoff, "The Inside View of Mencken's Mercury," *The New Republic*, 13 September 1954, pp. 18–22; "First H. L. Mencken, Now G. J. Nathan," *Worcester* (Mass.) *Gazette*, October 1954, in HLM clippings scrapbook, EPFL; HLM to AAK, 9, 15, and 22 March and 26 April 1955, EPFL; Alistair Cooke, *Six Men*, p. 116; HLM to AAK, 26 April 1955, NYPL; and AAK to HLM, 6 July 1955, EPFL.

"His plans did": Rosalind Lohrfinck to AAK, 26 September 1952, NYPL; AAK to HLM, 17 October 1952, EPFL; and AAK, "Alfred A. Knopf on Mencken" (ms.), G pamphlet collection, EPFL.

p. 529. "It was the": HLM, *Diary*, 14 July 1943 and 12 August 1948, pp. 267, 456.

"About the time": William Manchester, "America's Sam Johnson," and Alistair Cooke, "The Baltimore Fox," *Saturday Review*, 10 September 1955, pp. 11–13, 63–65; Gerald W. Johnson, "His Laughter Cleared the Air," *BS*, 11 September 1955; Edgar Kemler, "The Bright Twilight of H. L. Mencken," *The New York Times Magazine*, 12 September 1955; and AM to CM, 24 September 1955, EPFL.

"Mencken was genuinely": HLM, quoted by Robert Durr, "The Last Days of H. L. Mencken," *Yale Review*, Autumn 1958, p. 72; Sanki Ichikawa to HLM, 10 September 1955, NYPL; Rosalind Lohrfinck to AAK, 13 September 1955, NYPL; Lohrfinck to Gerald W. Johnson, 12 September 1955, EPFL; Edgar Kemler, "The Bright Twilight," p. 14; Hedda Hopper to HLM, 26 September 1955, NYPL; and Lohrfinck to Hopper, 30 September 1955, NYPL.

"Not long after": Rosalind Lohrfinck to Arthur Hawks, 19 September 1955, EPFL; LC, SNC diary, 25–27 May, 17 September, and 26 November 1955; Lohrfinck to Edwin F. A. Morgan, 19 September 1955, EPFL; AM to CM, 24 September 1955, EPFL; AM to GM, 14 June 1955, EPFL; AM to Dr. Philip Wagley, 8 July 1955, EPFL.

p. 530.  "In nearly every": HLM, *HD*, p. 9; and Evelyn Durant to HLM, 3 January 1955, EPFL.

p. 531.  "As late fall": AM to GM, 15 October 1955, EPFL; Rosalind Lohrfinck to Olga Owens (20 December 1955) and James Bready (28 December 1955), EPFL; LC, SNC diary, 26 November and [December] 1955; Lohrfinck to AAK, 15 and 17 December 1955, NYPL; AAK to HLM, 19 December 1955, NYPL; and HLM to AAK, 10 January 1956, NYPL.

"As 1956 dawned": Rosalind Lohrfinck to Clarissa Flugel, 8 January 1956, EPFL; Lohrfinck to Victor T. Reno, 1 December 1955, NYPL; Lohrfinck to GJN, 20 January 1956, NYPL; HLM to Judy Brilhart, 25 January 1956, *Letters of H. L. Mencken*, p. 506; LC, SNC diary, 14 January 1956; and AM, medical notes, 12 January 1956, EPFL.

"But principally he": AAK, in "Borzoi Books," [January 1956], HLM pamphlet collection, EPFL; Robert McHugh, "Mencken Eyes Book and Critics," *BS*, 26 January 1956; and Mark Schorer to Rosalind Lohrfinck, 27 January 1956, NYPL.

p. 532.  "The day after": LC, SNC diary, 28 January 1956; and author's interview with Elise Cheslock.

"Death did not": HLM to Anna Hildebrandt, 14 May 1936, EPFL; LC, SNC diary, 29 January 1956; and photostat of HLM death certificate, 31 January 1956, F pamphlet collction, EPFL. Louis Cheslock later puzzled further over Mencken's remark the night of his death that he would not see him again. Adding to his puzzlement was an incident related to him much later by a friend who had come upon a note in Mencken's papers instructing his brother to take from his pants pocket a key that would unlock a box in his desk—a box containing "ample money" for any necessities—and also reminding August not to let Gertrude change the terms of his funeral. The note itself is now nowhere to be found among the Mencken papers at the Enoch Pratt Free Library, but along with the statement to Cheslock that he would not see his friend again, it suggests Mencken's certainty in the winter of 1956 that he would not last much longer.

"In preparing for": HLM, *Diary*, 2 June 1943, p. 254; HLM, *Prejudices, VI*, p. 103; HLM to R. Meyers, 15 February 1937, NYPL; HLM, *"HD:* Additions," p. 99; and LC, SNC diary, miscellaneous notes.

p. 533.  "Mencken's first request": "H. L. Mencken, Author, Dies at 75," *BS*, 30 January 1956; Hamilton Owens, "HLM's Pungent Pen a Challenge to Orthodoxy," *BS*, 30 January 1956; Rosalind Lohrfinck to C. R. Bradish, 6 March 1956, NYPL; LC, SNC diary, [February 1956], miscellaneous notes; and AM, "Reminiscences," pp. 38–39. Cheslock states that he himself said the few words at the service, but all other accounts, including printed ones, suggest that Hamilton Owens spoke the words.

"After that there": HLM, "AN, 1925" (NYPL); and HLM, promotional pamphlet for Loudon Park Cemetery, D pamphlet collection, 1902, EPFL.

## Coda: The Posthumous Life of H. L. Mencken

p. 536. "Hardly had August": "The Scoffer Witherith Away" and other editorials, February 1956, HLM clippings scrapbook, EPFL; "Mencken Is Still a Storm Center," *BS*, 29 February 1956; and FBI file 61-1286, Bode collection, EPFL.

"'God is the'": HLM, *MR*, pp. 24, 148, 207; Edward Weeks, "Voice Undaunted," *The Atlantic*, June 1956, p. 74; AAK, "Alfred A. Knopf on Mencken" (ms.), G pamphlet collection, EPFL; and JB, "Prejudices According to Mencken," *The New York Times Book Review*, 20 May 1956, p. 124.

p. 537. "That bin was": HLM, *A Carnival of Buncombe*, ed. Malcolm Moos (Johns Hopkins University Press, 1956); AM, "Reminiscences," p. 21; and Charles Angoff, *H. L. Mencken: A Portrait from Memory*, especially pp. 9, 101.

"Mencken's friends, Knopf": AAK to Arthur Schlesinger (July 1956), William Feather (2 July 1956), and Huntington Cairns (22 April 1964), all in "About Mencken" file, EPFL; Robert Molloy, review of *A Portrait from Memory*, *Chicago Sunday Tribune*, 1 July 1956, and Stanley Walker, review in New York *Herald Tribune Book Review*, 17 June 1956, both in HLM clippings scrapbook, EPFL; and author's interview with Lawrence Spivak.

p. 538. "Angoff was to": Charles Angoff, "Mencken: Prejudices and Prophecies," *Saturday Review*, 10 August 1963, pp. 44–45, and "H. L. Mencken," *South Atlantic Quarterly*, Spring 1964, pp. 227–39; AAK to Robert Sarnoff, 11 July 1956, "About Mencken" file, EPFL; Angoff, letter to *The New Republic*, 18 November 1957, pp. 3, 23; Gerald W. Johnson, "Oh, For Mencken Now," *The New Republic*, 30 September 1957, p. 11; and William Manchester and Arthur Schlesinger, letters to *The New Republic*, 2 December 1957, p. 23, and 16 December 1957, p. 23.

"Mencken's other staunchest": HLM, last will and testament, dated 28 September 1954, F pamphlet collection, EPFL; *New York Times* report of 15 February 1956, HLM clippings scrapbook, EPFL; AM to Ruth Mencken, 10 April 1956, EPFL; AM to Virginia Mencken Morrison, [August 1956], EFPL; and LC, SNC diary, 11 February and 9 April 1956.

"In the spring": Janet Clark to GM, 5 May 1956, EPFL; GM to AM, 5, 9, 13, 18, and 25 July 1956, EPFL; AM to GM, 23 July 1956, EPFL.

p. 539. "Certainly he would": Van Wyck Brooks, *Days of the Phoenix*, p. 69.

"Within a decade": Betty Adler correspondence with MB, GH, and MD, 1960s–1970s, EPFL; MB to Adler, 3 November 1968, EPFL.

p. 540. "But Marion was": MB to Betty Adler, 15 December 1968, 3 and 18 July 1971, miscellaneous letters, 1960s, and 1971–72, *passim*, EPFL; MB to EB, [n.d.], NYPL; and MB obituary, *The Washington Post*, 15 March 1975, Bode collection, EPFL.

p. 541. "Hood was also": GH to Betty Adler, 29 March and 21 October 1968 and 27 November 1969, EPFL. Pringle's letters were donated to the Beinecke Library in 1990.

"It is curious": MB to Betty Adler, 15 December 1968 and [n.d.—1966], EPFL; MD to Betty Adler, 15 December 1971, EPFL; and Huntington Cairns to AM, 27 May 1959 and 7 October 1963, AM file, EPFL.

p. 542. "In September 1980": AAK, "For Henry with Love," *The Atlantic*, May 1959, pp. 50–54; and AAK, "H. L. Mencken: A Memoir," in John Dorsey, ed., *On Mencken* (Alfred A. Knopf, 1980), pp. 283–313.

"No member of": AM to GM, 24 July 1953 and 19 September 1956, EPFL; GM to AM, 27 September 1956, EPFL; AM, "Reminiscences," pp. 60ff; author's interviews with Elise Cheslock, Olga Owens, and R. P. Harriss; and "Anna Gertrude Mencken and Virginia Mencken Morrison," *Menckeniana*, Winter 1980, p. 3.

"The significance of ": "Anna Gertrude Mencken and Virginia Mencken Morrison," p. 3; and "Plane Crash Kills Young Executive," *Lancaster* (Pa.) *New Era*, 14 November 1974.

p. 543. "The events of ": Walter Lippmann, "H. L. Mencken," *Saturday Review*, 11 December 1926, p. 414; Charles Fecher, *A Study of Mencken's Thought*, p. 319.

"The release of ": HLM, note accompanying diary manuscript; and HLM to FHG, 27 July 1934, NYPL.

p. 544. "Kazin's portrait of "; Alfred Kazin, "Mencken and the Great American Boob," *The New York Review of Books*, 26 February 1987, pp. 8–11.

"The impassioned response": Charles Fecher, introduction to *Diary*, p. xix; Neil Grauer, "Mencken's Shocker," *BES*, 4 December 1989; Garry Wills, "The Ugly American," *The New Republic*, 19 February 1990, pp. 31–34; and review in *The Boston Globe*, 6 December 1989, quoted in Fecher, "Firestorm: The Publication of HLM's Diary," *Menckeniana*, Spring 1990, p. 2.

p. 545. "But the widespread": Jonathan Yardley, "Mencken's Unsurprising Prejudices," *The Washington Post*, 11 December 1989; Russell Baker, "Prejudices Without the Mask," *The New York Times*, 13 December 1989; William Manchester, "The Diary of H. L. Mencken," *The New York Times Book Review*, 4 February 1990, p. 33; and Arthur Miller and others, "Celebrating Mencken," *The New York Review of Books*, 15 March 1990, p. 53.

"The debate continued": Joseph Epstein, "Mencken on Trial," *Commentary*, April 1990, pp. 31–39; Gore Vidal, "The Essential Mencken," *The Nation*, 26 August–2 September 1991, pp. 228–33.

p. 546. " 'Human life is' ": HLM, *MR*, p. 11; and Clare Leighton, "Cynical Fantasy," p. 2.

p. 547. " 'Here I stand' ": HLM, *Prejudices, III*, p. 11.

# INDEX

# PERMISSIONS

Grateful acknowledgment is made to the following for permission to use both published and unpublished material:

*Beinecke Library of Yale University and Joseph Solomon, Gallet Dreyer & Berkey:* Letters between Aileen Pringle and H. L. Mencken. Used by permission.

*Mrs. Louis Cheslock:* Excerpts from the Saturday Night Club diary of Louis Cheslock. Used by permission.

*Laetitia Kelly Coolidge:* Letters of Dr. Howard Kelly to H. L. Mencken. Used by permission.

*Emory University:* Excerpts from correspondence between Gretchen Hood and H. L. Mencken housed at the Woodruff Library. Used by permission.

*The Enoch Pratt Free Library:* Excerpts from unpublished and certain published works and letters of H. L. Mencken. Used by permission of the Enoch Pratt Free Library in accordance with the terms of the will of Henry Louis Mencken.

*The Enoch Pratt Free Library and The University of Alabama Press:* Excerpts from letters by H. L. Mencken from *Ich Küss die Hand: The Letters of H. L. Mencken to Gretchen Hood,* edited by Peter W. Dowell. Reprinted by permission.

*Ruth Goodman Goetz:* Letters from Philip Goodman to H. L. Mencken. Used by permission.

*Goucher College:* Correspondence between Sara Haardt and H. L. Mencken. Used by permission.

*Arthur J. Gutman:* H. L. Mencken letters from his private collection. Used by permission.

*Alfred A. Knopf, Inc.:* Excerpts from the following works by H. L. Mencken: *The American Language, 4th Edition* and *Supplements 1 & 2, Prejudices, First Series* through *Sixth Series, In Defense of Women, Notes on Democracy, Treatise on the Gods, Treatise on Right and Wrong, Happy Days, Newspaper Days, Heathen Days,* and *Minority Report.* Reprinted by permission.

*William A. Koshland:* Letters from Alfred A. and Blanche Knopf to H. L. Mencken. Used by permission.

*David Leighton:* Letters of Clare Leighton to H. L. Mencken. Used by permission.

*Camella Mayfield:* Letters of Sara Mayfield to H. L. Mencken. Used by permission.

*The New York Public Library:* Excerpts from the literary correspondence of H. L. Mencken. Used by permission.

## About the Author

FRED HOBSON was born in North Carolina. After obtaining degrees from the University of North Carolina at Chapel Hill and Duke University, he worked as an editorial writer for the Winston-Salem *Journal and Sentinel*. He has been a professor of American Literature at the University of Alabama, Louisiana State University, and the University of North Carolina at Chapel Hill, where he teaches at present. In addition to being co-editor of the *Southern Review* and the *Southern Literary Journal*, he has written several books about the South, among them *Serpent in Eden: H. L. Mencken and the South, Tell About the South*, which won the Jules Landry Award, and *South-Watching: Selected Essays of Gerald W. Johnson*, which won the Lillian Smith Award. He and his wife live in Chapel Hill, North Carolina.

## About the Type

This book was set in a digital version of Bodoni Book, a typeface named after Giambattista Bodoni, an Italian printer and type designer of the late eighteenth and early nineteenth century. It is not actually one of Bodoni's fonts but a modern version based on his style and manner and is distinguished by a marked contrast between the thick and thin elements of the letters.